Ubuntu 15.04 Server with systemd

Administration and Reference

to

Larisa and Aleina

Ubuntu 15.04 Server with systemd: Administration and Reference

Richard Petersen

Surfing Turtle Press

Alameda, CA

www.surfingturtlepress.com

Please send inquires to: editor@surfingturtlepress.com

ISBN-13 978-1-936280-98-8

ISBN 1-936280-98-1

Preface

This book is designed as an Ubuntu 15.04 Server administration and reference source, covering the Ubuntu servers and their support applications. Server tools are covered as well as the underlying configuration files and system implementations. The emphasis is on what administrators will need to know to perform key server support and management tasks. Coverage of the systemd service management system is integrated into the book, replacing the deprecated Upstart system. Topics covered include software management, systemd service management, AppArmor security, OpenSSH, and the Network Time Protocol. Key servers are examined, including Web, FTP, CUPS printing, NFS, and Samba Windows shares. Network support servers and applications covered include the Squid proxy server, the Domain Name System (BIND) server, DHCP, distributed network file systems, IPtables firewalls, and cloud computing.

The book is organized into five parts: getting started, services, shared resources, network support, and shells.

Part 1 focuses on basic tasks such as installing the Ubuntu Server CD, managing software from the Ubuntu repository, and basic usage for the desktop and the command line interfaces.

Part 2 examines Internet servers as well as how services are managed by systemd using unit files. Configuration and implementation of the Postfix mail server, the vsftpd FTP server, the Apache Web server, as well as news and database servers are covered in detail.

Part 3 deals with servers that provide shared resources on a local network or the Internet. Services examined include the CUPS printing server, NFS Linux network file server, and Samba Windows file and printing server, the GFS distributed file system, and cloud computing services supported by Ubuntu.

Part 4 covers servers that provide network support, like the Squid proxy server, the Bind Domain Name System (DNS) server, DHCP servers, and the IPtables and FirewallD firewalls. Key networking operations are also examined like IPv6 auto-configuration, TPC/IP networking, and network monitoring tools.

Part 5 provides a review of shell commands, including those used for managing files, as well as shell scripts, variables, and configuration files. The Ubuntu Server CD only installs a command line interface, with no desktop. To manage your system and its files you will need to know the shell commands.

Overview

Part 1: Getting Started

Part 2: Services

Part 3: Shared Resources

Part 4: Network Support

Part 5: Shells

Contents

Part 4: Network Support

Part 5: Shells

Part 1: Getting Started

Introduction

Installation

Usage Basics

Software Management

ubuntu

1. Introduction to Ubuntu Linux

Ubuntu releases
Ubuntu Editions
Ubuntu 15.04 Server Installation Options
Ubuntu 15.04
Ubuntu Software
Ubuntu Help and Documentation

Ubuntu Linux is currently one of the most popular end-user Linux distributions (**www.ubuntu.com**). Ubuntu Linux is managed by the Ubuntu foundation, which is sponsored by Canonical, Ltd (**www.canonical.com**), a commercial organization that supports and promotes open source projects. Ubuntu is based on Debian Linux, one of the oldest Linux distributions, which is dedicated to incorporating cutting-edge developments and features (**www.debian.org**). Mark Shuttleworth, a South African and Debian Linux developer, initiated the Ubuntu project. Debian Linux is primarily a Linux development project, trying out new features. Ubuntu provides a Debian-based Linux distribution that is stable, reliable, and easy to use.

Ubuntu is designed as a Linux operating system that can be used easily by everyone. The name Ubuntu means "humanity to others." As the Ubuntu project describes it: "Ubuntu is an African word meaning 'Humanity to others", or "I am what I am because of who we all are." The Ubuntu distribution brings the spirit of Ubuntu to the software world."

The official Ubuntu philosophy lists the following principles.

1. Every computer user should have the freedom to download, run, copy, distribute study, share, change, and improve their software for any purpose, without paying licensing fees.
2. Every computer user should be able to use their software in the language of their choice.
3. Every computer user should be given every opportunity to use software, even if they work under a disability.

The emphasis on language reflects Ubuntu's international scope. It is meant to be a global distribution that does not focus on any single market. Language support has been integrated into Linux in general by its internationalization projects, denoted by the term i18n. You can find information about il8n at **http://www.openi18n.org**.

Making software available to all users involves both full accessibility supports for users with disabilities, as well as seamless integration of software access using online repositories, making massive amounts of software available to all users at the touch of a button. Ubuntu also makes full use of Linux's automatic device detection ability, greatly simplifying installation as well as access to removable devices and attached storage.

Ubuntu aims to provide a fully supported and reliable, open source and free, easy to use and modify, Linux operating system. Ubuntu makes the following promises about its distribution.

Ubuntu will always be free of charge, including enterprise releases and security updates.

Ubuntu comes with full commercial support from Canonical and hundreds of companies around the world.

Ubuntu includes the very best translations and accessibility infrastructure that the free software community has to offer.

Ubuntu CDs and DVDs contain only free software applications; we encourage you to use free and open source software, improve it and pass it on (Ubuntu repositories contain some proprietary software like vendor graphics drivers that is also free).

Ubuntu provides both long-term and short-term support releases. Long-term support releases (LTS), such as Ubuntu 12.04, are released every two years. Short-term releases, such as 15.04, are provided every six months between the LTS versions. They are designed to make available the latest applications and support for the newest hardware. Each has its own nickname, like Vivid Vervet for the 15.04 release. The long-term support releases are supported for three years for desktops and five years for servers, whereas short-term support releases are supported for 18 months. In addition, Canonical provides limited commercial support for companies that purchase it.

Installing Ubuntu is easy to do. A core set of applications are installed, and you can add to them as you wish. Following installation, additional software can be downloaded from online repositories. There are only a few install screens, which move quickly through default partitioning, user setup, and time settings. Hardware components, such as graphics cards and network connections, are configured and detected automatically.

All Linux software for Ubuntu is currently available from online repositories. You can download applications for desktops, Internet servers, office suites, and programming packages, among others. Software packages are distributed primarily through the official Ubuntu repository. Downloads and updates are handled automatically by your desktop software manager and updater.

Ubuntu Server

Those who want to run Ubuntu as a server in order to provide an Internet service such as a Web site, would use the Ubuntu Server edition. The Ubuntu Server is a collection of Linux servers, like those for a Web or FTP site, as well as networking support like a DNS server. The Ubuntu Server CD will install the Ubuntu versions of the Linux servers, with a command line interface. Keeping just the command line interface provides significant efficiency gains for intensely used servers. The server edition also provides Cloud computer support. Ubuntu maintains its own site for the server edition at:

```
http://www.ubuntu.com/server/
```

You can download the Server edition from:

```
http://www.ubuntu.com/download/server/
```

The **http://releases.ubuntu.com** site holds Ubuntu Server CD download configuration files for BitTorrent, jigdo, and metalink downloads from multiple mirrors, and zsync files for synchronizing downloads.

For more detailed information on configuration and management check the Ubuntu Server Guide for Ubuntu 15.04 at:

```
https://help.ubuntu.com/stable/serverguide/index.html
```

The Server edition provides only a simple command line interface; it does not install the desktop. It is designed primarily to run servers. You could, however, just install the servers individually on a standard Ubuntu Desktop, and then install the optimized Ubuntu linux server kernel for use on the desktop. You do not have to install the Server edition to install and run servers.

Ubuntu 15.04 Server Installation Alternatives and Options

There are several ways to install the Ubuntu server software. It is recommended that you install using the Ubuntu Server CD. This release holds a version of the Linux kernel that has been optimized for use by servers. The Server CD though does not install a desktop. You are provided the command line interface only. The aim is to provide a streamlined and efficient server with as little overhead as possible. Desktops, with their X Windows System, include a lot of overhead.

One important drawback to the Server CD is that, without the desktop, you will not be able to use many of the desktop server configuration tools. These tools often provide a very effective and simple way to configure your servers. Ubuntu will perform basic automatic configuration designed for Ubuntu. With the just the command line interface, though, you will have to perform any additional configuration using the command line editors, working directly on the various server configuration files.

Server on the desktop installation

As an alternative you could install the Desktop DVD and then just install the server kernel and the server packages from the Ubuntu repository, instead of from the Server CD. All the servers are available on the Ubuntu repository, as well as the optimized server kernel.

The name of the server kernel meta package is:

```
linux-server
```

Once installed, an entry will be placed for it in the GRUB menu. Your desktop kernel will remain. You can choose to boot with either.

This configuration still starts up the X Windows System, involving much more overhead. You end up running much more software than the servers actually need to use.

If you are running servers for a small or home network, the overhead involved with the desktop is not significant. Most likely your servers will be lightly used. At the same time the additional support provided by the desktop server configuration tools would be extremely helpful.

Desktop on the Server installation

You could install the Server CD and then later install the Ubuntu desktop from the Ubuntu repository. This would provide you with the optimized server kernel, and still give you desktop support. You can install either the complete Ubuntu desktop or just the minimal GNOME desktop interface.

Minimal GNOME desktop

If you want to install just a minimal GNOME desktop, you would install the GNOME core, xauth, and xorg (X server) package. The following command will install the core GNOME desktop, GNOME without few added applications. Be sure to update your package listing first. It is recommended, though, that you install the Ubuntu desktop instead, for greater compatibility.

```
sudo apt-get update
sudo apt-get install gnome-core xauth xorg
```

The gnome-core package is now dependent on the GNOME GDM Display Manager (**lightdm** package), which it will install, running the X server. The initial default desktop will be Ubuntu, which is not installed, so change the desktop to GNOME in the login window.

Other than the GNOME preference tools and the text editor, no additional software is installed, including administrative tools. You may want to install the Synaptic Package Manager (software management), the GNOME terminal, GNOME system tools (user and time management), gnome-utils (log viewer), the GNOME disk utility, and the update manager as shown here.

```
sudo apt-get install synaptic gnome-terminal gnome-system-tools gnome-utils
gnome-disk-utility update-manager
```

In addition, there are several administrative tools you may want, like system-config-printer-gnome, system-config-samba, and gnome-nettool.

```
sudo apt-get install system-config-printer-gnome system-config-samba gnome-nettool
```

The basic GNOME theme is installed. If you want to use the Ubuntu Ambiance or Radiance themes, install the **light-themes** package, and then open Applications | System Tools | System Settings, Appearance, and choose the Themes tab to change to the Ubuntu Ambiance or Radiance themes.

```
sudo apt-get install light-themes
```

Should you want to use the Hardware drivers, you can install **jockey-gtk**. For a Web browser you can install the **firefox** or **epiphany-browser** packages.

```
sudo apt-get install firefox
```

ubuntu-desktop

For desktop features, it is recommended that you install the entire Ubuntu desktop. The Ubuntu desktop will install the complete set of desktop packages, including multimedia and graphics packages, which you may have no use for on your server. The added packages do not degrade the server; they just take up additional disk space (about 1 GB or more). At the same time, the Ubuntu desktop also installs all the administrative packages you may want to use, like the Synaptic Package Manager, Network Manager, User and Group management, and the Update manager.

You install the Ubuntu desktop using the **ubuntu-desktop** meta-package and the **tasksel** software management tool (you could also use **apt-get**). Run **tasksel** with the **sudo** command and then use the arrow keys to move to the Ubuntu Desktop entry and press the spacebar. Then tab to the OK button and press ENTER.

```
sudo tasksel
```

You also could use **apt-get** with the **ubuntu-desktop** meta-package, as shown here.

```
sudo apt-get install ubuntu-desktop
```

Download and setup can take an hour or more. You then logout and restart your system. The LightDM will start up as shown in Figure 3-2.

Note: You could also perform installations of the KDE or XFCE desktops, using either of them instead of GNOME. For XFCE install **xfce4** with **xauth** and **xorg**. For a minimal KDE desktop, install the **kdebase** package with **xauth** and **xorg**. For the complete KDE desktop, including the KDM login screen, install the **kubuntu-desktop** package.

Server install options

To recap, your options are:

Server cd only with server optimized kernel, but using the command line interface alone. No support or access to server desktop configuration tools.

Server cd first, giving you the server optimized kernel, and then installing the minimal GNOME desktop from the Ubuntu repository (**gnome-core**, **xauth**, **xorg**), which installs the GDM display manager. Install added packages you may want, like **gnome-utils**, **gnome-system-tools**, **gnome-nettool**, and **light-themes**.

Server cd first, giving you the server optimized kernel, and then installing the Ubuntu Desktop from the Ubuntu repository (**ubuntu-desktop**). Will implement automatic X Window System startup for LightDM.

Desktop DVD first, and then install server kernel (**linux-server**) and server packages from the Ubuntu repository using Synaptic Package Manager. You will always have the X Window System running as additional overhead. But, you can use server desktop configuration tools and desktop editors. Efficiency degradation would be minor for a small or home network.

Choose the option that works best for you. Keep in mind that you do not need the Server cd to run servers. All the servers on the Server cd are available on the Ubuntu repository and can be run from any desktop install. What you would lose is the optimized server kernel, which is not needed for small or home networks, or which you can install and use later.

Also, unless you are performing a professional install or are comfortable with editing configuration files directly, you should not underestimate the help that server desktop configuration tools can provide. There are very good tools for local network servers like NFS, CUPS, and Samba. There are few for Internet servers like Apache and FTP, and most of these are too simple with few options. For most heavy duty Internet servers, direct editing of server configuration files will be required.

Ubuntu 15.04 Features

Check the Ubuntu Release Notes for an explanation of changes. For the Ubuntu server, there are key changes to the Apache Web server.

`https://wiki.ubuntu.com/VividVervet/ReleaseNotes`

Ubuntu 15.04 Server includes the following features.

There are key changes to the configuration directories and files for the Apache 2.4 Web server.

systemd replaces SysVinit and Upstart as the system and session manager. systemd uses unit file located in the **/lib/systemd/system** and **/etc/systemd/system** directories to manage services, filesystems, and device.

Some sevices, such as Apache, still install SysV init scripts in the **/etc/init.d** directory. These are used to generate systemd files automatically, which are placed in the **/run/system/generator.late** directory.

Ubuntu 15.04 server images are available on the Amazon EC2 cloud, and are listed on the Ubuntu Cloud Images site at: **http://cloud-images.ubuntu.com**. A Web browser is required.

Ubuntu 15.04 server images are available for use on the Ubuntu OpenStack and the Amazon EC2 cloud: **http://www.ubuntu.com/ cloud** and **https://help.ubuntu.com/community/EC2StartersGuide**.

Metal as a Service (MAAS) allows you to deploy, manage, log, and monitor multiple services. It is designed for use on enterprise data centers, and installs provisioning,

Security features: see **https://wiki.ubuntu.com/Security/Features** for documentation, including topics like AppArmor, firewalls, filesystem encryption, and hardware security (hardening).

Managing Systems with Landscape

Landscape is Ubuntu's administration and monitoring management service accessed through a hosted Web interface. You can register online with Ubuntu for the Landscape service. With Landscape you can administer, monitor, and maintain machines on your network, as well as install and update hosts software. You can find out more about Landscape at:

`http://www.ubuntu.com/management`

Machines can be organized into groups, letting you install packages on different groups. Your custom repository can be accessed directly with Landscape, using it to install software on your machines. You can also manage users and servers, adding and removing users, as well as starting and stopping servers.

Landscape also installs its own monitoring application on each machine, providing reports on usage, hardware status, and performance. You can also manage processes, detecting those that use the most resources.

In addition, Landscape supports cloud computing, letting you manage instances of a system on a cloud as you would machines on your network. Landscape can manage Ubuntu instances on the Amazon EC2 cloud and on the Ubuntu Cloud Infrastructure.

Ubuntu Linux Help and Documentation

A great deal of help and documentation is available online for Ubuntu, ranging from detailed install procedures to beginner questions (see Table 1-1). The documentation for Ubuntu 15.04 is located at **https://help.ubuntu.com/15.04/**. This site includes the Ubuntu Server Guide. The Firefox Web browser start page displays links for two major help sites: Ubuntu documentation at **https://help.ubuntu.com** and Ubuntu Community at **http://community.ubuntu.com**. For answers to commonly asked questions check **http://askubuntu.com/**. It provides detailed answers to many technical issues.

For detailed online support use the Ubuntu forums at **http://ubuntuforums.org**. In addition, there are blog and news sites as well as the standard Linux documentation. Ubuntu Community features Ubuntu documentation, support, blogs, and news. A Contribute section links to sites where you can contribute to development, artwork, documentation, and support.

For mailing lists, check **https://lists.ubuntu.com**. There are lists for categories like Ubuntu announcements, community support for specific editions, and development for areas like the desktop, servers, or mobile implementation. For more specialized tasks like Samba support and LAMP server installation, check **http://www.ubuntugeek.com**.

Site	Description
https://help.ubuntu.com	Help for the desktop, server, and installation
http://packages.ubuntu.com	Ubuntu software package list and search
http://ubuntuforums.org	Ubuntu forums
http:/askubuntu.com/	Answers to commonly asked questions
http://www.tldp.org	Linux Documentation Project Web site
http://community.ubuntu.com/	Links to Documentation, Support, News, and Blogs
https://lists.ubuntu.com	Ubuntu mailing lists

Table 1-1: Ubuntu help and documentation

help.ubuntu.com

Ubuntu-specific documentation is available at **https://help.ubuntu.com**. Here on listed links you can find specific documentation for different releases. Always check the release help page first for documentation, though it may be sparse and cover mainly changed areas. The Ubuntu LTS release usually includes desktop, installation, and server guides. For 15.04 the Documentation section provides the Ubuntu Desktop Guide (Ubuntu Desktop Help) and the Ubuntu Server Guide.

One of the more helpful pages is the Community Contributed Documentation page, **https://help.ubuntu.com/community**. Here you will find detailed documentation on installation of Ubuntu releases, using the desktop, installing software, and configuring devices. Always check the page for your Ubuntu release first.

ubuntuforums.org

Ubuntu forums provide detailed online support and discussion for users (**http://ubuntuforums.org**). An Absolute Beginner section provides an area where new users can obtain answers to questions. Sticky threads include both quick and complete guides to installation for the current Ubuntu release. You can use the search feature to find discussions on your topic of interest. The main support categories section covers specific support areas like networking, multimedia, laptops, security, and 64-bit support.

Other community discussions cover ongoing work such as virtualization, art and design, gaming, education and science, Wine, assistive technology, and the Ubuntu cloud. Here you will also find community announcements and news.

The forum community discussion is where you can talk about anything else. The **http://ubuntuforums.org/** site also provides a gallery page for posted screenshots as well as RSS feeds for specific forums.

Linux documentation

The Linux Documentation Project (LDP) has developed a complete set of Linux manuals. The documentation is available at the LDP home site at **http://www.tldp.org**. The Linux documentation for your installed software will be available at your **/usr/share/doc** directory.

ubuntu®

2. Installing the Ubuntu Server

Installing Ubuntu Linux has become a very simple procedure with just a few screens with default entries for easy installation. A pre-selected collection of software is already installed. Most of your devices, like your monitor and network connection, are detected automatically. The most difficult part would be a manual partitioning of the hard drive, but you can use a Guided partitioning for installs that use an entire hard disk, as is usually the case.

For Server specific installation details be sure to check the Ubuntu Server Guide Installation section at:

```
https://help.ubuntu.com/stable/serverguide/installation.html
```

For very detailed key installation topics, from obtaining the CD to starting up the system for the first time, as well as appendices on partitioning and automatic installs, check the Ubuntu Installation Guide/Installing Ubuntu 15.04 (Ubuntu documentation | Ubuntu 15.04 | Installing Ubuntu) at:

```
https://help.ubuntu.com/15.04/installation-guide/index.html
```

The Ubuntu Server CD uses a text-based interface. This particular guide does not take you through the steps. Instead, it details key installation topics like booting the install disk and preparing your hard disk.

The basic install procedures are covered in this chapter, though you should consult the Server install and Installation guide for more detailed information.

Upgrading

You can upgrade directly from the Ubuntu 15.04 release. First, install the **update-manager-core** package, if not installed already. Then edit the **/etc/update-manager/release-upgrades** file and modify the Prompt option.

```
sudo nano /etc/update-manager/release-upgrades
```

Set the Prompt option to normal.

```
Prompt = normal
```

Then run the **do-release-upgrade** command with the **-d** option. This operation will perform any needed system configuration changes.

```
sudo do-release-upgrade -d
```

Ubuntu Server CD

The Ubuntu server CD is designed for hardware servers, systems that will run only servers and not perform any other tasks like desktop applications. The Ubuntu desktops are not installed. You will be presented with just a command line interface and command line tools like the nano editor to manage your server configuration. You will have to know how to edit server configuration files manually, typing in your entries.

Server software, though, does not have to be installed from the Server CD. You can directly download and install any server from the Ubuntu repository. Should you wish, you can install the Ubuntu desktop and then use GNOME based desktop tools like Synaptic Package Manager of the Ubuntu Software Center to install the servers you want. You can also use desktop server configuration tools to manage your servers. These are not available on a direct Server CD install.

The downside of installing from the desktop is that you incur the overhead of running the desktop interface, namely GNOME. Most commercial and professional enterprise servers are time-critical, managing a massive number of transactions. A desktop interface can seriously degrade performance. However, for a simple home or local server, which would have relatively few transactions, the desktop would incur little or no overhead. It would also make managing your server much easier.

Getting the Install Server CD

You can download the Ubuntu Server CD from:

`http://www.ubuntu.com/download/server`

You can also download the Ubuntu Server CD directly from:

`http://releases.ubuntu.com/vivid/`

The Ubuntu Server CD has both 32 and 64-bit versions. If you want to use the 64-bit version, be sure you have a CPU that is 64-bit compatible (as are most current CPUs). The 64-bit version is faster.

The Ubuntu DVD includes both desktop and server applications. You can download it from:

`http://cdimages.ubuntu.com/releases/vivid/release/`

You can download the Server CD directly, or by using the BitTorrent, Jigdo, Metalinks, or Zsync download methods. The Server CD download files for these methods are located at:

`http://releases.ubuntu.com/vivid/`

For BitTorrent use a BitTorrent client such as transmission or ktorrent.

See the Jigdo Download HowTo page at **http://help.ubuntu.com** for details on using Jigdo.

`https://help.ubuntu.com/community/JigdoDownloadHowto`

For information about using metalink with Ubuntu see:

`https://wiki.ubuntu.com/MetalinkIsoDownloads`

Installing Ubuntu from the Server CD

The server install CD includes all the servers available for use on Linux. These include the Samba Windows network server, mail servers, and DNS servers. All these are also included with the Install DVD. The Server CD is designed for stripped down servers that are used to just run servers, not provide any desktop support. In fact, the GNOME and KDE desktops are not included or installed with the Server CD. This is a very specialized server installation.

The Server CD uses a text based install interface, with TABs, spacebar, and arrow keys used to make selections. Before the software is installed, a Software selection screen is displayed which lets you select the servers you want to install. Use the arrow keys to move to a selection, and the spacebar to make a selection.

When you start up a server installation, you will be using the command line interface. The desktop is not installed. Desktops are considered unnecessary overhead for a server. The user enters a user name at the Ubuntu login prompt, followed by the password at the password prompt.

Installing Linux involves several processes, beginning with creating Linux partitions, and then loading the Linux software, selecting a time zone, and creating new user accounts. The installation program used on Ubuntu is a screen-based program that takes you through all these processes, step-by-step, as one continuous procedure. You can use the keyboard to make selections. You can also use TAB, the arrow keys, SPACEBAR, and ENTER to make selections. The TAB key moves you to the GO Back and Continue buttons at the bottom of the screen.

When you finish with a screen, either press ENTER or tab to the Continue button at the bottom, and then press ENTER to move to the next screen. If you need to move back to the previous screen, tab to the Go Back button and press ENTER. You have little to do other than make selections and choose options.

Tip: To boot from a CD-ROM or DVD-ROM, you may first have to change the boot sequence setting in your computer's BIOS so that the computer will try to boot first from the CD-ROM. This requires some technical ability and knowledge of how to set your motherboard's BIOS configuration.

Installation Overview

Installation is a straightforward process. A screen-based installation is very easy to use.

Most systems today already meet hardware requirements and have automatic connections to the Internet (DHCP).

They also support booting a DVD-ROM or CD-ROM disc, though this support may have to be explicitly configured in the system BIOS.

Also, if you know how you want Linux installed on your hard disk partitions, or if you are performing a simple update that uses the same partitions, installing Ubuntu is a fairly simple process. Ubuntu features an automatic partitioning function that will perform the partitioning for you.

A preconfigured set of packages are installed, along with the servers you want installed.

For a quick installation you can simply start up the installation process, by placing your Server CD disc in your optical drive and starting up your system. Installation is a simple matter of following the instructions in each window as you progress. Installation follows seven easy steps:

1. **Language Selection** A default is chosen for you, like English, so you can usually just press ENTER.
2. **Location** Choose your country
3. **Keyboard Layout** You can choose to automatically detect the layout by pressing some keys, or choose one from a list, first by country and then by type. A default is chosen for you; you can usually press ENTER.

4. **Network Detection**. Automatic DHCP configuration or manual configuration. You will be prompted to enter a host name.
5. **Time Zone** Select your time zone.
6. **User name** Set up a user name for your computer, as well as a password for that user.
7. **Prepare partitions** Disks are scanned and the partitioner starts up. For automatic partitioning you have the option of using a Guided partition, which will set up your partitions for you. You can choose to use LVM or LVM encrypted file systems. You have the option to perform manual partitioning, setting up partitions yourself.
8. The base system is then installed.
9. **Select server software** Choose the server packages you want installed. LAMP includes the Apache Web server and the MySQL database server.
10. **Finish the Installation** After the install, you will be asked to remove your DVD/CD-ROM. You then press ENTER.

Starting the Installation Program

If your computer can boot from the DVD/CD-ROM, you can start the installation directly from the CD-ROMs or the DVD-ROM. Just place the CD-ROM in the CD-ROM drive, or the DVD-ROM in the DVD drive, before you start your computer. After you turn on or restart your computer, the installation program will start up.

The Ubuntu Server CD is designed for installing the server. The installation program will present you with a menu listing the following options (see Figure 2-1):

```
Install Ubuntu Server
Multiple server install with MAAS
Check disc for defects
Test memory
Boot from first hard disk
Rescue broken system
```

"Install Ubuntu Server" will start the installation (see the next section).

"Multiple server install with MAAS" enlists a server with a Metal on a Service (MAAS), which can be used to manage the server. See **https://wiki.ubuntu.com/ServerTeam/MAAS**. Provides cloud support of networked servers.

"Check disc for defects" will check if your CD burn was faulty.

"Test Memory" will check your memory.

"Boot from first hard disk" will let your CD work as boot loader, starting up an operating system on the first hard disk, if one is installed. Use it to boot a system that the boot loader is not accessing for some reason.

"Rescue a broken system" will start Ubuntu and let you mount a broken system. You can then make changes to the system configuration.

Figure 2-1: Install disk start menu for Server CD

Along the bottom of the screen are options you can set for the installation process. These are accessible with the function keys, 1 through 6.

```
F1 Help F2 Language F3 Keymap F4 Vga F5 Accessibility F6 Other Options
```

A description of these options is listed here:

Help Boot parameters and install prerequisites

Languages List of languages, popup menu

Keymap Languages for keyboard, popup menu

Modes Lists possible install modes: Normal.

Accessibility Contrast setting, Magnifier, On screen keyboard, and Braille support

Other options, Opens an editable text line listing the options of the current selected menu choice. You can add other options here, or modify or remove existing ones. The menu lists several specialized options like Expert mode, acpi=off, noapic, nolapic, edd=on, nodmraid (no hardware RAID), nomodeset, and Free Software only. Press ESC to activate to the main menu. The Expert mode will provide more detailed control over your installation.

Use the arrow keys to move from one menu entry to another, and then press ENTER to select the entry. Should you need to add options, press the F6 key A command line is displayed where you can enter the options. Current options will already be listed. Use the backspace key to delete and arrow keys to move through the line. Press the ESC key to return to the menu.

Starting the Ubuntu Installation

Your system then detects your hardware, providing any configuration specifications that may be needed. For example, if you have an IDE CD-RW or DVD-RW drive, it will be configured automatically.

Keys	Action
TAB	Move to Continue, OK, Yes, No, and Go Back buttons
ENTER	Execute a selected button
Arrow, up and down	Move to selections on a menu
Arrow, left and right	Move between Go Back and Continue buttons on some screens
PageUp and PageDown	Move through listings a page at a time

Table 2-1: Installation Keys

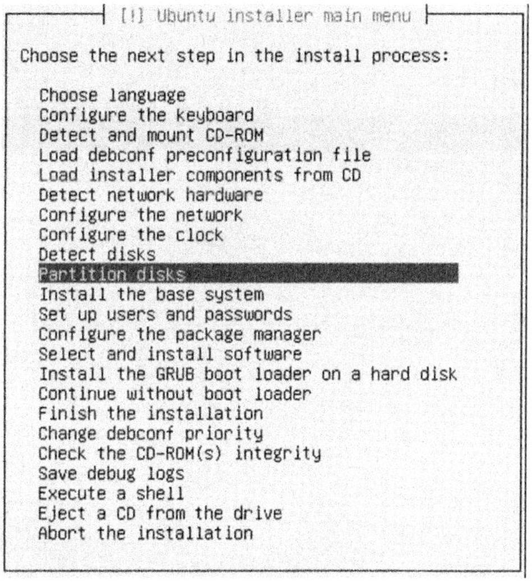

Figure 2-2: Installer main menu

As each screen appears in the installation, default entries will be already selected, usually by the auto-probing capability of the installation program. Selected entries will appear highlighted. If these entries are correct, you can simply press ENTER to accept them and go on to the next screen. Some screens will display a Continue button. Use the Tab key to move to that button. Many screens will also have a Go Back button. The Tab key will cycle through to the Continue and Go Back buttons. On some screens you can also use the arrow keys to move between the Go Back and Continue buttons. The install keys are listed in Table 2-1.

At any time during the install process, you can Tab to the Go Back key and press ENTER to display the "Ubuntu installer main menu" listing a complete set of install tasks (see Figure 2-2). This menu will include added tasks like installing the Grub boot loader.

Language and Keyboard

First, you select your Language (see Figure 2-3). Use the up/down arrow keys and PageUp/PageDown keys to move through the list. Press the ENTER key when you have reached your selection. The detected default will already be selected. If correct, just press ENTER.

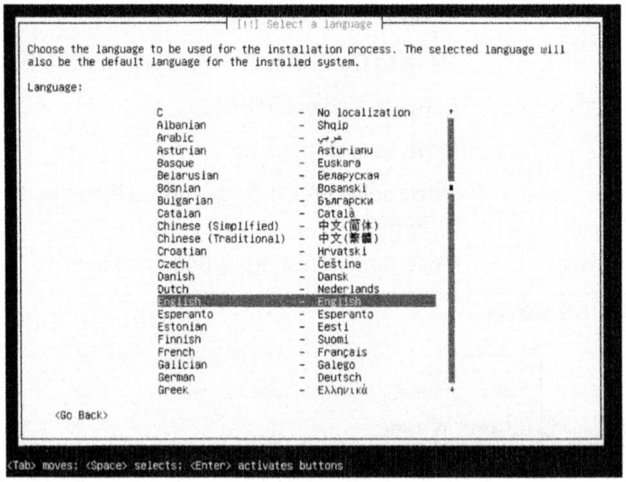

Figure 2-3: Language

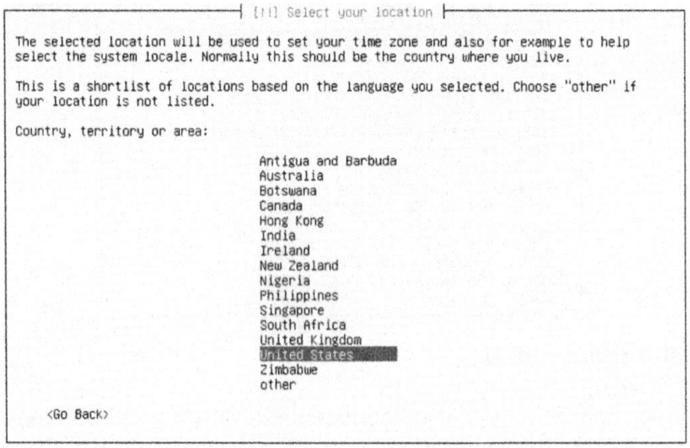

Figure 2-4: location

Then, select your location, country or region (see Figure 2-4). Use up/down arrow keys to move to a selection. Press the ENTER key to make your selection and move on to the next screen.

You will then be asked to select a keyboard. First you are asked if you want to detect it automatically by typing keys. The default response is NO and you can press ENTER to move to a manual selection screen. The default keyboard will be selected already, such as U.S. English (see Figure 2-5).

If there is more than one keyboard layout for your region, another screen lists them and you are prompted to select one. The USA keyboard will have several keyboard selections such as Macintosh, Dvorak, or International, as well as the standard. Your hardware is then detected.

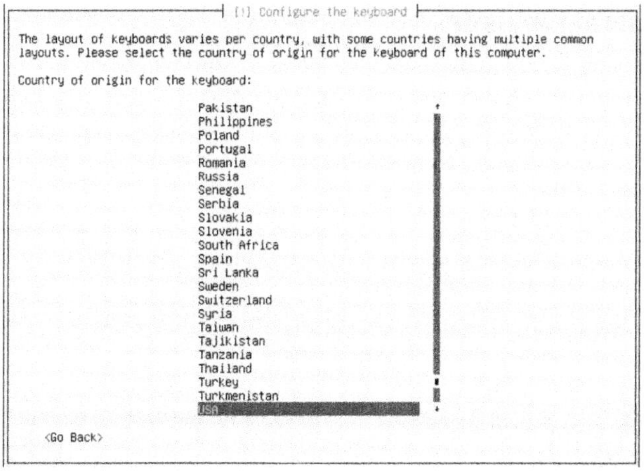

Figure 2-5: Keyboard Layout

Network Configuration and Cobbler

You then configure your network interface. If you have multiple hardware network connections, you are asked to choose one (usually the Ethernet connection, eth0). If you are using a DCHP server to configure your network information, you will be prompted just to enter a host name for your server (see Figure 2-6).

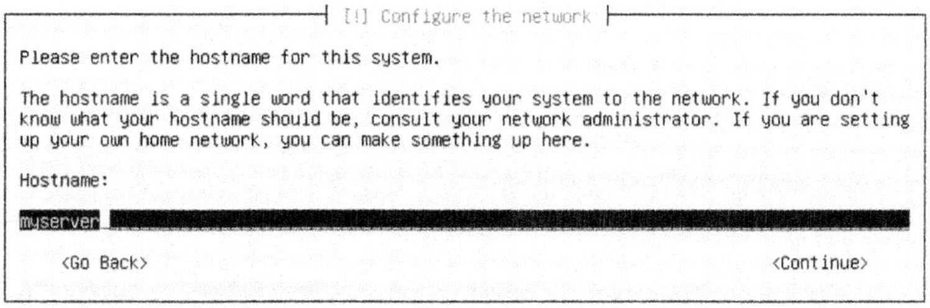

Figure 2-6: Network Configuration

If you are using a fixed IP address for your server, select Go Back and select the "Configure network manually" entry to configure your network information manually. Screens that follow prompt for:

IP address for the server

Your network netmask

IP address for the network gateway (address for router connected to the Internet)

IP addresses for the name servers (DNS servers)

Your server's host name

If you choose to install using the "Multiple server install with MAAS ", you will be prompted to enter the connection and access information for your MAAS server.

Create administrative user

On the following screens you will enter the user's full name, the user login name and that user's password (see Figures 2-7, 2-8, and 2-9). The user you are creating will have administrative access, allowing you to change your system configuration, add new users and printers, and install new software. You are also asked if you want to encrypt your home directory, adding a further level of security (see Figure 2-10).

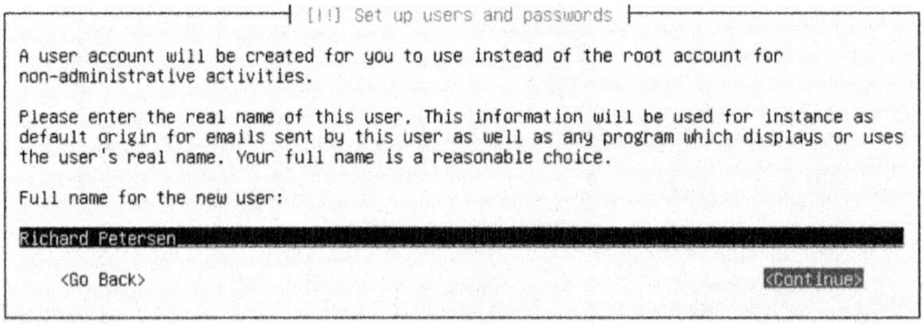

Figure 2-7: create user

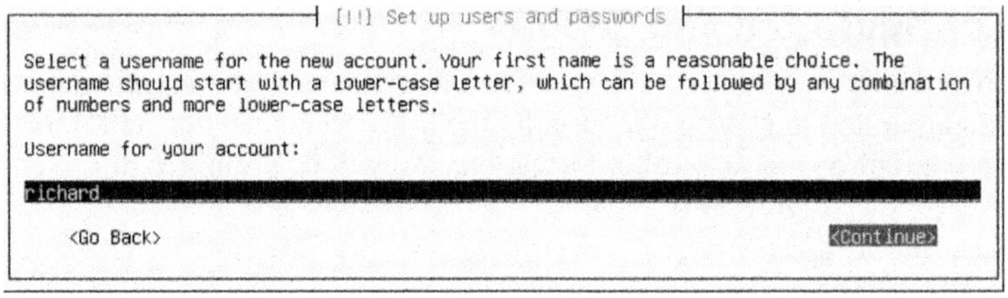

Figure 2-8: create user name

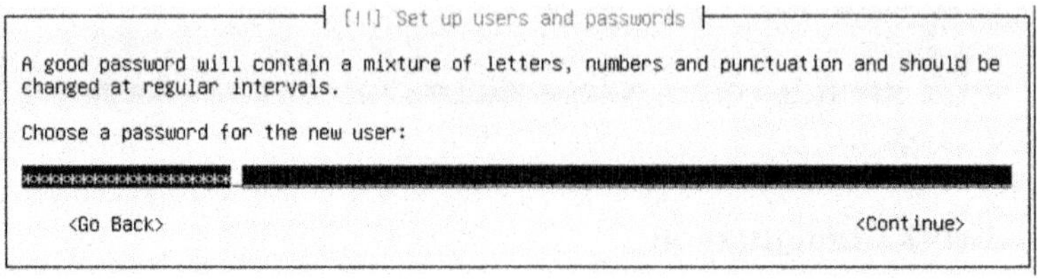

Figure 2-9: create user password

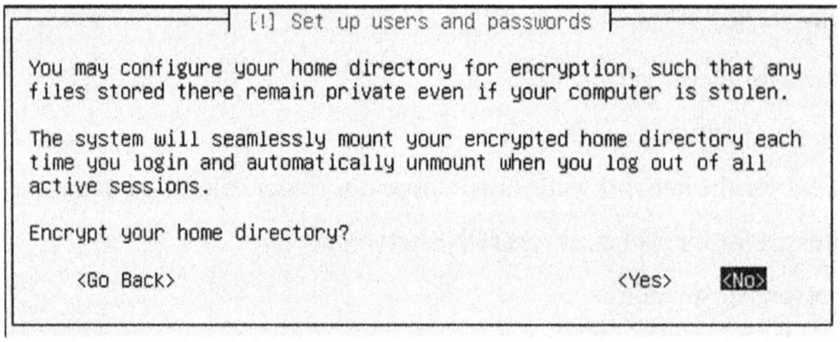

Figure 2-10: Encrypted private directory

Time Zone

You then choose your time zone (see Figure 2-11). The time zone is detected from the network time server, and you are prompted to confirm. If it is not correct, you can choose No to select from a list of time zones.

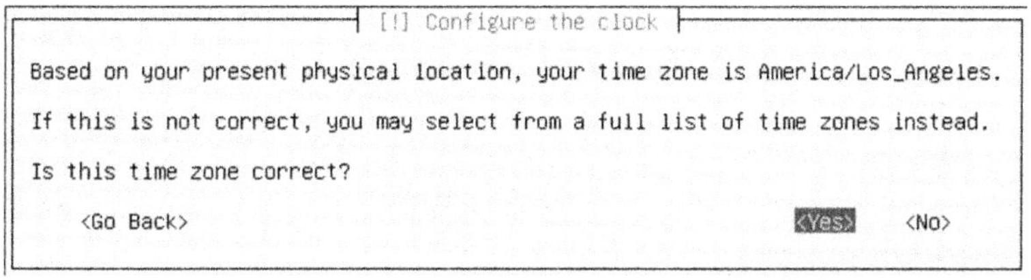

Figure 2-11: Time Zone

Partitions

Then you are asked to designate the Linux partitions and hard disk configurations you want to use on your hard drives. For LVM partitions, an LVM Group has to be set up before you can configure any partitions. This means that the partition table is written to before you configure your partitions. This action cannot be reversed. This is true for both Guided LVM and manual LVM partitioning.

If you are setting up standard partitions manually, instead of LVM partitions, partitions will be changed or formatted at the end of the partitioning process. At the end of the partitioning procedure, you will be asked explicitly to write the partition changes to your disk. You can opt out of the installation at any time until that point, and your original partitions will remain untouched.

The partition options will change according to the number of hard disks on your system. If you have several hard disks, they will be listed. You can also select the disk on which to install Ubuntu.

Guided Partitioning with LVM

Ubuntu provides automatic partitioning options if you just want to use available drives and free space for your Linux system. LVM, RAID, and encrypted file systems are supported.

The Ubuntu Server provides guided options, setting up default configurations for an entire disk. You will have to have an entire blank disk free for use for your Ubuntu server (see Figure 2-12). Each is preceded with the term Guided. These are:

Guided - use the entire disk

Guided - use the entire disk and set up LVM

Guided - use the entire disk and set up encrypted LVM.

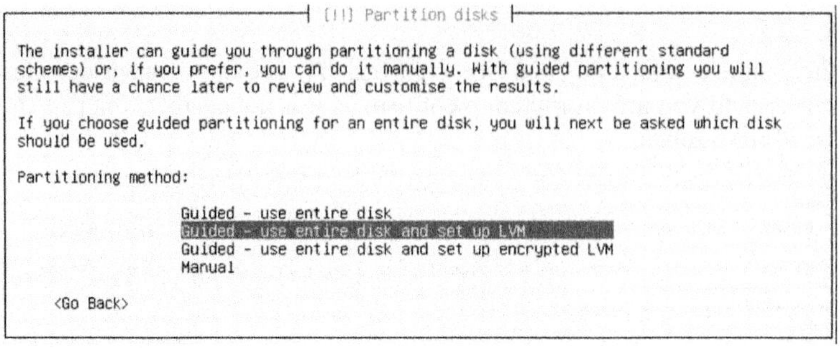

Figure 2-12: Partition options

If your disk is already partitioned, and the partitions have significant unused space, another option is displayed that allows you to resize the disk. The partition to be resized will be listed, usually the last partition. Be warned that resizing can take a very long time.

Guided - resize SCSI1 (0,0,0), partition #5 (sda) and use freed space

If you already have a Linux partition set up on your hard disk, and want to overwrite that existing Linux partition, an option is displayed that allows you to reuse that partition.

Guided - reuse partition SCSI1 (0,0,0), partition #5 (sda)

If you disk has a large amount of continuous unused (free) space, you are given the option to use it.

Guided - use the largest continuous free space

Windows and Linux **/home** partitions will **not** be overwritten in a Guided partition. The Guided option, though, requires free space on your hard disk on which to install your system.

If you are not sure exactly how your partitions will be formatted, and you have several partitions on your system that you want to preserve, you may want to select the Manual option so you can choose the specific partitions you want to use, designating them for formatting and installation.

If you selected a Guided option, you are then asked to select the disk to set up the partitions on (see Figure 2-13).

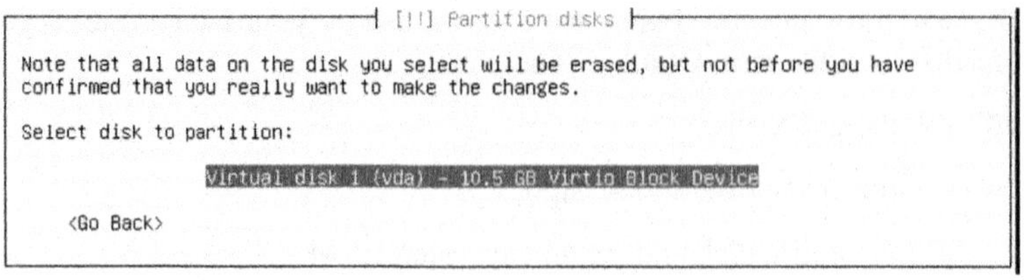

Figure 2-13: Selecting hard disk for partitioning

The default Guided partitioning will set up two partitions, one as the **swap** partition and an **ext4** partition for the entire file system (/).

A default LVM partitioning will set up an **ext2** file system for the boot directory, and then an LVM file system (Group) with two LVM volumes, one for the swap partition and one for the root (the Ubuntu system except for the **boot** directory).

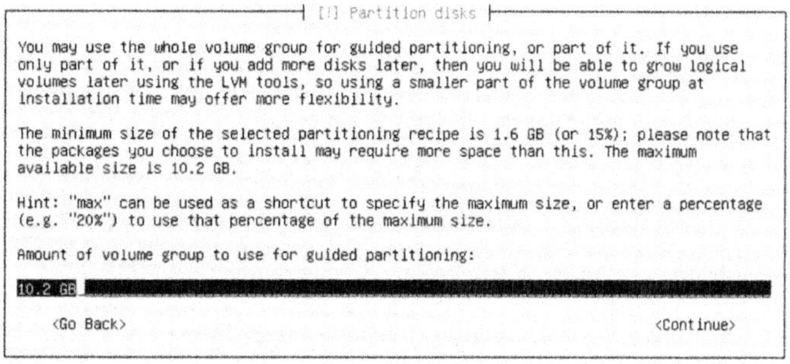

Figure 2-14: LVM partition size

Encrypted LVM will add a further prompt for the password for your encrypted file systems. Your LVM root and swap files systems will be encrypted, but not your boot file systems. Whenever your systems boots up, you will be prompted to enter the passphrase for your encrypted file systems. Encryption adds a further level of security, especially for publicly accessed file systems like those used for servers. The effect on performance is negligible.

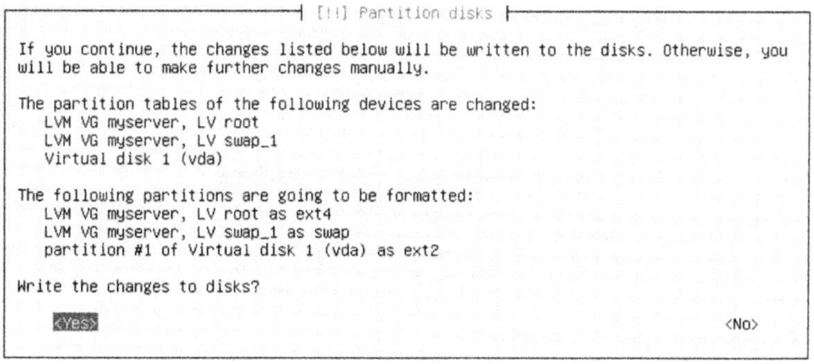

Figure 2-15: Creating partitions

With LVM Guided partitions, you also will be given the option to set the size for your overall partition use. This option is designed to let you leave free space on a large hard drive. This allows you to use that space for partitions that you can later add to the LVM group, expanding your space as needed. The default size will be set to use the entire hard disk (see Figure 2-14).

Before the partitions are created, the partition configuration is displayed and you are prompted to accept them. This is your last chance to back out of the partitioning (see Figure 2-15). The No button will be selected by default. If the listed changes are correct, tab to the Yes button and press ENTER to make your changes.

Tip: If you already have a Linux system, you will most likely have several Linux partitions already. Some of these may be used for just the system software, such as the boot and root partitions. These should be formatted. Others may have extensive user files, such as a **/home** partition that normally holds user home directories and all the files they have created. You should *not* format such partitions.

Manual Partitioning

To manually configure your hard drive, first plan what partitions you want to set up and what their size should be. You can set up different partitions for any directory on your system. Many systems set up separate partitions for **/home**, **/var**, **/srv**, as well as / (root) and **/boot**. You will, of course, need a swap partition.

/var directory holds data that constantly changes like printer spool files.

/srv directory holds server data, like Web server pages and FTP sites

/home directory holds users files along with any user data.

/ the root directory is the system directory. All other file systems and partitions attach to it.

/boot the boot directory holds the Linux kernel and the boot configuration. You will need a separate boot partition if you are using LVM partitions for your root partition. The boot directory cannot be on an LVM partition.

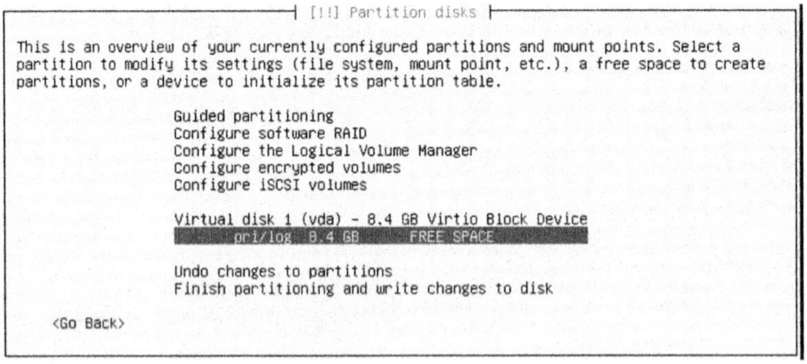

Figure 2-16: Selecting disk to partition

Except for the boot partition, all of these can be LVM volumes. LVM volumes may work better than ordinary ext4 partitions, since you can expand or replace them easily. With a standard ext4 partition you are limited to the size you specify when you first set up your partition. The following example sets up two basic partitions, one swap partition and another for the root system. First you select the disk on which to create the partition (see Figure 2-16).

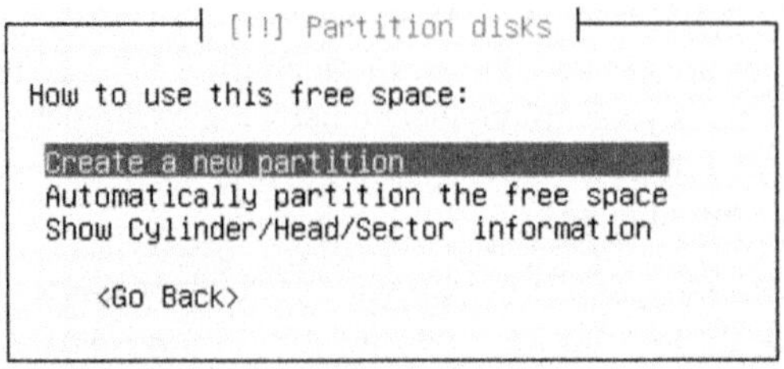

Figure 2-17: Choosing to create a partition

Then you choose the method of partitioning. You can create a partition manually, or just automatically partition the free space (see Figure 2-17).

Upon choosing to create a new partition, you are prompted to enter the size. The remaining free space will be selected by default. Specify the size of the partition in either MB or GB. The term max will use all remaining free space. Then choose whether it should be primary or logical, and then at the end or beginning of the disk. (see Figure 2-18).

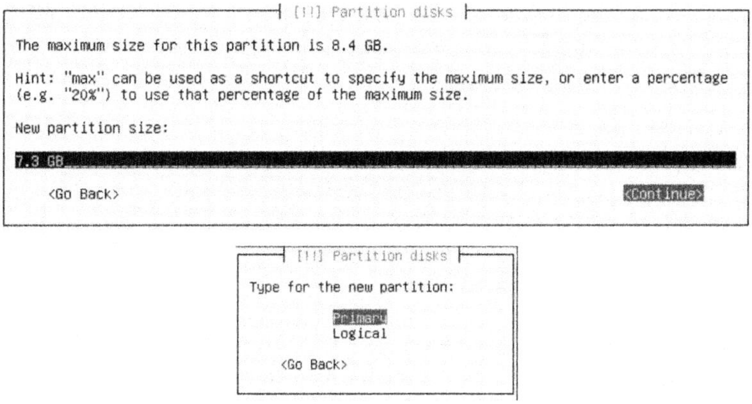

Figure 2-18: Selecting the partition size

On the partition settings screen you will specify the mount point, file system type (Use as), and the label. Pressing the ENTER key on the Use as entry will display a dialog listing file system types from which to choose. A standard Linux partition would use ext4, a swap partition would use swap area, and an LVM partition would use "Physical volume for LVM".

In Figure 2-19, a root system partition is set up. The type is ext4, mount point is the root, /, and the label is minute.

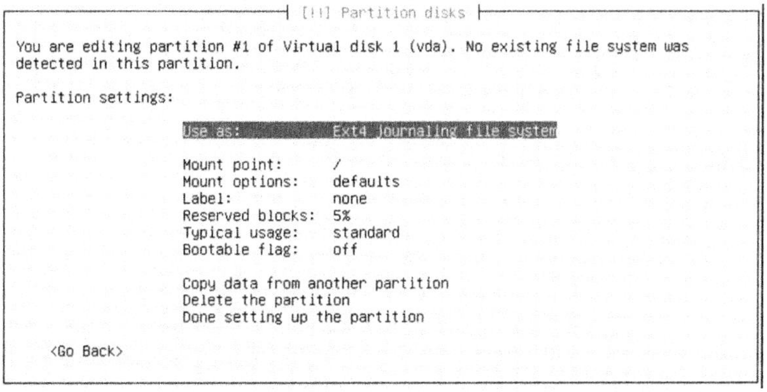

Figure 2-19: Partition configuration

Note: With manual partitioning you can also set up software RAID devices. First create RAID partitions, then on the Partition Disks page an entry will be listed to Configure RAID devices. Choose this entry and then create an MD drive, selecting the RAID partitions to use for the drive, as well as the RAID type.

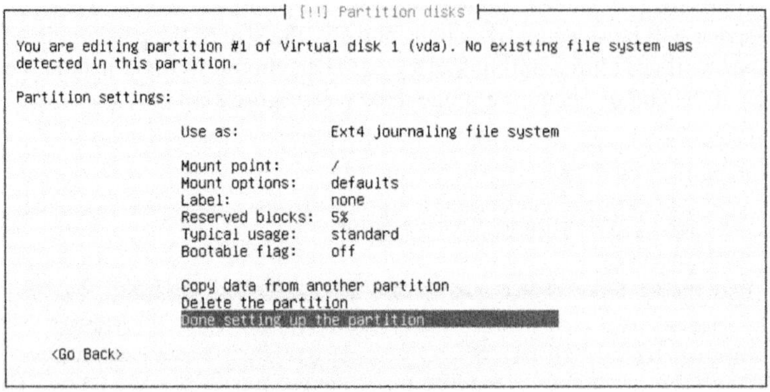

Figure 2-20: Manually created partitions

If you are setting up an LVM partition, select "physical volume for LVM" for the Use as option. The Partitions disk screen will then have an added entry for "Configure the Logical Volume Manager." Choose this to set up your volume group and its logical volumes. You are first prompted to create a volume group, specifying its device and a label. Then create the logical volumes (Create a logical volume). Enter a label and the size for each. You then return to the partitioner, which will list all your logical volumes. Select and press enter on each to then select a file system type and mount point (a swap partition will not have a mount point).

For the mount point, a dialog will list common mount points, like / for the root file system, **/home** for users, and **/boot** for a boot partition.

When you are ready, move to the last option and press ENTER, "Done setting up the partition."

When finished, your partitions will be displayed under your disk entry (see Figure 2-20). To actually create the partitions, move to the last entry and press ENTER, "Finish partitioning and write changes to disk." A dialog is displayed showing the partitions that will be formatted, similar to Figure 2-15. Tab to the Yes button and press ENTER to make your partition changes.

Reuse existing Linux partitions on a hard drive

If you already have a hard drive with Linux partitions that you want to reuse, choose the "Manual" option on the "Partition disks" screen. In this case, you have a hard disk you are already using for Linux, with partitions already set up on the hard drive for your Ubuntu systems. However, you do not want to keep any of the data on those partitions. In effect, you just want to reuse those partitions for the new release, creating an entirely new install, but with the old partitions. With this action, all current data on those partitions will be destroyed. This procedure avoids having to change the partition table on the hard drive. You just keep the partitions you already have. In this case, you wish to overwrite existing partitions, erasing all the data on them.

This procedure is used often for users that have already backed up their data, and just want to create a fresh install on their hard disk with the new release. Also, a Linux system could be configured to save data on a partition separate from the root partition, like a separate partition for the **/home** directories. In this case, you would only need to overwrite the root partition, leaving the other Linux partitions alone.

The Manual "Partition Disks" screen will list your current partitions, showing each partition's number, size, and file system type. Use the arrow key to move the partition you want to reuse, and press ENTER. The "Partition settings" screen is displayed for this partition (see Figure 2-19). The Use as: entry will be set to "do not use." Press ENTER to display a list of file system types, for the root system use Ext4. To overwrite the partition, move to the next entry for "Format the partition" and press ENTER to toggle to the "yes, format it" option. Move to the Mountpoints entry and press ENTER, then select the root file system entry on the list displayed, and press ENTER. Then move to the "Done setting up the partition" entry and press ENTER to return to the list of partitions. You will see the partition entry for your root partition shown the ext4 file system type and / as the mount point.

Then move to the last entry, "Finish partitioning and write changes to the disk" and press ENTER. A final warning screen is displayed prompting you to write the changes to the disk and listing the changes to be made (see Figure 2-15). If correct, tab to the Yes button and press ENTER.

Select server software: Package Tasks

The base system is then installed (see Figure 2-21).

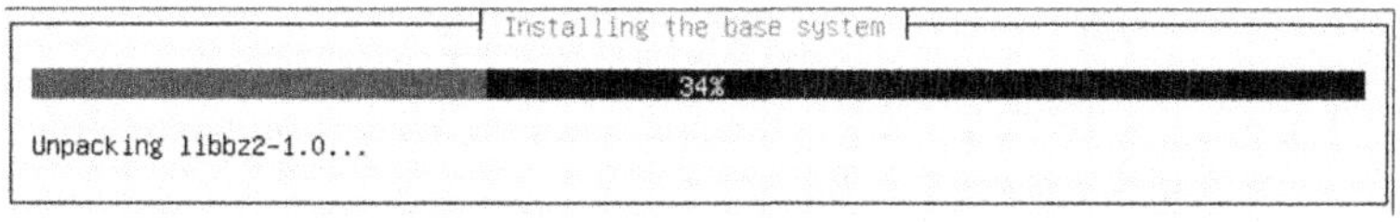

Figure 2-21: install base system

For access to the Ubuntu online repository, you are prompted to enter an http proxy server, should your network connection require it.

You are then prompted to select options for managing upgrades (see Figure 2-22). You can choose no automatic updates, install security updates automatically, or to use Ubuntu's Landscape service to perform automatic updates. The "No automatic updates" option will require that an administrator log in and choose to perform updates. The "Install security updates automatically" option will install the unattended-upgrades package, which will automatically perform security updates.

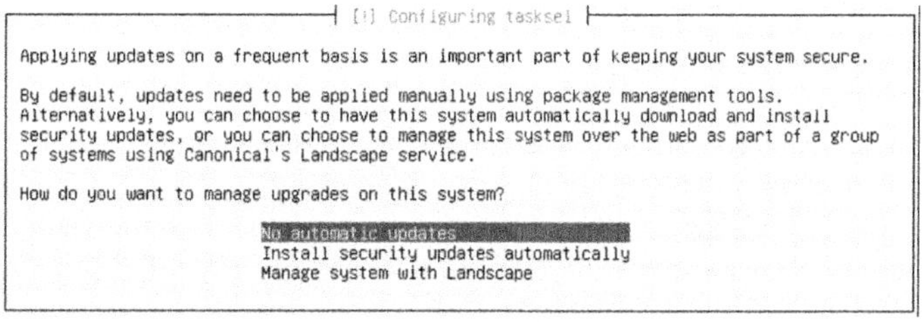

Figure 2-22: Select software upgrade options

On a Software Selection screen, you are prompted to select the servers you want installed (see Figure 2-23). Use the Arrow keys to move to a selection and press the spacebar to select it. The options are listed here.

DNS server This is the BIND Domain Name Service server (see Chapter 15).

Lamp server The LAMP server sets up a Web server with supporting software. It includes the Apache Web server, MySQL database server, and the PHP server for Web support (**L**inux, **A**pache, **M**ySQL, **and PHP**) (see Chapters 8 and 9).

Mail server This is the Postfix mail server. (see Chapter 6).

OpenSSH server This is the SSH (Secure SHell) server used for secure encrypted transmissions.

PostgreSQL database This is an optional database server (see Chapter 9).

Print server This is the CUPS print server (see Chapter 10).

Samba file server This is the SAMBA file server which provides access to shared directories and printers on a Windows network (see Chapter 12).

Tomcat Java server This is the Tomcat implementation of the JAVA Servlet and Java Server Pages (JSP) support for Web applications.

Virtual Machine host This is the kernel-based virtual machine server, KVM (libvirt).

Ubuntu Desktop USB This is USB image for installing the Ubuntu Desktop on a USB drive.

Manual package selection Select the particular packages you want. You can select additional packages you want installed.

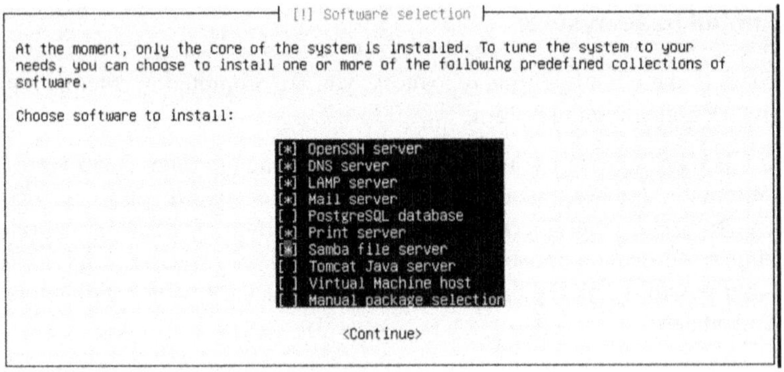

Figure 2-23: Select server packages

The "Manual package selection" entry will start up the Aptitude package manager and let you select individual packages to be installed, rather than using the server and meta package categories. See Chapter 4 for a description of how to use Aptitude. Use the + sign to mark a package for installation, and - to remove it. Use the ENTER and arrow keys to navigate the package lists, and **q** to close a tab. **?** lists all commands. You will see a package entry change to green with an **i** character, indicating that it is marked for installation. When you are ready, press **g** to display a preview screen listing your selections, then press **g** again to perform all the package installs. When finished, press **q** to return to the install program.

After selecting your server packages, tab to the Continue button and press ENTER. Your system and the selected software is then installed

During installation, for MySQL (LAMP), you are prompted for a password. For Postfix (Mail server), you are prompted to select the type of configuration. For the Internet option, you will need to enter the domain name for your server's network.

If other operating systems are present on your system, they will be detected and listed in the "Configure grub-pc" screen. If all the other operating systems are listed correctly, you can install the boot loader. The Yes button will be selected, press ENTER to continue. If you wish to use the older LILO boot loader instead or not to use any boot loader, tab to the Go Back button and press ENTER to list the "Ubuntu installer main menu" (see Figure 2-2). Here you can choose to install LILO or not to install any boot loader.

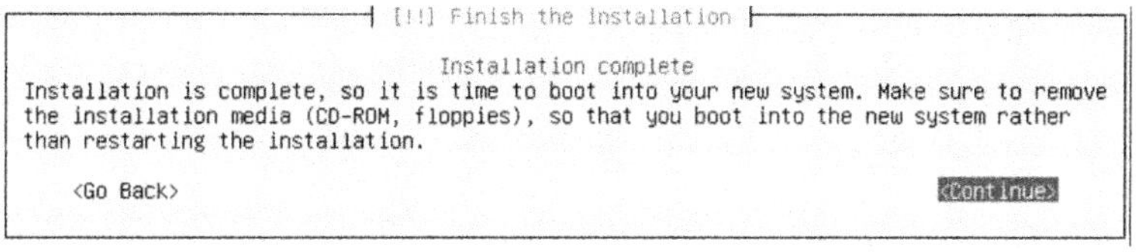

Figure 2-24: Finishing install

Remaining configuration and boot loader installation is performed for you. If another operating system is detected on your disk (like Windows), you will be prompted to install the boot loader on the master boot record. The installation then finishes. The server disk is ejected and you are prompted to reboot (see Figure 2-24).

Note: JeOS is no longer supported. Instead press F4 at the Ubuntu Server install screen.

Recovery, rescue, and boot loader re-install

Ubuntu provides the means to start up systems that have failed for some reason. A system that may boot but fails to start up, can be started in a recovery mode, already set up for you as an entry on your boot loader menu. A system that you cannot even boot may require work that is more advanced. You can access such a broken system using the Server CD.

Recovery

If for some reason your system is not able to start up, it may be due to conflicting configurations, libraries, or applications. On the GRUB menu first choose the "Advanced options or Ubuntu" to open the advanced options menu. Then select the recovery mode entry, the Ubuntu kernel entry with the (recovery mode) label attached to the end, as shown here.

```
Ubuntu, with Linux 3.19.0-15-generic (recovery mode)
```

This will start up a menu where you can use the arrow and ENTER keys to select from several recovery options (see Figure 2-25). These include resume, fsck, remount, and root. Short descriptions for each item are displayed on the menu.

The root option will start up Ubuntu as the root user with a command line shell prompt. In this case, you can boot your Linux system in a recovery mode and then edit configuration files with a text editor such as Vi and nano, remove the suspect libraries, or reinstall damaged software with **apt-get**.

If you forget your password, you can select the Recovery mode from the GRUB menu, then choose the "Drop to root shell prompt" entry. Then run the **passwd** command with the user name. You will be prompted to re-enter the password for that user. You can then run the halt command to shut down the system. When you restart, the new password will work.

The resume entry will start up Ubuntu normally, but in the command line mode.

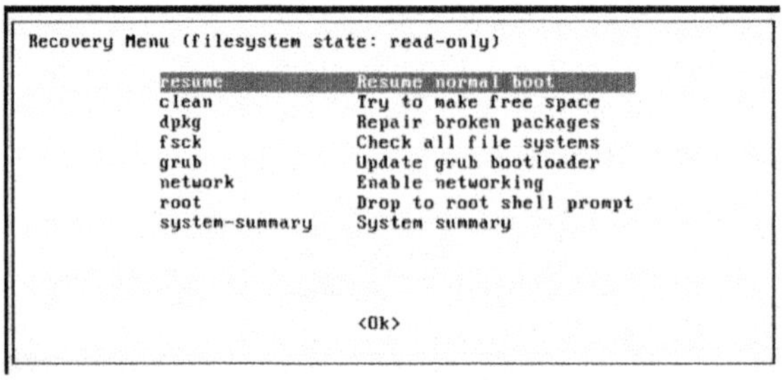

Figure 2-25: Recovery menu

To rescue a broken system, choose the **root** entry. Your broken system will be mounted and made accessible with a command line interface. You can then use command line operations and editors to fix configuration files.

Rescue a broken system with the Ubuntu Server CD

If you are not able to start up your system from your hard disk install, you can boot up with the Server CD and choose "Rescue a broken system" from the Start up menu (see Figure 2-1). Follow the prompts to start up your system, choosing a language, location, keyboard, hostname, and time zone. Select the file system when requested. The "Enter rescue mode" screen appears which provides options to mount your system (see Figure 2-26). Your broken system will be mounted and made accessible with a command line interface. You can then use command line operations and editors to fix configuration files.

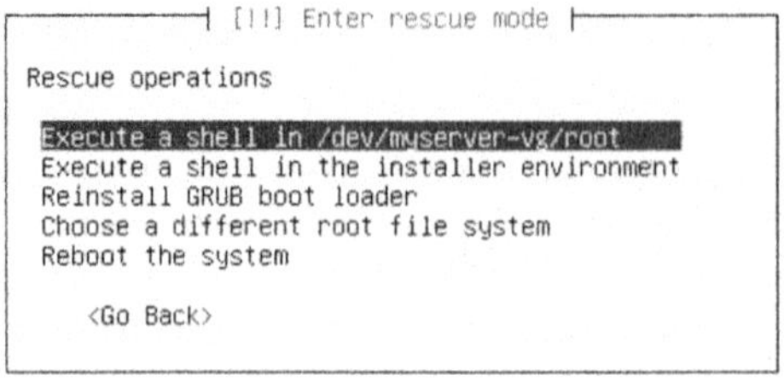

Figure 2-26: Server CD rescue mode choices

Re-Installing the Boot Loader

If you have a multiple-boot system, that runs both Windows and Linux on the same machine, you may run into a situation where you have to re-install your GRUB boot loader. This problem occurs if your Windows system completely crashes beyond repair and you have to install a new version of Windows, if you added Windows to your machine after having installed Linux, or if you upgraded to a new version of Windows. A Windows installation will automatically overwrite your boot loader (alternatively, you could install your boot loader on your Linux partition instead of the master boot record, MBR). You will no longer be able to access your Linux system.

You can manually reinstall your boot loader, using your Ubuntu Desktop DVD. The procedure is more complicated, as you have to mount your Ubuntu system. On the Ubuntu LiveCD, you can use GParted to find out what partition your Ubuntu system uses (Applications | Other | Partition). In a terminal window (Applications | Accessories | Terminal), create a directory on which to mount the system.

```
sudo mkdir myubuntu
```

Then mount it, making sure you have the correct file system type and partition name (usually **/dev/sda5** on dual boot systems).

```
sudo mount -t ext4 /dev/sda5  myubuntu
```

Then, use **grub-install** and the device name of your first partition to install the boot loader, with the **--root-directory** option to specify the directory where you mounted your Ubuntu file system. The **--root-directory** option requires a full path name, which for the Ubuntu LiveCD would be **/home/ubuntu** for the home directory. Using the **myubuntu** directory this example, the full patch name of the Ubuntu file system would be **/home/ubuntu/myubuntu**. You would then enter the following grub-install command.

```
sudo grub-install --root-directory=/home/ubuntu/myubuntu /dev/sda
```

This will re-install your current GRUB boot loader. You can then reboot, and the GRUB boot loader will start up.

Metal as a Service (MAAS)

MAAS allows you to manage hardware servers as if they were virtual servers (physical provisioning). You can find out more about MASS at:

```
http://www.ubuntu.com/cloud/orchestration/deployment
```

Check the Ubuntu MAAS page for information on how to set up a MAAS service.

```
https://wiki.ubuntu.com/ServerTeam/MAAS
```

MAAS uses a DHCP server to connect to your hardware machines (nodes). To set up MAAS, you install it using the Ubuntu Server CD, choosing the second install option.

```
Ubuntu MAAS Installation or Enlistment.
```

You will be prompted to either create a new MAAS server or connect to one you already have running (enlistment). Upon creating a new MAAS server, a dialog notifies you that the MAAS server is installed on your system, and displays the IP address with /MAAS as the URL.

```
http://192.168.0.5/MAAS
```

When you first restart your system with MAAS installed, you will have to set up a MAAS administrative user, using the following command.

```
maas createsuperuser
```

You then have to setup either a dedicated MAAS DHCP server, or modify your current DHCP server to support MAAS. For a dedicated MAAS DCHP server, install the mass-dhcp package. You will have to specify the IP address range for your nodes, the gateway they use, and the network domain.

You can then use the **mass-import-isos** command to import Ubuntu images. Then add nodes to your MAAS service using the Ubuntu Server CD to enlist the node, or use PXE to enlist them from the MAAS dashboard (Web interface). For more information see:

```
https://wiki.ubuntu.com/ServerTeam/MAAS/AddNodes
```

From the MAAS administration account, you then accept and commission the nodes.

```
http://ip-address/MAAS
```

You can then use JuJu with MAAS to deploy and manage cloud services

```
https://wiki.ubuntu.com/ServerTeam/MAAS/Juju
```

First, you create a MAAS API key for JuJu (MAAS Preferences dialog, Add Key entry). Create a JuJu directory (.juju) and configure in it an **envronments.yaml** file. The Ubuntu example is shown here.

```
environments:
 maas:
  type: maas
  maas-server: 'http:// maas.server.ip:80/MAAS'
  maas-oauth: '${maas-api-key}'
  admin-secret: 'nothing'
  default-series: vivid
```

You will then generate an SSH key for the JuJu node (ssh-keygen) and then run the JuJu bootstrap command to allocate a node to the JuJu environment.

```
juju bootstrap
```

3. Usage Basics: Login, Interfaces, and Help

Ubuntu Server startup

Grub selection and editing

The Command Line Interface

Accessing Linux from the Command Line Interface

Help Resources accessible from the command line

Using the Desktop Interface

The Ubuntu Unity Desktop

Network Connections: wired and wireless

Terminal window

The Ubuntu Help Center

Using Linux has become an almost intuitive process, with easy-to-use interfaces, including graphical logins and desktops like GNOME and KDE. Even the standard Linux command line interface has become more user-friendly, with editable commands, history lists, and cursor-based tools. To start using Linux, you have to know how to access your Linux system and, once you are on the system, how to execute commands and run applications.

Linux is noted for providing easy access to extensive help documentation. It is easy to obtain information quickly about any Linux command and utility while logged in to the system. You can access an online manual that describes each command or obtain help that provides more detailed explanations of different Linux features. A complete set of manuals provided by the Linux Documentation Project is included on your system and is available to browse through or print. Both the GNOME and KDE desktops provide help systems with easy access to desktop, system, and application help files.

It is possible to first install the Ubuntu server, and then later install the Ubuntu desktop. This would provide you with all the configuration files for the Ubuntu server, as well as the desktop configuration tools available for those servers.

Ubuntu Server startup

If you installed from the server disk, no desktop is installed. When you start up, a command line interface is presented. The startup procedure uses tty1, the terminal one device, presenting a command line interface. Like the desktop, the Ubuntu server edition uses Plymouth for start up. On tty1, Plymouth will not display any start up messages. Start up messages are displayed on terminal 7, tty7, which you can access by pressing **Alt-F7**. The messages are logged in the **/etc/log/boot** file.

Ubuntu now uses the systemd login manager, logind, to manage logins and sessions, replacing consolekit which is no longer supported. You can configure login manager options with the **/etc/systemd/logind.conf** file. You can set options such as the number of terminals (default is 6), the idle action, and hardware key operations, such as the power key. Check the **logind.conf** man page for details.

The startup procedure provides no interactive support by default. This is an issue if you have file system mount problems, where **fsck** is run to check or fix file systems. To enable interactive support, edit the GRUB boot entry as described in the next section, and add the splash option, then boot. The Plymouth start up splash screen is shown, and you are notified and prompted for any filesystem mount problems. To make the Plymouth splash screen the default, add the **splash** option to the **/etc/default/grub** file.

The login prompt then prompts you to enter your user name. This is the user name you set up during installation (see Figure 3-1).

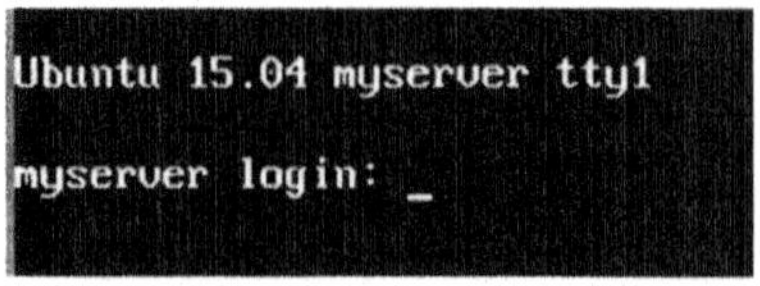

Figure 3-1: Server login prompt

After you enter your user name, you will be prompted to enter the password. Once logged in, you can then run commands. Basic server status information will be displayed such as the system load and the number of users logged in (see Figure 3-2).

To shut down the system enter the **halt** command with the **sudo** command. You will be prompted to enter your password.

```
sudo halt
```

From the login prompt, you can reboot your system with the Ctrl-Alt-Del keys.

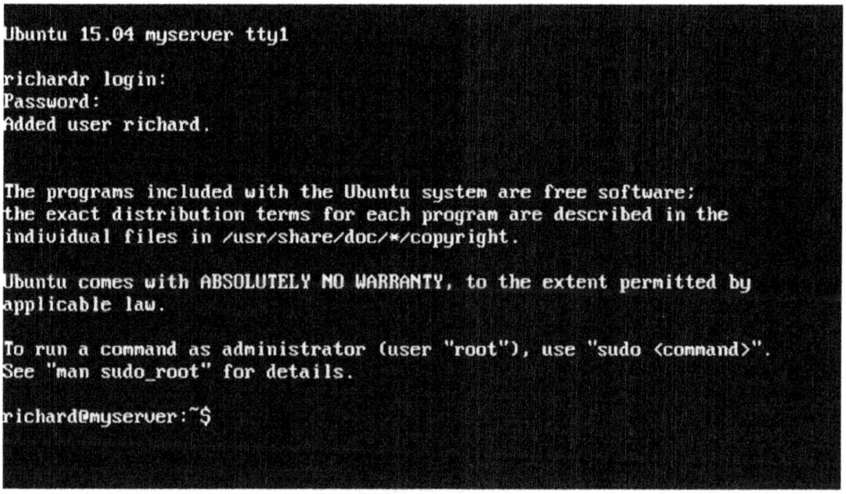

Figure 3-2: Server login

Grub selection and editing

If you have installed more than one operating system or wish to use the recovery kernel, you can select it using the GRUB menu.

If no other operating system is detected, by default, access to the GRUB menu is disabled. Disabling of the GRUB menu will also deny access to the recovery option. To enable the GRUB menu, you first have to edit the GRUB configuration file and comment out or modify the GRUB_HIDDEN_TIMEOUT option. By default this option set to 0, effectively disabling GRUB menu access.

```
GRUB_HIDDEN_TIMEOUT=0
```

If you want the GRUB menu displayed each time you start up, just comment out this line using a preceding # character.

```
#GRUB_HIDDEN_TIMEOUT=0
```

For the standard server installation and for systems with other operating systems installed, this entry will be commented out already (see Figure 3-3). Each time you start up, the GRUB menu will be displayed for a few seconds, allowing you to make selections.

If you only want the menu displayed when you choose to access it, change the numeric value to the number of seconds to wait. Pressing the ESC key in that time period will display the GRUB menu. On systems with other operating systems already installed, this option will be commented out. To enable the option, first remove the preceding # comment character. The following example waits for 10 seconds.

```
GRUB_HIDDEN_TIMEOUT=10
```

The GRUB configuration file is **/etc/default/grub**. You can edit it from the Server command line interface with a text editor like vi, emacs, or nano. The nano editor provides a simple cursor-based interface for easy editing. Use **Ctrl-o** to write changes and **Ctrl-x** to exit.

```
sudo nano /etc/default/grub
```

Once you have made your changes, you must run the **update-grub** command to implement the configuration changes.

```
sudo update-grub
```

In Figure 3-3, the GRUB_HIDDEN_TIMEOUT option has been commented out.

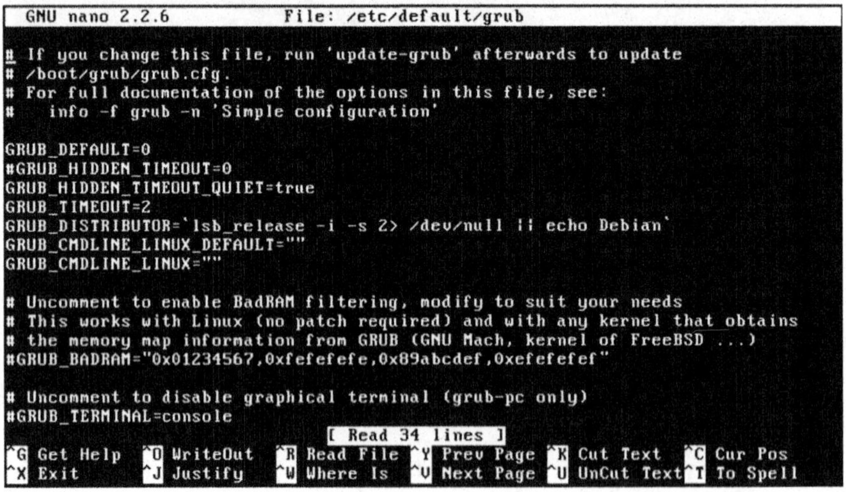

Figure 3-3: Editing the /etc/default/grub file with the nano editor

When enabled, the GRUB menu is displayed for several seconds at startup, before loading the default operating system automatically. Press an arrow key to have GRUB wait until you have made a selection. Your GRUB menu is displayed as shown in Figure 3-4.

The GRUB menu lists Ubuntu and other operating systems installed on your hard drive such as Windows. Use the arrow keys to move to the entry you want and press ENTER. Press the **e** key to edit a GRUB entry (see Figure 3-5).

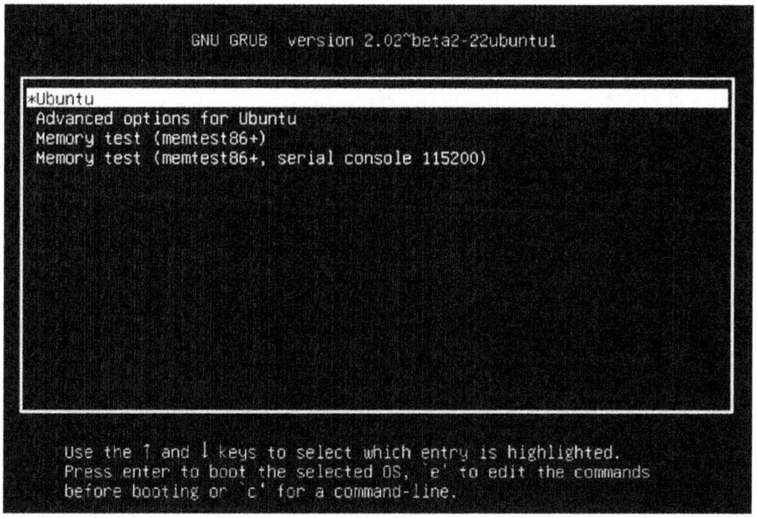

Figure 3-4: Ubuntu GRUB menu

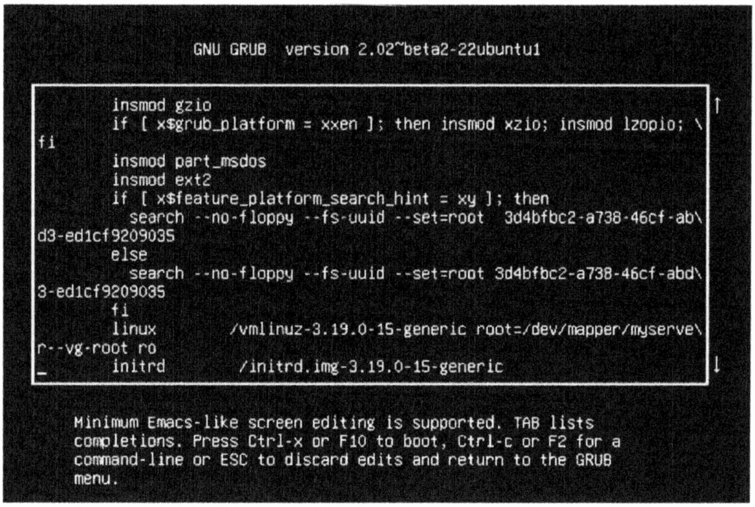

Figure 3-5: Editing a GRUB menu item

To change a particular line, use the arrow keys to move to the line. You can use the arrow keys to move along the line. The Backspace key will delete characters, and simply typing will insert characters. All changes are temporary. Permanent changes can only be made by directly editing the GURB configuration files: the **/etc/default/grub** file and those in the **/etc/grub.d** directory, and then running the **sudo update-grub** command.

The Command Line Interface

The Ubuntu server CD, for efficiency reasons, will not install a desktop interface. Instead, you use the traditional UNIX command line interface, accessing your system from a login prompt and typing commands from your keyboard on a command line.

Accessing Ubuntu from the Command Line Interface

For the command line interface, you are initially given a login prompt. The login prompt is preceded by the hostname you gave your system. In this example, the hostname is **turtle-server**. When you finish using Linux, you first log out. Linux then displays exactly the same login prompt, waiting for you or another user to log in again. This is the equivalent of the login window provided by the LightDM. You can then log in to another account.

Once you log in to an account, you can enter and execute commands. Logging in to your Linux account involves two steps: entering your username and then entering your password. Type the username for your user account. If you make a mistake, you can erase characters with the BACKSPACE key. In the next example, the user enters the username **richard** and is then prompted to enter the password:

```
Ubuntu 15.04 my-server tty1

my-server login: richard
Password:
```

When you type in your password, it does not appear on the screen. This is to protect your password from being seen by others. If you enter either the username or the password incorrectly, the system will respond with the error message "Login incorrect" and will ask for your username again, starting the login process over. You can then reenter your username and password.

Once you enter your username and password correctly, you are logged in to the system. Your command line prompt is displayed, waiting for you to enter a command. Notice the command line prompt is a dollar sign ($). In Ubuntu, your prompt is preceded by the user and the hostname. Both are bounded by a set of brackets.

```
[richard@turtle-server]$
```

To end your session, issue the **`logout`** or **`exit`** command. This returns you to the login prompt, and Linux waits for another user to log in.

```
[richard@turtle-server]$ logout
```

To, instead, shut down your system from the command line, you enter the **`halt`** command. This command will log you out and shut down the system. It requires administrative access.

```
$ sudo halt
```

Using the Command Line Interface

When using the command line interface, you are given a simple prompt at which you type in a command. Even when you are using a desktop like GNOME, you sometimes need to execute commands on a command line. You can do so in a terminal window, which is accessed from the desktop's dash's Accessories category as Terminal.

Linux commands make extensive use of options and arguments. Be careful to place your arguments and options in their correct order on the command line. The format for a Linux command is the command name followed by options, and then by arguments, as shown here:

```
$ command-name options arguments
```

An *option* is a one-letter code preceded by one or two hyphens, which modifies the type of action the command takes. Options and arguments may or may not be optional, depending on the command. For example, the **ls** command can take an option, **-s**. The **ls** command displays a listing of files in your directory, and the **-s** option adds the size of each file in blocks. You enter the command and its option on the command line as follows:

```
$ ls -s
```

If you are uncertain what format and options a command uses, you can check the command syntax quickly by displaying its man page. Most commands have a man page. Just enter the **man** command with the command name as an argument.

An *argument* is data the command may need to execute its task. In many cases, this is a filename. An argument is entered as a word on the command line that appears after any options. For example, to display the contents of a file, you can use the **more** command with the file's name as its argument. The **less** or **more** command used with the filename **mydata** would be entered on the command line as follows:

```
$ less mydata
```

The command line is actually a buffer of text you can edit. Before you press ENTER to execute the command, you can edit the command on the command line. The editing capabilities provide a way to correct mistakes you may make when typing a command and its options. The BACKSPACE key lets you erase the character you just typed (the one to the left of the cursor) and the DEL key lets you erase one character to the right of the cursor. With this character-erasing capability, you can BACKSPACE over the entire line if you want, erasing what you entered. CTRL-U erases the whole command line and lets you to start over again at the prompt.

You can use the UP ARROW key to redisplay your last-executed command. You can then re-execute that command, or you can edit it and execute the modified command. This is helpful when you have to repeat certain operations, such as editing the same file. This is also helpful when you have already executed a command you entered incorrectly.

Accessing USB drives from the Command line Interface on a Server.

When you attach a USB drive it is detected automatically, but not mounted. A message will be displayed indicating the device name for the drive. If you have one hard drive, which would be labeled device **sda**, then the USB device would be **sdb**. USB drives are normally formatted as **vfat** file systems. Your file system would be located on the first file system on the USB drive, which would be **sdb1** in this example.

To access the USB drive you have to create a directory on which to mount it. Then use the mount command to mount the file system. You only create the directory once. Use the **mkdir** command to create the directory.

```
mkdir myusb
```

To mount a USB drive to that directory, enter a mount command with the **vfat** type, mounting the **/dev/sdb1** device to the **myusb** directory. You have to have administrative access, so you need to use the **sudo** command.

```
sudo mount  -t vfat   /dev/sdb1  myusb
```

You can then access the USB drive by accessing the **myusb** directory.

```
$ cd myusb
$ ls
```

Write operations would still have to be run with administrative access.

```
sudo cp mydata  myusb
```

To write whole directories and their subdirectories, you need to add the **-R** option to **cp**.

```
sudo cp -R mydatadir  myusb
```

Once finished with the USB drive, be sure to first unmount it before removing it.

```
sudo umount /dev/sdb1
```

The USB drive's directory cannot be your working directory.

Setting the date and time

You can set the system date and time either manually or by referencing an Internet time server. You could also use your local hardware clock. To set the system time manually, you use the **date** command. The date command has several options for adjusting both the date and time. You can set the time by month or minutes with the **--set** option. You can use a sequence of numbers to set a specific time beginning with the month, day, hour, minute, and year. The following sets the date to July 22, 8:15 AM 2008.

```
sudo date 072208152008
```

The date command also has formatting options for the day, month, or year.

To use a time server, you use the **ntpdate** command and the address of the time server.

```
sudo ntpdate  ntp.ubuntu.com
```

To access the hardware clock, you use the **hwclock** command. The command itself will display the hardware clock time.

```
hwclock
```

The **--hctosys** option will set the system clock using the hardware clock's time, and the **--systohc** option resets the hardware clock using the system time. Use the **--set** and **--date** options to set the hardware clock to a certain time.

```
sudo hwclock --systohc
```

The time zone was set when you installed your system. If you need to change it, you can copy a new time zone from the files in the **/usr/share/zoneinfo** subdirectories. They are arranged by location and city. Copy the new time zone to the **/etc/localtime** file.

```
sudo cp /usr/share/zoneinfo/Europe/London  /etc/localtime
```

Editing files with the command line interface: text editors

If you are using the command line interface only, you will often have to edit configuration files directly to configure your system and servers. You will have to use a command-line based editor to perform your editing tasks. Most command line editors provide a screen-based interface that makes displaying and editing a file fairly simple. Two standard command line editors are installed by default on your system, **vi** and **nano**. Several common command line text editors are listed in Table 3-1. The commands you use to start the editors are also the editor names, in lower case, like **vi** for the Vi editor, **nano**, **joe**, and **emacs** for Emacs.

The **vi** editor is the standard editor used on most Linux and UNIX systems. It can be very difficult to use by people accustomed to a desktop editor. The **nano** editor is much easier to use, featuring a screen-based interface that you can navigate with arrow keys. If you do not already know **vi**, you may want to use **nano** instead.

The nano editor is a simple screen-based editor that lets you visually edit your file, using arrow and page keys to move around the file. You use control keys to perform actions. **Ctrl-x** will exit and prompt you to save the file, **Ctrl-o** will save it.

Editor	Description
vi	The Vi editor, difficult to use, considered the standard editor on Linux ad UNIX system, installed by default
nano	Easy to use screen based editor, installed by default
emacs	Powerful and complex screen-based editor, though easier to use than Vi, Ubuntu repository
vim	Easier to use version of vi, Ubuntu repository
joe	Simple screen based editor similar to Emacs, Universe repository
the	Screen based editor similar to Emacs, Universe repository
ne	Simple screen based editor similar to nano, Universe repository
aee	Simple screen based editor similar to nano, Universe repository

Table 3-1: Command line interface text editors

Start nano with the **nano** command. To edit a configuration file you will need administrative access. You would start nano with the **sudo** command. Figure 3-6 shows the nano editor being used to edit the **/etc/network/interfaces** file. To edit a configuration file like **/etc/network/interfaces** you would enter the following.

```
sudo nano /etc/network/interfaces
```

More powerful editors you may find helpful are vim and emacs. You will have to first install them. The **vim** editor provides a slightly easier interface for vi. Emacs provides an interface similar to **nano**, but much more complex.

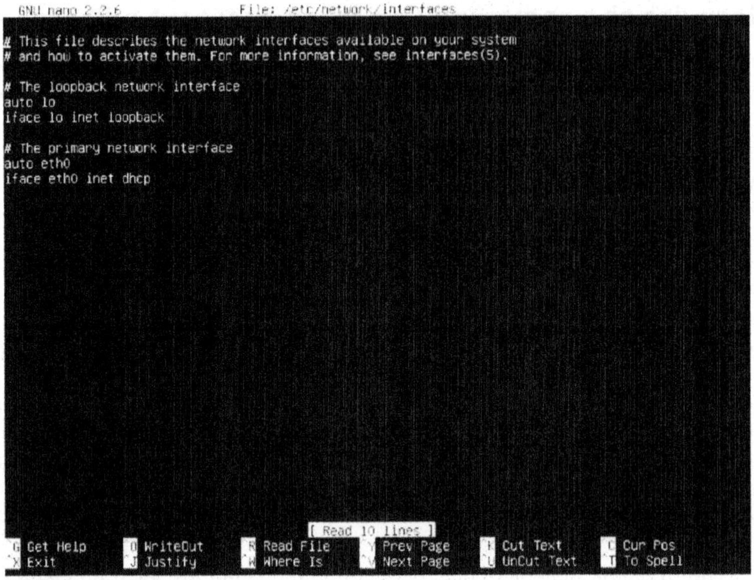

Figure 3-6: Editing with nano

Other simple screen-based editors you may find helpful are **joe**, **aee**, **ne**, and **the**. All are available on the Universe repository. **joe** and **the** are similar to Emacs. **ne** and **aee** are more like **nano**.

Help Resources accessible from the command line

There are several different resources you can access for help on your system. If you have installed a desktop, you can use the Ubuntu help center. The Ubuntu server CD will not install the desktop. You will have access to command line help tools, like the man and info pages. The **/usr/share/doc** directory will hold any documentation installed for applications. For many servers, like the Bind server, these include helpful examples or Web-based manuals. Often the documentation for applications like servers are included in a separate software package, usually with the suffix **-doc** in the name, like **bind9-doc** for the DNS BIND documentation.

A great deal of support documentation is already installed on your system, as well as accessible from online sources.

If you need to ask a question, you can obtain help support at **http://answers.launchpad.net** and **http://askubuntu.com**. Here you can submit your question, as well as check answered questions.

Application Documentation

On your system, the **/usr/share/doc** directory contains documentation files installed by each application. Within each directory, you can usually find HOW-TO, README, and INSTALL documents for that application. Some documentation will include detailed manuals. Many applications have separate documentation packages, usually with the **-doc** suffix, like **bind9-doc**.

Such documentation may be located under their package name, instead of their application name, like **/usr/share/doc/bind9-doc** for the DNS server documentation.

The Man Pages

You can also access the Man pages, which are manuals for Linux commands available from the command line interface, using the **man** command. Enter **man** with the command on which you want information. The following example asks for information on the **ls** command:

```
$ man ls
```

Pressing the SPACEBAR key advances you to the next page. Pressing the **b** key moves you back a page. When you finish, press the **q** key to quit the Man utility and return to the command line. You activate a search by pressing either the slash (/) or question mark (?). The / searches forward; the ? searches backward. When you press the /, a line opens at the bottom of your screen, and you then enter a word to search for. Press ENTER to activate the search. You can repeat the same search by pressing the N key. You needn't reenter the pattern.

The Info Pages

Online documentation for GNU applications, such as the gcc compiler and the Emacs editor, also exist as info pages. You can also access this documentation by entering the command **info**. This brings up a special screen listing different GNU applications. The info interface has its own set of commands. You can learn more about it by entering **info info** at the command prompt. Typing **m** opens a line at the bottom of the screen where you can enter the first few letters of the application. Pressing ENTER brings up the info file on that application.

Using the Ubuntu Desktop Interface

The Ubuntu desktop will install the complete set of desktop packages, including multimedia and graphics packages you may have no use for on your server. The Ubuntu desktop also installs all the administrative packages you may want to use, like the Synaptic Package Manager, the Ubuntu Software Center, Network Manager, User and Group management, and the Update manager.

You can install the Ubuntu desktop on a server system using the **ubuntu-desktop** meta-package and the **tasksel** software management tool. Run **tasksel** with the **sudo** command, then use the arrow keys to move to the Ubuntu Desktop entry and press the spacebar. Then tab to the OK button and press ENTER. You could also add **ubuntu-desktop** as a parameter to **tasksel** to install the desktop directly, as shown here.

```
sudo tasksel ubuntu-desktop
```

You also could use **apt-get** with the **ubuntu-desktop** meta-package, as shown here.

```
sudo apt-get install ubuntu-desktop
```

Download and setup can take an hour or more. You then logout and restart your system. The LightDM will start up as shown in Figure 3-7.

The Light Display Manager: LightDM

The graphical login interface displays a login window with a box, listing a menu of usernames. The currently selected user name displays a text box where you enter your password. Upon pressing ENTER, you log in to the selected account and your desktop starts up.

Graphical logins are handled by the Light Display Manager (LightDM). The LightDM manages the login interface along with authenticating a user password and username, and then starts up a selected desktop.

From the LightDM, you can shift to the command line interface with the CTRL-ALT-F1 keys, and then shift back to the LightDM with the CTRL-ALT-F7 keys. The keys F1 through F6 provide different command line terminals, as in CTRL-ALT-F3 for the third command line terminal.

Figure 3-7: LightDM Login Screen with user list

When the LightDM starts up, it shows a listing of users (see Figure 3-7). A session (power icon) menu at the top right of the screen shows the entries Suspend, Restart, and Shut Down. The time is displayed next to the Power icon. Passing the mouse over the time expands it to the calendar, showing the date. Next to the time, the sound menu lets you adjust or mute the sound. The network menu lets you configure network access. The keyboard menu lets you choose a keyboard. The accessibility menu displays options such as the on-screen keyboard, high contrast, and the screen reader.

You can use the arrow keys to move through the list of users. For the selected user, you are prompted to enter the user's password (see Figure 3-8). Once the password is entered, press ENTER, or click the arrow to the right. The desktop then starts up.

Figure 3-8: LightDM Login Screen: password entry

The Guest Session user has no password, just a simple Log In button. The Remote Login user prompts for an email address and password, as shown here.

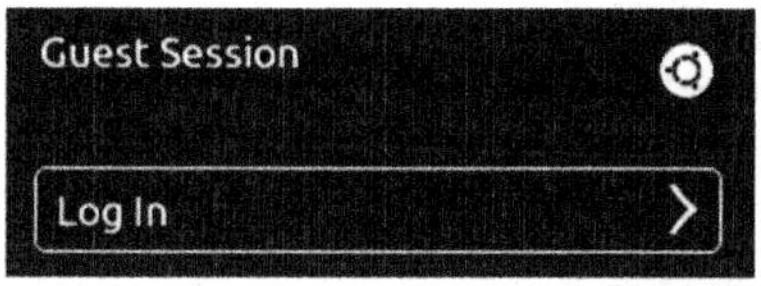

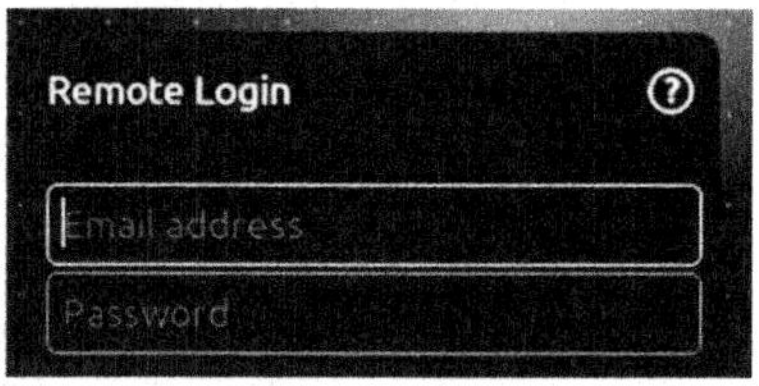

If you have installed more than one desktop interface, such as Kubuntu, an Ubuntu icon appears to the right of the user name. Click on it to display a menu (see Figure 3-9) from which you can select the desktop interface you want to start up. The menu shows all installed possible desktop interfaces. Here you can choose KDE to use the KDE Desktop. The KDE option is not shown unless you have already installed KDE. The interface you selected in your previous login is chosen automatically. Once you have made your choice, click the OK entry, or the back arrow to return to the user listing with the password text box. The icon for the desktop you have chosen is displayed next to your name. Enter your password and press ENTER to start up Ubuntu with the chosen interface.

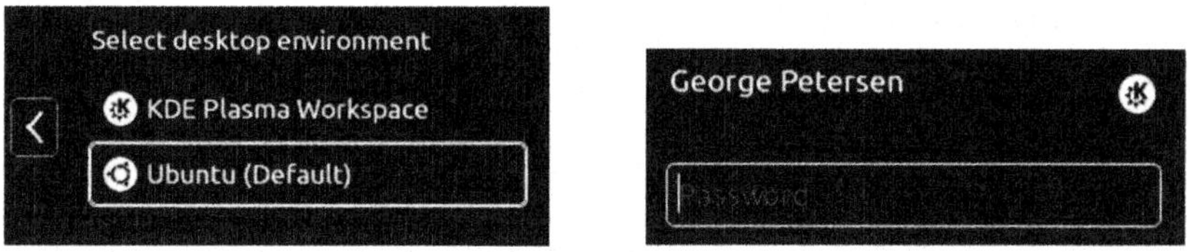

Figure 3-9: LightDM Login screen with desktop choices

If you log out from a user desktop, you will return to the LightDM login screen. To shut down your Ubuntu system, select the Shut Down entry in the session menu (power icon, top right). You can also shut down the system directly from the Ubuntu desktop by clicking the session icon on the top panel to the right. The desktop Session menu is displayed with entries for Lock Screen, Log Out, Restart, Suspend, and Shut Down.

Tip: To restart the system from the login screen using the keyboard, you first have to enter the command line interface. Press Ctrl-Alt-F1 to enter the command line interface, then press Ctrl-Alt-Del to restart the system.

The Session menu and the User Switcher

The Ubuntu desktop displays a Session menu on the right side of the top panel as the sprocket power icon (see Figure 3-10). You will usually use the Session menu to log out, restart, or shut down your system. The last section of the menu shows entries for Log Out, Suspend, Restart, and Shutdown. The Log Out entry logs out of your session and returns to the Login screen. From the menu, you can also shut down or restart your system directly from the desktop. To restart, choose Restart entry. Use the Lock entry to lock desktop access.

A System Settings entry opens the GNOME 3 System Settings dialog from which you can access desktop administrative tools such as those for users, mouse and touchpad, and Bluetooth. Guest Session allows a guest login.

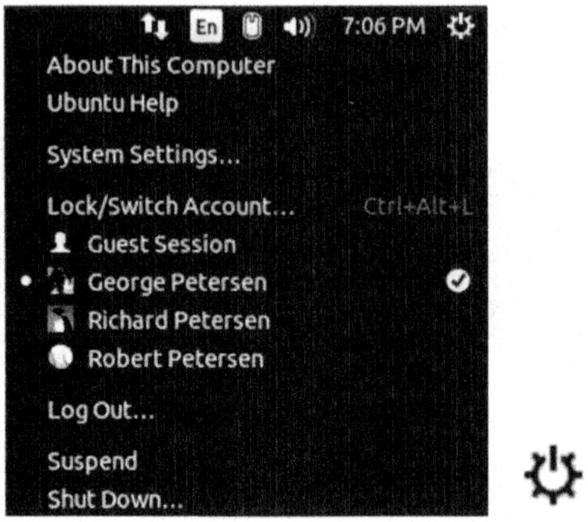

Figure 3-10: Desktop Session menu with single user and multiple users configured

The User Switcher is integrated into the Session menu. It is no longer a separate menu, as in previous releases. The User Switcher entries list other users on the system. It lets you switch to another user without having to log out or end your current user session. The user switching operations will keep you logged in while you log in to another user. Your active programs will continue to run in the background.

If your system has more than one user set up, then the Lock entry becomes the "Lock/Switch Account" entry, and lets you log in from the lock screen as a user not currently logged in. Additional users are also listed below the Lock/Switch Account entry (see Figure 3-10). Users already logged in will have a check mark next to their names. The current user has a dot preceding its name. Selecting one of these user entries suspends your current session (though applications continue to run), and starts up the login screen with the user list positioned at that user.

If you log out of a user you have switched to (Log Out entry), LightDM login screen will start up letting you log in as a different user. If you choose to switch to a user already logged in, then the login dialog for the lock screen will appear for that user. From the loc*k* screen, you can log in (Unlock), or choose to switch to another user (Switch User). A logged in user's original session will continue with the same open windows and applications running when the user switched off.

You can easily switch back and forth between logged-in users, with all users retaining their session from where they left off. When you switch off from a user, that user's running programs will continue in the background.

Guest login

Ubuntu supports a guest account, allowing you to let other users use your system, without having to give them a user account of their own or use someone else's. It is designed for situations like letting someone use your laptop to check a Web site quickly. The Guest login is accessible from the Session menu as the Guest Session entry (see Figure 3-9). The guest user is immediately placed on their own desktop as the guest user, while your account remains locked. The guest user name will appear on the User Switcher menu icon on the top panel. Upon logging out from the guest account, the LightDM login screen is displayed, letting you log in to your own account again. The guest user can also use the User Switcher menu to switch to another user, while the guest session remains logged in. This way the guest user's work is retained, while you access another user or your own account. You can then switch back to the guest user. The guest user's open windows and work will be restored.

Lock Screen

You can choose to lock your screen and suspend your system by choosing the Lock entry in the Session menu, or by pressing Ctrl-Alt-L. To start up again, press the spacebar and the Lock Screen dialog appears (see Figure 3-11). This is the same as the login screen, with only a single entry for your user name and the password prompt. Enter your password to start up your desktop session again.

From the lock screen, you also can switch to another user by clicking the Session button at the top right of the screen to open a menu with entries for other users. Select one to open the LightDM login screen at that user.

Figure 3-11: Lock Screen

Shut down and Logging out

To shut down from the Ubuntu desktop, click the session icon (power sprockets) on the right side of the top panel to open the Session menu. The Shut down options are displayed at the bottom of the menu: Log out, Suspend, and Shut Down (see Figure 3-10). To log out, you can use the Session menu Log Out entry, which returns you to the login screen where you login again as a different user. Restart is an option on the Shut Down dialog.

There are several ways to shut down your system:

Session menu: select one of the shut down options (see Figure 3-10).

Press the power button on your computer. This opens a menu with shutdown options (see Figure 3-13).

Should your display freeze or become corrupted, one safe way to shut down and restart is to press a command line interface key (like CTRL-ALT-F1) to revert to the command line interface, and then press CTRL-ALT-DEL to restart. You can also log in on the command line interface (terminal) and then enter the **sudo shutdown -h now** command.

When you select the Shut Down, Suspend, or Log Out entry from the Session menu, the appropriate dialog is displayed. From the Shut Down dialog you can also choose to restart (see Figure 3-12). From the Log Out dialog you can also choose to lock.

Figure 3-12: Shut Down and Restart dialog

You can also press your computer power button to shut down, restart, or suspend your system, which displays a shut down dialog with menu entries for Lock, Suspend, Restart, and Shut Down (see Figure 3-13).

Figure 3-13: Shut down dialog

Use Suspend to stop your system temporarily, using little or no power. Press the space key to redisplay the locked login screen where you can access your account again and continue your session from where you left off.

The Ubuntu Desktop (Unity)

Ubuntu 15.04 supports two major different desktop interfaces: Ubuntu and Kubuntu. The Ubuntu Desktop DVD installs Ubuntu. The Ubuntu desktop uses the Ubuntu Unity interface.

Ubuntu prefers hardware acceleration support provided by the appropriate display driver. If your current graphics driver does not support hardware acceleration, you will be logged in using acceleration simulation with LLVMpipe on OpenGL running on the CPU. This can result in a slower system.

The Kubuntu DVD installs the KDE desktop interface. You can also install KDE on an Ubuntu desktop system using the Ubuntu Software Center KDE meta-packages: **kubuntu-desktop** or **kubuntu-full**. Although the GNOME and KDE interfaces appear similar, they are very different desktop interfaces with separate tools for selecting preferences.

Ubuntu uses the Ubuntu Ambiance theme for its interface, with the Ubuntu screen background and menu icons as its default (see Figure 3-11). Another Ubuntu theme is available called Radiance. Ambience is a darker color theme, while Radiance uses lighter colors. The Ambiance theme is used in the examples in this book. You can change to the Radiance theme on the Appearance dialog's Look tab's Theme menu. The Appearance tool is accessible from the Customization dash and from System Settings.

Key press	Action
SHIFT	Move a file or directory, default
CTRL	Copy a file or directory
CTRL-SHIFT	Create a link for a file or directory
F2	Rename selected file or directory
CTRL-ALT-Arrow (right, left, up, down)	Move to a different desktop
CTRL-w	Close current window
ALT-spacebar	Open window menu for window operations
ALT-F2	Open Run command box
ALT-F1	Open Applications menu
Ctrl-F	Find file

Table 3-2: Window and File Manager Keyboard shortcuts

The Ambience and Radiance themes place the window control buttons (close, maximize, and minimize buttons) on the left side of a window title bar, as shown here. There are three window buttons: an x for close, a dash (-) for minimize, and a square for maximize. The close button is highlighted in orange.

window buttons 

To move a window, click and drag its title bar. Each window supports Minimize, Maximize, and Close buttons located on the left side of the title bar. Double-clicking the title bar will maximize the window. Many keyboard operations are also similar, as listed in Table 3-2.

Ubuntu Unity

Logging in to the Ubuntu desktop uses the Ubuntu Unity interface. Unity is designed to make the best use of screen space, placing a launcher on the left side to free up vertical space, making the window menu bar part of the top panel, along with indicator menus for Network Manager, sound volume, messaging, time and date, and the Session menu (see Figure 3-14).

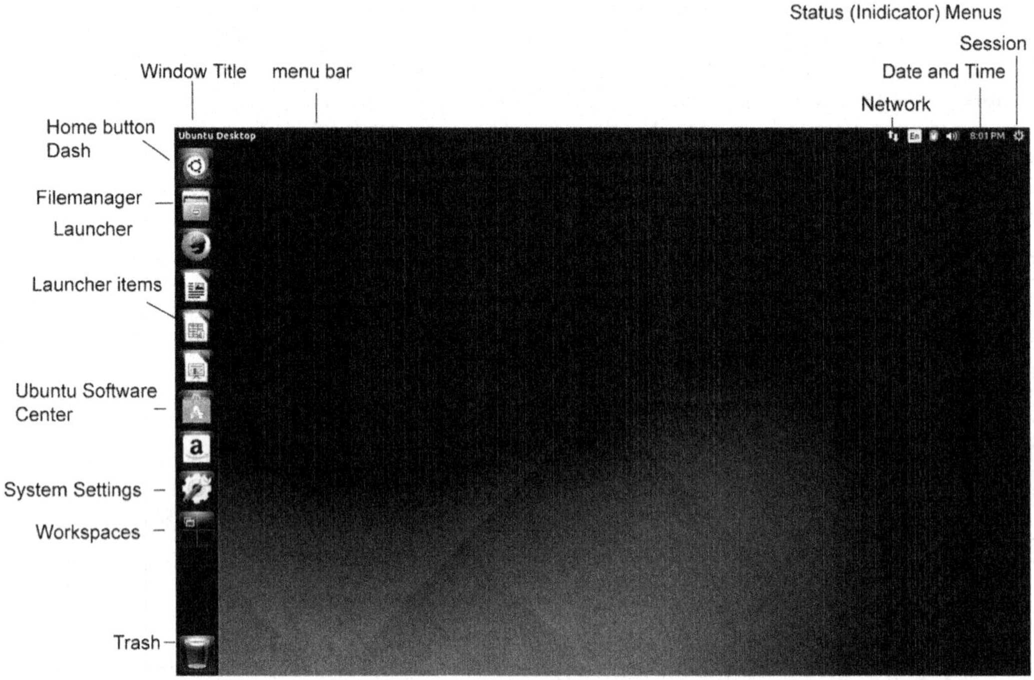

Figure 3-14: Ubuntu Unity interface

The Unity interface features a Launcher for applications and tasks, with icons for the dash home, the home folder, the Firefox browser, LibreOffice applications (Writer, Calc, and Impress), the Ubuntu Software Center, and System Settings. There are also icons for accessing workspaces and the trash. You can use the System Settings Appearance tool to configure changes to your Unity interface, such as Launcher hiding options and the size of the Launcher item icons.

The dash home button at the top of the Launcher (Ubuntu logo) opens the dash, displaying a search box to let you search for applications (see Figure 3-15). At the bottom of the dash are icons for different lenses: home, applications, files & folders, videos, music, and pictures. If you configure access to an online account such as Facebook, a social networking lens is also displayed. Click on an icon to open that lens. Clicking on the applications button (books) opens the Applications dash with a filter menu for accessing different application categories, such as Internet, Multimedia, and System. Applications are organized into the most frequently used, those installed, and those available for download, which connects directly to the Ubuntu Software Center.

You can close the dash by clicking the dash close button (**x**) located at the top left side of the panel, or by pressing the ESC key. You can expand it to full-screen by clicking the square button at the lower right corner of the dash.

The top panel displays the applications menu and the indicator menus. The left side of the top panel is the application menu, showing the menu bar for the currently selected open window.

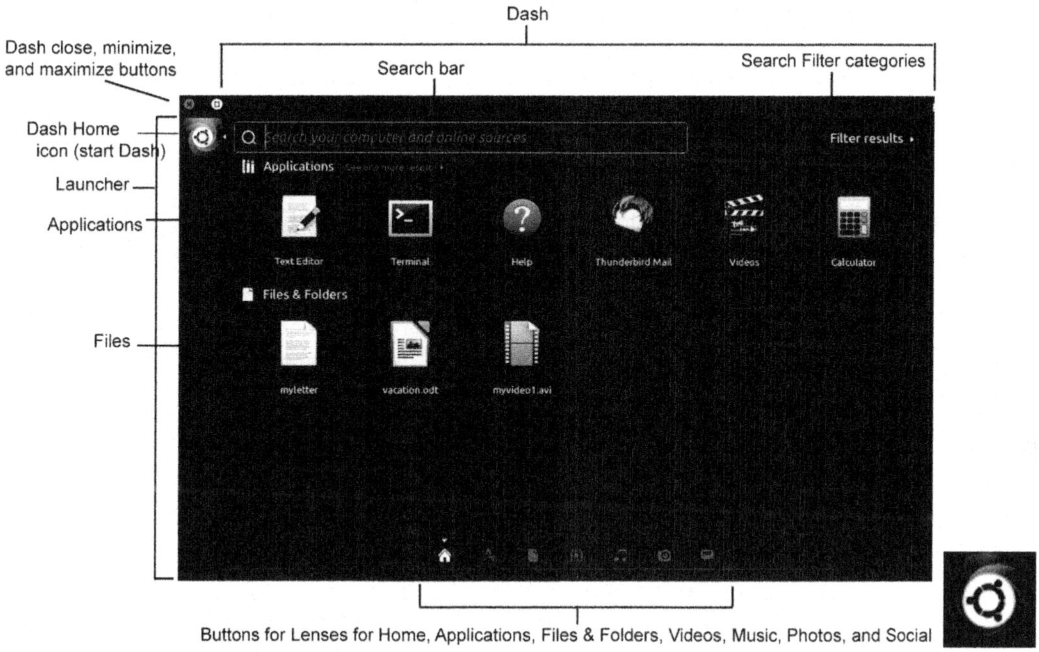

Figure 3-15: Unity Dash

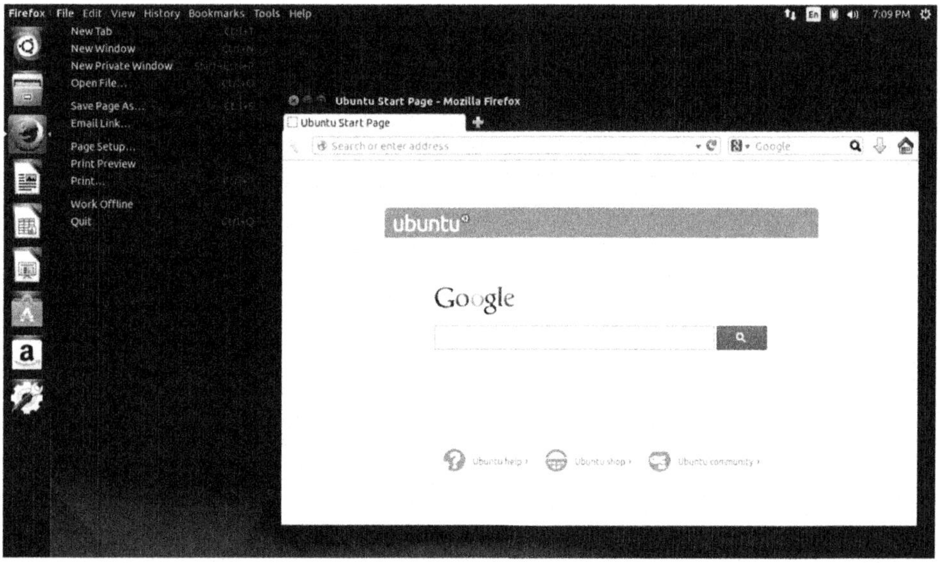

Figure 3-16: Ubuntu Unity interface with selected window and applications menu

The right side of the top panel holds indicator menus for the network manager, sound volume, messaging, Date and time, the User Switcher, and the Session menu (configuration tools and shut down options).

By default, application menus are now displayed in a window's title bar. You can change it to the top bar's menu bar in the Behavior tab of the System Settings Appearance dialog. Then, when you click on a window, its title is displayed on the top panel. When you move your mouse to the left side of the top panel (the menu bar), that window's menu bar is displayed (see Figure 3-16).

With Unity, Icons have become much more important for identifying an application. Instead of names on menus, users focus more on the icon in the Launcher and on the Dash. Table 3-3 lists the default launcher item icons.

Icon	Launcher item
	Dash home
	Home Folder
	Firefox Web browser
	Libre Office Writer
	Libre Office Calc
	Libre Office Impress
	Ubuntu Software Center
	System Settings
	Workspace Switcher
	Trash

Table 3-3: Ubuntu Unity Launcher default items and icons

Gnome file manager (Nautilus)

Ubuntu (Unity) uses the Nautilus file manager. You can access your home folder from its entry in the Go menu, or by clicking the Home Folder item in the Launcher. A file manager window opens showing your home directory. Your home directory will already have default directories created for commonly used files. These include Pictures, Documents, Music, Videos, and Downloads.

Your office applications will automatically save files to the Documents directory by default. Image and photo applications place image files in the Pictures directory. The Desktop folder will hold all files and directories saved to your desktop. When you download a file, it is placed in the Downloads directory.

The file manager window displays several components, including a toolbar and a sidebar showing devices, file systems, bookmarks, and folders. Use view and tools menus, accessible from button on the right side of the toolbar, to manage files and folders (zoom, sorting, folder creation, and bookmarks). When you open a new folder, the same window is used to display it, and you can use the forward and back arrows to move through previously opened directories. The location bar displays folder buttons showing your current folder and its parent folders. You can click on a parent folder to move to it. Figure 3-17 shows the file manager window. From the Files menu on the desktop applications menu bar (top bar), you can open a new file manager window, access an ftp site, enter path name (location), or manage bookmarks.

The file manager also supports tabs. You can open up several folders in the same file manager window. To open a new tab, select New Tab from the File menu or press **Ctrl-t**. You can use the entries in the Tabs menu to move from one tab to another, or to rearrange tabs. You also can use the Ctrl-PageUp and Ctrl-PageDown keys to move from one tab to another. Use the Shift-Ctrl-PageUp and Shift-Ctrl-PageDown keys to rearrange the tabs.

The file manager supports full drag-and-drop capabilities using combinations of key presses and mouse clicks. You can drag folders, icons, and applications to the desktop or other file manager windows open to other folders. The move operation is the default drag operation (you can also press the SHIFT key while dragging). To copy files, press the CTRL key and then click-and-drag before releasing the mouse button. To create a link (short cut), hold down both the CTRL and SHIFT keys while dragging the icon to where you want the link to appear, such as the desktop.

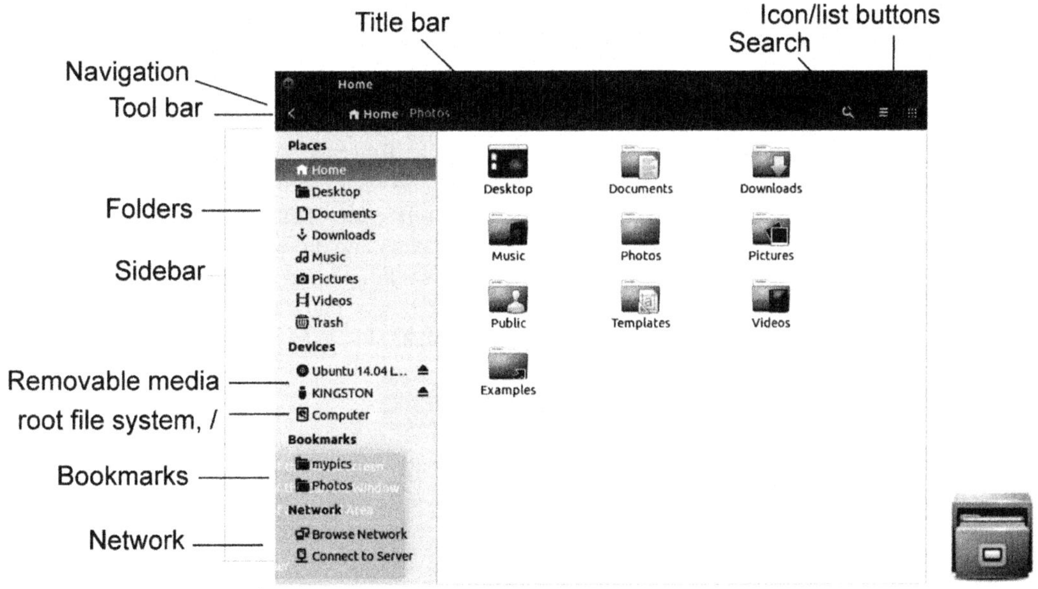

Figure 3-17: File manager for home folder

Note: The K Desktop Environment (KDE) displays a panel at the bottom of the screen that looks very similar to one displayed on the top of the GNOME desktop. The file manager appears slightly different but operates much the same way as the GNOME file manager.

Network Connections from the desktop

Network connections will be set up for you by Network Manager, which will detect your network connections automatically, both wired and wireless. Network Manager provides status information for your connection, and allows you to switch easily from one configured connection to another as needed. For initial configuration, it detects as much information as possible about the new connection.

Wired connections will be started automatically. For wireless connections, when a user logs in, Network Manager selects the connection preferred by that user. The user can choose the wireless connection to use from a menu of detected wireless networks.

The network menu displays a Network Manager icon on the top panel to the right. The Network Manager icon will vary according to the type of connection and your connection status. An Ethernet (wired) connection would display two arrows pointing in opposite directions. A wireless connection will display a staggered wave graph (see Figure 3-18). If no connection is active (wireless or wired), an empty wave graph is displayed. When Network Manager makes a wired or wireless connection, it displays a pulsing staggered wave graph. If you have both a wired and wireless connection, and the wired connection is active, the wired connection image (opposite arrows) will be displayed.

Figure 3-18: Network Manager wired, wireless, and disconnected icons.

Network Manager wired connections

For computers connected to a wired network, like an Ethernet connection, Network Manager will automatically detect the network connection and establish a connection. Most networks use DHCP to provide network information like an IP address and network DNS server automatically. With this kind of connection, Network Manager can connect automatically to your network whenever you start your system. The network connection would be labeled something like Wired connection 1, eth0 being the actual Ethernet network device name on your system. When you connect, a connection established message is displayed, as shown here.

The Network Manager panel icon will display the arrows pointed in opposite directions, as shown here.

The Network Manager menu displays your wired connection, shown here as Wired connection 1.

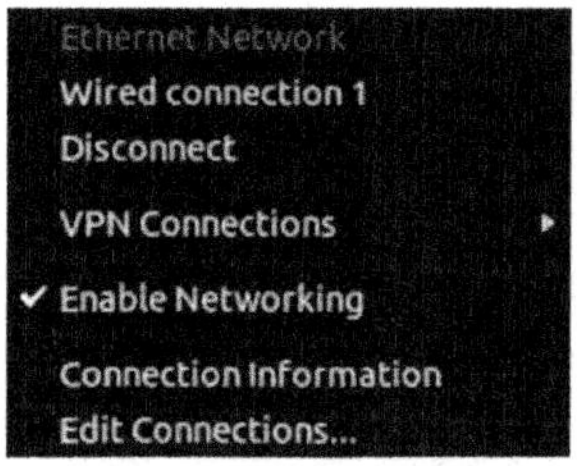

To disconnect your wired connection, you can choose the Disconnect entry on this menu. The menu will then show that you are disconnected. The wired connection will be displayed as a connection option. To reconnect later, choose an available wired connection, in this example Wired connection 1.

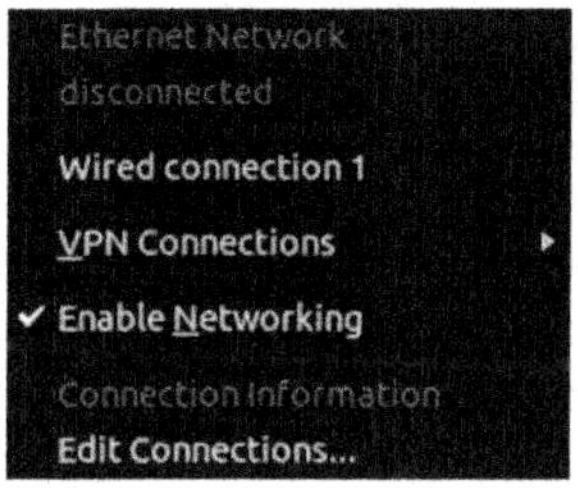

Network Manager wireless connections

With multiple wireless access points for Internet connections, a system could have several different network connections to choose from, instead of a single-line connection like DSL or cable. This is particularly true for notebook computers that could access different wireless connections at different locations. Instead of manually configuring a new connection each time one is encountered, the Network Manager tool can configure and select a connection to use automatically.

Network Manager will scan for wireless connections, checking for Extended Service Set Identifiers (ESSIDs). If an ESSID identifies a previously used connection, then it is selected. If several are found, then the recently used one is chosen. If only a new connection is available, then Network Manager waits for the user to choose one. A connection is selected only if the user is logged in.

Open the Network Manager menu to see a list of all possible network connections, including all available wireless connections (see Figure 3-19). Wireless entries display the name of the wireless network and a wave graph showing the strength of its signal. Computers with both wired and wireless devices show entries for both Wired Network and Wireless Networks. Computers with a wireless device only show entries for Wireless Networks. You can disable the display of wireless networks by selecting Enable Wireless from the menu. The check mark next to this entry is removed, and wireless detection is disabled. To re-activate your wireless connections, click the Enable Wireless entry again. A checkmark is displayed next to the entry and your wireless connections are now listed in the Network Manager menu.

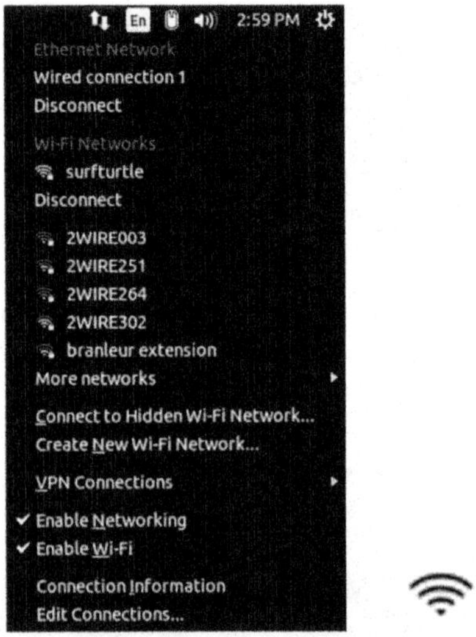

Figure 3-19: Network Manager connections menu: wired and wireless

Note: If a computer has both wired (Ethernet or dial-up) and wireless connection devices, as most laptops have, then you will see entries for both Wired and Wireless networks.

To connect to a wireless network, find its network entry in the Network Manager menu and click on it. If this the first time you are trying to connect to that network, you will be prompted to enter connection information: the wireless security and passphrase. The type of wireless security used by the network will be detected and displayed for you. If it is incorrect, you can use the drop-down menu to select the correct method. The entries will change depending on the method chosen. The WPA passphrase is one of the more common methods. Figure 3-20 shows the prompt for the passphrase to a wireless network that uses the WPA security method. A checkbox lets you see the passphrase should you need to check that you are entering it correctly. Click Connect to activate the connection.

Figure 3-20: Network Manager wireless authentication

Once connected, a message is displayed indicating that the connection has been established, as shown here.

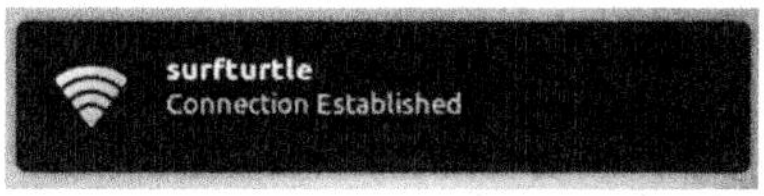

To disconnect from a particular wireless network, on the Network Manager menu click on the Disconnect option under the wireless entry.

When you connect to a wireless network for the first time, a configuration entry will be made for the wireless connection in the Wireless tab of the Network Connections dialog accessible from the System dash.

The very first time you make a wireless connection, you will be prompted to set up a keyring. The keyring holds your wireless connection passphrase, allowing you to connect to a wireless network without having to re-enter the network passphrase each time. You will be asked to create a keyring password for accessing the keyring. This is a one-time operation. Once the keyring is set up, any additional wireless connection passphrases will be added to it. When you first log in and try to connect to a wireless network, you will be prompted for your keyring password.

On KDE, clicking the Network Manager icon on the Plasma panel displays the KDE Network Manager widget. Interfaces are listed on the left, and connections on the right. To see a list of wireless connections, click the WLAN Interface icon on the left. Information about the WLAN interface is displayed with a list of possible wireless connections shown on the right side. Click the one you want to use to open an Add Network Connection dialog displaying the Wireless Security tab, where you can choose the type of security and enter the password. If you have not already set up a KDE Wallet password, you are prompted to do so now. This will allow automatic access to the connection later. You are then connected. You can click the Show Less button to hide all connections except the active one. Click Show More to see all possible connections, allowing you to switch to a different one. The Manage Connections button opens the KDE Network Manager dialog where you can manage all your connections.

Wireless connections can also be hidden. These are wireless connections that do not broadcast an SSID, making them undetectable by an automatic scan. To connect to a hidden wireless network, select "Connect to hidden wireless network" on the Network Manager menu. The Connection drop-down menu will select the New entry. If you have set up any hidden connections previously, they also are listed in the Connection drop-down menu. For a New connection, enter the wireless network name and select a security method. You are prompted in either case for your network keyring password.

Network Manager options

The network menu also provides options for editing your connection, shutting off your connection (Enable Networking and Enable Wireless), disabling all network access (Enable Networking), or viewing information about the connection, as shown here. On Ubuntu (Unity), these entries are included on the Network Manager menu. A computer with both wired and wireless connections will have entries to Enable Networking and Enable Wireless. Selecting Enable Wireless will disconnect only the wireless connections, leaving the wired connection active. The Enable Wireless checkbox will become unchecked and a message will be displayed telling you that your wireless connection is disconnected. Selecting Enable Networking will disable your wired connection, along with any wireless connections. Do this to work offline, without any network access.

A computer with only a wired network device (no wireless) will only show an Enable Networking entry. Selecting it will disconnect you from any network access, allowing you to work offline.

Setting up shared directories on the desktop (nautilus-share)

The GNOME desktop also provides an easy way to set up shared folders. The nautilus-share package (installed by default with the desktop) provides automatic configuration and access using Samba and NFS. You first have to install the Samba and NFS servers.

To share a folder on your Ubuntu system, right-click on it and select Sharing Options. This opens a window where you can allow sharing, and decide whether to permit modifying, adding, or deleting files in the folder (see Figure 3-21). You can also use the Share tab on the file's properties dialog. You can allow access to anyone who does not also have an account on your system (guest). Once you have made your selections, click the Create Share button. You can later change the sharing options if you want.

For a user to create a share, they have to have permission to do so. New users are not given this permission by default. On the Users and Group's Advanced dialog's Privileges tab set the "Share files with the local network" option.

Figure 3-21: Folder Sharing Options

To allow access by other users, permissions on the folder will have to be changed. You are prompted to allow Nautilus to make these changes for you. Just click the "Add the permissions automatically" button (see Figure 3-21).

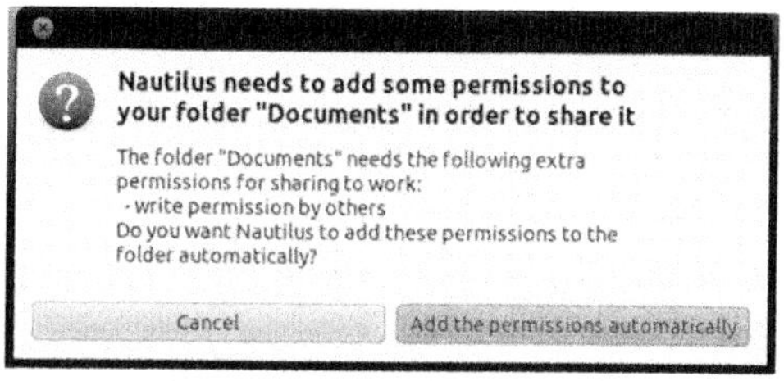

Figure 3-22 Folder Sharing permissions prompt

Note: If you are running a firewall, be sure to configure access for the NFS and Samba services, including browsing support. Otherwise, access to your shared folders by other computers may be blocked.

Folders that are shared display a sharing emblem next to their icon on a file manager window.

To allow other computers to access your folders be sure the sharing servers are installed: Samba for Windows systems and NFS (**nfs-kernelserver**) for Linux/Unix systems. The servers are configured and run for you automatically. You will not be able to share folders until these servers are installed. If your sharing servers are not installed, you will be prompted to install them the first time you try to share a folder (see Figure 3-23). Click the Install service button. The Samba servers will be downloaded and installed. You are then prompted to restart your desktop session. Click the Restart session button. You are now placed in the LightDM login screen. Log in again and then open the folder sharing dialog for the folder you want to share (Sharing Options).

Figure 3-23: Prompt to install sharing service (Samba and NFS)

Note: To share folders (directories) with other Linux systems on your network, you use the NFS service (**nfs-kernelserver**). For Windows systems you use the Samba service (**samba**). For Samba configuration you can use **system-config-samba**.

You can also install the Samba server directly with the Synaptic Package Manager (**samba** package) and from the Ubuntu Software Center | System | SMB/CIFS file, print, and login server for Unix (samba). Two servers are installed and run using the **smbd** and **nmbd** service scripts in the **/etc/init.d** directory (the **samba** service script is not longer used). The **smbd** server is the Samba server, and the **nmbd** server is the network discovery server.

Should the Samba server fail to start, you can start it manually in a terminal window with the commands:

```
sudo service nmbd start
sudo service smbd start
```

You can check the current status with the **status** option and restart with the **restart** option:

```
sudo service nmbd status
sudo service smbd status
```

When first installed, Samba imports the user accounts already configured on your Ubuntu system. Corresponding Windows users with the same user name and password as an Ubuntu account on your Ubuntu system are connected automatically to the Ubuntu shared folders. Should the Windows user have a different password, that user is prompted on Windows to enter a user name and password. This is an Ubuntu user name and password. In the case of a Windows user with the same user name but different password, the user would enter in the same user name with Ubuntu user password, not the Windows password.

Access is granted to all shares by any user. Should you want to implement restricted access by specific users and passwords, you would have to configure user level access using a Samba configuration tool, such as system-config-samba, as discussed in the next section.

To change the sharing permissions for a folder later, open the folder's Properties window and select the Share tab. When you make a change, a Modify Share button is displayed. Click it to make the changes.

Note: Avahi (installed with the desktop) provides your Ubuntu desktop with immediate access to any shared Windows directories. But, Windows or Linux clients can only access your shared Ubuntu directories through Samba and NFS.

Terminal Window on the desktop

The Terminal window allows you to enter Linux commands on a command line, accessible as Terminal, from the Applications lens | Accessories filter. It also provides you with a shell interface for using shell commands instead of your desktop. The command line is editable, allowing you to use the backspace key to erase characters on the line. Pressing a key will insert that character. You can use the left and right arrow keys to move anywhere on the line, and then press keys to insert characters, or use backspace to delete characters (see Figure 3-24). Folders, files, and executable files are color-coded: black for files, blue for folders, green for executable files, and aqua for links. Shared folders are displayed with a green background.

The terminal window will remember the previous commands you entered. Use the up and down arrows to have those commands displayed in turn on the command line. Press the ENTER key to re-execute the currently displayed command. You can even edit a previous command before running it, allowing you to execute a modified version of a previous command. This can be helpful if you need to re-execute a complex command with a different argument, or if you mistyped a complex command and want to correct it without having to re-type the entire command. The terminal window will display all your previous interactions and commands for that session. Use the scrollbar to see any previous commands you ran and their displayed results.

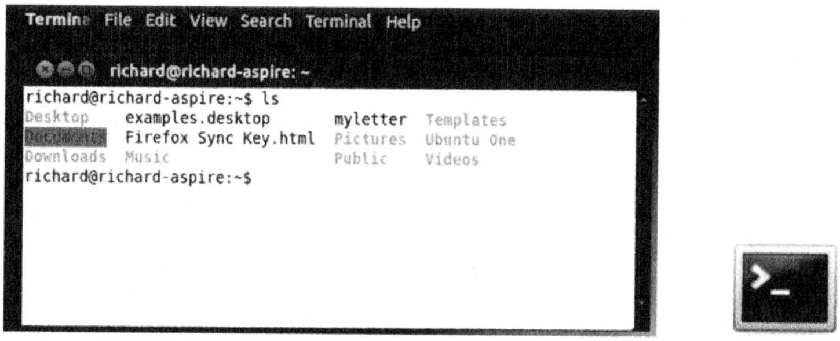

Figure 3-24: Terminal Window

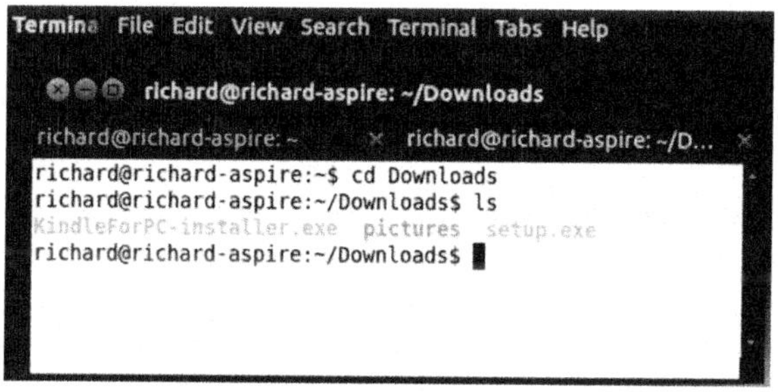

Figure 3-25: Terminal Window with tabs

You can open as many terminal windows as you want, each working in its own shell. Instead of opening a separate window for each new shell, you can open several shells in the same window, using tabs. Select Open Tab from the File menu to open a new tab (**Shift-Ctrl-t**). Each tab runs a separate shell, letting you enter different commands in each. You can use the Tabs menu to move to different tabs, or just click on its tab to select it. The Tab menu is displayed on the toolbar only if multiple tabs are open. For a single window, the Tab menu is not shown (see Figure 3-24).

The terminal window also supports desktop cut/copy and paste operations. You can copy a line from a Web page and paste it to the terminal window (you can use the Paste entry on the Terminal window's Edit menu, or press **Shift-Ctrl-v**). The command will appear and you can press ENTER to execute the command. This is useful for command line operations displayed on an instructional Web page. Instead of typing in a complex command yourself, just select and copy from the Web page directly, and then paste to the Terminal window. You can also perform any edits on the command, if needed, before executing it.

You can customize terminal windows using profiles. A default profile is set up already. You can create new ones with customized preferences. To customize your terminal window, select Profile Preferences from the Edit menu. This opens a window for setting your profile options with tabs for General, Title and Command, Colors, Background, Scrolling, and Compatibility. The window title lists your current profile. This will be the **default** profile if you have not set up and selected another profile (see Figure 3-26).

To create a new profile, choose New Profile from the File menu. This opens a Profiles window listing current profiles. Click the New button to open the New Profile window where you can enter the profile name, and select any profile to base it on. The default profile will be chosen initially. To edit a profile, select Profiles from the Edit menu to open the Profile window. Choose the one you want to edit, then click the Edit button to open the Editing Profile window for that profile.

On the General tab, you can select the default size of a terminal window in text rows and columns.

The Scrolling tab specifies the number of command lines your terminal history will keep. These are the lines you can move back through and select to re-execute. You can set this to unlimited to keep all the commands. You can also place the scrollbar on the right or left side.

Your terminal window will be set up to use a black background with white text. You can edit the profile to change the background and text colors on the Colors tab. De-select the "Use colors from system theme" entry. This enables the "Built-in schemes" menu from which you can select a "Black on white" display. Other color combinations are also listed, such as "Black on light yellow" and "Green on black." The Custom option lets you choose your own text and background colors. The colors on your open terminal window will change according to your selection, allowing you to see how the color choices will look.

Should you want a transparent or image background, use the Background tab. Initially the background will be set to a solid color (the colors chosen on the Colors tab). To use an image instead, select the Background image entry, then choose an image file. For a transparent background, choose the Transparent background entry and then set the amount of shading (none is completely transparent and maximum shows no transparency).

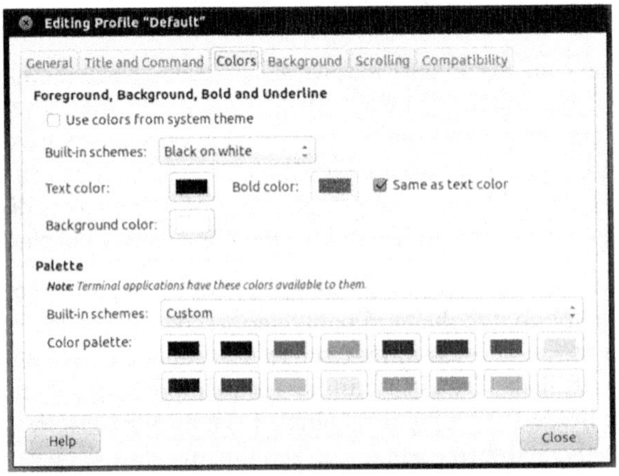

Figure 3-26: Terminal Window Profile configuration

System Settings

You can configure desktop settings and perform most administrative tasks using the administration tools listed in the GNOME System Settings dialog, accessible from the session menu and the Launcher. System Settings organizes tools into Personal, Hardware, and System categories (see Figure 3-27).

Setting	Description
Appearance	Desktop Backgrounds, Themes, and Launcher behavior configuration.
Assistive Technologies	Enables features like accessible login and keyboard screen.
Backup	Deja Dup backup tool
Bluetooth	Bluetooth detection and configuration
Brightness and Lock	Set screen brightness and the inactivity time to dim or lock the screen.
Color	Set the color profile for a device
Details	System and hardware information, default applications, and defaults for removable media.
Displays	Change your screen resolution, refresh rate, and screen orientation.
Keyboard	Configure repeat key sensitivity, and keys for special tasks.
Language Support	Language selection
Landscape Service	Canonical's Landscape commercial management service
Mouse and Touchpad	Mouse and touchpad configuration: select hand orientation, speed, and accessibility.
Network	Lets you turn wired and wireless networks on and off. You can access an available wireless network and proxy configuration
Online Accounts	Configure online accounts for use by social networking applications.
Power	Set the power options for laptop inactivity.
Printers	Printer configuration with system-config-printer (see Chapter 10)
Sound	Configure sound effects, output volume, sound device options, input volume, and sound application settings.
Time & Date	Set the time and date, including time zone, along with clock display options.
Security & Privacy	Manage when to require a password, your history logs, and search options.
Software & Updates	Manage repositories and drivers (Additional Drivers tab)
Text Entry	Configure your keyboard: selecting options, models, and typing breaks, accessibility features like slow, bounce, and sticky keys.
Universal Access	Set Universal access settings for the screen reader, text size, contrast, visual alerts, screen keyboard, and keypad based mouse.
User Accounts	Manage users, a GNOME 3 tool
Wacom Graphics tablet	Wacom graphics tablet configuration

Table 3-4: Desktop System Settings

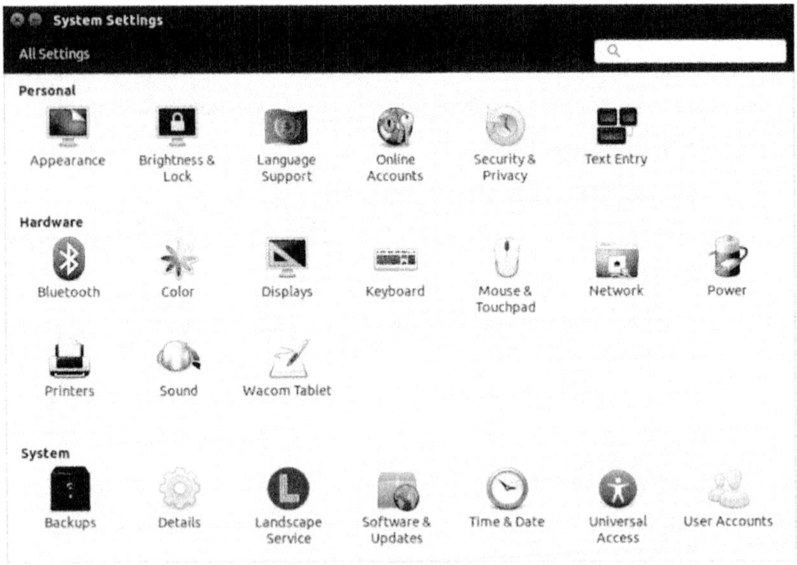

Figure 3-27: System Settings dialog

Many invoke the Ubuntu supported system tools available from previous releases such as Sound (PulseAudio) and Printing (system-config-printer). Others use the new GNOME 3 configuration and administrative tools such as Brightness, User Accounts, and Power. The Color tool lets you choose color schemes for different devices such as scanners, cameras, and printers. System Settings tools will open with an "All Settings" button at the top, which you can click to return to the System Settings dialog. Table 3-4 lists the System Settings tools.

Ubuntu Help Center on the desktop

A great deal of support documentation is already installed on your system, and is accessible from online sources. The GNOME and KDE desktops feature Help systems that use a browser-like interface to display help files. The Help browsers support the Ubuntu Help Center, which provides Ubuntu specific help.

If you need to ask a question, you can choose Help | Get online help to access the Ubuntu help support at **https://answers.launchpad.net** and at **http://askubuntu.com**. Here you can submit your question, and check answered questions about Ubuntu.

Ubuntu Desktop Guide

To start the Ubuntu Desktop Guide, choose "Ubuntu Help" from the Session menu. The Guide displays several links covering Ubuntu topics (see Figure 3-28). Unity topics covered include the Launcher, the Dash, indicator menus, window management, and workspace access.You can use the right and left arrows to move through the previous documentation you displayed. You can also search for topics. The search box displays the name of the current document. Clicking on the search bar lets you enter a search term. Press ENTER to display the results. You can also add bookmarks for documents and search results by clicking the yellow start button at the right of the search box (or choosing "Add Bookmark" from the Bookmarks menu).

Figure 3-28: Ubuntu Desktop Guide

These pages are organized more like frequently asked questions documents with more detailed headings, designed to provide a clearer understanding of what the document is about (see Figure 3-29). The Sound, video, and pictures link opens a page with entries like "Why won't DVDs play" and "My new iPod won't work."

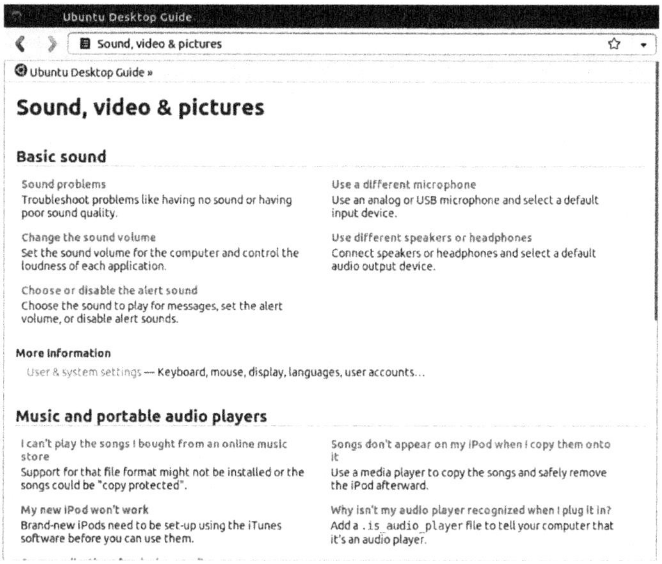

Figure 3-29: Ubuntu Desktop Guide topics

Help documents will include helpful links such as an install link that opens the Ubuntu Software Center showing the software you have to install, or a link to a user guide for a relevant application (see Figure 3-30). At the bottom of most pages, a More Information section will have links for more detailed information.

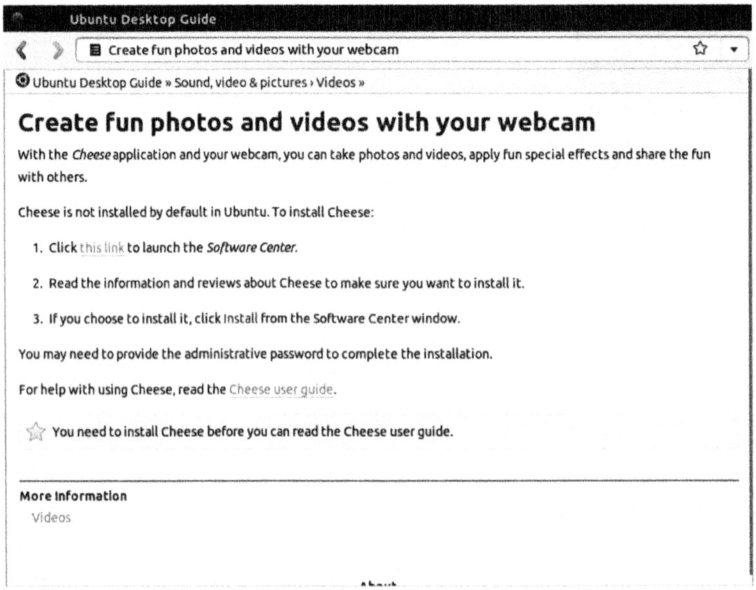

Figure 3-30: Ubuntu Desktop Guide page

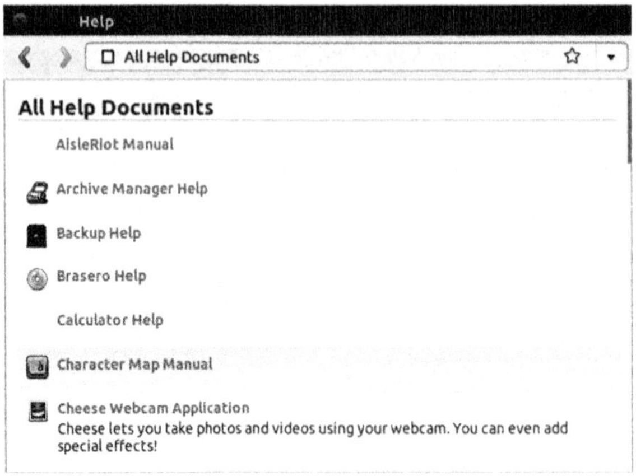

Figure 3-31: Ubuntu Help, All Documents

If you want to see the available application help documents, choose All Documents from the Help application's Go menu. You will see application manuals installed applications such as the Shotwell, Synaptic package manager, Totem movie player, the Ubuntu Software Center, and Rhythmbox (see Figure 3-31).

ubuntu

4. Managing Software

Ubuntu Package Management Software
Ubuntu Software Repositories
tasksel
Aptitude
Managing software with APT: apt-get
Command Line Search and Information
Source code files
Managing Software from the desktop
Synaptic Package Manager
Update Software
Managing non-repository packages with dpkg
Installing Software from Compressed Archives: .tar.gz
Checking Software Package Digital Signatures

Installing software is an administrative function performed by a user with administrative access. Unless you chose to install all your packages during your installation, only some of the many applications and utilities available for users on Linux were installed on your system. On Ubuntu, you can easily install or remove software from your system with the **apt-get** command, or, from the desktop, the Synaptic Package Manager. Alternatively, you can install software by downloading and compiling its source code.

APT (Advanced Package Tool) is integrated as the primary installation package tool. When you install a package with **apt-get** , the Ubuntu Software Center, or the Synaptic Package Manager, APT will be invoked and it will automatically select and download the appropriate packages from the online repository.

A DEB software package includes all the files needed for a software application. A Linux software application often consists of several files that must be installed in different directories. The program itself is most likely placed in a directory called **/usr/bin**; online manual files go in another directory, and library files go in yet another directory.

When you select a package for download, APT will install any additional dependent (required) packages. APT will also install all recommended packages by default. Many software applications have additional features that rely on recommended packages.

Ubuntu Package Management Software

Though all Ubuntu software packages have the same DEB format, they can be managed and installed using different package management software tools. The primary software management tool is APT. Some tools will operate on the command line interface, while others only work on the desktop.

Check the Ubuntu Server Guide | Package Management for basic command line software operations and repository configuration.

`https://help.ubuntu.com/stable/serverguide/package-management.html`

Command Line interface tools

If you installed the Ubuntu Server CD, you will only have access to the following command line interface based tools.

tasksel Cursor-based screen for selecting package groups and particular servers. This tool will work on the command-line interface installed by the Ubuntu Server CD. You can also run it in a terminal window on a desktop. Use arrow keys to move to and entry, the spacebar to select it, the Tab key to move to the OK button. Press ENTER on the OK button to perform your installs.

aptitude Front end for tools like dpkg or apt-get, screen based, uses own database, **/var/lib/aptitude**.

apt-get primary command line tool to install, update, and remove software, uses own database, **/var/lib/apt/**, repository info at **/var/cache/apt**.

dpkg older command line tool to install, update, remove, and query software packages. Uses own database, **/var/lib/dpkg**, repository info at **/var/cache/apt**, the same as APT.

Desktop tools

If you installed the Ubuntu Desktop DVD or one of its variations like Kubuntu, you will have access to the following desktop interface tools, as well as using a terminal window to run the previously listed command line tools.

APT (Advanced Package Tool): The Synaptic Package Manager, the Ubuntu Software Center, update-manager, dpkg, and apt-get are front ends for APT.

Ubuntu Software Center: GNOME Graphical front end for managing packages, repository info at **/var/cache/apt**, same as APT

Update Manager: Ubuntu graphical front end for updating installed software, uses APT.

Synaptic Package Manager: Graphical front end for managing packages, repository info at **/var/cache/apt**, same as APT. Ubuntu no longer supports it.

Muon is the KDE software manager, a graphical front end for APT.

Ubuntu Software Repositories

There are four main components or sections to the Ubuntu repository: main, restricted, universe, and multiverse. These components are described in detail at:

`https://help.ubuntu.com/community/Repositories/Ubuntu`

A complete listing of software packages for the Ubuntu distribution, along with a search capability is located at:

`http://packages.ubuntu.com`

Repository Components

The following repository components are included in the main Ubuntu repository:

main: Officially supported Ubuntu software (canonical), includes GStreamer Good plug-ins.

restricted: Commonly used and required for many applications, but not open source or freely licensed, like proprietary graphics card drivers from Nvidia and ATI, needed for hardware support. Because they are not open source, they are not guaranteed to work.

universe: All open source Linux software not directly supported by Ubuntu includes GStreamer Bad plug-ins.

multiverse: Linux software that does not meet licensing requirements and is not considered essential. It may not necessarily work. For example, the GStreamer ugly package is in this repository. Check **http://www.ubuntu.com/about /about-ubuntu/licensing**.

Repositories

In addition to the Ubuntu repository, Ubuntu maintains several other repositories used primarily for maintenance and support for existing packages. The updates repository holds updated packages for a release. The security updates repository contains critical security package updates every system will need.

Ubuntu repository: Collection of Ubuntu-compliant software packages for releases organized into main, universe, multiverse, and restricted sections.

Updates: Updates for packages in the main repository, both main and restricted sections.

Backports: Software under development for the next Ubuntu release, but packaged for use in the current one. Not guaranteed or fully tested. Backports access is now enabled by default.

Security updates: Critical security fixes for main repository software.

Partners: Third party proprietary software tested to work on Ubuntu. You need to authorize access manually.

The Backports repository provides un-finalized or development versions for new and current software. They are not guaranteed to work, but may provide needed features.

Ubuntu Repository Configuration file: sources.list and sources.list.d

Repository configuration is managed by APT using configuration files in the **/etc/apt** directory. The **/etc/apt/sources.list** file holds repository entries. The main and restricted sections are enabled by default. An entry consists of a single line with the following format:

```
format  URI  release  section
```

The format is normally **deb**, for Debian package format. The URI (universal resource identifier) provides the location of the repository, such as an FTP or Web URL. The release name is the official name of a particular Ubuntu distribution like vivid or oneric. Ubuntu 15.04 has the name vivid. The section can be one or more terms that identify a section in that release's repository. There can be more than one term used to specify a section, like **main** and **restricted** to specify the restricted section in the Ubuntu repository. The Multiverse and Universe sections can be specified by single terms: **universe** and **multiverse**. You can also list individual packages if you want. The entry for the Vivid restricted section is shown here.

```
deb http://us.archive.ubuntu.com/ubuntu/  vivid  main restricted
```

Corresponding source code repositories will use a **deb-src** format.

```
deb-src http://us.archive.ubuntu.com/ubuntu/ vivid main restricted
```

The update repository for a section is referenced by the **-updates** suffix, as in **vivid-updates**.

```
deb http://us.archive.ubuntu.com/ubuntu/  vivid-updates  main restricted
```

The security repository for a section is referenced with the suffix **-security**, as **vivid-security**.

```
deb http://security.ubuntu.com/ubuntu/  vivid-security  main restricted
```

Both Universe and Multiverse repositories should already be enabled. Each will have an updates repository as well as corresponding source code repositories, like those shown here for Universe.

```
deb http://us.archive.ubuntu.com/ubuntu/ vivid universe
deb-src http://us.archive.ubuntu.com/ubuntu/ vivid universe
deb http://us.archive.ubuntu.com/ubuntu/ vivid-updates universe
deb-src http://us.archive.ubuntu.com/ubuntu/ vivid-updates universe
```

The Backports repository is now enabled by default on the Ubuntu server. It holds applications being developed for future Ubuntu releases and may not work well.

Comments begin with a # mark. You can add comments of your own if you wish. Commenting an entry effectively disables that component of a repository. Placing a # mark before a repository entry will effectively disable it.

Commented entries are included for the extras and Canonical partners repositories. The extras repository provides third party software. Partners include companies like Adobe, VMware, and Parallels.

Most entries, including third-party entries for Ubuntu partners, can be managed using Software & Updates. The backports entry requires that you edit the **sources.list** file. You can edit the file directly with the following command.

```
sudo nano /etc/apt/sources.list
```

Remove the # at the beginning of the line to activate a repository such as partners.

```
# deb http://archive.canonical.com/ubuntu/ vivid partner
```

Repository information does not have to be added to the **sources.list** file directly. It can also be placed in a text file in the **/etc/apt/sources.list.d** directory, which APT will read as if part of the **sources.list** file. Editing such an important file always involves the risk of incorrectly changing the entries.

Software Management with Tasksel, DEB, APT, and DKPG

Both the Debian distribution and Ubuntu use the Debian package format (DEB) for their software packages. Two basic package managers are available for use with Debian packages: the Advanced Package Tool (APT) and the Debian Package tool (dpkg). APT is designed to work with repositories and is used to install and maintain all your package installations on Ubuntu. Though you can install packages directly as single files with just dpkg, it is always advisable to use APT. Information and package files for Ubuntu compliant software can be obtained from **http://packages.ubuntu.com**.

You can also download source code versions of applications, and then compile and install them on your system. Where this process once was complex, it has been significantly streamlined with the use of configure *scripts.* Most current source code, including GNU software, is distributed with a configure script. The configure script automatically detects your system configuration and generates a Makefile, which is used to compile the application and create a binary file that is compatible with your system. In most cases, with a few Makefile operations you can compile and install complex source code on any system.

Installing from source code requires that supporting development libraries and source code header files be installed. You can do this separately for each major development platform, like GNOME, KDE, or just the kernel. Alternatively you can run the APT metapackage **build-essential** for all the Ubuntu development packages. You will only have to do this once.

```
sudo apt-get install build-essential
```

DEB Software Packages

A Debian package will automatically resolve dependencies, installing any other needed packages instead of simply reporting their absence. Packages are named with the software name, the version number, and the **.deb** extension. Check **http://www.us.debian.org/doc** for more information. File name format is as follows:

the package name

version number

distribution label and build number. Packages created specifically for Ubuntu will have the **ubuntu** label here. Attached to it will be the build number, the number of times the package was built for Ubuntu.

architecture The type of system on which the package runs, like i386 for Intel 32-bit x86 systems, or amd64 for both Intel and AMD 64-bit systems, x86_64.

package format. This is always **deb**

For example, the package name for 3dchess is 3dchess, with a version and build number 0.8.1-17, and an architecture amd64 for a 64 bit system.

```
3dchess_0.8.1-17_amd64.deb
```

The following package has an **ubuntu** label, a package specifically created for Ubuntu. The version number is 1.21 and build number is 11, with the Ubuntu label **ubuntu1**. The architecture is i386 for a 32-bit system.

```
icebreaker_1.21-11ubuntu1_i386.deb
```

Installing and Removing Software with tasksel

The easiest way to install server packages is to use tasksel, which will display a list of all your server metapackages, as well as all other meta-packages on your configured repositories. To run tasksel, enter the **tasksel** command at the shell prompt. If you are using a desktop, open a terminal window and enter the **tasksel** command.

```
sudo tasksel
```

Should you want to quit tasksel without installing or removing any software, tab to the OK button and press ENTER. The tasksel application ends, and you return to the shell prompt.

The tasksel tool displays a keyboard-based dialog listing the server and package collections (see Figure 4-1). Those already installed have an asterisk next to their entries. Use the arrow keys to move to an entry and press the spacebar to select it. When you have made all your selections, use the Tab key to move to the OK button. Then press the ENTER key to install the selected software.

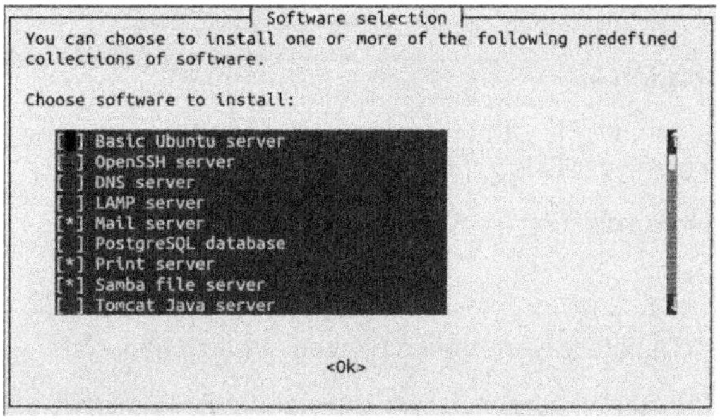

Figure 4-1: Tasksel server and meta package installation

You can also use tasksel to uninstall packages. Installed packages will have an asterisk next to them. Move to the package you want to remove and press the spacebar. The asterisk will disappear, leaving you with empty brackets. Tab to the OK button and press ENTER. An installation window is displayed, and the de-selected package collections are removed.

The last entry in the tasksel is Manual Page Selection. Selecting this entry opens the Aptitude package manager (discussed in the next section), which provides you with a screen-based interface to install, remove, and update individual packages.

The tasksel dialog displays an extensive list of package collections covering the Internet servers, the Ubuntu desktops and desktop derivatives, and even graphics and multimedia packages. The desktops will install a complete desktop system, such as the Ubuntu desktop which includes the LightDM. If you install a desktop, the X server and the desktop interface is started up automatically, just as if you installed from the Ubuntu desktop DVD, instead of from the server CD. You will still be using the server kernel, though.

If you already know the name of the server or package collection you want to install, you can use **tasksel** command with the **install** option and the package name to install the package directly. You would not have to use the screen interface. The package names are usually the same as those listed on the screen interface, but in lower case with a dash connecting the words, as in samba-server for Samba server. The option **--list-tasks** lists the server and meta package names with their associated descriptions used on the screen interface. The following command directly installs the Samba server.

```
sudo tasksel install samba-server
```

You can use the **remove** option to remove server or meta package. Check the tasksel Man page for a complete set of options. The following example removes the DNS server (BIND).

```
sudo tasksel remove dns-server
```

Managing software with Aptitude

The Aptitude software tool provides a keyboard based screen interface on command line interfaces for managing software. Because of its easy-to-use screen interface, Aptitude is a very effective package management tool for Ubuntu server installs that do not have a desktop.

Check the Ubuntu Server Guide | Package Management | Aptitude for basic operations.

```
https://help.ubuntu.com/stable/serverguide/aptitude.html
```

Key	Description
Ctrl-t	Access menu, the Ctrl-t will toggle between the menu and the main screen. Menu entries will also show equivalent key operations.
Arrow and Page up/down	Move to a selection
ENTER	Expand a category or open a package description
q	Quit the current screen. If only one screen is open, quit Aptitude
+	Mark a package for installation
-	Mark a package for removal
g g	Install and removed marked packages, the first g displays a preview showing what packages will be installed and removed. Pressing g again performs the actual install and remove operations. Press **q** on the preview screen to leave the preview and not perform any install and remove operations.
/	Search for a package, the Find operation
u	Update the package list
U	Mark packages to be updated for updating, use **g g** to perform the actual update.
?	Display the list of key commands
F6 and F7	Move forward and backward between tabs (screens)

Table 4-1: Aptitude key commands

A menu bar at the top lets you use your arrow keys to select menus and entries for package management, searching, and views (see Figure 4-2). You use the **Ctrl-t** keys to access the menu, and the arrow keys to move to different menus. To quit aptitude just press the **q** key if only one screen is open. Aptitude can have several screens open at the same time, though only one is shown at a time. The tabs for the screens are listed under the menubar. As you open a new screen, its label will be displayed below the menu. Pressing the **q** key will close the current screen, and, if there is only one screen open, will quit from Aptitude. To move from one tab screen to another, use the F6 and F7 keys. To see a listing of all the key commands, press the **?** key. Several commonly used key commands are listed in Table 4-1.

You start Aptitude by entering the **sudo aptitude** command on the command line. On desktops open a terminal window.

```
sudo aptitude
```

The screen will have two main views, the top one listing packages by category, and the bottom one displaying information about a selected package or category. On the top view, use the arrow keys to move to an entry, and then press the ENTER key to expand an entry. Categories will expand to a package listing, and packages will open a detailed description, along with a listing of dependent packages. Use the + key to mark a package for installation, and the - key to mark an installed package for removal. You can also use the Package menu's Install and Remove entries.

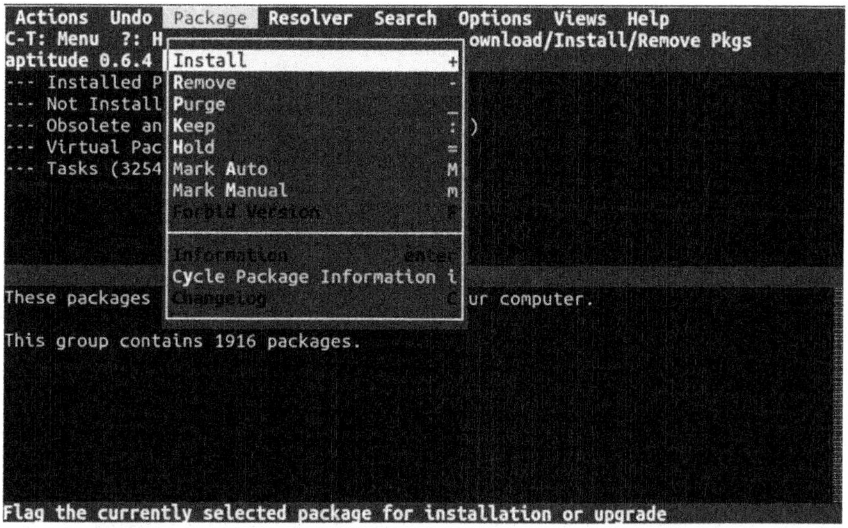

Figure 4-2: Aptitude package manager

Codes	Description
i	Installed package
c	Package not installed, but package configuration remains on system
p	Purged from system
v	Virtual package
B	Broken package
u	Unpacked files, but package not yet configured
C	Half-configured - Configuration failed and requires fix
H	Half-installed - Removal failed and requires fix

Table 4-2: Aptitude package codes

Each package entry begins with a letter denoting the package state. Uninstalled packages will be labeled with a **p** indicating a purged package, one not on the system. Installed packages will have the letter **i**. Packages marked for installation or removal will have an additional letter indicating an action yet to be taken. When a package is marked for installation it will have both a **p** and **i** (see Figure 4-3), as shown here for the **alien** package entry. Table 4-2 lists the package codes for Aptitude.

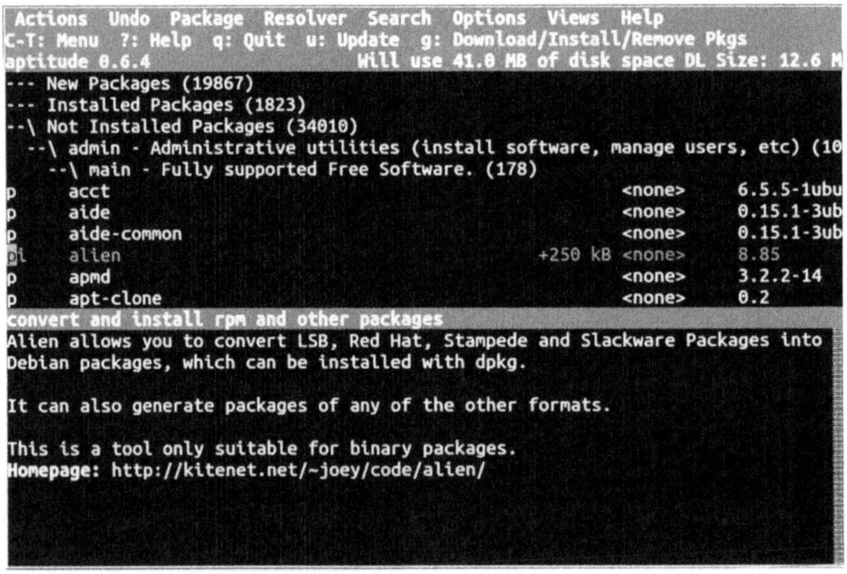

Figure 4-3: Aptitude: selecting packages

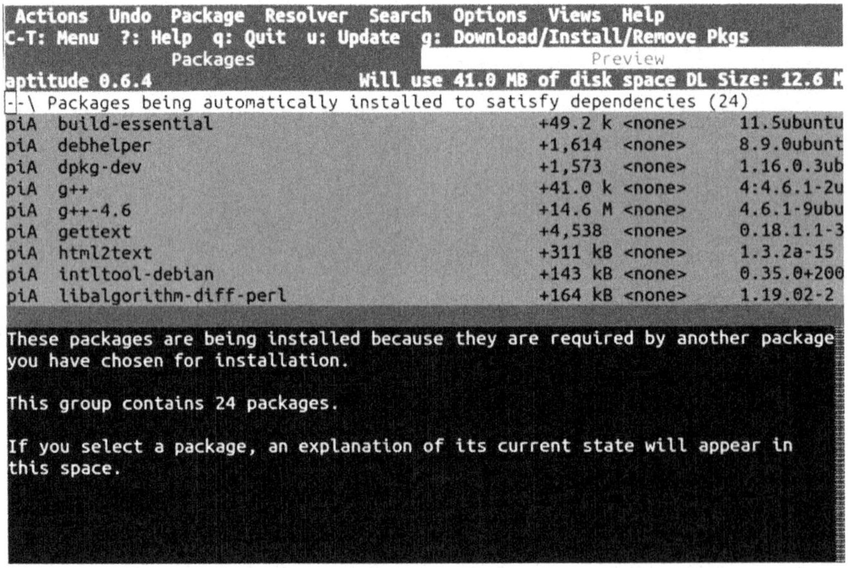

Figure 4-4: Aptitude: installing packages

Once you have selected packages for installation (or removal), press the **g** key. A preview of the packages to be installed and removed will be listed (see Figure 4-4). Then press the **g** key again; you will need to press **g** twice to install. Aptitude will change to the shell interface, displaying the download, unpack, and setup messages as packages are being installed. You will then be prompted to press return (the ENTER key), to return to the Aptitude interface. To install you could also select the Actions | Install/remove packages menu entry twice.

If you know the package name, you can search for it to locate it more easily. To open a search window, press the / key (or from the menubar (**Ctrl-t**) use the right arrow key to move to the Search menu and select Find). Type in your search and press ENTER. The selected package will be listed and highlighted.

In Figure 4-4, you will also see that two tabs (screens) are actually open, Packages and Preview. The Preview tab is currently displayed. You can use the F7 and F6 keys to move to the other tab (Packages) and back again. Use the q key to close a tab. With the Preview tab open, pressing **q** will quit and close the Preview screen.

Managing software with APT

APT is designed to work with repositories, and will handle any dependencies for you. It uses **dpkg** to install and remove individual packages, but can also determine what dependent packages need to be installed, as well as query and download packages from repositories. Several popular tools for APT let you manage your software easily, like the Synaptic Package Manager, the Ubuntu Software Center, and aptitude. The Ubuntu Software Center and the Synaptic Package Manager rely on a desktop interface like GNOME. If you are using the command line interface, you can use **apt-get** to manage packages. Using the **apt-get** command on the command line you can install, update, and remove packages. Check the **apt-get** man page for a detailed listing of **apt-get** commands (see Table 4-3).

```
apt-get command package
```

Command	Description
update	Download and resynchronize the package listing of available and updated packages for APT supported repositories. APT repositories updated are those specified in /etc/apt/sources.list
upgrade	Update packages, install new versions of installed packages if available.
dist-upgrade	Update (upgrade) all your installed packages to a new release
install	Install a specific package, using its package name, not full package file name.
remove	Remove a software package from your system.
source	Download and extract a source code package
check	Check for broken dependencies
clean	Removes the downloaded packages held in the repository cache on your system. Used to free up disk space.

Table 4-3: apt-get commands

The **apt-get** command takes two arguments: the command to perform and the name of the package. Other APT package tools follow the same format. The command is a term such as **install** for installing packages, or **remove** to uninstall a package. Use the **install**, **remove**, or **update** commands respectively. You only need to specify the software name, not the package's full file name. APT will determine that. To install the alien package you would use:

```
sudo apt-get install alien
```

To make sure that **apt-get** has current repository information, use the **apt-get update** command.

```
sudo apt-get update
```

To remove packages, you use the **remove** command.

```
sudo apt-get remove alien
```

You can use the **-s** option to check the install operation without performing the actual installation. This allows you to check whether any dependency problems exist. For remove operations you can use **-s** to find out first what dependent packages will also be removed.

```
sudo apt-get remove -s alien
```

A complete log of all install, remove, and update operations are kept in the **/var/log/dpkg.log** file. You can consult this file to find out exactly what files were installed or removed.

Configuration for APT is held in the **/etc/apt** directory. Here the **sources.list** file lists the distribution repositories from where packages are installed. Source lists for additional third-party repositories are kept in the **/etc/sources.list.d** directory. GPG (GNU Privacy Guard) database files hold validation keys for those repositories. Specific options for **apt-get** are can be found in the **/etc/apt.conf** file or in various files located in the **/etc/apt.conf.d** directory.

Updating packages (Upgrading) with apt-get

The **apt-get** tool also lets you easily update your entire system at once. The terms update and upgrade are used differently from other software tools. In **apt-get**, the **update** command just updates your package listing, checking for packages that may need to install newer versions, but not installing those versions. Technically, it updates the package list that APT uses to determine what packages need to be updated. The term upgrade is used to denote the actual update of a software package; a new version is downloaded and installed. What is referred to as updating by **apt-get**, other package managers refer to as obtaining the list of software packages to be updated. In **apt-get**, upgrading is what other package managers refer to as performing updates.

TIP: The terms **update** and **upgrade** can be confusing when used with **apt-get**. The **update** operation updates the Apt package list only, whereas an **upgrade** actually downloads and installs updated packages.

Upgrading is a simple matter of running **apt-get** with the **upgrade** command. With no package specified, using **apt-get** with the **upgrade** command will upgrade your entire system. Add the **-u** option to list packages as they are upgraded. First, make sure your repository information (package list) is up to date with the **update** command, then issue the **upgrade** command.

```
sudo apt-get update
sudo apt-get -u upgrade
```

For automatic updates, install the **unattended-upgrades** package if you have not done so already.

```
sudo apt-get install unattended-upgrades
```

Security updates are enabled by default. To configure updates, you edit the **/etc/apt/apt.conf.d/50unattended-upgrades** file.

```
sudo nano /etc/apt/apt.conf.d/50unattended-upgrades
```

To allow updates, remove the preceding comment characters (//) from the "${distro_id} ${distro_codename}-updates" entry in the **Unattended-Upgrade::Allowed-Origins** section.

```
Unattended-Upgrade::Allowed-Origins {
        "${distro_id} ${distro_codename}-security";
//      "${distro_id} ${distro_codename}-updates";
//      "${distro_id} ${distro_codename}-proposed";
//      "${distro_id} ${distro_codename}-backports";
};
```

In the **/etc/apt/apt.conf.d/10periodic** file you can specify the frequency of the updates as well as the download and package list update frequency.

```
APT::Periodic::Update-Package-Lists "1";
APT::Periodic::Download-Upgradeable-Packages "1";
APT::Periodic::AutocleanInterval "7";
APT::Periodic::Unattended-Upgrade "1";
```

To be notified of updates, install the **apticron** package.

```
sudo apt-get install apticron
```

Edit the **/etc/apticron/apticron.conf** file to set notification options such as the email address to sent notification messages to.

Command Line Search and Information: dpkg-query and apt-cache tools

The **dpkg-query** command lets you list detailed information about your packages. It operates on the command line (terminal window). Use **dpkg-query** with the **-l** option to list all your packages.

```
dpkg-query -l
```

The **dpkg** command can operate as a front end for **dpkg-query**, detecting its options to perform the appropriate task. The preceding command could also be run as:

```
dpkg -l
```

Listing a particular package requires and exact match on the package name, unless you use pattern matching operators. The following command lists the **wine** package (Windows Compatibility Layer).

```
dpkg-query -l wine
```

A pattern matching operator, such as *, placed after a pattern will display any packages beginning with the specified pattern. The pattern with operators needs to be placed in single quotation marks to prevent an attempt by the shell to use the pattern to match on filenames on your current directory. The following example finds all packages beginning with the pattern "wine". This would include packages with names such as **wine-doc** and **wine-utils**.

```
dpkg-query -l 'wine*'
```

You can further refine the results by using **grep** to perform an additional search. The following operation first outputs all packages beginning with **wine**, and from those results, the **grep** operations lists only those with the pattern **dev** in their name, such as **wine-dev**.

```
dpkg -l  'wine*' | grep 'dev'
```

Use the **-L** option to list only the files that a package has installed.

```
dpkg-query  -L  wine
```

To see the status information about a package, including its dependencies and configuration files, use the **-s** option. Fields will include Status, Section, Architecture, Version, Depends (dependent packages), Suggests, Conflicts (conflicting packages), and Conffiles (configuration files).

```
dpkg-query -s  wine
```

The status information will also provide suggested dependencies. These are packages not installed, but likely to be used. For the wine package, the **msttcorefonts** Windows fonts package is suggested.

```
dpkg-query  -s  wine | grep Suggests
```

Use the **-S** option to determine to which package a particular file belongs to.

```
dpkg-query  -S  filename
```

You can also obtain information with the **apt-cache** tool. Use the search command with **apt-cache** to perform a search.

```
apt-cache search wine
```

To find dependencies for a particular package, use the **depends** command.

```
apt-cache depends wine
```

To display just the package description, use the **show** command.

```
apt-cache show wine
```

Note: With the Aptitude software manager, you can use the **aptitude** command with the **search** and **show** options to find and display information about packages.

Source code files

Though you can install source code files directly, the best way to install one is to use **apt-get**. Use the **source** command with the package name. Packages will be downloaded and extracted.

```
sudo apt-get source alien
```

The **--download** option lets you just download the source package without extracting it. The **--compile** option will download, extract, compile, and package the source code into a Debian binary package, ready for installation.

No dependent packages will be downloaded. If you have a software package that requires any dependent packages to run, you will have to download and compile those also. To obtain needed dependent files, use the **build-dep** option. All your dependent files will be located and downloaded for you automatically.

```
sudo apt-get build-dep alien
```

Managing Software from the Ubuntu Desktop

If you have install the Ubuntu desktop (either from the Server install or directly from a Desktop DVD), you can use desktop-based software management tools for installing, updating, and removing software.

Repositories managed from Ubuntu Desktop: Software & Updates

If you have installed a desktop interface, you can manage your repositories with the Software & Updates dialog (formerly Software Sources), allowing you to enable or disable repository sections, as well as add new entries. This dialog edits the **/etc/apt/sources.list** file directly. You can access Software & Updates from the Applications lens, System filter. You can also access it on the Ubuntu Software Center from the Edit menu, and on the Synaptic Package Manager from the Settings menu as the Repositories entry. The Software & Updates dialog displays five tabs: Ubuntu Software, Other Software, Updates, Authentication, and Statistics (see Figure 4-5). The Ubuntu Software tab lists all the Ubuntu repository section entries. These include the main repository, universe, restricted, and multiverse, as well as source code. Those that are enabled will be checked. Initially all of them, except the source code, will be enabled. You can enable or disable a repository section by checking or un-checking its entry. You can select the repository server to use from the "Download from" drop-down menu.

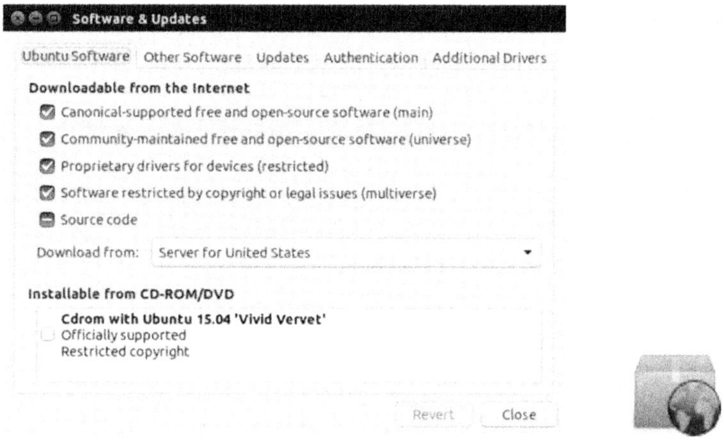

Figure 4-5: Software & Updates Ubuntu Software repository sections.

On the Other Software tab, you can add repositories for third-party software (see Figure 4-6). The repository for Ubuntu partners will already be listed, but not checked. Check that entry if you want access to software from the Partners repository such as Adobe reader. To add a third-party repository manually, click the Add Volume button. This opens a dialog where you enter the complete APT entry, starting with the deb format, followed by the URL, release, and sections or packages. This is the line as it will appear in the **/etc/apt/sources.list** file. Once entered, click the Add Source button.

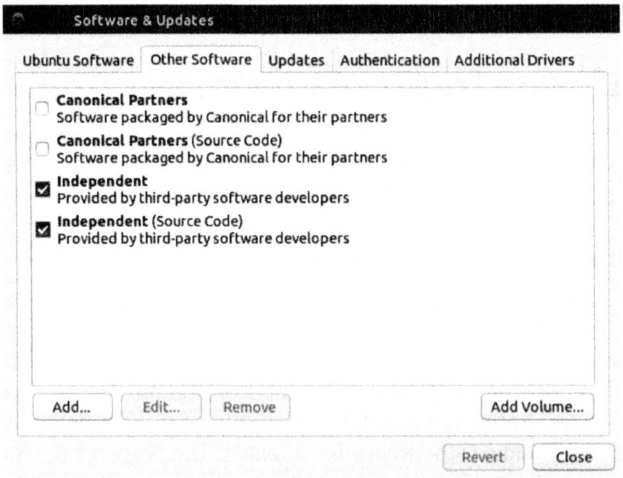

Figure 4-6: Software & Updates Other Software configuration

The Updates tab lets you configure how updates are handled (see Figure 4-7). The tab specifies both your update repositories and how automatic updates are managed. You have the option to install Important Security Updates (vivid-security), Recommended Updates (vivid-updates), Pre-released Updates (vivid-proposed), and Unsupported Updates (vivid-backports). The Important Security and Recommended updates will already be selected; these cover updates for the entire Ubuntu repository. Pre-released and unsupported updates are useful if you have installed any packages from the backports or pre-release repositories.

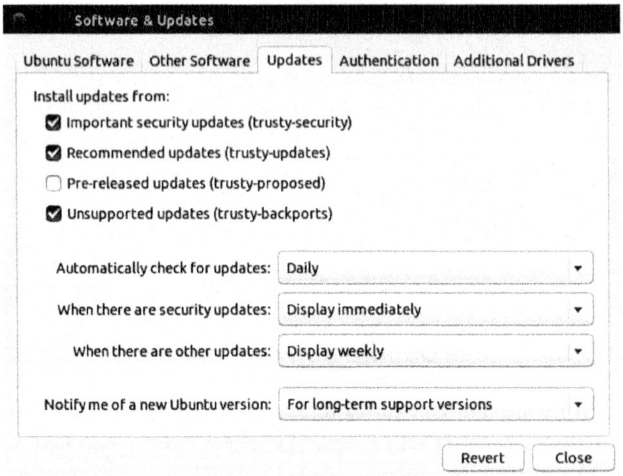

Figure 4-7: Software & Updates Update configuration

Your system is already configured to check for updates automatically on a daily basis. You can opt not to check for updates at all by un-checking the "Check for updates" check box. You also have options for how updates are handled. You can install any security updates automatically, without confirmation. You can download updates in the background. Or you can just be notified of available updates, and then choose to install them when you want. The options are exclusive.

On this tab, you also can choose what releases to be notified of: the LTS releases only, all releases, or none.

The Authentication tab shows the repository software signature keys that are installed on your system (see Figure 4-8). Ubuntu requires a signature key for any package that it installs. Signature keys for all the Ubuntu repositories are installed, and are listed on this tab, including your CD/DVD disc.

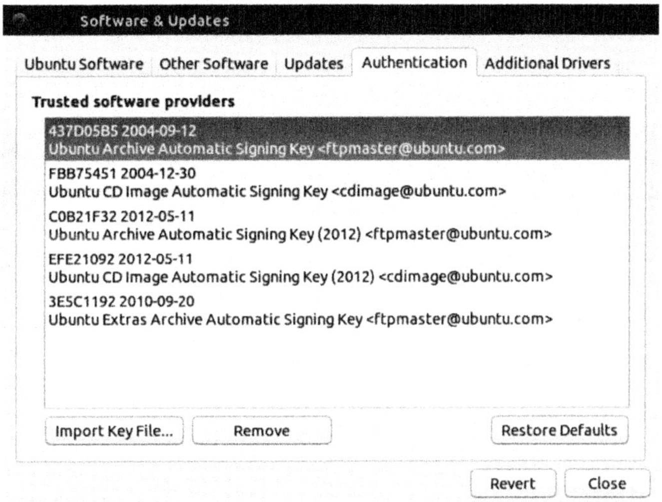

Figure 4-8: Software & Updates Authentication, package signature keys

Most other third party or customized repositories will provide a signature key file for you to download and import. You can add such keys manually from the Authentication tab. Click the Import Key File to open a file browser where you can select the downloaded key file. This procedure is the same as the **apt-key add** operation. Both add keys that APT then uses to verify DEB software packages downloaded from repositories before it installs them.

After you have made changes and click the Close button, the Software & Updates tool will notify you that your software package information is out of date, displaying a Reload button. Click the Reload button to make the new repositories or components available on your package managers, like the Ubuntu Software Center and the Synaptic Package Manager. You also can reload your repository configuration by running **apt-get update**, clicking the Reload button on the Synaptic Package Manager, or clicking the Check button on the Software updater.

Managing Packages with the Ubuntu Software Center

To perform simple installation and removal of software, you can use the Ubuntu Software Center, which is the primary supported package manager for Ubuntu. The Ubuntu Software Center is designed to be the centralized utility for managing all your software. The Ubuntu Software Center is also a store for commercial Ubuntu applications. For more details on the Ubuntu Software

Center, open the Ubuntu Help dialog by choosing Ubuntu Software Center Help from the Ubuntu Software Center's Help menu.

To use the Ubuntu Software Center, click the Ubuntu Software Center icon on the Launcher or from the System dash. The Ubuntu Software Center displays a toolbar, a side panel on the left showing categories and software lists (see Figure 4-9).

The "What's New" and "Top Rated" sections at the right provide a listing of new and popular applications. Click on an icon to display its information tab where you can install the application or link to its web site. Click the More button at the top right of each section to open a full listing of new and top-rated software. The "Recommended For You" feature lists applications you may be interested in based on software you have installed. Click the "Turn on Recommendations" link to turn this feature on (also, you can choose Turn On Recommendations from the View menu).

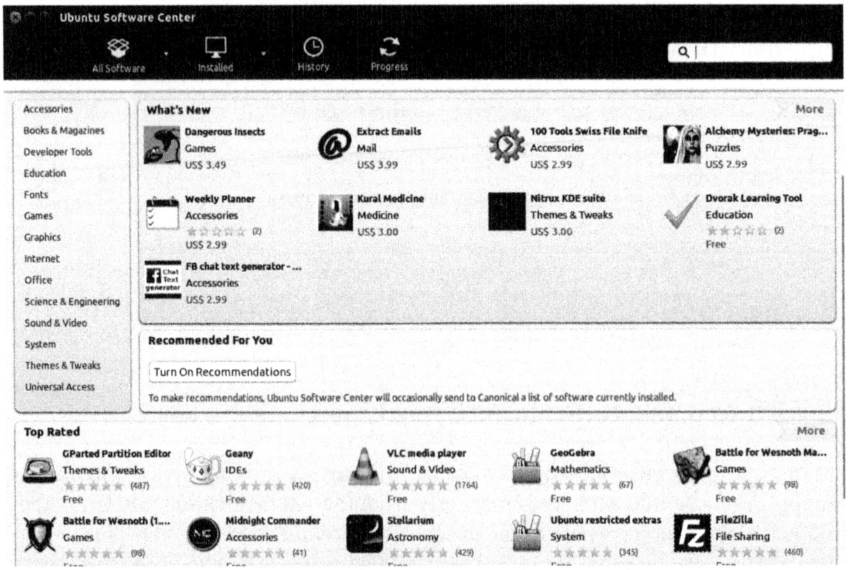

Figure 4-9: Ubuntu Software Center

The toolbar provides forward and back buttons for moving through previously viewed software listing and search results. On the toolbar, software icons and menus let you choose the software categories you want to view or search. The All Software icon displays all available software. A drop-down menu to the right of the icon lets you limit your views and searches to certain software categories such as "Provided by Ubuntu" for Ubuntu supported software, "Canonical Partners" for software available from Ubuntu partners like Adobe, and "For Purchase" for software you can purchase.

Clicking the All Software icon displays the listing of software categories, such as Office, Graphics, Internet, and System on a left sidebar. Clicking on a category will list the available software with a brief description of each (see Figure 4-10). Some categories will have subcategories such as Drawing and Viewers for Graphics (see Figure 4-11). You can scroll down the list to find the package you want. Installed software will have a green check mark emblem displayed on their small icon. To display the sidebar of software categories again, just click on the All Software button.

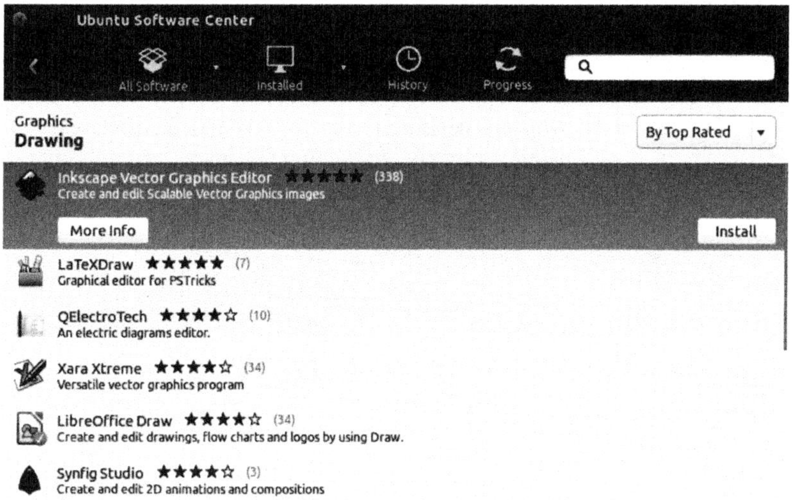

Figure 4-10: Ubuntu Software Center package listing

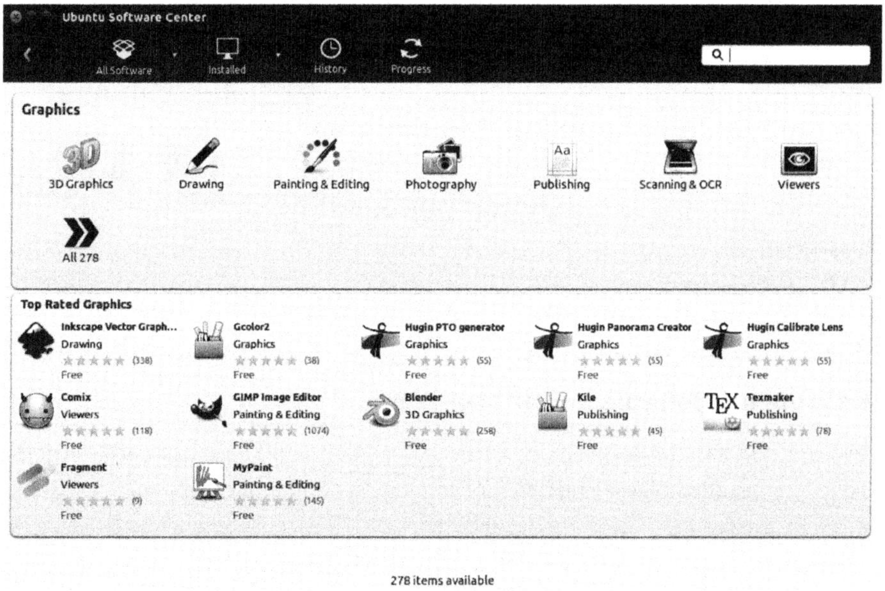

Figure 4-11: Ubuntu Software Center sub-categories

To install a package, first locate it. Once you have found your package, you can click it to display an Install button on the right side, which you click to install (see Figure 4-10). An install process entry is displayed on the left sidebar as the package is installed.

Should you want more information about a package, click the More Info button to open a new tab for that application. The application tab for an uninstalled package will have an Install button and display a detailed description of the application, along with the License and Price, if any (see Figure 4-12). For software on the Ubuntu repository, most have an Open Source license and the software is free. You can click the Website link to access the application's Web site, which may provide detailed documentation. If an application thumbnail is displayed, you can click on it to display the full image. Under the Add-ons heading is a list of associated software designed to work with your application. Packages installed already are marked. To install an additional software package, click on its checkbox. An Apply Changes button appears above the Add-ons list, which you then click.

Figure 4-12: Ubuntu Software Center application

The "People Also Installed" section lists applications that others users who installed the package have also installed. These popular applications are similar or complementary to the package.

Version, License, size, and update information are then listed. The update information indicates whether it is supported by the Ubuntu repository. If Canonical does not provide critical updates, the package is part of the Universe or Multiverse repositories. User reviews follow, providing information about the software's stability and usefulness.

You also can install the application from this page by clicking the Install button (if the application is already installed, a Remove button is shown). You are prompted to enter your password. You also can choose the Install item on the File menu to install the application (File | Install).

A progress bar on the Info page will show the download and install progress. A "Progress" icon also appears in the toolbar. Clicking on it displays the progress bar and the package name (see Figure 4-13). When installation takes place, the Launcher item for that application is placed on the Launcher. A progress bar on the Launcher item shows the install progress (see Figure 4-13). When installation is finished, the Launcher item is placed on the Launcher for that session. You can have it stay on the Launcher permanently by choosing "Lock to launcher" entry on its quicklist.

Figure 4-13: Ubuntu Software Center and Launcher item download and install progress

When finished, the application page displays a Remove button and a green check mark with the installed label and the date (see Figure 4-14). The entry in the list of applications also will have a green checkmark emblem indicating that the application is installed.

Figure 4-14: Ubuntu Software Center installed application

To remove a package, first locate it in the package lists and select it. A Remove button will appear which you can click to remove it. You also can use the Remove button on the application's Info page.

You can perform a search using the Search box. The search is performed on the description and the package name. To remove the search list and return to the All Software page, click the x button icon on the right side of the search box. Searches can be carried out within categories and subcategories. To search globally, search from the "All Software" page. In Figure 4-15 all vector related applications are listed.

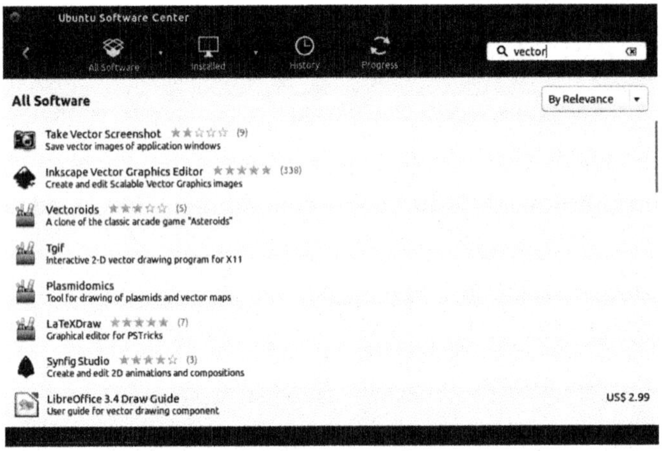

Figure 4-15: Ubuntu Software Center search

If you have selected a category and are displaying a category page like Graphics, then the search will be performed only on the packages in that category. In Figure 4-16 only vector applications in the Graphics | Drawing subcategory are listed.

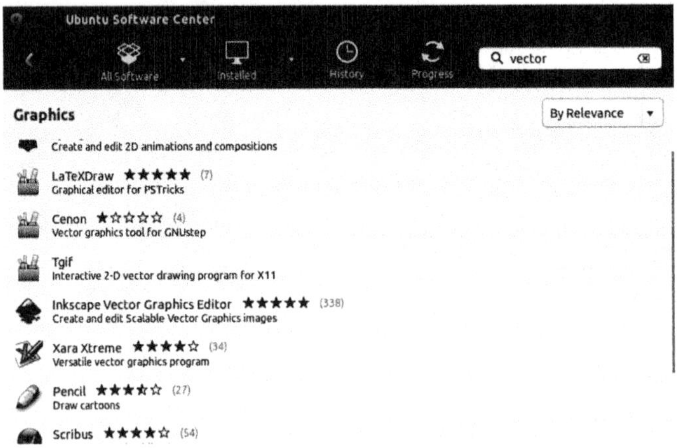

Figure 4-16: Ubuntu Software Center search within a category

On the Ubuntu Software Center toolbar, the Installed icon lists installed software, with a drop-down menu for installed Ubuntu, Partner, and Purchased software. Software categories such as Graphics and Office are listed, which you can expand to show those packages installed (see Figure 4-17).

On the toolbar, the History icon displays a list of all package changes, installations, updates, and removals.

The Ubuntu Software Center is a front end for the APT package manager. When you install a package with the Ubuntu Software Center, APT is invoked and automatically selects and downloads the package from the appropriate online repository.

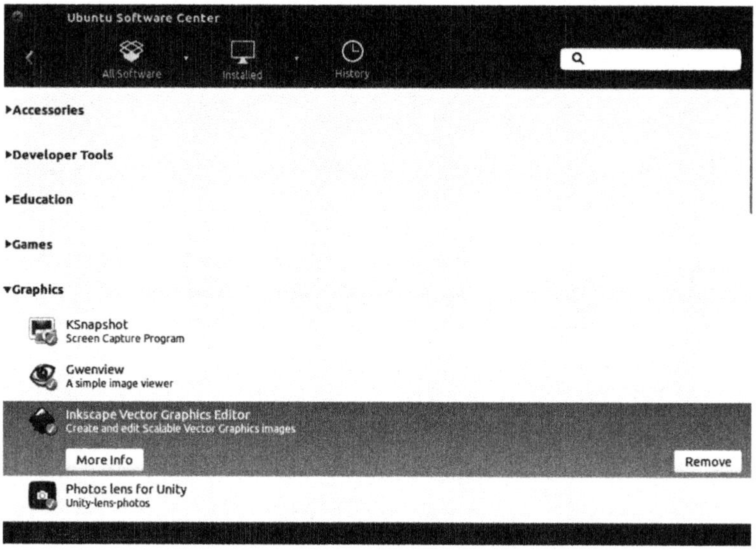

Figure 4-17: Ubuntu Software Center installed software

The packages listed in the Ubuntu Software Center are set up using the **app-install-data** packages, accessible through the Synaptic Package Manager. The **app-install-data** and **app-install-data-partner** packages will already be installed. These list the commonly used packages on the Ubuntu repository. In addition, you can install the **app-install-data-edubuntu** package to list edubuntu educational packages.

Synaptic Package Manager

The Synaptic Package Manager has been replaced by the Ubuntu Software Center as the primary package manager. It is not installed by default. Synaptic is no longer supported by Ubuntu, though support is still provided by the Ubuntu community. Packages are listed by name and include supporting packages like libraries and system critical packages. Once installed, you can access the Synaptic Package Manager on the System dash.

The Synaptic Package Manager displays three panes: a side pane for listing software categories and buttons, a top pane for listing software packages, and a bottom pane for displaying a selected package's description. When a package is selected, the description pane also displays a Get

Screenshot button. Clicking this button will download and display an image of the application, if there is one. Click the Get Changelog button to display a window listing the application changes.

Buttons at the lower left of the Synaptic Package Manager window provide options for organizing and refining the list of packages shown (see Figure 4-18). Five options are available: Sections, Status, Origin, Custom Filters, and Search results. The dialog pane above the buttons changes depending on which option you choose. Clicking the Sections button will list section categories for your software such as Base System, Communications, and Development. The Status button will list options for installed and not installed software. The Origin button shows entries for different repositories and their sections, as well as those locally installed (manual or disc based installations). Custom filters lets you choose a filter to use for listing packages. You can create your own filter and use it to display selected packages. Search results will list your current and previous searches, letting you move from one to the other.

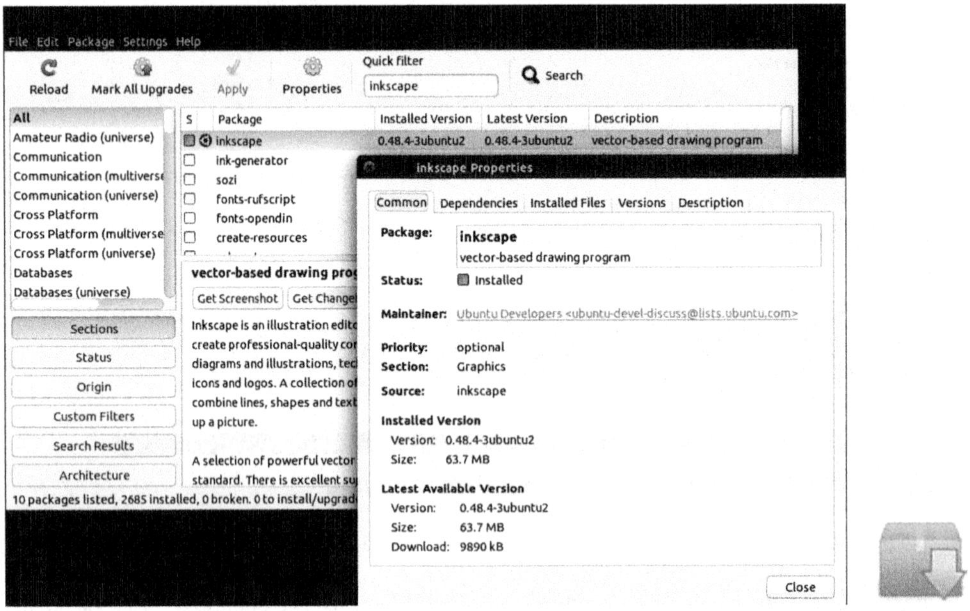

Figure 4-18: Synaptic Package Manager: Quick search

The Sections option is selected by default (see Figure 4-19). You can choose to list all packages, or refine your listing using categories provided in the pane. The All entry in this pane will list all available packages. Packages are organized into categories such as Base System, Cross Platform, and Communications. Each category is, in turn, subdivided by multiverse, universe, and restricted software.

To perform a quick search, enter the pattern to be searched for in the "Quick search" box and the results will appear. In Figure 4-18 the *inkscape* pattern is used to locate the Inkscape graphics software. Quick searches will be performed within selected sections. Selecting different sections applies your quick search pattern to the packages in that section. Clicking on the Editors section with an inkscape search pattern would give no results, since Inkscape is not an editor package.

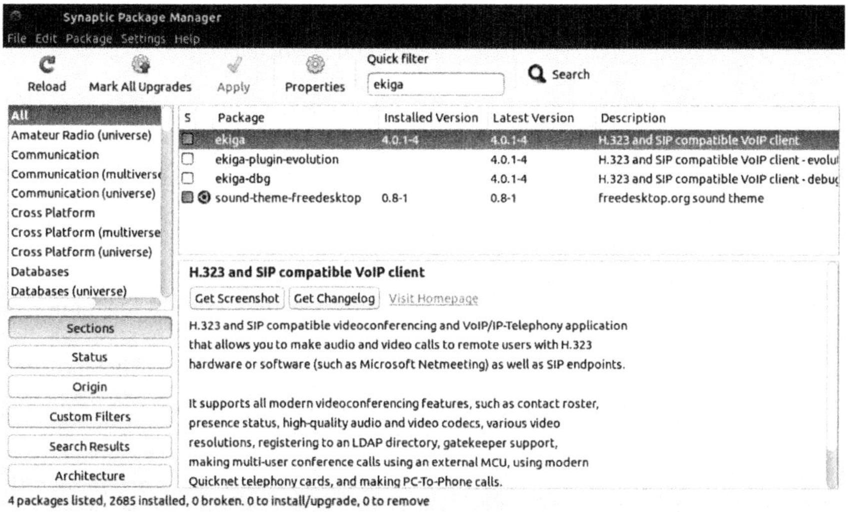

Figure 4-19: Synaptic Package Manager: Sections

Status entries further refine installed software as manual or as upgradeable (see Figure 4-20). Local software consists of packages you download and install manually.

With the Origin options, Ubuntu-compliant repositories may further refine access according to multiverse, universe, and restricted software. A main section selects Ubuntu-supported software.

Figure 4-20: Synaptic Package Manager: Status

To perform more detailed searches, you can use the Search tool. Click the Search button on the toolbar to open a Search dialog with a text box where you can enter search terms. A pop-up menu lets you specify what features of a package to search, such as the "Description and Name" feature. You can search other package features like the Name, the maintainer name (Maintainer), the package version (Version), packages it may depend on (Dependencies), or associated packages (Provided Packages). A list of searches will be displayed in Search Results. You can move back and forth between search results by clicking on the search entries in this listing.

Properties

To find out information about a package, select the package and click the Properties button. This opens a window with Common, Dependencies, Installed Files, Versions, and Description tabs. The Common tab provides section, versions, and maintainer information. The Installed Files tab shows you exactly what files are installed, which is useful for finding the exact location, and names for configuration files, as well as commands. The Description tab displays detailed information about the software. The Dependencies tab shows all dependent software packages needed by this software, usually libraries.

Installing packages

Before installing software, you should press the Reload button to load the most recent package lists from the active repositories.

To install a package, right-click on its name to display a pop-up menu and select the Mark for installation entry. Should any dependent packages exist, a dialog opens listing those packages. Click the Mark button in the dialog to mark those packages for installation. The package entry's check box will then be marked in the Synaptic Package Manager window.

Once you have selected the packages you want to install, click the Apply button on the toolbar to begin the installation process. A Summary dialog opens showing all the packages to be installed. You have the option to download the package files. The number of packages to be installed is listed, along with the size of the download and the amount of disk space used. Click the Apply button on the Summary dialog to download and install the packages. A download window will then appear showing the progress of your package installations. You can choose to show the progress of individual packages, which opens a terminal window listing each package as it is downloaded and installed.

Once downloaded, the dialog name changes to Installing Software. You can choose to have the dialog close automatically when finished. Sometimes installation requires user input to configure the software. You will be prompted to enter the information if necessary.

When you right-click a package name, you also see options for Mark Suggested for Installation, or Mark Recommended for Installation. These will mark applications that can enhance your selected software, though they are not essential. If there are no suggested or recommended packages for that application, then these entries will be grayed out.

Certain software, like desktops or office suites that require a significant number of packages, can be selected all at once using metapackages. A metapackage has configuration files that select, download, and configure the range of packages needed for such complex software. For example, the **kubuntu-desktop** meta package will install the entire Kubuntu desktop (Sections | Meta Packages).

Removing packages

To remove a package, first locate it. Then right-click it and select the "Mark package for removal" entry. This will leave configuration files untouched. Alternatively, you can mark a package for complete removal, which will also remove any configuration files, "Mark for Complete Removal." Dependent packages will not be removed.

Once you have marked packages for removal, click the Apply button. A summary dialog displays the packages that will be removed. Click Apply to remove them.

The Synaptic Package Manager may not remove dependent packages, especially shared libraries that might be used by other applications. This means that your system could have installed packages that are never being used. Their continued presence will not harm anything.

Note: You can further refine your search for packages on the Synaptic Package Manager by creating search filters. Select the Settings | Filters menu entry to open the Filters window. To create a new filter, click the New button located just below the filter listing.

Updating Ubuntu with Software Updater

New updates are continually being prepared for particular software packages as well as system components. These are posted as updates you can download from software repositories and install on your system. These include new versions of applications, servers, and even the kernel. Such updates may range from single software packages to whole components. Updating your Ubuntu system is a very simple procedure, using Software Updater, a graphical update interface for APT.

The Software Updater item appears on the Launcher when updates are available. You can invoke the update from its quicklist, as shown here:

When invoked from the quicklist, the Software Updater icon shows a progress bar. When finished, a dialog indicating the update completion or the need for a restart is shown.

You can also start the Software Updater manually from the Applications lens System filter, or by clicking on the Software Updater Launcher icon, which appears when updates are avialable. When manually invoked, the Software Updater displays a simple dialog displays the amount to be downloaded with "Remind Me Later" and "Install Now" buttons (see Figure 4-21). A manual update gives you more control over the update, letting you choose packages to install.

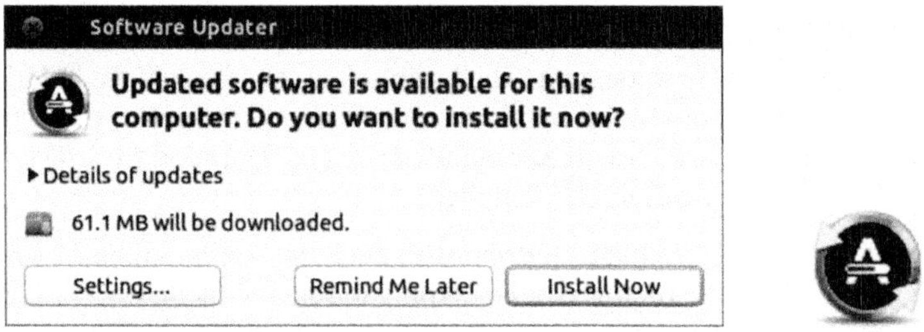

Figure 4-21: Software Updater with selected packages

To see actual packages to be updated, click the "Details of updates" arrow. Packages are organized into application categories such as Ubuntu base for the Linux OS packages, Firefox for Firefox updates, and LibreOffice for office updates. You can expand these to individual packages. The check boxes for each entry lets you de-select any particular packages you do not want to update (see Figure 4-6). Packages are organized according to importance, beginning with Important security updates and followed by Recommended updates. You should always install the security updates. All the APT-compatible repositories that are configured on your system will be checked for updates.

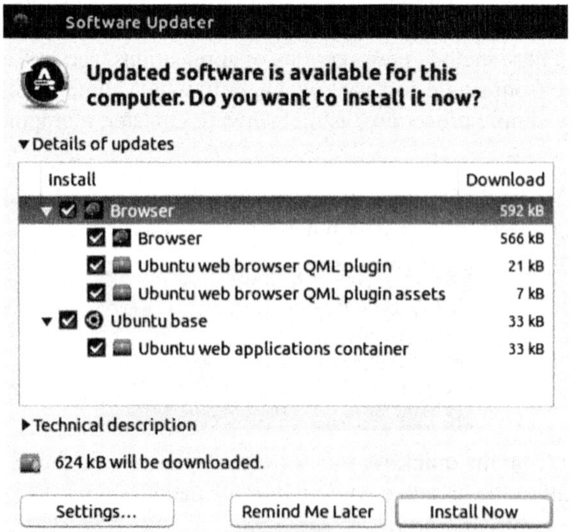

Figure 4-22: Details of updates

To see a detailed description of a particular update, select the update and then click the "Technical description" arrow (see Figure 4-23). Two tabs are displayed: Changes and Description. The Changes tab lists detailed update information, and Description provides information about the software.

Click the Install Now button to start updating. The packages will be downloaded from their appropriate repository. Once downloaded, the packages are updated.

Figure 4-23: Details of updates, Technical description

When downloading and installing, a dialog appears showing the download and install progress (see Figure 4-24). You can choose to show progress for individual files. A window will open up that lists each file and its progress. Once downloaded, the updates are installed. Click the Details arrow to see install messages for particular software packages. The Software Updater Launcher item will also show a progress bar for the install process and the number of updates, as shown in Figure 4-24).

Figure 4-24: Download updates

When the update completes, Software updater will display a message saying that your system is up-to-date. If a critical package was installed such as a new kernel, you will be prompted to restart your system. The power icon will turn red as a warning, and the Session menu will have the added entry "Restart required."

Installing Software from the Applications Dash

You can install software packages directly from the Applications lens on the dash. This is perhaps the easiest and simplest way to install software, if you already know the name of the software you want. Open the dash and click the Applications lens, and then perform a search for the application you want. Use the "Filter results" buttons to search within a particular category, such as Office or Internet. Results are listed under the "More suggestions" heading (see Figure 4-25). A label indicates whether it is free or not.

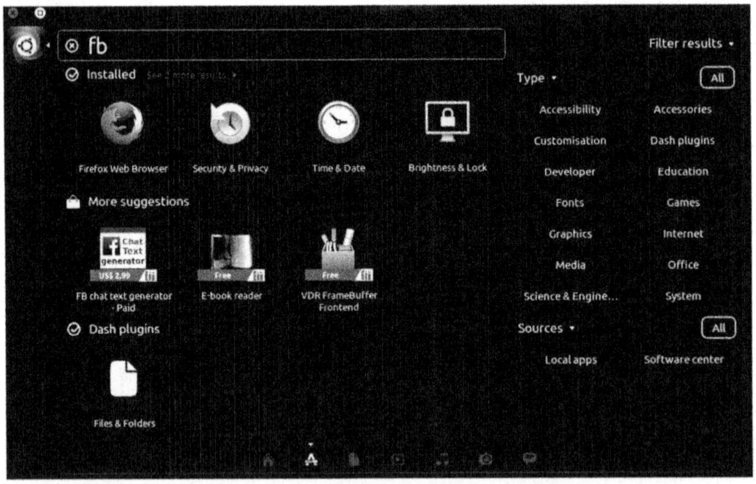

Figure 4-25: Searching for software on the Dash, Applications lens

Click on the application icon to open the information for it on the dash. An image of the application window is shown, along with a description and version number (see Figure 4-26). There is a button for the development Web site. Software available on from the Ubuntu repositories will have a "Free Download" button. Click the button to start the download and installation. You are prompted first for your administrative password. As the download and install proceeds, an icon for the application appears on the launcher with a progress bar (see Figure 4-26). Passing the mouse over the icon displays an Installing status message.

Figure 4-26: Application to install from the dash

Ubuntu Software Center for separate DEB packages

You can also use the Ubuntu Software Center to perform an installation of a single DEB software package. Usually these packages are downloaded directly from a Web site and have few or no dependent packages. When you use your browser to download a particular package, you will be prompted to open it with Ubuntu Software Center. The Ubuntu Software Center opens to an install page for that software package, displaying information about the package and checking to see if it is compatible with your system. Click the Install button to download and install the package. It is advisable to use the Ubuntu Software Center to install a manually downloaded package.

You could also first download the package, and then later select it from your file manager window (usually the Downloads folder). Double clicking should open the package with the Ubuntu Software Center. You can also right-click and choose to open it with the Ubuntu Software Center.

Software Package Types

Ubuntu uses Debian-compliant software packages (DEB), whose filenames have a **.deb** extension. Other packages, such as those in the form of source code that you need to compile, may be distributed as compressed archives. These commonly have the extension **.tar.gz**, **.tgz**, or **.tar.bz2**. Packages with the **.rpm** extension are Red Hat Package software packages used on Red Hat, Fedora, SuSE and other Linux distributions that use RPM packages. They are not compatible directly with Ubuntu. You can use the **alien** command to convert most RPM packages to DEB packages that you can then install on Ubuntu. Table 4-2 lists several common file extensions that you will find for the great variety of Linux software packages available. You can download any Ubuntu-compliant deb package, as well as the original source code package, as single files, directly from **http://packages.ubuntu.com**.

Managing non-repository packages with dpkg

You can use **dpkg** to install a software package you have downloaded directly as a simple package file. In this case, you are not installing from a repository. Instead, you have manually downloaded the package file from a Web or FTP site to a folder on your system. Such a situation would be rare, reserved for software not available on the Ubuntu repository or any APT enabled repository. Keep in mind that most software is already on your Ubuntu or an APT enabled repositories. Check there first for the software package before performing a direct download, and install with **dpkg**. The **dpkg** configuration files are located in the **/etc/dpkg** directory. Configuration is held in the **dpkg.cfg** file. See the **dpkg** man page for a detailed listing of options.

One situation for which you would use **dpkg**, is for packages you have built yourself, like packages you created when converting a package in another format to a Debian package (DEB). This is the case when converting a RPM package (Red Hat Package Manager) to a Debian package format.

For **dpkg**, you use the **-i** option to install a package and **-r** to remove it.

```
sudo dpkg -i package.deb
```

The major failing for **dpkg** is that it provides no dependency support. It will inform you of needed dependencies, but you will have to install them separately. **dpkg** installs only the specified package. It is ideal for packages that have no dependencies.

You use the **-I** option to obtain package information directly from the DEB package file.

```
sudo dpkg -I package.deb
```

To remove a package you use the **-r** option with the package software name. You do not need version or extension information like **.386** or **.deb**. With **dpkg**, when removing a package with dependencies, you first have to remove all its dependencies manually. You will not be able to uninstall the package until you do this. Software configuration files are not removed.

```
sudo dpkg -r packagename
```

Extension	Package type
.deb	A Debian/Ubuntu Linux package
.gz	A **gzip**-compressed file (use **gunzip** to decompress)
.bz2	A **bzip2**-compressed file (use **bunzip2** to decompress; also use the **j** option with **tar**, as in **xvjf**)
.tar	A tar archive file (use **tar** with **xvf** to extract)
.tar.gz	A **gzip**-compressed **tar** archive file (use **gunzip** to decompress and **tar** to extract; use the **z** option with **tar**, as in **xvzf**, to both decompress and extract in one step)
.tar.bz2	A **bzip2**-compressed **tar** archive file (extract with **tar -xvzj**)
.tz	A **tar** archive file compressed with the **compress** command
.Z	A file compressed with the **compress** command (use the **decompress** command to decompress)
.bin	A self-extracting software file
.rpm	A software package created with the Red Hat Software Package Manager, used on Fedora, Red Hat, Centos, and SuSE distributions

Table 4-4: Linux Software Package File Extensions

If you install a package that requires dependencies, and then fail to install these dependencies, your install database will be marked as having broken packages. In this case, APT will not allow new packages to be installed until the broken packages are fixed. You can enter the **apt-get** command with the **-f** and install options to fix all broken packages at once.

```
sudo apt-get -f install
```

Installing Software from Compressed Archives: .tar.gz

Linux software applications in the form of source code are available at different sites on the Internet. You can download any of this software and install it on your system. Recent releases are often available in the form of compressed archive files. Applications will always be downloadable as compressed archives if they don't have a DEB (Ubuntu) version.

Decompressing and Extracting Software

Before you unpack the archive, move it to the directory where you want it. When source code files are unpacked, they generate their own subdirectories from which you can compile and install the software. Once the package is installed, you can delete this directory, keeping the original source code package file (**.tar.gz**). For example, the file **antigrav_0.0.3.orig.tar** unpacks to a subdirectory called **antigrav_0.0.3.orig**. In certain cases, the software package that contains precompiled binaries is designed to unpack directly into the system subdirectory where it will be used.

Though you can decompress and extract software in separate operations, you will find that the more common approach is to perform both actions with a single command. The **tar** utility provides decompression options you can use to have **tar** first decompress a file for you, invoking the specified decompression utility. The **z** option automatically invokes **gunzip** to unpack a **.gz** file, and the **j** option unpacks a **.bz2** file. Use the **Z** option for **.Z** files. For example, to combine the decompressing and unpacking operation for a **tar.gz** file into one **tar** command, insert a **z** option to the option list, **xzvf**. The next example shows how you can combine decompression and extraction in one step:

```
tar xvzf antigrav_0.0.3.orig.tar.gz
```

For a **.bz2**-compressed archive, you use the **j** option instead of the **z** option.

```
tar xvjf antigrav_0.0.3.orig.tar.bz2
```

Files ending with **.bin** are self-extracting archives. Run the bin file as if it were a command. You may have to use **chmod** to make it executable. Then enter the file as a command on a command line, with ./ attached to the beginning of the file name.

```
sudo chmod 755 package
```

The extraction process creates a subdirectory consisting of the name and release of the software. In the preceding example, the extraction created a subdirectory called **antigrav_0.0.3.orig**. You can change to this subdirectory and examine its files, such as the **README** and **INSTALL** files.

```
cd antigrav_0.0.3.orig
```

Installation of your software may differ for each package. Instructions are usually provided along with an installation program. Be sure to consult the **README** and **INSTALL** files, if included.

Compiling Software

Some software may be in the form of source code that you need to compile before you can install it. This is particularly true of programs designed for cross-platform implementations. Programs designed to run on various Linux and UNIX systems may be distributed as source code that is downloaded and compiled in those different systems. Compiling such software has been greatly simplified in recent years by the use of configuration scripts that automatically detect a given system's hardware and software configuration and then allow you to compile the program accordingly. For example, the name of the C compiler on a system could be **gcc** or **cc**. Configuration scripts detect which is present and select it for use in the program compilation.

Note: Some software will run using scripting languages like Python, instead of programming language code like C++. These may require only a setup operation (a setup command), not compiling. Once installed, they will run directly using the scripting language interpreter, like Python.

A configure script works by generating a customized Makefile, designed for that particular system. A Makefile contains detailed commands to compile a program, including any preprocessing, links to required libraries, and the compilation of program components in their proper order. Many Makefiles for complex applications may have to access several software subdirectories, each with separate components to compile. The use of configure and Makefile scripts vastly automates the compile process, reducing the procedure to a few simple steps.

First, change to the directory where the software's source code has been extracted, as shown in this example:

```
# cd /usr/local/src/antigrav_0.0.3.orig
```

Before you compile software, read the **README** or **INSTALL** files included with it. These give you detailed instructions on how to compile and install this particular program.

Most software can be compiled and installed in three simple steps. Their first step is the ./**configure** command, which generates your customized Makefile. The second step is the **make** command, which uses a Makefile in your working directory (in this case, the Makefile you just generated with the ./**configure** command) to compile your software. The final step also uses the **make** command, but this time with the **install** option. The Makefile generated by the ./**configure** command also may contain instructions for installing the software on your system. Using the **install** option runs just those installation commands. To perform the installation, you have to be logged in as the root user, giving you the ability to add software files to system directories as needed. If the software uses configuration scripts, compiling and installing usually involves only the following three simple commands:

```
./configure
make
make install
```

In the preceding example, the./**configure** command performs configuration detection. The **make** command performs the actual compiling, using a Makefile script generated by the ./**configure** operation. The **make install** command installs the program on your system, placing the executable program in a directory, such as **/usr/local/bin**, and any configuration files in **/etc**. Any shared libraries it created may go into **/usr/local/lib**.

Once you have compiled and installed your application, and you have checked that it is working properly, you can remove the source code directory that was created when you extracted the software. You can keep the archive file (**tar**) in case you need to extract the software again. Use **rm** with the **-rf** options so that all subdirectories will be deleted and you do not have to confirm each deletion.

Tip: Be sure to remember to place the period and slash before the **configure** command. The ./ references a command in the current working directory, rather than another Linux command with the same name.

Certain software may have specific options set up for the ./**configure** operation. To find out what these are, you use the ./**configure** command with the **--help** option:

```
./configure --help
```

A useful common option is the **-prefix** option, which lets you specify the install directory:

```
./configure -prefix=/usr/bin
```

Note: If you are compiling an X, GNOME, or KDE-based program, be sure their development libraries have been installed.

Checking Software Package Digital Signatures

One very effective use for digital signatures is to verify that a software package has not been tampered with. A software package could be intercepted in transmission and some of its system-level files changed or substituted. Software packages from your distribution, as well as those by reputable GNU and Linux projects, are digitally signed. The signature provides modification digest information with which to check the integrity of the package. The digital signature may be included with the package file or posted as a separate file. To import a key that APT can use to check a software package, you use the **apt-key** command. APT will automatically check for digital signatures. To check the digital signature of a software package file that is not part of the APT repository system, you use the **gpg** command with the **--verify** option. These would include packages like those made available as compressed archives, **.tar.gz**, whereas APT can check all DEB packages itself.

Importing Software Public keys with apt-key

First, however, you will need to make sure that you have the signer's public key. The digital signature was encrypted with the software distributor's private key; that distributor is the signer. Once you have that signer's public key, you can check any data you receive from them. In the case of third party software repositories, you have to install their public key. Once the key is installed, you do not have to install it again.

Ubuntu includes and installs its public keys with its distribution. For any packages on the Ubuntu repositories, the needed public keys are already installed and checked by APT automatically. With other sites, you may need to download the public key from their site and install it. You may also have to add repository support to access their Ubuntu compatible software. Once downloaded, you can then use the **apt-key** command to install the public key for use by APT in software verification. Ubuntu uses the **apt-key** command to maintain public keys for software packages. Use the **apt-key** command with the **add** option to add the key. To actually access the software repository you would have to also install its APT configuration file in the **/etc/apt/sources.list.d** directory.

Checking Software Compressed Archives

Many software packages in the form of compressed archives, **.tar.gz** or **tar.bz2**, will provide signatures in separate files that end with the **.sig** extension. To check these, you use the **gpg** command with the **--verify** option. For example, the most recent Sendmail package is distributed in the form of a compressed archive, **.tar.gz**. Its digital signature is provided in a separate **.sig** file. First, you download and install the public key for Sendmail software obtained from the Sendmail website (the key may have the year as part of its name). Sendmail has combined all its keys into one armored text file, **PGPKEYS**.

```
gpg --import PGPKEYS
```

You can also use the **gpg** command with the **--search-key** and **--keyserver** options to import the key. Keys matching the search term will be displayed in a numbered list. You will be prompted to enter the number of the key you want. The 2007 Sendmail key from the results from the following example would be 7. This is the key used for 2007 released software.

```
gpg  --keyserver pgp.mit.edu  --search-keys Sendmail
```

Instead of using **gpg**, you could use Encryptions and Password Keys application to find and import the key (Accessories | Encryption and Password Keys).

To check a software archive, a **tar.gz**, file, you need to also download its digital signature files. For the compressed archive (**.tar.gz**) you can use the **.sig** file ending in **.gz.sig**, and for the uncompressed archive use **.tar.sig**. Then, with the **gpg** command and the **--verify** option, use the digital signature in the **.sig** file to check the authenticity and integrity of the software compressed archive.

```
$ gpg --verify sendmail.8.14.2.tar.gz.sig sendmail.8.14.2.tar.gz
gpg: Signature made Wed 31 Oct 2007 08:23:07 PM PDT using RSA key ID 7093B841
gpg: Good signature from "Sendmail Signing Key/2007 <sendmail@Sendmail.ORG>"$
```

You can also specify just the signature file, and **gpg** will automatically search for and select a file of the same name, but without the **.sig** or **.asc** extension.

```
gpg --verify sendmail.8.14.2.tar.gz.sig
```

In the future, when you download any software from the Sendmail site that uses this key, you just have to perform the **--verify** operation. Bear in mind, though, that different software packages from the same site may use different keys. You will have to make sure that you have imported and signed the appropriate key for the software you are checking.

Tip: You can use the **--fingerprint** option to check a key's validity if you wish. If you are confident that the key is valid, you can then sign it with the **--sign-key** command.

Part 2: Services

Managing Services

Mail Servers

FTP Servers

Web Servers

News and Database Servers

ubuntu

5. Managing Services with systemd

systemd
systemd unit files: /lib/systemd/system
special targets (runlevels)
managing services
Network Time Protocol, NTP
AppArmor security
OpenSSH

A single Linux system can provide several different kinds of services, ranging from security to administration, and including more obvious Internet services like web and FTP sites, e-mail, and printing. Security tools, such as the Secure Shell (SSH) and Kerberos run as services, along with administrative network tools, such as Dynamic Host Control Protocol (DHCP) and Lightweight Directory Access Protocol (LDAP). The network connection interface is, itself, a service that you can restart at will. Each service operates as a continually running daemon looking for requests for its particular services. In the case of a web service, the requests come from remote users. You can turn services on or off by starting or shutting down their daemons.

System start up is managed by the **systemd** service. The original System V init system for starting individual services has been phased out. The Upstart service used in previous Ubuntu releases has been deprecated. For information about changing from Upstart to systemd see:

```
https://wiki.ubuntu.com/SystemdForUpstartUsers
```

systemd

Linux systems traditionally used the Unix System V init daemon to manage services by setting up runlevels at which they could be started or shutdown. Linux has since replaced the SystemV init daemon with the **systemd** init daemon. Whereas the System V init daemon would start certain services when the entire system started up or shut down using shell scripts run in sequence, **systemd** is uses sockets for all system tasks and services. **systemd** sets up sockets for daemons and coordinates between them as they start up. This allows **systemd** to start daemons at the same time (in parallel). Should one daemon require support from another, **systemd** coordinates the data from their sockets (buffering), so that one daemon receives the information from another daemon that it needs to continue. This parallel start up compatibility allows for very fast boot times.

In effect, you can think of **systemd** as a combination of System V init scripts and the inetd daemon (xinetd), using socket activation applied to all system start up tasks and to network servers. The socket activation design was originally inspired by the inetd service that used sockets (AT_INET) to start internet daemons when requested. The socket activation design was used by in Apple's OS X system to apply to all sockets (AF_UNIX). This allowed all start up processes to start at the same time in parallel, making for very fast boot times. Sockets are set up and managed by **systemd**. When D-BUS needs to write to journald (logging), it writes to the systemd-journald socket set up and managed by **systemd**. It does not have to communicate directly with journald. This means that services no longer have to be started and shutdown in a particular sequence as they were under System V. They can all start and stop at the same time. Also, as **systemd** controls the socket, if a service fails, it socket remains in place. The service can be restarted using the same socket with no loss of information. **systemd** manages all types of sockets including UNIX (system), INET (network), NETLINK (devices), FIFO (pipes), and POSIX (messages). See the following for more details:

```
http://fedoraproject.org/wiki/Systemd
https://wiki.ubuntu.com/systemd
http://www.freedesktop.org/wiki/Software/systemd/
```

systemd sets up sockets for all system tasks and services. Configuration for systemd tasks are defined in unit files in **/lib/systemd/system** directory. In this respect, **systemd** files replace the entries that used to be in the Sys V init's **/etc/inittab** file. **systemd** also has its own versions of **shutdown**, **reboot**, **halt**, **init**, and **telinit**, each with their own man page.

systemd is entirely compatible with both System V scripts in the **/etc/init.d** directory and the **/etc/fstab** file. The SystemV scripts and **/etc/fstab** are treated as additional configuration files for **systemd** to work with. If System V scripts are present in the **/etc/init.d** directory, it will use them to generated a corresponding unit configuration file, if there are no corresponding **systemd** unit configuration files already. **systemd** configuration always takes precedence. **systemd** will also, if needed, use the start and stop priority files in the System V init **/etc/rc.d** directories to determine dependencies. Entries in **/etc/fstab** are used to generate corresponding **systemd** unit files that are then used to manage file systems. **systemd** also supports snapshots that allow restoring services to a previous state.

The systemd configuration (**.service**) files are located in the **/lib/systemd/system** directory and are considered system files that you should not modify. It is possible to copy them to the /etc/systemd/system directory and make changes to the copies. File in the **/etc/systemd/system** file take precedence. The configuration file for the logind daemon, **logind.conf**, is located in the **/etc/systemd** directory. Some software, like the Apache Web server, do not yet have systemd service files. systemd automatically generates service files for then in the **/var/run/systemd/generator.late** directory.

Ubuntu also uses systemd services for time (**timedated**), location (**localed**), login (**logind**), and hostname (**hostnamed**) (**systemd-services** package). They can be managed with corresponding systemd control applications: **timedatectl**, **localectl**, and **hostnamectl**. Ubuntu uses the shim daemon (systemd-shim) to interface systemd daemons through Dbus. Configuration files located at **/etc/dbus-1/system.d**.

systemd basic configuration files

You can configure **systemd** for system, login manager, users, and, journal service using the configuration files located in the **/etc/systemd** directory. When run for a system service, systemd uses the **system.conf** file, otherwise it uses the **user.conf** file. You can set options such as the log level (LogLevel) and resource size limits. See the man page for **systemd.conf** (system.conf and user.conf), **logind.conf**, and **journald.conf** for details on the options available.

units

systemd organizes tasks into units, each with a unit configuration file. There are several types of units (see Table 5-1). A unit file will have an extension to its name that specifies the type of unit it is. Service types have the extension **.service**, and mount types have the extension **.mount**. The service type performs much the same function as System V init scripts. Services can be stopped, started and restarted. The **systemctl** command will list all units, including the ones it generates.

Units can also be used for socket, device, and mount tasks. The socket type implements the kind of connection used for inetd and xinetd, allowing you to start a service on demand. The device type references devices as detected by udev. The mount type manages a file system's mount point, and automount activates that mount point should it be automounted. An automount unit file has a corresponding mount unit file, which it uses to mount a file system. Similarly, a socket type usually has a corresponding service type used to perform a task for that socket.

Within each unit are directives that control a service, socket, device, or mount point. Some directives are unique to the type of unit. These are listed in the man page for that service, such as **systemd.service** for the service unit, or **systemd.mount** for a mount unit (see Table 5-1).

```
man systemd.service
```

Options common to units are listed in the **systemd.exec** and **systemd.unit** pages. The **systemd.unit** page lists directives common to all units such as Wants, Conflicts, Before, SourcePath, and Also. The **systemd.exec** pages list options for the execution of a program for a unit, such as the starting of a server daemon. These include options such as User, group, WorkingDirectory, Nice, Umask, and Environment. The **systemd.exec** page covers options for service, socket, mount, and swap units. The **systemd.directives** man page provides a listing of all systemd unit options and the man page for each option.

Unit Type	Unit Man page	Description
`service`	systemd.service	Services such as servers, which can be started and stopped
`socket`	systemd.socket	Socket for services (allows for inetd like services, AF_INET)
`device`	systemd.device	Devices
`mount`	systemd.mount	File system mount points
`automount`	systemd.automount	Automount point for File system. Use with mount units.
`target`	systemd.target	Group units
`path`	systemd.path	Manage directories
`snapshot`	systemd.snapshot	Created by systemd using the **systemctl snapshot** command to save runtime states of systemd. Use **systemctl isolate** to restore a state.
`swap`	systemd.swap	Swap unit file generated by systemd for the swap file system.
`timer`	systemd.timer	Time-based activation of a unit. Corresponds to a service file. Time formats are specified on the **systemd.time** man page.
	systemd.unit	Man page with configuration options common to all units
	systemd.exec	Man page for execution environment options for service, socket, mount, and swap units
	systemd.special	Man page for systemd special targets such as multi-user.target and printer.target.
	systemd.time	Time and date formats for **systemd**
	systemd.directives	Listing of all systemd options and the man page they are described on.

Table 5-1: systemd unit types and man pages

The target unit is used to group units. For example, targets are used to emulate runlevels. A multi-user target groups units (services) together that, in System V, would run on runlevel 3. In effect, targets group those services that run on a certain runlevel for a certain task. The printer target activates the CUPS service, and the graphical target emulates runlevel 5. A target can also be used to reference other targets. A default target designated the default runlevel. Some unit files are automatically generated by **systemd**. For example, operations specified in the **/etc/fstab** are performed by mount units, which are automatically generated from the fstab entries.

Units can be dependent on one another, where one unit may require the activation of other units. This dependency is specified using directories with the **.wants** extension. For example, the **poweroff.target** is dependent on the **plymouth-poweroff** service. The directory **poweroff.target.wants** has a symbolic links to this service. Should you want a service dependent on your graphical desktop, you can add symbolic links to it in the **graphical.target.wants** directory.

It is important to distinguish between the wants directories in the **/etc/systemd/system** directory and those in the **/lib/systemd/system** directory. Those in the **/lib/systemd** directory are set up by your system and should be left alone. To manage your own dependencies, you can set up corresponding wants directories in the **/etc/systemd/system** directory. The **/etc/systemd** directory always takes priority. For example, in the **/etc/systemd/system/multi-user.target.wants** directory you can place links to services that you want started up for the multi-user.target (runlevel 3). Your system automatically installs links for services you enable, such as **ufw.service** and **vsftpd.service**. These are all links to the actual service files in the **/lib/systemd/system** directory. The **multi-user.target.wants** directory holds a link to **ufw.sevice**, starting up the firewall. The **printer.target.wants** directory has a link to the cups service.

Disabling a service removes its link from its wants directory in **/etc/systemd/system**. For example, disabling the vsftpd service removes its link from the **/etc/systemd/system/multi-user.target.wants** directory. The original service file, in this case **vsftpd.service**, remains in the **/lib/systemd/system** directory. If you enable the service again, a link for it is added to the **/etc/systemd/system/multi-user.target.wants** directory.

The **/etc/systemd/system** directory also hold links to services. The **/etc/systemd/system/syslog.service** file is a link to **/lib/systemd/system/rsyslog.service.** The **/etc/systemd/system/dbus-org.freedesktop.Avahi.service** link references **/lib/systemd/system/avahi-daemon.service.**

To manage **systemd** you can use **systemctl**. The older service management tool, **service**, has been modified to use **systemctl** to perform actions on services such as starting and stopping.

unit file syntax

A unit file is organized into sections designated by keywords enclosed in brackets. All units have a unit section, **[Unit]**, and an install section, **[Install]**. The options for these sections are descript in the **systemd.unit** Man page. Comments can be written by beginning a line with # or **;** character. See Table 5-2 for a listing of commonly used Unit and Install section options.

The Unit section of a unit file holds generic information about a unit. The Description option provides information about the task the unit manages, such as the Vsftpd server as shown here.

```
Description=vsftpd FTP server
```

The Documentation option lists URIs for the application's documentation.

```
Documentation=man:dhcpd(8)
```

Note: The syntax for unit file is base on **.desktop** files, which in turn are inspired by Windows ini files. The .desktop type of file conforms to the XDB Desktop Entry Specification.

Types of dependencies can be specified using the Before, After, Requires, Wants, and Conflicts options in the unit section. After and Before configure the ordering of a unit. In the following After option in the **vsftpd.service** file, the vsft[d service is started after networking.

```
After= network.target
```

Unit options	Description
`[Unit]`	
`Description`	Description of the unit.
`Documentation`	URIs referencing documentation.
`Requires`	Units required by the service. This is strict requirement. If the required units fail, so will the unit.
`Wants`	Units wanted by the service. This is not a strict requirement. If the required units fail, the unit will still start up. Same functionality as the wants directories.
`Conflicts`	Negative unit dependency. Starting the unit stops the listed units in the Conflicts option.
`Before`	Unit ordering. Unit starts before the units listed.
`After`	Unit ordering. Unit waits until the units listed start.
`OnFailure`	Units to be run if unit fails.
`SourcePath`	File the configuration was generated from, such as the mount unit files generated from **/etc/fstab**.
`[Install]`	
`WantedBy`	Sets up the unit's symbolic link in listed unit's .wants subdirectory. When the listed unit is activated, so is the unit. This is not a strict requirement.
`RequiredBY`	Sets up the unit's symbolic link in listed unit's .requires subdirectory. When the listed unit is activated, so is the unit. This is a strong requirement.
`Alias`	Additional names the unit is installed under. The aliases are implemented as symbolic links to the unit file.
`Also`	Additional units to install with this unit.

Table 5-1: systemd Unit and Install section options (common to all units, systemd.unit)

The Requires option sets up a dependency between units. This is a strong dependency. If one fails so does the other. In the following Requires option from the **graphical.target** unit file, the graphical target can only be started if the multi-user and rescue targets are activated.

```
After=multi-user.target display-manager.service rescue.service rescue.target
```

The Wants option sets up a weaker dependency, requiring activation, but not triggering failure should it occur. This is the case with the graphical target and the display manager service like GDM.

```
Wants=display-manager.service
```

Several condition options are available such as ConditionACPower which, if true, checks to see if a system is using AC power. In the following example, ConditionPathExists checks for the existence of a file with runtime options for the dhcp server in the **/etc/default** directory.

```
ConditionPathExists=/etc/default/isc-dhcp-server
```

Some unit files are automatically generated by systemd, allowing you to use older configuration methods. For example, the unit file used to manage the mounting of your file systems is generated from the configuration information in the **/etc/fstab** file. The SourcePath option specifies the configuration file used to generate the unit file. The SourcePath option for the **boot.mount** unit file is shown here.

```
SourcePath=/etc/fstab
```

The Install section provides installation information for the unit. The WantedBy and RequiredBy options specify units that this unit wants or requires. For service units managing servers like Vsftpd and the DCHP servers, the install section has a WantedBy option for the **multi-user.target**. This has the effect of running the server at runlevels 2, 3, 4, and 5. When the multi-user target becomes activated so does that unit.

```
WantedBy=multi-user.target
```

The WantedBy option is implemented by setting up a link to the unit in a wants subdirectory for the wanted by unit. For the **multi-user.target** unit, a subdirectory called **multi-user.target.wants** has symbolic links in to all the units that want it, such as **vsftpd.service** for the vsfptd FTP service. These wants symbolic links are set up in the **/etc/systemd/system** directory, which can be changed as you enable and disable a service. Disabling a service removes the link. RequiredBy is a much stronger dependency.

The Alias option lists other unit names that could reference this unit. In the **ssh.service** file you will find an Alias option for **sshd.service**.

```
Alias=sshd.service
```

The Also option lists other unit that should be activated when this unit is started. The CUPS service has an Also option to start the CUPS socket and path.

```
Also=cups.socket cups.path
```

Different types of units have their own options. Service, socket, target, and path units all have options appropriate for their tasks.

special targets

A target file groups units for services, mounts, sockets, and devices. **systemd** has a set of special target files designed for specific purposes (see Table 5-3). Some are used for on demand services such as bluetooth and printer. When a bluetooth device is connected the bluetooth target becomes active. When you connect a printer, the printer target is activated which, in turn, activates the CUPS print server. The sound target is activated when the system starts and runs all sound-related units. See the **special.target** Man page for more details.

There are several special target files that are designed to fulfill the function of runlevels in System V (see Table 5-4). These include the rescue, multi-user, and graphical targets. On boot, **systemd** activates the default target, which is a link to a special target, such as **multi-user.target** and **graphical.target**. You can override the default target with a **systemd.unit** kernel command line option in the GRUB.

The following will start up the rescue target.

```
systemd.unit=rescue.target
```

On the GRUB startup menu, you could edit the kernel boot line and add the following option to boot to the command line instead of the desktop.

```
systemd.unit=multi-user.target
```

The following will start up the rescue target.

```
systemd.unit=rescue.target
```

Special units	Description
`basic.target`	Units to be run at early boot
`bluetooth.target`	Starts when a bluetooth device becomes active
`printer.target`	Starts printer service when a printer is attached.
`sound.target`	Starts when sound device is detected, usually at boot.
`display-manager.service`	Link to display service such as LightDM or KDM.
`ctrl-alt-del.target`	Activated when the user presses Ctrl-Alt-Del keys, this is a link to the reboot.target which reboots the system.
`system-update.target`	Implements an offline system update. After downloading, the updates are performed when your system reboots, at which time it detects the presence of the target.

Table 5-3: special units

Special RunlevelTargets	Description
`default.target`	References special target to be activated on boot
`rescue.target`	Starts up base system and rescue shell
`emergency.target`	Starts base system, with option to start full system
`multi-user.target`	Starts up command line interface, multi-user and non-graphical (similar to runlevel 3)
`graphical.target`	Start graphical interface (desktop) (similar to runlevel 5)

Table 5-4: special runlevel targets (boot)

On the GRUB startup menu, you could edit the kernel boot line and add the following option to boot to the command line instead of the desktop.

```
systemd.unit=multi-user.target
```

You could also simply add a 3 as in previous releases, as runlevel links also reference the special targets in **systemd**. The 3 would reference the runlevel 3 target, which links to the multi-user target. A copy of the **multi-user.target** file follows. The multi-user target requires the basic target which load the basic system (Requires). It conflicts with the rescue target (Conflicts), and it is run after the basic target. It can be isolated allowing you to switch special targets (AllowIsolate).

multi-user.target

```
[Unit]
Description=Multi-User System
Documentation=man:systemd.special(7)
Requires=basic.target
Conflicts=rescue.service rescue.target
After=basic.target rescue.service rescue.target
AllowIsolate=yes
```

The **graphical.target** depends on the **multi-user.target**. A copy of the **graphical.target** unit file follows. It requires that the **multi-user.target** be activated (Requires). Anything run for the multi-user target, including servers, is also run for the graphical target, the desktop. The desktop target is run after the **multi-user.target** (After). It is not run for the **rescue.target** (Conflicts). It also wants the display-manager service to run (GDM or KDM) (Wants). You can isolate it to switch to another target (AllowIsolate). .

graphical.target

```
[Unit]
Description=Graphical Interface
Documentation=man:systemd.special(7)
Requires=multi-user.target
Wants=display-manager.service
Conflicts=rescue.service rescue.target
After=multi-user.target rescue.service rescue.target display-manager.service
AllowIsolate=yes
```

Modifying unit files: /etc/systemd/system

systemd uses unit files to manage devices, mounts, and services. These are located in the **/lib/systemd/system** directory and are considered system files that you should not modify. Instead, to modify a unit file, you should copy it to the **/etc/systemd/system** directory. Unit files in this directory take precedence over those in the **/lib/systemd/system** directory. You can then modify the unit file version in **/etc/systemd/system**. Use a **cp** command to copy the file. The following command copies the Samba service unit file.

```
cp /lib/systemd/system/vsftpd.service    /etc/systemd/system/vsftpd.service
```

If you just want to add unit options to a unit file, not changing the original options in the **/lib/systemd/system** version, you do not have to copy the original unit file. Instead, you can set up a corresponding new unit file in **/etc/systemd/system** that has an include options that reads in the original unit file from **/lib/systemd/system**. Then, in the new **/etc/systemd/system** file, you can add the new systemd options.

Keep in mind that most runtime options for a service application, such as the Vsftpd server, are still held in the appropriate **/etc/default** file, such as **/etc/default/vsftpd**. This file is read by the service when it is activated.

The actual enabling or disabling of services such as vsftpd, is handled through symbolic links set up or removed from the **multi-user.target.wants** directory in the **/etc/systemd/system** directory. This is considered a user based modification appropriate for **/etc/systemd/system**.

Execution Environment Options

The unit files of type service, sockets, mount, and swap share the same options for the execution environment of the unit (see Table 5-5). These are found in the unit section for that type such as **[Service]** for service units or **[Socket]** for socket unit. With these options you can set features such as the working directory (WorkingDirectory), the file mode creation mask (UMask), and the system logging level (SysLogLevel). Nice sets the default scheduling priority level. User specifies the user id for the processes the unit runs.

```
User=mysql
```

Exec options	Description
`WorkingDirectory`	Sets the working directory for an application.
`RootDirectory`	Root directory for an application
`User, Group`	Application's user and group ids.
`Nice`	Sets priority for an application
`CPUSchedulingPriority`	CPU Scheduling priority for the applications.
`UMask`	File mode creation mask, default is 022.
`Environment`	Set environment variables for an application.
`StandardOutput`	Direct standard output a connection such as log, console, or null.
`SysLogLevel`	System logging level such as warn, alert, info, or debug.
`DeviceAllow, DeviceDeny`	Control applications access to a device.
`ControlGroup`	Assign application to a control group.

Table 5-5: systemd exec options (Service, Socket, Mount, Swap) (systemd.exec)

service unit files

A service unit file is used to run applications and commands such as the Samba (smb) and Web (httpd) servers. They have a **[Service]** section with options specified in the **systemd.service** Man page. See Table 5-6 for a listing of several common service options. A service unit file has the extension **.service** and the prefix is the name of the server program, such as **isc-dhcp-server.service** for the DHCP server and **vsftpd.service** for the Very Secure FTP server. Table 5-7 lists several popular servers.

A copy of the Vsftpd service unit file, **vsftpd.service**, follows. The Vsfptd FTP service is started after the network has started. The server program to run is specified, **/usr/sbin/vsftpd** (ExecStart). The service is installed by the **multi-user.target** (WantedBy), when the system starts up.

vsftpd.service

```
[Unit]
Description=vsftpd FTP server
After=network.target

[Service]
Type=simple
ExecStart=/usr/sbin/vsftpd /etc/vsftpd.conf
ExecReload=/bin/kill -HUP $MAINPID
ExecStartPre=-/bin/mkdir -p /var/run/vsftpd/empty

[Install]
WantedBy=multi-user.target
```

Service options	Description
`ExecStart`	Commands to execute when service starts, such as running an application or server.
`Type`	Startup type such as simple (the default), forking, dbus, notify, or idle
`ExecStartPre`, `ExecStartPost`	Commands executed before and after the ExecStart command.
`TimeStartSec`	Time to wait before starting the ExecStart command.
`Restart`	Restart when the ExecStart command end.
`PermissionsStartOnly`	Boolean value, If true the permission based options are applied, such as User.
`RootDirectoryStartOnly`	Boolean value, if true, the RootDirectory option applies only to the ExecStart option.

Table 5-6: systemd service options [Service] (systemd.service)

The **bind9.service** file is even simpler, incorporating configuration references into the program command. It is run after the network service, and is started by the **multi-user.target**.

bind9.service

```
[Unit]
Description=BIND Domain Name Server
Documentation=man:named(8)
After=network.target
[Service]
ExecStart=/usr/sbin/named -f -u bind
ExecReload=/usr/sbin/rndc reload
ExecStop=/usr/sbin/rndc stop
[Install]
WantedBy=multi-user.target
```

Service unit files	Description
`apache2`	Apache Web server
`bind9`	Bind 9 DNS server
`cups`	The CUPS printer daemon
`isc-dhcp-server`	Dynamic Host Configuration Protocol daemon
`mysql`	MySQL database server
`network`	Operations to start up or shut down your network connections.
`nis`	The NIS server
`nfs-server`	Network Filesystem
`postfix`	Postfix mail server
`sendmail`	The Sendmail MTA daemon
`smbd`	Samba for Windows hosts
`squid3`	Squid proxy-cache server
`ssh`	Secure Shell daemon
`systemd-journald`	System logging daemon
`vsftpd`	Very Secure FTP server
`ufw`	Controls the UFW firewall

Table 5-7: Collection of Service unit files

System V Scripts and generated systemd service files: /etc/init.d and /run/systemd/generator.late

Some services are not yet configured natively for use by systemd. They are installed without a systemd service file. Instead a SysV script is installed in the **/etc/init.d** directory. The **systemd-sysv-generator** tool automatically reads this script and generates a corresponding systemd unit file in the **/var/run/systemd/generator.late** directory, which, in turn, will use the script to manage the service. For Ubuntu 15.04, the Apache Web server is such a service, with an apache2 script in **/etc/init.d** and a corresponding systemd service file in the **/var/run/systemd/generator.late** directory. A copy of the **apache2.service** unit service file follows. It is started before the runlevel targets, which are links to the multi-user and graphical targets (Before), which is the equivalent of runlevels 2,3,4, and 5. It is run after network, remote file system mounts, and name service lookup. The server program is run using the **/etc/init.d/apache2** script (ExecStart). The same script is used to reload and stop the server but with different options (ExecReload and ExecStop).

There are **.target.wants** directories for different runlevels in the **/run/systemd/generator.late** directory, which hold links for the services active for a given runlevel. These runlevel target wants directories reference the runlevel targets, which, in turn, are simply links to the systemd multi-user and graphical targets.

apache2.service

```
# Automatically generated by systemd-sysv-generator

[Unit]
Documentation=man:systemd-sysv-generator(8)
SourcePath=/etc/init.d/apache2
Description=LSB: Apache2 web server
Before=runlevel2.target runlevel3.target runlevel4.target runlevel5.target
shutdown.target
After=local-fs.target remote-fs.target network-online.target systemd-journald-
dev-log.socket nss-lookup.target
Wants=network-online.target
Conflicts=shutdown.target

[Service]
Type=forking
Restart=no
TimeoutSec=5min
IgnoreSIGPIPE=no
KillMode=process
GuessMainPID=no
RemainAfterExit=yes
ExecStart=/etc/init.d/apache2 start
ExecStop=/etc/init.d/apache2 stop
ExecReload=/etc/init.d/apache2 reload
```

On Demand and Standalone Services (socket)

The On Demand activation of services, formerly implemented by inetd, is the default in systemd. Should you want a standalone service, you can specify that it is wanted by a special target so that it will be started up at boot time, instead of when it is first activated. In the Install section of a service unit file, a WantedBy option specifying the multi-user target will start the service at boot, making it a standalone service. In the following, the service is wanted by the multi-user.target. To put it another way, the service starts at runlevels 2, 3, 4, and 5. Note that the graphical target (5) is dependent on (Requires) the multi-user target (2, 3, and 4), so by specifying the multi-user target, the service is also started with the graphical target.

```
 [Install]
WantedBy=multi-user.target
```

The Bluetooth service only wants the **bluetooth.target** which is only activated if a bluetooth device is present. It is not started at boot.

```
[Install]
WantedBy=bluetooth.target
```

Should you want the service started at all runlevels.

```
[Install]
WantedBy=basic.target
```

To emulate an on-demand server service, as inetd used to do, you would use a **.socket** file to compliment a **.service** file. This is the case with CUPS, which has a cups service file and corresponding cups socket file. The WantedBy option for **sockets.target** ties the socket to the special target **sockets.target**, which makes the unit socket-activated.

The Socket section lists options for the socket, usually what socket to listen on (ListenStream). The **systemd.socket** Man page lists socket options. Table 5-8 lists common options.

Socket options	Description
`ListenStream`	Address to listen on for a stream. The address can be a port number, path name for a socket device, or an IPv4 or IPv6 address with a port number.
`Accept`	If true, service instance is set up for each connection; if false, only one service instance is set up for all connections
`MaxConnections`	Maxminum number of connections for a service
`Service`	Service unit to run when socket is active. Default is a service name that is the same as the socket name.

Table 5-8: systemd socket file options [Socket] (systemd.socket)

cups.socket

```
[Unit]
Description=CUPS Scheduler

[Socket]
ListenStream=/var/run/cups/cups.sock

[Install]
WantedBy=sockets.target
```

cups.service

```
[Unit]
Description=CUPS Scheduler
Documentation=man:cupsd(8)

[Service]
ExecStart=/usr/sbin/cupsd -l
Type=simple

[Install]
Also=cups.socket cups.path
WantedBy=printer.target
```

Path units

systemd uses path units to monitor a path. Sometimes a service unit has a corresponding path unit to monitor directories, as is the case with **cups.path** and **cups.service**. Options for the Path section are listed in Table 5-9 and on the **systemd.path** Man page. The **cups.path** unit file is shown here. The PathExists option checks if the printer spool files exist.

cups.path

```
[Unit]
Description=CUPS Scheduler

[Path]
PathExists=/var/cache/cups/org.cups.cupsd

[Install]
WantedBy=multi-user.target
```

path options	Description
PathExists	Activates if a file exists
PathExistsGlob	Activates if there exists a file matching a pattern, such as any file in a specified directory.
PathModified	Activates if a file has been modified

Table 5-9: path option (systemd.path)

Template unit files

There is a special type of unit file called a template file, which allow for the generation of several unit files at runtime using one template file. Templates are used for services that generate instances of a service such as a getty terminal, an OpenVPN connection, and an rsync connection. A template file name ends with an @ sign. If a corresponding unit file is not found for a service, **systemd** will check to see if there is template file that can be applied to it. **systemd** matches the service name with the template name. It then generates an instance unit file for that particular service.

For example, a terminal uses the getty service (get TTY). As you do not know how many terminals you may use, they are generated automatically using the **getty@.service** unit file.

In the configuration file, the **%I** specifier is used to substitute for the service name. Given the service name **getty@tty3**, the **%I** specifier substitutes for **tty3**.

```
ExecStart=-/sbin/agetty --noclear %I $TERM
```

The **getty@.service** template file is shown here.

getty@.service

```
[Unit]
Description=Getty on %I
Documentation=man:agetty(8) man:systemd-getty-generator(8)
Documentation=http://0pointer.de/blog/projects/serial-console.html
After=systemd-user-sessions.service plymouth-quit-wait.service
After=rc-local.service

# If additional gettys are spawned during boot then we should make
# sure that this is synchronized before getty.target, even though
# getty.target didn't actually pull it in.
Before=getty.target
IgnoreOnIsolate=yes
```

```
# On systems without virtual consoles, don't start any getty. Note
# that serial gettys are covered by serial-getty@.service, not this
# unit.
ConditionPathExists=/dev/tty0

[Service]
# the VT is cleared by TTYVTDisallocate
ExecStart=-/sbin/agetty --noclear %I $TERM
Type=idle
Restart=always
RestartSec=0
UtmpIdentifier=%I
TTYPath=/dev/%I
TTYReset=yes
TTYVHangup=yes
TTYVTDisallocate=yes
KillMode=process
IgnoreSIGPIPE=no
SendSIGHUP=yes

# Unset locale for the console getty since the console has problems
# displaying some internationalized messages.
Environment=LANG= LANGUAGE= LC_CTYPE= LC_NUMERIC= LC_TIME= LC_COLLATE=
LC_MONETARY= LC_MESSAGES= LC_PAPER= LC_NAME= LC_ADDRESS= LC_TELEPHONE=
LC_MEASUREMENT= LC_IDENTIFICATION=

[Install]
WantedBy=getty.target
DefaultInstance=tty1
```

Runlevels and Special Targets

Under the old System V, a Linux system could run in different levels, called **runlevels**, depending on the capabilities you want to give it. Under System V, Linux had several runlevels, numbered from 0 to 6. When you power up your system, you enter the default runlevel. Runlevels 0, 1, and 6 are special runlevels that perform specific functions. Runlevel 0 was the power-down state. Runlevel 6 was the reboot state—it shuts down the system and reboots. Runlevel 1 was the single-user state, which allowed access only to the superuser and does not run any network services.

systemd uses special targets instead of runlevels create the same effect as runlevels, grouping services to run for specified targets. Runlevels are no longer directly implemented. There are two major special targets: multi-user and graphical. The multi-user target is similar to runlevel 3, providing you with a command line login. The graphical target is similar to runlevel 5, providing you with a graphical login and interface.

You set the default target (runlevel) by linking a target's **systemd** service file to the **systemd** default target file. This operation replaces the way inittab was used to specify a default runlevel in previous releases. The **inittab** file is no longer used. The following makes the graphical interface the default (runlevel 5).

```
ln -s /lib/systemd/system/graphicl.target  /etc/systemd/system/default.target
```

systemd does provide compatibility support for runlevels. Runlevel compatibility is implemented using symbolic links in **/lib/system/systemd** directory to **systemd** targets. The **runlevel0.target** link references the systemd **poweroff.target**. Runlevel 2, 3, and 4 targets all link to the same **multi-user.target** (command line interface). The **runlevel6.target** links to the reboot target, and **runlevel5.target** links to **graphical.target** (desktop interface). The runlevels and their targets are listed in Table 5-10.

System Runlevel links	systemd targets
runlevel0	poweroff.target
runlevel1	rescue.target
runlevel2	multi-user.target
runlevel3	multi-user.target
runlevel4	multi-user.target.
runlevel5	graphical.target.
runlevel6	reboot.target

Table 5-10: System Runlevels (States)

You can still use the **runlevel** command to see what state you are currently running in. It lists the previous state followed by the current one. If you have not changed states, the previous state will be listed as N, indicating no previous state. This is the case for the state you boot up in. In the next example, the system is running in state 3, with no previous state change:

```
# runlevel
N 3
```

Changing runlevels can be helpful if you have problems at a particular runlevel. For example, if your video card is not installed properly, then any attempt to start up in runlevel 5 (graphical.target) will likely fail, as this level immediately starts your graphical interface. Instead, you should use the command line interface, runlevel 3 (multi-user.target), to fix your video card installation.

No matter what runlevel you start in, you can change from one runlevel to another with the **telinit** command. If your default runlevel is 3, you power up in runlevel 3, but you can change to, say, runlevel 5 with **telinit 5**. The command **telinit 0** shuts down your system. In the next example, the **telinit** command changes to runlevel 1, the administrative state:

```
telinit 1
```

Before **systemd** was implemented, you could also use **init** to also change runlevels. With **systemd**, both **telinit** and **init** are now **systemd** emulation versions of the original Unix commands. The **telinit** command is always used to change runlevels. If you use **init** with a runlevel number, it now merely invokes **telinit** to make the change.

Alternatively you can use the systemctl command directly to change runlevels (targets). The **systemctl** command with the isolate option and the name of the target file changes to that target (runlevel). The following command changes to the multi-user target.

```
sudo systemctl isolate multi-user.target
```

You could also use the runlevel link instead.

```
sudo systemctl isolate runlevel3.target
```

This is what the telinit command actually does.

systemd and automatically mounting file systems: /etc/fstab

The **systemd** unit files with the extension **.mount** can be used to mount file systems automatically. Normally systemd will read the /etc/fstab for mount information. If a mount unit file exists in the **/etc/systemd** directory, it takes precedence, but **/etc/fstab** takes precedence over any unit mount files in the **/lib/systemd** directory. The **/etc/fstab** file is used for mount configuration information. Most of the options for a mount unit file correspond to those of the **/etc/fstab** file, specifying the device path name, the mount point, file system type, and mount options (see Table 5-11). In fact, the entries in the **/etc/fstab** file are converted to mount unit files at boot, which are then used by systemd to perform the actual mount operations. These mount unit files are created by the systemd-fstab-generator and can be found in the **/run/systemd/generator** directory.

The following fstab file entries have corresponding mount files created in the **/run/systemd/generator** directory: **boot.mount** for the boot file system (**boot-efi.mount** for a EUFI boot system), **home.mount** for the home file system, and **-.mount** for the root file system. For the swap file system a swap unit file is generated.

```
UUID=1059a-4a86-4072-982e-000717229b9f / ext4   errors=remount-ro   0 1
UUID-=5537-AF41 /boot/efi    vfat    umask=0077   0 1
UUID=147b-4a86-4072-982e-000717229b6g /home ext4   default   0 1
UUID=cba958e4-4a86-4072-982e-000717228355 none     swap    sw    0 0
```

For this example, the **-.mount** file used for the root file system will have the following mount options. The root directory is represented in the mount file name as a dash, -, instead of a slash, /. The mount options are listed in a **[Mount]** section.

```
[Mount]
What=/dev/disk/by-uuid/1059a-4a86-4072-982e-000717229b9f
Where=/
Type=ext4
Options=errors=remount-ro
```

The **home.mount** file references partition for the home file system and mounts it to the **/home** directory.

```
[Mount]
What=/dev/disk/by-uuid/147b-4a86-4072-982e-000717229b6g
Where=/home
Type=ext4
FsckPassNo=2
```

The **boot.mount** file mounts the ext4 file system that holds the kernel in the **/boot** directory.

```
[Mount]
What=/dev/disk/by-uuid/e759aa59-4a86-4072-982e-000717229b4a
Where=/boot
Type=ext4
FsckPassNo=2
```

The **boot-efi.mount** file mounts the vfat efi file system that holds the boot information.

```
[Mount]
What=/dev/disk/by-uuid/5537-AF41
Where=/boot/efi
Type=vfat
Options=umask=0077
```

mount options	Description
`What`	Path of the device
`Where`	Directory of the mount point.
`Type`	File system type
`Options`	Mount options
`DirectoryMode`	Permissions for created file system mount directories
`TimeoutSec`	Time to wait for a mount operation to finish
automount options	**Description**
`Where`	Mount point for the file system. If it does not exist, it will be created.
`DirectoryMode`	Permissions for any directories created.

Table 5-11: systemd mount and automount file options [Mount] [Automount]

All the unit files will designate the **/etc/fstab** file as the SourcePath, the file from which the configuration was generated from.

```
SourcePath=/etc/fstab
```

All are mounted before any local file systems.

```
Before=local-fs.target
```

Local and remote file systems are distinguished by Wants options in their unit files for **local-fs.target** or **remote-fs.target**.

A mount unit file has to be named for the mount point it references. The path name slashes are replaced by dashes in the unit name. For example, the **proc-fs-nfsd.mount** file references the mount point **/proc/fs/nfsd**. The root path name, /, becomes simple a dash, -.

For file systems to be automatically mounted when accessed you can use the automount unit type. An automount unit must have a corresponding mount unit of the same name.

The **systemd-fsck@service** file provides a file system check with fsck, using the disk name as an argument.

```
RequiresOverridable=system-fsck@dev-disk-by\x2duuid-5537\x2dAF41.service
After=system-fsck@dev-disk-by\x2duuid-5537\x2dAF41.service
```

systemd slice and scope units

The slice and scope units are designed to group units to more easily control their processes and resources. The scope units are generated by systemd to manage a process and its sub processes. An example of a scope unit is a user session scope that groups the processes for a user session together. A slice is used to manage resources for processes, such as the machine slice for virtual machines, the system slice for system services, and the user slice for usr sessions.

System V: /etc/init.d

The SysVinit support for services is no longer implemented. There are no **rc.d** scripts for starting services. **systemd** manages all services directly. Check the README file in the **/etc/init.d** directory. For a very few system tasks, you may find System V scripts in the **/etc/init.d** directory. **systemd** will read these scripts as configuration information for a service, generating a corresponding unit configuration file for it. The unit file, in turn, may use the **init.d** script to start, stop, and restart the service. Should there be a unit file already in existence, that unit file is used and the System V script is ignored.

For Ubuntu 15.04, some servers use unit files generated from System V scripts in the **/etc/init.d** directory. These include Apache (apache2), Samba (smbd and nmbd), Postfix (postfix), NIS (nis), and Squid (squid3). The unit files are generated by systemd-sysv-generator and located in the **/var/run/systemd/generator.late** directory.

An **rc-local.service** unit file in the **/lib/systemd/system** directory will run a **/etc/rc.local** file, if present. This is to maintain compatibility with older System V configuration.

Shutdown and Poweroff

You can use the **shutdown** and **poweroff** commands to power down the system. The **shutdown** command provides more options. Keep in mind that the **shutdown** command used is the **systemd** version, which will use **poweroff.target** to actually shutdown the system. The **poweroff** command with the **-f** option forces a shutdown, with the **--reboot** option, it reboots the system.

```
poweroff
```

The **shutdown** command has a time argument that gives users on the system a warning before you power down. You can specify an exact time to shut down, or a period of minutes from the current time. The exact time is specified by *hh***:***mm* for the hour and minutes. The period of time is indicated by a **+** and the number of minutes.

The **shutdown** command takes several options with which you can specify how you want your system shut down. The `-h` option, which stands for halt, simply shuts down the system, whereas the `-r` option shuts down the system and then reboots it. In the next example, the system is shut down after ten minutes:

```
shutdown -h +10
```

To shut down the system immediately, you can use `+0` or the word `now`. The shutdown options are listed in Table 5-12. The following example shuts down the system immediately and then reboots:

```
shutdown -r now
```

With the **shutdown** command, you can include a warning message to be sent to all users currently logged in, giving them time to finish what they are doing before you shut them down.

```
shutdown -h +5 "System needs a rest"
```

If you do not specify either the `-h` or the `-r` options, the **shutdown** command shuts down the multi-user mode and shifts you to an administrative single-user mode. In effect, your system state changes from 3 (multi-user state) to 1 (administrative single-user state). Only the root user is active, allowing the root user to perform any necessary system administrative operations with which other users might interfere.

Note: the halt command now merely halts the system, it does not turn it off.

Command	Description
`shutdown [-rkhncft]` *time* [*warning*]	Shuts the system down after the specified time period, issuing warnings to users; you can specify a warning message of your own after the time argument; if neither `-h` nor `-r` is specified to shut down the system, the system sets to the administrative mode, runlevel state 1.
Argument	
Time	Has two possible formats: it can be an absolute time in the format *hh:mm,* with *hh* as the hour (one or two digits) and *mm* as the minute (in two digits); it can also be in the format *+m,* with *m* as the number of minutes to wait; the word `now` is an alias for `+0`.
Option	
`-t` *sec*	Tells `init` to wait *sec* seconds between sending processes the warning and the kill signals, before changing to another runlevel.
`-k`	Doesn't actually shut down; only sends the warning messages to everybody.
`-r`	Reboots after shutdown, runlevel state 6.
`-h`	Halts after shutdown, runlevel state 0.
`-n`	Doesn't call `init` to do the shutdown; you do it yourself.
`-f`	Skips file system checking (fsck) on reboot.
`-c`	Cancels an already running shutdown; no time argument.

Table 5-12: System Shutdown Options

Managing Services

You can select certain services to run and the special target (runlevel) at which to run them. Most services are servers like a Web server or FTP server. Other services provide security, such as SSH or Kerberos. You can decide which services to use with the **systemctl** or **service** tools.

Enabling services: starting a service automatically at boot

Services such as the Apache Web server, Samba server, and the FTP server are now handled by the **systemd** daemon. You can manage services using the **systemctl** command. The older **service** command is simply a front end to the **systemctl** command.

To have a service start up at boot, you need to first enable it using the **systemctl** tool as the root user. Use the **enable** command to enable the service. The following command enables the vsftpd server and the Samba server (**smb**). The **systemctl** command uses the service's service configuration file located at the **/lib/systemd/system or /etc/systemd/system** directory.

```
sudo systemctl enable vsftpd.service
sudo systemctl enable smb
```

Managing services manually

Use the start, stop, and restart command with **systemctl** to manually start, stop, and restart a service. The enable command only starts up a service automatically. You could choose to start it manually using the **start** command. You can stop and restart a service any time using the **stop** and **restart** commands. The **condrestart** command only starts the server if it is already stopped. Use the **status** command to check the current status of service.

```
sudo systemctl start vsftpd
sudo systemctl restart vsftpd
sudo systemctl condrestart vsftpd
sudo systemctl stop vsftpd
sudo systemctl status vsftpd
```

You can also use **service** to start, stop, or restart a service. It is simply a front end for the **systemctl** command which performs the actual operation using **systemd**.

```
service start vsftpd
```

The service Command

The **service** command is now simply a front end for the **systemctl** command which performs the actual operation using **systemd**. The **service** command cannot enable or disable services. It only performs management operations such as stop, restart, and status. To start and stop services manually, you can use the **`service`** command. With the **`service`** command, you enter the service name with the **`stop`** argument to stop it, the **`start`** argument to start it, and the **`restart`** argument to restart it. The **`service`** command is run from a Terminal window. You will have to first login as the **root** user, using the **su** command, or use the **sudo** command, if configured. The following will start the **vsftod** FTP service.

```
sudo service vsftpd start
```

The **systemd** version of the **service** command actually invokes the **systemctl** command to run the service's **systemd .service** unit file in **/lib/systemd/system**. If a service is not enabled, **systemd** will enable it. You can perform the same operations as the **service** command, using the **systemctl** command. The following is the equivalent of the previous command.

```
sudo systemctl vsftpd vsftpd
```

Note: Upstart had been deprecated.

/etc/default

The **/etc/default** directory holds scripts for setting runtime options when a service starts up. For example, the **/etc/default/apache2** script sets cache cleaning options. The **/etc/default/ufw** scripts sets firewall default policies. You can edit these scripts and change the values assigned to options, changing the behavior of a service.

Service Startup Management with rcconf

Ubuntu provides the **rcconf** (Debian) toos which you can use to start or stop services when you boot up your system (see Figure 5-1). The **rcconf** tool was developed by Debian and is used on Debian, Ubuntu, and similar distributions. The rcconf works both for System V init service scripts located in the **/etc/init.d** directory and for systemd service files, changing appropriate links the the **/etc/systemd/multi-user.target.wants** directory.

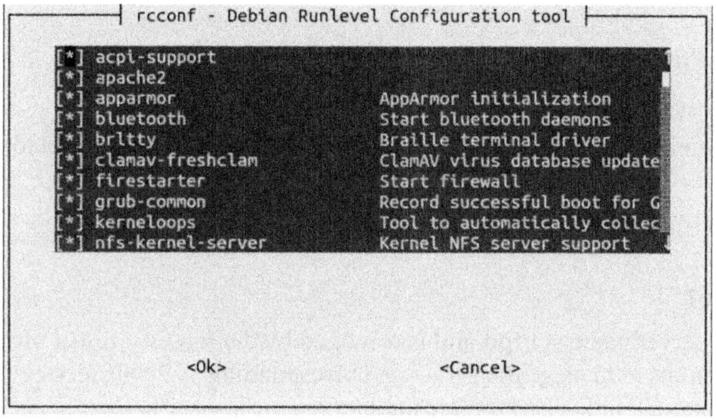

Figure 5-1: rcconf service management

The **rcconf** is run from a terminal window or from the command line, and provides an easy cursor-based interface for using arrow keys and the spacebar to turn services on or off.

```
sudo rcconf
```

Network Time Protocol, NTP

For servers to run correctly, they need to always have the correct time. Internet time servers worldwide provide the time in the form of the Universal Time Coordinated (UTC). Local time is then calculated using the local system's local time zone. The time is obtained from Internet time servers from an Internet connection. You have the option of using a local hardware clock instead, though this may be much less accurate.

Normally, the time on a host machine is kept in a Time of Year chip (TOY) that maintains the time when the machine is off. Its time is used when the machine is rebooted. A host using the Network Time Protocol then adjusts the time, using the time obtained from an Internet time server. If there is a discrepancy of more than 1000 seconds (about 15 minutes), the system administrator is required to manually set the time. Time servers in the public network are organized in stratum levels, the highest being 1. Time servers from a lower stratum obtain the time from those in the next higher level.

For servers on your local network, you may want to set up your own time server, insuring that all your servers are using a synchronized time. If all your servers are running on a single host system that is directly connected to the Internet and accessing an Internet time server, you will not need to set up a separate time server. You can use the **ntpdate** command to update directly from an Internet time server.

```
sudo ntpdate ntp.ubuntu.com
```

If the servers are on different host systems, then you may want a time server to insure their times are synchronized. Alternatively, you could just use the **ntpdate** command to update those hosts directly at given intervals. You could set up a cron job to perform the **ntpdate** operation automatically.

There are packages on the Ubuntu repository for both the NTP server and its documentation. You can install them with **apt-get**, **aptitude**, or (from the desktop) the Synaptic Package Manager.

```
ntp
ntp-doc
```

The documentation will be located in the /usr/share/doc/ntp-doc directory in Web page format.

```
/usr/share/doc/ntp-doc/html/index.html
```

The ntp server

The NTP server name is **ntpd** and is managed by the **/etc/init.d/ntp** script. Use the start, stop, and restart options to manage the server. A corresponding systemd service file, **ntp.service**, is generated in the /run/systemd/generator.late directory. s

```
sudo service ntp start
```

Your host systems can then be configured to use NTP and access your NTP time server.

To check the status of your time server, you can use the **ntpq** command. With the **-p** option is displays the current status.

```
ntpq -p
```

The ntp.conf configuration file

The NTP server configuration file is **/etc/ntp.conf**. This file lists the Internet time servers that your own time server used to deterring the time. Check the **ntp.conf** Man page for a complete listing of the NTP server configuration directives.

In the **ntp.conf** file, the server directive specifies the Internet time server's Internet address that your NTP server uses to access the time. There is a default entry for the Ubuntu time server, but you can add more server entries for other time servers.

```
server ntp.ubuntu.com
```

NTP access controls

Access control to the NTP server is determined by the restrict directives. An NTP server is accessible from the Internet, anyone can access it. You can specify access options and the addresses of hosts allowed access. The **default** option lets you specify the set of default options. The **noquery**, **notrust**, **nopeer**, and **nomodify** option deny all access. The **notrust** option will not trust hosts unless specifically allowed access. The **nomodify** option prevents any modification of the time server. The **noquery** option will not even allow queries from other hosts, unless specifically allowed.

```
restrict -4 default kod notrap nomodify nopeer noquery
```

The default **/etc/ntp.conf** file is shown here.

```
#/etc/ntp.conf, configuration for ntpd: see ntp.conf(5) for help
driftfile /ver/lib/ntp/ntp.drift

#Enable this if you want statistics to be logged.
#statsdir /var/log/ntpstats/
statistics loopstats peerstats clockstats
filegen loopstats file loopstats type day enable
filegen peerstats file peerstats type day enable
filegen clockstats file clockstats type day enable
# Use Servers from the NTP Pool Project. Approved by Ubuntu Technical Board
# on 2011-02-08 (LP: #104525). See http://www.pool.ntp.org/join.html for
# more information
server 0.ubuntu.pool.ntp.org
server 1.ubuntu.pool.ntp.org
server 2.ubuntu.pool.ntp.org
server 3.ubuntu.pool.ntp.org

# Use Ubuntu's ntp server as fallback
server ntp.ubuntu.com

# Access control configuration; see
# /usr/share/doc/ntp-doc/html/accopt.html for
# details.  The web page <http://support.ntp.org/bin/view/Support/AccessRestrictions>
# might also be helpful.
#
# Note that "restrict" applies to both servers and clients, so a configuration
# that might be intended to block requests from certain clients could also end
# up blocking replies from your own upstream servers.

# By default, exchange time with everybody, but don't allow configuration.
restrict -4 default kod notrap nomodify nopeer noquery
restrict -6 default kod notrap nomodify nopeer noquery

# Local users may interrogate the ntp server more closely.
restrict 127.0.0.1
restrict ::1

# Clients from this (example!) subnet have unlimited access, but only if
# cryptographically authenticated.
#restrict 192.168.123.0 mask 255.255.255.0 notrust

# If you want to provide time to your local subnet, change the next
# line. (Again, the address is an example only.)
#broadcast 192.168.123.255

# If you want to listen to time broadcasts on your local subnet,
# de-comment the next lines. Please do this only if you trust everybody
# on the network!
#disable auth
#broadcastclient
```

Then local users, users on the same host that is running the NTP server, are allowed to access the NTP server. Addresses are specified for both IPv4 and IPv6 local host, **127.0.0.1** and **::1**.

```
restrict 127.0.0.1
restrict ::1
```

To allow access from hosts on a private local network, you can use the restrict directive to specify the local network address and mask. The following allows access to a local network, 192.168.123, with a network mask of 255.255.255.0 to determine the range of allowable host addresses.

```
restrict 192.168.123.0 mask 255.255.255.0
```

If you want to require the use of encrypted keys for access, add the **notrust** option. Use **ntp-keygen** to generate the required public/private keys.

You can also run the time server in broadcast mode where the time is broadcasted to your network clients (this can involve security risks). Use the broadcast directive and your network's broadcast address. Your host systems need to have the **broadcastclient** setting set, which will listen for time broadcasts.

```
broadcast 192.168.123.255
```

NTP clock support

You can also list a reference to the local hardware clock, and have that clock be used if your connection to the Internet time server should fail. The hardware clock is references by the IP address that has the prefix 127.127 followed by the clock type and instance, as in 127.127.1.1. The type for the local clock is 1.

```
server 127.127.1.1
```

The **fudge** directive is used to specify the time for a hardware clock, passing time parameters for that clock's driver.

AppArmor security

Ubuntu installs AppArmor as its default security system. AppArmor (Application Armor) is designed as an alternative to SELinux (Security-Enhanced Linux, **http://www.nsa.gov/research/selinux/** and **http://selinuxproject.org/page/Main_Page**). It is much less complicated, but makes use of the same kernel support provided for SELinux. AppArmor is a simple method for implementing mandatory access controls (MAC) for specified Linux applications. It is used primarily for servers like Samba, the CUPS print servers, and the time server. In this respect it is much more limited in scope than SELinux, which tries to cover every object. Instead of labeling each object, which SELinux does, AppArmor identifies an object by its path name. The object does not have to be touched. Originally developed by Immunix and later supported for a time by Novell (OpenSUSE), AppArmor is available under the GNU Public License. You can find out more about AppArmor at **http://en.opensuse.org/Apparmor**.

AppArmor works by setting up a profile for supported applications. Essentially, this is a security policy similar to SELinux policies. A profile defines what an application can access and use on the system. Ubuntu will install the apparmor and apparmor-utils packages (Ubuntu main repository). Also available are the **apparmor-profiles** (Universe repository) and **apparmor-doc** packages.

AppArmor is still installed with the **/etc/init.d/apparmor** script. You can use the **service** or **systemctl** commands to start, stop, and restart AppArmor.

```
sudo service apparmor start
```

Currently, the generated systemd service file, **apparmor.service** (/run/systemd/generator.late), uses the **/etc/init.d/apparmor** script to manage Apparmor.

AppArmor utilities

The **appArmor-utils** packages installs several AppArmor tools, including **enforce**, which enables AppArmor and **complain**, which instructs AppArmor to just issue warning messages (see Table 5-13). The **unconfined** tool will list applications that have no AppArmor profiles. The **audit** tool will turn on AppArmor message logging for an application (uses enforce mode).

The **apparmor_status** tool will display current profile information. The **--complaining** options lists only those in complain mode, and **--enforced** for those in enforcing mode.

```
sudo apparmor_status
```

Utility	Description
apparmor_status	Status information about AppArmor policies
aa-audit *applications*	Enable logging for AppArmor messages for specified applications
aa-complain	Set AppArmor to complain mode
aa-enforce	Set AppArmor to enforce mode
aa-autodep *application*	Generate a basic profile for new applications
aa-logprof	Analyzes AppArmor complain messages for a profile, and suggests profile modifications
aa-genprof *application*	Generate profile for an application
aa-unconfined	Lists applications not controlled by AppArmor (no profiles)

Table 5-13: AppArmor Utilities

The **aa-logprof** tool will analyze AppArmor logs to determine if any changes are needed in any of the application profiles. Suggested changes will be presented and the user can allow (**A**) or deny them (**D**). In complain mode, allow is the default, and in enforce mode, deny is the default. You can also make your own changes with the new (**N**) option. Should you want the change applied to all files and directories in a suggested path, you can select the glob option (**G**), essentially replacing the last directory or file in a path with the * global file matching symbol.

The **aa-autodep** tool will generate a basic AppArmor profile for a new or unconfined application. If you want a more effective profile, you can use **aa-genprof** to analyze the application's use and generate profile controls accordingly.

The **aa-genprof** tool will update or generate a detailed profile for a specified application. **aa-genprof** will first set the profile to complain mode. You then start up the application and use it, generating complain mode log messages on that use. Then, v**genprof** prompts you to either scan the complain messages to further refine the profile (**S**), or to finish (**F**). When scanned, different violations are detected and the user is prompted to allow or deny recommended controls. You can then repeat the scan operation until you feel the profile is acceptable. Select finish (**F**) to finalize the profile and quit.

AppArmor configuration

AppArmor configuration is located in the **/etc/apparmor** directory. Configurations for different profiles are located in the **/etc/apparmor.d** directory. Loaded profile configuration file have the name of their path, using periods instead of slashes to separate directory names. The profile file for the **smbd** (Samba) application is **usr.sbin.smbd**. For CUPS (**cupsd**) it is **usr.sbin.cupsd**. For the time server it is **user.sbin.ntpd**. Additional profiles like the Samba and Apache profiles are installed with the **apparmor-profiles** package (not installed by default).

```
sudo apt-get install apparmor-profiles
```

Configuration rules for AppArmor profiles consist of a path and permissions allowable on that path. A detailed explanation of AppArmor rules and permissions can be found in the **apparmor.d** Man page, including a profile example. A path ending in a * matching symbol will select all the files in that directory. The ** symbol selects all files and subdirectories. All file matching operations are supported (* **[]** ?). Permissions include **r** (read), **w** (write), **x** (execute), and **l** (link). The **u** permission allows unconstrained access. The following entry allows all the files and subdirectories in the **/var/log/samba/cores/smdb** directory to be written to.

```
/var/log/samba/cores/smbd/** rw,
```

The **/etc/apparmor.d/abstractions** directory has files with profile rules that are common to different profiles. Rules from these files are read into actual profiles using the **include** directive. There are abstractions for applications like audio, samba, and video. Some abstractions will include yet other more general abstractions, like those for the X server (**X**) or GNOME (**gnome**). For example, the profile for the Samba smbd server, **usr.sbin.smbd**, will have a include directive for the **samba** abstraction. This abstraction holds rules common to both the **smbd** and **nmbd** servers, both used by the Samba service. The <> used in an **include** directive indicates the **/etc/apparmor.d** directory. A list of abstraction files can be found in the **apparmor.d** Man page. The **include** directive begins with a # character.

```
#include <abstractions/samba>
```

In some cases, a profile may need access to some files in a directory that it normally should not have access to. In this case it may need to use a sub-profile to allow access. In effect, the application changes hats, taking on permissions it does not have in the original profile.

The **armor-profiles** package will activate several commonly used profiles, setting up profile files for them in the **/etc/apparmor.d** directory, like those for samba (**usr.sbin.nmbd** and **usr.sbin.smbd**), the Dovecot mail pop and imap server (**usr.sbin.dovecot**), and Avahi (**usr.sbin.avahi-daemon**).

The package also will provide profile default files for numerous applications in the **/usr/share/doc/apparmor-profiles/extras** directory, such as the vsftpd FTP server (**usr.sbin.vsftpd**), the ClamAV virus scanner (**usr.bin.freshclam**), and the Squid proxy server (**usr.sbin.squid**). Some service applications are located in the **/usr/lib** directory, and will have

usr.lib prefix such as those for the Postfix server, which uses several profiles, beginning with **usr.lib.postfix**. To use these extra profiles, copy them to the **/etc/apparmor.d** directory. The following example copies the profile for the vsftpd FTP server.

```
sudo cp /usr/share/doc/apparmor-profiles/extras/usr.sbin.vsftpd  /etc/apparmor.d
```

Remote Administration

For remote administration you can use the OpenSSH and Puppet. OpenSSH lets you remotely control and transfer files securely over your network. Puppet lets you manage remote configuration of services.

Puppet

Puppet allows you to configure remote systems automatically, even though they may be running different linux distributions with varying configuration files. Instead of configuring each system on a network manually, you can use Puppet to configure them automatically. Puppet abstracts administration tasks as resources in a resource abstraction layer (RAL). You then specify basic values or operations for a particular resource using a Puppet configuration language. Administration types include services, files, users, and groups. For example, you could use puppet to perform an update for a service (server) on systems using different package managers such as APT or Synaptic.

Puppet configuration can become very complex. Once set up though is fully automates configuration changes across all your networked systems. For detailed documentation and guides see the following.

```
http://docs.puppetlabs.com/
```

Puppet configuration is located in the **/etc/puppet** directory. Puppet operations on services are specified in modules programmed in the init.pp file located in a **manifests** directory. In the Ubuntu example for Apache (Ubuntu Server Guide, Puppet), the apache module is created in the init.pp file in:

```
/etc/puppet/modules/apache2/manifests/init.pp
```

On Ubuntu, clients use the puppet client (**puppet** package) and the server uses the puppetmaster daemon (**puppetmaster** package).

On puppet clients, use the **service** command to manually start and stop the **puppet** service. For the server, enable the **puppetmaster** service.

On the firewall add access for the Puppet port, 8140.

For the client, the puppet runtime configuration is set in the **/etc/default/puppet** file. Here you set the daemon to start by setting the **START** variable to yes

If your network is running a DNS server, you can set up a CNAME puppet entry for the puppet server. The puppet clients can then use the CNAME to locate the puppet server.

```
puppet   IN   CNAME   turtle.mytrek.com
```

You could also add a host entry for the puppet server in each client's **/etc/host** file.

On the server, the puppetmaster configuration in **/etc/default/puppetmaster** file lets you set port entries and the log service. Default entries are commented out. Remove the comment character, #, to enable.

When you first set up a client server puppet connection, the client and server have to sign the client's SSL certificate. First run puppet on the client. On the server run the **puppet cert --list** command to see the clients certificate request. Then use **puppet cert --sign** to sign the certificate.

The Secure Shell: OpenSSH

Although a firewall can protect a network from attempts to break into it from the outside, the problem of securing legitimate communications to the network from outside sources still exists. A particular problem is one of users who want to connect to your network remotely. Such connections could be monitored, and information such as passwords and user IDs used when the user logs in to your network could be copied and used later to break in. One solution is to use SSH for remote logins and other kinds of remote connections such as FTP transfers. SSH encrypts any communications between the remote user and a system on your network.

The SSH protocol has become an official Internet Engineering Task Force (IETF) standard. A free and open source version is developed and maintained by the OpenSSH project, currently supported by the OpenBSD project. OpenSSH is the version supplied with most Linux distributions, including Ubuntu. You can find out more about OpenSSH at **www.openssh.org**, where you can download the most recent version, though your distribution will provide current RPM versions.

SSH secures connections by both authenticating users and encrypting their transmissions. The authentication process is handled with public key encryption. Once authenticated, transmissions are encrypted by a cipher agreed upon by the SSH server and client for use in a particular session. SSH supports multiple ciphers. Authentication is applied to both hosts and users. SSH first authenticates a particular host, verifying that it is a valid SSH host that can be securely communicated with. Then the user is authenticated, verifying that the user is who they say they are.

Encryption

The public key encryption used in SSH authentication makes use of two keys: a public key and a private key. The public key is used to encrypt data, while the private key decrypts it. Each host or user has its own public and private keys. The public key is distributed to other hosts, who can then use it to encrypt authenticated data that only the host's private key can decrypt. For example, when a host sends data to a user on another system, the host encrypts the authentication data with a public key, which it previously received from that user. The data can be decrypted only by the user's corresponding private key. The public key can safely be sent in the open from one host to another, allowing it to be installed safely on different hosts. You can think of the process as taking place between a client and a server. When the client sends data to the server, it first encrypts the data using the server's public key. The server can then decrypt the data using its own private key.

It is recommended that SSH transmissions be authenticated with public-private keys controlled by passphrases. Unlike PGP, SSH uses public-key encryption for the authentication process only. Once authenticated, participants agree on a common cipher to use to encrypt transmissions. Authentication will verify the identity of the participants. Each user who intends to use SSH to access a remote account first needs to create the public and private keys along with a passphrase to use for the authentication process. A user then sends their public key to the remote account they want to access and installs the public key on that account. When the user attempts to access the remote account, that account can then use the user's public key to authenticate that the user is who they claim to be. The process assumes that the remote account has set up its own SSH private and public key. For the user to access the remote account, they will have to know the remote account's SSH passphrase. SSH is often used in situations where a user has two or more accounts located on different systems and wants to be able to securely access them from each other. In that case, the user already has access to each account and can install SSH on each, giving each its own private and public keys along with their passphrases.

Authentication

The mechanics of authentication in SSH version 1 and version 2 differ slightly. However, the procedure on the part of users is the same. Essentially, a user creates both public and private keys. For this you use the **`ssh-keygen`** command. The user's public key then has to be distributed to those users that the original user wants access to. Often this is an account a user has on another host. A passphrase further protects access. The original user will need to know the other user's passphrase to access it.

SSH version 1 uses RSA authentication. When a remote user tries to log in to an account, that account is checked to see if it has the remote user's public key. That public key is then used to encrypt a challenge (usually a random number) that can be decrypted only by the remote user's private key. When the remote user receives the encrypted challenge, that user decrypts the challenge with its private key. SSH version 2 can use either RSA or DSA authentication. The remote user will first encrypt a session identifier using its private key, signing it. The encrypted session identifier is then decrypted by the account using the remote user's public key. The session identifier has been previously set up by SSH for that session.

SSH authentication is first carried out with the host, and then with users. Each host has its own host keys, public and private keys used for authentication. Once the host is authenticated, the user is queried. Each user has their own public and private keys. Users on an SSH server who want to receive connections from remote users will have to keep a list of those remote user's public keys. Similarly, an SSH host will maintain a list of public keys for other SSH hosts.

SSH Packages, Tools, and Server

SSH is implemented on Linux systems with OpenSSH. The full set of OpenSSH packages includes the OpenSSH meta-package (ssh), the OpenSSH server (openssh-server), and the OpenSSH client (openssh-clients). These packages also require OpenSSL (openssl), which installs the cryptographic libraries that SSH uses.

The SSH tools are listed in Table 5-7. They include several client programs such as **scp**, **ssh**, as well as the **ssh** server. The **ssh** server (**sshd**) provides secure connections to anyone from the outside using the **ssh** client to connect. Several configuration utilities are also included, such as **ssh-add**, which adds valid hosts to the authentication agent, and **ssh-keygen**, which generates the keys used for encryption.

For version 2, names of the actual tools have a *2* suffix. Version 1 tools have a *1* as their suffix. During installation, however, links are set for each tool to use only the name with the suffix.

For example, if you have installed version 2, there is a link called **scp** to the **scp2** application. You can then use the link to invoke the tool. Using **scp** starts **scp2**. Table 5-14 specifies only the link names, as these are the same for each version. Some applications, such as **sftp**, are available only with version 2.

You can start, stop, and restart the server manually with the service or systemctl commands.

```
sudo service sshd restart
```

Application	Description
ssh	SSH client
sshd	SSH server (daemon)
sftp	SSH FTP client, Secure File Transfer Program. Version 2 only. Use `?` to list sftp commands(SFTP protocol)
sftp-server	SSH FTP server. Version 2 only (SFTP protocol)
scp	SSH copy command client
ssh-keygen	Utility for generating keys. `-h` for help
ssh-keyscan	Tool to automatically gather public host keys to generate ssh_known_hosts files
ssh-add	Adds RSD and DSA identities to the authentication agent
ssh-agent	SSH authentication agent that holds private keys for public key authentication (RSA, DSA)
ssh-askpass	X Window System utility for querying passwords, invoked by **`ssh-add`** (openssh-askpass)
ssh-askpass-gnome	GNOME utility for querying passwords, invoked by **`ssh-add`**
ssh-signer	Signs host-based authentication packets. Version 2 only. Must be suid root (performed by installation)
slogin	Remote login (version 1)

Table 5-14: SSH Tools

You have to configure your firewall to allow access to the ssh service. The services is set up to operate using the TCP protocol on port 22, tcp/22. If you are managing your IPTables firewall directly, you could manage access directly by adding the following IPtables rule. This accepts input on port 22 for TCP/IP protocol packages.

```
iptables -A INPUT -p tcp --dport 22 -j ACCEPT
```

SSH Setup

Using SSH involves creating your own public and private keys and then distributing your public key to other users you want to access. These can be different users or simply user accounts of your own that you have on remote systems. Often people remotely log in from a local client to an account on a remote server, perhaps from a home computer to a company computer. Your home computer would be your client account, and the account on your company computer would be your server account. On your client account, you need to generate your public and private keys and then place a copy of your public key in the server account. You can do this by simply e-mailing the key file or copying the file from a floppy disk. Once the account on your server has a copy of your client user's public key, you can access the server account from your client account. You will be also prompted for the server account's passphrase. You will have to know this to access that account. Figure 5-2 illustrates the SSH setup that allows a user **george** to access the account **cecelia**.

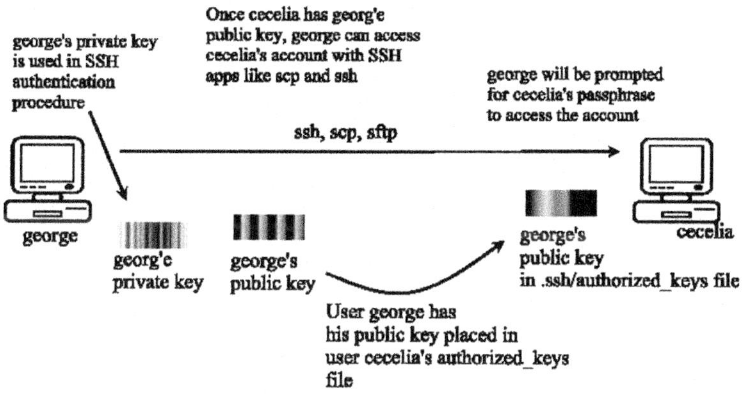

Figure 5-2: SSH setup and access

To allow you to use SSH to access other accounts:

You must create public and private keys on your account along with a passphrase. You will need to use this passphrase to access your account from another account.

You must distribute your public key to other accounts you want to access, placing them in the **.ssh/authorized_keys** file.

Other accounts also have to set up public and private keys along with a passphrase.

You must know the other account's passphrase to access it.

Creating SSH Keys with ssh-keygen

You create your public and private keys using the **`ssh-keygen`** command. You need to specify the kind of encryption you want to use. You can use either DSA or RSA encryption. Specify the type using the **`-t`** option and the encryption name in lowercase (**`dsa`** or **`rsa`**). In the following example, the user creates a key with the RSA encryption:

```
ssh-keygen -t rsa
```

The **`ssh-keygen`** command prompts you for a passphrase, which it will use as a kind of password to protect your private key. The passphrase should be several words long. You are also prompted to enter a filename for the keys. If you do not enter one, SSH will use its defaults. The public key will be given the extension **.pub**. The **ssh-keygen** command generates the public key and places it in your **.ssh/id_dsa.pub** or **.ssh/id_rsa.pub** file, depending on the type of key you specified; it places the private key in the corresponding **.ssh/id_dsa** or **.ssh/id_rsa** file.

File	Description
$HOME/.ssh/known_hosts	Records host keys for all hosts the user has logged in to (that are not in **/etc/ssh/ssh_known_hosts**).
$HOME/.ssh/random_seed	Seeds the random number generator.
$HOME/.ssh/id_rsa	Contains the RSA authentication identity of the user.
$HOME/.ssh/id_dsa	Contains the DSA authentication identity of the user.
$HOME/.ssh/id_rsa.pub	Contains the RSA public key for authentication. The contents of this file should be added to **$HOME/.ssh/authorized_keys** on all machines where you want to log in using RSA authentication.
$HOME/.ssh/id_dsa.pub	Contains the DSA public key for authentication.
$HOME/.ssh/config	the per-user configuration file.
$HOME/.ssh/authorized_keys	Lists the RSA or DSA keys that can be used for logging in as this user.
/etc/ssh/ssh_known_hosts	Contains the system-wide list of known host keys.
/etc/ssh/ssh_config	Contains the system-wide configuration file. This file provides defaults for those values not specified in the user's configuration file.
/etc/ssh/sshd_config	Contains the SSH server configuration file.
/etc/ssh/sshrc	Contains the system default. Commands in this file are executed by ssh when the user logs in just before the user's shell (or command) is started.
$HOME/.ssh/rc	Contains commands executed by ssh when the user logs in just before the user's shell (or command) is started.

Table 5-15: SSH Configuration Files

If you need to change your passphrase, you can do so with the **ssh-keygen** command and the **-p** option. Each user will have their own SSH configuration directory, called **.ssh**, located in their own home directory. The public and private keys, as well as SSH configuration files, are placed here. If you build from the source code, the **make install** operation will automatically run **ssh-keygen**. Table 5-15 lists the SSH configuration files.

Authorized Keys

A public key is used to authenticate a user and its host. You use the public key on a remote system to allow that user access. The public key is placed in the remote user account's **.ssh/authorized_keys** file. Recall that the public key is held in the **.ssh/id_dsa.pub** file. If a user wants to log in remotely from a local account to an account on a remote system, they would first place their public key in the **.ssh/authorized_keys** file in the account on the remote system they want to access. If the user **larisa** on **turtle.mytrek.com** wants to access the **aleina** account on

rabbit.mytrek.com, **larisa**'s public key from **/home/larisa/.ssh/id_dsa.pub** first must be placed in **aleina**'s **authorized_keys** file, **/home/aleina/.ssh/authorized_keys**. User **larisa** can send the key or have it copied over. A simple cat operation can append a key to the authorized key file. In the next example, the user adds the public key for **aleina** in the **larisa.pub** file to the authorized key file. The **larisa.pub** file is a copy of the **/home/larisa/.ssh/id_dsa.pub** file that the user received earlier.

```
cat larisa.pub >>  .ssh/authorized_keys
```

Note: You can also use seahorse to create and manage SSH keys.

Note: The **.ssh/identity** filename is used in SSH version 1; it may be installed by default on older distribution versions. SSH version 2 uses a different filename, **.ssh/id_dsa** or **.ssh/id_rsa**, depending on whether RSA or DSA authentication is used.

Loading Keys

If you regularly make connections to a variety of remote hosts, you can use the **ssh-agent** command to place private keys in memory where they can be accessed quickly to decrypt received transmissions. The **ssh-agent** command is intended for use at the beginning of a login session. For GNOME, you can use the openssh-askpass-gnome utility, invoked by **ssh-add**, which allows you to enter a password when you log in to GNOME. GNOME will automatically supply that password whenever you use an SSH client.

Although the **ssh-agent** command enables you to use private keys in memory, you also must specifically load your private keys into memory using the **ssh-add** command. **ssh-add** with no arguments loads your private key from your **.ssh/id_dsa** or **.ssh/id_rsa.pub** file. You are prompted for your passphrase for this private key. To remove the key from memory, use **ssh-add** with the **-d** option. If you have several private keys, you can load them all into memory. **ssh-add** with the **-l** option lists those currently loaded.

SSH Clients

SSH was originally designed to replace remote access operations, such as rlogin, rcp, and Telnet, which perform no encryption and introduce security risks. You can also use SSH to encode X server sessions as well as FTP transmissions (sftp). The ssh-clients package contains corresponding SSH clients to replace these applications. With **slogin** or **ssh**, you can log in from a remote host to execute commands and run applications, much as you can with rlogin and rsh. With **scp**, you can copy files between the remote host and a network host, just as with rcp. With **sftp**, you can transfer FTP files secured by encryption.

ssh

With **ssh** you can remotely log in from a local client to a remote system on your network operating as the SSH server. The term local client here refers to one outside the network, such as your home computer, and the term remote refers to a host system on the network to which you are connecting. In effect, you connect from your local system to the remote network host. It is designed to replace rlogin, which performs remote logins, and rsh, which executes remote commands. With ssh, you can log in from a local site to a remote host on your network and then send commands to be executed on that host. The **ssh** command is also capable of supporting X Window System connections. This feature is automatically enabled if you make an ssh connection from an X Window System environment, such as GNOME or KDE. A connection is set up for you between the local X server and the remote X server. The remote host sets up a dummy X server and sends any X Window System data through it to your local system to be processed by your own local X server.

The ssh login operation function is much like the **`rlogin`** command. You enter the **`ssh`** command with the address of the remote host, followed by a `-l` option and the login name (username) of the remote account you are logging in to. The following example logs in to the **aleina** user account on the **rabbit.mytrek.com** host:

```
ssh rabbit.mytrek.com -l aleina
```

You can also use the username in an address format with ssh, as in

```
ssh aleian@rabbit.mytrek.com
```

The following listing shows how the user **george** accesses the **cecelia** account on **turtle.mytrek.com**:

```
[george@turtle george]$ ssh turtle.mytrek.com -l cecelia
cecelia@turtle.mytrek.com's password:
[cecelia@turtle cecelia]$
```

A variety of options are available to enable you to configure your connection. Most have corresponding configuration options that can be set in the configuration file. For example, with the `-c` option, you can designate which encryption method you want to use, for instance, **`idea`**, **`des`**, **`blowfish`**, or **`arcfour`**. With the `-i` option, you can select a particular private key to use. The `-C` option enables you to have transmissions compressed at specified levels (see the **`ssh`** Man page for a complete list of options).

scp

You use **scp** to copy files from one host to another on a network. Designed to replace rcp, **scp** uses **ssh** to transfer data and employs the same authentication and encryption methods. If authentication requires it, **scp** requests a password or passphrase. The **scp** program operates much like rcp. Directories and files on remote hosts are specified using the username and the host address before the filename or directory. The username specifies the remote user account that **scp** is accessing, and the host is the remote system where that account is located. You separate the user from the host address with an @, and you separate the host address from the file or directory name with a colon. The following example copies the file **party** from a user's current directory to the user **aleina**'s **birthday** directory, located on the **rabbit.mytrek.com** host:

```
scp party aleina@rabbit.mytrek.com:/birthday/party
```

Of particular interest is the `-r` option (recursive) option, which enables you to copy whole directories. See the **`scp`** Man page for a complete list of options. In the next example, the user copies the entire **reports** directory to the user **justin**'s **projects** directory:

```
scp -r reports justin@rabbit.mytrek.com:/projects
```

In the next example, the user **george** copies the **mydoc1** file from the user **cecelia**'s home directory:

```
[george@turtle george]$ scp cecelia@turtle.mytrek.com:mydoc1  .
cecelia@turtle.mytrek.com's password:
mydoc1     0% |                            |    0 --:--
ETA
mydoc1   100% |****************************|  17 00:00
[george@turtle george]$
```

From a Windows system, you can also use **scp** clients such as **winscp**, which will interact with Linux scp-enabled systems.

sftp and sftp-server

With **sftp**, you can transfer FTP files secured by encryption. The **sftp** program uses the same commands as **ftp**. This client, which works only with ssh version 2, operates much like **ftp**, with many of the same commands. Use **sftp** instead of **ftp** to invoke the sftp client.

```
sftp download.ubuntu.com
```

To use the sftp client to connect to an FTP server, that server needs to be operating the sftp-server application. The ssh server invokes sftp-server to provide encrypted FTP transmissions to those using the sftp client. The sftp server and client use the SSH File Transfer Protocol (SFTP) to perform FTP operations securely.

Port Forwarding (Tunneling)

If, for some reason, you can connect to a secure host only by going through an insecure host, ssh provides a feature called port forwarding. With port forwarding, you can secure the insecure segment of your connection. This involves simply specifying the port at which the insecure host is to connect to the secure one. This sets up a direct connection between the local host and the remote host, through the intermediary insecure host. Encrypted data is passed through directly. This process is referred to as tunneling, creating a secure tunnel of encrypted data through connected servers.

You can set up port forwarding to a port on the remote system or to one on your local system. To forward a port on the remote system to a port on your local system, use **ssh** with the **-R** option, followed by an argument holding the local port, the remote host address, and the remote port to be forwarded, each separated from the next by a colon. This works by allocating a socket to listen to the port on the remote side. Whenever a connection is made to this port, the connection is forwarded over the secure channel, and a connection is made to a remote port from the local machine. In the following example, port 22 on the local system is connected to port 23 on the **rabbit.mytrek.com** remote system:

```
ssh -R 22:rabbit.mytrek.com:23
```

To forward a port on your local system to a port on a remote system, use the **ssh -L** option, followed by an argument holding the local port, the remote host address, and the remote port to be forwarded, each two arguments separated by a colon. A socket is allocated to listen to the port on the local side. Whenever a connection is made to this port, the connection is forwarded over the secure channel and a connection is made to the remote port on the remote machine. In the following example, port 22 on the local system is connected to port 23 on the **rabbit.mytrek.com** remote system:

```
ssh -L 22:rabbit.mytrek.com:23
```

You can use the LocalForward and RemoteForward options in your **.ssh/ssh_config** file to set up port forwarding for particular hosts or to specify a default for all hosts you connect to.

SSH Configuration

The SSH configuration file for each user is in their **.ssh/ssh_config** file. The **/etc/ssh/ssh_config** file is used to set site-wide defaults. In the configuration file, you can set various options, as listed in the **ssh_config** Man document. The configuration file is designed to specify options for different remote hosts to which you might connect. It is organized into segments, where each segment begins with the keyword `HOST`, followed by the IP address of the host. The following lines hold the options you have set for that host. A segment ends at the next `HOST` entry. Of particular interest are the `User` and `Cipher` options. Use the `User` option to specify the names of users on the remote system who are allowed access. With the `Cipher` option, you can select which encryption method to use for a particular host. Encryption methods include triple-DES (3DES) , Arcfour (RSA's RC4), and Advanced Encryption Standard (AES). The following example allows access from **larisa** at **turtle.mytrek.com** and uses 3des encryption for transmissions:

```
Host turtle.mytrek.com
    User larisa
    Compression no
    Cipher 3des
```

Most standard options, including ciphers are already listed as commented entries. Remove the # to activate.

```
#   Ciphers aes128-ctr,aes192-ctr,aes256-ctr,arcfour256,arcfour128,aes128-
cbc,3des-cbc
```

To specify global options that apply to any host you connect to, create a `HOST` entry with the asterisk as its host, `HOST *`. This entry must be placed at the end of the configuration file because an option is changed only the first time it is set. Any subsequent entries for an option are ignored. Because a host matches on both its own entry and the global one, its specific entry should come before the global entry. The asterisk (`*`) and the question mark (`?`) are both wildcard matching operators that enable you to specify a group of hosts with the same suffix or prefix.

```
Host *
  PasswordAuthentication yes
  ConnectTimeout 0
  Cipher 3des
```

The protocol option lets you specify what version of SSH to use, 1, 2, or both. By default, both protocols are acceptable, for backward compatibility. You can restrict use to just the more advanced and secure SSH2 protocol by changing the Protocol option to just 2.

```
Protocol 2
```

You use the **/etc/ssh/sshd_config** file to configure an SSH server. Here you will find server options like the port to use, password requirement, and PAM usage.

ubuntu

6. Mail Servers

Mail servers provide Internet users with electronic mail services. They have their own TCP/IP protocols such as the Simple Mail Transfer Protocol (SMTP), the Post Office Protocol (POP), and the Internet Mail Access Protocol (IMAP). Messages are sent across the Internet through mail servers that service local domains. A *domain* can be seen as a subnet of the larger Internet, with its own server to handle mail messages sent from or received for users on that subnet. When a user mails a message, it is first sent from his or her host system to the mail server. The mail server then sends the message to another mail server on the Internet, the one servicing the subnet on which the recipient user is located. The receiving mail server then sends the message to the recipient's host system.

At each stage, a different type of operation takes place using different agents (programs). A mail user agent (MUA) is a mail client program, such as Evolution, Thunderbird, Kmail, or mail. With an MUA, a user composes a mail message and sends it. Then a mail transfer agent (MTA) transports the messages over the Internet. MTAs are mail servers that use SMTP to send messages across the Internet from one mail server to another, transporting them among subnets. On Ubuntu, the commonly used MTAs are Postfix and Exim. These are mail server daemons that constantly check for incoming messages from other mail servers and send outgoing messages to appropriate servers (see Table 6-1). Incoming messages received by a mail server are distributed to a user with mail delivery agents (MDAs). Ubuntu supports the procmail and dovecot MDAs, taking messages received by the mail server and delivering them to user accounts. Dovecot refers to its delivery function as an LDA (Local Delivery Agent) which is the same as MDA.

Ubuntu now bundles both dovecot and Postfix into a meta package to install both the MTA and LDA, as well as dovecot IMAP and POP servers, into the **dovecot-postfix** package. Install this package to set up a fully functional mail server.

For those systems not supported by a mail server directly, a mail retrieval agent (MRA), like fetchmail, will manually retrieve mail from a remote mail server and direct the mail to the system's mail clients (MUAs).

Mail Transport Agents

On Ubuntu you can install and configure the Exim, Postfix, or Sendmail mail servers. You can also set up your Linux system to run a POP server. POP servers hold users' mail until they log in to access their messages, instead of having mail sent to their hosts directly. The two recommended MTAs are Exim and Postfix, both in the main Ubuntu repository. Sendmail is also available from the Universe repository.

Exim is a fast and flexible MTA similar to Sendmail. Developed at the University of Cambridge, it has a very different implementation than Sendmail. You can find out more about Exim at **http://wiki.debian.org/PkgExim4** and at **http://www.exim.org**. Exim is a Debian Linux project. Ubuntu, as a version a Debian Linux, implements Exim reliably.

Courier (Universe repository) is a fast, small, and secure MTA that maintains some compatibility with Sendmail. The Courier software package also includes POP, IMAP, and webmail servers along with mailing list services. It supports extensive authentication methods including shadow passwords, PAM, and LDAP.

Qmail (Multiverse repository) is also a fast and secure MTA, but it has little compatibility with Sendmail. It has its own configuration and maintenance files. Like Postfix, it has a modular design, using a different program for each mail task. It also focuses on security, speed, and easy configuration.

Agent	Description
Postfix	Fast, easy-to-configure, and secure mail transfer agent compatible with Sendmail and designed to replace it (Ubuntu repository) **www.postfix.org**
Exim	MTA based on smail3 (Ubuntu repository) **www.exim.org**
Sendmail	Sendmail mail transfer agent, supported by the Sendmail consortium (Universe repository) **www.sendmail.org**
Courier	Courier MTA (Universe repository) **www.courier-mta.org**
Qmail	Fast, flexible, and secure MTA with its own implementation and competitive with Postfix (Multiverse repository) **www.qmail.org**

Table 6-1: Mail Transfer Agents

Postfix

Postfix is a fast, secure, and flexible MTA designed to replace Sendmail while maintaining as much compatibility as possible. Written by Wietse Venema and originally released as the IBM Secure Mailer, it is now available under the GNU license (**www.postfix.org**). Postfix was created with security in mind, treating all incoming mail as potential security risks. Postfix uses many of the same Sendmail directories and files and makes use of Sendmail wrappers, letting Sendmail clients interact seamlessly with Postfix servers. Postfix is also easier to configure than Sendmail, using its own configuration file.

Check the Ubuntu Server Guide | Email Services | Postfix for basic configuration.

`https://help.ubuntu.com/stable/serverguide/postfix.html`

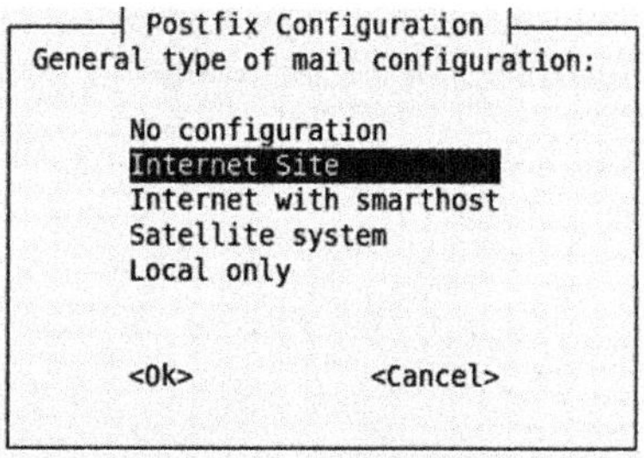

Figure 6-1: Postfix standard configuration selection

Postfix is available on the main Ubuntu repository. When you install Postfix, two configuration screens will appear to prompt you for the kind of installation you want. The first screen asks you select a standard configuration, with Internet site already selected as the default (see Figure 6-1). You can choose from Internet site, Internet with smarthost, Satellite system, Local, or No configuration. If you install using the desktop (Synaptic Package Manager or Ubuntu Software Center), the screen will look different, but the prompts will be the same.

Instead of one large program, Postfix is implemented as a collection of smaller programs, each designed to perform a specific mail-related task. A Postfix master daemon runs continuously and manages the use of the other Postfix daemons, running them only as needed. A **bounce** daemon handles undeliverable mail, a **trivial-rewrite** daemon redirects messages, and the **showq** daemon provides information on the print queues.

The options are as follows:

Internet site: The default configuration. Mail server interacts directly with the Internet. Mail sent directly with SMTP.

Internet site with smarthost: Mail server for a local network that, in turn, uses an ISP mail server to interact with the Internet. Mail is received and sent to and from the ISP mail server with mail server access tools like fetchmail. Mail can be received, but not sent, directly from the Internet.

Local only: System only mail server (no network access) for users on the mail server's system (localhost).

No configuration: No configuration to standard configuration files (requires detailed configuration on your part).

Satellite system: Outgoing forwarding mail server for sent mail only (no received mail).

The following configuration screen will prompt you for your system mail name, displaying your computer host name as the default.

Several other support packages are also available on the Ubuntu repository for Postfix. These include the Postfix documentation with examples (**postfix-doc**), LDAP (**postfix-ldap**), PGSQL (**postfix-pgsql**) and MySQL (**postfix-mysql**), as well as Postfix greylisting support (**postgrey**).

Postfix is managed by **systemd** using the **/run/system/generator.late/postfix.service** unit file. The file is generated by the systemd-sysv-generator from the **/etc/init.d/postfix** script. Postfix is started as a standalone daemon for the multi-user and graphical targets (runlevel targets 2, 3, 4, and 5) (Before). The **/etc/init.d/postfix** script is used to start, stop, and reload the server (ExecStart, ExecReload, and ExecStop).

postfix.service

```
[# Automatically generated by systemd-sysv-generator

[Unit]
Documentation=man:systemd-sysv-generator(8)
SourcePath=/etc/init.d/postfix
Description=LSB: Postfix Mail Transport Agent
Before=runlevel2.target runlevel3.target runlevel4.target runlevel5.target
shutdown.target mail-transport-agent.target
After=local-fs.target remote-fs.target systemd-journald-dev-log.socket nss-
lookup.target network-online.target time-sync.target postgresql.service
mysql.service clamav-daemon.service postgrey.service spamassassin.service
saslauthd.service dovecot.service
Wants=mail-transport-agent.target network-online.target
Conflicts=shutdown.target

[Service]
Type=forking
Restart=no
TimeoutSec=5min
IgnoreSIGPIPE=no
KillMode=process
GuessMainPID=no
RemainAfterExit=yes
ExecStart=/etc/init.d/postfix start
ExecStop=/etc/init.d/postfix stop
ExecReload=/etc/init.d/postfix reload
```

Postfix Commands

Several Postfix commands allow you to manage your server tasks. The **`sendmail`** command sends messages. You use **`mailq`** to display the status of your mail queues. The **`newaliases`** command takes mail aliases listed in the aliases files and stores them in a database file that can be used by Postfix.

The **`postmap`** command is used to maintain various database files used by Postfix, such as the alias file for mail aliases and the access file that restricts messages received by the server. You can also implement these database files as SQL databases like MySQL, allowing for easier management. The **mysql_table** Man page provides detailed information on how to configure SQL database support (check **pgsql_table** for Postgresql database support). You could also use LDAP instead of SQL (**ldap_table**).

In addition, Postfix provides lower-level tools, all beginning with the term **`post`**, such as the **`postalias`** command, which maintains the alias database, and **`postcat`**, which displays print queue files.

Quick configuration with dpkg-reconfigure

Instead of manually editing the **main.cf** file directly, you can perform an automatic configuration using the **dpkg-reconfigure** command. With the postfix option, **dpkg-reconfigure** will run a series of screens prompting you to enter basic Postfix configuration options. As when you first installed Postfix, you are prompted to enter the configuration type and the system mail name. Additional screens let you enter more detailed options, like the administrator account and the domains supported.

Before you use the **dpkg-reconfigure** command, be sure to back up your **main.cf** file, with a command like the following. The **dpkg-reconfigure** operation will replace the **main.cf** file entirely.

```
sudo cp /etc/postfix/main.cf  mainback.cf
```

You can then start up the **dpkg-reconfigure** operation in terminal window or from the command line with the following command.

```
sudo dpkg-reconfigure postfix
```

The **dpkg-reconfigure** operation uses a screen-based keyboard interface. Use the TAB key to move to the button labels at the bottom of the screen. Use the ENTER key to select a button. Some screens will display menus, from which you can select an entry using the arrow keys and then, using the TAB key move to the OK button to choose it. You can use the ESC key to move back to the previous screen. The screens are as follows.

Welcome screen with configuration descriptions and configuration type (see Figure 6-2). Choose a configuration type (usually you would select Internet).

Enter the system mail name (the hostname of your current system will already be entered), see Figure 6-3.

Enter the user that will be the Postfix administrator.

Enter the domains that this mail server supports (the final destination (your current host and domain are entered for you. You should change this to the network domain that this mail server is meant to serve), see Figure 6-4.

You are then asked if you want to force synchronous updates. "No" will be selected by default. Normally you do not need synchronous updates. The ext4 file system used on all Ubuntu systems supports journaling, which easily recovers from any crashes.

You are then asked to specify the networks for which the server will relay mail. IP address entries will already be displayed for your local host (IPv4 and IPv6 versions). To use the postfix default, leave this entry blank.

You can then specify a limit to your mailbox files, 0 is no limit (the default). A size limit can prevent large email attachments.

You then have the option to change the character used for the local address. The default is the plus sign (+) and is already entered. Normally you would use this sign.

You are then given the option to choose which IP protocol to use. The default is the one already in use on your system and will be selected already. You can choose to use IPV4, IPV6, or both (all).

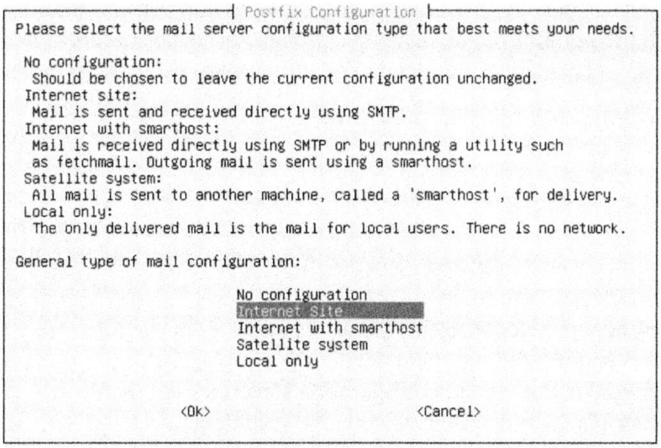

Figure 6-2: Postfix dpkg-reconfigure, first screen (press TAB and ENTER)

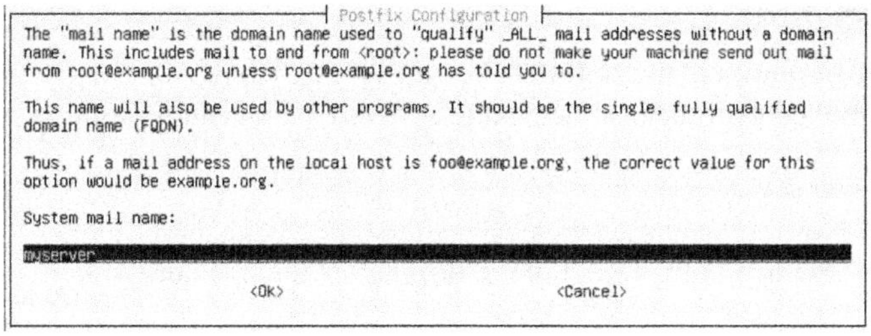

Figure 6-3: Postfix dpkg-reconfigure, administrator user

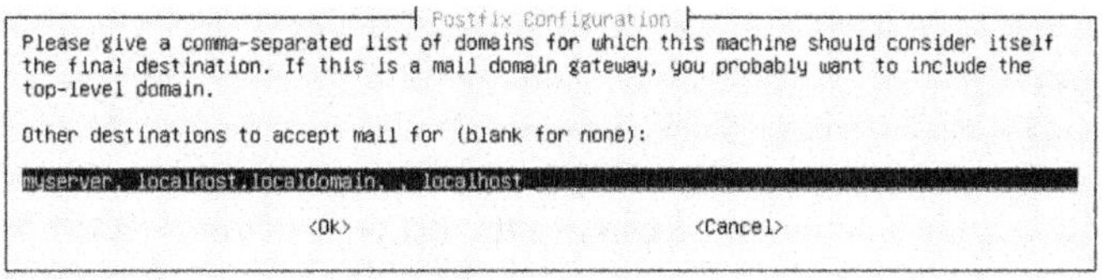

Figure 6-4: Postfix dpkg-reconfigure, domains

Postfix Configuration: /etc/postfix/main.cf

Postfix configuration is handled by setting parameters in its configuration file, **main.cf**. In addition, a **master.cf** file holds parameters for running Postfix services, and **dynamicmaps.cf** file for additional runtime capabilities.

A default **/etc/postfix/main.cf** file is installed with Postfix, with most of the essential configuration values already set. Parameter names tend to be user-friendly. For example, directory locations are specified by parameters ending in the term `directory`, such as `queue_directory` for the location of Postfix queues and `daemon_directory` for the location of the Postfix daemons. Defaults are already implemented for most parameters. For example, defaults are set for particular resource controls, such as message size, time limits, and the number of allowed messages per queue. You can edit the **main.cf** file to change the parameter values to meet your own needs. After making any changes, you need only to reload the configuration using the **`postfix reload`** command:

```
postfix reload
```

The Ubuntu main.cf file

Ubuntu installs a customized version of **main.cf**, using only a few options, several of which are Debian specific.

The **myorigin** parameter specifies the origin address for e-mail sent by the server. On Debian/Ubuntu this is commented out. On Ubuntu, the **myorigin** value is set to the **myhostname** value, which you entered in the second configuration screen during the Postfix installation. This is the host name for your mail server. Alternatively, the commented entry is set to the file that holds the host name, the same value as **myhostname**. If enabled, the entry line would read the origin address from a designated file, like **/etc/mailname**.

```
#myorigin=/etc/mailname
```

One of the first lines in the **main.cf** file will set the banner. On the Ubuntu version, the term Ubuntu is displayed with the host name and software name (**mail_name** is set to Postfix).

```
smtpd_banner = $myhostname ESMTP $mail_name (Ubuntu)
```

Several of the Ubuntu entries are designed to make your server more efficient. For efficiency purposes, the **biff** option is set to no, turning off the biff notification operation for the mail server.

```
biff = no
```

The **append_dot_mydomain** option adds the domain name to the email address. This operation is now handled by mail clients (MUA) like Thunderbird and Evolution. Ubuntu turns it off.

```
# appending .domain is the MUA's job.
append_dot_mydomain = no
```

Ubuntu will include a commented entry to the **delay_warning_time** option. This option will notify the sender of undelivered mail after a specified time period. The time period default is four hours.

```
# Uncomment the next line to generate "delayed mail" warnings
#delay_warning_time = 4h
```

The **readme_directory** option specifies the location of the Postfix documentation. On Ubuntu, Postfix documentation is held in the **postfix-doc** package which is installed separately. If the package is not installed, the option will be set to no. If installed, the location is set to **/etc/share/doc/postfix**.

```
readme_directory = /usr/share/doc/postfix
```

The html_directory entry holds the location of documentation in the Web page format.

```
html_directory = /usr/share/doc/postfix/html
```

Several TLS options are specified to provide Secure Socket Layer (SSL) security. See the following section on SMTP Authentication.

Network options are then set, including **myhostname**, **mydestination**, and **mynetworks**. These were set up during configuration. **myhostname** is the server URL, **mydestination** is a list of domains supported by the server, and **mynetworks** is the list of supported networks. The **alias_maps** directive specifies the file that holds aliases associated with users, like that for postmaster. The **alias database** specifies the file that holds aliases for destination addresses. Usually these are the same file, **/etc/aliases**. The **relay_host** directive is used if you are using another mail server to send and receive mail. This is empty if your mails server sends and receives mail directly.

```
myhostname = my-server
alias_maps = hash:/etc/aliases
alias_database = hash:/etc/aliases
mydestination = my-server, localhost.localdomain, localhost
relayhost =
mynetworks = 127.0.0.0/8 [::ffff:127.0.0.0]/104 [::1]/128
```

To easily control spam, relay restrictions are put in place with **smtpd_relay_restrictions** for relay operation. With Postfix 2.10, relay restrictions are specified with their own options, instead of using recipient restrictions. Relay operations are allowed from local networks (**permit_mynetworks**), from authenticated sources (Simple Authentication and Security Layer, SASL) (**permit_sasl_authenticated**), and rejects unauthorized destinations (**defer_unauth_destination**).

```
smptd_relay_restrictions = permit_mynetworks permit_sasl_authenticated
defer_unauth_destination
```

Then several mailbox configuration entries are listed. The **mailbox_size** directive is used to restrict the size of user's mailbox files, the files that hold their messages. It is set to 0 by default, meaning an unlimited size. The **recipient_delimiter** character is usually set to +.

```
mailbox_size_limit = 0
recipient_delimiter = +
```

Then certain basic network options are set. The **inet_interfaces** directive specifies the network device that supports the mail server. Usually this is set to all.

```
inet_interfaces = all
```

The Ubuntu server default **main.cf** file is shown here without the Mail User Agent options:

```
# See /usr/share/postfix/main.cf.dist for a commented, more complete version

# Debian specific:  Specifying a file name will cause the first
# line of that file to be used as the name.  The Debian default
# is /etc/mailname.
#myorigin = /etc/mailname

smtpd_banner = $myhostname ESMTP $mail_name (Ubuntu)
biff = no
```

```
# appending .domain is the MUA's job.
append_dot_mydomain = no

# Uncomment the next line to generate "delayed mail" warnings
#delay_warning_time = 4h

readme_directory = /usr/share/doc/postfix

# TLS parameters
smtpd_tls_cert_file = /etc/ssl/certs/ssl-cert-snakeoil.pem
smtpd_tls_key_file = /etc/ssl/private/ssl-cert-snakeoil.key
smtpd_use_tls = yes
smtpd_tls_session_cache_database = btree:${data_directory}/smtpd_scache
smtp_tls_session_cache_database = btree:${data_directory}/smtp_scache

# See /usr/share/doc/postfix/TLS_README.gz in the postfix-doc package for
# information on enabling SSL in the smtp client.

smptd_relay_restrictions = permit_mynetworks permit_sasl_authenticated
defer_unauth_destination
myhostname = myserver
alias_maps = hash:/etc/aliases
alias_database = hash:/etc/aliases
mydestination = my-server, localhost.localdomain, , localhost
relayhost =
mynetworks = 127.0.0.0/8 [::ffff:127.0.0.0]/104 [::1]/128
mailbox_size_limit = 0
mailbox_command = procmail -a "$EXTENSION"
recipient_delimiter = +
inet_interfaces = all
inet_protocols = all
html_directory = /usr/share/doc/postfix/html
```

SMTP Authentication

Several TLS options in the **main.cf** file provide Secure Socket Layer (SSL) security for the SMTP server (outgoing mail). Encryption uses Transport Layer Security (TLS), which is the current version of SSL. These options have the prefix **smtpd_tls**. The **smtpd_tls_cert_file** and **smtpd_tls_key_file** options specify the files for the TLS certificate and SSL key in the **/etc/ssl** directory. The **smtpd_use_tls** option is set to yes to enable the use of TLS encryption. The two **tls_session_cache_database** options designate a secure cache to hold passwords for the extent of a session.

```
# TLS parameters
smtpd_tls_cert_file = /etc/ssl/certs/ssl-mail.pem
smtpd_tls_key_file = /etc/ssl/private/ssl-mail.key
smtpd_use_tls = yes
smtpd_tls_session_cache_database = btree:${data_directory}/smtpd_scache
smtp_tls_session_cache_database = btree:${data_directory}/smtp_scache
```

For an actual mail server, you should obtain a certificate and key for that server, and set the **smtpd_tls_cert_file** and **smtpd_tls_key_file** options to the new certificate and key files.

https://help.ubuntu.com/stable/serverguide/certificates-and-security.html

Mail User Agent Options and Authentication

When you install a Mail User Agent like dovecot or procmail, several options will be added to the **main.cf** file, denoting the MUA installed and specifying security options to use. The **mailbox_command** directive specifies the mail delivery agent to use for delivering mail to user's mailboxes (be sure one is installed, **dovecot** or **procmail**). If you install procmail, it will be listed.

```
mailbox_command = procmail -a "$EXTENSION"
```

If you have installed dovecot, then it will be used instead.

```
mailbox_command = /usr/lib/dovecot/deliver -c /etc/dovecot/conf.d/01-mail-stack-delivery.conf -m "${EXTENSION}"
```

The **home_mailbox** specifies the subdirectory for mailboxes.

```
home_mailbox = Maildir/
```

For MUA Authentication it is recommended that you install **dovecot-postfix** package. This will implement SASL security for mail clients, as well as use dovecot for your mail delivery agent.

For MUA support, dovecot will add several **smtpd_sasl** options to provide MUA security. The **smtpd_sasl_auth_enable** option will enable SASL security. The **smtpd_sasl_type** option specifies the MUA used, such as dovecot. **smtpd_sasl_security_options** will list nonanonymous to deny anonymous use. **smtpd_sasl_local_domain** is set to the server host name.

The **smtpd_recipient_restrictions** option sets several conditions for accepting mail, such as **reject_unknown_sender_domain**, **permit_mynetworks**, and **reject_unauth_destination**. The **smtpd_sender_restrictions** place restrictions on outgoing mail, like **reject_unknown_sender_domain**.

In additions, the MUA also has its own **smtpd_tls** options such as smtpd_tls_received_header, smtpd_tls_mandatory_ciphers, and smtpd_tls_auth_only.

```
smtpd_sasl_auth_enable = yes
smtpd_sasl_type = dovecot
smtpd_sasl_path = private/dovecot-auth
smtpd_sasl_authenticated_header = yes
smtpd_sasl_security_options = noanonymous
smtpd_sasl_local_domain = $myhostname
broken_sasl_auth_clients = yes
smtpd_recipient_restrictions = reject_unknown_sender_domain,
reject_unknown_recipient_domain, reject_unauth_pipelining, permit_mynetworks,
permit_sasl_authenticated, reject_unauth_destination
smtpd_sender_restrictions = reject_unknown_sender_domain
smtp_use_tls = yes
smtpd_tls_received_header = yes
smtpd_tls_mandatory_protocols = SSLv3, TLSv1
smtpd_tls_mandatory_ciphers = medium
smtpd_tls_auth_only = yes
tls_random_source = dev:/dev/urandom
```

Postfix directives for main.cf

Postfix provides an extensive set of configuration directives letting you set up more complex configurations. The **/usr/share/postfix** directory has sample **main.cf** files listing available directives, many with detailed comments (install **postfix-doc**). You can find the complete version of **main.cf** with detailed comments at:

```
/usr/share/postfix/main.cf.dist
```

Network Parameters

You will most likely need to set several network parameters. To ease this process, Postfix defines parameters that hold key network information, such as **myhostname**, which holds the hostname of your system, and **mydomain**, which holds the domain name of your network. For example, **myhostname** would be set to the host **turtle.mytrek.com**, whereas **mydomain** would be just **mytrek.com**. Parameters like **myhostname** and **mydomain** are themselves used as values assigned to other parameters. On Ubuntu, **myhostname** will be set to the system mail name you entered in the second configuration screen during the Postfix installation. In the next example, **myhostname** and **mydomain** are set to the host the mail server is running on and its network domain:

```
myhostname=turtle.mytrek.com
mydomain=mytrek.com
```

The **myorigin** parameter specifies the origin address for e-mail sent by the server. On Debian/Ubuntu this is commented out. It is set to the file that holds the host name, the same value as **myhostname**. You could assign the value of myhostname to it directly as shown here and described in the **main.cf.dist** sample version:

```
myorigin=$myhostname
```

On Ubuntu/Debian, the line would, instead, read the origin address from a designated file, like **/etc/mailname**.

```
#myorigin=/etc/mailname
```

If you are using a single system directly attached to the Internet, you may want to keep this configuration, labeling mail as being sent by your host. However, if your system is operating as a gateway for a network, your mail server is sending out mail from different hosts on that network. You may wish to change the origin address to the domain name, so that mail is perceived as sent from the domain.

```
myorigin=$mydomain
```

The **inet_protocols** option specifies the IP protocol to use. This can be IPV4, IPV6, or all for both.

```
inet_protocols = ipv4
```

Local Networks

The **mydestination** parameter holds the list of domains that your mail server will receive mail for. By default, these include **localhost** and your system's hostname.

```
mydestination = $myhostname localhost.$mydomain
```

If you want the mail server to receive mail for an entire local network, you need to also specify its domain name. That way, the server can receive mail addressed just to the domain, instead of your specific host.

```
mydestination = $myhostname localhost.$mydomain $mydomain
```

Also, if your host goes by other hostnames and there are DNS records identifying your host by those names, you need to specify those names as well. For example, your host could also be a web server to which mail could be directed. A host **turtle.mytrek.com** may also be identified as the website **mytrek.com**. Both names would have to be listed in the **mydestination** parameter.

```
mydestination = $myhostname localhost.$mydomain $mydomain www.$mydomain
```

If your system is a gateway for one or more local networks, you can specify them with the **mynetworks** parameter. This allows your mail server to relay mail addressed to those networks. Networks are specified using their IP addresses. The **relay_domains** parameter lets you specify domain addresses of networks for which you can relay messages. By default, this is set to **mydestination**:

```
mynetworks=192.168.0.0
relay_domains=$mydestination
```

Hosts within the local network connected to the Internet by a gateway need to know the identity of the relay host (the mail server). You set this with the **relayhost** parameter. Also, **myorigin** should be set to just **mydomain**. If there is a DNS server identifying the gateway as the mail server, you can just set **relayhost** to the value of **mydomain**. If not, then **relayhost** should be set to the specific hostname of the gateway/mail server. If your local network is not running a DNS server, be sure to set **disable_dns_lookups** to **yes**.

```
relay_host=$mydomain
```

Direct Connections

If your system is directly connected to the Internet and you use an ISP (Internet service provider) for receiving mail, you can configure Postfix as a null client to only send mail. Set the **relay_host** parameter to just your own domain name. Also, in the **master.cf** file, comment out the SMTP server and local delivery agent entries.

```
relayhost = $mydomain
```

Masquerading

If your mail server is operating on a gateway for a local network and you want to hide the hosts in that network, you can opt to masquerade the local hosts, letting it appear that all mail is coming from the domain in general, instead of a particular host. To set this option, you use the **masquerade_domains** parameter. In the following example, all mail sent by a local host such as **rabbit.mytrek.com** will be addressed as coming from **mytrek.com**. Thus a message sent by the user **chris@rabbit.mytrek.com** is sent out as coming from **chris@mytrek.com**:

```
masquerade_domains = $mydomain
```

Received mail is not masqueraded by default. This allows Postfix to still deliver received mail to particular hosts. If you want received mail to also be masqueraded, you have to add the

envelope_recipients parameter to the list of values assigned to the **masquerade_class** parameter. In that case, Postfix will no longer be able to deliver received mail.

Virtual Domains and Virtual Accounts

If your network has implemented virtual domains, you will need to set up a virtual domain table and specify that table with the **virtual_maps** option. Setting up a table is a simple matter of listing virtual names and their real addresses in a text file such as **/etc/postfix/virtual**. Then use the **postmap** command to create a Postfix table:

```
postmap /etc/postfix/virtual
```

In the **main.cf** file, specify the table with the **virtual_maps** parameter. Postfix will then use this table to look up virtual domains.

```
virtual_maps = hash:/etc/postfix/virtual
```

Note: See the Postfix FAQ at **http://postfix.org** for detailed information on how to set up Postfix for a gateway, a local workstation, or a host directly connected to the Internet (null server).

Instead of using mail accounts for actual users on a system, you can set up virtual accounts. Virtual accounts can be managed either in standard Postfix text files, in SQL databases, or as LDAP entries. SQL databases are preferred for managing a large number of virtual accounts. For SQL support, you first create tables in a MySQL database for domains (the virtual domains), users (user accounts), and forwarding (aliases). Corresponding virtual domain configuration files will list information like the database, tables, and host to use, such as a **mysql_virt.cf** for SQL database access and **mysql_users.cf** for accessing the user table. Check the documentation at **http://www.postfix.org** for detailed information.

Postfix Greylisting Policy Server

Postfix also supports greylisting with the Postfix Greylisting Policy Server. Greylisting blocks spammers based on their mailing methods rather than content, relying on the idea that spammers will not attempt retries if rejected (**greylisting.org**). Messages from new previously unknown sources are rejected, whereupon a valid MTA will retry, whereas a spammer will not. To support the Greylisting Policy Server, Postfix is configured to delegate Policy access to a server. In the **/etc/postfix** directory you can use the **postgrey_whitelist** files to exclude email addresses from greylisting.

The Greylisting Policy Server is run as a standalone server, using its own startup script. The postgrey Man page provides detailed information about the server's options.

Controlling User and Host Access

With an access file, you can control access by certain users, hosts, and domains. The access file works much like the one used for Sendmail. Entries are made in a text file beginning with the user, host, or domain name or address, followed by an action to take. A user, host, or domain can be accepted, rejected with no message, or rejected with a message. Once entries are made, they can be installed in a Postfix database file with the **postmap** command:

```
postmap /etc/postfix/access
```

You can then use the access file in various Postfix operations to control clients, recipients, and senders.

Access can also be controlled by use of the Mail Abuse Prevention System (MAPS), which provides the RBL+ service, a collection of mail address DNS-based databases (**mail-abuse.com**). These databases, like the Realtime Blackhole List (RBL), list mail addresses that are known be used by mail abusers. A domain or host is matched against a list maintained by the service, which can be accessed on a local server or directly from an online site. Various Postfix operations let you use MAPS databases to control access by clients, recipients, or senders.

Header and Body Checks

With the **header_checks** parameter, you can specify a Postfix table where you can list criteria for rejecting messages. Check the **/etc/postfix/header_checks** file for details. The criteria are patterns that can match message headers. You can have matching messages rejected, rejected with a reply, simply deleted, or logged with a warning. You have the option of taking several actions, including REJECT, DISCARD, WARN, HOLD, and IGNORE.

```
header_checks = regexp:/etc/postfix/header_checks
```

The database, in this case **/etc/postfix/header_checks**, will have lines, each with a regular expression and a corresponding action. The regular expression can either be a standard regular expression as denoted by **regexp** in the **header_checks** parameter, or conform to a Perl Compatible Regular Expression, **prece**.

The **body_checks** parameter lets you check the body of text messages, line by line, using regular expressions and actions like those used for **header_checks** in a **/etc/postfix/body_checks** file.

Controlling Client, Senders, and Recipients

Combined with Dovecot, Postfix defines sender and recipient controls in the **/etc/postfix/main.cf** file a shown here.

```
smtpd_recipient_restrictions = reject_unknown_sender_domain,
   reject_unknown_recipient_domain, reject_unauth_pipelining, permit_mynetworks,
   permit_sasl_authenticated, reject_unauth_destination
smtpd_sender_restrictions = reject_unknown_sender_domain
```

You could also configure Postfix with added or different client, sender, and recipient options. With the **smtpd_client_restrictions** parameter, you can restrict access to the mail server by certain clients. Restrictions you can apply include **reject_unknown_client_hostname**, which will reject any clients with unresolved addresses; **permit_mynetworks**, which allows access by any clients defined by **mynetworks**; and **check_client_access**, which will check an access database to see if a client should be accepted or rejected. The **reject_rbl_client** and **reject_rhsbl_client** parameters will reject clients from specified domains.

```
smtpd_client_restrictions = permit_mynetworks, \
          reject_unknown_client, check_client_access, reject_maps_rbl
```

The **reject_rbl_client** restriction rejects domain addresses according to a specified MAPS service. The site can be an online site or a local one set up to provide the service. The **reject_rhsbl_client** restriction rejects host addresses.

```
smtpd_client_restrictions = reject_rbl_client relays.mail-abuse.org
```

To implement restrictions from an access file, you can use the **hash** directive and the name of the file.

```
smtpd_client_restrictions = hash:/etc/postfix/access
```

The corresponding **smtpd_sender_restrictions** parameter works much the same way as its client counterpart but controls access from specific senders. It has many of the same restrictions but adds **reject_non_fqdn_sender**, which will reject any mail header without a fully qualified domain name, and **reject_sender_login_mismatch**, which will require sender verification. The **reject_rhsbl_sender** restriction rejects domain addresses according to a specified MAPS service.

The **smtpd_recipient_restrictions** parameter will restrict the recipients the server will accept mail for. Restrictions include **permit_auth_destination**, which allows authorized messages, and **reject_unauth_destination**, which rejects unauthorized messages. The **check_recipient_access** restriction checks local networks for a recipient address. The **reject_unknown_recipient_domain** restriction rejects recipient addresses with no DNS entry. The **reject_rhsbl_recipient** restriction rejects domain addresses according to a specified MAPS service.

You can further refine restrictions with parameters such as **smtpd_helo_restrictions**, which requires a HELO command from a client. Restriction parameters include **reject_invalid_hostname**, which checks for faulty syntax, **reject_unknown_hostname**, for hosts with no DNS entry, and **reject_non_fqdn_hostname** for hosts whose names are not fully qualified. The **strict_rfc821_envelopes** parameter will implement strict envelope protocol compliance.

Note: Sendmail operates as a server to both receive and send mail messages. Sendmail listens for any mail messages received from other hosts and addressed to users on the network hosts it serves and, at the same time, handles messages users are sending out to remote users, determining what hosts to send them to. You can learn more about Sendmail at **http://www.sendmail.org**, including online documentation and current software packages. You can also obtain a commercial version from **http://www.sendmail.com**.

POP and IMAP Server: Dovecot

The protocols Internet Mail Access Protocol (IMAP) and Post Office Protocol (POP) allow a remote server to hold mail for users who can fetch their mail from it when they are ready. Unlike procmail, which delivers mail messages directly to a user account on a Linux system, the IMAP and POP protocols hold mail until a user accesses an account on the IMAP or POP server. The servers then transfer any received messages to the user's local mailbox. Such servers are often used by ISPs to provide Internet mail services for users. Instead of being sent directly to a user's machine, the mail resides in the IMAP or POP server until it's retrieved. Ubuntu installs Dovecot as its recommended IMAP and POP servers. It will be installed as part of the **dovecot-postfix** package, and used by Postfix as the delivery agent. Other popular IMAP and POP servers available are Qpopper, the Qmail POP server, the Washington University POP and IMAP servers, and the Courier POP and IMAP servers.

You can access the POP server from different hosts; however, when you do, all the messages are transferred to that host. They are not kept on the POP server (though you can set an option to keep them). The POP server simply forwards your messages to the requesting host. When you access your messages from a certain computer, they will be transferred to that computer and erased from the POP server. If you access your POP server again from a different computer, those previous messages will be gone.

The Internet Mail Access Protocol (IMAP) allows a remote server to hold mail for users who can log in to access their mail. Unlike the POP servers, IMAP servers retain user mail messages. Users can even save their mail on the IMAP mail server. This has the advantage of keeping a user's mail in one centralized location accessible anywhere on the network. Users can log in to the mail server from any host on the network and read, send, and save their mail.

Unlike POP, IMAP allows users to set up multiple folders on their mail server in which they can organize their mail. IMAP also supports the use of shared folders to which several users can access mail on a given topic.

Dovecot

Dovecot is a combination IMAP and POP server, as well as an LDA (Local Delivery Agent). Using its own indexing methods, Dovecot is able to handle a great deal of e-mail traffic. It features support for SSL, along with numerous authentication methods. Password database support includes shadow passwords, LDAP, PAM, and MySQL. Dovecot is available in POP, IMAP, common packages, and the **dovecot-postfix** meta package, on the Ubuntu main repository. Dovecot can function as a local delivery agent for the major mail servers, including Postfix, Exim, and Sendmail. For detailed configuration information check **http://wiki.dovecot.org/**. For information about the Dovecot LDA check **http://wiki.dovecot.org/LDA**.

The dovecot configuration files are located in the **/etc/dovecot** directory. The main configuration file is **/etc/dovecot/dovecot.conf**, which includes configuration files located in the **conf.d** subdirectory such as **10-logging.conf**, **10-ssl.conf**, **10-auth.conf**, and **10-mail.conf**. Options specific to **imap** and **pop3** are placed in their own files. Corresponding copies are placed in the **/usr/share/dovecot/conf.d** directory. These are some basic settings to configure:

protocols This can be set to `imap` and `pop3`, as well as `imaps` and `pop3s` for SSL-encrypted connections. Protocols are listed in the **/usr/share/dovecot/protocols.d** directory.

listen This can be set to IPv4 or IPv4 addresses on which to listen for connections. The * character indicates all IPv4 network interfaces, and **[::]** on all IPv6 interfaces.

Authentication processes are listed in the **10-auth.conf** file in the **/etc/dovecot/conf.d** directory.

mechanism in **10-auth.conf** file is plain by default. The digest-MD5 and cran-MD5 methods are supported, but they are not needed if you are using SSL.

mail_location The default mail storage method and location (**/etc/dovecot/conf.d/10-mail.conf** file).

On Ubuntu, the standard dovecot configuration options are set up in the **.conf** file. These files are read in at the end of the **dovecot.conf** file as part of the dovecot configuration. It will set the **protocols**, **ssl**, and **mail_location** options, as well as set options for the IMAP, POP3, and LDA.

```
!include conf.d/*.conf
```

Dovecot supports either mailbox or maildir (IMAP) storage formats. The mailbox format uses single large mailbox files to hold several mail messages. This will be the user's **mbox** file at **/var/mail**. Updates can be time consuming. The maildir format uses a separate file for each message, making updates much more efficient. You can configure Dovecot to use a maildir format by setting the `mail_location` option to use a **maildir** setting, specifying the directory to use. The `%u` symbol can be used to represent the user name, `%h` for the home directory. Messages will be stored in a user's **maildir** directory instead of an **mbox** file. Be sure to create the **maildir** directory and give it read, write, and execute access The default **maildir** entry in the**10-mail.conf** file uses the **mail** subdirectory in the user's home directory, but for inboxes uses the **/var/mail** directory with a subdirectory for the user .

```
mail_location=mbox:~/mail:INBOX=/var/mail/%u
```

Alternatively you could place mail in separate files instead of an mbox file in the user's home directory.

```
mail_location=maildir:~/Maildir
```

If you have installed Postfix, then dovecot configures the user mail directory with the **home_mailbox** option in the **/etc/posfix/main.cf** file. This sets the mail box directory to the **Maildir** directory in the user's home directory.

```
home_mailbox = Maildir/
```

Other POP and IMAP Servers

Many distributions also include the Cyrus IMAP server, which you can install and use instead of Dovecot. In addition, several other IMAP and POP servers are available for use on Linux:

The **University of Washington** POP and IMAP servers (**ftp://ftp.cac.washington.edu/imap**) are part of the University of Washington's **ipopd** package (Universe repository). The POP server daemons are called **ipop2d** and **ipop3d**. Your Linux system runs as a POP2 and POP3 server for your network.

The **Cyrus IMAP** server (**http://cyrusimap.web.cmu.edu**) features security controls and authentication, using a private mailbox structure that is easily scalable (Universe repository). Designed to be run on dedicated mail servers, it is supported and maintained by Carnegie Mellon. The name of the Cyrus IMAP server daemon is **imapd**.

The **Courier-IMAP** server (**http://courier-mta.org**) is a small, fast IMAP server that provides extensive authentication support including LDAP and PAM (Universe repository).

Spam: SpamAssassin

With SpamAssassin, you can filter sent and received e-mail for spam. The filter examines both headers and content, drawing on rules designed to detect common spam messages. When they are detected, it then tags the message as spam, so that a mail client can then discard it. SpamAssassin will also report spam messages to spam detection databases. The version of SpamAssassin distributed for Linux is the open source version developed by the Apache project, located at **http://spamassassin.apache.org**. There you can find detailed documentation, FAQs, mailing lists, and even a listing of the tests that SpamAssassin performs.

Note: For dovecot IMAP server you can use **dovecot-antispam** plugin to implement spam detection.

SpamAssassin rule files are located at **/usr/share/spamassassin**. The files contain rules for running tests such as detecting the fake hello in the header. Configuration files for SpamAssassin are located at **/etc/spamassassin**. The **local.cf** file lists system-wide SpamAssassin options such as how to rewrite headers. The **init.pre** file holds spam system configurations. Server options such as enabling SpamAssassin, are listed in the **/etc/default spamassassin** file.

Users can set their own SpamAssassin option in their **.spamassassin/user_prefs** file. Common options include `required_scorei`, which sets a threshold for classifying a message as SPAM, numerous whitelist and blacklist options that accept and reject messages from certain users and domains, and tagging options that either rewrite or just add SPAM labels. Check the **Mail::SpamAssassin::Conf** man page for details.

Configuring Postfix for use with SpamAssassin can be complicated. A helpful tool for this task is **amavisd-new**, an interface between a mail transport agent like Exim or Postfix and content checkers like SpamAssassin and virus checkers. Check **http://www.ijs.si/software/amavisd/** for more details.

Mail Filtering: Amavisd-new

See the Ubuntu Server Guide for information on how to set up mail filtering. ,.

```
https://help.ubuntu.com/stable/serverguide/mail-filtering.html
```

On Ubuntu you can set up mail filtering using Amavisd-new, which invokes the ClamAV virus protection utility and SpamAssassin to filter mail. You can also use external filters such as opendkim for Sendmail and python-policy-spf for Postfix. Avmadvisd-new which calls filtering tools as needed. First, a message is filtered using an external filters such as opnedkim or python-policy-spf (Postfix will use both), then Amavisd-new has the message scanned by ClamAV for viruses, followed by an analysis by SpamAssassin to see if it is spam. Only then does Amavisd-new allow the message to be placed in the in box.

To implement mail filtering, be sure you have installed amavisd-new, spamassassin, and clamav, along with the external filters.

```
sudo apt-get install amavisd-new spamassassin clamav-daemon
sudo apt-get install opendkim postfix-policyd-spf-python
```

Ubuntu also recommends that you install supporting applications such as pyzor, razor, and the extraction utilities if you have not already done so (arg, capextract, cpio, lha, nomarch, pax, rar, unrar, unzip, zip).

Add the clamav user to the amavis group to allow amavis to use clamav to scan files.

```
sudo adduser calmav amavis
sudo adduser amavis clamav
```

Enable spamassassin by editing the spamassassin configuration file, **/etc/default/spamassassin**, and setting the ENABLED entry to 1.

```
ENABLED=1
```

Then start spamassassin.

```
sudo service spamassasin start
```

You can then configure Amavisd-new using files in the **/etc/amavis/conf.d** directory. To activate virus detection and spamassassin, edit the **/etc/amavis/conf.d/15_content_filter_mode** file and uncomment the lines for virus detection and spamassassin as indicated by the comments.

Ubuntu also recommends that you disable the bounce response for spam emails by settings the **final_spam_destiny** option in the **20_debian_defaults** file to D_DISCARD instead of D_BOUNCE. You can also adjust the level of spam detection

```
$final_spam_destiny  =  D_DISCARD;
```

Should your mail server DNS address be different from the DNS MX record, you have to specify the mail server's domain name in the **50_user** file. If your server supports different domains, you would list them in the local_domain_acl directive.

Amavisd-new also supports whitelists for domains and subdomains with valid Domain Keys (DKIM whitelists). These are configures in the **40-policy_banks** file.

Mailing Lists: Mailman

Mailman provides a Web interface for managing email mailing lists used for email discussions and newsletters. It supports Postfix, Sendmail, Exim, and Qmail mail servers. To use mailman you configure the Apache Web server to run a mailman virtual Web server. A default Apache configuration file for a mailman Web host is located at **/etc/mailman/apache.conf**. You can copy this file to the Apache **sites-available** directory as **mailman.conf.** ,

```
sudo cp /etc/mailman/apache.conf /etc/apache2/sites-available/mailman.conf
```

Simply enable the mailman virtual host with the **a2ensite** command and then restart Apache.

```
sudo a2ensite mailman.conf
sudo service apache2 restart
```

For Postfix, you have to specify the mailing list domain, in the **/etc/postfix/main.cf** file. You can use the **postconf –e** command to add the mailman configuration entries.

```
sudo postconf -e 'relay_domains = lists.example.com'
sudo postconf -e 'transport_maps = hash:/etc/postfix/transport'
sudo postconf -e 'mailman_destination_recipient_limit = 1'
```

In the **/etc/postfix/transport** file specify the domain for the mailman lists.

```
lists.example.com       mailman:
```

Then rebuild the transport map.

```
sudo postmap -v /etc/postfix/transport
```

You can then start the mailman server.

```
sudo service mailman start
```

Use the **newlist** command to create a default mailing list.

```
sudo newlist mailman
```

The mailman Web server is managed using CGI scripts in the **/usr/lib/chi-bin/mailman** directory. Administrators can access mailman at (*hostnane* is the name of your machine):

```
http://hostname/cgi-bin/mailman/admin
```

Users can access the mailing list at:

```
http://hostname/cgi-bin/mailman/listinfo
```

7. FTP

- FTP Servers
- Anonymous FTP: vsftpd
- The FTP User Account: anonymous
- The Very Secure FTP Server
- vsftpd Virtual Hosts
- rsync and FTP

The File Transfer Protocol (FTP) is designed to transfer large files across a network from one system to another. Like most Internet operations, FTP works on a client/server model. FTP client programs can enable users to transfer files to and from a remote system running an FTP server program. Any Linux system can operate as an FTP server. It has to run only the server software—an FTP daemon with the appropriate configuration. Transfers are made between user accounts on client and server systems. A user on the remote system has to log in to an account on a server and can then transfer files to and from that account's directories only. A special kind of user account named ftp, allows any user to log in to it with the username "anonymous." This account has its own set of directories and files that are considered public, available to anyone on the network who wants to download them. The numerous FTP sites on the Internet are FTP servers supporting FTP user accounts with anonymous login. Any Linux system can be configured to support anonymous FTP access, turning them into network FTP sites. Such sites can work on an intranet or on the Internet.

FTP Servers

FTP server software consists of an FTP daemon and configuration files. The *daemon* is a program that continuously checks for FTP requests from remote users. When a request is received, it manages a login, sets up the connection to the requested user account, and executes any FTP commands the remote user sends. For anonymous FTP access, the FTP daemon allows the remote user to log in to the FTP account using **anonymous** as the username. The user then has access to the directories and files set up for the FTP account. As a further security measure, however, the daemon changes the root directory for that session to be the FTP home directory. This hides the rest of the system from the remote user. Normally, any user on a system can move around to any directories open to him or her. A user logging in with anonymous FTP can see only the FTP home directory and its subdirectories. The remainder of the system is hidden from that user. This effect is achieved by the `chroot` operation (discussed later) that literally changes the system root directory for that user to that of the FTP directory. By default, the FTP server also requires a user to be using a valid shell. It checks for a list of valid shells in the **/etc/shells** file. Most daemons have options for turning off this feature.

FTP Servers	Site
Very Secure FTP Server (vsftpd)	**vsftpd.beasts.org**
ProFTPD	**proftpd.org**
PureFTP	**pureftpd.org**
Washington University web server (WU-FTPD)	**wu-ftpd.org**

Table 7-1: FTP Servers

Available Servers

Several FTP servers are available for use on Linux systems (see Table 7-1). Three of the more common servers include **vsftpd**, **pureftpd**, and **proftpd**. The Very Secure FTP Server provides a simple and very secure FTP server (**vsftpd** package). The Pure FTPD servers is a lightweight, fast, and secure FTP server, based upon Troll-FTPd (**pure-ftpd** package), **http://pureftpd.org**. ProFTPD is a popular FTP daemon based on an Apache web server design (**proftpd-basic** package). It features simplified configuration and support for virtual FTP hosts,

http://proftpd.org. Another FTP daemon, the Washington University FTP server, was the standard server used before vsftpd (**wu-ftpd** package).

You can only have one FTP server installed. Should you decide to install another, the currently installed one will be removed.

FTP Users

Normal users with accounts on an FTP server can gain full FTP access simply by logging into their accounts. Such users can access and transfer files directly from their own accounts or any directories they may have access to. You can also create users, known as guest users that have restricted access to the FTP publicly accessible directories. This involves setting standard user restrictions, with the FTP public directory as their home directory. Users can also log in as anonymous users, allowing anyone on the network or Internet to access files on an FTP server.

Anonymous FTP: vsftpd

An anonymous FTP site is essentially a special kind of user on your system with publicly accessible directories and files in its home directory. Anyone can log in to this account and access its files. Because anyone can log in to an anonymous FTP account, you must be careful to restrict a remote FTP user to only the files on that anonymous FTP directory. Normally, a user's files are interconnected to the entire file structure of your system. Normal users have write access that lets them create or delete files and directories. The anonymous FTP files and directories can be configured in such a way that the rest of the file system is hidden from them and remote users are given only read access.

An FTP site is made up of an FTP user account, an FTP home directory, and controlled access to selected configuration and support files. Most distributions have already set up an FTP user account when you installed your system. Within the FTP home directory, you then have a publicly accessible directory that holds the files you want to make available to remote users. This directory usually has the name **pub**, for public.

The FTP User Account: anonymous

To allow anonymous FTP access by other users to your system, you must have a user account named *FTP*. Ubuntu has already created this account for you. You can then place restrictions on the FTP account to keep any remote FTP users from accessing any other part of your system. The entry for this account in your **/etc/passwd** file is set up to prevent normal user access to it. The following is the entry you find in your **/etc/passwd** file on Ubuntu that sets up an FTP login as an anonymous user:

```
ftp:x:117:134:ftp daemon,,,:/srv/ftp:/bin/false
```

The **x** in the password field blocks the account, which prevents any other users from gaining access to it, thereby gaining control over its files or access to other parts of your system. The user ID, 117, is a unique ID. The comment field is "ftp daemon". The login directory is **/srv/ftp**. A location commonly used for servers is the **/srv** directory. When FTP users log in to your system, they are placed in this directory.

Should you want to change your FTP server to use a different directory, you would simply change the FTP user's home directory to be that new directory. You can use the **usermod** command with the **-d** option to make the change. First be sure to create the new directory. In the following example the FTP directory is changed to **/srv/myftp**.

```
sudo mkdir /srv/myftp
sudo usermod -d /srv/myftp  ftp
```

The FTP home directory is owned by the root user, not by the FTP user. The FTP user has no administrative control over the FTP home directory. Use the `ls -d` command to check on the ownership of the FTP directory.

```
ls -ld /srv/ftp
```

If you set up a different FTP directory, be sure to change a directory's ownership. You use the `chown` command, as shown in this example for a **myftp** directory:

```
sudo chown root.nogroup /srv/myftp
```

The permission for the FTP directory is set to 755; read, write and execute permission for the root user, but only read and execute permission for everyone else. If you create your own FTP directory, be sure to change the permissions on that directory to 755. Use the chmod command.

```
sudo chmod 755 /srv/myftp
```

An important part of protecting your system is preventing remote users from using any commands or programs not in the restricted directories. For example, you would not let a user use your `ls` command to list filenames, because `ls` is located in your **/bin** directory. At the same time, you want to let the FTP user list filenames using an `ls` command. Newer FTP daemons such as **vsftpd** and ProFTPD solve this problem by creating secure access to needed system commands and files, while restricting remote users to only the FTP site's directories.

Another, more traditional solution is to create copies of certain system directories and files needed by remote users, and to place them in the **ftp** directory where users can access them. A **bin** directory is placed in the **ftp** directory and remote users are restricted to it, instead of the system's **bin** directory. Whenever they use the `ls` command, remote users are using the one in **ftp/bin**, not the one you use in **/bin**. To set up such support, you would make a new **bin** directory in the **ftp** directory, and then make a copy of the `ls` command and place it in **ftp/bin**. Do this for any commands you want to make available to FTP users. Then create an **ftp/etc** directory to hold a copy of your **passwd** and **group** files. Again, the idea is to prevent any access to the original files in the **/etc** directory by FTP users. The **ftp/etc/passwd** file should be edited to remove any entries for regular users on your system. All other entries should have their passwords set to **x** to block access. For the **group** file, remove all user groups and set all passwords to **x**. Create an **ftp/lib** directory, and then make copies of the libraries you need to run the commands you placed in the **bin** directory.

Anonymous FTP Files

A directory named **pub**, located in the FTP home directory, usually holds the files you are making available for downloading by remote FTP users. When FTP users log in, they are placed in the FTP home directory (**/srv/ftp**), and they can then change to the **pub** directory to start accessing those files (**/srv/ftp/pub**). Within the **pub** directory, you can add as many files and directories as you want. You can even designate some directories as upload directories, enabling FTP users to transfer files to your system.

In each subdirectory set up under the **pub** directory to hold FTP files, you should create a **README** file and an **INDEX** file as a courtesy to FTP users. The **README** file contains a brief description of the kind of files held in this directory. The **INDEX** file contains a listing of the files and a description of what each one holds.

The Very Secure FTP Server

The Very Secure FTP Server (vsftpd) is small, fast, easy, and secure. It is designed to avoid the overhead of large FTP server applications, while maintaining a very high level of security. It can also handle a very large workload, managing high traffic levels on an FTP site. It is perhaps best for sites where many anonymous and guest users will be downloading the same files. This FTP server is the supported server for Ubuntu, available on the Ubuntu main repository and provided with critical updates.

The Very Secure FTP Server is inherently designed to provide as much security as possible, taking full advantage of UNIX and Linux operating system features. The server is separated into privileged and unprivileged processes. The unprivileged process receives all FTP requests, interpreting them and then sending them over a socket to the privileged process, which then securely filters all requests. Even the privileged process does not run with full root capabilities, using only those that are necessary to perform its tasks. In addition, the Very Secure FTP Server uses its own version of directory commands like `ls`, instead of the system's versions.

Check the Ubuntu Server Guide | File Servers | FTP Servers for basic configuration.

```
https://help.ubuntu.com/stable/serverguide/ftp-server.html
```

See Table 7-2 for a list of vsftpd configuration and support files.

File	Description
/etc/ftpusers	Users always denied access
vsftpd.user_list	Specified users denied access (allowed access if `userlist_deny` is **NO**)
vsftpd.chroot_list	Local users allowed access (denied access if `chroot_local_user` is on)
/etc/vsftpd.conf	vsftpd configuration file
/etc/pam.d/vsftpd	PAM vsftpd script
/lib/systemd/system/vsftpd.service	Service file for vsftpd server, standalone
/home/ftp	Anonymous FTP directory

Table 7-2: Configuration and support files for vsftpd

The Very Secure FTP server package is **vsftpd**. Use **apt-get**, **aptitude**, or the Synaptic Package Manager to install it. The package also installs anonymous FTP support.

```
sudo apt-get install vsftpd
```

The Very Secure FTP Server is managed by **systemd** using the **vsftpd.service** unit file, shown here. It is a simple file that is run after the network starts (After), and is started by the **multi-**

user.target (runlevels 2, 3, 4, and 5) (WantedBy). It is run by the **/usr/sbin/vsftpd** command with reads the **/etc/vsftpd/vsftpd.conf file** for configuration.

vsftpd.service

```
[Unit]
Description=vsftpd FTP server
After=network.target

[Service]
Type=simple
ExecStart=/usr/sbin/vsftpd /etc/vsftpd.conf
ExecReload=/bin/kill -HUP $MAINPID
ExecStartPre=-/bin/mkdir -p /var/run/vsftpd/empty

[Install]
WantedBy=multi-user.target
```

Running vsftpd

The Very Secure FTP Server's daemon is named **vsftpd**. It is designed to be run as a stand-alone server, which can be started and stopped using the **/lib/systemd/system/vsftpd.service** server script. To start, stop, and restart **vsftpd**, you can use the **service** command. If you previously enabled another FTP server such as ProFTPD, be sure to disable it first. You can start, stop, and restart the **vsftpd** server using the **service** script. Whenever you make changes to your configuration, be sure to restart the FTP server to make the changes take effect.

```
sudo service vsftpd restart
```

The anonymous FTP directory will be **ftp** user's home directory, **/srv/ftp**. Here will be located the file and directories for an anonymous FTP server.

Firewall access

To allow firewall access to the FTP port, usually port 21, you should enable access using a firewall configuration tool like ufw (desktop).

For the **ufw** default firewall, you would use the following command. The ufw firewall maintains its IPtables files in **/etc/ufw**. You can also use the Gufw tool (desktop) to add access on the Preconfigured tab for the FTP port, port 21.

```
sudo ufw allow tcp/21
```

If you are managing your IPtables firewall directly, you could manage access directly by adding the following IPtables rule. This accepts input on port 21 for TCP/IP protocol packages.

```
iptables -A INPUT -p tcp --dport 21 -j ACCEPT
```

Configuring vsftpd

You configure **vsftpd** using one configuration file, **/etc/vsftpd.conf**. Configuration options are simple and kept to a minimum. The **vsftpd.conf** file contains a set of directives where an option is assigned a value (there are no spaces around the = sign). Options can be on and off flags assigned a **YES** or **NO** value, features that take a numeric value, or ones that are assigned a string (see Table

7-3). A default **vsftpd.conf** file is installed in the **/etc** directory. This file lists some of the commonly used options available with detailed explanations for each. Those that are not used are commented out with a preceding # character. Option names are very understandable. For example, **anon_upload_enable** allows anonymous users to upload files; whereas **anon_mkdir_write_enable** lets anonymous users create directories. The Man page for **vsftpd.conf** lists all options, providing a detailed explanation for each.

The vsftpd server runs as the nobody user for unsecured tasks. The nobody user is used by various services. You can change this to a user dedicated to FTP server, something like **ftpsecure**. Set the user name in the **nopriv_user** option.

```
nopriv_user=ftpsecure
```

Enabling Standalone Access

To run **vsftpd** as a standalone server, set the listen option to **YES**. This instructs **vsftpd** to continually listen on its assigned port for requests. You can specify the port it listens on with the **listen_port** option.

```
listen=YES
```

To listen on an IPv6 socket you remove the comment for the **listen_ipv6** option.

```
#listen_ipv6=YES
```

Enabling Login Access

In the following example taken from the **vsftpd.conf** file, anonymous FTP is enabled by assigning the **YES** value to the **anonymous_enable** option. Be aware that if you disable this option by commenting it out, the default is to enable anonymouse FTP. The **local_enable** option allows local users on your system to use the FTP server.

```
# Allow anonymous FTP? (Beware - allowed by default if you comment this out).
anonymous_enable=YES
#
# Uncomment this to allow local users to log in.
local_enable=YES
```

Should you want to let anonymous users log in without providing a password, you can set **no_anon_password** to YES.

Local User Permissions

A variety of user permissions control how local users can access files on the server. If you want to allow local users to create, rename, and delete files and directories on their account, you have to enable write access with the **write_enable** option. This way, any files they upload, they can also delete. Literally, the **write_enable** option activates a range of commands for changing the file system, including creating, renaming, and deleting both files and directories. With **user_config_dir** you can configure specific users.

```
write_enable=YES
```

You can further specify the permissions for uploaded files using the **local_umask** option (022 is the recommended default set in **vsftpd.conf**, turning off the write permission for other users and giving you read, write, and execute for the owner; and read and execute for all other users, a 755 permission setting).

```
local_umask=022
```

Option	Description
`listen`	Set standalone mode
`listen_port`	Specify port for standalone mode
`anonymous_enable`	Enable anonymous user access
`local_enable`	Enable access by local users
`write_enable`	Enable write access by local users (modify and create files)
`no_anon_password`	Specify whether anonymous users must submit a password
`anon_upload_enable`	Enable uploading by anonymous users
`anon_mkdir_write_enable`	Allow anonymous users to create directories
`aonon_world_readable_only`	Make uploaded files read-only to all users
`idle_session_timeout`	Set time limit in seconds for idle sessions
`data_connection_timeouts`	Set time limit in seconds for failed connections
`dirmessage_enable`	Display directory messages
`ftpd_banner`	Display FTP login message
`xferlog_enable`	Enable logging of transmission transactions
`xferlog_file`	Specify log file
`deny_email_enable`	Enable denying anonymous users, whose e-mail addresses are specified in **vsftpd.banned**
`userlist_enable`	Deny access to users specified in the **vsftp.user_list** file
`userlist_file`	Deny or allow users access depending on setting of `userlist_deny`
`userlist_deny`	When set to **YES**, **userlist_file** deny list users access.
`chroot_list_enable`	Restrict users to their home directories
`chroot_list_file`	Allow users access to home directories. Unless `chroot_local_user` is set to **YES**, this file contains a list of users not allowed access to their home directories
`chroot_local_user`	Allow access by all users to their home directories
`pam_service_name`	Specify PAM script
`ls_recurse_enable`	Enable recursive listing
`user_config_dir`	Directory for user specific configurability

Table 7-3: Configuration Options for vsftpd.conf

Because ASCII uploads entail certain security risks, they are turned off by default. However, if you are uploading large text files, you may want to enable them in special cases. Use **ascii_upload_enable** to allow ASCII uploads.

Anonymous User Permissions

You can also allow anonymous users to upload and delete files, as well as create or remove directories. Uploading by anonymous users is enabled with the **anon_upload_enable** option. To let anonymous users also rename or delete their files, you set the **anon_other_write_enable** option. To let them create directories, you set the **anon_mkdir_write_enable** option.

```
anon_upload_enable=YES
anon_other_write_enable=YES
anon_mkdir_write_enable=YES
```

The **anon_world_readable_only** option will make uploaded files read-only (downloadable), restricting write access to the user that created them. Only the user who uploaded a file can delete it.

All uploaded files are owned by the anonymous FTP user. You can have the files owned by another user, adding greater possible security. In effect, the actual user owning the uploaded files becomes hidden from anonymous users. To enable this option, use **chown_uploads** and specify the new user with **chown_username**. Never make the user an administrative user like **root**.

```
chown_uploads=YES
chown_username=myftp
```

The upload directory itself should be given write permission by other users.

```
sudo chmod 777 /srv/ftp/upload
```

You can control the kind of access that users have to files with the **anon_umask** option, setting default read/write permissions f or uploaded files. The default is 077, which gives read/write/execute permission to the owner only (700). To allow all users read access, you set the umask to 022, where the 2 turns off write permission but sets read and execute permission (755). The value 000 allows both read, write, and execute for all users.

Messages

The **dirmessage_enable** option allows a message held in a directory's **.message** file to be displayed whenever a user accesses that directory. The **ftpd_banner** option lets you set up your own FTP login message. The default is shown here:

```
ftpd_banner=Welcome to blah FTP service.
```

Logging

A set of **xferlog** options control logging. You can enable logging, as well as specify the format and the location of the file.

```
xferlog_enable=YES
```

Use **xferlog_file** option to specify the log file you want to use. The default is shown here:

```
xferlog_file=/var/log/vsftpd.log
```

You can choose to save entries in the standard ftpd xferlog format.

```
xferlog_std_format=YES
```

Connection Time Limits

To efficiently control the workload on a server, you can set time limits on idle users and failed transmissions. The **idle_session_timeout** option will cut off idle users after a specified time, and **data_connection_timeouts** will cut off failed data connections. The defaults are shown here:

```
idle_session_timeout=600
data_connection_timeout=120
```

vsftpd Access Controls

Certain options control access to the FTP site. As previously noted, the **anonymous_enable** option allows anonymous users access, and **local_enable** permits local users to log in to their accounts. Files set up to control access will have a **vsftpd.** prefix, like **vsftpd.banned_emails** for email addresses of banned anonymous users.

Denying Access

The **deny_email_enable** option lets you deny access by anonymous users, and the **banned_email_file** option designates the file (usually **vstfpd.banned_emails**) that holds the e-mail addresses of those users. The **/etc/ftpusers** file lists those users that can never be accessed. These are usually system users like **root**, **mail**, and **nobody**.

User Access

The **userlist_enable** option controls access by users, denying access to those listed in the file designated by the **userlist_file** option (usually **vsftpd.user_list**). If, instead, you want to restrict access to just certain select users, you can change the meaning and usage of the **vsftpd.user_list** file to indicate only those users allowed access, instead of those denied access. To do this, you set the **userlist_deny** option to **NO** (its default is **YES**). Only users listed in the **vsftpd.user_list** file will be granted access to the FTP site.

User Restrictions

The **chroot_list_enable** option controls access by local users, letting them access only their home directories, while restricting system access. The **chroot_list_file** option designates the file (usually **vstfpd.chroot**) that lists those users allowed access. You can allow access by all local users with the **chroot_local_user** option.

```
chroot_local_users=YES
```

If this option is set, then the file designated by **chroot_list_file** will have an inverse meaning, listing those users not allowed access. In the following example, access by local users is limited to those listed in **vsftpd.chroot**:

```
chroot_list_enable=YES
chroot_list_file=/etc/vsftpd.chroot_list
```

On Ubuntu the **secure_chroot_dir** option is used to specify a non-user secure non-writeable directory used when FTP does not require file system access.

```
secure_chroot_dir=/var/run/vsftpd/empty
```

User Authentication and SSL Encryption

The **vsftpd** server makes use of the PAM service to authenticate local users that are remotely accessing their accounts through FTP. In the **vsftpd.conf** file, the PAM script used for the server is specified with the **pam_service_name** option.

```
pam_service_name=vsftpd
```

In the **etc/pam.d** directory, you will find a PAM file named **vsftpd** with entries for controlling access to the **vsftpd** server. PAM is currently set up to authenticate users with valid accounts, as well as deny access to users in the **/etc/ftpusers** file. The default **/etc/pam.d/vsftpd** file is shown here:

```
# Standard behavior for ftpd(8)
auth required  pam_listfile.so  item=user sense=deny  file=/etc/ftpusers  onerr=succeed
# Note: vsftpd handles anonymouse logins on its own. Do not enable pam_ftp.so.
# Standard pam includes
@include common-account
@include common-session
@include common-auth
auth   required   pam_shells.so
```

The `rsa_cert_file` option specifies the location of the RSA certificate file, and the `rsa_private_key_file` option specifies the SSL encryption key to use for SSL connections.

```
rsa_cert_file=/etc/ssl/certs/ssl-cert-snakeoil.pem
rsa_private_key_file=/etc/ssl/private/ssl-cert-snakeoil.key
```

Command Access

Command usage is highly restricted by vsftpd. Most options for the **ls** command that lists files are not allowed. Only the asterisk file-matching operation is supported. To enable recursive listing of files in subdirectories, you have to enable the use of the **-R** option by setting the **ls_recurse_enable** option to **YES**. Some clients will assume that the recursive option is enabled.

vsftpd Virtual Hosts

Though the capability is not inherently built in to vsftpd, you can configure and set up the vsftpd server to support virtual hosts. Virtual hosting is where a single FTP server operates as if it has two or more IP addresses. Several IP addresses can then be used to access the same server. The server will then use a separate FTP user directory and files for each host. With **vsftpd**, this involves manually creating separate FTP users and directories for each virtual host, along with separate vsftpd configuration files for each virtual host in the **/etc/** directory. You can set up virtual hosts for running vsftpd. You can set up virtual hosts for running vsftpd either as a standalone server, or with systemd, or even xinetd. You will have to create an FTP user and directory for each host.

Virtual Hosts on a standalone server

On Ubuntu, **vsftpd** is configured to run as a standalone service. Adding virtual hosts is a simple matter of creating a separate vsftpd configuration file for each virtual host. Then run an instance of **vsftpd** for each using a different configuration file. The configuration files are placed in the **/etc** directory and can have the prefix **vsftpd-**, and in **/etc/vsftpd-mysite1.conf**. In the configuration file, use the **listen_address** option to specify which IP address that virtual host will use.

```
listen_address=192.168.0.5
```

When you run vsftpd, specify the configuration file to use.

```
sudo service vsftpd /etc/vsftpd-mysite1.conf
```

See the **/usr/share/doc/vsftpd/examples/INTERNET_SITE_NOINETD** directory for more information.

You will, of course, have to set up a user and a directory for each virtual host. For example, for the first virtual host you could use **mysite1** and use the directory **/srv/mysite1**. Be sure to set root ownership and the appropriate permissions.

```
sudo useradd -d /srv/mysite1 mysite1
sudo chown root.root /srv/mysite1
sudo chmod a+rx /srv/mysite1
sudo unmask 022
sudo mkdir /srv/mysite1/pub
```

Virtual Hosts with xinetd

Currently, vsftpd as installed on Ubuntu supports the older xinetd. You will first have to install the xinetd package. If you wish to run **vsftpd** as a **xinetd** service, you have to create a separate **xinetd** service script for each host in the **/etc/xinetd.d** directory. In effect, you have several **vsftpd** services running in parallel for each separate virtual host. Check the following file in **/usr/share/doc/vsftpd** for information on how to set up virtual hosts with **xinetd**.

```
/usr/share/doc/vsftpd/examples/VIRTUAL_HOSTS/README
```

Create an FTP user for each host. Create directories for each host (you can use the one already set up for one of the users). For example, for the first virtual host, you could use **FTP-host1**. Be sure to set root ownership and the appropriate permissions.

```
sudo useradd -d /srv/ftp-host1 FTP-host1
sudo chown root.root /srv/ftp-host1
sudo chmod a+rx /srv/ftp-host1
sudo umask 022
mkdir /srv/ftp-host1/pub
```

Set up two corresponding vsftpd service scripts in the **/etc/xinetd.d** directory. The **vsftpd** directory in **/usr/share/doc/vsftpd/examples/INTERNET_SITE** has an **xinetd** example script, `vsftpd.xinetd`. You can copy it to the **/etc/xinetd.d** directory and give it a name for the virtual host, like **vsftpd-host1**. Make a copy for each virtual host. Within each, add a **`bind`** entry to specify the IP address the virtual host will respond to.

```
bind  192.168.0.34
```

Within the same scripts, add a **`server_args`** entry specifying the name of the configuration file to use.

```
server_args = vsftpd-host1.conf
```

Within the **/etc** directory, create separate configuration files for each virtual host, using the same name specified in **server_args**, like **vsftpd-host1.conf**. Within each, specify the FTP user you created for each, using the **`ftp_username`** entry.

```
ftp_username = FTP-host1
```

Once you have finished your configuration, restart **xinetd** to restart the **vsftpd** server.

```
sudo service xinetd restart
```

vsftpd Virtual Hosts with systemd

As currently installed, vsftpd does not support virtual hosts using systemd directly. But you can set up the appropriate service and target files to have systemd run vsftpd virtual hosts. The **vsftpd@.service** systemd template file reads the configuration files listed in the **/etc/vsftpd** directory. The **vsfptd@.service** file is shown here.

vsftpd@.service

```
[Unit]
Description=Vsftpd ftp daemon
After=network.target
PartOf=vsftpd.target

[Service]
Type=forking
ExecStart=/usr/sbin/vsftpd /etc/vsftpd/%i.conf

[Install]
WantedBy=vsftpd.target
```

The following example uses two IP addresses for an FTP server. Create an FTP user for each host. Create directories for each host (you can use the one already set up for one of the users). For example, for the first virtual host you could use **FTP-host1**. Be sure to set root ownership and the appropriate permissions.

```
useradd -d /var/ftp-host1 FTP-host1
chown root.root /var/ftp-host1
chmod a+rx /var/ftp-host1
umask 022
mkdir /var/ftp-host1/pub
```

Within the **/etc/vsftpd** directory, create separate configuration files for each virtual host. Within each, specify the FTP user you created for each, using the **`ftp_username`** entry.

```
ftp_username = FTP-host1
```

The **vsftpd@.service** file needs a corresponding target file, **vsftpd.target**, which provides group configuration of all the vsftpd servers you start with the **vsftpd@.service** file. The **vsftpd.target** file starts the servers after the network.target file (network service files) and it is wanted by multi-user.target.

vsftpd.target

```
[Unit]
Description=FTP daemon
After=network.target

[Install]
WantedBy=multi-user.target
```

vsftpd Virtual Users

Virtual users can be implemented by making use of PAM to authenticate authorized users. In effect, you are allowing access to certain users, while not having to actually set up accounts for them on the FTP server system. First, create a PAM login database file to use along with a PAM file in the **/etc/pam.d** directory that will access the database (for sample files and documentation check **/usr/share/doc/vsftpd/examples/VIRTUAL_USERS**). Then create a virtual FTP user along with corresponding directories that the virtual users will access. In the **vsftpd.conf** file, you disable anonymous FTP:

```
anonymous_enable=NO
local_enable=YES
```

Then enable guest access:

```
guest_enable=YES
guest_username=virtual
```

For more refined user control, you can set up a user configuration directory with files for different permissions for each user. Set the **user_config_dir** option in the **/etc/vsftpd.conf** file to the directory that will hold user configuration files. For example:

```
user_config_dir=/etc/vsftpd_user_conf
```

Be sure to create that directory.

```
sudo mkdir /etc/vsftpd_user_conf
```

In separate files named with a user name, enter the vsftpd permissions and options you want for that user. See **/usr/share/doc/vsftpd/examples/VIRTUAL_USERS_2** for more information.

Using FTP with rsync

Many FTP servers also support rsync operations using **rsync** as a daemon. This allows intelligent incremental updates of files from an FTP server. You can update multiple files in a directory or a single file such as a large ISO image.

Accessing FTP Sites with rsync

To access the FTP server running an rsync server, you enter the **rsync** command, and following the hostname, you enter a double colon and then either the path of the directory you want to access or one of the FTP server's modules. In the following example, the user updates a local **myproject** directory from the one on the **mytrek.com** FTP site:

```
sudo rsync ftp.mytrek.com::/home/ftp/pub/myproject  /home/myproject
```

To find out what directories are supported by rsync, you check for rsync modules on that site. These are defined by the site's **/etc/rsyncd.conf** configuration file. A *module* is just a directory with all its subdirectories. To find available modules, you enter the FTP site with a double colon only.

```
sudo rsync ftp.mytrek.com::
ftp
```

This tells you that the **ftp.mytrek.com** site has an FTP module. To list the files and directories on the module, you can use the **rsync** command with the **-r** option.

```
rsync -r ftp.mytrek.com::ftp
```

Many sites that run the rsync server will have an rsync protocol that will already be set to access the available rsync module (directory). You can even use **rsync** to update just a single file, such as an ISO image that may have been changed.

Configuring an rsync Server

To configure your FTP server to let clients use rsync on your site, you need to first run rsync as a server. First configure rsync to run as a server. The rsync configuration file is **/etc/default/rsync**. Set the **RSYNC_ENABLE** entry to **true**.

```
RSYNC_ENABLE=true
```

If you make any configuration changes, be sure to restart the **rsync** server with the **service** command.

```
sudo service rsync restart
```

When run as a daemon, rsync will read the **/etc/rsyncd.conf** file for its configuration options. Here you can specify FTP options such as the location for the FTP site files. There is no default configuration file set up for you in the **/etc** directory. You will have to create one. You could copy a default version from the **/usr/share/doc/rsync/**examples directory.

```
sudo cp /usr/share/doc/rsync/examples/rsyncd.conf  /etc
```

The configuration file is segmented into modules, each with its own options. A module is a symbolic representation of an exported tree (a directory and its subdirectories). The module name is enclosed in brackets, for instance, **[ftp]** for an FTP module. You can enter options for that module, as by using the path option to specify the location of your FTP site directories and files (**/srv/ftp** is the default for the vsftpd server). The user and group IDs can be specified with the **uid** and **gid** options. The default is nobody. A sample FTP module heading with the **vsftpd** path setting is shown here:

```
[ftp]
        comment = public archive
        path = /srv/ftp
```

The sample version of **rsyncd.conf** will have an ftp module set up for you with default values assigned. Many less common options will be commented out with a # character.

For more restricted access, you can add an **auth users** option to specify authorized users; rsync will allow anonymous access to all users by default. The **hosts allow** and **hosts deny** access controls limit access for specific hosts. Access to areas on the FTP site by rsync can be further controlled using a secrets file, such as **/etc/rsyncd.secrets**. This is a colon-separated list of user names and passwords.

```
aleina:mypass3
larisa:yourp5
```

A corresponding module to the controlled area would look like this:

```
[specialftp]
        comment = special projects
        path = /var/projects/special
        command = restricted access
        auth users = aleina,larisa
        secrets file = /etc/rsyncd.secrets
```

If you are on your FTP server and want to see what modules will be made available, you can run `rsync` with the `localhost` option and nothing following the double colon.

```
$ rsync localhost::
ftp             public archive
specialftp      special projects
```

Remote users can find out what modules you have by entering your hostname and double colon only.

```
rsync ftp.mytrek.com::
```

rsync Mirroring

Some sites will allow you to use rsync to perform mirroring operations. With rsync you do not have to copy the entire site, just those files that have been changed. The following example mirrors the mytrek FTP site to the **/srv/ftp/mirror/mytrek** directory on a local system:

```
rsync -a --delete ftp.mytrek.com::ftp /srv/ftp/mirror/mytrek
```

The `-a` option is archive mode, which includes several other options, such as `-r` (recursive) to include all subdirectories, `-t` to preserves file times and dates, `-l` recreate symbolic links, and `-p` to preserve all permissions. In addition, the `--delete` option is added to delete files that don't exist on the sending side, removing obsolete files.

ProFTPD

ProFTPD is based on the same design as the Apache web server, implementing a similar simplified configuration structure and supporting such flexible features as virtual hosting. ProFTPD is an open source project made available under a GPL license. At **proftpd.org** you can find detailed documentation including FAQs, user manuals, and sample configurations. Check the site for new releases and updates. ProFTPD is available on the Universe repository as **proftpd-basic** and **proftpd-doc**, with additional authentication modules for mysql, ldap, odbc, sqlite, and pgsql.

You cannot have both vsftpd and ProFTPD installed at the same time. If you install ProFTPD, then vsftpd will be removed.

When you install ProFTPD you are prompted to choose to install it as a standalone or inetd server. Configuration files are located in the **/etc/proftpd** directory. The primary configuration file is **/etc/proftpd/proftpd.conf**. Virtual servers are configured in the **virtual.conf** file. Modules have their own configuration files such as **sql.conf** and **ldap.conf**. You can choose what modules to load in the **modules.conf** file.

ubuntu

8. Web Servers

The primary web server for Ubuntu is Apache, which has almost become the standard web server for all Linux distributions. It is a very powerful, stable, and fairly easy-to-configure server. Ubuntu provides default configuration for the Apache, making it usable as soon as it is installed.

Check the Ubuntu Server Guide | Web Servers | HTTPD for basic configuration.

```
https://help.ubuntu.com/stable/serverguide/httpd.html
```

Note: The Zope Application server for Web development is also included on the main Ubuntu repository. Zope application server (**http://zope.org**) is an open source web server with integrated security, web-based administration and development, and database interface features. It was developed by the Zope Corporation, which also developed the Python programming language.

Apache Web Server

The Apache web server is a full-featured, free HTTP (Web) server, developed and maintained by the Apache Server Project. The aim of the project is to provide a reliable, efficient, and easily extensible Web server, with free open source code made available under its own Apache Software License. The server software includes the server daemon, configuration files, management tools, and documentation. The Apache Server Project is maintained by a core group of volunteer programmers and supported by a great many contributors worldwide. The Apache Server Project is one of several projects currently supported by the Apache Software Foundation (formerly known as the Apache Group). This nonprofit organization provides financial, legal, and organizational support for various Apache Open Source software projects, including the Apache HTTPD Server, Java Apache, Jakarta, and XML-Apache. The website for the Apache Software Foundation is **http://apache.org**. Table 8-1 lists several Apache-related websites.

Apache was originally based on the NCSA web server developed at the National Center for Supercomputing Applications, University of Illinois, Urbana-Champaign. Apache has since emerged as a server in its own right, and become one of the most popular Web servers in use. Although originally developed for Linux and UNIX systems, Apache has become a cross-platform application with Windows and OS/2 versions. Apache provides online support and documentation for its web server at **http://httpd.apache.org**. An HTML-based manual also is provided with the server installation.

Website	Description
http://apache.org	Apache Software Foundation
http://httpd.apache.org	Apache HTTP Server Project
http://jakarta.apache.org	Jakarta Apache Project
http://apache-gui.com	Apache GUI Project
http://php.net	PHP Hypertext Preprocessor, embedded web page programming language
http://zope.org	Zope application server

Table 8-1: Apache-Related Websites

Java: Apache Jakarta Project

The Apache Jakarta Project supports the development of Open Source Java software; its website is located at **http://jakarta.apache.org**. Currently, the Jakarta supports numerous projects, including libraries, tools, frameworks, engines, and server applications. Tomcat is an open source implementation of the Java Servlet and JavaServer Pages specifications. Tomcat is designed for use in Apache servers. JMeter is a Java desktop tool used to test performance of server resources, such as server lets and CGI scripts. Velocity is a template engine that provides easy access to Java objects. Watchdog is a tool that checks the compatibility of servlet containers. Struts, Cactus, and Tapestry are Java frameworks, established methods for developing Java web applications.

LAMP

During installation, you can install the Apache Web server as part of the LAMP collection of packages. LAMP stands for Linux Apache MySQL and PHP. It consists essentially of the Web server (Apache) with database support (MySQL) and programming capability (PHP). For programming, PHP is selected by default, though you could use Python or Perl instead. Together they provide a commercially capable Web site, supporting multiple users and complex data with application support. For a basic informational Web site, you only need the Apache Web server.

The LAMP packages include the following from the Ubuntu main repository.

apache2 The Apache Web server and all supporting packages

mysql-server The MySQL database server

php5-mysql and **libapache2-mod-php5** The PHP support for MySQL and Apache

To install the LAMP package after installation, you would use the **tasksel** command in a terminal window with the install and lamp-server options.

```
sudo tasksel install lamp-server
```

To allow other hosts on your network to access your MySQL database, you have to set the MySQL server to accept access from the local network. You do this with the **bind-address** option in the **mysqld** section of the **/etc/mysql/my.cnf** configuration file. Initially, this option is set to the localhost, 127.0.0.1, allowing access only for your local machine. For a local network, you can change this to the IP address of your machine on that network, or the IP address of network device connected to the local network. If the address is allocated dynamically, comment out the bind-address entry. If you want to allow MySQL to use several interfaces, including **localhost**, you would set the bind-address to 0.0.0.0. This allows MySQL to use all your network interfaces.

Ubuntu Apache Installation

Ubuntu will provide you with the option of installing the Apache web server during the Ubuntu Server CD installation (LAMP package). Alternatively, you can install the Apache web server later as the **apache2** package (see the Ubuntu Software Center, the Synaptic Package Manager, or **apt-get**). All the necessary directories and configuration files are automatically generated for you. Then, whenever you run Linux, your system is already a fully functional website. Every time you start your system, the web server will also start up, running continuously. On Ubuntu, the directory reserved for your website data files is **/var/www**. Place your web pages in this directory. Your system is already configured to operate as a web server. All you need to do is perform any needed network server configuration, and then designate the files and directories open to remote users. Once your website is connected to a network, remote users can access it.

Directories and Files	Description
.htaccess	Directory-based configuration files; an **.htaccess** file holds directives to control access to files within the directory in which it is located
/var/www	Directory for Apache Web site HTML files, location of the default server HTML files. Virtual sites will be located here
/etc/apache2	Directory for Apache web server configuration files
/etc/init.d/apache2	Apache Web server script for start up and shut down
/etc/default/apache2	Apache Web start up configuration
/usr/sbin	Location of the Apache web server program file and utilities
/usr/share/doc/apache2-doc	Apache web server manual, **apache2-doc** package
/var/log/apache2	Location of Apache log files
/usr/lib/apache2	Directory holding Apache modules
/usr/lib/cgi-bin	Directory holding Web CGI scripts
/var/cache/apache2	Directory holding Apache cache

Table 8-2: Apache Web Server Files and Directories

The web server normally sets up your website in the **/var/www** directory. A simple **index.html** test page is installed for you to check if your Web server is working. Your configuration files are located in a different directory, **/etc/apache2**. Table 8-2 lists the various Apache web server directories and configuration files.

Application	Description
apache2ctl	Control start, stop, and restart the apache server
a2enmod	Enable an Apache module
a2dismod	Disable an Apache module
a2enconf	Enable an Apache configuration file in **conf-available**
a2disconf	Disable an Apache configuration file in **conf-available**
a2ensite	Enable a Web site, loading its configuration file
a2dissite	Disable an Apache Web site
/etc/init.d/apache2	Script designed for Ubuntu to start, stop, and restart server, invokes **apache2ctl**. Managed by systemd.

Table 8-3: Apache management tools

The Apache manual is installed from the **apacha2-doc** package, and is placed in the **/usr/share/doc/apache2-doc/manual** directory in html format. You can access it with any browser as:

```
http://localhost/manual/index.html
```

Apache also installs several management applications, such as **apache2ctl** for starting and stopping the server, **a2ensite** for activating a Web site, and **a2enmod** for enabling particular modules. The **/etc/init.d/apache2** script is designed to safely run **apache2ctl**, and should be used to actually start and stop the server manually. Table 8-3 lists the applications.

The Apache server is managed by **systemd** using the **apache2.service** unit file in the **/run/systemd/generator.late** directory. This file is generated by systemd-sysv-generator using the **/etc/init.d/apache2** file. The server is started after the network and file system mounts (After). The **/etc/init.d/apache2** script is used to start, stop, and restart the sever (ExecStart, ExecStop, ExecReload). It is run after the **multi-user** and **graphical targets** (runlevel targets 2, 3, 4, and 5) (After).

apache2.service

```
# Automatically generated by systemd-sysv-generator

[Unit]
Documentation=man:systemd-sysv-generator(8)
SourcePath=/etc/init.d/apache2
Description=LSB: Apache2 web server
Before=runlevel2.target runlevel3.target runlevel4.target runlevel5.target
shutdown.target
After=local-fs.target remote-fs.target network-online.target systemd-journald-
dev-log.socket nss-lookup.target
Wants=network-online.target
Conflicts=shutdown.target

[Service]
Type=forking
Restart=no
TimeoutSec=5min
IgnoreSIGPIPE=no
KillMode=process
GuessMainPID=no
RemainAfterExit=yes
ExecStart=/etc/init.d/apache2 start
ExecStop=/etc/init.d/apache2 stop
ExecReload=/etc/init.d/apache2 reload
```

Apache Multiprocessing Modules: MPM

Apache now uses architecture with multiprocessing modules (MPMs), which are designed to customize Apache to different operating systems, as well as handle certain multiprocessing operations. For the main MPM, a Linux system uses the prefork, worker, or event MPM, whereas Windows uses the mpm_winnt MPM. The prefork is a standard MPM module designed to be compatible with older UNIX and Linux systems, particularly those that do not support threading. Currently Ubuntu uses the worker modules. You can configure the workload parameters for both in their module configuration files in the **mods-available** directory: the **mpm_prefork.conf**, **mpm_worker.conf**, and **mpm_event.conf** files.

Starting and Stopping the Web Server

On Ubuntu, Apache is installed as a standalone server, continually running. Your system will use an init script to automatically start up the web server daemon, invoking it whenever you start your system. An init script for the web server called **apache2** is in the **/etc/init.d** directory. This script uses the `apache2ctl` tool to manage the apache server, allowing you to start, stop, and restart the server from the command line. The **apache2** init script takes several arguments: `start` to start the server, `stop` to stop it, and `restart` to shut down and restart the server.

To check your web server, start your web browser on the host that is running the Web server, and use localhost as the domain name. Your Web server will be providing access on port 80. You would enter **http://localhost/**. You can also just enter your host name, like **http://turtle**. If you already have an Internet domain name address already supported by DNS servers, you could use that instead. This should display the home page you placed in your web root directory. A test page **index.html** file is set up for you that will display the words, It Works. Your Web site will be located in the **/var/www** directory. Here is where you would place the Web pages for your Web site.

As you configure your Web site, you will need to reload your configuration settings and restart the Web server, so that the new settings will take effect. You can do this by running the **apache2** service script first with the **reload** option, and then with the **restart** option. Use the service command to invoke the **apache2** script.

```
sudo service apache2 reload
sudo service apache2 restart
```

You also can use the apache2 script to start and stop the Web server using the start and stop options.

```
sudo service apache2 start
```

With the **status** option you can check if your Web server is running already.

The apache2 script also can be used to run the **htcacheclean** daemon, which will periodically check and clean the disk cache used by the Web server. Use the **start-htcacheclean** option to start the htcacheclean server, and **stop-htcacheclean** to stop it.

```
sudo service apache2 start-htcacheclean
```

Once you have your server running, you can check its performance with the `ab` benchmarking tool, also provided by Apache. `ab` shows you how many requests at a time your server can handle. It takes as its argument the website URL. Options include `-v`, which enables you to control the level of detail displayed; `-n`, which specifies the number of requests to handle (default is 1); and `-t`, which specifies a time limit.

```
ab -v -n localhost/index.htm.
```

Apache Configuration

Configuration directives are run from the **apache2.conf** configuration file. A documented version of the **apache2.conf** configuration file is installed automatically in **/etc/apache2/apache2.conf**. It contains detailed descriptions and default entries for global Apache directives. Though the **apache2.conf** file runs the entire configuration, it does so by including the contents of other configuration files. In effect, Apache configuration is distributed among other configuration files tailored for specific tasks. Configuration files for Apache are listed in Table 8-4.

File or Directory	Description
apache2.conf	Apache web server configuration file, will run all other configuration files
conf-available	Directory holding specialized and local configuration files
conf-enabled	Active configuration files, links to their configuration files in conf-available Read by apache2.conf
ports.conf	Directives for defining the port the Web server will use
envvars	Variable definitions used by apache2.conf and other scripts, defines user, groups, and pid for Apache
mods-available	Configuration files for particular modules, including their directives Also includes modules.
mods-enabled	Active modules, links to their configuration files in mods-available Read by apache2.conf
sites-available	Configuration files for particular sites, including Directory directives
sites-enabled	Active sites, links to their configuration files in sites-available. Read by apache2.conf

Table 8-4: Apache configuration files in the /etc/apache2 directory.

The **apache2.conf** file is configured to include and run all the directives in the **ports.conf**, **envvars**, all the configuration files linked to in the **/etc/apache2/conf-enabled** and **/etc/apache2/mods-enabled** directories, and all the configuration files linked to in the **/etc/apache2/sites-enabled** directory. The **/etc/apache2/ports.conf** file holds the port directives determining what port Apache will use (normally 80). The **/etc/apache2/envvars** file holds variable definitions such as APACHE_LOG_DIR, which are used by Apache tools, site configuration files, and scripts like **apache2ctl**. Currently these include user and group definitions for running Apache.

Any of the directives in the main configuration files can be overridden on a per-directory basis using an **.htaccess** file located within a directory. Although originally designed only for access directives, the **.htaccess** file can also hold any resource directives, enabling you to tailor how web pages are displayed in a particular directory. You can configure access to **.htaccess** files in the **apache2.conf** file. In addition, default start-up settings for **htcacheclean** are set up in the **/etc/default/apache2** file for managing the Web server cache.

Module configuration files

Many directives that once resided in the apache core are now placed in respective modules and MPMs. With this modular design, several directives have been dropped, such as ServerType. Available modules and their configuration files are located in the **/etc/apache2/mods-available** directory. The enabled modules are listed in the /**etc/apache2/mods-enabled** directory as links to their corresponding modules in the **mods-available** directory. A module is disabled by removing its link. Use the **a2enmod** command to enable a module, and the **a2dismod** command to disable a module. These commands work by adding or removing links for available modules in the **/etc/apache2/mods-enabled** directory...

Modules will have both a **.conf** and **.load** configuration file. For example, the SSL module has both an **ssl.conf** and **ssl.load** file The **.conf** file holds directives for configuring the module, and the **.load** file holds the LoadModule directive for performing the actual load operation, specifying the location and name of the module. Their corresponding links in the **mods-enabled** directory also have **.conf** and **.load** extensions.

Configuration files in conf-available

Additional configuration files, not associated with a particular module, are located in the **/etc/apache2/conf-available** directory. Sometimes these are links to configuration files set up by other applications. The configuration files have the extension **.conf**, such as **security.conf**. The configuration files are not active unless enabled. The enabled configuration files are listed in the **/etc/apache2/conf-enabled** directory as links to their corresponding modules in the **conf-available** directory. The links also have the same **.conf** extension. A configuration file is disabled by removing its link. Use the **a2enconf** command to enable a module, and the **a2disconf** command to disable a module. These commands work by adding or removing links for available modules in the **/etc/apache2/conf-enabled** directory.

Site configuration files

All sites on the Web server are configured as virtual hosts, with a special site called default for the main Web server. Normally you would create your site as a virtual host, reserving the default for administration. Virtual hosts can then be enabled or disabled, letting you turn access to a site on and off. You use the **a2dissite** and **a2ensite** commands to enable or disable sites. .

The configuration files for sites you have set up on your server are listed in the **/etc/apache2/sites-available** directory. Configuration files will contain Directory directives specifying the location of the site and controls and features you have set up for it. The **000-default.conf** file holds configuration directives for the default Web server, such as the directory directives locating the default site at **/var/www/html**. All site configuration files have the extension **.conf**. To make a site accessible, a link to its configuration file must be created in the **/etc/apache2/sites-enabled** directory. Use the **ensite** command to create such a link. There will already be a link for the **default** site (**000-default.conf**). The links also have a **.conf** extension.

Apache Configuration Directives

Apache configuration takes the form of directives entered into the Apache configuration files (**/etc/apache2**). With these directives, you can enter basic configuration information, such as your server name, or perform more complex operations, such as implementing virtual hosts. The design is flexible enough to enable you to define configuration features for particular directories and different virtual hosts. Apache has a variety of different directives performing operations as diverse as controlling directory access, assigning file icon formats, and creating log files. Most directives set values such as `DirectoryRoot`, which holds the root directory for the server's web pages, or `Port`, which holds the port on the system that the server listens on for requests. The syntax for a simple directive is shown here:

```
directive option option ...
```

Certain directives create blocks able to hold directives that apply to specific server components (also referred to as block directives). For example, the **Directory** directive is used to define a block within which you place directives that apply only to a particular directory. Block directives are entered in pairs: a beginning directive and a terminating directive. The terminating directive defines the end of the block and consists of the same name beginning with a slash. Block directives take an argument that specifies the particular object to which the directives apply. For the **Directory** block directive, you must specify a directory name to which it will apply. The **<Directory** *mydir*> block directive creates a block whose directives within it apply to the *mydir* directory. The block is terminated by a **</Directory>** directive. The **<VirtualHost** *hostaddress*> block directive is used to configure a specific virtual web server, and must include the IP or domain name address used for that server. **</VirtualHost>** is its terminating directive. Any directives you place within this block are applied to that virtual web server. The **<Limit** *method*> directive specifies the kind of access method you want to limit, such as GET or POST. The access control directives located within the block list the controls you are placing on those methods. The syntax for a block directive is as follows:

```
<block-directive option ... >
 directive option ...
 directive option ...
</block-directive>
```

Global directives are placed in one of the main configuration files. Directives for particular sites are located in that site's configuration file in **/etc/apache2/sites-available** directory. Directory directives in those files can be used to configure a particular directory. However, Apache also makes use of directory-based configuration files. Any Web site directory may have its own **.htaccess** file that holds directives to configure only that directory. If your site has many directories, or if any directories have special configuration needs, you can place their configuration directives in their **.htaccess** files, instead of filling the main configuration file with specific **Directory** directives for each one. You also can control what directives in an **.htaccess** file take precedence over those in the main configuration files. If your site allows user or client-controlled directories, you may want to monitor or disable the use of **.htaccess** files in them. It is possible for directives in an **.htaccess** file to override those in the standard configuration files unless disabled with AllowOverride directives.

You can find a listing of Apache web configuration directives both at the Apache website, **http://httpd.apache.org/docs/2.4/mod/quickreference.html** and, if you have installed the **apache2-doc** package, on your own system as **http://localhost/manual/en/mod/quickreference.htm**l.

Access controls: require

With access control directive **require** you can control access to your website by remote users and hosts (see Table 8-5) . With Apache 2.4, the **require** directive replaces the **allow**, **order**, **deny**, and **satisfy** directives used in Apache 2.2. It is implemented by the **mod_authz_host** module. Access can be granted or denied. The **all** term refers to all hosts. The **require** directive can be used globally to control access to the entire site or placed within **Directory** directives to control access to individual directives. In the following example, all users are allowed access:

```
require all granted
```

The **require** directive performs authentication on users. Authentication can refer to all users (**all**), specific users (**user**), groups (**group**), the domain name of a host the users are on (**host**), IP address (**ip**) of a host, and even an expression (**expr**), HTTP method (**method**), or environment variable (**env**). In most cases it is used to determine access by all users (**all**), or those from specified hosts (**host** or **ip**).

Directory blocks

A Directory block begins with a **<Directory** *pathname*> directive, where *pathname* is the directory to be configured. The ending directive uses the same <> symbols, but with a slash preceding the word "Directory": **</Directory>**. Directives placed within this block apply only to the specified directory. The following example denies access to only the **mypics** directory by requests from **www.myvids.com**.

```
<Directory /var/www/mypics>
    Require all granted
    Require host www.myvids.com denied
</Directory>
```

With the **Options** directive, you can enable certain features in a directory, such as the use of symbolic links, automatic indexing, execution of CGI scripts, and content negotiation. The default is the **All** option, which turns on all features except content negotiation (**Multiviews**). The following example enables automatic indexing (**Indexes**), symbolic links (**FollowSymLinks**), and content negotiation (**Multiviews**). A simple **index.html** file has been placed in the **/var/www** directory to disable automatic indexing (Indexes) for that top level directory (DocumentRoot). The Indexes option can be a security risk.

```
Options Indexes FollowSymLinks Multiviews
```

Configurations made by directives in main configuration files or in upper-level directories are inherited by lower-level directories. Directives for a particular directory held in **.htaccess** files and Directory blocks can be allowed to override those configurations. This capability can be controlled by the **AllowOverride** directive. With the **all** argument, **.htaccess** files can override any previous configurations. The **None** argument disallows overrides, effectively disabling the **.htaccess** file. You can further control the override of specific groups of directives. **AuthConfig** enables use of authorization directives, **FileInfo** is for type directives, **Indexes** is for indexing directives, **Limit** is for access control directives, and **Options** is for the options directive.

```
AllowOverride all
```

Authentication

Your web server can also control access on a per-user or per-group basis to particular directories on your website. You can require various levels for authentication. Access can be limited to particular users and require passwords, or expanded to allow members of a group access. You can dispense with passwords altogether or set up an anonymous type of access, as used with FTP.

To apply authentication directives to a certain directory, you place those directives within either a **Directory** block or the directory's **.htaccess** file. Use the **require** directive to determine what users can access the directory. You can list particular users or groups. The **AuthName** directive provides the authentication realm to the user, the name used to identify the particular set of resources accessed by this authentication process. The **AuthType** directive specifies the type of authentication, such as basic or digest. A **require** directive requires also **AuthType**, **AuthName**, and directives specifying the locations of group and user authentication files. In the following example, only the users **george**, **robert**, and **mark** are allowed access to the **newpics** directory:

```
<Directory /var/www/newpics
     AuthType Basic
     AuthName Newpics
     AuthUserFile /web/users
     AuthGroupFile /web/groups
     <Limit GET POST>
           require users george robert mark
     </Limit>
</Directory>
```

To set up anonymous access for a directory, place the **Anonymous** directive with the user anonymous as its argument in the directory's Directory block or **.htaccess** file. You can also use the **Anonymous** directive to provide access to particular users without requiring passwords from them.

Apache maintains its own user and group authentication files, specifying what users and groups are allowed access to which directories. These files are normally simple flat files, such as your system's password and group files. They can become large, however, possibly slowing down authentication lookups. As an alternative, many sites have used database management files in place of these flat files. Database methods are then used to access the files, providing a faster response time. Apache has directives for specifying the authentication files, depending on the type of file you are using. The **AuthUserfile** and **AuthGroupFile** directives are used to specify the locations of authentication files that have a standard flat file format. The **AuthDBUserFile** and **AuthDBGroupFile** directives are used for DB database files, and the **AuthDBMGUserFile** and **AuthDBMGGroupFile** are used for DBMG database files.

The programs **htdigest**, **htpasswd**, and **htdbm** are tools provided with the Apache software package for creating and maintaining *user authentication files,* which are user password files listing users who have access to specific directories or resources on your website. The **htdigest** and **htpasswd** programs manage a simple flat file of user authentication records, whereas **htdbm** uses a more complex database management format. If your user list is extensive, you may want to use a database file for fast lookups. **htdigest** takes as its arguments the authentication file, the realm, and the username, creating or updating the user entry. **htpasswd** can also employ encryption on the password. **htdbm** has an extensive set of options to add, delete, and update user entries. A variety of different database formats are used to set up such files. Three common ones are Berkeley DB2, NDBM, and GNU GBDM. **htdbm** looks for the system libraries for these formats in that order. Be careful to be consistent in using the same format for your authentication files.

Directory-level Configuration

One of the most flexible aspects of Apache is its ability to configure individual directories. With the **Directory** directive, you can define a block of directives that apply only to a particular directory (see Table 8-5). Such a directive can be placed in a site configuration file. Global default directives are located in the **apache2.conf** configuration file. You can also use an **.htaccess** file within a particular directory to hold configuration directives. Those directives are then applied only to that directory. The name **.htaccess** is set with the **AccessFileName** directive. You can change this if you want.

```
AccessFileName .htaccess
```

Directive	Description
require *user-authentication*	Authenticates users that can access a given directory or site. Authentication can refer to all users (**all**), userids (**user**), groups (**group**), domain name (**host**), IP address (**ip**), and even an expression, HTTP method, or environment variable.
require host *hosts*	Determines hosts (domain names) that can access a given directory.
require ip *addresses*	Determines hosts (IP addresses) that can access a given directory.
require all granted	Grant access to all hosts
require all denied	Deny access to all hosts
<Files *filename***>** ... **</Files>**	Provides for access control by filename. Similar to the **<Directory>** directive and **<Location>** directive. **<Files>** sections are processed in the order they appear in the configuration file, after the **<Directory>** sections and **.htaccess** files are read, but before **<Location>** sections. **<Files>** can be nested inside **<Directory>** sections to restrict the portion of the file system to which they apply.
<FilesMatch *regex***>** ... **</FilesMatch>**	Provides for access control by filename like the **<Files>** directive, but uses a regular expression.
<Limit *method method* ... **>** ... **</Limit>**	**<Limit>** and **</Limit>** specify a group of access control directives that apply only to the specified access methods, any valid HTTP method. Access control directives appearing outside a **<Limit>** directive apply to all access methods. Method names are GET, POST, PUT, DELETE, CONNECT, and OPTIONS.
<LimitExcept *method method* ... **>** ... **</LimitExcept>**	**<LimitExcept>** and **</LimitExcept>** specify a group of access control directives, which then apply to any HTTP access method *not* listed in the arguments.
<Location *URL***>** ... **</Location>**	The **<Location>** directive provides for access control by URL. Similar to the **<Directory>** directive.
<LocationMatch *regex***>** ... **</LocationMatch>**	Provides access control by URL, in an identical manner to **<Location>**, using a regular expression as an argument.
LimitRequestBody *number*	Limits the size of an HTTP request message body.

Table 8-5: Access Control Directives

A Directory block begins with a **`<Directory`** *pathname*> directive, where *pathname* is the directory to be configured. The ending directive uses the same <> symbols, but with a slash preceding the word "Directory": **`</Directory>`**. Directives placed within this block apply only to the specified directory.

With the **Options** directive, you can enable certain features in a directory, such as the use of symbolic links, automatic indexing, execution of CGI scripts, and content negotiation. The default is the **`All`** option, which turns on all features except content negotiation (**Multiviews**). The following example enables automatic indexing (**`Indexes`**), symbolic links (**`FollowSymLinks`**), and content negotiation (**`Multiviews`**).

```
Options Indexes FollowSymLinks Multiviews
```

Configurations made by directives in main configuration files or in upper-level directories are inherited by lower-level directories. Directives for a particular directory held in **.htaccess** files and Directory blocks can be allowed to override those configurations. This capability can be controlled by the **AllowOverride** directive. With the `all` argument, **.htaccess** files can override any previous configurations. The `none` argument disallows overrides, effectively disabling the **.htaccess** file. You can further control the override of specific groups of directives. **AuthConfig** enables use of authorization directives, **FileInfo** is for type directives, **Indexes** is for indexing directives, **Limit** is for access control directives, and **Options** is for the options directive.

```
AllowOverride all
```

When given a URL for a directory instead of an HTML file, and when no default web page is in the directory, Apache creates a page on the fly and displays it. This is usually only a listing of the different files in the directory. In effect, Apache indexes the items in the directory for you. You can set several options for generating and displaying such an index using **IndexOptions**. With **FancyIndexing**, web page items are displayed with icons and column headers that can be used to sort the listing. With **VersionSort** items are sorted alphabetically and numerically. **NameWidth** sets column width, with the * value setting the width as needed. **Charset** sets the character set, usually UTF-8. For a complete list of options see **http://httpd.apache.org/docs/2.2/mod/mod_autoindex.html#indexoptions**

```
IndexOptions FancyIndexing VersionSort NameWidth=* HTMLTable Charset=UTF-8
```

Global Configuration: apache2.conf, ports.conf, and envvars

The Apache configuration places global settings in the **apache2.conf** file, as well as the **ports.conf** and **envvars** files. Configuration for particular modules is located in the **modules-conf** directory. The global settings control the basic operation and performance of the web server. Here is where you set configuration locations, process ID files, timing, ports, environmental variable definitions, and default directory controls.

The **ServerRoot** directive specifies where your web server configuration files and modules are kept. This server root directory is then used as a prefix to other directory entries.

```
ServerRoot "/etc/apache2"
```

The server's process ID (PID) file is set by **PidFile**. On Ubuntu, the Process ID file is defined by APACHE_PID_FILE variable in the **/etc/apache2/envvars** file.

```
PidFile ${APACHE_PID_FILE}
```

Connection and request timing is handled by **Timeout**, **KeepAlive**, **MaxKeepAlive**, and **KeepAliveTimeout** directives. **Timeout** is the time in seconds that the web server times out a send or receive request. **KeepAlive** allows persistent connections, several requests from a client on the same connection. This is turned off by default. **KeepAliveRequests** sets the maximum number of requests on a persistent connection. **KeepAliveTimeout** is the time that a given connection to a client is kept open to receive more requests from that client.

Additional directives set user and group, local directory configuration files, and logs. The User and Group directives set the User and Group that run the Apache server. The

APACHE_RUN_USERS and the APACHE_RUN_GROUP variables are set in the **/etc/apache2/envvars** file. The name of the user and group is **www-data**.

```
User ${APACHE_RUN_USERS}
Group ${APACHE_RUN_GROUP}
```

The **Listen** directive will bind the server to a specific port or IP address. By default this is port 80. The Listen directive is defined in the **/etc/apache2/ports.conf** file.

```
Listen 80
```

Directory security defaults in apache2.conf

One of the most flexible aspects of Apache is its ability to configure individual directories. With the **Directory** directive, you can define a block of directives that apply only to a particular directory. Such a directive can be placed in the **apache2.conf** configuration file.

You can also use an **.htaccess** file within a particular directory to hold configuration directives. Those directives are then applied only to that directory. The name ".htaccess" is set with the **AccessFileName** directive. You can change this if you want.

```
AccessFileName .htaccess
```

Several default Directory blocks are defined in the **apache2.conf** file to control access to your Web site. All of them prevent the use of **.htaccess** files in their directories by setting the AllowOverride directive to none.

```
  AllowOverride None
```

For the Web site's root directory, /, symbolic links are allowed.

```
<Directory />
    Options FollowSymLinks
    AllowOverride None
    Require all denied
</Directory>

<Directory /usr/share>
    AllowOverride None
    Require all granted
</Directory>
```

Then the directory block is defined for the Web site directory, **/var/www/**. This is the location for all the Web site files. The "Require all granted" directive will allow anyone to access the files. Keep in mind that the Web site's document directory is defined by the DocumentRoot directive as **/var/www/html** in the site's sites-available configuration file.

```
<Directory "/var/www">
    Options Indexes FollowSymLinks
    AllowOverride None
    Require all granted
</Directory>
```

An additional commented directive is listed for the srv directory, should you want to enable it.

```
#<Directory "/srv ">
#    Options Indexes FollowSymLinks
#    AllowOverride None
#    Require all granted
#</Directory>
```

The Options directive specifies options to display default indexes, allows symbolic links, and supports MultiViews. The Indexes option will list files, should there be no default page for the directory (DirectoryIndex). MultiViews supports content negotiation, like using a particular language or a preferred image type.

```
  Options Indexes FollowSymLinks MultiViews
```

To deny access to the **.htaccess** files by Web clients, a FilesMatch block is defined with the access control directives "Require all denied", which denies access to all users. The FilesMatch directive references any file beginning with **.ht** (the period is quoted with a backslash). The FilesMatch directive allows the use of regular expressions, in this case, the ^ expression. The </FilesMatch> entry ends the <Files> block.

```
<FilesMatch ~ "^\.ht">
    Require all denied
</Files>
```

logs

For efficiency, the HostnameLookups operation is turned off. HostnameLookups, if turned on, would log all Web clients, generating a DNS server search for each client that accesses the Web server.

```
HostnameLookups Off
```

ErrorLog specifies the location of the log file (APACHE_LOG_DIR is set in the **/etc/apache2/envvars** file).

```
ErrorLog ${APACHE_LOG_DIR}/error.log
```

LogLevel sets the level at which messages should be logged. The warn level is usually used, though you can choose others like notice, info, debug, as well as more serious ones like crit, alert, and emerg.

```
LogLevel warn
```

The LogFormat directive defines some nicknames to be used with the CustomLog directive, like host_combined, common, and referrer. These are the formats in which messages are saved in the log file. The formats use substitution symbols like **%h** for the host, **%t** for the time, and **%u** for the user. The following defines a common format that displays the host, remote logname, user, time, the first line of the request in quotes, status, and size. The substitution characters are listed at **http://httpd.apache.org/docs/2.3/mod/mod_log_config.html**.

```
LogFormat "%h %l %u %t \"%r\" %>s %O" common
```

The CustomLog directive defines a default log for virtual hosts that don't define one. It is now defined in the **/etc/apache2/conf-available/other-vhosts-access-log** file, which is read by the **apache2.conf** file. The format used is the **vhost_combined** format.

```
CustomLog ${APACHE_LOG_DIR}/other_vhosts_access.log   vhost_combined
```

Included files in apache2.conf

The **apache2.conf** file will include all module, port, and site configuration files with the **Include** and **IncludeOptional** directives. Specialized configurations will be located in the **conf-available** directory.

```
# Include module configuration:
IncludeOptional mods-enabled/*.load
IncludeOptional mods-enabled/*.conf
# Include ports listing
Include ports.conf
# Include generic snippets of statements
IncludeOptional conf-enabled/*.conf
# Include the virtual host configurations:
IncludeOptional sites-enabled/*.conf
```

MPM Configuration: mods-available

Configuration settings for MPM prefork, worker, and event modules let you tailor your Apache web server to your workload demands. Default entries will already be set for a standard web server operating under a light load. You can modify these settings for different demands. These setting are located in the **mods-available** directory in the **mpm_prefork.conf**, **mpm_worker.conf**, and **mpm_event.conf** files. A link in the **mods-enabled** directory shows the one enabled, usually the **mpm_prefork** module. Use **a2enmod** to enable the module you want.

Three MPM modules commonly available to UNIX and Linux systems are prefork, worker, and event. The prefork module supports one thread per process, which maintains compatibility with older systems and modules. The worker module supports multiple threads for each process, placing a much lower load on system resources. The event module serves more requests simultaneously. They share several of the same directives, such as **StartServer** and **MaxRequestPerChild**. Ubuntu currently uses the worker modules.

Apache runs a single parent process with as many child processes as are needed to handle requests. Configuration for MPM modules focuses on the number of processes that should be available. The prefork module will list server numbers as a process is started for each server; the worker module will control threads, since it uses threads for each process. The **StartServer** directive lists the number of server processes to start for both modules. This will normally be larger for the prefork than for the worker module.

In the prefork module (**mpm_prefork.conf**) you need to set minimum and maximum settings for spare servers. **MaxClients** sets the maximum number of servers that can be started, and **ServerLimit** sets the number of servers allowed. The **MaxRequestsPerChild** sets the maximum number of requests allowed for a server.

```
<IfModule mpm_prefork_module>
    StartServers           5
    MinSpareServers        5
    MaxSpareServers       10
    MaxClients           150
    MaxRequestsPerChild    0
</IfModule>
```

The directives serve as a kind of throttle on the web server access, controlling processes to keep available, and limiting the resources that can be used. In the prefork configuration, the **StartServer** is set number to 5, and the spare minimum to 5, with the maximum spare as 20. This means that initially 5 server processes will be started up and will wait for requests, along with 5 spare processes. When server processes are no longer being used, they will be terminated until the number of these spare processes is less than 10. The maximum number of server processes that can be started is 150.

In the worker MPM (**mpm_worker.conf**), only 2 server processes are initially started (StartServer). Spare threads are set at 25 and 75. The maximum number of threads is set at 150, with the threads per child at 25. **MaxClients** sets the maximum number of client threads, and **ThreadsPerChild** sets the number of threads for each server. **MaxRequestsPerChild** limits the maximum number of requests for a server.

```
<IfModule mpm_worker_module>
    StartServers          2
    MinSpareThreads      25
    MaxSpareThreads      75
    ThreadLimit          64
    ThreadsPerChild      25
    MaxClients          150
    MaxRequestsPerChild   0
</IfModule>
```

The event MPM is based on the worker MPM and has the same configuration. It is designed to pass off processing to supporting threads, freeing up the main threads to handle new requests.

Error Messages: conf-available/localized-error-pages.conf

Configured in the **conf-available/localized-error-pages** file, and included in the **apache2.conf** file with other **conf-available** files, are directives for internationalized error messages. The LanguagePriority directive lets you rank the languages to use. The mod_alias, mod_include, and mod_negotiation modules have to be loaded. The Alias and Directory directives specify the error directory as **/usr/share/apache2/error**. Here you will find **.var** files for different error messages, like HTTP_BAD_GATEWAY.html.var. These **.var** files contain configuration for displaying the messages in the languages specified by LanguagePriority directive. Some of the key internationalization error directives are shown here:

```
Alias /error/ "/usr/share/apache2/error'
LanguagePriority en cs de es fr it nl sv pg-br ro
ErrorDocument 502 /error/HTTP_BAD_GATEWAY.html.var
```

Security: conf-available/security.conf

Configured in the **conf-available/security** file, and included in the **apache2.conf** file with other **conf-available** files, are directives for site security. Most entries are commented out. ServerTokens determines the content of the site's response header. On Ubuntu, it is set to OS to return the operating system type. ServerSignature is set to On, which adds server version and hostname information for server generated pages. TraceEnable is set to Off to disable trace requests.

cgi-bin: conf-available/serve-cgi-bin.conf

Configured in the **conf-available/serve-cgi-bin** file, and included in the **apache2.conf** file with other **conf-available** files, are directives for site cgi-bin directory access. The cgi-bin directory holds the Web site's executable scripts like the CGI (Common Gateway Interface) and SSI (Server Side Includes) scripts. An alias is set up for the cgi-bin directory, which is actually located at **/usr/lib/cgi-bin**.

```
ScriptAlias /cgi-bin/ /usr/lib/cgi-bin/
```

Controls are then placed on the **/usr/lib/cgi-bin** directory. All users are allowed access. Options designate that CGI programs can be executed and symbolic links are allowed if the owner's match. Multiviews are not allowed. The ExeCGI option allows the execution of CGI scripts. The + and - signs are used to indicate whether an option is turned on or off. If you use a + and - sign for one option, you have to use them for all.

```
<Directory "/usr/lib/cgi-bin">
  AllowOverride None
  Options +ExecCGI -MultiViews +SymLinksIfOwnerMatch
  Require all granted
</Directory>
```

The configuration file will also check for the existence of the **mod_cgi** and **mod_cgid** modules, defining the ENABLE_USR_LIB_CGI_BIN variable if found..

Documentation: conf-available/apache2-doc.conf

If you installed the **apache-doc** package, documentation is set up for you at **/usr/share/doc/apache2-doc**. The configuration file for the apache documentation is at **/etc/apache2/conf-available/apache2-doc.conf**. The manual directory is aliased **(/usr/share/doc/apache2-doc/manual**) and controls are set up to allow access from all users.

```
Alias /manual/ /usr/share/doc/apache2-doc/manual/

<Directory "/usr/share/doc/apache2-doc/manual/">
    Options Indexes FollowSymLinks
    AllowOverride None
    Require all granted
    AddDefaultCharset off
</Directory>
```

Site-Level Configuration Directives

Site specific information is kept in the site's configuration files in **/etc/apache2/sites-available** directory. The **000-default.conf** site configuration file will hold directives for the main server. A **default-ssl.conf** file holds configuration for a main server with SSL support. The site configuration files hold site-specific information like Directory directives for their Web pages and server information like the administrator address. Authentication controls can be placed on particular directives. You can use the default configuration file as a partial model.

The site configuration files begin with few directives. Most global, module, and default directives are already enabled by the **apache2.conf** file, the added configuration files (**conf-available** directory), and the module configuration files (**modules-conf** directory). The actual site configuration file initially has only a few directives. You can add ones that you want to apply to that site.

A site configuration begins with a **VirtualHost** directive. The directive can name a particular IP address of a site or ***:80** for the main server (you can use a fully qualified domain name instead of the IP address, but this is not recommended). The directive block ends with a **</VirtualHost>** directive at the end of the file. Your site specific directives like Directory directives are placed within the block. Keep in mind that all the site level configurations that are enabled will be read directly as if they were part of one large **apache2.conf** file.

```
<VirtualHost *:80>
</VirtualHost>
```

The following is an example of the **ServerAdmin** directive used to set the address where users can send mail for administrative issues. The default entry is **webmaster@localhost**. You can replace this with the address you want to use to receive system administration mail.

```
ServerAdmin webmaster@localhost
```

The **DocumentRoot** directive specifies where the Web server's HTML files are located. On Ubuntu this is the **/var/www/html** directory.

```
DocumentRoot /var/www/html
```

The ServerName directive (not used for the default host) determines the name of the virtual host.

```
ServerName www.example.com
```

Virtual Hosting on Apache

All sites are treated as virtual hosts configured by their site configuration files in **/etc/apashe2/sites-available** directory. In effect, the server can act as several servers, each hosted website appearing separate to outside users.

Apache supports both IP address–based and name-based virtual hosting. IP address–based virtual hosts use valid registered IP addresses, whereas name-based virtual hosts use fully qualified domain addresses. These domain addresses are provided by the host header from the requesting browser. The server can then determine the correct virtual host to use on the basis of the domain name alone. See **http://httpd.apache.org** for more information.

You can enable or disable a virtual site with the **a2dissite** and **a2ensite** commands. . Enabled sites are listed as symbolic links in the **/etc/apache2/sites-enabled** directory.

Virtual Host for main server: 000-default.conf

The main server must also have a virtual host configuration. This is set up by Ubuntu as the default configuration in the sites-available directory, **/etc/apache2/sites-available/000-default**. For the main server, the **VirtualHost** directive uses an * as its name with its port, 80. The directive block begins with **<VirtualHost *:80>** and ends with **</VirtualHost>**. The DocumentRoot is set to **/var/www/**, the location of the Web server's HTML files and subdirectories.

```
<VirtualHost *:80>
 ServerAdmin webmaster@localhost
 DocumentRoot /var/www/html
...
</VirtualHost>
```

For logging, the ErrorLog location is specified and the LogLevel is set at warn. The log display format used is combined (APACHE_LOG_DIR is defined in **/etc/apache2/envvars**).

```
  LogLevel warn
  ErrorLog ${APACHE_LOG_DIR}/error.log
  CustomLog ${APACHE_LOG_DIR}/access.log combined
```

Should you have an alias for your main host, you can specify that using an added Virtual host directive that also uses the *:80 name, but with the alias as the ServerName. The following example sets up the default for the main Web server host as well as an alias, **www.turtle.com** and **www.turtle.org**.

```
<VirtualHost *:80>
 ServerName www.turtle.com
 ServerAdmin webmaster@mail.turtle.com
 DocumentRoot /var/www/html
</VirtualHost>

<VirtualHost 192.168.1.5>
 ServerName www.turtle.org
 ServerAdmin webmaster@mail.turtle.com
 DocumentRoot /var/www/html
</VirtualHost>
```

You may want to modify the **/etc/apache2/sites-available/000-default.conf** configuration file to reflect the server name and mail address you want to use for your site.

A copy of the **/etc/apache2/sites-available/000-default.conf** file is shown here.

```
<VirtualHost *:80>
  ServerAdmin webmaster@localhost

  DocumentRoot /var/www/html

  # Possible values include: debug, info, notice, warn, error, crit,
  # alert, emerg.
  # LogLevel warn

  ErrorLog ${APACHE_LOG_DIR}/error.log
  CustomLog ${APACHE_LOG_DIR}/access.log combined

</VirtualHost>
```

Site and Global Configuration

It may be the case that certain directives that are configured globally, you may want to configure just for particular sites. This would entail turning off their global configuration, and enabling them on a site by site basis. As an example, access to the cgi-bin directory is currently global, with its **conf-available/serve-cgi-bin.conf** file enabled by a link to it in the **conf-enabled** directory. If you only want a few sites to have access to the **cgi-bin** directory, instead of all of them (global), you would disable the global link. Then, in the **sites-available** files for those sites you want to give access to the cgi-bin directory, you would insert an **include** statement for the serve-cgi-bin.conf file.

Use the **a2disconf** command to disable the global use of the configuration file. This removes its link in the **/etc/apache2/conf-enabled** directory.

```
a2disconf serve-cgi-bin.conf
```

Add the following include statement to the site files for the sites you want to have access to the cgi-bin directory.

```
include conf-available/serve-cgi-bin.conf
```

Virtual Host for main server: default-ssl.conf

The **default-ssl.conf** file has the same entries as the default site file, but adds directives for SSL. The directives are explained with detailed comments. Several directives are commented out, which you can enable as you need them, like those for the certificate authority, revocation lists, client authentication, SSL options, and access control. The virtual host is set to use port 443, **<Virtualhost_default_:443>**.

In the SSL Engine Switch section, SSL is enabled.

```
SSLEngine on
```

A self-signed SLL certificate is specified

```
SSLCertificateFile    /etc/ssl/certs/ssl-cert-snakeoil.pem
SSLCertificateKeyFile /etc/ssl/private/ssl-cert-snakeoil.key
```

SSL options are applied to the Web site files and the cgi-bin.

```
<FilesMatch "\.(cgi|shtml|phtml|php)$">
    SSLOptions +StdEnvVars
  </FilesMatch>
  <Directory /usr/lib/cgi-bin>
    SSLOptions +StdEnvVars
  </Directory>
```

For an SSL enabled Web server to work you will need an SSL certificate and key specific to your Web site to implement SSL encryption. See the followings section in the Ubuntu Server Guide for details:

```
https://help.ubuntu.com/stable/serverguide/certificates-and-security.html
```

Creating Virtual Hosts

The easiest way to create a new Virtual host is to copy the default file, giving it the name of the new Web site. Then edit the file to add the ServerName directive with the domain name of the Web site. Be sure to change the ServerAdmin, DocumentRoot, ErrorLog, and CustomLog directives. You also could remove the document directives. The following example implements a name-based virtual host, **www.mypics.com**. A subdirectory for the Web site has to be created in the **/var/www** directory, in this case, **/var/www/mypics/**, with the DocumentRoot at

/var/www/mypics/. The Directory directive now references the **/var/www/mypics/** directory. The **/usr/share/doc** Directory directives are not needed. If you wanted to allow the use of **.htaccess** files on this site you would change the AllowOverride directive to **all**. You also have to add a subdirectory in the Apache log directory for the logs such as **/var/log/apache2/mypics**, (APACHE_LOG_DIR). Basic steps would include the following:

Create a configuration file in **/etc/apache2/sites-available**

Create a directory for the Web site documents at **/var/www/**

Create a subdirectory for the Web site log files at **/var/log/apache2/**

If your virtual host is referenced by other domain names, you can specify them with the **ServerAlias** directive, listing the domain names within the selected **VirtualHost** block.

```
ServerAlias www.greatpics.org
```

A sample configuration file called here **mypics** would be placed in the **sites-available** directory. The file is shown here with ServerName and ServerAlias directives included.

```
<VirtualHost *:80>
 ServerName www.mypics.com
 ServerAdmin webmaster@mail.mypics.com
 ServerAlias www.greatpics.org
 DocumentRoot /var/www/mypics/


  <Directory /var/www/mypics/>
    Options Indexes FollowSymLinks MultiViews
    AllowOverride None
    Require all granted
  </Directory>

  ErrorLog ${APACHE_LOG_DIR}/mypics/error_log
  LogLevel warn
  CustomLog ${APACHE_LOG_DIR}/mypics/access.log combined

</VirtualHost>
```

Once configured, you would then activate the site with the **a2ensite** command.

```
sudo a2ensite mypics
```

Name-based Virtual Hosts

The Apache default configuration described in the previous section uses name-based virtual hosting. With name-based virtual hosting, you can support any number of virtual hosts using no additional IP addresses. With only a single IP address for your machine, you can still support an unlimited number of virtual hosts. Such a capability is made possible by the HTTP/1.1 protocol, which lets a server identify the name by which it is being accessed. This method requires the client, the remote user, to use a browser that supports the HTTP/1.1 protocol, as current browsers do. A browser using such a protocol can send a host header specifying the particular host to use on a machine.

If you are using a particular IP address for your Web site, you would use that address instead of the port number in the VirtualHost directive. To implement name-based virtual hosting for a particular IP address, you use a **VirtualHost** directive and a **NameVirtualHost** directive to specify the IP address you want to use for the virtual hosts. If your system has only one IP address, you need to use that address. Within the **VirtualHost** directives, you use the **ServerName** directive to specify the domain name you want to use for that host. Using **ServerName** to specify the domain name is important to avoid a DNS lookup. A DNS lookup failure disables the virtual host. The **VirtualHost** directives each take as their argument the same IP address specified in the **NameVirtualHost** directive. You use Apache directives within the **VirtualHost** blocks to configure each host separately. Name-based virtual hosting uses the domain name address specified in a host header to determine the virtual host to use. If no such information exists, the first host is used as the default.

Here, **www.mypics.com** and **www.myproj.org** are implemented as name-based virtual hosts instead of IP-based hosts. Though on Ubuntu these would be placed in separate sites-available files, they are shown here together to make for a clearer example, with directives for the main server added (turtle.mytrek.com).

```
ServerName turtle.mytrek.com
NameVirtualHost 192.168.1.5

<VirtualHost 192.168.1.5>
 ServerName www.mypics.com
 ServerAdmin webmaster@mail.mypics.com
 DocumentRoot /var/www/mypics/html
 ErrorLog /var/www/mypics/logs/error_log
 ...
</VirtualHost>

<VirtualHost 192.168.1.5>
 ServerName www.myproj.org
 ServerAdmin webmaster@mail.myproj.org
 DocumentRoot /var/www/myproj/html
 ErrorLog /var/www/myproj/logs/error_log
 ....
</VirtualHost>
```

If your system has only one IP address, implementing virtual hosts prevents access to your main server with that address. You could no longer use your main server as a Web server directly; you could use it only indirectly to manage your virtual host. You could configure a virtual host to manage your main server's Web pages. You would then use your main server to support a set of virtual hosts that would function as Web sites, rather than the main server operating as one site directly. This is the approach implemented by Ubuntu for the Apache Web server.

If your machine has two or more IP addresses, you can use one for the main server and the other for your virtual hosts. You can even mix IP-based virtual hosts and name-based virtual hosts on your server. You can also use separate IP addresses to support different sets of virtual hosts.

Dynamic Virtual Hosting

If you have implemented many virtual hosts on your server that have the same configuration, you can use a technique called dynamic virtual hosting to have these virtual hosts generated dynamically. The code for implementing your virtual hosts becomes much smaller, and as a result, your server accesses them faster. Adding yet more virtual hosts becomes a simple matter of creating appropriate directories and adding entries for them in the DNS server.

To make dynamic virtual hosting work, the server uses commands in the **mod_vhost_alias** module (supported in Apache version 1.3.6 and up) to rewrite both the server name and the document root to those of the appropriate virtual server (for older Apache versions before 1.3.6, you use the mod_rewrite module). Dynamic virtual hosting can be either name-based or IP-based. In either case, you have to set the **UseCanonicalName** directive in such a way as to allow the server to use the virtual hostname instead of the server's own name. For name-based hosting, simply turn off **UseCanonicalName**. This allows your server to obtain the hostname from the host header of the user request. For IP-based hosting, you set the **UseCanonicalName** directive to DNS. This allows the server to look up the host in the DNS server.

```
UseCanonicalName Off
UseCanonicalName DNS
```

You then have to enable the server to locate the different document root directories and CGI bin directories for your various virtual hosts. You use the **VirtualDocumentRoot** directive to specify the template for virtual host directories. For example, if you place the different host directories in the **/var/www/hosts** directory, you can then set the **VirtualDocumentRoot** directive accordingly.

```
VirtualDocumentRoot /var/www/hosts/%0/html
```

The %0 will be replaced with the virtual host's name when that virtual host is accessed. It is important that you create the dynamic virtual host's directory using that host's name. For example, for a dynamic virtual host called **www.mygolf.org**, you first create a directory named **/var/www/hosts/www.mygolf.org**, and then create subdirectories for the document root and CGI programs, as in **/var/www/hosts/www.mygolf.org/html**. For the CGI directory, use the **VirtualScriptAlias** directive to specify the CGI subdirectory you use.

```
VirtualScriptAlias /var/www/hosts/%0/cgi-bin
```

A simple example of name-based dynamic virtual hosting directives follows:

```
UseCanonicalName Off
VirtualDocumentRoot /var/www/hosts/%0/html
VirtualScriptAlias /var/www/hosts/%0/cgi-bin
```

A request for **www.mygolf.com/html/mypage** evaluates to

```
/var/www/hosts/www.mygolf.com/html/mypage
```

A simple example of dynamic virtual hosting is shown here:

```
UseCanonicalName Off
NameVirtualHost 192.168.1.5

<VirtualHost 192.168.1.5>
 ServerName www.mygolf.com
 ServerAdmin webmaster@mail.mygolf.com
 VirtualDocumentRoot /var/www/hosts/%0/html
 VirtualScriptAlias /var/www/hosts/%0/cgi-bin
```

```
...
</VirtualHost>
```

To implement IP-based dynamic virtual hosting instead, set the **UseCanonicalName** to DNS instead of Off.

```
UseCanonicalName DNS
VirtualDocumentRoot /var/www/hosts/%0/html
VirtualScriptAlias /var/www/hosts/%0/cgi-bin
```

Interpolated Strings

The mod_vhost_alias module supports various interpolated strings, each beginning with a % symbol and followed by a number. The `%0` symbol references the entire web address. `%1` references only the first segment, `%2` references the second, `%-1` references the last part, and `%2+` references from the second part on. For example, to use only the second part of a web address for the directory name, use the following directives:

```
VirtualDocumentRoot /var/www/hosts/%2/html
VirtualScriptAlias /var/www/hosts/%2/cgi-bin
```

In this case, a request made for **www.mygolf.com/html/mypage** uses only the second part of the web address. This would be "mygolf" in **www.mygolf.com**, and would evaluate to

```
/var/www/hosts/mygolf/html/mypage
```

If you used `%2+` instead, as in **/var/www/hosts/%2/html**, the request for **www.mygolf.com/html/mypage** would evaluate to

```
/var/www/hosts/mygolf.com/html/mypage
```

The same method works for IP addresses, where `%1` references the first IP address segment, `%2` references the second, and so on.

Logs for Dynamic Virtual Hosts

One drawback of dynamic virtual hosting is that you can set up only one log for all your hosts. However, you can create your own shell program to simply cut out the entries for the different hosts in that log.

```
LogFormat "%V %h %l %u %t \"%r\" %s %b" vcommon
CustomLog logs/access_log vcommon
```

Note: Apache also supports IP address–based virtual hosting. Your server must have a different IP address for each virtual host. Your machine can have separate physical network connections for each one. You can configure Apache to run a separate daemon for each virtual host, separately listening for each IP address, or you can have a single daemon running that listens for requests for all the virtual hosts. To set up a single daemon to manage all virtual hosts, use **VirtualHost** directives. To set up a separate daemon for each host, also use the **Listen** directive.

9. News and Database Services

Newsgroup servers are used for setting up newsgroups for local networks or for supporting the Internet's Usenet News service. Database servers are being used to manage large collections of data on local networks as well as for Internet services.

News Servers

News servers provide Internet users with Usenet news services. They have their own TCP/IP protocol, the Network News Transfer Protocol (NNTP). On most Linux systems, the InterNetNews (INN) news server is used to provide news services (**http://www.isc.org**). INN news servers access Usenet newsfeeds, providing news clients on your network with the full range of newsgroups and articles. Newsgroup articles are transferred using NNTP, and servers that support this protocol are known as *NNTP servers.* INN was written by Rich Salz and is currently maintained and supported by the Internet Software Consortium (ISC). You can download current versions from its website at **http://www.isc.org**. The documentation directory for INN in **/usr/share/doc** contains extensive samples. The primary program for INN is the **innd** daemon. There are two versions of INN, a smaller INN used for local networks, and a much more complex INN2 used for large networks. Ubuntu uses INN.

INN also includes several support programs to provide maintenance and crash recovery and to perform statistical analysis on server performance and usage. **cleanfeed** implements spam protection, and **innreport** generates INN reports based on logs. INN also features a strong filter system for screening unwanted articles.

Note: Leafnode is an NNTP news server designed for small networks that may have slow connections to the Internet. You can install the Leafnode software package (**leafnode**) using **apt-get** or the Synaptic Package Manager. Documentation is available at **http://leafnode.org**. Along with the Leafnode NNTP server, the software package includes several utilities such as Fetchnews, Texpire, and NewsQ that send, delete, and display news articles. **slrnpull** is a simple single-user version of Leafnode that can be used only with the slrn newsreader.

Database Servers: MySQL and PostgreSQL

Two fully functional database servers are included with most Linux distributions, MySQL and PostgreSQL. MySQL is by far the more popular of the two, though PostgreSQL is noted for providing more features. You can learn more about these products through the sites listed in Table 9-1. Check the Ubuntu Server Guide | Databases for basic configuration.

`https://help.ubuntu.com/stable/serverguide/databases.html`

Relational Database Structure

MySQL and PostgreSQL both use a relational database structure. In a relational database, data is placed in tables, with identifier fields used to relate the data to entries in other tables. Each row in the table is a record, each with a unique identifier, like a record number. The connections between records in different tables are implemented by special tables that associate the unique identifiers from records in one table with those of another.

Database	Resource	Packages
MySQL	**http://mysql.com**	**mysql-server** **mysql-client**
PostgreSQL	**http://postgresql.org**	**postgresql**

Table 9-1: Database Resources

A simple, single-table database has no need for a unique identifier. A simple address book listing names and addresses is an example of a single-table database. However, most databases access complex information of different types, related in various ways. Instead of having large records with repeated information, you divide the data among different tables, each holding the unique instance of the data. This way, data is not repeated; you have only one table that holds a single record for a person's name, rather than repeating that person's name each time the data references him or her. The relational organization then takes on the task of relating one piece of data to another. This way, you can store a great deal of information using relatively small database files.

Though there are many ways to implement a relational database, a simple rule of thumb is to organize data into tables where you have a unique instance of each item of data. Each record is given a unique identifier, usually a number. To associate the records in one table with another, you create tables that associate their identifiers.

The Structured Query Language (SQL) is used by most relational database management systems (RDBMSs), including both MySQL and PostgreSQL. The following command will create the database:

```
CREATE DATABASE myphotos
```

Before performing any operations on a database, you first access it with the USE command.

```
USE myphotos
```

The tables are created using the CREATE TABLE command; the fields for each table are listed within parentheses following the table name. For each field, you need to specify a name, data type, and other options, such as whether it can have a null value or not.

```
CREATE TABLE names (
    personid INT(5) UNSIGNED NOT NULL,
    name VARCHAR(20) NOT NULL,
    street VARCHAR(30) NOT NULL,
    phone CHAR(8)
     );
```

MySQL

MySQL is structured on a client/server model with a server daemon (**mysqld**) filling requests from client programs. MySQL is designed for speed, reliability, and ease of use. It is meant to be a fast database management system for large databases and, at the same time, a reliable one, suitable for intensive use. To create databases, you use the standard SQL language. User access can be controlled by assigning privileges.

On Ubuntu you can install MySQL server and client packages, along with numerous MySQL configuration packages for certain services like Postfix, Exim, and Apache. The packages to install are **mysql-client**, **mysql-common**, and **mysql-server**. Documentation is held in the **mysql-doc** package and installed at **/usr/share/doc/mysql-doc**.

MySQL is managed by **systemd** using the **/lib/systemd/system/mysql.service** unit file. For the service file you can create a version of it in the **/etc/systemd/system** directory, which includes the original version. You would create a version in **/etc/systemd/system** that includes the system version in **/lib/systemd/system**. Then you add a Service section with added options, as shown here.

/etc/systemd/system/mysql.service

```
.include /lib/systemd/system/mysqld.service
 [Service]
  LimitNOFILE=10000
```

Alternatively you can create a **.conf** in the **/etc/systemd/system/mysql.service.d** directory.

The **mysql.service** file is shown here.

mysql.service

```
# MySQL systemd service file

[Unit]
Description=MySQL Community Server
After=network.target
After=syslog.target

[Install]
WantedBy=multi-user.target

[Service]
User=mysql
Group=mysql
PermissionsStartOnly=true
ExecStartPre=/usr/share/mysql/mysql-systemd-start pre
ExecStart=/usr/bin/mysqld_safe
ExecStartPost=/usr/share/mysql/mysql-systemd-start post
TimeoutSec=600
Restart=on-failure
RuntimeDirectory=mysqld
RuntimeDirectoryMode=755
```

MySQL Configuration

The MySQL supports three different configuration files, one for global settings, another for server-specific settings, and an optional one for user-customized settings.

The **/etc/mysql/my.cnf** configuration file is used for global settings applied to both clients and servers. It is a link the **/etc/mysql/mysql.cnf** file, which includes configuration files from the **/etc/mysql/conf.d** and the **/etc/mysql/mysql.conf.d** directories. The **conf.d** directory hold the **mysql.cnf** file, which provides user configuration, and the **mysql.conf.d** directory holds the **mysqld.cnf** file, which holds server configuration.

The **/etc/mysql/mysql.conf.d/mysqld.cnf** file provides the MySQL server settings.

The **.my.cnf** file allows users to customize their access to MySQL. It is located in a user's home directory. Note that this is a dot file.

Global Configuration:/etc/mysql/mysql.conf.d/mysqld.cnf

MySQL specifies options according to different groups, usually the names of server tools. The options are arranged in group segments. The group name is placed within brackets, and options applied to it follow. A selection of MySQL directives in the **mysqld** section of the **/etc/mysql/mysql.conf.d/mysqld.cnf** file is shown here:

```
[mysqld]
user = mysql
pid-file = /var/run/mysqld/mysqld.pid
socket = /var/run/mysqld/mysqld.sock
port = 3306
basedir = /usr
datadir = /var/lib/mysql
tmpdir = /tmp
bind-address = 127.0.0.1
log_error = /var/log/mysql/errorlog
expire_logs_days = 10
max_binlog_size = 100M
```

Options are set up according to groups that control different behaviors of the MySQL server: `mysqld` for the daemon and `mysqld_safe` for the MySQL startup script. The `datadir` directory, **/var/lib/mysql**, is where your database files will be placed. Server tools and daemons are located in the `basedir` directory, **/usr**, and the user that MySQL will run as, has the name **mysql**, as specified in the `user` option.

A **mysql_safe** group will set up options to be sent to clients, such as the port and socket to use to access the MySQL database.

```
[mysqld_safe]
port=3306
socket=/var/run/mysqld/mysqld.sock
```

To see what options are currently set for both client and server, you run `mysqld` directly with the `--help` option.

```
/usr/libexec/mysqld --help
```

MySQL networking

The network services for which MySQL databases are used, such as the Apache Web server, require that hosts on your network be allowed to access a MySQL database. In effect, the MySQL database can operate as a network database server. To allow other hosts on your network to access your MySQL database, you have to set the MySQL to accept access from a network source. You do this with the **bind-address** option in the **mysqld** section of the **/etc/mysql/my.cnf**

configuration file. Initially this is set to the localhost, 127.0.0.1, allowing access only for your local machine.

```
bind-address = 127.0.0.1
```

If the address is allocated dynamically by a DHCP server, comment out the bind-address entry with a # sign. If the bind-address option is not set, the default is to allow any access. This is also a quick way to enable network access to MySQL databases used by a network server like the Apache Web server.

```
# bind-address = 127.0.0.1
```

To allow access from a specific local network, you can change the bind-address entry to the IP address of your machine on that network. Should your local network access on your machine use an additional dedicated network device, you can use the IP address of that network device.

```
bind-address = 192.168.0.52
```

If you want to allow MySQL to use several network interfaces, including **localhost**, you would set the bind-address to 0.0.0.0. This allows MySQL to use all your network interfaces.

```
bind-address = 0.0.0.0
```

To deny any kind of network access, including localhost, you can use the skip-networking option.

```
skip-networking
```

Also, make sure that your firewall has enabled access on the port that the MySQL server is using. The default port for MySQL is 3306.

For the **ufw** default firewall, you would use the following command. The ufw firewall maintains its IPtables files in **/etc/ufw**. You can also use the Gufw tool (desktop) to add access on the Simple tab for port 3306.

```
sudo ufw allow 3306/tcp
```

If you are managing your IPtables firewall directly, you could manage access directly by adding the following IPtables rule. This accepts input on port 3306 for TCP/IP protocol packages.

```
iptables -A INPUT -p tcp --dport 3306 -j ACCEPT
```

User Configuration: .my.cnf

Users who access the database server will have their own configuration file in their home directory: **.my.cnf**. Here the user can specify connection options, such as the password used to access the database and the connection timeouts.

```
 [client]
password=mypassword

[mysql]
no-auto-rehash
set-variable = connect_timeout=2

[mysql-hotcopy]
interactive-timeout
```

MySQL Tools

MySQL provides a variety of tools (as shown in Table 9-2), including server, client, and administrative tools. Backups can be handled with the **mysqldump** command. The **mysqlshow** command will display a database, just as issuing the SQL command **SELECT *.*** does, and **mysqlimport** can import text files, just like LOAD INFILE.

Command	Description
mysqld	MySQL server
mysql	MySQL client
mysqladmin	Creates and administers databases
mysqldump	Database backup
mysqlimport	Imports text files
mysqlshow	Displays databases

Table 9-2: MySQL Commands

To manage your MySQL database, you use **mysql** as the **root** user. The **mysql** client starts up the MySQL monitor. As the root user, you can enter administrative commands to create databases and database tables, add or remove entries, and carry out standard client tasks such as displaying data. Open a terminal window. Then enter the **mysql** command with the **-u root** and the **-p** option. You will be prompted for a MySQL password. When you installed MySQL server, you were prompted to enter a password. This is the password you need to use to access the MySQL monitor.

```
mysql -u root -p
mysql>
```

MySQL Management with mysql and mysqladmin

This command will start a MySQL monitor shell with a **mysql>** prompt. Be sure to end your commands with a semicolon; otherwise, the monitor will provide an indented arrow prompt waiting for added arguments. In the monitor, the semicolon, not the ENTER key, ends commands, however, once you enter the semi-colon, you then press the ENTER key to execute the command.

Once the **mysql** client has started, you can use the **status** command to check the status of your server and **show databases** to list current databases.

```
mysql> status;
mysql> show databases;
```

A mysql database is initialy set up for its own management.

PostgreSQL

PostgreSQL is based on the POSTGRESQL database management system, though it uses SQL as its query language. POSTGRESQL is a next-generation research prototype developed at the University of California, Berkeley. You can learn more about it from the PostgreSQL website at

http://www.postgresql.org. PostgreSQL is an open source project, developed under the GPL license. You can install PostgreSQL using the **postgresql** package.

PostgreSQL is often used to provide database support for Internet servers with heavy demands, such as web servers. With a few simple commands, you can create relational database tables. Use the **`createuser`** command to create a PostgreSQL user with which you can log in to the server. You can then create a database with the **`createdb`** command and construct relational tables using the **create table** directive. With an **`insert`** command, you can add records and then view them with the **`select`** command. Access to the server by remote users is controlled by entries in the **pg_hba.conf** file located in PostgreSQL directory, usually at **/var/lib/pgsql**.

Part 3: Shared Resources

Print Services: CUPS

Network File System (NFS), Network Information System (NIS), Distributed File System (GFS)

Samba (Windows)

Cloud Computing

ubuntu

10. Print Services

Printer Services: CUPS

Printer Devices and Configuration

Installing Printers

CUPS Configuration files

CUPS Command Line Print Clients

CUPS Command Line Administrative Tools

Print services have become an integrated part of every Linux system. They allow you to use any printer on your system or network. Once treated as devices attached to a system directly, printers are now treated as network resources managed by print servers. In the case of a single printer attached directly to a system, the networking features become transparent and the printer appears as just one more device. On the other hand, you could easily use a print server's networking capability to let several systems access the same printer. Although printer installation is almost automatic on most Linux distributions, it helps to understand the underlying process. Printing sites and resources are listed in Table 10-1.

CUPS

The Common Unix Printing System (CUPS) provides printing services, developed by Apple as an open source project, and is freely available under the GNU Public License. CUPS is the primary print server for most Linux distributions, including Ubuntu. The CUPS site at **http://cups.org** provides detailed documentation on installing and managing printers. CUPS is based on the Internet Printing Protocol (IPP), which was designed to establish a printing standard for the Internet (for more information, see **http://pwg.org/ipp**). Whereas the older line printer (LPD) based printing systems focused primarily on line printers, an IPP-based system provides networking, PostScript, and web support. CUPS works like an Internet server and employs a configuration setup much like that of the Apache web server. Its network support lets clients directly access printers on remote servers, without having to configure the printers themselves. Configuration needs to be maintained only on the print servers. With **libgnomecups**, GNOME provides integrated support for CUPS, allowing GNOME-based applications to directly access CUPS printers.

Resource	Description
http://cups.org	Common Unix Printing System
http://pwg.org/ipp	Internet Printing Protocol
http://lprng.sourceforge.net/	LPRng print server (Universe repository)

Table 10-1: Print Resources

Once you have installed your printers and configured your print server, you can print and manage your print queue using print clients. A variety of print configuration tools are available for the CUPS server such as system-config-printer, the CUPS configuration tool, and various line printing tools such as `lpq` and `lpc`, described in detail later in this chapter. Check the Ubuntu Server Guide | File Servers | CUPS - Print Server for basic configuration.

`https://help.ubuntu.com/stable/serverguide/cups.html`

CUPS is managed by systemd using an on demand socket implementation with **cups.service**, **cups.socket**, and **cups.path** files. In addition, a special **printer.target** unit detects when a printer is connected to your system. The **cups.service** file runs the CUPS server, **/usr/sbin/cupsd** (ExecStart). It is run when the **printer.target** is activated, which happens when a user connects a printer (WantedBy). The **cups.socket** unit file has CUPS listen for request at the CUPS socket, **/var/run/cups/cups.sock** (ListenStream). In effect, CUPS runs like the old inetd daemons, activated only when requested. The **cups.path** unit sets up CUPS print directories at **/var/spool/cups** (PathExistsGlob) when the system starts up (WantedBy=multi-user.target).

cups.service

```
[Unit]
Description=CUPS Scheduler
Documentation=man:cupsd(8)

[Service]
ExecStart=/usr/sbin/cupsd -l
Type=simple

[Install]
Also=cups.socket cups.path
WantedBy=printer.target
```

cups.socket

```
[Unit]
Description=CUPS Scheduler

[Socket]
ListenStream=/var/run/cups/cups.sock

[Install]
WantedBy=sockets.target
```

cups.path

```
[Unit]
Description=CUPS Scheduler

[Path]
PathExists=/var/cache/cups/org.cups.cupsd

[Install]
WantedBy=multi-user.target
```

cups-browsed.service

```
[Unit]
Description=Make remote CUPS printers available locally
After=cups.service avahi-daemon.service
Wants=cups.service avahi-daemon.service

[Service]
ExecStart=/usr/sbin/cups-browsed

[Install]
WantedBy=multi-user.target
```

Note: Line Printer, Next Generation (LPRng) was the traditional print server for Linux and UNIX systems, but it has since been dropped from many Linux distributions. You can find out more about LPRng at **http://lprng.sourceforge.net/**.

Printer Devices and Configuration

Before you can use any printer, you first have to install it on a Linux system on your network. A local printer is installed directly on your own system. This involves creating an entry for the printer in a printer configuration file that defines the kind of printer it is, along with other features such as the device file and spool directory it uses. On CUPS, the printer configuration file is **/etc/cups/printers.conf**. Installing a printer is fairly simple. You determine which device file to use for the printer and the configuration entries for it.

Tip: If you cannot find the drivers for your printer, you may be able to download them from OpenPrinting database at **http://www.openprinting.org/drivers**. The site maintains an extensive listing of drivers.

Printer Device Files

Linux dynamically creates the device names for printers that are installed. USB-connected printers will be treated as a removable device that can easily be attached to other connections and still be recognized. For older printers connected to a particular port, dedicated device files will be generated. As an example, for parallel printers, the device names will be **lp0**, **lp1**, **lp2**, and so on. The number used in these names corresponds to a parallel port on your PC; **lp0** references the LPT1 parallel port and **lp1** references the LPT2 parallel port. Serial printers will use serial ports, referenced by the device files like **ttyS0**, **ttyS1**, **ttyS2**, and so on.

Printer URI (Universal Resource Identifier)

Printers can be local or remote. Both are referenced using Universal Resource Identifiers (URI). URIs support both network protocols used to communicate with remote printers, and device connections used to reference local printers.

Remote printers are referenced by the protocol used to communicate with it, like **ipp** for the Internet Printing Protocol used for UNIX network printers, **smb** for the Samba protocol used for Windows network printers, and **lpd** for the older LPRng Unix servers. Their URIs are similar to a Web URL, indicating the network address of the system the printer is connected to.

```
ipp://mytsuff.com/printers/queue1
smb://guest@lizard/myhp
```

For attached local printers, especially older ones, the URI will use the device connection and the device name. The **usb:** prefix is used for USB printers, **parallel**: for older printers connected to a parallel port, **serial:** for printers connected to a serial port, and **scsi:** for SCSI connected printers.

In the CUPS **/etc/cups/printers.conf** file the DeviceURI entry will reference the URI for a printer. For USB printers, the URI uses **usb:**.

```
DeviceURI usb://Canon/S330
```

Spool Directories

When your system prints a file, it makes use of special directories called *spool directories.* A *print job* is a file to be printed. When you send a file to a printer, a copy of it is made and placed in a spool directory set up for that printer. The location of the spool directory is obtained from the printer's entry in its configuration file. On Linux, the spool directory is located at **/var/spool/cups** under a directory with the name of the printer. For example, the spool directory for the **myepson** printer would be located at **/var/spool/cups/myepson**. The spool directory contains several files for managing print jobs. Some files use the name of the printer as their extension. For example, the **myepson** printer has the files **control.myepson**, which provides printer queue control, and **active.myepson** for the active print job, as well as **log.myepson,** which is the log file.

CUPS start and restart: cups init script

You can start, stop, and restart CUPS using the **service** command and the **cups** script. When you make changes or install printers, be sure to restart CUPS to have your changes take effect. You can use the following command:

```
sudo service cups restart
```

The CUPS server is configured to start up when your system boots. The **/etc/default/cups** script holds start up options for the cups server, such as the LOAD_LP_MODULE option to load the parallel printer driver module.

Installing Printers

Several tools are available for installing CUPS printers. The easiest method is to use the Ubuntu **system-config-printer** tool on a desktop system. You can also use the CUPS Web browser-based configuration tools, included with the CUPS software (will work with **lynx** command line browser). Or you can just edit the CUPS printer configuration files directly.

Configuring Printers on the Desktop with system-config-printer

Printers are detected and configured automatically. For removable printers, like a USB printer, a printer icon will appear on the panel as soon as you connect your USB printer, as your printer is detected and configured. If a driver is available for your printer, it will be selected automatically for you and a setup message will appear. If the driver is not available, a Missing printer driver notification is displayed, and a New Printer dialog opens where you can choose your driver.

system-config-printer

To change your configuration or to add a remote printer, you can use the printer configuration tool, system-config-printer. This utility enables you to select the appropriate driver for your printer, as well as set print options, such as paper size and print resolutions. You can configure a printer connected directly to your local computer or a printer on a remote system on your network. You can start system-config-printer by choosing Printers in the Applications lens System filter.

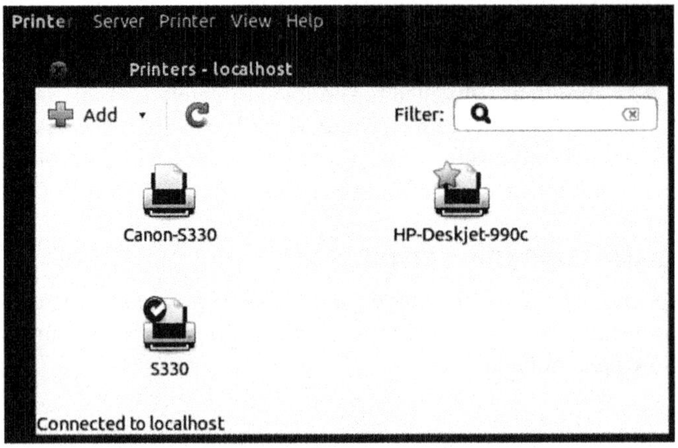

Figure 10-1: system-config-printer tool

The Printing configuration window displays icons for installed printers (see Figure 10-1). The menu bar has menus for Server configuration and selection, Printer features like its properties and the print queue, printer classes, and viewing discovered printers. A toolbar has buttons for adding new printers manually and refreshing print configuration. A Filter search box lets you display only printers matching a search pattern. Click on the x icon in the search box to clear the pattern. Clicking on the Looking glass icon in the File search box will display a pop-up menu that will let you search on Name, Description, Location, and Manufacturer/Model. You can save searches as a search group.

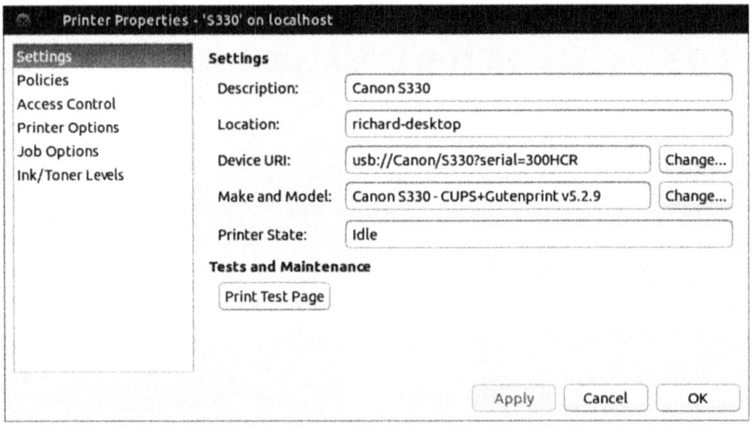

Figure 10-2: Printer properties window

To see the printer settings such as printer and job options, access controls, and policies, double-click on the printer icon or right-click and select Properties. The Printer Properties window opens up with six tabs: Settings, Policies, Access Control, Printer Options, Job Options, and Ink/Toner Levels (see Figure 10-2).

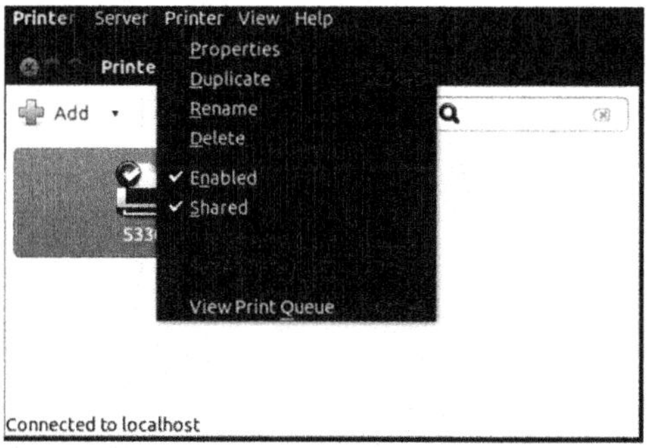

Figure 10-3: Printer configuration window Printer menu

The Printing configuration window's Printer menu lets you rename the printer, enable or disable it, and make it a shared printer. Select the printer icon and then click the Printer menu (see Figure 10-3). You can also display the Printer menu by right-clicking on a printer icon. The Delete entry will remove a printer configuration. Use the Set As Default entry to make the printer a system-wide or your personal default printer. The properties entry opens the printer properties window for that printer. You can also access the print queue for the selected printer. If the printer is already a default, the Set As Default entry is shaded out.

When print jobs are waiting in the print queue, a printer icon will appear on the top panel. Clicking on this icon opens the Document Print Status window listing the pending print jobs. You can also open this window from the system-config-printer's Printer menu, View Print Queue item (Printer | View Print Queue). On the Document Print Status window, you can change a job's queue position as well as stop or delete a job (see Figure 10-4). From the job menu you can cancel, hold (stop), release (restart), or reprint a print job. Reprint is only available if you have set the preserve jobs option in the printer settings Advanced dialog. You can also authenticate a job. From the View menu, you can choose to display just-printed jobs and refresh the queue.

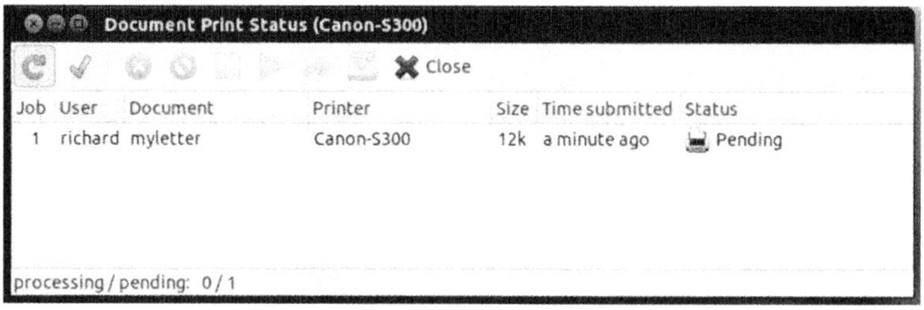

Figure 10-4: Printer queue

To check the server settings, select Settings from the Server menu. This opens a new window showing the CUPS printer server settings (see Figure 10-5). The Advanced expand button displays job history and browser server options. If you want to allow reprinting, then select the "Preserve job files (allow reprinting)" option.

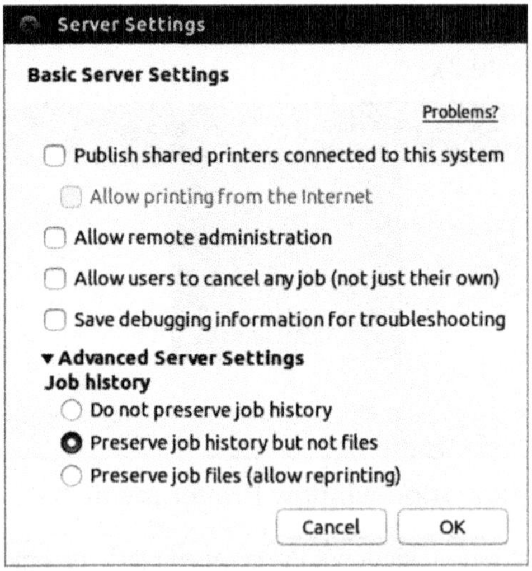

Figure 10-5: Server Settings

Figure 10-6: Selecting a CUPS server

To select a particular CUPS server, select the Connect entry in the Server menu. This opens a "Connect to CUPS Server" window with a drop down menu listing all current CUPS servers from which to choose (see Figure 10-6).

Editing Printer Configuration

To edit an installed printer, double click its icon in the Printer configuration window, or right-click and select the Properties entry. This opens a Printer Properties window for that printer. A sidebar lists configuration tabs. Click on one to display that tab. There are configuration tabs for Settings, Policies, Access Control, Printer Options, Job Options, and Ink/Toner Levels (see Figure 10-8).

Once you have made changes, you can click Apply to save your changes and restart the printer daemon. You can test your printer using the Tests and Maintenance tasks on the Settings tab. The Print Test Page prints a page, whereas the Print Self-Test Page also checks the printer hardware such as ink-jet heads.

Figure 10-7: Printer Options

On the Settings tab you can change configuration settings like the driver and the printer name, and run test pages (see Figure 10-2). Should you need to change the selected driver, click on the Change button next to the Make and Model entry to open printer model and driver windows like those described in the "Add new printer manually" section. There you can specify the model and driver you want to use, even loading your own driver. Should you have to change the device URI (location and protocol), you can click the Change button to the right of the Device URI entry to open a "Change Device URI" dialog.

The Policies tab lets you enable and disable the printer, determine if it is to be shared, and whether to let it accept jobs or not (you also can enable or share the printer from the Printer menu). You can also specify an error policy, which specifies whether to retry or abort the print job, or stop the printer should an error occur. You can choose to print banners at the start or end indicating the level of security for a document, like confidential and secret.

The Access Control tab lets you to deny access to certain users.

The Printer Options tab is where you set particular printing features like paper size and type, print quality, and the input tray to use (see Figure 10-7).

On the Job Options tab you can select default printing features (see Figure 10-8) such as the number of copies, orientation, and single or double sided printing. Options are arranged into three categories: Common Options, Image Options, and Text Options. Only the more common options are displayed. Each category has an expand button that will display all the options for that category. Double sided, output order, and media are all expanded options in the Common Options category.

The Ink/Toner Levels tab will display Ink or Toner levels for supported printers, along with status messages.

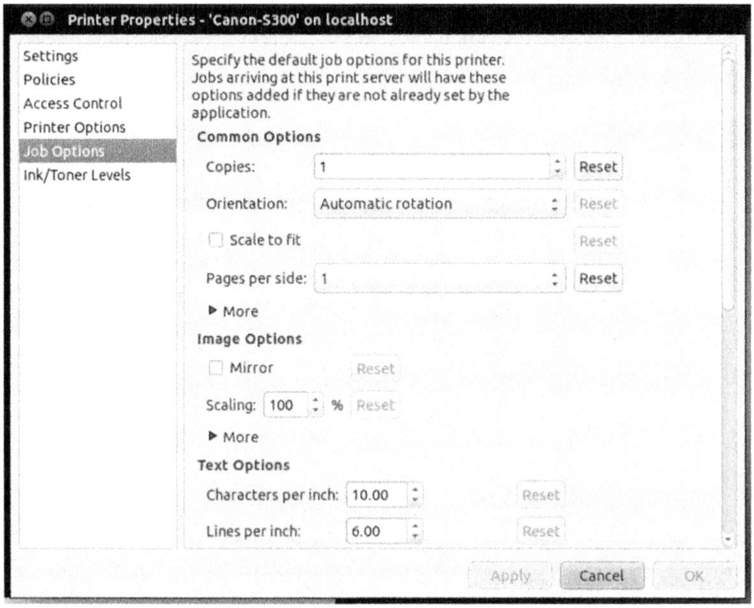

Figure 10-8: Jobs Options

Default System-wide and Personal Printers

To make a printer the default printer, either right-click on the printer icon and select "Set As Default", or single click on the printer icon and then from the Printer configuration window's Printer menu select the "Set As Default" entry (see Figure 10-3). A Set Default Printer dialog open with options for setting the system-wide default or setting the personal default (see Figure 10-9). The system-wide default printer is the default for the system served by your CUPS server.

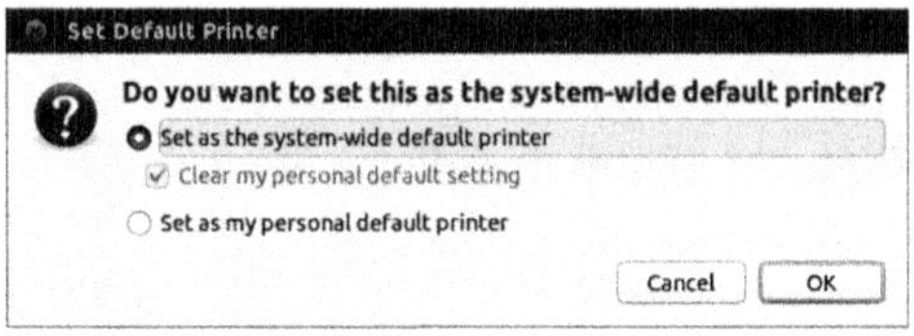

Figure 10-9: Set Default Printer

The system-wide default printer will have a green check mark emblem on its printer icon in the Printing configuration window.

Should you wish to use a different printer yourself (user-specific) as your default printer, you can designate it as your personal default. To make a printer your personal default, select the entry "Set as my personal default printer" in the Set Default Printer dialog. A personal emblem, a yellow star, will appear on the printer's icon in the Printer configuration window. In Figure 10-10, the Canon-S300 printer is the system-wide default, whereas the HP-DeskJet printer is the personal default.

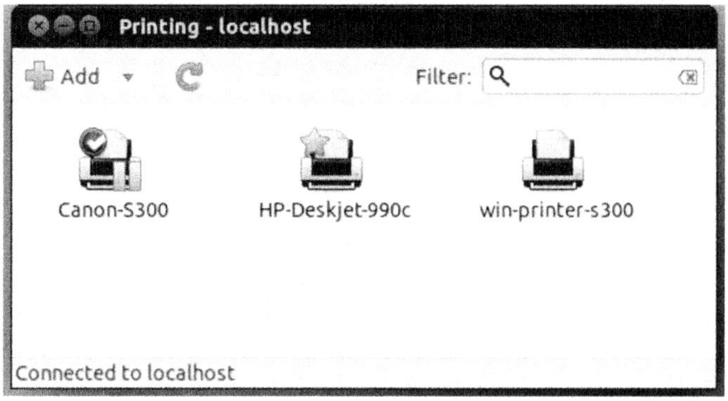

Figure 10-10: System-wide and personal default printers

Printer Classes

The Class entry in the Server | New menu lets you create a printer class. You can access the New menu from the Server menu or from the Add button. This feature lets you select a group of printers to print a job, instead of selecting just one. That way, if one printer is busy or down, another printer can be selected automatically to perform the job. Installed printers can be assigned to different classes. When you click the Class entry in the New menu, a New Class window opens. Here you can enter the name for the class, any comments, and the location (your host name is entered by default). The next screen lists available printers on right side (Other printers) and the printers you assigned to the class on the left side (Printers in this class). Use the arrow button to add or remove printers to the class. Click Apply when finished. Tabs for a selected class are much the same as for a printer, with a Members tab instead of a Printer Options tab. In the Members tab you can change which printers belong to the class

Adding New Printers Manually

Printers are detected automatically, though in the case of older printers and network printers, you may need to add the printer manually. In this case click the Add button and select Printer. A New Printer window opens, displaying a series of dialog boxes where you select the connection, model, drivers, and printer name with location.

On the Select Device dialog, select the appropriate printer connection information. Connected local printer brands will already be listed by name, such as Canon. For remote printers you will specify the type of network connection, like "Windows printers via Samba" for printers connected to a Windows system, "AppSocket/HP Direct" for HP printers connected directly to your network, and the "Internet Printing Protocol (ipp)" for printers on Linux and Unix systems on your network. These connections are displayed under the Network Printer heading. Click the expansion arrow to display them.

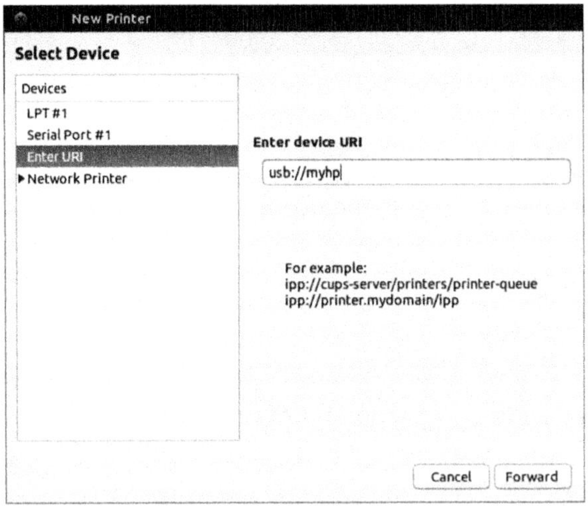

Figure 10-11: Selecting a new printer connection

For most connected printers, your connection is usually determined by udev, which now manages all devices. A USB printer will simply be described as a USB printer, using the usb URI designation (see Figure 10-11). For an older local printer, you may have to choose the port the printer is connected to, such as LPT1 for the first parallel port used for older parallel printers, or Serial Port #1 for a printer connected to the first serial port. To add a USB printer manually, you would select the "Enter URI" Entry and enter the URI consisting of the prefix **usb://** and the name you want to give to the printer, like **usb://myepson**.

A search is conducted for the appropriate driver, including downloadable drivers. If the driver is found, the Choose Driver screen is displayed with the appropriate driver manufacturer already selected for you. You need only click the forward button. On the next screen, also labeled Choose Driver, the printer models and drivers files are listed and the appropriate one is already selected for you. Just click the Forward button. The Describe Printer screen is then displayed where you can enter the Printer Name, Description, and Location. These are ways you can personally identify a printer. Then click Apply.

If the printer driver is not detected or is detected incorrectly, on the Choose Driver screen you have the options to choose the driver from the printer database, from a PPD driver file, or from a search of the OpenPrinting online repository. The selection display will change according to which option you choose.

The database option lists possible manufacturers. Use your mouse to select the one you want (see Figure 3-12).

The search option displays a search box for make and model. Enter both the make (printer manufacturer) and part of the model name (See figure 3-13). The search results will be available in the Printer model drop down menu. Select the one you want. Then click Forward.

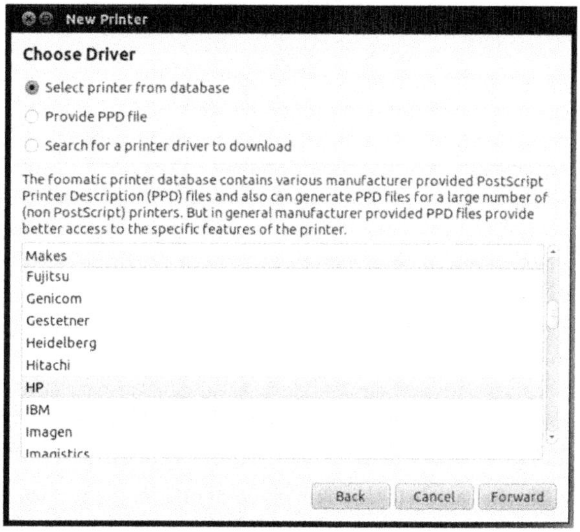

Figure 10-12: Printer manufacturer for new printers

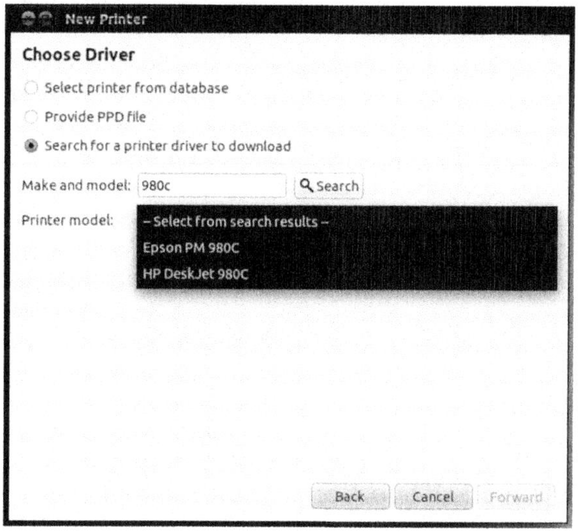

Figure 10-13: Searching for a printer driver from the OpenPrinting repository

The PPD file option displays a file location button that opens a Select file dialog you can use to locate the PPD file on your system.

If you are selecting a printer from the database, on the next screen you select that manufacturer's model along with its driver (see Figure 10-14). For some older printer, though the driver can be located on the online repository, you will still choose it from the local database (the drivers are the same). The selected drivers for your printer will be listed. If there are added options for your printer, the Installable Options screen lists them allowing you to check the ones you want.

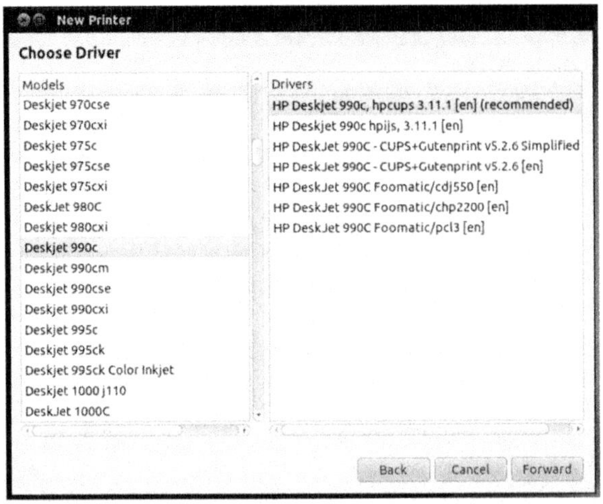

Figure 10-14: Printer Model and driver for new printers using local database

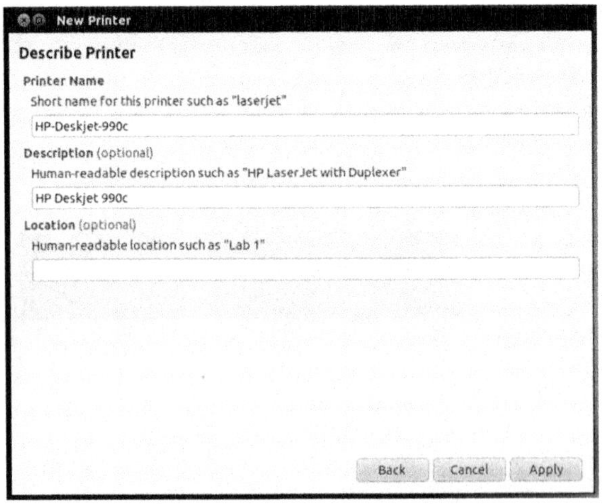

Figure 10-15: Printer Name and Location for new printers

You can then enter your printer name and location (see Figure 10-15). These will be entered for you using the printer model and your system's host name. You can change the printer name to anything you want. When ready, click Apply. You will be prompted to print a test page. An icon for your printer will be displayed in the Printing configuration window. You are now ready to print.

Note: KDE 4 provides a printer configuration interface for CUPS. Access it on the System Settings Advanced tab, or from Applications | System | Printer Configuration). Configuration is similar to system-config-printer.

CUPS Web Browser-based configuration tool

One of the easiest ways to configure and install printers with CUPS is to use the CUPS configuration Web interface, a web browser–based tool. The CUPS configuration interface is a web-based tool that can also manage printers and print jobs. A web page is displayed with tabs for managing jobs and printers, and performing administrative tasks. You can access the CUPS configuration tool using the **localhost** address and specifying port **631**. Enter the following URL into your web browser:

```
http://localhost:631
```

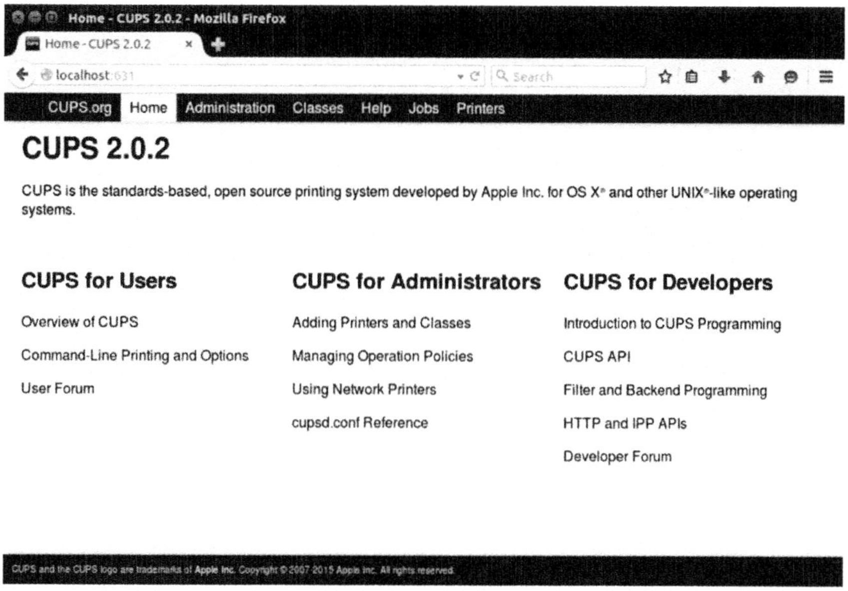

Figure 10-16: CUPS Web-based Configuration Tool: Home tab

You can also can use this CUPS configuration interface with a command line Web browser like **elinks** (install **elinks** first). This allows you to configure a printer from the command line interface. Use the ENTER key to display menus and make selections, and arrow keys to navigate.

```
elinks localhost:631
```

Entering the **localhost:631** URL in your Web browser opens the Home screen for the CUPS Web interface. There are tabs for various sections, as well as links for specialized tasks like adding printers or obtaining help (see Figure 10-16). Tabs include Administration, Classes, Online Help, Jobs, and Printers. You can manage and add printers on the Administration tab. The Printers tab will list installed printers with buttons for accessing their print queues, printer options, and job options, among others. The Jobs tab lists your print jobs and lets you manage them.

When you try to make any changes for the first time during the session, you will first be asked to enter the administrator's username (your user name) and password (your user password), just as you would for the **sudo** command.

The Administration tab displays segments for Printers, Classes, Jobs, and the Server (see Figure 10-17). The server section is where you allow printer sharing. Buttons allow you to view logs and change settings.

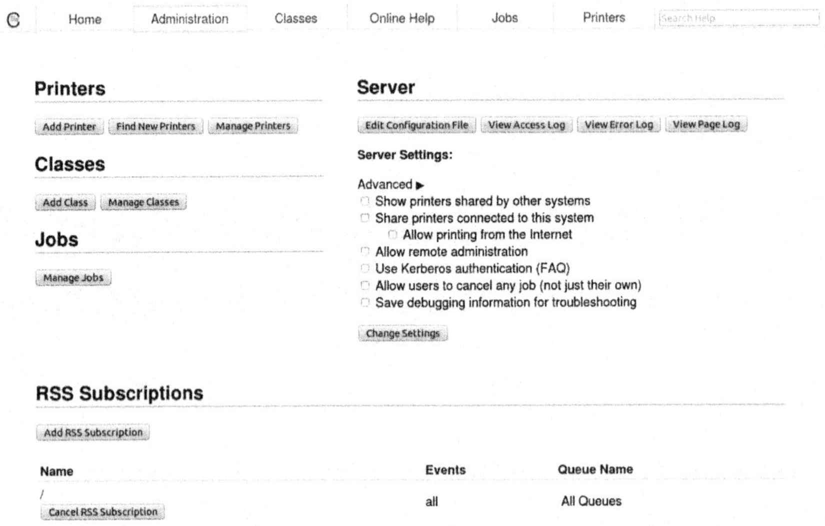

Figure 10-17: CUPS Web-based Configuration Tool: Administration tab

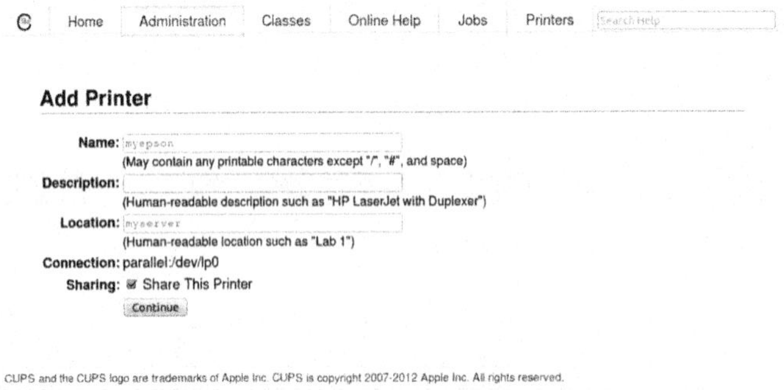

Figure 10-18: Adding a new printer: CUP Web Interface

With the CUPS configuration tool, you install a printer on CUPS through a series of Web pages, each of which requests different information. To install a printer, click the Add Printer button either on the Home page or the Administration page. You must first specify the protocol. On the next screen you enter a URI to use for the printer. For a local printer this is the protocol and the host name. A page is displayed where you enter the printer name and location (see Figure 10-18). A Sharing entry lets you choose to share the printer. The location is the host to which the printer is connected. The procedure is similar to **system-config-printer**. Subsequent pages will prompt you to enter the make and model of the printer, which you select from available listings. You can also load a PPD driver file instead, if you have one. Click the Add Printer button when read. On the following page you then set default options for your printer, like paper size and type, color, print quality, and resolution.

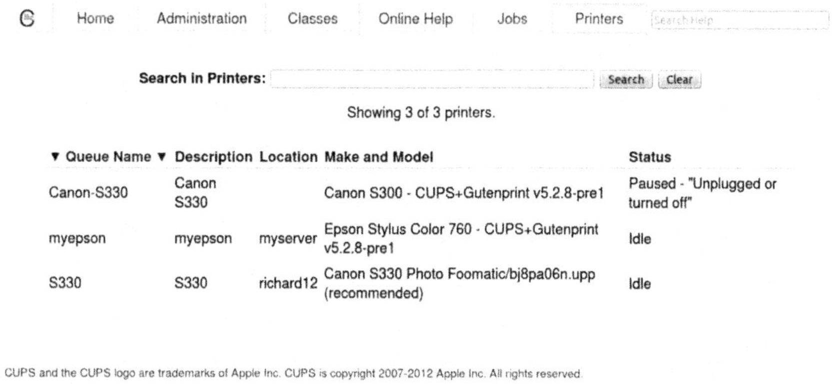

Figure 10-19: CUPS Web-based Configuration Tool: Printers tab

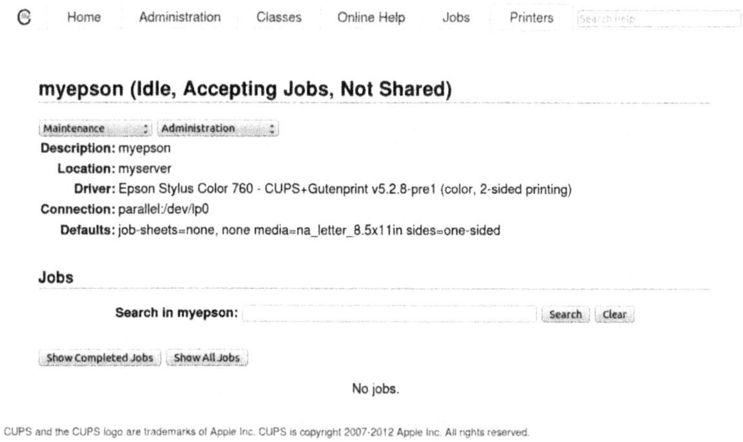

Figure 10-20: CUPS Web-based Configuration Tool: Managing Printers

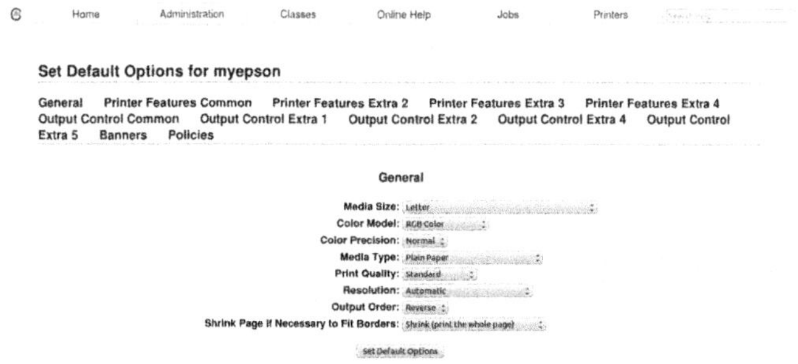

Figure 10-21: CUPS Web-based Configuration Tool: Printer Options

To manage a printer, click the Printers tab or the Manage Printers button in the Administration page. The Printers page will list your installed printers (see Figure 10-19). Clicking a printer link opens a page for managing your jobs and performing administrative tasks (see Figure 10-20). From the Maintenance drop down menu lets you perform printer and job tasks like pausing the printer, printing a test page, and canceling all jobs. The Administration menu lets you modify the printer, delete it, and set default options. Choosing the Administration menu's Set Default Options entry displays a page can configure how your printer prints (see Figure 10-21). Links at the top of the page display pages for setting certain options like general options, output control, banners, and extra features such as printer direction, ink type, color density, and drop size. The general options are listed first, where you can set basic features like the resolution and paper size.

Note: You can perform all administrative tasks from the command line using the **lpadmin** command. See the CUPS documentation for more details.

Configuring Remote Printers on CUPS

To install a remote printer that is attached to a Windows system or another Linux system running CUPS, you specify its location by using special URL protocols. For another CUPS printer on a remote host, the protocol used is **ipp**, for Internet Printing Protocol, whereas for a Windows printer, it would be **smb**. Older UNIX or Linux systems using LPRng would use the **lpd** protocol.

To use the CUPS configuration tool to install a remote printer, specify the remote printer network protocol on the initial Add Printer page. You can choose from Windows, Internet Printing Protocol (other UNIX or Linux systems), Apple and HP JetDirect connected printers, and the older LPD line printers (see Figure 10-22). If a network printer is connected currently, it may be listed in the Discovered Network Printers list.

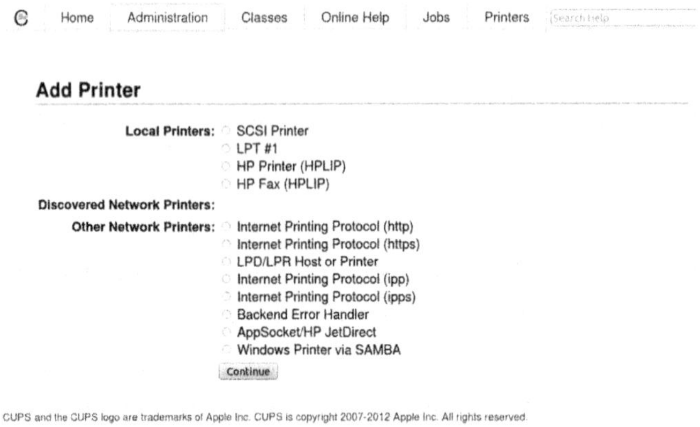

Figure 10-22: CUPS Web-based Configuration Tool: Network Printers

Configuring Remote Printers on the Desktop with system-config-printer

You specify a printer location using special URI protocols. For a locally attached USB printer, the USB URI is **usb**. For another CUPS printer on a remote host, the protocol used is **ipp**, for Internet Printing Protocol, whereas for a Windows printer, it would be **smb**. Older UNIX or Linux systems using LPRng would use the **lpd** protocol.

You can use system-config-printer to set up a remote printer on Linux, UNIX, or Windows networks. When you add a new printer or edit one, the New Printer dialog will list possible remote connection types under the Network entry. When you select a remote connection entry, a pane will be displayed to the right where you can enter configuration information.

To find any connected printers on your network automatically, click the Find Network Printer entry. Enter the host name of the system the remote printer is connected to, then click the Find button. The host is searched and the detected printers are displayed as entries under the Network Printer heading (see Figure 10-23).

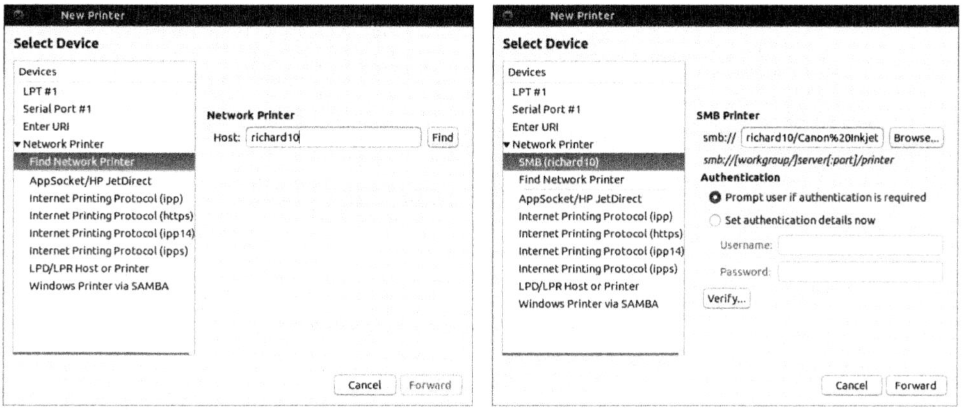

Figure 10-23: Finding a network printer

To configure a specific type of printer, choose from the available entries. For a remote Linux or UNIX printer, select either Internet Printing Protocol (ipp), which is used for newer systems, or LPD/LPR Host or Printer, which is used for older systems. Both panes display entries for the Host name and the queue. For the Host name, enter the hostname for the system that controls the printer. For an Apple or HP jet direct printer on your network, select the AppSocket/HP jetDirect entry.

A "Windows printer via Samba" printer is one located on a Windows network (see Figure 10-24). You need to specify the Windows server (host name or IP address), the name of the share, the name of the printer's workgroup, and the username and password. The format of the printer SMB URL is shown on the SMP Printer pane. The share is the hostname and printer name in the **smb** URI format *//workgroup/hostname/printername.* The workgroup is the windows network workgroup that the printer belongs to. On small networks there is usually only one. The hostname is the computer where the printer is located. The username and password can be for the printer resource itself, or for access by a particular user. The pane will display a box at the top where you can enter the share host and printer name as a **smb** URI.

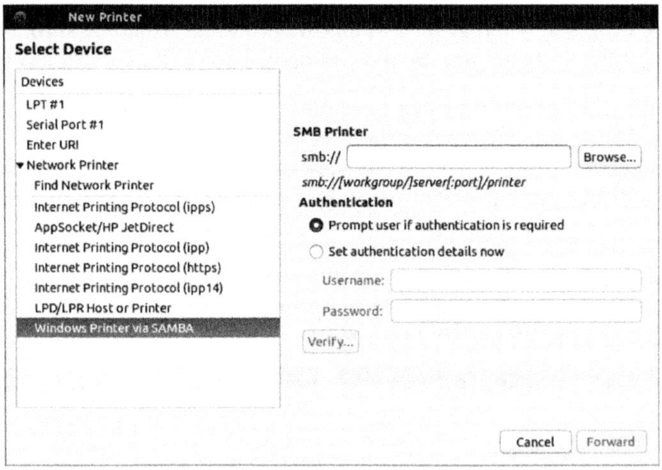

Figure 10-24: Selecting a Windows printer

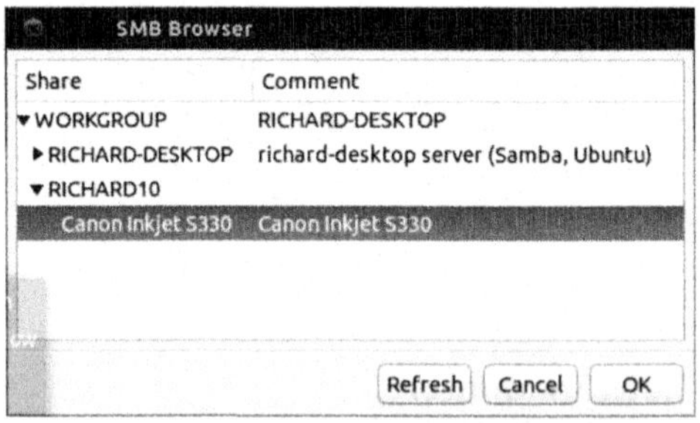

Figure 10-25: SMB Browser, selecting a remote windows printer

Instead of manually entering the URI for a printer, you can use the Browse button to choose from a list of detected Windows printers on your network. Click the Browse button to open a SMB Browser window, where you can select the printer from a listing of Windows hosts (see Figure 10-25). For example, if your Windows network is WORKGROUP, then the entry WORKGROUP will be shown, which you can then expand to list all the Windows hosts on that network (if your network is MSHOME, then that is what will be listed). If you are using a firewall, be sure to turn it off before browsing a Windows workgroup for a printer, unless the firewall is already configured to allow Samba access.

When you make your selection, the corresponding URI will show up in the **smb://** box (See Figure 10-26). You also can enter in any needed Samba authentication, if required, like user name or password. Check "Authentication required" to allow you to enter the Samba Username and Password.

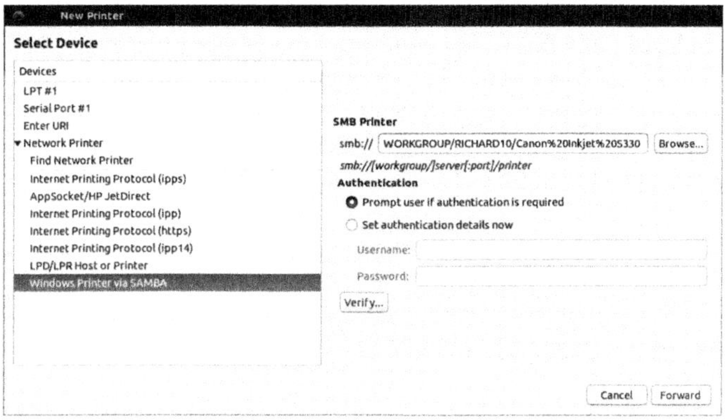

Figure 10-26: Remote Windows printer connection configuration

You then continue with install screens for the printer model, driver, and name. Once installed, you can then access the printer properties just as you would any printer (see Figure 10-27).

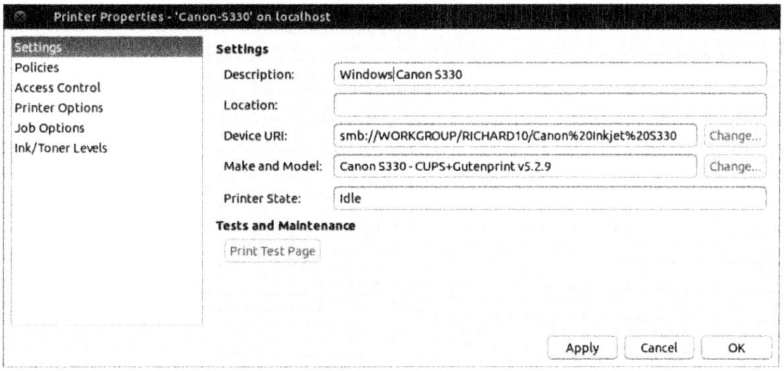

Figure 10-27: Remote Windows printer Settings

To access an SMB shared remote printer, you need to install Samba and have the Server Message Block services enabled using the **smbd** and **nmbd** daemons. The Samba service will be enabled by default. You can use the **service** command to restart, stop, and start the services. Printer sharing must be enabled on the Windows network.

```
sudo service smbd restart
sudo service nmbd restart
```

Configuring remote printers manually

In the **printers.conf** file, for a remote printer, instead of listing the device, the DeviceURI entry, will have an Internet address, along with its protocol. For example, a remote printer on a CUPS server (**ipp**) would be indicated as shown here (a Windows printer would use the **smb** protocol):

```
DeviceURI ipp://mytsuff.com/printers/queue1
```

For a Windows printer, you first need to install, configure, and run Samba (CUPS uses Samba to access Windows printers). When you install the Windows printer on CUPS, you specify its location using the URL protocol **smb**. The username of the user allowed to log in to the printer is entered before the hostname and separated from the hostname by an @ sign. On most configurations, this is the **guest** user. The location entry for a Windows printer called **myhp** attached to a Windows host named **lizard** is shown next. Its Samba share reference would be **//lizard/myhp**:

```
DeviceURI smb://guest@lizard/myhp
```

To enable CUPS on Samba, you also have to set the printing option in the **/etc/samba/smb.conf** file to **cups**, as shown here:

```
printing = cups
printcap name = cups
```

Note: To configure a shared Linux printer for access by Windows hosts, you need to configure it as a SMB shared printer. You do this with Samba.

CUPS Printer Classes

CUPS lets you select a group of printers to print a job, instead of selecting just one. If one printer is busy or down, another printer can be selected automatically to print the job. Such groupings of printers are called *classes.* Once you have installed your printers, you can group them into different classes. For example, you may want to group all inkjet printers into one class and laser printers to another, or you may want to group printers connected to one specific printer server in their own class.

You can create classes on the CUPS Configuration tool Administration tab by clicking the Add Class button. On the Add Class page you enter the name of the class, its location and then select the printers to add to the class from the Members list. The class will then show up on the Classes tab, showing its members and status.

As previously noted, on system-config-printer, you can set up classes for printers. The Class entry in the Server | New menu lets you create a printer class. You can access the New menu from the Server menu or from the Add button. You can also select a printer or set of printers and choose "Create class" from the Printer menu, automatically adding them to the new class.

CUPS Configuration files

CUPS configuration files are placed in the **/etc/cups** directory. These files are listed in Table 10-2. The **classes.conf** and **printers.conf** files can be managed by the web interface. The **printers.conf** file contains the configuration information for the different printers you have installed. Any of these files can be edited manually, if you want. Some applications will have their own configuration files like **acroread.conf** for the Adobe Reader.

Filename	Description
classes.conf	Contains configurations for different local printer classes
client.conf	Lists specific options for specified clients
cupsd.conf	Configures the CUPS server, **cupsd**
printers.conf	Contains printer configurations for available local printers
cups-files.conf	File and directories used by CUPS
cups-browsed.conf	Access to remote and local printers
subscriptions.conf	Subscription controls for printer and print job information

Table 10-2: CUPS Configuration Files

cupsd.conf

The CUPS server is configured with the **cupsd.conf** file located in **/etc/cups**. You must edit configuration options manually; the server is not configured with the web interface. Your installation of CUPS installs a commented version of the **cupsd.conf** file with each option listed, though most options will be commented out. Commented lines are preceded with a # symbol. Each option is documented in detail. The server configuration uses an Apache web server syntax consisting of a set of directives. As with Apache, several of these directives can group other directives into blocks.

For a detailed explanation of cupsd.conf directives check the CUPS documentation for cupsd.conf. You can also reference this documentation from the Online Help page | References link on the CUPS browser-based administration tool, **http://localhost:631**.

```
http://www.cups.org/documentation.php/doc-1.7/ref-cupsd-conf.html
```

The **cupsd.conf** file begins with setting.

```
LogLevel warn
```

On Ubuntu CUPS logging in disables.

```
MaxLogSize 0
```

The Listen directives set the machine and socket on which to receive connections. These are set by default to the local machine, localhost port 631. If you are using a dedicated network interface for connecting to a local network, you would add the network card's IP address, allowing access from machines on your network.

```
# Only listen for connections from the local machine.
Listen localhost:631
Listen /var/run/cups/cups.sock
```

Browsing directives allows your local printers to be detected on your network, enabling them to be shared. For shared printing, the Browsing directive is set to on (it is set to Off by default). A BrowseOrder of allow, deny will deny all browse transmissions, then first check the BrowseAllow directives for exceptions. A reverse order (deny, allow) does the opposite, accepting all browse transmissions, and first checks for those denied by BrowseDeny directives. The default

cupsd.conf file has a BrowseOrder allow, deny directive followed by a BrowseAllow directive, which is set to **all**. To limit this to a particular network, use the IP address of the network instead of **all**. The BrowseLocalProtocols lists the network protocols to use for advertising the printers on a local network. The BrowseAddress directive will make your local printers available as shared printers on the specified network. It is set to @LOCAL to allow access on your local network. You can add other BrowseAddress directives to allow access by other networks.

```
# Show shared printers on the local network.
Browsing On
BrowseOrder allow,deny
BrowseAllow all
BrowseLocalProtocols CUPS dnssd
BrowseAddress @LOCAL
```

CUPS supports both Basic and Digest forms of authentication, specified in the **AuthType** directive. Basic authentication requires a user and password. For example, to use the web interface, you are prompted to enter the root user and the root user password. Digest authentication makes use of user and password information kept in the CUPS **/etc/cups/passwd.md5** file, using MD5 versions of a user and password for authentication. In addition, CUPS also supports a BasicDigest and Negotiate authentication. BasicDigest will use the CUPS md5 password file for basic authentication. Negotiate will use Kerberos authentication. The default authentication type is set, using the DefaultAuthType directive, set to Basic.

```
# Default authentication type, when authentication is required...
DefaultAuthType Basic
```

The Web interface setting is set to yes.

```
WebInterface Yes
```

Location Directives

Certain directives allow you to place access controls on specific locations. These can be printers or resources, such as the administrative tool or the spool directories. Location controls are implemented with the **Location** directive. There are several Location directives that control access. The first controls access to the server root directory, /. The Order allow, deny entry activates restrictions on access by remote systems. If there are no following Allow or Deny entries then the default is to deny all. There is an implied Allow localhost with the "Order allow, deny" directive, always giving access to the local machine. In effect, access here is denied to all systems, allowing access only by the local system.

```
# Restrict access to the server...
<Location />
  Order allow,deny
</Location>
```

Another **Location** directive is used to restrict administrative access, the **/admin** resource. The **Order allow,deny** directive denies access to all systems, except for the local machine.

```
# Restrict access to the admin pages...
<Location /admin>
  Order allow,deny
</Location>
```

`Allow from` and `Deny from` directives can permit or deny access from specific hosts and networks. If you wanted to just allow access to a particular machine, you would use an Allow from directive with the machine's IP address. CUPS also uses **@LOCAL** to indicate you local network, and **IF(*name*)** for a particular network interface (*name* is the device name of the interface) used to access a network. Should you want to allow administrative access by all other systems on your local network, you can add the **Allow from @LOCAL**. If you add an **Allow** directive, you also have to explicitly add the **Allow localhost** to insure access by your local machine.

```
# Restrict access to the admin pages...
<Location /admin>
  Allow from localhost
  Allow from @LOCAL
  Order allow,deny
</Location>
```

The following entry would allow access from a particular machine.

```
  Allow From 192.168.0.5
```

The next location directive restricts access to the CUPS configuration files, **/admin/conf**. The **AuthType default** directive refers to the default set by DefaultAuthType. The **Require user** directive references the **SystemGroup** directive, **@SYSTEM** (defined in the **cups-files.conf** file). Only users from that group are allowed access.

```
# Restrict access to configuration files...
<Location /admin/conf>
  AuthType Default
  Require user @SYSTEM
  Order allow,deny
</Location>
```

Default Operation Policy: Limit Directives

A default operation policy is then defined for access to basic administration, printer, print job, and owner operations. The default operation policy section begins with the **<Policy default>** directive. Limit directives are used to implement the directives for each kind of operation. Job operations covers tasks like sending a document, restarting a job, suspending a job, and restarting a job. Administrative tasks include modifying a printer configuration, deleting a printer, managing printer classes, and setting the default printer. Printer operations govern tasks like pausing a printer, enabling or disabling a printer, and shutting down a printer. The owner operations consist of just canceling a job and authenticating access to a job.

See the CUPS documentation on managing operations policies for more details.

```
http://www.cups.org/documentation.php/doc-1.6/policies.html
```

On all the default **Limit** directives, access is allowed only by the local machine (localhost), **Order allow,deny**.

The policy section begins with access controls for user and job information. The default for **JobPrivateAccess** limits access to owner, system, and access control lists. **JobPrivateValues** specifies values made private, such as the job name, originating host, and originating user. **SubscriptionPrivateAccess** and **SubscriptionPrivateValues** specify access for subscription attributes such notifications of printer events like job completed or job stopped.

Limit directive are set up to create and print jobs.

```
<Limit Create-Job Print-Job Print-URI Validate-Job>
  Order deny,allow
</Limit>
```

Both the administrative and printer **Limit** directives are set to the **AuthType default** and limited to access by an administrative users, **Require user @SYSTEM**. The administrative directive is shown here.

```
# All administration operations require an administrator to authenticate...
<Limit CUPS-Add-Modify-Printer CUPS-Delete-Printer CUPS-Add-Modify-Class CUPS-
Delete-Class CUPS-Set-Default CUPS-Get-Devices>
   AuthType Default
   Require user @SYSTEM
   Order deny,allow
</Limit>
```

Both the job related and owner Limit directives require either owner or administrative authentication, **Require user @OWNER @SYSTEM**. The **Owner Limit** directive is shown here.

```
# Only the owner or an administrator can cancel or authenticate a job...
<Limit Cancel-Job CUPS-Authenticate-Job>
  Require user @OWNER @SYSTEM
  Order deny,allow
</Limit>
```

For all other tasks, **<Limit All>**, access is restricted to the local machine (localhost).

```
<Limit All>
 Order deny,allow
</Limit>
```

The **AuthClass** directive can be used within a **Limit** directive to specify the printer class allowed access. The **System** class includes the root, sys, and system users.

An authenticated set of policy directives follows the default policy, with similar entries and an added AuthType entry in the Limit directive to create and print jobs.

```
<Limit Create-Job Print-Job Print-URI Validate-Job>
  AuthType Default
  Order deny,allow
</Limit>
```

cupsctl

You can use the **cupsctl** command to modify your cupsd.conf file, rather than editing the file directly. Check the **cupsctl** Man page for details. The **cupsctl** command with no options will display current settings.

```
cupsctl
```

The changes you can make with this command are limited turning off remote administration or disabling shared printing. The major options you can set are:

remote-admin Enable or disable remote administration

remote-any Enable or disable remote printing

remote-printers Enable or disable the display of remote printers

share-printers Enable or disable sharing of local printers with other systems

printers.conf

Configured information for a printer will be stored in the **/etc/cups/printers.conf** file. You can examine this file directly, even making changes. Here is an example of a printer configuration entry. The **DeviceURI** entry specifies the device used, in this case a USB printer. It is currently idle, with no jobs:

```
# Printer configuration file for CUPS
# Written by cupsd
<Printer mycannon>
Info Cannon s330
Location richard-server
MakeModel Canon S330
DeviceURI usb://Canon/S330
State Idle
StateTime 1166554036
Accepting Yes
Shared Yes
ColorManaged Yes
JobSheets none none
QuotaPeriod 0
PageLimit 0
KLimit 0
OpPolicy default
ErrorPolicy retry-job
</Printer>
```

subscriptions.conf

Configured information for printer and job information is located in the **/etc/cups/subscriptions.conf** file. Those receiving the information are specified by the **SubscriptionPrivateAccess** and **SubscriptionPrivateValues** directives in the policy section of the **cupd.conf** file. The **Events** directive specifies notifications of events to be sent, events such as job-completed, printer-stopped, and server-started. The **Owner** directive lists the users for this subscription. **LeaseDuration** is the time the subscription remains valid (0 value is the life of the print job or forever). **Interval** is the time between notifications. **Recipient** is the recipient URI for the notification. In the following example it is dbus:// (your desktop). You can find a complete list of directives and events at:

```
http://www.cups.org/documentation.php/ref-subscriptions-conf.html
```

A sample **subscriptions.conf** file is shown here:

```
# Subscription configuration file for CUPS v1.5.4
# Written by cupsd on 2013-03-13 14:13
NextSubscriptionId 119
<Subscription 118>
Events printer-state-changed printer-restarted printer-shutdown printer-stopped
printer-added printer-deleted job-state-changed job-created job-completed job-
stopped
Owner richard
Recipient dbus://
LeaseDuration 3600
Interval 0
ExpirationTime 1363212783
NextEventId 1
</Subscription>
```

cups-files.conf

The files and directories that CUPS uses to manage print jobs can be configured in the **/etc/cups/cups-files.conf** file. The ErrorLog directive specified the CUPS error log file.

```
ErrorLog  /var/log/cups/error_log
```

The SystemGroup directive defines the users referenced by @SYSTEM in **cupsd.conf**.

```
SystemGroup lpadmin
```

cups-browsed.conf

The cups-browsed.conf file configures the cups-browsed daemon, used for browsing remote and local printers. The BrowseRemoteProtocoals defines the protocols to use.

```
BrowseRemoteProtocols  dnssd cups
```

The BrowseAllow directive can be used to restrict browsing to specified servers or networks.

```
BrowseAllow 192.168.1.0/24
```

The CreateIPPPrinterQueues directive allows the detection of non-CUPS IPP printers.

CUPS Command Line Print Clients

Once a print job is placed in a print queue, you can use any of several print clients to manage the jobs on your printer or printers, such as system-config-printer and the CUPS Printer Configuration tool. You can also use several command line print CUPS clients, which include the **`lpr`**, **`lpc`**, **`lpq`**, and **`lprm`** commands. With these clients, you can print documents, list a print queue, reorder it, and remove print jobs, effectively canceling them. For network connections, CUPS features an encryption option for its commands, **`-E`**, to encrypt print jobs and print information sent from a network. Table 10-3 shows various printer commands.

Note: The command line clients have the same name, and much the same syntax, as the older LPR and LPRng command line clients used in Unix and older Linux systems.

lpr

The **lpr** client submits a job, and **lpd** then takes it in turn, and places it on the appropriate print queue; **lpr** takes as its argument the name of a file. If no printer is specified, the default printer is used. The **-P** option lets you specify a particular printer. In the next example, the user first prints the file **preface** and then prints the file **report** to the printer with the name **myepson**:

```
$ lpr preface
$ lpr -P myepson report
```

Printer Management	Description
GNOME Print Manager	GNOME print queue management tool (CUPS)
CUPS Configuration Tool	Prints, manages, and configures CUPS
`lpr` *options file-list*	Prints a file, copies the file to the printer's spool directory, and places it on the print queue to be printed in turn. `-P` *printer* prints the file on the specified printer
`lpq` *options*	Displays the print jobs in the print queue. `-P` *printer* prints the queue for the specified printer `-l` prints a detailed listing
`lpstat` *options*	Displays printer status
`lprm` *options printjob-id* `or` *printer*	Removes a print job from the print queue. You identify a particular print job by its number as listed by `lpq`. `-P` *printer* removes all print jobs for the specified printer
`lpc`	Manages your printers. At the `lpc>` prompt, you can enter commands to check the status of your printers and take other actions

Table 10-3: CUPS Print Clients

lpc

You can use **lpc** to enable or disable printers, reorder their print queues, and re-execute configuration files. To use **lpc**, enter the command **lpc** at the shell prompt. You will see an **lpc>** prompt, where you can enter **lpc** commands to manage your printers and reorder their jobs. The **status** command with the name of the printer displays whether the printer is ready, how many print jobs it has, and so on. The **stop** and **start** commands can stop a printer and start it back up. The printers shown depend on the printers configured for a particular print server. A printer configured on CUPS will appear only if you have switched to CUPS.

```
$ lpc
lpc> status myepson
myepson:
 printer is on device 'usb' speed -1
 queuing is enabled
 printing is enabled
 1 entry in spool area
```

lpq and lpstat

You can manage the print queue using the **lpq** and **lprm** commands. The **lpq** command lists the print jobs currently on the print queue. With the **-P** option and the printer name, you can list the jobs for a particular printer. If you specify a username, you can list the print jobs for that user. With the **-l** option, **lpq** displays detailed information about each job. If you want information on a specific job, simply use that job's ID number with **lpq**. To check the status of a printer, use **lpstat**.

```
$ lpq
myepson is ready and printing
Rank    Owner  Jobs  File(s)            Total Size
active  chris    1   report             1024
```

lprm

The **lprm** command lets you remove a print job from the queue, erasing the job before it can be printed. The **lprm** command takes many of the same options as **lpq**. To remove a specific job, use **lprm** with the job number. To remove all printing jobs for a particular printer, use the **-P** option with the printer name. **lprm** with no options removes the job printing currently. The following command removes the first print job in the queue (use **lpq** to obtain the job number):

```
lprm 1
```

CUPS Command Line Administrative Tools

CUPS provides command line administrative tools such as **lpadmin**, **lpoptions**, **lpinfo**, **cupsenable**, **cupsdisable**, **accept**, and **reject** (**cups-client** package). The **cupsenable** and **cupsdisable** commands start and stop print queues directly, whereas the **accept** and **reject** commands start and stop particular jobs. The **lpinfo** command provides information about printers, and **lpoptions** lets you set printing options. The **lpadmin** command lets you perform administrative tasks such as adding printers and changing configurations. CUPS administrative tools are listed in Table 10-4.

You can use the **lpadmin** command either to set the default printer or configure various options for a printer. You can use the **-d** option to specify a particular printer as the default destination. Here **myepson** is made the default printer:

```
lpadmin -d myepson
```

The **-p** option lets you designate a printer for which to set various options. The following example sets printer description information:

```
lpadmin -p myepson  -D  Epson550
```

Certain options let you control per-user quotas for print jobs. The **job-k-limit** option sets the size of a job allowed per user, **job-page-limit** sets the page limit for a job, and **job-quota-period** limits the number of jobs with a specified time frame. The following command set a page limit of 100 for each user:

```
lpadmin -p myepson  -o job-page-limit=100
```

Administration Tool	Description
`lpadmin`	CUPS printer configuration
`lpoptions`	Sets printing options
`cupsenable`	Activates a printer
`cupsdisable`	Stops a printer
`accept`	Allows a printer to accept new jobs
`reject`	Prevents a printer from accepting print jobs
`lpinfo`	Lists CUPS devices available

Table 10-4: CUPS Administrative Tools

lpadmin

User access control is determined with the `-u` option with an `allow` or `deny` list. Users allowed access are listed following the `allow`: entry, and those denied access are listed with a `deny`: entry. Here access is granted to **chris** but denied to **aleina** and **larisa**.

```
lpadmin -p myepson -u allow:chris  deny:aleina,larisa
```

Use `all` or `none` to permit or deny access to all or no users. You can create exceptions by using `all` or `none` in combination with user-specific access. The following example allows access to all users except **justin**:

```
lpadmin -p myepson  -u allow:all   deny:justin
```

lpoptions

The `lpoptions` command lets you set printing options and defaults that mostly govern how your print jobs will be printed. For example, you can set the color or page format to be used with a particular printer. The `-l` option lists current options for a printer, and the `-p` option designates a printer (you can also set the default printer to use with the `-d` option). The following command lists the current options for the myepson printer.

```
lpoptions -p myepson -l
```

Printer options are set using the `-o` option along with the option name and value, `-o` *option=value.* You can remove a printer option with the `-r` option. For example, to print on both sides of your sheets, you can set the `sides` option to `two-sided`:

```
lpoptions -p myepson -o sides=two-sided
```

To remove the option, use `-r`.

```
lpoptions -p myepson -r sides
```

To display a listing of available options, check the standard printing options in the CUPS Software Manual at **http://cups.org**.

cupsenable and cupsdisable

The `cupsenable` command starts a printer, and the `cupsdisable` command stops it. With the `-c` option, you can cancel all jobs on the printer's queue, and the `-r` option broadcasts a message explaining the shutdown. This command disables the printer named **myepson.**

```
cupsdisable myepson
```

These are CUPS versions of the System V **enable** and **disable** commands, renamed to avoid conflicts.

accept and reject

The `accept` and `reject` commands let you control access to the printer queues for specific printers. The `reject` command prevents a printer from accepting jobs, whereas `accept` allows new print jobs. The following command prevents the **myepson** printer from accepting print jobs:

```
reject myepson
```

The Man pages for accept and reject are **cupsaccept** and **cupsreject**. These names are also links to the **accept** and **reject** commands, allowing you to use them instead.

lpinfo

The `lpinfo` command is a handy tool for letting you know what CUPS devices and drivers are available on your system. Use the `-v` option for devices and the `-m` option for drivers.

```
lpinfo -m
```

11. Network File Systems, Network Information System, and Distributed Network File Systems: NFS, NIS, and GFS

Network File Systems: NFS and /etc/exports

Setting up NFS Directories with shares-admin: Shared Folders

NFS Configuration: /etc/exports

Controlling Accessing to NFS Servers

Mounting NFS File Systems: NFS Clients

Network Information Service: NIS

Name Service Switch: nsswitch.conf

Red Hat Global File System (GFS and GFS 2)

Linux provides several tools for accessing files on remote systems connected to a network. The Network File System (NFS) enables you to connect to and directly access resources such as files or devices like CD-ROMs that reside on another machine. The new version, NFS4, provides greater security, with access allowed by your firewall. The Network Information Service (NIS) maintains configuration files for all systems on a network.

Distributed Network File Systems build on the basic concept of NFS as well as RAID techniques to create a file system implemented on multiple hosts across a large network, in effect, distributing the same file system among different hosts. The primary implementation used on most Linux systems, including Ubuntu, is Red Hat's Global File System (GFS).

Network File Systems: NFS and /etc/exports

NFS enables you to mount a file system on a remote computer as if it were local to your own system. You can then directly access any of the files on that remote file system. This has the advantage of allowing different systems on a network to access the same files directly, without each having to keep its own copy. Only one copy will be on a remote file system, which each computer can then access. You can find out more about NFS at its website at **http://nfs.sourceforge.net**.

To set up the NFS service for your system, install the **nfs-kernel-server**, **nfs-common**, and **portmap** packages (selecting just the **nfs-kernel-server** will select the others automatically).

```
sudo apt-get install nfs-kernel-server
```

NFS Daemons

NFS operates over a TCP/IP network using Remote Procedure Calls (RPC) to manage file systems. The remote computer that holds the file system makes it available to other computers on the network. It does so by exporting the file system, which entails making entries in an NFS configuration file called **/etc/exports**, as well as by running several daemons to support access by other systems. These include **rpc.mountd**, **rpc.nfsd**, and **rpc.gssd**. Access to your NFS server can be controlled by the **/etc/hosts.allow** and **/etc/hosts.deny** files. The NFS server daemons provided in the **nfs-kernel-server** package are listed here. You can configure options in the **/etc/default/nfs-kernel-server** file.

rpc.nfsd Receives NFS requests from remote systems and translates them into requests for the local system.

rpc.mountd Performs requested mount and unmount operations.

rpc.svcgssd Performs security for rpc operations (rpcsec_gss protocol).

Additional NFS support daemons are provided by the nfs-common package. You can configure options in the **/etc/default/nfs-common** file.

rpc.gssd Client support for the rpcsec_gss protocol for gss-api security in NFSv4.

rpc.idmapd Maps user and group IDs to names.

rpc.statd Provides locking services when a remote host reboots.

The **portmap** server converts remote procedure calls program number to appropriate port numbers.

The NFS daemons are managed by **systemd** using several service unit files located in **/lib/systemd/system**. The NFS daemons and their **systemd** unit files are listed in Table 11-1.

The **nfs-server.service** file is shown here. Runtime configuration information is read from **/etc/default/nfs-kernel-server** (EnvironmentFile).

nfs-server.service

```
[Unit]
Description=NFS server and services
DefaultDependencies=no
Requires= network.target proc-fs-nfsd.mount rpcbind.target
Requires= nfs-mountd.service
Wants=nfs-idmapd.service

After= local-fs.target
After= network.target proc-fs-nfsd.mount rpcbind.target nfs-mountd.service
After= nfs-idmapd.service rpc-statd.service
Before= rpc-statd-notify.service

# GSS services dependencies and ordering
Wants=auth-rpcgss-module.service
After=rpc-gssd.service gssproxy.service rpc-svcgssd.service

# start/stop server before/after client
Before=remote-fs-pre.target

Wants=nfs-config.service
After=nfs-config.service

[Service]
EnvironmentFile=-/run/sysconfig/nfs-utils

Type=oneshot
RemainAfterExit=yes
ExecStartPre=/usr/sbin/exportfs -r
ExecStart=/usr/sbin/rpc.nfsd $RPCNFSDARGS
ExecStop=/usr/sbin/rpc.nfsd 0
ExecStopPost=/usr/sbin/exportfs -au
ExecStopPost=/usr/sbin/exportfs -f

ExecReload=/usr/sbin/exportfs -r

[Install]
WantedBy=multi-user.target
```

Use the **service** command to start, stop, and restart the NFS server manually.

```
sudo service nfs-kernel-server start
```

The corresponding **systemd** unit files for the, **mountd** and **idmapd** daemons, will run these daemons.

To see if NFS is actually running, you can use the **rpcinfo** command with the **-p** option. You should see entries for **mountd** and **nfs**. If not, NFS is not running.

Option for the **nfsd**, **mountd**, **nfsd**, and **svcgssd** daemons are set in the **/etc/default/nfs-kernel-server** file, where you can set options, such as the number of servers, server priority, ports, and whether to use svcgsssd.

/etc/default/nfs-kernel-server

```
# Number of servers to start up
# To disable nfsv4 on the server, specify '--no-nfs-version 4' here
RPCNFSDCOUNT=8

# Runtime priority of server (see nice(1))
RPCNFSDPRIORITY=0

# Options for rpc.mountd.
# If you have a port-based firewall, you might want to set up
# a fixed port here using the --port option. For more information,
# see rpc.mountd(8) or http://wiki.debian.org/?SecuringNFS
RPCMOUNTDOPTS=--manage-gids

# Do you want to start the svcgssd daemon? It is only required for Kerberos
# exports. Valid alternatives are "yes" and "no"; the default is "no".
NEED_SVCGSSD=

# Options for rpc.svcgssd.
RPCSVCGSSDOPTS=

# Options for rpc.nfsd.
RPCNFSDOPTS=
```

The **rpc.statd**, **rpc.idmapd**, and **rpc.gssd** daemons can be accessed using the **service** command.

```
sudo service statd restart
sudo service idmapd restart
sudo service gssd restarr
```

To configure whether to start up the **statd**, **idmapd**, and **gssd** daemons, you set options in the **/etc/default/nfs-common** file. By default, the **statd** and **idmapd** daemons are started up.

/etc/default/nfs-common

```
# If you do not set values for the NEED_ options, they will be attempted
# autodetected; this should be sufficient for most people. Valid alternatives
# for the NEED_ options are "yes" and "no".

# Do you want to start the statd daemon? It is not needed for NFSv4.
NEED_STATD=

# Options for rpc.statd.
#   Should rpc.statd listen on a specific port? This is especially useful
#   when you have a port-based firewall. To use a fixed port, set this
#   this variable to a statd argument like: "--port 4000 --outgoing-port 4001".
```

```
#   For more information, see rpc.statd(8) or http://wiki.debian.org/?SecuringNFS
STATDOPTS=

# Do you want to start the idmapd daemon? It is only needed for NFSv4.
NEED_IDMAPD=

# Do you want to start the gssd daemon? It is required for Kerberos mounts.
NEED_GSSD=
```

Setting up NFS Directories on the Desktop with shares-admin

You can set up an NFS shared folder easily using the **shares-admin** tool, which is part of the **gnome-system-tools** package. This package is no longer supported by Ubuntu and is part of the Universe repository. You can install it from the Ubuntu Software Center's System list. The menu entry for shares-admin is Shared Folders, and is hidden by default. Use Main Menu to activate it, checking it under the Other menu. To have the item appear on the Unity System Dash, you may have to log out and log in again. Then choose Shared Folders on the System dash. You can also enter the **shares-admin** command in a terminal window, without the **sudo** or **gksu** commands.

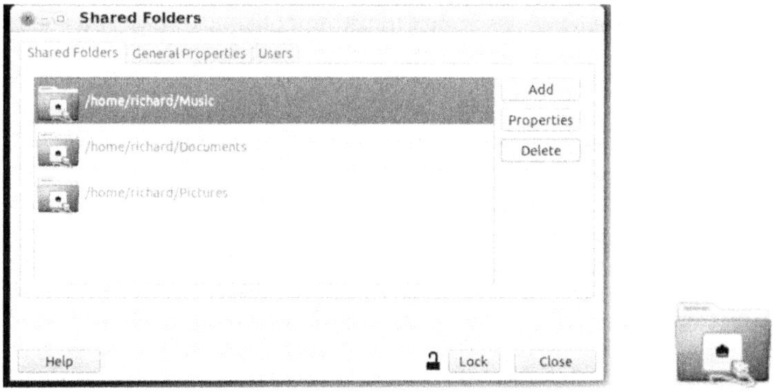

Figure 11-1: Shared Folders tool

The Shared Folders window has three tabs: Shared Folders, General Properties, and Users (see Figure 11-1). On the General tab you specify the Windows workgroup name, and a WINS server is there is one (see Figure 15-30). On Shared Folders, user access can be configured, but only for all the shares. Use the Users tab to specify which user can have access to the shared folders (see Figure 11-2).

Figure 11-2: Shared Folders User tab

To use shares-admin to manage NFS directories, you first have to unlock it, providing you with administrative access. Click the bottom-left lock button labeled "**Lock**". A PolicyKit authorization dialog will appear, prompting you to enter your password. Upon entering your password, the button label will change to "Click to prevent changes", and you can now add or modify NFS directories.

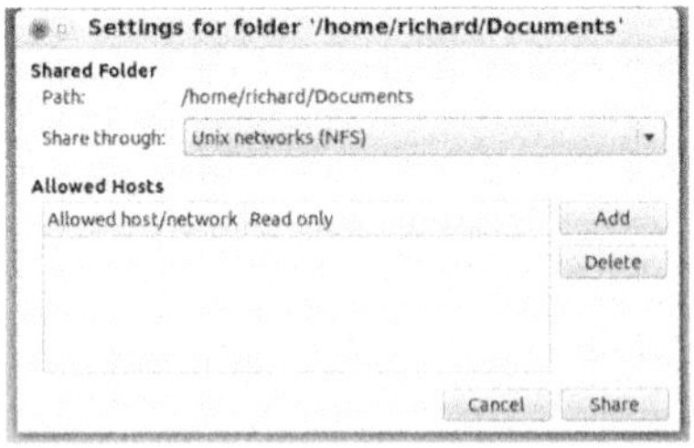

Figure 11-3: Adding a new shared folder

To add a new shared folder, click the Add button to open a Share Folder window (see Figure 11-3). On the Path pop-up menu, select the folder you want to share. If the one you want is not listed, select Other to open a file browser for the entire system. You then select the server to share through. For NFS select Unix networks (NFS).

You then select the host or network to allow access to this folder (see Figure 11-4). Click Add to open the Add Allowed hosts window. Here you can select a host name, IP address, or network address, and then enter the name or address. You can also specify read only, otherwise access is writeable.

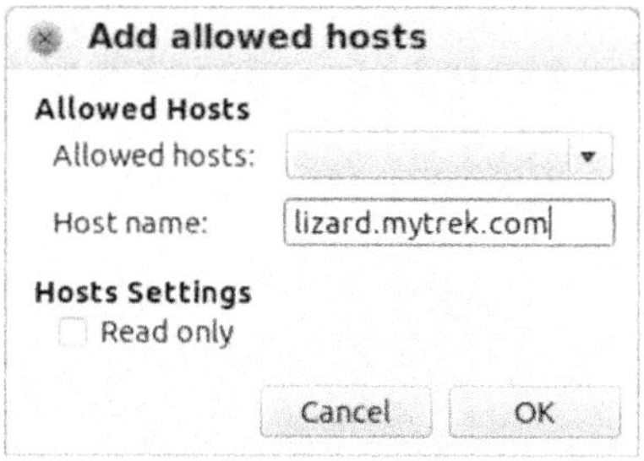

Figure 11-4: Specifying allowed hosts or networks

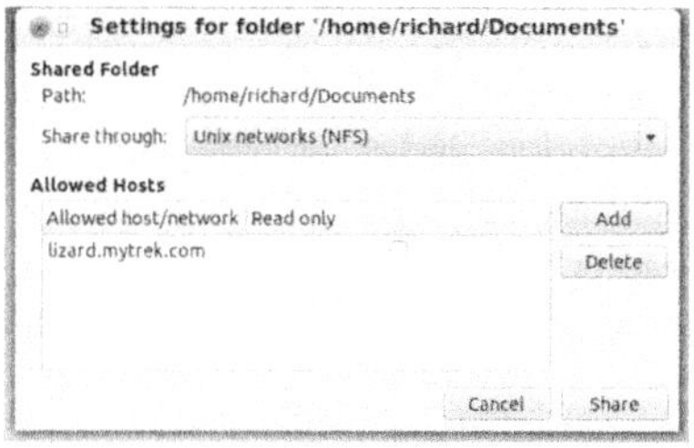

Figure 11-5: Share Folder with host access

The allowed host will then appear in the Share Folder dialog (see Figure 11-5). You can add more hosts, or delete others to deny access. When finished, click the Share button. The shared folder will then appear in the Shared Folders window.

NFS Configuration: /etc/exports

An entry in the **/etc/exports** file specifies the file system to be exported as well as the hosts on the network that can access it. For the file system, enter its mountpoint (the directory to which it was mounted on the host system). This is followed by a list of hosts that can access this file system along with options to control that access. A comma-separated list of export options placed within a set of parentheses may follow each host. For example, you might want to give one host read-only access and another read and write access. If the options are preceded by an `*` symbol, they are applied to any host. A list of options is provided in Table 11-1. The format of an entry in the **/etc/exports** file is shown here:

```
directory-pathname    host-designation(options)
```

NFS Host Entries

You can have several host entries for the same directory, each with access to that directory:

```
directory-pathname    host(options) host(options)   host(options)
```

You have a great deal of flexibility when specifying hosts. For hosts within your domain, you can just use the hostname, whereas for those outside, you need to use a fully qualified domain name. You can also use just the host's IP address. Instead of a single host, you can reference all the hosts within a specific domain, allowing access by an entire network. A simple way to do this is to use the * for the host segment, followed by the domain name for the network, such as ***.mytrek.com** for all the hosts in the **mytrek.com** network. Instead of domain names, you can use IP network addresses with a CNDR format where you specify the netmask to indicate a range of IP addresses. You can also use an NIS netgroup name to reference a collection of hosts. The NIS netgroup name is preceded by an @ sign.

```
directory      host(options)
directory      *(options)
directory      *.domain(options)
directory      192.168.1.0/255.255.255.0(options)
directory      @netgroup(options)
```

NFS Options

Options in **/etc/exports** operate as permissions to control access to exported directories. Read-only access is set with the **ro** option, and read/write with the **rw** option. The **sync** and **async** options specify whether a write operation is performed immediately (**sync**) or when the server is ready to handle it (**async**). By default, write requests are checked to see if they are related, and if so, they are written together (**wdelay**). This can degrade performance. You can override this default with **no_wdelay** and have writes executed as they are requested. If two directories are exported, where one is the subdirectory of another, the subdirectory is not accessible unless it is explicitly mounted (**hide**). In other words, mounting the parent directory does not make the subdirectory accessible. The subdirectory remains hidden until it is also mounted. You can overcome this restriction with the **no_hide** option (though this can cause problems with some file systems).

If an exported directory is actually a subdirectory in a larger file system, its parent directories are checked to make sure that the subdirectory is the valid directory (**subtree_check**). This option works well with read-only file systems, but can cause problems for write-enabled file systems, where filenames and directories can be changed. You can cancel this check with the **no_subtree_check** option.

NFS User-Level Access

Along with general options, are options that apply to user-level access. As a security measure, the client's root user is treated as an anonymous user by the NFS server. This is known as *squashing* the user. In the case of the client root user, squashing prevents the client from attempting to appear as the NFS server's root user. Should you want a particular client's root user to have root-level control over the NFS server, you can specify the **no_root_squash** option. To prevent any client user from attempting to appear as a user on the NFS server, you can classify them as anonymous users (the **all_squash** option). Such anonymous users can access only directories and files that are part of the anonymous group.

Normally, if a user on a client system has a user account on the NFS server, that user can mount and access files on the NFS server. However, NFS requires the User ID for the user be the same on both systems. If this is not the case, the user is considered to be two different users. To overcome this problem, you can use an NIS service, maintaining User ID information in just one place, the NIS password file (see the following section for information on NIS).

General Option	Description
`secure`	Requires that requests originate on secure ports, those less than 1024 This is on by default
`insecure`	Turns off the **`secure`** option
`ro`	Allows only read-only access. This is the default
`rw`	Allows read/write access
`sync`	Performs all writes when requested. This is the default
`async`	Performs all writes when the server is ready
`no_wdelay`	Performs writes immediately, not checking to see if they are related
`wdelay`	Checks to see if writes are related, and if so, waits to perform them together. Can degrade performance. This is the default.
`hide`	Automatically hides an exported directory that is the subdirectory of another exported directory
`subtree_check`	Checks parent directories in a file system to validate an exported subdirectory. This is the default.
`no_subtree_check`	Does not check parent directories in a file system to validate an exported subdirectory
`insecure_locks`	Does not require authentication of locking requests. Used for older NFS versions
User ID Mapping	**Description**
`all_squash`	Maps all UIDs and GIDs to the anonymous user. Useful for NFS-exported public FTP directories, news spool directories, and so forth
`no_all_squash`	The opposite option to **`all_squash`**. This is the default setting.
`root_squash`	Maps requests from remote root user to the anonymous UID/GID. This is the default.
`no_root_squash`	Turns off root squashing. Allows the root user to access as the remote root
`anonuid`	Sets explicitly the UID and GID of the anonymous account used for **`all_squash`** and **`root_squash`** options. The defaults are nobody and nogroup

Table 11-1: The /etc/exports Options

NFSv4

NFS version 4 is the latest version of the NFS protocol with enhanced features, such as greater security, reliability, and speed. Most of the commands are the same as the earlier version, with a few changes. For example, when you mount an NFSv4 file system, you need to specify the **nfs4** file type. Also, for NFSv4, in the **/etc/exports** file, you can use the **`fsid=0`** option to specify the root export location.

```
/home/richlp          *(fsid=0,ro,sync)
```

The preceding entry lets you mount the file system to the **/home/richlp** directory without having to specify it in the mount operation.

```
mount -t nfs4  rabbit.mytrek.com:/  /home/dylan/projects
```

NFSv4 also supports the RPCSEC_GSS (Remote Procedure Call Security, Generic Security Services) security mechanism which provides for private/public keys, encryption, and authentication with support for Kerberos. Kerberos comes in two flavors: **krb5i** with validates the integrity of the data, and **krb5p** which encrypts all requests, but involves a performance hit. Samples for using the GSS and Kerberos security are listed as comments in the **/etc/exports** file. Instead of specifying a remote location, the rpcsec_gss protocol (**gss**) is used with **krb5i** security, **gss/krb5i**. The directory mounted in the sample is the **/srv/nfs4/homes** directory, which you could set up if you want.

```
# /srv/nfs4/homes  gss/krb5i(rw,sync,no_subtree_check)
```

NFS /etc/exports Example

Examples of entries in an **/etc/exports** file are shown here. Read-only access is given to all hosts to the file system mounted on the **/srv/pub** directory. Users, however, are treated as anonymous users (**all_squash**). The **/srv** directory is used usually for server managed directories and file systems. In the next entry, read and write access is given to the **lizard.mytrek.com** computer for the file system mounted on the **/home/mypics** directory. The next entry allows access by **rabbit.mytrek.com** to the NFS server's CD-ROM, using only read access. The last entry allows anyone secure access to **/home/richlp**.

/etc/exports

```
/srv/pub               *(ro,insecure,all_squash,sync)
/home/mypics         lizard.mytrek.com(rw,sync)
/media/cdrom          rabbit.mytrek.com(ro,sync)
/home/richlp          *(secure,sync)
```

The default **/etc/options** file shows examples for using NFSv2, NFSv3, and NFSv4 formats.

/etc/exports

```
# /etc/exports: the access control list for filesystems which may be exported
#               to NFS clients.  See exports(5).
#
# Example for NFSv2 and NFSv3:
# /srv/homes     hostname1(rw,sync,no_subtree_check)  hostname2(ro,sync,no_subtree_check)
#
# Example for NFSv4:
# /srv/nfs4        gss/krb5i(rw,sync,fsid=0,crossmnt,no_subtree_check)
# /srv/nfs4/homes  gss/krb5i(rw,sync,no_subtree_check)
#
```

Applying Changes

Each time your system starts up the NFS server (usually when the system starts up), the **/etc/exports** file will be read and any directories specified will be exported. When a directory is exported, an entry for it is made in the **/var/lib/nfs/xtab** file. It is this file that NFS reads and uses to perform the actual exports. Entries are read from **/etc/exports** and corresponding entries made in **/var/lib/nfs/xtab**. The **xtab** file maintains the list of actual exports.

If you want to export added entries in the **/etc/exports** file immediately, without rebooting, you can use the **exportfs** command with the **-a** option. It is helpful to add the **-v** option to display the actions that NFS is taking. Use the same options to effect any changes you make to the **/etc/exports** file.

```
exportfs -a -v
```

If you make changes to the **/etc/exports** file, you can use the **-r** option to re-export its entries. The **-r** option will re-sync the **/var/lib/nfs/xtab** file with the **/etc/exports** entries, removing any other exports or any with different options.

```
exportfs -r -v
```

To export added entries and re-export changed ones, you can combine the **-r** and **-a** options.

```
exportfs -r -a -v
```

Manually Exporting File Systems

You can also use the **exportfs** command to export file systems manually instead of using entries for them in the **/etc/exports** file. Export entries will be added to the **/var/lib/nfs/xtab** file directly. With the **-o** option, you can list various permissions and then follow them with the host and file system to export. The host and file system are separated by a colon. For example, to export the **/home/myprojects** directory manually to **golf.mytrek.com** with the permissions **ro** and **insecure**, you use the following:

```
exportfs -o rw,insecure golf.mytrek.com:/home/myprojects
```

You can also use **exportfs** to un-export a directory that has already been exported, either manually or by the **/etc/exports** file. Just use the **-u** option with the host and the directory exported. The entry for the export will be removed from the **/var/lib/nfs/xtab** file. The following example will un-export the **/home/foodstuff** directory that was exported to **lizard.mytrek.com**:

```
exportfs -u lizard.mytrek.com:/home/foodstuff
```

Controlling Accessing to NFS Servers

You can use several methods to control access to your NFS server, such as using **hosts.allow** and **hosts.deny** to permit or deny access, as well as using your firewall to intercept access.

/etc/hosts.allow and /etc/hosts.deny

The **/etc/hosts.allow** and **/etc/hosts.deny** files are used to restrict access to services provided by your server to hosts on your network or on the Internet (if accessible). For example, you can use the **hosts.allow** file to permit access by certain hosts to your FTP server. Entries in the **hosts.deny** file explicitly deny access to certain hosts. For NFS, you can provide the same kind of security by controlling access to specific NFS daemons. The entries in the **hosts.allow** file are the same you specified in the **shares-admin** tool's Add Allow hosts window (Share Folder).

Portmap Service

The first line of defense is to control access to the portmapper service. The portmapper tells hosts where the NFS services can be found on the system. Restricting access does not allow a remote host to even locate NFS. For a strong level of security, you should deny access to all hosts except those that are explicitly allowed. In the **hosts.deny** file, you should place the following entry, denying access to all hosts by default. ALL is a special keyword denoting all hosts.

```
portmap:ALL
```

The portmapper service is referenced with the **portmap** name. You can set options manually in the **/etc/default/portmap** file.

In the **hosts.allow** file, you can then enter the hosts on your network, or any others that you want to permit access to your NFS server. Again, specify the portmapper service and then list the IP addresses of the hosts you are permitting access. You can list specific IP addresses or a network range using a netmask. The following example allows access only by hosts in the local network, 192.168.0.0, and to the host 10.0.0.43. You can separate addresses with commas:

```
portmap: 192.168.0.0/255.255.255.0, 10.0.0.43
```

The portmapper is also used by other services such as NIS. If you close all access to the portmapper in **hosts.deny**, you will also need to allow access to NIS services in **hosts.allow**, if you are running them. These include ypbind and ypserver. In addition, you may have to add entries for remote commands like `ruptime` and `rusers`, if you are supporting them.

It is also advisable to add the same level of control for specific NFS services. In the **hosts.deny** file, you add entries for each service, as shown here:

```
mountd:ALL
statd:ALL
```

Then, in the **hosts.allow** file, you can add entries for each service:

```
mountd:  192.168.0.0/255.255.255.0, 10.0.0.43
statd:   192.168.0.0/255.255.255.0, 10.0.0.43
```

Netfilter Rules

You can further control access using Netfilter to check transmissions from certain hosts on the ports used by NFS services. The portmapper uses port 111, and nfsd uses 2049. Netfilter is helpful if you have a private network that has an Internet connection and you want to protect it from the Internet. Usually a specific network device, such as an Ethernet card, is dedicated to the Internet connection. The following examples assume that device **eth1** is connected to the Internet. Any packets attempting access on port 111 or 2049 are refused.

```
iptables -A INPUT -i eth1 -p 111 -j DENY
iptables -A INPUT -i eth1 -p 2049 -j DENY
```

To enable NFS for your local network, you will have to allow packet fragments. Assuming that **eth0** is the device used for the local network, you could use the following example:

```
iptables -A INPUT -i eth0 -f -j ACCEPT
```

Mounting NFS File Systems: NFS Clients

Once NFS makes directories available to different hosts, those hosts can then mount those directories on their own systems and access them. The host needs to be able to operate as an NFS client. Current Linux kernels all have NFS client capability built in. This means that any NFS client can mount a remote NFS directory that it has access to by performing a simple mount operation.

Option	Description
`rsize=`*n*	The number of bytes NFS uses when reading files from an NFS server. The default is 1,024 bytes. A size of 8,192 can greatly improve performance.
`wsize=`*n*	The number of bytes NFS uses when writing files to an NFS server. The default is 1,024 bytes. A size of 8,192 can greatly improve performance.
`timeo=`*n*	The value in tenths of a second before sending the first retransmission after a timeout. The default value is seven-tenths of a second.
`retry=`*n*	The number of minutes to retry an NFS mount operation before giving up. The default is 10,000 minutes (one week).
`retrans=`*n*	The number of retransmissions or minor timeouts for an NFS mount operation before a major timeout (default is 3). At that time, the connection is canceled or a "server not responding" message is displayed.
`soft`	Mount system using soft mount.
`hard`	Mount system using hard mount. This is the default.
`intr`	Allows NFS to interrupt the file operation and return to the calling program. The default is not to allow file operations to be interrupted.
`bg`	If the first mount attempt times out, continues trying the mount in the background. The default is to fail without backgrounding.
`tcp`	Mounts the NFS file system using the TCP protocol, instead of the default UDP protocol.

Table 11-2: NFS Mount Options

Mounting NFS Automatically: /etc/fstab

You can mount an NFS directory either by an entry in the **/etc/fstab** file or by an explicit `mount` command. You have your NFS file systems mounted automatically by placing entries for them in the **/etc/fstab** file. An NFS entry in the **/etc/fstab** file has a mount type of NFS. An NFS file system name consists of the hostname of the computer on which it is located, followed by the pathname of the directory where it is mounted. The two are separated by a colon. For example, **rabbit.trek.com:/home/project** specifies a file system mounted at **/home/project** on the **rabbit.trek.com** computer. The format for an NFS entry in the **/etc/fstab** file follows. The file type for NFS versions 1 through 3 is **nfs**, whereas for NFS version 4 it is **nfs4**.

```
host:remote-directory    local-directory    nfs   options   0   0
```

You can also include several NFS-specific mount options with your NFS entry. You can specify the size of datagrams sent back and forth, and the amount of time your computer waits for a response from the host system. You can also specify whether a file system is to be hard-mounted or soft-mounted. For a *hard-mounted* file system, your computer continually tries to make contact if for some reason the remote system fails to respond. A *soft-mounted* file system, after a specified interval, gives up trying to make contact and issues an error message. A hard mount is the default. A system making a hard-mount attempt that continues to fail will stop responding to user input as it tries continually to achieve the mount. For this reason, soft mounts may be preferable, as they will simply stop attempting a mount that continually fails. Table 11-2 and the Man pages for **mount** contain a listing of these NFS client options. They differ from the NFS server options indicated previously.

An example of an NFS entry follows. The remote system is **rabbit.mytrek.com**, and the file system is mounted on **/home/projects**. This file system is to be mounted on the local system as the **/home/dylan/projects** directory. The **/home/dylan/projects** directory must already be created on the local system. The type of system is NFS, and the **timeo** option specifies the local system waits up to 20 tenths of a second (two seconds) for a response. The mount is a soft mount and can be interrupted by NFS.

```
rabbit.mytrek.com:/home/projects /home/dylan/projects  nfs  soft,intr,timeo=20
```

Mounting NFS Manually: mount

You can also use the **mount** command with the **-t nfs** option to mount an NFS file system explicitly. For a NFSv4 file system you use **-t nfs4**. To mount the previous entry explicitly, use the following command:

```
mount -t nfs -o soft,intr,timeo=20  rabbit.mytrek.com:/home/projects  /home/dylan/projects
```

You can, of course, unmount an NFS directory with the **umount** command. You can specify either the local mountpoint or the remote host and directory, as shown here:

```
umount /home/dylan/projects
umount  rabbit.mytrek.com:/home/projects
```

Mounting NFS on Demand: autofs

You can also mount NFS file systems using the automount service, autofs (**autofs** package). This requires added configuration on the client's part. The autofs service will mount a file system only when you try to access it. A directory change operation (**cd**) to a specified directory will trigger the mount operation, mounting the remote file system at that time.

The autofs service is configured using a master file to list map files, which in turn lists the file systems to be mounted. The **/etc/auto.master** file is the autofs master file. The master file will list the root pathnames where file systems can be mounted, along with a map file for each of those pathnames. The map file will then list a key (subdirectory), mount options, and the file systems that can be mounted in that root pathname directory. On some distributions, the **/auto** directory is already implemented as the root pathname for file systems automatically mounted. You can add your own file systems in the **/etc/auto.master** file along with your own map files, if you wish. You will find that the **/etc/auto.master** file contains the following entry for the **/auto** directory, listing **auto.misc** as its map file:

```
/auto    auto.misc   --timeout 60
```

Following the map file, you can add options, as shown in the preceding example. The **timeout** option specifies the number of seconds of inactivity to wait before trying to automatically unmount.

In the map file, you list the key, the mount options, and the file system to be mounted. The key will be the subdirectory on the local system where the file system is mounted. For example, to mount the **/home/projects** directory on the **rabbit.mytrek.com** host to the **/auto/projects** directory, use the following entry:

```
projects  soft,intr,timeo=20   rabbit.mytrek.com:/home/projects
```

You can also create a new entry in the master file for an NFS file system, as shown here:

```
/myprojects    auto.myprojects    --timeout 60
```

You then create an **/etc/auto.myprojects** file and place entries in it for NFS files system mounts, like the following:

```
dylan     soft,intr,rw    rabbit.mytrek.com:/home/projects
newgame   soft,intr,ro    lizard.mytrek.com:/home/supergame
```

Network Information Service: NIS

On networks supporting NFS, many resources and devices are shared by the same systems. Normally, each system needs its own configuration files for each device or resource. Changes entail updating each system individually. However, NFS provides a special service called the Network Information System (NIS) that maintains such configuration files for the entire network. For changes, you need only to update the NIS files. NIS works for information required for most administrative tasks, such as those relating to users, network access, or devices. For example, you can maintain user and password information with an NIS service, having only to update those NIS password files.

The NIS service is configured for use by the **/etc/nsswitch** configuration file. Here are some standard entries:

```
passwd:              compat
shadow:              compat
networks:            files
protocols:           db files
```

Note: NIS+ is a more advanced form of NIS that provides support for encryption and authentication. However, it is more difficult to administer.

NIS was developed by Sun Microsystems and was originally known as Sun's Yellow Pages (YP). NIS files are kept on an NIS server (NIS servers are still sometimes referred to as YP servers). Individual systems on a network use NIS clients to make requests from the NIS server. The NIS server maintains its information on special database files called *maps.* Linux versions exist for both NIS clients and servers. Linux NIS clients easily connect to any network using NIS.

Note: Instead of NIS, many networks now use LDAP to manage user information and authentication.

The NIS client is installed as part of the initial installation on most Linux distributions. NIS client programs are ypbind (the NIS client daemon), ypwhich, ypcat, yppoll, ypmatch, yppasswd, and ypset. Each has its own Man page with details of its use. The NIS server programs are ypserv (the NIS server), ypinit, yppasswdd, yppush, ypxfr, and netgroup—each also with its own Man page. When you install the NIS server (**nis** package) you will be prompted to enter an NIS domain, listing your host name as the default.

The NIS server is managed by **systemd** using the **nis.service** unit files in the **/run/systemd/generator.late** directory. It is generated by systemd-sysv-generator using the **/etc/init.d/nis** script. The **ypbind.service** and **ypserv.service** files are links to the **nis.service** file.

nis.service

```
# Automatically generated by systemd-sysv-generator

[Unit]
Documentation=man:systemd-sysv-generator(8)
SourcePath=/etc/init.d/nis
Description=LSB: Start NIS client and server daemons.
Before=runlevel2.target runlevel3.target runlevel4.target runlevel5.target
After=network-online.target rpcbind.target
Wants=network-online.target

[Service]
Type=forking
Restart=no
TimeoutSec=5min
IgnoreSIGPIPE=no
KillMode=process
GuessMainPID=no
RemainAfterExit=yes
ExecStart=/etc/init.d/nis start
ExecStop=/etc/init.d/nis stop
ExecReload=/etc/init.d/nis reload
```

/etc/nsswitch.conf: Name Service Switch

Different functions in the standard C Library must be configured to operate on your Linux system. Previously, database-like services, such as password support and name services like NIS or DNS, directly accessed these functions, using a fixed search order. For GNU C Library 2.*x*, used on current versions of Linux, this configuration is carried out by a scheme called the Name Service Switch (NSS), which is based on the method of the same name used by Sun Microsystems Solaris 2 OS. The database sources and their lookup order are listed in the **/etc/nsswitch.conf** file.

The **/etc/nsswitch.conf** file holds entries for the different configuration files that can be controlled by NSS. The system configuration files that NSS supports are listed in Table 11-3. An entry consists of two fields: the service and the configuration specification. The service consists of the configuration file followed by a colon. The second field is the configuration specification for that file, which holds instructions on how the lookup procedure will work. The configuration specification can contain service specifications and action items. Service specifications are the services to search. Currently, valid service specifications are nis, nis-plus, files, db, dns, and compat (see Table 11-4). Not all are valid for each configuration file. For example, the dns service is valid only for the **hosts** file, whereas nis is valid for all files. The following example will first check the local **/etc/password** file and then NIS.

```
passwd:   files nisplus
```

File	Description
ethers	Ethernet numbers
group	Groups of users
hosts	Hostnames and numbers
netgroup	Network-wide list of hosts and users, used for access rules; C libraries before glibc 2.1 only support netgroups over NIS
network	Network names and numbers
passwd	User passwords
protocols	Network protocols
publickey	Public and secret keys for SecureRPC used by NFS and NIS+
rpc	Remote procedure call names and numbers
services	Network services
shadow	Shadow user passwords

Table 11-3: NSS-Supported databases

For more refined access to passwd, group, and shadow sources, you can use the + and - symbols in file entries to determine if the entry can be accessed by the nsswitch service. The **compat** service provides a compatible mode that will check for such entries. With no such entries, the nis service will be used for all entries. The **compat** service can only be applied to the passwd, group, and shadow databases. This provides the equivalent of the files and nis services.

If your passwd, group, and shadow files already have + and - entries, and you need to have the file entries take precedence over the nis service, you can specify the files database before the compat entry.

```
passwd:   files compat
```

An action item specifies the action to take for a specific service. An action item is placed within brackets after a service. A configuration specification can list several services, each with its own action item. In the following example, the entry for the **hosts** file has a configuration specification that says to check the **/etc/hosts** files and **mdns4_minimal** service and, if not found, to check the DNS server and the **mdns4** service (multicast DNS name resolution).

```
hosts: files mdns4_minimal [NOTFOUND=return] dns mdns4
```

Service	Description
files	Checks corresponding **/etc** file for the configuration (for example, **/etc/hosts** for hosts); this service is valid for all files
db	Checks corresponding **/var/db** databases for the configuration; valid for all files except **netgroup**
compat	Provides **nis** and **files** services, with compatibility support for + and - entries. Valid only for **passwd**, **group**, and **shadow** files
dns	Checks the DNS service; valid only for **hosts** file
nis	Checks the NIS service; valid for all files
nisplus	NIS version 3
hesiod	Uses Hesiod for lookup

Table 11-4: NSS Configuration Services

An action item consists of a status and an action. The status holds a possible result of a service lookup, and the action is the action to take if the status is true. Currently, the possible status values are SUCCESS, NOTFOUND, UNAVAIL, and TRYAGAIN (service temporarily unavailable). The possible actions are return and continue: return stops the lookup process for the configuration file, whereas continue continues on to the next listed service. In the preceding example, if the record is not found in NIS, the lookup process ends.

Shown here is a copy of the **/etc/nsswitch.conf** file, which lists commonly used entries. Comments and commented-out entries begin with a **#** sign:

/etc/nsswitch.conf

```
# /etc/nsswitch.conf
#
# Example configuration of GNU Name Service Switch functionality.
# If you have the `glibc-doc-reference' and `info' packages installed, try:
# `info libc "Name Service Switch"' for information about this file.

passwd:         compat
group:          compat
shadow:         compat

hosts:          files mdns4_minimal [NOTFOUND=return] dns
networks:       files

protocols:      db files
services:       db files
ethers:         db files
rpc:            db files

netgroup:       nis
```

Distributed Network File Systems

For very large distributed systems like Linux clusters, Linux also supports distributed network file systems, such as Oracle Cluster File System for Linux (OCFS2), Lustre, the Gluster Storage Platform (GlusterFS), and Red Hat Global File System (GFS and GFS 2). These systems build on the basic concept of NFS as well as RAID techniques to create a file system implemented on multiple hosts across a large network, in effect, distributing the same file system among different hosts at a very low level (see Table 11-5). You can think of it as a kind of RAID array implemented across network hosts instead of just a single system. Instead of each host relying on its own file systems on its own hard drive, they all share the same distributed file system that uses hard drives collected on different distributed servers. This provides far more efficient use of storage available to the hosts, as well as providing for more centralized management of file system use.

A distributed network file system builds on the basic concept of NFS as well as RAID techniques to create a file system implemented on multiple hosts across a large network, in effect, distributing the same file system among different hosts at a very low level. You can think of it as a kind of RAID array implemented across network hosts instead of just a single system. That is, instead of each host relying on its own file systems on its own hard drive, they all share the same distributed file system that uses hard drives collected on different distributed servers. This provides far greater efficient use of storage available to the hosts and provides for more centralized management of file system use. GFS can be run either directly connected to a SAN (storage area network) or using GNBD (Global Network Block Device) storage connected over a LAN. The best performance is obtained from a SAN connection, whereas a GNBD format can be implemented easily using the storage on LAN (Ethernet)–connected systems. As with RAID devices, mirroring, failover, and redundancy can help protect and recover data.

Website	Name
http://fedoraproject.org/wiki/Features/Cluster	Fedora Cluster status and links
http:// www.corosync.org	Corosync Cluster Engine
http://clusterlabs.org/	Pacemaker cluster services and PCS documentation
http://oss.oracle.com/projects/ocfs2/	OCFS2, Oracle Cluster File System for Linux
https://access.redhat.com/knowledge/docs/en-US/Red_Hat_Enterprise_Linux/6/html/High_Availability_Add-On_Overview/index.html	Red Hat High Availability Addon
http://www.gluster.org	Gluster Storage Platform
http://wiki.lustre.org	Lustre cluster file system

Table 11-5: Distributed File Systems

The Red Hat Global File System (GFS2) is the preferred distributed file system for Ubuntu. GFS separates the physical implementation from the logical format. A GFS appears as a set of logical volumes on one seamless logical device that can be mounted easily to any directory on your Linux file system. The logical volumes are created and managed by the Cluster Logical Volume Manager (CLVM), which is a cluster-enabled LVM. Physically, the file system is constructed from different storage resources, known as cluster nodes, distributed across your network. The administrator manages these nodes, providing needed mirroring or storage expansion. Should a node fail, GFS can fence a system off until it has recovered the node. Setting up a GFS requires planning. You have to determine ahead of time different settings like the number and names of your Global File Systems, the nodes that will be able to mount the file systems, fencing methods, and the partitions and disks to use.

The Red Hat Global File System (GFS2), the Gluster Storage Platform (GlusterFS), and the Oracle Cluster File System for Linux (OCFS2) are available from the Ubuntu repository. GlusterFS is open source and freely available, though support can be purchased commercially. On Ubuntu it is installed with the **glusterfs-server**, **glusterfs-common**, and **glusterfs-client** packages. See the GlusterFS site for more details, **http://www.gluster.org**, and commercial support is available at **http://www.gluster.com**. Configuration is located at **/etc/glusterfs** and is started using the **glusterfsd** init script in **/etc/init.d**. Detailed examples are located in the **/usr/share/doc/glusterfs-server** directory.

The OCFS2 cluster file system is provided by Oracle as open source software. You can install it with the **ocfs2-tools** and **ocfs2-tools-dev** packages. The **ocfs2console** package installs a graphical management interface which you can run with the **ocfs2console** command in a terminal window. You can use it to configure, mount, format, and check your OCFS2 file systems. You can find out more about OCFS2 at **http://oss.oracle.com/projects/ocfs2/**.

Note: The Parallel Virtual File System (PVFS) implements a distributed network file system using a management server that manages the files system on different I/O servers. Management servers maintain the file system information, including access permissions, directory structure, and metadata information, **http://www.pvfs.org**.

Corosync Cluster Engine

The Corosync Cluster Engine is a "user space kernel" for clustering services. It provides the basis of communication, membership, and other services used in clustering environments., **www.corosync.org**. This is an open source Linux project. Ubuntu provides Ubuntu compliant binaries in the **corosync** and **corosynclib** packages. Corosync packages include **corosync**, **corosync-cfgtool** (a configuration tool), and **corosync-keygen**. Corosync is managed by systemd using the **corosync.service** unit file, which starts the Corosync service for the multi-user.target using the **corosync** script located at **/usr/share/corosync**. You can use the **service** command to start and stop corosync.

It separates the core infrastructure from the clustering services. Derived from the OpenAIS project, Corosync provides the underlying cluster infrastructure rather than API.

You can find out more about Corosync at:

```
http://www.corosync.org/
```

Corosync is a plug-in cluster engine with a modular design. Modules, known as service engines, are plugged in to the Corosync engine to make use of Corosync cluster services. Corosync components include Totem communications protocol which is based on the OpenAIS virtual synchrony communications model, a live component replacement (LCR) plugin system, an object database for the service engines and their configuration, a logging system, and inter-process communications (IPC) manager. Service engine modules include configuration for LDAP and corosync/openeais file format, the cluster manager (**pacemaker**) operates as part of corosync, both fence and fence agents.

Corosync is configured by the **/etc/corosync.conf** configuration file. Currently there are four directives, forming blocks, within which options can be specified. They are the same as those used for OpenAIS. The four directives are totem for the Totem protocol, logging, amf for the AMF service, and event for the event service. See the **corosync.conf** man page for a complete description of directives and options.

Corosync uses its own protocol called Totem to perform multicast communications. Totem configuration is specified in the **totem** directive of the **corosync.conf** file as shown here.

```
totem {
     version: 2
     secauth: off
     threads: 0
     interface {
          ringnumber: 0
          bindnetaddr: 192.168.1.1
          mcastaddr: 226.94.1.1
          mcastport: 5405
     }
}
```

Pacemaker

To manage your clusters you use a cluster manager. The recommended one for Ubuntu is the Pacemaker Cluster Resource Manager (**pacemaker** and **pcs** packages). The older **cman** cluster manager has been deprecated. The pacemaker package installs the pacemaker service. The **pcs** package installs the pacemaker configuration service. Pacemaker can work with Redhat's GFS2, Oracle's OCFS2, and with Cluster LVM (CLVM2). On Ubuntu you would normally use GFS2.

Pacemaker is managed by **systemd** using the **pacemaker.service** unit file, which is generated from a pacemaker System V script in **/etc/init.d**.

Once installed, you can use the Pacemaker Configuration Service (pcs) to manage your clusters. The pcs daemon is managed by **systemd** using the **pcsd.service** unit file. You can use **pcs** commands to setup and manage your clusters.

Check the Pacemaker Web site for detailed documentation on Pacemaker and Corosync for PCS.

```
http://clusterlabs.org
```

Red Hat Global File System (GFS)

Red Hat provides the Global File System (GFS) as an open source freely available distributed network file system. The original GFS version has been replaced with the new version of GFS, GFS 2, which uses a similar set of configuration and management tools, as well as native kernel support. Instead of a variety of seemingly unrelated packages. Native kernel support for GFS 2 provides much of the kernel-level operations. GFS 2 now works through the Corosync Cluster Engine. You would use Corosync cluster commands for your cluster. GFS2 tools have been placed in the **gfs2-utils**, package, and the Distributed Lock Manager (DLM) commands in the **dlm** package.

Many former cluster packages and applications have been deprecated with Ubuntu, including cman, rgmanager, openais, heartbeat, luci, and system-config-cluster. Though lower level GFS commands are available in the **gfs2-utils** package, you are expected to use Corosync and Pacemaker commands to manage your clusters.

To run a cluster, you need both a cluster manager and locking mechanism. Pacemaker with the Distributed Lock Manager (**dlm**) implements cluster management and locking. Pacemaker manages connections between cluster devices and services, using **dlm** to provide locking. The **dlm** locking mechanism operates as a daemon with supporting libraries.

To set up a GFS 2 file system, you first need to create cluster devices using the physical volumes and organizing them into logical volumes. You use the CLVM (Clustering Logical Volume Manager) to set up logical volumes from physical partitions (in the past you used a volume manager called pool to do this). You can then install GFS file systems on these logical volumes directly. CLVM operates like LVM, using the same commands. It works over a distributed network and requires that the **clvmd** server be running (**clvm** package).

Several GFS commands manage the file system, such as **gfs2_mount** for mounting file systems, **gfs2_mkfs** to make a GFS file system, **gfs2_fsck** to check and repair, and **gfs2_grow** to expand a file system. Check their respective Man pages for detailed descriptions. The GFS commands for managing GFS file systems are listed in Table 11-6.

To mount a GFS file system, you use the **mount** command specifying **gfs2** as the mount type, as in

```
mount  -t gfs2  /dev/vg0/mgfs  /mygfs
```

This will invoke the **gfs2_mount** tool to perform the mount operation. Several GFS-specific mount options are also available, specified with the **-o** option, such as **lockproto** to specify a different lock protocol and **acl** to enable ACL support.

To check the status of a file system, you can use **gfs2_fsck**. This tool operates much like fsck, checking for corrupt systems and attempting repairs. You must first unmount the file system before you can use **gfs2_fsck** on it.

Should you add available space to the device on which a GFS file system resides, you can use **gfs2_grow** to expand the file system to that available space. It can be run on just one node to expand the entire cluster. If you want journaling, you first have to add journal files with the **gfs2_jadd** tool. **gfs2_grow** can only be run on a mounted GFS file system.

Journal files for GFS are installed in space outside of the GFS file system, but on the same device. After creating a GFS file system, you can run **gfs2_add** to add the journal files for it. If you are expanding a current GFS file system, you need to run **gfs2_add** first. Like **gfs2_grow**, **gfs2_add** can only be run on mounted file systems. With the **setfacl** command you can set permissions for files and directories.

Command	Description
`dlm_tool`	Distributed Lock Manager, implemented as a kernel module.
`gfs2_fsck`	The GFS 2 file system checker
`gfs2_grow`	Grows a GFS 2 file system
`gfs2_jadd`	Adds a journal to a GFS 2 file system
`mkfs.gfs2`	Makes a GFS 2 file system
`gfs2_quota`	Manipulates GFS 2 disk quotas
`gfs2_edit`	Edit a GFS 2 file system
`getfacl`	Gets the ACL permissions for a file or directory
`setfacl`	Sets access control (ACL) for a file or directory

Table 11-6: GFS2 Tools

To create new file systems on the cluster devices, you use the **gfs2_mkfs** command and mount them with the **-t gfs2** option. The following command creates a GFS file system on the **/dev/gv0/mgfs** and then mounts it to the **/mygfs** directory. For **gfs2_mkfs**, the **-t** option indicates the lock table used and the **-p** option specifies the lock protocol. The **-j** option specifies the number of journals, and the **-p** option specifies the lock protocol to use.

```
gfs2_mkfs  -t mycluster:mygfs  -p lock_dlm  -j 2   /dev/vg0/mgfs
mount -t gfs /dev/vg0/mgfs /gfs1
```

To have the **gfs** service script mount the GFS file system for you, you need to place an entry for it in the **/etc/fstab** file. If you do not want the file system automatically mounted, add the **noauto** option.

```
/dev/vg0/mgfs    /mygfs    gfs2   noauto,defaults   0   0
```

GFS also supports access controls. You can restrict access by users or groups to certain files or directories, specifying read or write permissions. With the **setfacl** command you can set permissions for files and directories. You use the **-m** option to modify an ACL permission and **-x** to delete it. The **getfacl** obtains the current permissions for file or directory. The following sets read access by the user **dylan** to **myfile**.

```
setfacl -m u:dylan:r myfile
```

12. Samba

With Samba, you can connect your Windows clients on a Microsoft Windows network to services such as shared files, systems, and printers controlled by the Linux Samba server and, at the same time, allow Linux systems to access shared files and printers on Windows systems. Samba is a collection of Linux tools that allow you to communicate with Windows systems over a Windows network. In effect, Samba allows a Linux system or network to act as if it were a Windows server, using the same protocols as used in a Windows network. Whereas most UNIX and Linux systems use the TCP/IP protocol for networking, Microsoft networking with Windows uses a different protocol, called the Server Message Block (SMB) protocol that implements a local area network (LAN) of PCs running Windows. SMB makes use of a network interface called Network Basic Input Output System (NetBIOS) that allows Windows PCs to share resources, such as printers and disk space. One Windows PC on such a network can access a folder on another Windows PC's disk drive as if the folder were its own. SMB was originally designed for small LANs. To connect it to larger networks, including those with UNIX systems, Microsoft developed the Common Internet File System (CIFS), which still uses SMB and NetBIOS for Windows networking.

Wanting to connect his Linux system to a Windows PC, Andrew Tridgell wrote a SMB client and server that he called Samba. Samba allows UNIX and Linux systems to connect a Windows network as if they were Windows PCs. UNIX systems can share resources on Windows systems as if they were just another Windows PC. Windows PCs can also access resources on UNIX systems as if they were Windows systems. Samba, in effect, has become a professional-level, open source, and free version of CIFS. It also runs much faster than CIFS. Samba lets you use a Linux or UNIX server as a network server for a group of Windows machines operating on a Windows network. You can also use it to share files on your Linux system with other Windows PCs, or to access files on a Windows PC from your Linux system, as well as between Windows PCs. On Linux systems, the **cifs** file system type enables you, in effect, to mount a remote SMB-shared directory on your own file system. You can then access it as if it were a directory on your local system.

Package name	Description
samba	The Samba server
samba-common	Samba Ubuntu configuration files and support tools
samba-doc	Documentation for Samba, including examples
samba-doc-pdf	PDF versions for Samba documentation
smbclient	Samba clients for accessing Windows shares
smbfs	Mount and unmount tools for Samba shares
system-config-samba	Samba desktop configuration tool from Red Hat
kdenetwork-filesharing	Samba sharing configuration on KDE
gnome-system-tools	**shares-admin** Samba sharing configuration on GNOME (deprecated)
nautilus-share	Quick sharing configuration using the GNOME Nautilus file manager

Table 12-1: Samba packages on Ubuntu

You can obtain extensive documentation from the Samba Web and FTP sites at **http://www.samba.org**. Samba HOW-TO documentation is also available at **http://www.tldp.org**.

Extensive documentation is provided with the software package and installed on your system in the **/usr/share/doc/samba-doc** directory. Be sure to install the **samba-doc** package. The **htmldocs** subdirectory holds various documentation resources. All are in Web page format. Documentation includes the HOWTO, By Example, Using Samba, and Developers Guide. The examples include sample **smb.conf** files for different kinds of configuration. For PDF versions install the **samba-doc-pdf** package, which will be located at **/usr/share/doc/samba-doc-pdf**.

On Ubuntu, Samba software is organized into several packages, with configuration tools such as system-config-samba in separate packages (see Table 12-1). By selecting the samba server package, necessary supporting packages such as smbclient and samba-common will be automatically selected. Documentation and configuration tools have to be selected manually. Samba software packages can be obtained from the Ubuntu repositories using apt-get or the Synaptic Package Manager.

Check the Ubuntu Server Guide | Windows Networking for basic configuration and management.

```
https://help.ubuntu.com/stable/serverguide/windows-networking.html
```

Samba Applications

The Samba software package consists of two server daemons and several utility programs (see Table 12-2). The **smbd** daemon provides file and printer services to SMB clients and other systems, such as Windows, that support SMB. The **nmbd** daemon provides NetBIOS name resolution and service browser support. Additional packages provide support tools, like **smbclient** which provides FTP-like access by Linux clients to Samba services. The **mount.cifs** and **umount.cifs** commands enable Linux clients to mount and unmount Samba shared directories (used by the `mount` command with the `-t cifs` option). The **smbstatus** utility displays the current status of the SMB server and who is using it. You use **testparm** to test your Samba configuration. `smbtar` is a shell script that backs up SMB/CIFS-shared resources directly to a Unix tape drive. The **nmblookup** command will map the NetBIOS name of a Windows PC to its IP address.

Basic Samba configuration support is already provided by nautilus-share and shares-admin (GNOME). For a more complex configuration, you can use system-config-samba, a GNOME desktop tool with which you can set up secure access to Samba shares. Configuration files are kept in the **/etc/samba** directory.

Samba provides four main services: file and printer services, authentication and authorization, name resolution, and service announcement. The SMB daemon, **smbd**, provides the file and printer services, as well as authentication and authorization for those services. This means users on the network can share files and printers. You can control access to these services by requiring that users provide a password. When users try to access a shared directory, they are prompted for the password (user mode). The *user* mode provides a different password for each user. Samba maintains its own password file for this purpose: **/etc/samba/smbpasswd**.

Name resolution and service announcements are handled by the nmbd server. Name resolution essentially resolves NetBIOS names with IP addresses. Service announcements, also known as *browsing,* are the way a list of services available on the network is made known to the connected Windows PCs (and Linux PCs connected through Samba).

Samba also includes the **winbind** daemon, which allows Samba servers to use authentication services provided by a Windows domain. Instead of a Samba server maintaining its own set of users to allow access, it can make use of a Windows domain authentication service to authenticate users.

Application	Description
nautilus-share	Basic file sharing configuration built in to the GNOME Nautilus file manager
system-config-samba	Samba configuration tool (provided by Red Hat) for configuring **smb.conf** with a GNOME desktop interface
shares-admin	Older GNOME Samba configuration tool (deprecated), enter **shares-admin** in a terminal window
smbd	Samba server daemon that provides file and printer services to SMB clients
nmbd	Samba daemon that provides NetBIOS name resolution and service browser support
winbind	Uses authentication services provided by Windows domain
mount.cifs	Mounts Samba share directories on Linux clients (used by the `mount` command with the `-t cifs` option)
smbpasswd	Changes SMB-encrypted passwords on Samba servers
pdbedit	Edit the Samba users database file. This is a Secure Accounts Manager (SAM) database.
tdbbackup	Backup the Samba **.tdb** database files.
smbcontrol	Send the Samba servers administrative messages, like shutdown or close-share.
smbstatus	Displays the current status of the SMB network connections
testparm	Tests the Samba configuration file, **smb.conf**
nmblookup	Maps the NetBIOS name of a Windows PC to its IP address
/etc/default/samba	Samba startup options

Table 12-2: Samba Server Applications

Starting up and accessing Samba

Once installed, Samba is normally configured to start up automatically. You can turn this option on or off using **rcconf**. For a simple Samba configuration, you can use Ubuntu system-config-samba to configure your **/etc/samba/smb.conf** file. If you make changes, you must restart the Samba server for them to take effect. To restart Samba with your new configuration, use the **service** command. The start, stop, and restart options will start, stop, and restart the server. Run the following command from a terminal window to restart Samba.

```
sudo service smbd restart
sudo service nmbd restart
```

The Samba server consists of two daemons: **smb** and **nmb**. You may have to first enable and then start these daemons using the **service** command as the **root** user. At the prompt (on the desktop open a terminal window), access the root user with the **sudo** command, and then enter a **systemctl** command for the **smb** and **nmb** servers with the **enable** command to enable the server, and then use the **service** command with the **start** command to start it. Once enabled, the server should start automatically whenever your system starts up. Samba is managed by **systemd**.

```
sudo systemctl nmb enable
sudo systemctl smb enable
service nmb start
service smb start
```

In Ubuntu 15.04, Samba is managed by **systemd** using the **smb.service** and **nmb.service** unit files in **/run/systemd/generator.late** directory. These files are generated for systemd by the systemd-sysv-generator tool, which generates the unit files from the sysv init files for samba in the **/etc/init.d** directory. The **smb.service** file is shown here. Samba is started after the, networking, file system mounts, and the Cups service (After). It is started before the **multi-user.target** (the runlevel 2, 3, 4 targets are links to the muli-user target) (Before). On the desktop the **graphical.target** is added (runlevel5.target). The service is started using the **smbd** script in the /etc/init.d directory (ExecStart).

smb.service

```
# Automatically generated by systemd-sysv-generator

[Unit]
Documentation=man:systemd-sysv-generator(8)
SourcePath=/etc/init.d/smbd
Description=LSB: start Samba SMB/CIFS daemon (smbd)
Before=runlevel2.target runlevel3.target runlevel4.target runlevel5.target
shutdown.target
After=network-online.target local-fs.target remote-fs.target slapd.service
cups.service
Wants=network-online.target
Conflicts=shutdown.target

[Service]
Type=forking
Restart=no
TimeoutSec=5min
IgnoreSIGPIPE=no
KillMode=process
GuessMainPID=no
RemainAfterExit=yes
ExecStart=/etc/init.d/smbd start
ExecStop=/etc/init.d/smbd stop
ExecReload=/etc/init.d/smbd reload
```

The NMB daemon is started after networking (After). It starts the nmbd server using the **/etc/init.d/nmbd** script.

nmb.service

```
# Automatically generated by systemd-sysv-generator

[Unit]
Documentation=man:systemd-sysv-generator(8)
SourcePath=/etc/init.d/nmbd
Description=LSB: start Samba NetBIOS nameserver (nmbd)
Before=runlevel2.target runlevel3.target runlevel4.target runlevel5.target
shutdown.target smbd.service
After=network-online.target local-fs.target remote-fs.target
Wants=network-online.target
Conflicts=shutdown.target

[Service]
Type=forking
Restart=no
TimeoutSec=5min
IgnoreSIGPIPE=no
KillMode=process
GuessMainPID=no
RemainAfterExit=yes
ExecStart=/etc/init.d/nmbd start
ExecStop=/etc/init.d/nmbd stop
```

Firewall access

The IPtables firewall prevents browsing Samba and Windows shares from your Linux desktop. To work around this restriction, you need to make sure your firewall treats Samba as a trusted service. To allow firewall access to the Samba ports you should enable access using a firewall configuration tool like ufw. The Samba ports are 125/TCP, 137/UDP, and 138/UDP. In addition, Samba uses the Microsoft Service Discovery service which uses port 445/TCP.

On the command line interface, using the UFW default firewall, you would use the following **ufw** commands. The UFW firewall maintains its IPtables files in **/etc/ufw**.

```
ufw allow 135/tcp
ufw allow 137:138/udp
ufw allow 445/tcp
```

If you are working from a desktop interface, you can use the Gufw tool to set the Samba ports for the UFW firewall. You will have to add the ports as simple rules (see Chapter 17). On the desktop, the UFW firewall blocks remote file browsing from the desktop for Samba (the Places | Network window), because browsing uses additional broadcast packets that have not been allowed. You have to add a rule to allow access to anywhere from port **137/udp** or enter the following command. The rule restricts broadcasts to the local network. Most private networks use the network address **192.168.0.0/24**, as specified in this example (see Chapter 17).

```
sudo ufw allow from 192.168.0.0/24 port 137 proto udp
```

If you are managing your IPtables firewall directly, you could manage access by adding the following IPtables rule. This accepts input on ports 137, 138, and 139 for TCP/IP protocol packages.

```
iptables -A INPUT -p tcp --dport 135 -j ACCEPT
iptables -A INPUT -p udp --dport 137-138 -j ACCEPT
iptables -A INPUT -p tcp --dport 445 -j ACCEPT
```

Setting Up Samba with system-config-samba (desktop)

On the Ubuntu desktop, directory shares can be set up easily using the folder sharing capability of the GNOME file manager (nautilus-share), see Chapter 3. For more complex configuration you can either edit the **/etc/samba/samba.conf** file or use a desktop configuration tool like system-config-samba configuration. On Ubuntu, the **system-config-samba** tool (see Figure 12-1) provides a basic configuration. The system-config-samba tool is not directly supported by Ubuntu, but is available on the Universe repository. Install the system-config-samba package using the Synaptic Package Manager or from the Ubuntu Software Center | System Tools | Samba.

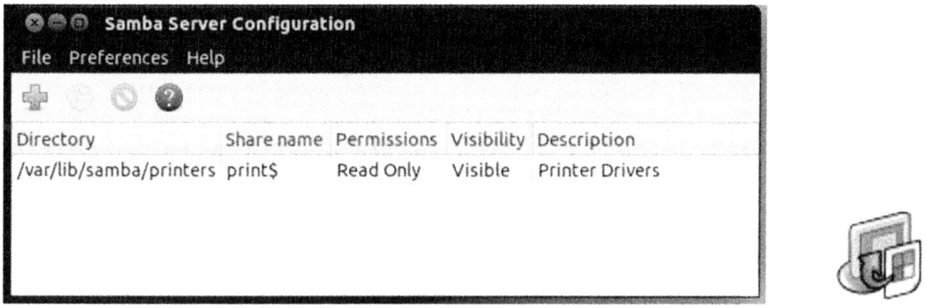

Figure 12-1: Samba server configuration with system-config-samba

Note: If you have already set up file sharing for Windows systems using the Nautilus sharing capability, the configuration information for those Samba shares will be displayed by system-config-samba.

Once installed, on Unity you can open system-config-samba from the Applications | Customization or System dashes as Samba.

Samba Server Configuration

You will first have to configure the Samba server, designating users that can have access to shared resources like directories and printers. On the Samba Preferences menu, select Server Settings to open the Server Settings dialog.

On the Basic tab, enter the name of your Windows network workgroup (see Figure 12-2). The default names given by Windows are MSHOME or WORKGROUP. Use the workgroup name already given to your Windows network. For home networks, you can decide on your own. Just make sure all your computers use the same workgroup name. On a Windows system, the Control Panel's System application will show you the Windows workgroup name. The description is the name you want displayed for your Samba server on your Windows systems. Windows 7 home networks will work with Samba without any special configuration.

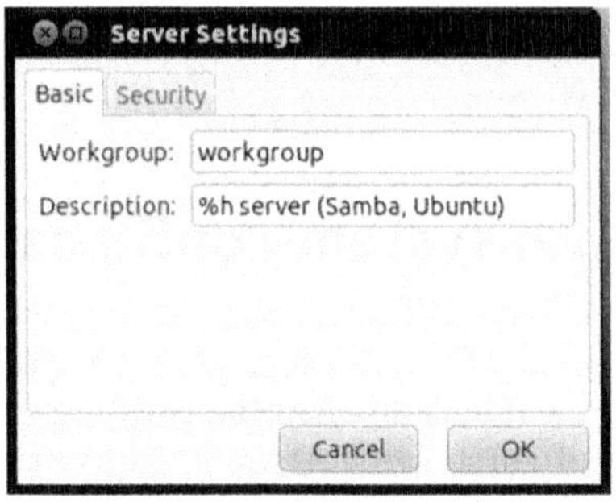

Figure 12-2: Samba Server Settings, Basic tab

On the Security tab you can select the kind of authentication you want to use (see Figure 12-3). The authentication mode specifies the access level, which can be user, server (separate authentication server), ADS (Kerberos realm), or domain (Windows domain controller). User-level access restricts access by user password. Normally, you would elect to encrypt passwords, rather than have them passed over your network in plain text. The Guest user is the name of the account used to allow access to shares or printers that you want open to any user, without having to provide a password. The pop-up menu will list all your current users, with "No Guest Account" as the selected default. Unless you want to provide access by everyone to a share, you would not have a Guest account.

Figure 12-3: Samba Server Settings, Security tab

Samba Users

For user authentication, you will want to associate a Windows user with a particular Linux account. Select Samba Users in the Preferences menu to open the Samba Users dialog (see Figure 12-4). Ubuntu users who were set up on your system when you installed Samba are listed already, using their user names and password for access by Windows users. If you want to add a new Samba user, click Add User to open the Create New Samba User window. There you can select the Unix Username from a pop-up menu, and then enter the Windows Username and the Samba password to be used for that user (see Figure 12-5). The Unix Username menu lists all the users on your Samba server. Samba maintains its own set of passwords that users on other computers will need to access a Samba share. When a Windows user wants to access a Samba share, they will have to provide their Samba password. If you use a Windows user name with spaces, enclose it within quotes.

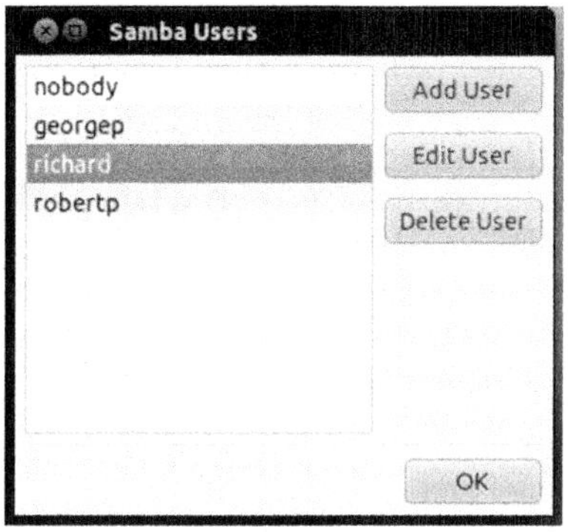

Figure 12-4: Samba Users

Once you create a Samba user, its name will appear in the list of Samba users on the Samba Users window. To later modify or delete a Samba user, use the same Samba Users window, select the user from the list, and click the Edit User button to change entries like the password, or click the Delete User button to remove the Samba user.

Note: If a password prompt prevents you from accessing a Windows share on Windows 7 from your Ubuntu system, you may have to uninstall the "Windows Live Sign In Assistant" on your Windows 7 system.

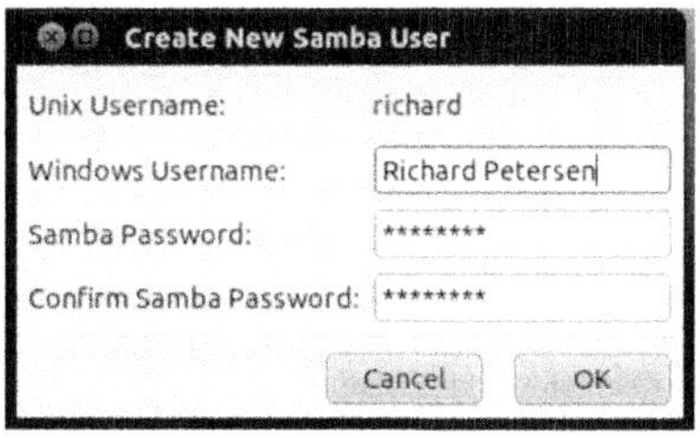

Figure 12-5: Create a new samba user

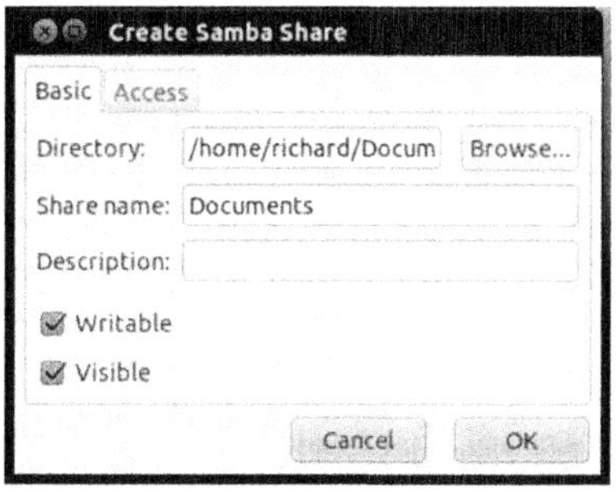

Figure 12-6: New Samba Share, Basic tab

Samba Shares

To set up a simple share, click Add Share in the Samba Server Configuration window, which opens a Create Samba Share window (see Figure 12-6).

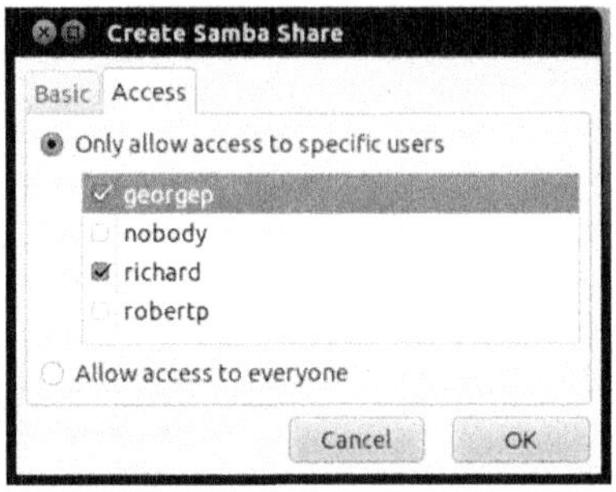

Figure 12-7: Samba share, Access tab

On the Basic tab, select the Linux directory to share (click Browse to find it), and then specify whether it will be writable and visible.

On the Access tab you can choose to open the share to everyone, or just for specific users (see Figure 12-7). All Samba users on your system are listed with check boxes where you can select those you want to give access.

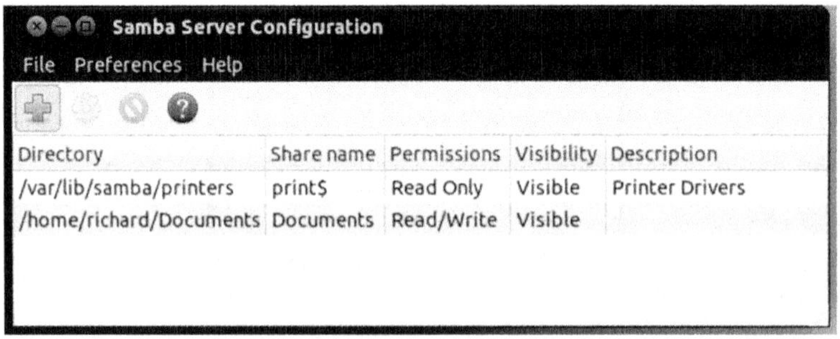

Figure 12-8: Samba with shares

Your new share will be displayed in the Samba Server Configuration window (see Figure 12-8). The share's directory, share name, its visibility, read/write permissions, and description are shown. To modify a share later, click on its entry and then click on the Properties button (or double-click). This opens an Edit samba share window with the same Basic and Access tabs you used to create the share.

Configuring Samba Access from Windows

To set up a connection for a Windows client, you need to specify the Windows workgroup name and configure the password. The workgroup name is the name that appears in the My Network Places on Windows 2000, NT, and XP (or in the Entire Network window in the Network Neighborhood on earlier Windows versions). On Vista and Windows 7, this is simply called Network. To set the workgroup name on Windows XP, open System on the Control Panel, and on the Computer Name panel, click the Change button for the Rename Or Change Domain Entry. This opens a dialog with a setting for the Workgroup, where you can enter the workgroup name. The default may be WORKGROUP or MSHOME. You can set up your own workgroup name, but all your computers would have to be configured to use that name.

On your Ubuntu Samba server, you will specify the network name in the server Settings window on system-config-samba. Alternatively, you can manually enter the network name in the **smb.conf** file, specifying the workgroup name in the `workgroup=` entry in the `global` section. The workgroup name should be uppercase and contain no spaces. The default name used on Windows XP systems is a simple WORKGROUP. The **smb.conf** `workgroup` entry would then look like this:

```
workgroup = WORKGROUP
```

Accessing Samba Shares from Windows

On a Windows client, you will see the Samba server listed when you select View Workgroups Computers from My Network Places (network on Vista). The Samba server will have, as a name, the description you gave it in your Samba configuration. Opening the icon will display a window with all the configured shares and printers on that Samba server.

When Windows users want to access a new share on the Linux system, they open their My Network Places (network on Vista) and then "Add a network place" to add a network place entry for the share, or View workgroup computers to see computers on your Windows network. Selecting the Linux Samba server will display your Samba shares. To access the share, the user will be required to enter in the user name and the Samba password. You have the option of having the username and password remembered for automatic access.

You will also need to make sure that your Windows system has enabled TCP/IP networking. This may already be the case if your Windows client is connected to a Microsoft network. If you need to connect a Windows system directly to a TCP/IP network that your Linux Samba server is running on, you should check that TCP/IP networking is enabled on that Windows system. This involves making sure that the Microsoft Network client and the TCP/IP protocol are installed, and that your network interface card (NIC adapter) is configured to use TCP/IP. The procedures differ slightly on Windows 7, Vista, 2000 and XP.

Sharing Windows Directories and Printers with Samba Clients

To manage directory shares, open the Computer Management tool in the Administrative window in the Control Panel. Click Shared Folders and there you can see the Shares, Sessions, and Open folders. To add a new share, click the Shares folder and then click the Action menu and select New File Share. The Sessions and Open folders' Action menus let you disconnect active sessions and folders.

Sharing Windows Directories

To share a directory, right-click the directory and select Sharing from the pop-up menu (Sharing And Security on Windows XP). Click Share This Folder and then enter the share name, the name by which the directory will be known by Samba. You can specify whether you want to allow others to change files on the share. You can also specify a user limit (maximum allowed is the default). You can further click the Permissions button to control access by users. Here, you can specify which users will have access, as well as the type of access. For example, you could allow only read access to the directory.

Sharing Windows Printers

To share a printer, locate the printer in the Printers window and right-click it, selecting the Sharing As option. This opens the Sharing panel, where you can click the Shared As button and enter the name under which the printer will be known by other hosts. For example, on the Windows client named lizard, to have a printer called Epson Stylus Color shared as myepson, the Sharing panel for this printer would have the Shared As button selected and the name myepson entered. Then when the user double-clicks the lizard icon in the Computers Near Me window, the printer icon labeled myepson will appear.

For a Linux system to use this printer, it will have be first configured as a remote Windows printer on that Linux system. You can do this easily with the **system-config-printer** tool (see Chapter 10).

User-Level Security

For stand alone servers, Samba provides primarily user-level security, requiring users on remote systems to log in using Samba-registered passwords. User-level security requires the use of Windows encrypted passwords. Windows uses its own methods of encryption. For Samba to handle such passwords, it has to maintain its own Windows-compatible password database. It cannot use the Linux password databases. Windows also uses additional information for the login process like where the user logged in.

User-level security requires that each user who wants to login to a Samba share from a Windows system have a corresponding user account on the Samba server. These are the users listed in the system-config-samba Samba Users window (see Figure 12-4). In addition, this account has to have a separate Samba password with which to log in to the Samba share. In effect, the user becomes a Samba user.

The account on the Samba server does not need to use the same username as that used on the Windows system. A Windows username can be specified for a Samba user. On system-config-samba, the Create New Samba User window lets you enter a Windows username in the Windows Username entry (see Figure 12-5). This mapping of windows users to Samba (Linux) users is listed in the **/etc/smbusers** file. The following maps the Windows user **rpetersen** to the Samba (Linux) user **richard**.

```
richard = rpetersen
```

When the Windows user in Windows tries to access the Samba share, the user will be prompt to login. The Windows user would then enter **rpetersen** as the user name and the Samba password that was set up for **richard**. On system-config-samba, this is the Samba password entered in the Samba Password entries in the Create New Samba Users window (see Figure 12-5)

User-level security is managed by password back-end databases. By default, the **tdbsam** back-end database is used. This is a **tdb** database file (trivial data base) that stores Samba passwords along with Windows extended information. The tdbsam database is designed for small networks. For systems using LDAP to manage users, you can use the LDAP-enabled back-end, **ldbsam**. The **ldbsam** database is designed for larger networks. The **smbpasswd** file previously used is still available, but it is included only for backward compatibility. The default configuration entries for user access in the **smb.conf file** are shown here, though, for a standalone server, user security is used and assumed. The security option will not be listed in the **smb.conf** file.

```
security = user
passdb backend = tdbsam
```

The **username map** option specifies the file used to associate Windows and Linux users. Windows users can use the Windows user name to login as the associated user. The username map file is usually **/etc/samba/smbusers**.

```
username map = /etc/samba/smbusers
```

If you are using an LDAP-enabled Samba database, ldbsam, you would use special LDAP Samba tools to manage users. These are provided in the **smbldap-tools** package. They are prefixed with the term smbldap. There are tools for adding, modifying, and deleting users and groups like **smbldap-useradd**, **smbldap-userdelete**, and **smbldap-groupmod**. You use the **sbmldap-passwd** command to manage Samba passwords with LDAP. The **smbldap-userinfo** command is used to obtain information about a user. You configure your LDAP Samba tools support using the **/etc/smbldap-tools/smbldap.conf** file.

Samba also provides its own Samba password Pluggable Authentication Module (PAM) module, **pam_smbpass.so**. With this module, you provide PAM authentication support for Samba passwords, enabling the use of Windows hosts on a PAM-controlled network. The module could be used for authentication and password management configured in your PAM **samba** file. The following entries in the PAM **samba** file would implement PAM authentication and passwords using the Samba password database:

```
auth required pam_smbpass.so nodelay
password required pam_smbpass.so nodelay
```

Be sure to enable PAM in the **smb.conf** file:

```
obey pam restrictions = yes
```

Samba Passwords: smbpasswd

With user-level security, access to Samba server resources by a Windows client is allowed only to users on that client. The username and Samba password used to access the Samba server must be registered in the Samba password database.

Note: If you are using the older smbpasswd file, you can use the `mksmbpasswd.sh` script to generate a smbpasswd file made up of all the users listed in your **/etc/passwd** file. You pipe the contents of the passwd file to `mksmbpasswd.sh` and then use redirection (>) to create the file.

You can use either system-config-samba or the smbpasswd tool to manage Samba passwords. On system-config-samba you use the Samba Users window (Preferences | Samba Users) to add or edit passwords (see Figure 12-4). Alternatively, you can use the `smbpasswd` command in a terminal window to add, or later change, passwords. To add or change a password for a particular user, you use the `smbpasswd` command with the username:

```
$ smbpasswd dylan
New SMB Password: new-password
Repeat New SMB Password: new-password
```

Users can use **smbpasswd** to change their own passwords. The following example shows how you would use **smbpasswd** to change your Samba password. If you have no Samba password, you can press the ENTER key.

```
$ smbpasswd
Old SMB password: old-password
New SMB Password: new-password
Repeat New SMB Password: new-password
```

Should you want to use no passwords, you can use smbpasswd with the **-n** option. The **smb.conf** file will need to have the **null passwords** option set to yes.

If you are using the older smb passwords file, be sure that Samba is configured to use encrypted passwords. Set the **encrypt passwords** option to **yes** and specify the SMB password file.

Managing Samba Users: smbpasswd and pdbedit

To manage users you can use the **smbpasswd** command, the **pdbedit** tool, or system-config-samba. The **smbpasswd** command with the **-a** option will add a user and with the **-x** option will remove one. To enable or disable users you would use the **-e** and **-d** options.

```
smbpasswd -a aleina
```

The smbpasswd command will operate on either the older smbasswd file or the newer tdbsam backend database files. For the **tdbsam** backend database files you can use **pdbedit**. To add a user you would use the **-a** option and to remove a user you use the **-x** option.

```
pdbedit -a larisa
```

This is a command line tool with options for adding and removing users, as well as features like changing passwords and setting the home directory. You can also import or export the user entries to or from other back-end databases.

The **pdbedit** command lets you display more information about users. To display users from the back-end database you could use the **-L** option. Add the **-v** option for detailed information. For a particular user, add the user name.

```
pdbedit -Lv richard
```

For domain policies such as minimum password lengths or retries, you use the **-P** option.

```
pdbedit -P
```

You use the **-i** and **-e** options to import and export database entries. The following will import entries from the old **smbpasswd** file to the new **tdbsam** back-end database.

```
pdbedit -i smbpasswd -e tdbsam
```

If your system is using an LDAP-enabled Samba database, use the smbldap tools to manage users and groups.

The Samba smb.conf Configuration File

Samba configuration is held in the **smb.conf** file located in the **/etc/samba** directory. Samba configuration tools, such as system-config-samba, will maintain this file for you. Alternatively, you can manually edit the file directly, creating your own Samba configuration. You may have to do this if your Samba configuration proves to be very complex. Direct editing can provide more refined control over your shares.

You use the **testparm** command in a terminal window to check the syntax of any changes you have made to the **/etc/samba/smb.conf** file.

```
testparm
```

The file is separated into two basic parts: one for global options and the other for shared services. Shared services, also known as *shares,* can either be file space services (used by clients as an extension of their native file systems) or printable services (used by clients to access print services on the host running the server). The file space service is a directory to which clients are given access; they can use the space in it as an extension of their local file system. A printable service provides access by clients to print services, such as printers managed by the Samba server.

The **/etc/samba/smb.conf** file holds the configuration for the various shared resources, as well as global options that apply to all resources. Linux installs an **smb.conf** file in your **/etc/samba** directory. The file contains default settings used for Ubuntu. You can edit the file to customize your configuration to suit your needs. Comments are commented with a # sign and directives that are commented out to deactivate them, are commented with a semi-colon, **;**. You can remove a directive's initial semi-colon symbol to make it effective. For a complete listing of the Samba configuration parameters, check the Man page for **smb.conf**. An extensive set of sample **smb.conf** files is located in the **/usr/share/doc/samba-doc** directory in the **examples** subdirectory (install the **samba-doc** package).

The **smb.conf** file is organized into two main groups, Global Settings and Share Definitions, each labeled by a comment. The Global Settings section has several subsections for different settings: Browsing/Identification, Networking, Debugging/Accounting, Authentication, Domains, Printing, and Misc. They use shorter comment lines.

In the **smb.conf** file, global options are set first, followed by each shared resource's configuration. The basic organizing component of the **smb.conf** file is called a *section.* Each resource has its own section that holds its service name and definitions of its attributes. Even global options are placed in a section of their own, labeled `global`. For example, each section for a file space share consists of the directory and the access rights allowed to users of the file space. The section of each share is labeled with the name of the shared resource. Special sections, called `printers` and `homes`, provide default descriptions for user directories and printers accessible on the Samba server. Following the special sections, other sections are entered for specific services, namely access to specific directories or printers.

A section begins with a section label, consisting of the name of the shared resource encased in brackets. Other than the special sections, the section label can be any name you choose. Following the section label, on separate lines, different parameters for this service are entered. The parameters define the access rights to be granted to the user of the service. For example, for a directory, you may want it to be browseable, but read-only, and use a certain printer. Parameters are entered in the format *parameter name* = *value.* You can enter a comment by placing a semicolon at the beginning of the comment line.

A simple example of a section configuration follows. The section label is encased in brackets and followed by two parameter entries. The **path** parameter specifies the directory to which access is allowed. The **writeable** parameter specifies whether the user has write access to this directory and its file space.

```
[mysection]
 path = /home/chris
 writeable = true
```

A printer service has the same format but requires certain other parameters. The path parameter specifies the location of the printer spool directory. The **read-only** and **printable** parameters are set to **true**, indicating the service is read-only and printable. **public** indicates anyone can access the service.

```
[myprinter]
 path = /var/spool/samba
 read only = true
 printable = true
 public = true
```

Parameter entries can be synonymous yet use different entries with the same meaning. For example, **read only** = **no**, **writeable** = **yes**, and **write ok** = **yes** all mean the same thing, providing write access to the user.

Tip: The **writeable** option is an alias for the inverse of the **read only** option. The **writeable = yes** entry is the same as **read only = no** entry.

Variable Substitutions

For string values assigned to parameters, you can incorporate substitution operators. This provides greater flexibility in designating values that may be context-dependent, like usernames.

Variable	Description
%S	Name of the current service
%P	Root directory of the current service
%u	Username of the current service
%H	Home directory of the user
%h	Internet hostname on which Samba is running
%m	NetBIOS name of the client machine
%L	NetBIOS name of the server
%M	Internet name of the client machine
%I	IP address of the client machine

Table 12-3: Samba Substitution Variables

For example, suppose a service needs to use a separate directory for each user who logs in. The path for such directories could be specified using the **%u** variable that substitutes in the name of the current user. The string **path** = /**tmp**/**%u** would become **path** = /**tmp**/**justin** for the **justin** user and /**tmp**/**dylan** for the **dylan** user. Table 12-43 lists several of the more common substitution variables.

Global Settings

The Global Settings section determines configuration for the entire server, as well as specifying default entries to be used in the home and directory segments. In this section, you will find entries for the workgroup name, password configuration, and directory settings. Several of the more important entries are discussed here.

Browsing/Identification

The Workgroup entry specifies the workgroup name you want to give to your network. This is the workgroup name that appears on the Windows client's Network window. The default Workgroup entry in the **smb.conf** file is shown here:

```
[global]

# Change this to the workgroup/NT-domain name your Samba server will part of
 workgroup = WORKGROUP
```

The workgroup name has to be the same for each Windows client that the Samba server supports. On a Windows client, the workgroup name is usually found on the Network Identification or General tab in the System tool located in the Control Panel. On many clients, this is defaulted to WORKGROUP. This is also the default name specified in the **smb.conf** file. If you want to use another name, you have to change the **workgroup** entry in the **smb.conf** file accordingly. The **workgroup** entry in the **smb.conf** file and the workgroup name on each Windows client has to be the same. In this example the workgroup name is **mygroup**.

```
workgroup = mygroup
```

The server string entry holds the descriptive name you want displayed for the server on the client systems. On Windows systems, this is the name displayed on the Samba server icon. The default is Samba Server, but you can change this to any name you want.

```
# server string is the equivalent of the NT Description field
    server string = %h server (Samba, Ubuntu)
```

Note: You can also configure Samba to be a Primary Domain Controller (PDC) for Windows NT networks. As a PDC, Samba sets up the Windows domain that other systems will use, instead of participating in an already established workgroup.

Name service resolution is normally provided by the WINS server (Windows NetBIOS Name Service, nmbd). If your local network already has a WINS server, you can specify that instead. The commented default entry is shown here. Replace w.x.y.z with your network's WINS server name.

```
;   wins server = w.x.y.z
```

WINS server support by your Samba **nmbd** server would have to be turned off to avoid conflicts, turning your Samba name resolution server into just a client. The commented entry to turn off WINS support is shown here.

```
#   wins support = no
```

If your network also has its own Domain Name Service (DNS) server that it wants to use for name resolution, you can enable that instead. By default, this is turned off, as shown next. Change the no to yes to allow use of your network's DNS server for Windows name resolution. Also, WINS server support would have to be turned off.

```
   dns proxy = no
```

Networking

This subsection has interface directives for assigning a network interface device to a particular network to use for your server. The entries are commented out by default. The commented default entry is shown here for localhost on the first Ethernet device.

```
;   interfaces = 127.0.0.0/8 eth0
```

If the system your Samba server runs on is not protected by a firewall, or the firewall is running on the same system, you should also enable the following.

```
;   bind interfaces only = yes
```

Debugging/Accounting

This section has directives for setting up logging for the Samba server. The log file directive is configured with the **%m** substitution symbol so that a separate log file is set up for each machine that connects to the server.

```
log file = /var/log/samba/log.%m
```

The maximum size of a log file is set to 1000 lines.

```
max log size = 1000
```

To have Samba log only through syslog, set the syslg only option to yes.

```
syslog only = yes
```

The syslog directive is set to 0 to just log brief information to the system logs. Detailed logging is handled by the Samba server instead.

```
syslog = 0
```

The panic action directive notifies the administrator in case of a crash.

```
panic action = /usr/share/samba/panic-action %d
```

Authentication

The server role for the Samba server can be standalone, a member server, or a domain controller (primary, backup, or active directory). Usually the server is a standalone server. The server role determines the security. For standalone server the security is user, which requires a password logon.

```
server role = standalone server
```

Windows clients use encrypted passwords for the login process. Passwords are encrypted by default and managed by the password database. In the following entries, the security is set to the user-level (**user**), and the password database file uses **tdbsam**.

```
passdb backend = tdbsam
```

You can use the security option to specify the security: **user** (user password), **domain** (Windows domain), or **ads** (Kerberos) security. The **auto** setting is the default, which derives the security from the server role. If the server role is **standalone sever**, then the security is **user** and is not specified in the **smb.conf** file.

Support for Pluggable Authentication Modules (PAM) security is then turned on.

```
obey pam restrictions = yes
```

Sync unix password with smb password changes.

```
unix password sync = yes
```

When Samba passwords are changed, they need to be synced with UNIX passwords. The **unix password sync** directive turns on syncing, and the **passwd program** and **passwd chat** directives use the **passwd** command and specified prompts to change the password.

```
unix password sync = yes
passwd program = /usr/bin/passwd %u
passwd chat = *Enter\snew\s*\spassword:* %n\n *Retype\snew\s*\spassword:* %n\n
*password\supdated\successfully* .
```

PAM is also used for password changes by Samba clients.

```
pam password change = yes
```

As a security measure, you can restrict access to SMB services to certain specified local networks. On the host's network, type the network addresses of the local networks for which you want to permit access. To deny access to everyone in a network except a few particular hosts, you can use the EXCEPT option after the network address with the IP addresses of those hosts. The localhost (127) is always automatically included. The next example allows access to two local networks:

```
hosts allow = 192.168.1. 192.168.2.
```

The map to guest directive is set to bad user. This will allow any unknown users to login as guests. Samba users that fail to login though will not be allowed access, even as guests.

```
map to guest = bad user
```

Domains

The Domains subsection configures your Samba server as a Microsoft Public Domain Controller (PDC). All of these directives are commented out by default. See the section later in this chapter on Public Domain Controller on how to set up your Samba server as a PDC on a Microsoft network.

Printing

The **load printers** directive will automatically load your printer list..

```
load printers = yes
```

The **printing** directive specifies the printing server (CUPS is the default), and the printcap name directives designates the name of the printer configuration file.

```
printing = cups
printcap name = cups
```

There is a separate set of entries for LPRng and CUPS printing, with a printing and printcap name directive for each. Most systems now use CUPS, but some other systems may still use LPRng.

Misc

The Misc subsection has entries used to customize your server. Most are commented out, except for the **usershare** directive that allows users to create public shares. An include directive lets you set up configuration files for particular machines in the **/home/samba/etc** directory, that are then read when the machine connects.

```
;    include = /home/samba/etc/smb.conf.%m
```

The domain master directive is only used if your server operates as a PDC.

```
#    domain master = auto
```

There are also entries for those using the Winbind server, specifying the user and group id ranges, and the shell to use.

```
# Some defaults for winbind (make sure you're not using the ranges
# for something else.)
;    idmap uid = 10000-20000
;    idmap gid = 10000-20000
;    template shell = /bin/bash
```

The usershare directives allow non-root users to share folders. A commented entry for user max shares can be use to limit the number of shares a user can set up.

```
;        usershare max shares = 100
```

The **user allow guests** directive permits users to create public shares, allowing guests to access the shares.

```
# Allow users who've been granted usershare privileges to create
# public shares, not just authenticated ones
usershare allow guests = yes
```

You can use a guest user login to make resources available to anyone without requiring a password. A guest user login would handle any users who log in without a specific account. Samba is usually set up to use the **nobody** user as the guest user. Alternatively, you can set up and designate a specific user to use as the guest user. You can designate the guest user with the **guest ok** and **guest account** entries in the **smb.conf** file. Be sure to add the guest user to the password file (you can also set up the guest user on the system-config-samba Server Settings dialog, Security tab, Guest Account menu).

```
guest ok = yes
guest account = nobody
```

In addition, this section provides several performance tweaks, such as setting socket options for Linux systems.

Share Definitions

The Share Definitions part will hold sections for the definition of commonly used shares, as well as any shares you have set up yourself, like shared directories or printers. There are three special sections: homes, netlogon, and profiles that are used for special purposes.

Homes Section

The Homes section specifies default controls for accessing a user home directory through the SMB protocols by remote users. Setting the **browseable** entry to **no** prevents the client from listing the files in a file browser. The **read only** entry specifies whether users have read access to files in their home directories. The **create mask** and **directory mask** entries set default permissions for new files and directories. The permission is 0700, which allows owner read/write/ execute permission. The **valid users** entry uses the **%S** macro to map to the current service. You can add the **writeable** directive to allow write access.

```
writeable = yes
```

All these entries are commented out, disabling access to user home directories by default. To enable access to home directories, remove the semi-colon comment in front of each entry in the **smb.conf** file.

If you are setting up a PDC and chose to save user profiles in the user home directories, then the homes section and its entries have to be un-commented.

```
[homes]
 comment = Home Directories
 browseable = no
 read only = yes
 valid users = %S
 create mask = 0700
 directory mask = 0700
```

The printers and print$ Sections

The printers section specifies the default controls for accessing printers. These are used for printers for which no specific sections exist. Setting **browseable** to **no** simply hides the Printers section from the client, not the printers. The **path** entry specifies the location of the spool directory Samba will use for printer files. To enable printing at all, the **printable** entry must be set to yes. To allow guest users to print, set the **guest ok** entry to **yes**. The standard implementation of the Printers section is shown here:

```
[printers]
 comment = All Printers
 browseable = no
 path = /var/spool/samba
 guest ok = no
 printable = yes
 read only = yes
 create mask = 0700
```

The **print$** section, shown next, specifies where a Windows client can find a print driver on your Samba server. The printer drivers are located in the **/var/lib/samba/printers** directory and are read-only. The browseable, read-only, and guest directives are commented out. They can be enabled to allow browsing of the drivers. The **write list** directive would allow you to remotely administer the Windows print drivers. **lpadmin** is the name of your administrator group.

```
# Windows clients look for this share name as a source of downloadable
# printer drivers
[print$]
   comment = Printer Drivers
   path = /var/lib/samba/printers
  browseable = yes
  read only = yes
  guest ok = no
;  write list = root, @lpadmin
```

Shares

Sections for specific shared resources, such as directories on your system, are placed after the Homes and Printers sections. For a section defining a shared directory, enter a label for the share. Then, on separate lines, enter options for its pathname and the different permissions you want to set. In the `path` = *option,* specify the full pathname for the directory. The `comment` = *option* holds the label to be given the share. You can make a directory writeable, public, or read-only. You can control access to the directory with the **valid users** entry, which you can use to list those users permitted access. For those options not set, the defaults entered in the Global, Homes, and Printers segments are used.

The following example is the **myprojects** share. Here the **/myprojects** directory is defined as a share resource that is open to any user with guest access.

```
[myprojects]
     comment = Great Project Ideas
     path = /myprojects
     read only = no
     guest ok = yes
```

To limit access to certain users, you can list a set of valid users. Setting the `guest ok` option to `no` closes it off from access by others.

```
[mynewmusic]
 comment =  New Music
 path = /home/specialprojects
 valid users = mark, richard
 guest ok = no
 read only = no
```

The following example makes the Documents folder accessible and writeable to the georgep and richard users.

```
[Documents]
path = /home/richard/Documents
writeable = yes
browseable = yes
valid users = georgep, richard
```

To allow complete public access, set the **guest ok** entry to **yes**, with no valid users entry.

```
[newdocs]
comment =  New Documents
path = /home/newdocs
guest ok = yes
read only = no
```

To set up a directory that can be shared by more than one user, where each user has control of the files he or she creates, simply list the users in the Valid Users entry. Permissions for any created files are specified in the Advanced mode by the Create Mask entry (same as create mode). In this example, the permissions are set to 765, which provides read/write/execute access to owners, read/write access to members of the group, and only read/execute access to all others (the default is 744, read-only for group and other permission):

```
[myshare]
 comment = Writer's projects
 path = /usr/local/drafts
 valid users = Justin, chris, dylan
 guest ok = no
 read only = no
 create mask = 0765
```

Printer shares

Access to specific printers is defined in the Printers section of the **smb.conf** file. For a printer, you need to include the Printer and Printable entries, as well as specify the type of Printing server used. With the Printer entry, you name the printer, and by setting the Printable entry to yes, you allow it to print. You can control access to specific users with the **valid users** entry and by setting the Public entry to no. For public access, set the **public** entry to yes. For the CUPS server, set the printing option to **cups**.

The following example sets up a printer accessible to guest users. This opens the printer to use by any user on the network. Users need to have write-access to the printer's spool directory, located in **/var/spool/samba**. Keep in mind that any printer has to first be installed on your system. The following printer was already installed as **myhp**. You use the CUPS administrative tool to set up printers for the CUPS server. The Printing option can be inherited from the Printers share.

```
[myhp]
     path = /var/spool/samba
     read only = no
     guest ok = yes
     printable = yes
```

```
printer = myhp
oplocks = no
share modes = no
printing = cups
```

As with shares, you can restrict printer use to certain users, denying it to public access. The following example sets up a printer accessible only by the users **larisa** and **aleina** (you could add other users if you want). Users need to have write access to the printer's spool directory.

```
[larisalaser]

    path = /var/spool/samba
    read only = no
    valid users = larisa aleina
    guest ok = no
    printable = yes
    printing = cups
    printer = larisalaser
    oplocks = no
    share modes = no
```

Testing the Samba Configuration

After you make your changes to the **smb.conf** file, you can then use the **testparm** program to see if the entries are correctly entered. **testparm** checks the syntax and validity of Samba entries. By default, testparm checks the **/etc/samba/smb.conf** file. If you are using a different file as your configuration file, you can specify it as an argument to testparm. You can also have testparm check to see if a particular host has access to the service set up by the configuration file.

To check the real-time operation of your Samba server, you can log in to a user account on the Linux system running the Samba server and connect to the server.

Samba Public Domain Controller: Samba PDC

Samba can also operate as a Public Domain Controller (PDC). The domain controller will be registered and advertised on the network as the domain controller. The PDC provides a much more centralized way to control access to Samba shares. It provides the netlogon service and a NETLOGON share. The PDC will set up machine trust accounts for each Windows and Samba client. Though you can do this manually, Samba will do it for you automatically. Keep in mind that Samba cannot emulate a Microsoft Active PDC, but can emulate a Windows NT4 PDC. You can find out more about Samba PDC at:

```
http://us1.samba.org/samba/docs/man/Samba-HOWTO-Collection/samba-pdc.html
```

For basic configuration check the Ubuntu Server Guide | Windows Networking | Samba as a Domain Controller.

```
https://help.ubuntu.com/stable/serverguide/samba-dc.html
```

You will, of course, have to have the Samba server installed. Also make sure that **libpam-smbpass** is also installed.

Microsoft Domain Security

As noted in the Samba documentation, the primary benefit of Microsoft domain security is single-sign-on (SSO). In effect, logging into your user account also logs you into access to your entire network's shared resources. Instead of having to be separately authenticated any time you try to access a shared network resource, you are already authenticated. Authentication is managed using Security IDs (SID) that consists of a network ID (NID) and a relative ID (RID). The RID references your personal account. A separate RID is assigned to every account, even those for groups or system services. The SID is use to set up access control lists (ACL) the different shared resources on your network, allowing a resource to automatically identify you.

Essential Samba PDC configuration options

To configure your PDC, edit the **Domains** section in the **smb.conf** file. Here you will find entries for configuring your Samba PDC options. Certain other entries are found elsewhere. The domain master entry is located in the Misc section.

The essential PDC options are shown here.

```
workgroup = myworkgroup
domain logons = yes
domain master = yes
security = user
```

If the netbios name is different from the host name on which the server is run, you can add a **netbios name** option to specify it.

```
netbios name = myserver
```

Basic configuration

Like most Samba configurations, the PDC requires a Samba back-end. The **tdbsam** is already configured for you. The security level should be **user**. This is normally the default and should already be set. The **smb.conf** entries are shown here:

```
security = user
passdb backend = tdbsam
```

The PDC must also be designated the domain master. This entry is located in the Misc section, and is set to auto by default. For a PDC, set it to yes, and for a BDC (backup domain controller) set it to no.

```
domain master = yes
```

The PDC has browser functionality, with which it locates systems and shares on your network. These features are not present in the Ubuntu **smb.conf** file, but you can add them if needed. The **local master** option is use only if you already have another PDC that you want to operate as the local master. You could have several domain controllers operating on your network. Your Microsoft network holds an election to choose which should be the master. The **os level** sets the precedence for this PDC. It should be higher than 32 to gain preference over other domain controllers on your network, insuring this PDC's election as the primary master controller. The **preferred master** option starts the browser election on start up.

```
;       local master = no
os level = 33
preferred master = yes
```

Domain Logon configuration

Samba PDC uses the domain logons service whereby a user can log on to the network. The domain logon service is called the netlogon service by Microsoft. The samba share it uses is also called netlogon. To configure the domain logon service you set the **domain logons** option to yes, or if you set the **server role** option to "primary classic domain controller" or to "backup domain controller."

```
domain logons = yes
```

The logon path references the profile used for a user. The **%N** will be the server name, and the **%U** references the user name. Profiles can be set up either in a separate profiles share or in the user home directories. The following would reference user profiles in the profiles share. You would also have to define the profiles share by un-commenting the profiles share entries in the **smb.conf** file.

```
logon path = \\%N\Profiles\%U
```

If the profile is stored in the user's home directory instead of the Profiles share, you would uncomment the following entry instead. You will also have to allow access to user home directories, un-commenting the homes share entries.

```
logon path = \\%N\%U\profile
```

The **logon drive** and **logon home** specify the location of the user's home directory. The logon drive is set as the H: drive. The **%N** evaluates to the server name and **%U** to the user.

```
logon drive = H:
logon home = \\%N\%U
```

The login script can be one set by the system or by users.

```
# the login script name depends on the machine name
logon script = logon.cmd
```

You can then enable user add operations for adding users, groups, and machines to the PDC. The add machine entry allows Samba to automatically add trusted machine accounts for Windows systems when they first join the PDC controlled network.

```
add user script = /usr/sbin/adduser --quiet --disabled-password --gecos "" %u
add machine script  = /usr/sbin/useradd -g machines -c "%u machine account" -d
/var/lib/samba -s /bin/false %u
add group script = /usr/sbin/addgroup --force-badname %g
```

You then need to set up a netlogon share in the **smb.conf** file. This share holds the `netlogon` scripts—in this case, the **/var/lib/samba/netlogon** directory—which should not be writable, but should be accessible by all users (Guest OK). In the share definitions section of the **smb.conf** file you will find the **[netlogon]** section commented. Remove the semi-colon comments from the entry, as shown here.

```
# Un-comment the following and create the netlogon directory for Domain Logon
# (you need to configure Samba to act as a domain controller too.)
```

```
[netlogon]
comment = Network Logon Service
path = /home/samba/netlogon
guest ok = yes
read only = yes
```

If you choose to use a profiles share to store user profiles in, then you should enable the **profiles** share. Un-comment the following to define a **profiles** share. The entries are located just after the **netlogon** shares.

```
 [profiles]
comment = Users profiles
path = /home/samba/profiles
guest ok = no
browseable = no
create mask = 0600
directory mask = 0700
```

The **profile** share is where user netlogon profiles are stored. If, instead, you are using the user's home directories to store their profiles, you will not need to define and use a **profiles** share. If you choose to store user profiles in the user home directories, you would un-comment the **homes** share entries instead.

Accessing Samba Services with Clients

Client systems connected to the SMB network can access the shared services provided by the Samba server. Windows clients should be able to access shared directories and services automatically through the My Network Places or Network on a Windows desktop. For Linux systems connected to the same network, Samba services can be accessed using the GNOME Nautilus file manager and KDE file manager, as well as special Samba client programs.

With the Samba smbclient**,** a command line client, a local Linux system can connect to a shared directory on the Samba server and transfer files and run shell programs. Using the **`mount`** command with the **`-t cifs`** option, directories on the Samba server can be mounted to local directories on the Linux client. The **`cifs`** option invokes **mount.cifs** to mount the directory.

Accessing Windows Samba Shares from GNOME

You can use Nautilus (the GNOME file manager) to access your Samba shares. Select Places | Network to open the Network window, displays the icons for your network. In this window, open the Windows Network folder to list folders for your Windows network groups, such as WORKGROUP. Opening up a Windows group folder will list the hosts in that group. These will show host icons for your shared Windows hosts. Clicking a host icon will list all the shared resources on it.

Alternatively, you can start Nautilus in browser mode and enter the **smb:** protocol in the Location box to display all the Samba and Windows networks, from which you can access the Samba and Windows shares.

smbclient

The smbclient utility operates like FTP to access systems using the SMB protocols. With smbclient you can access SMB-shared services, either on the Samba server or on Windows systems. Many smbclient commands are similar to those of FTP, such as `mget` to transfer a file or `del` to delete a file. The smbclient program has several options for querying a remote system, as well as connecting to it. See the **smbclient** Man page for a complete list of options and commands. The smbclient program takes as its argument a server name and the service you want to access on that server. A double slash precedes the server name, and a single slash denotes the service. The service can be any shared resource, such as a directory or a printer. The server name is its NetBIOS name, which may or may not be the same as its IP name. For example, to specify the **myreports** shared directory on the server named **turtle.mytrek.com**, use **//turtle.mytrek.com/myreports**. If you must specify a pathname, use backslashes for Windows files and forward slashes for Unix/Linux files:

```
//server-name/service
```

You can also supply the password for accessing the service. Enter it as an argument following the service name. If you do not supply the password, you are prompted to enter it.

You can then add several options to access shares, such as the remote username or the list of services available. With the `-I` option, you can specify the system using its IP address. You use the `-U` option and a login name for the remote login name you want to use on the remote system. Attach % with the password if a password is required. With the `-L` option, you can obtain a list of the services provided on a server, such as shared directories or printers. The following command will list the shares available on the host **turtle.mytrek.com**:

```
smbclient -L turtle.mytrek.com
```

To access a particular directory on a remote system, enter the directory as an argument to the `smbclient` command, followed by any options. For Windows files, you use backslashes for the pathnames, and for Unix/Linux files, you use forward slashes. Once connected, an SMB prompt is displayed and you can use smbclient commands such as `get` and `put` to transfer files. The `quit` and `exit` commands quit the smbclient program. In the following example, smbclient accesses the directory **myreports** on the **turtle.mytrek.com** system, using the **dylan** login name:

```
smbclient //turtle.mytrek.com/myreports -I 192.168.0.1 -U dylan
```

In most cases, you can simply use the server name to reference the server, as shown here:

```
smbclient //turtle.mytrek.com/myreports -U dylan
```

If you are accessing the home directory of a particular account on the Samba server, you can simply specify the **homes** service. In the next example, the user accesses the home directory of the **aleina** account on the Samba server, after being prompted to enter that account's password:

```
smbclient //turtle.mytrek.com/homes -U aleina
```

You can also use smbclient to access shared resources located on Windows clients. Specify the computer name of the Windows client along with its shared folder. In the next example, the user accesses the **windata** folder on the Windows client named **lizard**. The folder is configured to allow access by anyone, so the user just presses the ENTER key at the password prompt.

```
$ smbclient //lizard/windata
```

Once logged in, you can execute smbclient commands to manage files and change directories. Shell commands can be executed with the ! operator. To transfer files, you can use the **mget** and **mput** commands, much as they are used in the FTP program. The **recurse** command enables you to turn on recursion to copy whole subdirectories at a time. You can use file-matching operators, referred to here as *masks,* to select a certain collection of files. The file-matching (mask) operators are *****, **[]**, and **?** (see Chapter 19). The default mask is *****, which matches everything. The following example uses **mget** to copy all files with a **.c** suffix, as in **myprog.c**:

```
smb> mget *.c
```

mount.cifs: mount -t cifs

Using the **mount** command with the **-t cifs** option, a Linux client can mount a shared directory onto its local system. The **cifs** option invokes the **mount.cifs** command to perform the mount operation. The syntax for the **mount.cifs** command is similar to that for the **smbclient** command, with many corresponding options. The **mount.cifs** command takes as its arguments the Samba server and shared directory, followed by the local directory where you want to mount the directory. Instead of using **mount.cifs** explicitly, you use the **mount** command with the file system type **cifs**. The **mount** command will then run the /**sbin**/**mount.cifs** command, which will invoke **smbclient** to mount the file system. The following example mounts the **myreports** directory onto the **/mnt/myreps** directory on the local system::

```
mount -t cifs //turtle.mytrek.com/myreports /mnt/myreps -U dylan
```

To unmount the directory, use the **umount** command with the **-t cifs** option and the directory name. This will invoke the **umount.cifs** command which performs the unmount operation.

```
umount -t cifs  /mnt/myreps
```

To mount the home directory of a particular user on the server, specify the **homes** service and the user's login name. The following example mounts the home directory of the user **larisa** to the **/home/chris/larisastuff** directory on the local system:

```
mount -t cifs //turtle.mytrek.com/homes /home/chris/larisastuff -U larisa
```

You can also mount shared folders on Windows clients. Specify the computer name of the Windows client along with its folder. If the folder name contains spaces, enclose it in single quotes. In the following example, the user mounts the **windata** folder on **lizard** as the **/mylinux** directory. For a folder with access to anyone, just press ENTER at the password prompt:

```
$ mount -t cifs //lizard/windata /mylinux
Password:
$ ls /mylinux
_hi_mynewdoc.doc_myreport.txt
```

To unmount the shared folder when you are finished with it, use the **umount** command and the **-t cifs** option.

```
umount -t cifs /mylinux
```

You could also specify a username and password as options, if user-level access is required:

```
mount -t cifs -o username=chris passwd=mypass //lizard/windata /mylinux
```

You can also use the cifs type in an **/etc/fstab** entry to have a Samba file system mounted automatically:

```
//lizard/windata /mylinux cifs defaults 0 0
```

13. Cloud Computing

Ubuntu features fully integrated support for cloud computing. Ubuntu provides private and public cloud support. The public cloud accesses the Amazon EC2 cloud system, and the private cloud sets up your own cloud computing service with the Ubuntu Enterprise Cloud software. Both use EC2 (Elastic Computing), which is the standard for cloud computing. Cloud support is still very much a work in progress. An overview of Ubuntu cloud computing with links is located at:

```
http://www.ubuntu.com/cloud/
```

You will need to use a Web browser to set up access and manage your cloud. Use either a command line browser like elinks or lynx, or, if you have installed the ubuntu desktop or basic GNOME interface, you can use Firefox or Epiphany.

Check the Amazon EC2 documentation for more details, including the User Guide and Getting Started guide at **http://docs.amazonwebservices.com**.

Public Cloud: Amazon EC2 Cloud

The Ubuntu 15.04 server edition provides support for access the Amazon EC2 cloud provided by Amazon Web Services (AWS). This is a commercial service that you have to sign up and pay for. Once you have access, you can then access an Amazon Machine Image (AMI) for an Ubuntu server and set up applications to run from the Amazon EC2 cloud. See the Ubuntu public cloud page for an overview.

```
http://www.ubuntu.com/cloud/
```

You can find out more about Amazon EC2 cloud at:

```
http://aws.amazon.com/ec2/
```

The EC2StartGUide shows how to set up access.

```
https://help.ubuntu.com/community/EC2StartersGuide
```

To find out what Ubuntu AMIs are available on Amazon, you can use the Ubuntu Cloud Images site at:

```
http://cloud-images.ubuntu.com
```

Cloud tools

You can install a tool to allow you to start and stop instances. The recommended tools are the Eucalyptus tools in the **euca2ools** package and the Amazon tools in the **ec2-api-tools** package. The Eucalyptus tool is an open source tool supported by Ubuntu.

Amazon EC2 tools

Alternatively, you can use the Amazon EC2 tools (Multiverse repository). The examples in this chapter use these tools.

First install the Amazon EC2 API package.

```
ec2-api-tools
```

There are an extensive number of EC2 tools provided by this package. A listing and explanation for these tools are located at:

```
http://docs.amazonwebservices.com/AWSEC2/latest/CommandLineReference/
```

Click on the API Command Line Tools Reference link on the left pane of this Web page. These explanations also apply to their Eucalyptus counterparts (**euca** prefix).

Eucalyptus tools

For the Eucalyptus tools, you install the euca2ools package.

```
euca2ools
```

The package installs several cloud management tools, beginning with the prefix **euca**. For examples check the man page for a command and also check the Eucalyptus User Guide at:

```
http://open.eucalyptus.com/wiki/Euca2oolsGuide
```

Proprietary management tools

You can also use proprietary management tools such as Canonical's Landscape, Rightscale cloud management service (**http://www.rightscale.com**), and the CohesiveFT Elastic cloud management support (**http://www.cohesiveft.com/**). Check this site for more information.

```
http://www.ubuntu.com/cloud/management
```

Setting up access

On the Amazon cloud, you can access a public Amazon Machine Image (AMI) for an Ubuntu 15.04 server system provided by Ubuntu. You will have to create an Amazon EC2 account, set up security, and then set up your cloud. Check the Ubuntu EC2 starter guide on how to set up access.

```
https://help.ubuntu.com/community/EC2StartersGuide
```

Create an account

To set up an Amazon EC2 account, you first have to have a basic Amazon account. Set one up if you do not already have one. Then sign in and set up an Amazon EC2 account at (click the Sign Up button):

```
http://aws.amazon.com/ec2
```

Set up Security:

To ensure access to the Amazon EC2 cloud, you have to make sure your security certificates and keys are installed and made available to the EC2 API tools that will manage your access to the AMI. You will create a certificate and private key on your AWS account. Click on the Account tab and choose Security Credentials. Click the **X.509 Certificates** tab. On this tab, click the "Create a new Certificate" link. This opens a dialog with buttons to download both a private key and certificate. Take note where you are downloading the certificate and private key. The private key file begins with the prefix **pk-** and the certificate file begins with **cert-**.

If you have set up an account already, but your Ubuntu system does not have access, you will have to generate a new certificate in order to download a private key. Sign in and click the Account tab, choosing the Security Credentials link. Click on the "X.509 Certificates" tab, and then click on the "Create a new Certificate" link. A dialog opens with buttons to download the Private key and the X.509 certificate.

Note your account ID which is listed at the bottom of the Security Credentials page.

You then set up three shell variables and export them to make them global. These are set up in your **.bashrc** file in your home directory. The variables hold the locations of your private key, Amazon certificate, and the JAVA OpenJDK.

EC2_PRIVATE_KEY	The location and name of your Amazon EC2 private key file
EC2_CERT	The location and name of your Amazon EC2 certificate file
JAVA_HOME	The location of the JAVA OpenJDK software

The EC2StartGUide provides an example format.

```
https://help.ubuntu.com/community/EC2StartersGuide
```

Here is the example.

```
export EC2_PRIVATE_KEY=$HOME/<where your private key is>/pk-XXXXXXXXXXXXXXXXXX.pem
export EC2_CERT=$HOME/<where your certificate is>/cert-XXXXXXXXXXXXXXXXXXXXXX.pem
export JAVA_HOME=/usr/lib/jvm/java-6-openjdk-amd64/
```

The name of the certificate and key files can be very complex. On the command line interface, a simple way to copy the file names is to list them with the **ls** command and save the names in a file that you can then copy and paste from in nano.

```
ls *.pem > mykeyname
nano mykeyname
```

To access the Ubuntu Server public AMI, you also have to generate an SSH key. Use the **ec2-add-keypair** command to create an SSH key. Be sure to save the output to a file, named in this example **myec2key.pem**. You can also set up the SSH keys using the AWS console.

```
ec2-add-keypair myec2key > myec2key.pem
```

Set the file permissions to 600.

```
chmod 600 myec2key.pem
```

Authorize access through the SHH port, port 22, using the **ec2-authorize** command.

```
ec2-authorize default -p 22
```

You can assign the SSH key you made to the EC2_KEYPAIR variable, and then use that variable to reference the key in your ec2 commands.

```
export EC2_KEYPAIR=<your keypair name> # name only, not the file name
```

In addition, you can specify the EC2 region site for your cloud instances. These are listed on the EC2StartersGuide Web page. For example, **us-east-1** indicates the Eastern US, and **eu-west-1** indicates Europe. The region site URL is assigned to the EC2_URL variable.

```
export EC2_URL=https://ec2.<your ec2 region>.amazonaws.com
```

You can then edit the **.bashrc** file, adding the EC2 variables at the end and copying and pasting the key file names.

```
nano .bashrc
```

On a desktop interface, you can edit the **.bashrc** file and copy and paste using gedit (View | Show Hidden Files).

A sample of the lines you would add is listed on the EC2StartersGuide Web page and is shown here, with example key and certificate names. In this example, the keys are in the user's HOME directory (**$HOME**), though you may want to place them in a more secure directory. On a desktop interface you could copy and paste directly from the Web page to the **.bashrc** file, being edited with gedit.

```
export EC2_KEYPAIR=myec2key # name only, not the file name
export EC2_URL=https://ec2.us-west-1.amazonaws.comexport
EC2_PRIVATE_KEY=$HOME/pk-ABCDE2MA6RCNEC7LCXEDULV7H6JBZZZZ.pem
export EC2_CERT=$HOME/cert-ABCDE2MA6RCNEC7LCXEDULV7H6JBZZZZ.pem
export JAVA_HOME=/usr/lib/jvm/java-6-openjdk-amd64/
```

Ubuntu AMI Cloud Images

The official AMI IDs for Ubuntu are listed using the Ubuntu Cloud Images site at:

```
http://cloud-images.ubuntu.com
```

The Cloud Images page requires that you have access to a Web browser.

Click on the folder with the release name you want, such as vivid for Ubuntu 15.04. This opens the page for the daily build folder. Click on the current folder for the latest link.

Clicking on Launch button opens the AWS Web console, prompting you to add an instance of the selected image.

Accessing the AMI with the ec2 commands

The EC2 Starter Guide describes the use of the Amazon EC2 tools (**ec2-api-tools**), but the examples also apply to the Eucalyptus EC2 tools (**euca2ools**). Just replace the **ec2** prefix for these tools with the **euca** prefix, as in **euca-describe-images** instead of **ec2-describe-images**.

You will first have to find the AMI ID for the Ubuntu Server AMI. You have to reference the AMI ID to access that image. The official AMI IDs for Ubuntu are listed on the Ubuntu Cloud Images site at:

```
http://cloud-images.ubuntu.com
```

The "ec2 command" column lists the actual ec2 command you have to enter to start the instance. It shows the ec2-run-instance command with the AMI ID and the cloud region.

To list all available Ubuntu images you can use the **ec2-describe-images** command with the **-a** option, and use **grep** to filter the results with the ubuntu pattern. These will include images posted by third parties, not just the official Ubuntu images.

```
ec2-describe-images -a | grep ubuntu
```

To list the current official Vivid Ubuntu AMI images, use the **ec2-describe-images** command and pipe the results through a series of **grep** operations beginning with a **099720109477/ubuntu-images/ubuntu-vivid** pattern. Be sure to specify the official Canonical user Amazon ID, 099720109477. Add a grep operation to show just the AMI images. This will display the original release Ubuntu images. You can add another **grep** operation to list just the 32 or 64 bit version.

```
ec2-describe-images -a | grep 099720109477/ubuntu/images/ubuntu-vivid
```

Add a grep operation for an **instance-store**, or **ebs** for an Elastic Block Store volume.

The images are periodically rebuilt, and have the name **images-testing** instead of just **images**. The latest (daily build) images have the name **daily**. You can add the image type and the date to narrow your search.

To access an Amazon Machine Image (AMI), you first run the instance using the **ec2-run-instances** command. You will have to specify the AMI image, the SSH keys you created (use the EC2_KEYPAIR variable), and the type (small or micro). For a 64 bit AMI specify the size. For 64 bit systems you can add the **-t c1.large** option.

The reservation and instance information is displayed.

Run the **ec2-describe-instances** command to find out your instance ID and the external host the instance is running on.

There are two lines; the second is lengthy and will wrap around. The first entry in the INSTANCE line is the instance ID, and begins with **i-** prefix. The AMI image follows, and then the external host name on which the instance is being run.

Once the AMI is running, you login using the **ssh** command, your private key, and the external host listed in the **ec2-describe-instances** output preceded with **ubuntu@**.

When finished, you can logout to return to your shell.

When you are finished, be sure to shut down your AMI instance with the **ec2-terminate-instances** command. Otherwise your AMI will continue to run and you will be charged for its use. For this command you use the instance ID listed in the **ec2-describe-instances** output.

```
ec2-terminate-instances <instance_id>
```

Use the **ec2-describe-instances** command to check the status of your AMI, as well as to make sure it is shut down.

Amazon AWS Management Console

If you have access to a desktop Web browser on your system, you can also use the AWS management console to manage and access your Amazon EC2 cloud. Click the EC2 tab to manage your AWS EC2 service. Tasks are listed in the Navigation panel organized by Instances, Images, EBS, and Networking & Security. You can create private keys (SSH) for access and launch instances of AMI images.

```
http://aws.amazon.com/console/
```

The easiest way to access Ubuntu Images is to use the Ubuntu Cloud Images site to first find the image you want, and then click on the Launch button, which is a link to open the AWS management console to configure an instance of that image. You are taken through the steps of creating and starting an instance, as well as creating a private key (SSH) to access the instance. Once the instance is created, you can manage it by clicking on the Instance link in the Navigation bar. You can terminate an instance, click its check box and then choose Terminate from the Instance Actions menu.

Information on creating an AMI

You can create your own AMI with the Amazon AMI tools. Install the ec2-ami-tools package.

```
ec2-ami-tools
```

To create an AMI, you use the **ec2-bundle-image** tool. You then use the **ec2-upload-bundle** tool to upload it to the Amazon EC2 cloud. The **/etc/ec2/amitools** directory will hold the EC2 certificate.

A listing and explanation for the EC2 AMI tools are located at:

```
http://docs.amazonwebservices.com/AWSEC2/latest/CommandLineReference/
```

Click on the AMI Tools Reference link on the left pane of this Web page.

Cloud-Init

The **cloud-init** package provides scripts for the configuration and customization of cloud instances. It applies to AMI images. It includes support for installing SSH key during instance initialization, login credentials (EC2 SSH keys), repository access, and to set your host name. The **/etc/cloud-init** directory holds the **cloud-config.cfg** configuration file specifying scripts to run, and a **templates** subdirectory for your hostname and Ubuntu repository configuration. See **https://help.ubuntu.com/community/CloudInit** for more details.

OpenStack

OpenStack is the private/public cloud software currently supported by Ubuntu, replacing Eucalyptus. You can find out more about OpenStack at:

```
http://www.openstack.org
```

Detail documentation, including the end user guide, is available at:

```
http://docs.openstack.org
```

You can use the OpenStack dashboard (horizon) to manage your cloud (Universe repository). It provides a Web interface for administering the OpenStack Nova cloud controller.

OpenStack comprises several services, including compute (Nova), storage (Cinder), and imaging (Glance), networking (Neutron), orchestration (Heat), and database support (Trove). The computer packages on Ubuntu begin with the term nova (Ubuntu main repository). OpenStack supports several kinds of hypervisors including KVM and Xen, as well as database backends such as MySQL and PostgreSQL. It also supports LDAP user databases.

Ubuntu Cloud

The Ubuntu Cloud refers to the full range of cloud software and services that Ubuntu offers. These include both Public cloud (instances of Ubuntu on public clouds such as the Amazon AWS), and Ubuntu OpenStack (OpenStack supported clouds that you can set up yourself). See:

```
http://www.ubuntu.com/cloud
```

The Ubuntu OpenStack refers to a cloud you can build yourself, using the OpenStack applications and servers provided by Ubuntu. An OpenStack cloud can be private, public, or a hybrid of both. They can be managed using Juju charms (apps).

In addition, the Ubuntu Advantage service (Cloud management) provides professional support for Ubuntu OpenStack. You can then use Landscape to manage your Ubuntu clouds. For more information see:

```
http://www.ubuntu.com/management
```

Note: The Ubuntu Enterprise Cloud and the Eucalyptus cloud software are no longer supported by Ubuntu.

Service Orchestration

To implement cloud application services, Canonical provides JuJu and Metal as a Service (MAAS). JuJu is a service orchestration toolset and MAAS provides hardware provisioning. With JuJu you can manage installation, configuration, and availability of your cloud services, with MAAS set up hardware resources for them. Juju (formerly Ensemble) is a service orchestration system, which provides the tools to configure, upgrade, and deploy cloud services (juju package, Universe repository). It allows you to monitor use and scale deployment of services. For more information see:

```
https://juju.ubuntu.com/
```

JuJu orchestrates application components such as dependencies on other software and various configuration settings, by combining them into an entity referred to as a charm. Using charms, JuJu can quickly manage a cloud service. A charm is basically a script, as set of instructions, for deploying a cloud service. Several are already available. With a JuJu charm you can easily deploy a cloud service, specifying the number of nodes to use and choosing the cloud service such as AmazonEC2 or OpenStack. Using a charm you can scale back the number of nodes, or shutdown the service quickly. You can find out more about JuJu at:

```
https://juju.ubuntu.com/
```

Notes: Ubuntu also provides Docker, a technology that allows any application to be deployed as a container that will run on any type of server (bare-metal, virtual machine, public, and Open Stack), **https://www.docker.io**.

Part 4: Network Support

Proxy Servers
Domain Name System
Network Auto-configuration and DHCP
Firewalls
Administering TCP/IP Networks

14. Proxy Servers: Squid

Configuring Client Browsers

The squid.conf File

Proxy Security

Proxy Caches

Logs

A proxy server operates as an intermediary between a local network and services available on a larger one, such as the Internet. Requests from local clients for web services can be handled by the proxy server, speeding transactions as well as controlling access. Proxy servers maintain current copies of commonly accessed web pages, speeding web access times by eliminating the need to access the original site constantly. They also perform security functions, protecting servers from unauthorized access.

Protocol	Description and Port
HTTP	Web pages, port 3128
FTP	FTP transfers through websites, port 3128
ICP	Internet Caching Protocol, port 3130
HTCP	Hypertext Caching Protocol, port 4827
CARP	Cache Array Routing Protocol
SNMP	Simple Network Management Protocol, port 3401
SSL	Secure Socket Layer

Table 14-1: Protocols Supported by Squid

Squid is a free, open source, proxy-caching server for web clients, designed to speed Internet access and provide security controls for web servers. It implements a proxy-caching service for web clients that caches web pages as users make requests. Copies of web pages accessed by users are kept in the Squid cache, and as requests are made, Squid checks to see if it has a current copy. If Squid does have a current copy, it returns the copy from its cache instead of querying the original site. If it does not have a current copy, it will retrieve one from the original site. Replacement algorithms periodically replace old objects in the cache. In this way, web browsers can then use the local Squid cache as a proxy HTTP server. Squid currently handles web pages supporting the HTTP, FTP, and SSL protocols (Squid cannot be used with FTP clients), each with an associated default port (see Table 14-1). It also supports ICP (Internet Cache Protocol), HTCP (Hypertext Caching Protocol) for web caching, and SNMP (Simple Network Management Protocol) for providing status information.

You can find out more about Squid at **http://squid-cache.org**. For detailed information, check the Squid FAQ and the user manual located at their website. The FAQ is also installed in your **/usr/share/doc** under the **squid** directory.

As a proxy, Squid does more than just cache web objects. It operates as an intermediary between the web browsers (clients) and the servers they access. Instead of connections being made directly to the server, a client connects to the proxy server. The proxy then relays requests to the web server. This is useful for situations where a web server is placed behind a firewall server, protecting it from outside access. The proxy is accessible on the firewall, which can then transfer requests and responses back and forth between the client and the web server. The design is often used to allow web servers to operate on protected local networks and still be accessible on the Internet. You can also use a Squid proxy to provide web access to the Internet by local hosts. Instead of using a gateway providing complete access to the Internet, local hosts can use a proxy to allow them just web access. You can also combine the two, allowing gateway access, but using the proxy server to provide more control for web access. In addition, the caching capabilities of Squid can provide local hosts with faster web access.

Technically, you could use a proxy server to simply manage traffic between a web server and the clients who want to communicate with it, without doing caching at all. Squid combines both capabilities as a proxy-caching server.

Squid also provides security capabilities that let you exercise control over hosts accessing your web server. You can deny access by certain hosts and allow access by others. Squid also supports the use of encrypted protocols such as SSL. Encrypted communications are tunneled (passed through without reading) through the Squid server directly to the web server.

Squid is supported and distributed under a GNU Public License by the National Laboratory for Applied Network Research (NLANR) at the University of California, San Diego. The work is based on the Harvest Project to create a web indexing system that includes a high-performance cache daemon called **cached**. You can obtain current source code versions and online documentation from the Squid home page at **http://squid-cache.org**. The Squid software package (squid) consists of the Squid server and several support scripts for services like LDAP and HTTP. You can also install the cache manager script called **`cachemgr.cgi`**, the **squid-cgi** package. The **`cachemgr.cgi`** script lets you view statistics for the Squid server as it runs. Squid version 2.7 is available on the main Ubuntu repository. You can also install the Squid 3 version (Universe repository), but updates are not supported by Canonical.

```
sudo apt-get install squid3
```

Check the Ubuntu Server Guide | Web Servers | Squid - Proxy Server for basic configuration.

```
https://help.ubuntu.com/stable/serverguide/squid.html
```

Also check the Ubuntu Community Documentation on Squid at:

```
https://help.ubuntu.com/community/Squid
```

The Squid server is managed by systemd using the **squid3.service** file, shown here. It is started for the multi-user.target (runlevels 2, 3, 4, and 5) (WantedBy). The **/usr/sbin/squid3** application is used to start, stop, and restart the server (ExecStart, ExecReload, ExecStop).

squid3.service

```
# Automatically generated by systemd-sysv-generator

[Unit]
Documentation=man:systemd-sysv-generator(8)
SourcePath=/etc/init.d/squid3
Description=LSB: Squid HTTP Proxy version 3.x
Before=runlevel2.target runlevel3.target runlevel4.target runlevel5.target
shutdown.target
After=network-online.target remote-fs.target systemd-journald-dev-log.socket nss-
lookup.target
Wants=network-online.target
Conflicts=shutdown.target

[Service]
Type=forking
Restart=no
TimeoutSec=5min
```

```
IgnoreSIGPIPE=no
KillMode=process
GuessMainPID=no
RemainAfterExit=yes
ExecStart=/etc/init.d/squid3 start
ExecStop=/etc/init.d/squid3 stop
ExecReload=/etc/init.d/squid3 reload
```

You can use the **service** command to manually stop, start, and restart the server.

```
service squid stop
```

Configuring Client Browsers

Squid supports both standard proxy caches and transparent caches. With a standard proxy cache, users will need to configure their browsers to specifically access the Squid server. A transparent cache, on the other hand, requires no browser configuration by users. The cache is transparent, allowing access as if it were a normal website. Transparent caches are implemented by IPtables, using net filtering to intercept requests and direct them to the proxy cache.

With a standard proxy cache, users need to specify their proxy server in their web browser configuration. For this, they will need the IP address of the host running the Squid proxy server as well as the port it is using. Proxies usually make use of port 3128. To configure use of a proxy server running on the private network, you enter the following. The proxy server is running on **turtle.mytrek.com** (192.168.0.1) and using port 3128.

```
192.168.0.1 3128
```

On Firefox, Mozilla, and Netscape, the user on the sample local network first selects the Proxy panel located in Preferences under the Edit menu. Then, in the Manual proxy configuration's View panel, you enter the previous information. The user will see entries for FTP, HTTP, and security proxies. For standard web access, enter the IP address in the FTP and web boxes. For their port boxes, enter **3128**.

For GNOME, select Network Proxy tab in the System Settings Network dialog, and for Konqueror on the KDE Desktop, select the Proxies panel on the Preferences | Web Browsing menu window. Here, you can enter the proxy server address and port numbers.

On Linux and UNIX systems, local hosts can set the **`http_proxy`** and **`ftp_proxy`** shell variables to configure access by Linux-supported web browsers such as Lynx. You can place these definitions in your **.profile** or **/etc/profile** file to have them automatically defined whenever you log in.

```
http_proxy=192.168.0.1:3128
ftp_proxy=192.168.0.1:3128
export http_proxy ftp_proxy
```

Alternatively, you can use the proxy's URL.

```
http_proxy=http://turtle.mytrek.com:3128
```

For the Elinks browser, you can specify a proxy in its configuration file, **/etc/elinks.conf**. Set both FTP and web proxy host options, as in:

```
protocol.http.proxy.host  turtle.mytrek.com:3128
protocol.ftp.proxy.host  turtle.mytrek.com:3128
```

Before a client on a local host can use the proxy server, access permission has to be given to it in the server's **squid.conf** file, described in the later section "Security." Access can easily be provided to an entire network. For the sample network used here, you would have to place the following entries in the **squid.conf** file. These are explained in detail in the following sections.

```
acl mylan src 192.168.0.0/255.255.255.0
http_access allow mylan
```

Tip: Web clients that need to access your Squid server as a standard proxy cache will need to know the server's address and the port for Squid's HTTP services, by default 3128.

The squid.conf File

The Squid configuration file is **squid.conf**, located in the **/etc/squid3** directory. In the **/etc/squid3/squid.conf** file, you set general options such as ports used, security options controlling access to the server, and cache options for configuring caching operations. The default version of **squid.conf** provided with Squid software includes detailed explanations of all standard entries, along with commented default entries. Entries consist of tags that specify different attributes. For example, **maximum_object_size** sets limits on objects transferred.

```
maximum_object_size 4 MB
```

As a proxy, Squid will use certain ports for specific services, such as port 3128 for HTTP services like web browsers. Default port numbers are already set for Squid. Should you need to use other ports, you can set them in the **/etc/squid3/squid.conf** file. The following entry shows how you set the web browser port:

```
http_port 3128
```

Note: Squid uses the Simple Network Management Protocol (SNMP) to provide status information and statistics to SNMP agents managing your network. You can control SNMP with the **snmp access** and **port** configurations in the **squid.conf** file.

Proxy Security

Squid can use its role as an intermediary between web clients and a web server to implement access controls, determining who can access the web server and how. Squid does this by checking access control lists (ACLs) of hosts and domains that have had controls placed on them. When it finds a web client from one of those hosts attempting to connect to the web server, it executes the control. Squid supports a number of controls with which it can deny or allow access to the web server by the remote host's web client (see Table 14-2). In effect, Squid sets up a firewall just for the web server.

The first step in configuring Squid security is to create ACLs. These are lists of hosts and domains for which you want to set up controls. You define ACLs using the **acl** command, creating a label for the systems on which you are setting controls. You then use commands such as **http_access** to define these controls. You can define a system, or a group of systems, by use of several **acl** options, such as the source IP address, the domain name, or even the time and date. For example, the **src** option is used to define a system or group of systems with a certain source address. To define a **mylan acl** entry for systems in a local network with the addresses 192.168.0.0 through 192.168.0.255, use the following ACL definition:

```
acl mylan src 192.168.0.0/255.255.255.0
```

Options	Description
src *ip-address/netmask*	Client's IP address
src *addr1-addr2/netmask*	Range of addresses
dst *ip-address/netmask*	Destination IP address
myip *ip-address/netmask*	Local socket IP address
srcdomain *domain*	Reverse lookup, client IP
dstdomain *domain*	Destination server from URL; for **dstdomain** and **dstdom_regex**, a reverse lookup is tried if an IP-based URL is used
srcdom_regex [-i] *expression*	Regular expression matching client name
dstdom_regex [-i] *expression*	Regular expression matching destination
time *[day-abbrevs] [h1:m1-h2:m2]*	Time as specified by day, hour, and minutes. Day abbreviations: S = Sunday, M = Monday, T = Tuesday, W = Wednesday, H = Thursday, F = Friday, A = Saturday
url_regex [-i] *expression*	Regular expression matching on whole URL
urlpath_regex [-i] *expression*	Regular expression matching on URL path
port *ports*	A specific port or range of ports
proto *protocol*	A specific protocol, such as HTTP or FTP
method *method*	Specific methods, such as GET and POST
browser [-i] *regexp*	Pattern match on user-agent header
ident *username*	String match on **ident** output
src_as *number*	Used for routing of requests to specific caches
dst_as *number*	Used for routing of requests to specific caches
proxy_auth *username*	List of valid usernames
snmp_community *string*	A community string to limit access to your SNMP agent

Table 14-2: Squid ACL Options

Once it is defined, you can use an ACL definition in a Squid option to specify a control you want to place on those systems. For example, to allow access by the mylan group of local systems to the web through the proxy, use an **http_access** option with the **allow** action specifying **mylan** as the **acl** definition to use, as shown here:

```
http_access allow mylan
```

The default **squid.conf** file provides entries for a recommended minimum configuration, beginning with entries for controlling access to your local net and server ports. Local net entries are listed for different local addresses (see Chapter 18).

```
acl localnet src 192.168.0.0.0/16  # RFC1918 possible internal network
```

Access is supported on the SSL port (443, 591, 873) and server ports such as 80 for the Web server and 21 for the FTP server are designated as safe.

```
acl SSL_ports  port 443          # https
acl SSL_ports  port 591          # filemaker
acl SSL_ports  port 873          # rsync
acl Safe_ports port 80           # http
acl Safe_ports port 21           # ftp
```

Default **http_access** entries deny access to outside users, and allow access by hosts on the local network and the local host (Squid server host). Access is also denied on ports not deemed safe or without SSL security. The **`http_access`** entries already defined in the **squid.conf** file are shown here.

```
http_access allow localhost manager
http_access deny manager
http_access deny !Safe_ports
http_access deny CONNECT !SSL_ports

http_access allow localhost

http_access deny all
```

By defining ACLs and using them in Squid options, you can tailor your website with the kind of security you want. You should add your own ACLs after the comment label located near the middle of the file after the http_access entries for safe ports, and before the http_access entries for the localnet and local host.

```
#
# INSERT YOUR OWN RULE(S) HERE TO ALLOW ACCESS FROM YOUR CLIENTS
#
```

The following example allows access to the web through the proxy by only the **mylan** group of local systems, denying access to all others. Two **`acl`** entries are set up: one for the local system and one for all others; **`http_access`** options first allow access to the local system and then deny access to all others.

```
acl mylan src 192.168.0.0/255.255.255.0
acl all src 0.0.0.0/0.0.0.0
http_access allow mylan
http_access deny all
```

Basic default entries that you will find in your **squid.conf** file, along with an entry for the **mylan** sample network, are shown here.

```
acl manager proto cache_object
acl localhost src 127.0.0.1/32 ::1
acl to_localhost dst 127.0.0.1/0.0.0.0/32  ::1
acl mylan src 192.168.0.0/255.255.255.0
acl SSL_ports port 443 563 873
```

The order of the **http_access** options is important. Squid starts from the first and works its way down, stopping at the first **http_access** option with an ACL entry that matches. In the preceding example, local systems that match the first **http_access** command are allowed, whereas others fall through to the second **http_access** command and are denied.

For systems using the proxy, you can also control what sites they can access. For a destination address, you create an **acl** entry with the **dst** qualifier. The **dst** qualifier takes as its argument the site address. Then you can create an **http_access** option to control access to that address. The following example denies access by anyone using the proxy to the destination site **rabbit.mytrek.com**. If you have a local network accessing the web through the proxy, you can use such commands to restrict access to certain sites.

```
acl myrabbit dst rabbit.mytrek.com
http_access deny myrabbit
```

Proxy Caches

Squid primarily uses the Internet Cache Protocol (ICP) to communicate with other web caches. It also provides support for the more experimental Hypertext Cache Protocol (HTCP) and the Cache Array Routing Protocol (CARP).

Using the ICP protocols, your Squid cache can connect to other Squid caches or other cache servers, such as Microsoft proxy server, Netscape proxy server, and Novell BorderManager. This way, if your network's Squid cache does not have a copy of a requested Web page, it can contact another cache to see if it is there instead of accessing the original site. You can configure Squid to connect to other Squid caches by connecting it to a cache hierarchy. Squid supports a hierarchy of caches denoted by the terms *child, sibling,* and *parent.* Sibling and child caches are accessible on the same level and are automatically queried whenever a request cannot be located in your own Squid's cache. If these queries fail, a parent cache is queried, which then searches its own child and sibling caches—or its own parent cache, if needed—and so on.

You can set up a cache hierarchy to connect to the main NLANR server by registering your cache using the following entries in your **squid.conf** file:

```
anounce_period 1 day
announce_host tracker.ircache.net
announce_port 3131
```

Use **cache_peer** to set up parent, sibling, and child connections to other caches. This option has five fields. The first two consist of the hostname or IP address of the queried cache and the cache type (parent, child, or sibling). The third and fourth are the HTTP and the ICP ports of that cache, usually 3128 and 3130. The last is used for cache_peer options such as proxy-only to not save fetched objects locally, no-query for those caches that do not support ICP, and weight, which assigns priority to a parent cache. The following example sets up a connection to a parent cache:

```
cache_peer sd.cache.nlanr.net parent 3128 3130
```

Squid provides several options for configuring cache memory. The **cache_mem** option sets the memory allocated primarily for objects currently in use (objects in transit). If available, the space can also be used for frequently accessed objects (hot objects) and failed requests (negative-cache objects). The default is 8MB. The following example sets it to 256MB:

```
cache_mem 256 MB
```

You can use the cache manager (**cachemgr.cgi**) to manage the cache and view statistics on the cache manager as it runs. To run the cache manager, use your browser to execute the **cachemgr.cgi** script (this script should be placed in your web server's **cgi-bin** directory).

Logs

Squid keeps several logs detailing access, cache performance, and error messages. The log files are located in the **/var/log/squid3** directory.

access.log holds requests sent to your proxy.

cache.log holds Squid server messages such as errors and startup messages.

store.log holds information about the Squid cache such as objects added or removed.

15. Domain Name System

The Domain Name System (DNS) is an Internet service that locates and translates domain names into their corresponding Internet Protocol (IP) addresses. All computers connected to the Internet are addressed using an IP address. Since an average user on a network might have to access many different hosts, keeping track of the IP addresses needed quickly became a problem. It was much easier to label hosts with names and use the names to access them. Names were associated with IP addresses. When a user used a name to access a host, the corresponding IP address was looked up first and then used to provide access.

With the changeover from IPv4 to IPv6 address, DNS servers will have some configuration differences. Both are covered here, though some topics will use IPv4 addressing for better clarity, as they are easier to represent.

Check the Ubuntu Server Guide | Domain Name Service (DNS) for basic configuration.

`https://help.ubuntu.com/stable/serverguide/dns.html`

DNS Address Translations

The process of translating IP addresses into associated names is fairly straightforward. Small networks can be set up easily, with just the basic configuration. The task becomes much more complex when you deal with larger networks and with the Internet. The sheer size of the task can make DNS configuration a complex operation.

Fully Qualified Domain Names

IP addresses were associated with corresponding names, called fully qualified domain names. A fully qualified domain name is composed of three or more segments. The first segment is the name that identifies the host, and the remaining segments are for the network in which the host is located. The network segments of a fully qualified domain name are usually referred to simply as the domain name, while the host part is referred to as the hostname (though this is also used to refer to the complete fully qualified domain name). In effect, subnets are referred to as domains. The fully qualified domain name **www.linux.org** could have an IPv4 address 198.182.196.56, where 198.182.196 is the network address and 56 is the host ID. Computers can be accessed only with an IP address, so a fully qualified domain name must first be translated into its corresponding IP address to be of any use. The parts of the IP address that make up the domain name and the hosts can vary.

IPv4 Addresses

The IP address may be implemented in either the newer IPv6 (Internet Protocol Version 6) format, or the older and more common IPv4 (Internet Protocol Version 4) format. Since the IPv4 addressing is much easier to read, that format will be used in these examples. In the older IPv4 format, the IP address consists of a number composed of four segments, separated by periods. Depending on the type of network, several of the first segments are used for the network address and one or more of the last segments are used for the host address. In a standard class C network used in smaller networks, the first three segments are the computer's network address and the last segment is the computer's host ID (as used in these examples). For example, in the address 192.168.0.2, 192.168.0 is the network address and 2 is the computer's host ID within that network. Together, they make up an IP address by which the computer can be addressed from anywhere on the Internet. IP addresses, though, are difficult to remember and easy to get wrong.

IPv6 Addressing

IPv6 addressing uses a very different approach designed to provide more flexibility and support for very large address spaces. There are three different types of IPv6 addresses, unicast, multicast, and anycast, of which unicast is the most commonly used. A unicast address is directed to a particular interface. There are several kinds of unicast addresses, depending on how the address is used. For example, you can have a global unicast address for access through the Internet or a unique-level unicast address for private networks.

Though consisting of 128 bits in eight segments (16 bits, 2 bytes, per segment), an IPv6 address is made up of several fields that conform roughly to the segments and capabilities of an IPv4 address: networking information, subnet information, and the interface identifier (host ID). The network information includes a format prefix indicating the type of network connection. In addition, a subnet identifier can be used to specify a local subnet. The network information takes up the first several segments; the remainder is used for the interface ID. The interface ID is a 64-bit (four-segment) Extended Unique Identifier (EUI-64) generated from a network device's Media Access Control (MAC) address. IP addresses are written in hexadecimal numbers, making them difficult to use. Each segment is separated from the next by a colon, and a set of consecutive segments with zero values can be left empty.

Manual Translations: /etc/hosts

Any computer on the Internet can maintain a file that manually associates IP addresses with domain names. On Linux and UNIX systems, this file is called the **/etc/hosts** file. Here, you can enter the IP addresses and domain names of computers you commonly access. Using this method, however, each computer needs a complete listing of all other computers on the Internet, and that listing must be updated constantly. Early on, this became clearly impractical for the Internet, though it is still feasible for small, isolated networks, as well as simple home networks.

DNS Servers

The Domain Name System has been implemented to deal with the task of translating the domain name of any computer on the Internet to its IP address. The task is carried out by interconnecting servers that manage the Domain Name System (also referred to as DNS servers or name servers). These DNS servers keep lists of fully qualified domain names and their IP addresses, matching one up with the other. This service that they provide to a network is referred to as the Domain Name System. The Internet is composed of many connected subnets called *domains,* each with its own Domain Name System (DNS) servers that keep track of all the fully qualified domain names and IP addresses for all the computers on its network. DNS servers are hierarchically linked to root servers, which, in turn, connect to other root servers and the DNS servers on their subnets throughout the Internet. The section of a network for which a given DNS server is responsible is called a *zone.* Although a zone may correspond to a domain, many zones may, in fact, be within a domain, each with its own name server. This is true for large domains where too many systems exist for one name server to manage.

DNS Operation

When a user enters a fully qualified domain name to access a remote host, a resolver program queries the local network's DNS server requesting the corresponding IP address for that remote host. With the IP address, the user can then access the remote host. In Figure 15-1, the user at **rabbit.mytrek.com** wants to connect to the remote host **lizard.mytrek.com**. The host **rabbit.mytrek.com** first sends a request to the network's DNS server, in this case **turtle.mytrek.com**, to look up the name **lizard.mytrek.com** and find its IP address. The DNS server at **turtle.mytrek.com** then returns the IP address for **lizard.mytrek.com**, 192.168.0.3, to the requesting host, **rabbit.mytrek.com**. With the IP address, the user at **rabbit.mytrek.com** can then connect to **lizard.mytrek.com**.

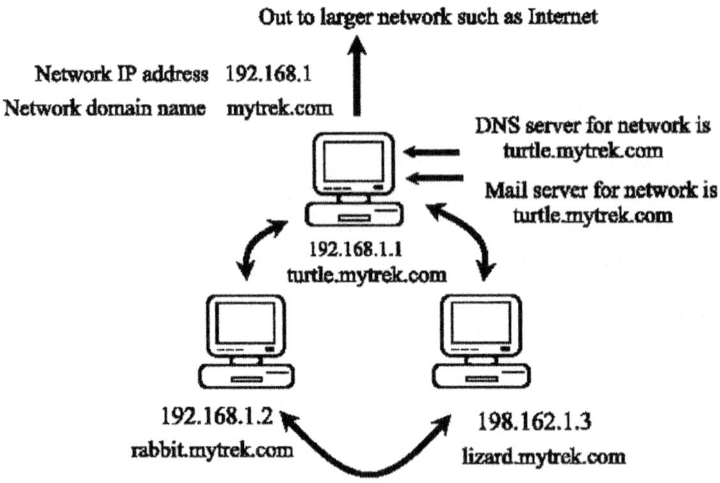

Figure 15-1: DNS server operation

DNS Clients: Resolvers

The names of the DNS servers that service a host's network are kept in the host's **/etc/resolv.conf** file. When setting up an Internet connection, the DNS servers, also referred to as name servers, provided by your Internet service provider (ISP) were placed in this file. These name servers resolve any fully qualified domain names that you use when you access different Internet sites. For example, when you enter a Web site name in your browser, the name is looked up by the name servers and the name's associated IP address is then used to access the site. In this file, the term **nameserver** references the IP address of a DNS server.

/etc/resolv.conf

```
search  mytrek.com   mytrain.com
nameserver  192.168.0.1
nameserver  192.168.0.3
```

Local Area Network Addressing

If you are setting up a DNS server for a local area network (LAN) that is not connected to the Internet, you should use a special set of IP numbers reserved for such local networks (also known as *private networks* or *intranets*). This is especially true if you are implementing IP masquerading, where only a gateway machine has an Internet address, and the others make use of that one address to connect to the Internet. The IPv4 and IPv6 protocols use different addressing formats for local addresses. Many local and home networks still use the IPv4 format, and this is the format used in the following local addressing example.

Address	Networks
10.0.0.0	Class A network
172.16.0.0–172.31.255.255	Class B network
192.168.0.0	Class C network
127.0.0.0	Loopback network (for system self-communication)

Table 15-1: Non-Internet Private Network IP Addresses

IPv4 Private Networks

IPv4 provides a range of private addresses for the three classes supported by IPv4. The class C IPv4 network numbers use the special network number 192.168. Numbers are also reserved for class A and class B non-Internet local networks. Table 15-1 lists these addresses. The possible addresses available span from 0 to 255 in the host segment of the address. For example, class B network addresses range from 172.16.0.0 to 172.16.255.255, giving you a total of 65,534 possible hosts. The class C network ranges from 192.168.0.0 to 192.168.255.255, giving you 254 possible subnetworks, each with 254 possible hosts. The number 127.0.0.0 is reserved for a system's loopback interface, which allows it to communicate with itself, as it enables users on the same system to send messages to each other.

These numbers were originally designed for class-based addressing. However, they can just as easily be used for Classless Interdomain Routing (CIDR) addressing, where you can create subnetworks with a smaller number of hosts. For example, the 254 hosts addressed in a class C network could be split into two subnetworks, each with 125 hosts.

IPv6 Private Networks

IPv6 supports private networks with unique-local addresses that provide the same functionality of IPv4 private addresses. The unique-local addresses have no public routing information. They cannot access the Internet. They are restricted to the site they are used on. The unique-local addresses use only three fields: a format prefix, subnet identifier, and interface identifier. A site-level address has the format prefix **fc00**. If you have no subnets, it will be set to 0. This will give you a network prefix of **fc00:0:0:0**. You can drop the set of empty zeros to give you **fc00::**. The interface ID field will hold the interface identification information, similar to the host ID information in IPv4.

```
fc00::          IPv6 unique-local prefix
```

The loopback device will have special address of **::1**, also known as localhost.

```
::1      IPv6 loopback network
```

Rather than using a special set of reserved addresses as IPv4 does, with IPv6 you only use the unique-local prefix, **fc00**, and the special loopback address, **::1**.

Tip: Once your network is set up, you can use ping6 or ping to see if it is working. The ping6 tool is designed for IPv6 addresses, whereas ping is used for IPv4.

Local Network Address Example Using IPv4

If you are setting up a LAN, such as a small business or home network, you are free to use class C IPv4 network (254 hosts or less), that have the special network number 192.168, as used in these examples. These are numbers for your local machines. You can set up a private network, such as an intranet, using network cards, such as Ethernet cards and Ethernet hubs, and then configure your machines with IP addresses starting from 192.168.0.1. The host segment can range from 1 to 254, where 255 is used for the broadcast address. If you have three machines on your home network, you can give them the addresses 192.168.0.1, 192.168.0.2, and 192.168.0.3. You can then set up domain name system services for your network by running a DNS server on one of the machines. This machine becomes your network's DNS server. You can then give your machines fully qualified domain names and configure your DNS server to translate the names to their corresponding IP addresses. As shown in Figure 15-1, for example, you could give the machine 192.168.0.1 the name **turtle.mytrek.com** and the machine 192.168.0.2 the name **rabbit.mytrek.com**. You can also implement Internet services on your network such as FTP, Web, and mail services by setting up servers for them on your machines. Then you can configure your DNS server to let users access those services using fully qualified domain names. For example, for the **mytrek.com** network, the Web server could be accessed using the name **www.mytrek.com**. Instead of a Domain Name System, you could have the **/etc/hosts** files in each machine contain the entire list of IP addresses and domain names for all the machines in your network. But in this case, for any changes, you would have to update each machine's **/etc/hosts** file.

BIND

The DNS server software currently in use on Linux systems is Berkeley Internet Name Domain (BIND). BIND was originally developed at the University of California, Berkeley, and is currently maintained and supported by the Internet Software Consortium (ISC). You can obtain BIND information and current software releases from its Web site at **www.isc.org**. Web page documentation and manuals are included with the software package. At that site you can also access the BIND Administration Manual for detailed configuration information. The BIND documentation directory, **bind9-doc**, in **/usr/share/doc** contains extensive documentation, including Web page manuals and examples. The Linux HOW-TO for the Domain Name System, DNS-HOWTO, provides detailed examples. Documentation, news, and DNS tools can be obtained from the DNS Resource Directory (DNSRD) at **www.dns.net/dnsrd**. The site includes extensive links and online documentation, including the *BIND Operations Guide (BOG).*

The DNS server packages on Ubuntu are:

```
bind9
bind9-doc
```

Note: The djbdns server, written by D.J. Bernstein, is designed specifically with security in mind, providing a set of small server daemons, each performing specialized tasks.

djbdns separates the name server, caching server, and zone transfer tasks into separate programs: tinydns (tinydns.org) implements the authoritative name server for a network, whereas dnscache implements a caching server that will resolve requests from DNS clients such as Web browsers.

BIND Servers and Tools

The BIND DNS server software consists of a name server daemon, several sample configuration files, and resolver libraries. As of 1998, a new version of BIND, beginning with the series number 8.*x,* implemented a new configuration file using a new syntax. Version 9.0 adds new security features and support for IPv6. Older versions, which begin with the number 4.*x,* use a different configuration file with an older syntax. Most distributions, including Ubuntu, currently install the newer 9.*x* version of BIND.

Tool	Description
`dig` *domain*	Domain Information Groper, tool to obtain information on a DNS server. Preferred over `nslookup`
`host` *hostname*	Simple lookup of hosts
`nslookup` *domain*	Tool to query DNS servers for information about domains and hosts
`named-checkconf`	BIND tool to check the syntax of your DNS configuration file, **/etc/named.conf**
`named-checkzone`	BIND tool to check the syntax of your DNS zone files
`nslint`	Tool to check the syntax of your DNS configuration and zone files
`rndc` *command*	Remote Name Daemon Controller, an administrative tool for managing a DNS server (version 9.*x*)
`ndc`	Name Daemon Controller (version 8.*x*)
`bind9`	Use the **/etc/init.d/bind9** script to start, stop, and restart the **named** server with the **service** command

Table 15-2: BIND Diagnostic and Administrative Tools

The name of the BIND name server daemon is **named**. To operate your machine as a name server, simply run the **named** daemon with the appropriate configuration. The **named** daemon listens for resolution requests and provides the correct IP address for the requested hostname. On Ubuntu, **named** runs as a stand-alone daemon, starting up when the system boots and constantly running. You can start, stop, and restart the daemon manually using the **service** command and the **bind9** script.

```
sudo service bind9 restart
```

You can also use the Remote Name Daemon Controller utility, rndc, provided with BIND (**bind9utils** package) to start, stop, restart, and check the status of the server as you test its configuration. rndc with the stop command stops **named** and, with the start command, starts it again, reading your **named.conf** file. rndc with the help command provides a list of all rndc commands. Configuration is set in the /**etc/rndc.conf** file. Once your name server is running, you can test it using the `dig` or `nslookup` utility, which queries a name server, providing information about hosts and domains. If you start **dig** with no arguments, it enters an interactive mode where you can issue different **dig** commands to refine your queries.

To check the syntax of your DNS server configuration and zone files, BIND provides the **named-checkconfig** and **named-checkzone** tools: **named-checkconfig** will check the syntax of DNS configuration file, **named.conf**, and **named-checkzone** will check a zone file's syntax. Other syntax checking tools are also available, such as **nslint**, which operates like the programming tool **lint**. Table 15-2 lists several DNS administrative tools.

The **named** daemon is managed by **systemd** using the **bind9.service** unit file. It is started for the multi-user.target (runlevels 2, 3, 4, and 5) (WantedBy). Runtime configuration is read from **/etc/default/bind9**. Though the **/usr/sbin/named** command starts the server (ExecStart), the **rndc** command is used to restart or stop the server (ExecReload and ExecStop).

bind9.service

```
[Unit]
Description=BIND Domain Name Server
Documentation=man:named(8)
After=network.target

[Service]
ExecStart=/usr/sbin/named -f -u bind
ExecReload=/usr/sbin/rndc reload
ExecStop=/usr/sbin/rndc stop

[Install]
WantedBy=multi-user.target
```

Note: The GADMIN-BIND configuration tool uses a different set of files that it sets up in the /var/named directory.

Domain Name System Configuration

You configure a DNS server using a configuration file, several zone files, and a cache file. The part of a network for which the name server is responsible is called a *zone.* A zone is not the same as a domain, because in a large domain you could have several zones, each with its own name server. You could also have one name server servicing several zones. In this case, each zone has its own zone file.

DNS Zones

The zone files hold resource records that provide hostname and IP address associations for computers on the network for which the DNS server is responsible. Zone files exist for the server's network and the local machine. Zone entries are defined in the **named.conf** file. Here, you place zone entries for your master, slave, and forward DNS servers. The most commonly used zone types are described here:

Master zone This is the primary zone file for the network supported by the DNS server. It holds the mappings from domain names to IP addresses for all the hosts on that network.

Slave zone These are references to other DNS servers for your network. Your network can have a master DNS server and several slave DNS servers to help carry the workload.

A slave DNS server automatically copies its configuration files, including all zone files, from the master DNS server. Any changes to the master configuration files trigger an automatic download of these files to the slave servers. In effect, you only have to manage the configuration files for the master DNS server, since they are automatically copied to the slave servers.

Forward zone The forward zone lists name servers outside your network that should be searched if your network's name server fails to resolve an address.

IN-ADDR.ARPA zone DNS can also provide reverse resolutions, where an IP address is used to determine the associated domain name address. Such lookups are provided by **IN-ADDR.ARPA** zone files. Each master zone file usually has a corresponding **IN-ADDR.ARPA** zone file to provide reverse resolution for that zone. For each master zone entry, a corresponding reverse mapping zone entry named **IN-ADDR.ARPA** also exists, as well as one for the localhost. This entry performs reverse mapping from an IP address to its domain name. The name of the zone entry uses the domain IP address, which is the IP address with segments listed starting from the host, instead of the network. So for the IP address 192.168.0.4, where 4 is the host address, the corresponding domain IP address is 4.0.168.192, listing the segments in reverse order. The reverse mapping for the localhost is 1.0.0.127.

IP6.ARPA zone This is the IPv6 equivalent of the **IN-ADDR.ARPA** zone, providing reverse resolution for that zone. The IP6.ARPA zone uses bit labels that provide a bit-level format that is easier to write, requiring no reverse calculation on the part of the DNS administrator.

IP6.INT zone This is the older form of the IPv6 IP6.ARPA zone, which is the equivalent of the IPv4 **IN-ADDR.ARPA** zone, providing reverse resolution for a zone. IP6.INT uses a nibble format to specify a reverse zone. In this format, a hexadecimal IPv6 address is segmented into each of its 32 hexadecimal numbers and listed in reverse order, each segment separated by a period.

Hint zone A hint zone specifies the root name servers and is denoted by a period (.). A DNS server is normally connected to a larger network, such as the Internet, which has its own DNS servers. DNS servers are connected this way hierarchically, with each server having its root servers to which it can send resolution queries. The root servers are designated in the hint zone.

DNS Servers Types

There are several kinds of DNS servers, each designed to perform a different type of task under the Domain Name System. The basic kind of DNS server is the *master* server. Each network must have at least one master server that is responsible for resolving names on the network. Large networks may need several DNS servers. Some of these can be slave servers that can be updated directly from a master server. Others may be *alternative master* servers that hosts in a network can use. Both are commonly referred to as *secondary* servers. For DNS requests a DNS server cannot resolve, the request can be forwarded to specific DNS servers outside the network, such as on the Internet. DNS servers in a network can be set up to perform this task, and are referred to as *forwarder* servers. To help bear the workload, local DNS servers can be set up within a network that operate as caching servers. Such a server merely collects DNS lookups from previous requests it sent to the main DNS server. Any repeated requests can then be answered by the caching server.

A server that can answer DNS queries for a given zone with authority is known as an *authoritative* server. An authoritative server holds the DNS configuration records for hosts in a zone that will associate each host's DNS name with an IP address. For example, a master server is an authoritative server. So are slave and stealth servers (see the list that follows). A caching server is not authoritative. It only holds whatever associations it picked up from other servers and cannot guarantee that the associations are valid.

Master server This is the primary DNS server for a zone.

Slave server A DNS server that receives zone information from the master server.

Forwarder server A server that forwards unresolved DNS requests to outside DNS servers. Can be used to keep other servers on a local network hidden from the Internet.

Caching only server Caches DNS information it receives from DNS servers and uses it to resolve local requests.

Stealth server A DNS server for a zone not listed as a name server by the master DNS server.

Location of Bind Server Files: /etc/bind/

Both the configuration and zone files used by BIND are placed in the **/etc/bind** directory. Zone files begin with the prefix db, as in **db.127** for the localhost zone file.

```
/etc/bind/named.conf          BIND configuration file
/etc/bind/db.*                BIND zone files
```

named.conf

The configuration file for the **named** daemon is **/etc/bind/named.conf**. It uses a flexible syntax similar to C programs. The format enables easy configuration of selected zones, enabling features such as access control lists and categorized logging. The **named.conf** file consists of BIND configuration statements with attached blocks within which specific options are listed. A configuration statement is followed by arguments and a block that is delimited with braces. Within the block are lines of option and feature entries. Each entry is terminated with a semicolon. Comments can use the C, C++, or Shell/Perl syntax: enclosing /* */, preceding //, or preceding #. The following example shows a zone statement followed by the zone name and a block of options that begin with an opening brace ({). Each option entry ends with a semicolon. The entire block ends with a closing brace, also followed by a semicolon. The format for a **named.conf** entry is show here, along with the different kinds of comments allowed. Tables 35-5, 35-6, and 35-7 list several commonly used statements and options.

```
// comments
/* comments */
# comments

statements {
 options and features; //comments
};
```

The following example shows a simple caching server entry:

```
// a caching only nameserver config
//
zone "." {
        type hint;
        file "named.ca";
        };
```

Once you have created your configuration file, you should check its syntax with the **named-checkconfig** tool. Enter the command on a shell command line. If you do not specify a configuration file, it will default to **/etc/bind/named.conf**.

```
named-checkconfig
```

The zone Statement

The zone statement is used to specify the domains that the name server will service. To create a zone statement, enter the keyword zone, followed by the name of the domain placed within double quotes. Do not place a period at the end of the domain name. In the following example, a period is within the domain name, but not at the end, "**mytrek.com**"; this differs from the zone file, which requires a period at the end of a complete domain name.

Type	Description
master	Primary DNS zone
slave	Slave DNS server; controlled by a master DNS server
hint	Set of root DNS Internet servers
forward	Forwards any queries in it to other servers
stub	Like a slave zone, but holds only names of DNS servers

Table 15-3: DNS BIND Zone Types

After the zone name, you can specify the class **in**, which stands for Internet. You can also leave it out, in which case in is assumed (there are only a few other esoteric classes that are rarely used). Within the zone block, you can place several options (see Table 15-3). Two essential options are type and file. The type option is used to specify the zone's type. The file option is used to specify the name of the zone file to be used for this zone. You can choose from several types of zones: master, slave, stub, forward, and hint. A *master* zone specifies that the zone holds master information and is authorized to act on it. A master server was called a primary server in the older 4.*x* BIND configuration. A *slave* zone indicates that the zone needs to update its data periodically from a specified master name server. Use this entry if your name server is operating as a secondary server for another primary (master) DNS server. A *stub* zone copies only other name server entries, instead of the entire zone. A *forward* zone directs all queries to name servers specified in a forwarders statement. A *hint* zone specifies the set of root name servers used by all Internet DNS servers. You can also specify several options that can override any global options set with the options statement. Table 15-3 lists the BIND zone types. The following example shows a simple zone statement for the **mytrek.com** domain. Its class is Internet (in), and its type is master. The name of its zone file is usually the same as the zone name, in this case, "**mytrek.com**."

```
zone "mytrek.com" in {
       type master;
       file "mytrek.com";
       };
```

Statement	Description
`/* comment */`	BIND comment in C syntax.
`// comment`	BIND comment in C++ syntax.
`# comment`	BIND comment in Unix shell and Perl syntax.
acl	Defines a named IP address matching list.
include	Includes a file, interpreting it as part of the **named.conf** file.
key	Specifies key information for use in authentication and authorization.
logging	Specifies what the server logs and where the log messages are sent.
options	Global server configuration options and defaults for other statements.
controls	Declares control channels to be used by the ndc utility.
server	Sets certain configuration options for the specified server basis.
sortlists	Gives preference to specified networks according to a queries source.
trusted-keys	Defines DNSSEC keys preconfigured into the server and implicitly trusted.
zone	Defines a zone.
view	Defines a view.

Table 15-4: BIND Configuration Statements

Configuration Statements

Other statements, such as acl, server, options, and logging, enable you to configure different features for your name server (see Table 15-4). The server statement defines the characteristics to be associated with a remote name server, such as the transfer method and key ID for transaction security. The control statement defines special control channels. The key statement defines a key ID to be used in a server statement that associates an authentication method with a particular name server (see "DNSSEC" later in this chapter). The logging statement is used to configure logging options for the name server, such as the maximum size of the log file and a severity level for messages. Table 15-5 lists the BIND statements.

The sortlists statement lets you specify preferences to be used when a query returns multiple responses. For example, you could give preference to your localhost network or to a private local network such a 192.168.0.0.

The options Statement

The options statement defines global options and can be used only once in the configuration file. An extensive number of options cover such components as forwarding, name checking, directory path names, access control, and zone transfers, among others (see Table 15-6).

A complete listing can be found in the BIND documentation. The options statement is listed in the **/etc/bind/named.conf.options** file. It is included in the **named.conf** file with an **include** statement.

```
include  "/etc/bind/named.conf.options"
```

Option	Description
`type`	Specifies a zone type.
`file`	Specifies the zone file for the zone.
`directory`	Specifies a directory for zone files.
`forwarders`	Lists hosts for DNS servers where requests are to be forwarded.
`masters`	Lists hosts for DNS master servers for a slave server.
`notify`	Allows master servers to notify their slave servers when the master zone data changes and updates are needed.
`allow-transfer`	Specifies which hosts are allowed to receive zone transfers.
`allow-query`	Specifies hosts that are allowed to make queries.
`allow-recursion`	Specifies hosts that are allowed to perform recursive queries on the server.

Table 15-5: Zone Options

The directory Option

An important option found in most configuration files is the directory option, which holds the location of links for the name server's zone and cache files on your system. The following example is taken from the **/etc/bind/named.conf.options** file, with sample entries added for forward servers. The example uses IPv4 addresses.

```
options {
        directory "/var/cache/bind";
        forwarders { 192.168.0.34;
                    192.168.0.47;
                   };
       };
```

The forwarders Option

Another commonly used global option is the forwarders option. With the forwarders option, you can list several DNS servers to which queries can be forwarded if they cannot be resolved by the local DNS server. This is helpful for local networks that may need to use a DNS server connected to the Internet. The forwarders option can also be placed in forward zone entries.

The notify Option

With the notify option turned on, the master zone DNS servers send messages to any slave DNS servers whenever their configuration has changed. The slave servers can then perform zone transfers in which they download the changed configuration files. Slave servers always use the DNS configuration files copied from their master DNS servers. The notify option takes one argument, yes or no, where yes is the default. With the no argument, you can have the master server not send out any messages to the slave servers, in effect preventing any zone transfers.

Option	Description
`sortlist`	Gives preference to specified networks according to a queries source.
`directory`	Specifies a directory for zone files.
`forwarders`	Lists hosts for DNS servers where requests are to be forwarded.
`allow-transfer`	Specifies which hosts are allowed to receive zone transfers.
`allow-query`	Specifies hosts that are allowed to make queries.
`allow-recursion`	Specifies hosts that are allowed to perform recursive queries on the server.
`notify`	Allows master servers to notify their slave servers when the master zone data changes and updates are needed.
`blackhole`	Option to eliminate denial response by `allow-query`.

Table 15-6: Bind Options for the options Statement

The named configuration files

BIND configuration uses three named configuration files for your zones and server options. These files are located in the **/etc/bind** directory.

named.conf The primary BIND configuration file. This file will read in the **named.conf.local**, the **named.conf.options**, and the **named.conf.default-zones** files. The DNS server actually only looks for the named.conf file.

named.conf.options This file includes global options for your DNS server.

named.conf.local Here you add your own zone configuration entries.

named.conf.default-zones This file lists the entries for the localhost and broadcast zones, used by a DNS server to access its own host.

The named.conf configuration file

The **named.conf** configuration file consist of three **include** statements for reading in the contents of the **named.conf.local**, the **named.conf.options**, and the **named.conf.default-zones** files. You should make any changes to these files, not to the **named.conf** file, though you can add changes to the **named.conf** file if you want. First the **named.conf.options** file is read to set global options, then the **named.conf.local** file which holds your DNS server zone statements, and then the **named.conf.default-zones** file which holds the standard zone definitions for root level access, the localhost, and broadcast. The **named.conf** file installed by the BIND server package to the **/etc/bind** directory is shown here. The file begins with comments using C++ syntax, //.

/etc/bind/named.conf

```
// This is the primary configuration file for the BIND DNS server named.
//
// Please read /usr/share/doc/bind9/README.Debian.gz for information on the
// structure of BIND configuration files in Debian, *BEFORE* you customize
// this configuration file.
//
// If you are just adding zones, please do that in /etc/bind/named.conf.local

include "/etc/bind/named.conf.options";
include "/etc/bind/named.conf.local";
include "/etc/bind/named.conf.default-zones";
```

The named.conf.options configuration file

The **named.conf.options** file contains an options statement with global options listed. The **directory** option sets the directory for the zone and cache files to **/var/cache/bind**. In this directory, you will find links to your zone files and reverse mapping files, along with the cache file, **named.ca**. The original files will be located in **/etc/bind**. The **forwarders** option can be used for your ISP DNS servers. The **dnssec-validation** option enables DNSSEC support.

/etc/bind/named.conf.options

```
options {
    directory "/var/cache/bind";

// If there is a firewall between you and nameservers you want
// to talk to, you may need to fix the firewall to allow multiple
// ports to talk.  See http://www.kb.cert.org/vuls/id/800113

// If your ISP provided one or more IP addresses for stable
// nameservers, you probably want to use them as forwarders.
// Uncomment the following block, and insert the addresses
// replacing the all-0's placeholder.

    // forwarders {
    //     0.0.0.0;
    // };

========================================================================
    // If BIND logs error messages about the root key being expired,
    // you will need to update your keys.  See https://www.isc.org/bind-keys
    //
========================================================================
    dnssec-validation auto;
    auth-nxdomain no;    # conform to RFC1035
    listen-on-v6 { any; };
    };
```

The named.conf.local configuration file

In the **named.conf.local** file you add the zone statements for your particular DNS server. Initially this file will be empty, except for a few comments.

A sample **named.conf.local** file follows.

```
//
// A simple BIND configuration
//

zone "mytrek.com" {
                    type master;
                    file "/etc/bind/db.mytrek.com";
                    };
zone "1.168.192.IN-ADDR.ARPA" {
                                type master;
                                file "/etc/bind/db.192.168.0";
                                };
```

The first zone statement defines a zone for the **mytrek.com** domain. Its type is master, and its zone file is named "**mytrek.com**." The next zone is used for reverse IP mapping of the previous zone. Its name is made up of a reverse listing of the **mytrek.com** domain's IP address with the term **IN-ADDR.ARPA** appended. The domain address for **mytrek.com** is 192.168.0, so the reverse is 1.168.192. The **IN-ADDR.ARPA** domain is a special domain that supports gateway location and Internet address–to–host mapping.

The **named.local.local** file is also where you would include the local address zone definitions for private non-Internet local addresses (those beginning with **192**, **10**, and **172.16** through **172.31)** (see Chapter 18). If you are not using them, you should include the dummy definitions for them located in the **zones.rfc1918** file.

```
include "/etc/bind/zones.rfc1918";
```

The named.conf.default-zones configuration file

The **named.conf** configuration file will read in any default zones from the **named.conf.default-zones** file, using the **include** directive. The zone statements in the **named.conf.default-zones** file will configure the localhost, broadcast, and root level zones.

You should not have to modify the **named.conf.default-zones** file. The **named.conf.default-zones** file installed by the BIND server package to the **/etc/bind** directory is shown here.

/etc/bind/named.conf.default-zones

```
// prime the server with knowledge of the root servers
zone "." {
     type hint;
     file "/etc/bind/db.root";
};

// be authoritative for the localhost forward and reverse zones, and for
// broadcast zones as per RFC 1912
```

```
zone "localhost" {
     type master;
     file "/etc/bind/db.local";
};

zone "127.in-addr.arpa" {
     type master;
     file "/etc/bind/db.127";
};

zone "0.in-addr.arpa" {
     type master;
     file "/etc/bind/db.0";
};

zone "255.in-addr.arpa" {
     type master;
     file "/etc/bind/db.255";
};
```

The "." zone is set up for accessing the root DNS servers, the **db.root** zone file.

The localhost zone statement configures the localhost network addresses. The **127** statement defines a reverse mapping zone for the loopback interface (localhost), the method used by the system to address itself and enable communication between local users on the system. The zone file for local host is **db.local**, and its reverse lookup file is **db.127**.

Two reverse lookup zones are then set up for the broadcast zone, 0 and 255, in the **db.0** and **db.255** zone files.

An IPv6 named.conf.local Example

The IPv6 version for the preceding **named.conf.local** file appears much the same, except that the IN-ADDR.ARPA domain is replaced by the IP6.ARPA domain in the reverse zone entries. IP6.ARPA uses bit labels providing bit-level specification for the address. This is simply the full hexadecimal address, including zeros, without intervening colons. You need to use IP6.ARPA format of the IPv6 address for both the **mytrek.com** domain and the localhost domain.

named.conf.local

```
//
// A simple BIND 9 configuration
//

zone "mytrek.com" {
                    type master;
                    file "/etc/bind/db.mytrek.com";
                    };

zone "\[xFC00000000000000/64].IP6.ARPA" {
                              type master;
                              file "/etc/bind/db.fc0";
                             };
```

Resource Records for Zone Files

Your name server holds domain name information about the hosts on your network in resource records placed in zone and reverse mapping files. Resource records are used to associate IP addresses with fully qualified domain names. You need a record for every computer in the zone that the name server services. A record takes up one line, though you can use parentheses to use several lines for a record, as is usually the case with SOA records. A resource record uses the Standard Resource Record Format as shown here:

```
name [<ttl>] [<class>] <type> <rdata> [<comment>]
```

Type	Description
A	An IPv4 host address, maps hostname to IPv4 address
AAAA	An IPv6 host address
A6	An IPv6 host address supporting chained addresses
NS	Authoritative name server for this zone
CNAME	Canonical name, used to define an alias for a hostname
SOA	Start of Authority, starts DNS entries in zone file, specifies name server for domain, and other features such as server contact and serial number
WKS	Well-known service description
PTR	Pointer record, for performing reverse domain name lookups, maps IP address to hostname
RP	Text string that contains contact information about a host
HINFO	Host information
MINFO	Mailbox or mail list information
MX	Mail exchanger, informs remote site of your zone's mail server
TXT	Text strings, usually information about a host
KEY	Domain private key
SIG	Resource record signature
NXT	Next resource record

Table 15-7: Domain Name System Resource Record Types

Here, *name* is the name for this record. It can be a domain name or a hostname (fully qualified domain name). If you specify only the hostname, the default domain is appended. If no name entry exists, the last specific name is used. If the @ symbol is used, the name server's domain name is used. *ttl* (time to live) is an optional entry that specifies how long the record is to be cached (the **$TTL** directive sets default). *class* is the class of the record. The class used in most resource record entries is IN, for Internet. By default, it is the same as that specified for the domain in the **named.conf** file. *type* is the type of the record. *rdata* is the resource record data. The following is an example of a resource record entry. The name is **rabbit.mytrek.com**, the class is Internet (IN), the type is a host address record (A), and the data is the IP address 192.168.0.2.

```
rabbit.mytrek.com.    IN   A   192.168.0.2
```

Resource Record Types

Different types of resource records exist for different kinds of hosts and name server operations (see Table 15-7 for a listing of resource record types). A, NS, MX, PTR, and CNAME are the types commonly used. A is used for host address records that match domain names with IP addresses. NS is used to reference a name server. MX specifies the host address of the mail server that services this zone. The name server has mail messages sent to that host. The PTR type is used for records that point to other resource records and is used for reverse mapping. CNAME is used to identify an alias for a host on your system.

Time To Live Directive and Field: $TTL

All zone files begin with a Time To Live directive, which specifies the time that a client should keep the provided DNS information before refreshing the information again from the DNS server. Realistically this should be at least a day, though if changes in the server are scheduled sooner, you can temporarily shorten the time, later restoring it. Each record, in fact, has a Time To Live value that can be explicitly indicated with the TTL field. This is the second field in a resource record. If no TTL field is specified in the record, then the default, as defined by the $TLL directive, can be used. The $TTL directive is placed at the beginning of each zone file. By default it will list the time in seconds, usually 86400, 24 hours.

```
$TTL 86400
```

You can also specify the time in days (d), hours (h), or minutes (m), as in

```
$TTL 2d3h
```

When used as a field, the TTL will be a time specified as the second field. In the following example, the turtle resource record can be cached for three days. This will override the default time in the TTL time directive:

```
turtle     3d     IN    A      192.168.0.1
```

Start of Authority: SOA

A zone or reverse mapping file always begins with a special resource record called the Start of Authority (SOA) record. This record specifies that all the following records are authoritative for this domain. It also holds information about the name server's domain, which is to be given to other name servers. An SOA record has the same format as other resource records, though its data segment is arranged differently. The format for an SOA record follows:

```
name {ttl} class SOA Origin Person-in-charge (
                                Serial number
                                Refresh
                                Retry
                                Expire
                                Minimum )
```

Each zone has its own SOA record. The SOA begins with the zone name specified in the **named.conf** zone entry. This is usually a domain name. An @ symbol is usually used for the name, and acts like a macro expanding to the domain name. The *class* is usually the Internet class, IN.

SOA is the type. Origin is the machine that is the origin of the records, usually the machine running your name server daemon. The person-in-charge is the e-mail address for the person managing the name server (use dots, not @, for the e-mail address, as this symbol is used for the domain name). Several configuration entries are placed in a block delimited with braces. The first is the *serial number.* You change the serial number when you add or change records, so that it is updated by other servers. The serial number can be any number, as long as it is incremented each time a change is made to any record in the zone. A common practice is to use the year-month-day-number for the serial number, where number is the number of changes in that day. For example, 2009120403 would be the year 2009, December 4, for the third change. Be sure to update it when making changes.

Refresh specifies the time interval for refreshing SOA information. *Retry* is the frequency for trying to contact an authoritative server. Expire is the length of time a secondary name server keeps information about a zone without updating it. Minimum is the length of time records in a zone live. The times are specified in the number of seconds.

The following example shows an SOA record. The machine running the name server is **turtle.mytrek.com,** and the e-mail address of the person responsible for the server is **hostmaster.turtle.mytrek.com**. Notice the periods at the ends of these names. For names with no periods, the domain name is appended. **turtle** would be the same as **turtle.mytrek.com**. When entering full hostnames, be sure to add the period so that the domain is not appended.

```
@ IN SOA turtle.mytrek.com. hostmaster.turtle.mytrek.com. (
                                1997022700 ; Serial
                                28800 ; Refresh
                                14400 ; Retry
                                3600000 ; Expire
                                86400 ) ; Minimum
```

Name Server: NS

The name server record specifies the name of the name server for this zone. These have a resource record type of NS. If you have more than one name server, list them in NS records. These records usually follow the SOA record. As they usually apply to the same domain as the SOA record, their name field is often left blank to inherit the server's domain name specified by the @ symbol in the previous SOA record.

```
          IN   NS      turtle.mytrek.com.
```

You can, if you wish, enter the domain name explicitly as shown here:

```
mytrek.com.  IN   NS     turtle.mytrek.com.
```

Address Record: A, AAAA, and A6

Resource records of type A are address records that associate a fully qualified domain name with an IP address. Often, only their hostname is specified. Any domain names without a terminating period automatically have the domain appended to them. Given the domain **mytrek.com**, the **turtle** name in the following example is expanded to **turtle.mytrek.com**:

```
rabbit.mytrek.com. IN    A       192.168.0.2
turtle             IN    A       192.168.0.1
```

BIND supports IPv6 addresses. IPv6 IP addresses have a very different format from that of the IPv4 addresses commonly used. Instead of the numerals arranged in four segments, IPv6 uses hexadecimal numbers arranged in seven segments. In the following example, **turtle.mytrek.com** is associated with a unique-local IPv6 address: **fc00::**. There are only three fields in a unique-local address: format prefix, subnet identifier, and interface identifier. The empty segments of the subnet identifier can be represented by an empty colon pair (::). The interface identifier follows, **8:800:200C:417A**.

```
turtle.mytrek.com. IN     AAAA    FC00::8:800:200C:417A
```

IPv6 also supports the use of IPv4 addresses as an interface identifier, instead of the MAC-derived identifier. The network information part of the IPv6 address would use IPv6 notation, and the remaining interface (host) identifier would use the full IPv4 address. These are known as mixed addresses. In the next example, **lizard.mytrek.com** is given a mixed address using IPv6 network information and IPv4 interface information. The IPv6 network information is for an IPv6 unique-local address.

```
lizard.mytrek.com. IN      AAAA        fc00::192.168.0.3
```

The AAAA record is used in most networks for an IPv6 record. An AAAA record operates much like a standard A address record, requiring a full IPv6 address. An A6 record is an experimental version of the IPv6 record. It can be more flexible, in that it does not require a full address. Instead you chain A6 records together, specifying just part of the address in each. For example, you could specify just an interface identifier for a host, letting the network information be provided by another IPv6 record (you can implement an A6 record with a full address, just like an AAAA record). In the next example, the first A6 record lists only the address for the interface identifier for the host **divit**. Following the address is the domain name, **mytrek.com**, whose address is to be used to complete **divit**'s address, providing network information. The next A6 record provides the network address information for **mytrek.com**.

```
divit.mygolf.com. IN    A6   0:0:0:0:1234:5678:3466:af1f  mytrek.com.
mytrek.com.       IN    A6   3ffe:8050:201:1860::
```

Mail Exchanger: MX

The Mail Exchanger record, MX, specifies the mail server that is used for this zone or for a particular host. The mail exchanger is the server to which mail for the host is sent. In the following example, the mail server is specified as **turtle.mytrek.com**. Any mail sent to the address for any machines in that zone will be sent to the mail server, which in turn will send it to the specific machines. For example, mail sent to a user on **rabbit.mytrek.com** will first be sent to **turtle.mytrek.com**, which will then send it on to **rabbit.mytrek.com**. In the following example, the host 192.168.0.1 (**turtle.mytrek.com**) is defined as the mail server for the **mytrek.com** domain:

```
mytrek.com. IN      MX   10   turtle.mytrek.com.
```

You could also inherit the domain name from the SOA record, leaving the domain name entry blank.

```
           IN      MX   turtle.mytrek.com.
```

You could use the IP address instead, but in larger networks, the domain name may be needed to search for and resolve the IP address of a particular machine, which could change.

```
mytrek.com. IN      MX   10   192.168.0.1
```

An MX record recognizes an additional field that specifies the ranking for a mail exchanger. If your zone has several mail servers, you can assign them different rankings in their MX records. The smaller number has a higher ranking. This way, if mail cannot reach the first mail server, it can be routed to an alternate server to reach the host. In the following example, mail for hosts on the **mytrek.com** domain is first routed to the mail server at 192.168.0.1 (**turtle.mytrek.com**), and if that fails, it is routed to the mail server at 192.168.0.2 (**rabbit.mytrek.com**).

```
mytrek.com. IN MX 10 turtle.mytrek.com.
            IN MX 20 rabbit.mytrek.com.
```

You can also specify a mail server for a particular host. In the following example, the mail server for **lizard.mytrek.com** is specified as **rabbit.mytrek.com**:

```
lizard.mytrek.com. IN      A       192.168.0.3
                   IN      MX  10  rabbit.mytrek.com.
```

Aliases: CNAME

Resource records of type CNAME are used to specify alias names for a host in the zone. Aliases are often used for machines running several different types of servers, such as both Web and FTP servers. They are also used to locate a host when it changes its name. In this case, the old name becomes an alias for the new name. In the following example, **ftp.mytrek.com** is an alias for a machine actually called **turtle.mytrek.com**:

```
ftp.mytrek.com. IN CNAME turtle.mytrek.com.
```

The term CNAME stands for canonical name. The canonical name is the actual name of the host. In the preceding example, the canonical name is **turtle.mytrek.com**. The alias, also known as the CNAME, is **ftp.mytrek.com**. In a CNAME entry, the alias points to the canonical name. Aliases cannot be used for NS (name server) or MX (mail server) entries. For those records, you need to use the original domain name or IP address.

A more stable way to implement aliases is simply to create another address record for a host or domain. You can have as many hostnames for the same IP address as you want, provided they are certified. For example, to make **www.mytrek.com** an alias for **turtle.mytrek.com**, you only have to add another address record for it, giving it the same IP address as **turtle.mytrek.com**.

```
turtle.mytrek.com. IN A 192.168.0.1
www.mytrek.com. IN A 192.168.0.1
```

Pointer Record: PTR

A PTR record is used to perform reverse mapping from an IP address to a host. PTR records are used in the reverse mapping files. The name entry holds a reversed IP address, and the data entry holds the name of the host. The following example maps the IP address 192.168.0.1 to **turtle.mytrek.com**:

```
1.1.168.192 IN PTR turtle.mytrek.com.
```

In a PTR record, you can specify just that last number segment of the address (the host address) and let DNS fill in the domain part of the address. In the next example, 1 has the domain address, 1.168.192, automatically added to give 1.1.168.192:

```
1 IN PTR turtle.mytrek.com.
```

Host Information: HINFO, RP, MINFO, and TXT

The HINFO, RP, MINFO, and TXT records are used to provide information about the host. The RP record enables you to specify the person responsible for a certain host. The HINFO record provides basic hardware and operating system identification. The TXT record is used to enter any text you want. MINFO provides a host's mail and mailbox information. These are used sparingly, as they may give too much information out about the server.

Zone Files

A DNS server uses several zone files covering different components of the DNS. Each zone uses two zone files: the principal zone file and a reverse mapping zone file. The *zone file* contains the resource records for hosts in the zone. A *reverse mapping file* contains records that provide reverse mapping of your domain name entries, enabling you to map from IP addresses to domain names. The name of the file used for the zone file can technically be any name, but on the Ubuntu server zone files, use the prefix **db**, as in **db.local** for the localhost zone. The name of the file is specified in the zone statement's file entry in the **named.conf** and **named.conf.local** files. If your server supports several zones, you may want to use a name that denotes the specific zone. The domain name is used as the name of the zone file. For example, the zone **mytrek.com** would have a zone file with the same name and the prefix **db**, as in **db.mytrek.com**. The zone file used in the following example is called **db.mytrek.com**. The reverse mapping file can also be any name, though it is usually the reverse IP address domain specified in its corresponding zone file. For example, in the case of **mytrek.com.zone** zone file, the reverse mapping file would be called **db.192.168.0**, the IP address of the **mytrek.com** domain defined in the **db.mytrek.com** zone file. This file would contain reverse mapping of all the host addresses in the domain, allowing their hostname addresses to be mapped to their corresponding IP addresses. In addition, BIND sets up a cache file and a reverse mapping file for the localhost. The cache file holds the resource records for the root name servers to which your name server connects. The cache file is called **db.root**. The localhost reverse mapping file, **db.local**, holds reverse IP resource records for the local loopback interface, localhost.

Once you have created your zone files, you should check their syntax with the **named-checkzone** tool. This tool requires that you specify both a zone and a zone file. In the following example, in the **/etc/bind** directory, the zone **mytrek.com** in the zone file **db.mytrek.com** is checked:

```
named-checkzone  mytrek.com db.mytrek.com
```

Zone Files for Internet Zones

A zone file holds resource records that follow a certain format. The file begins with general directives to define default domains or to include other resource record files. These are followed by a single SOA record, name server and domain resource records, and then resource records for the different hosts. Comments begin with a semicolon and can be placed throughout the file. The @ symbol operates like a special macro, representing the domain name of the zone to which the records apply. The @ symbol is used in the first field of a resource or SOA record as the zone's domain name. Multiple names can be specified using the * matching character. The first field in a resource record is the name of the domain to which it applies. If the name is left blank, the previous explicit name entry in another resource record is used automatically. This way, you can list several entries that apply to the same host without having to repeat the hostname. Any host or domain name used throughout this file that is not terminated with a period has the zone's domain appended to it. For example, if the zone's domain is **mytrek.com** and a resource record has only the name **rabbit** with no trailing period, the zone's domain is automatically appended to it, giving you **rabbit.mytrek.com.**. Be sure to include the trailing period whenever you enter the complete fully qualified domain name, **turtle.mytrek.com.**, for example.

Directives

You can also use several directives to set global attributes. $ORIGIN sets a default domain name to append to address names that do not end in a period. $INCLUDE includes a file. $GENERATE can generate records whose domain or IP addresses differ only by an iterated number. The $ORIGIN directive is often used to specify the root domain to use in address records. Be sure to include the trailing period. The following example sets the domain origin to **mytrek.com** and will be automatically appended to the **lizard** host name that follows:

```
$ORIGIN   mytrek.com.
lizard   IN   A    192.168.0.2
```

SOA Record

A zone file begins with an SOA record specifying the machine the name server is running on, among other specifications. The @ symbol is used for the name of the SOA record, denoting the zone's domain name. After the SOA, the name server resource records (NS) are listed. Just below the name server records are resource records for the domain itself. Resource records for host addresses (A), aliases (CNAME), and mail exchangers (MX) follow. The following example shows a sample zone file, which begins with an SOA record and is followed by an NS record, resource records for the domain, and then resource records for individual hosts:

db.turtle.mytrek.com

```
; Authoritative data for turle.mytrek.com
;
$TTL 86400
@ IN SOA turtle.mytrek.com. hostmaster.turtle.mytrek.com. (
                            93071200 ; Serial number
                               10800 ; Refresh 3 hours
                                3600 ; Retry 1 hour
                             3600000 ; Expire 1000 hours
                             86400 ) ; Minimum 24 hours

             IN      NS          turtle.mytrek.com.
             IN      A           192.168.0.1
             IN      MX    10    turtle.mytrek.com.
             IN      MX    15    rabbit.mytrek.com.

turtle       IN      A           192.168.0.1
```

```
        IN      HINFO   PC-686 LINUX
ftp     IN      CNAME   turtle.mytrek.com.
www     IN      A       192.168.0.1

rabbit  IN      A       192.168.0.2

lizard  IN      A       192.168.0.3
        IN      HINFO   MAC MACOS
```

The first two lines are comments about the server for which this zone file is used. Notice that the first two lines begin with a semicolon. The class for each of the resource records in this file is IN, indicating these are Internet records. The SOA record begins with an `@` symbol that stands for the zone's domain. In this example, it is **mytrek.com**. Any host or domain name used throughout this file that is not terminated with a period has this domain appended to it. For example, in the following resource record, **turtle** has no period, so it automatically expands to **turtle.mytrek.com**. The same happens for **rabbit** and **lizard**. These are read as **rabbit.mytrek.com** and **lizard.mytrek.com**. Also, in the SOA, notice that the e-mail address for hostmaster uses a period instead of an `@` symbol; `@` is a special symbol in zone files and cannot be used for any other purpose.

Nameserver Record

The next resource record specifies the name server for this zone. Here, it is **mytrek.com.**. Notice the name for this resource record is blank. If the name is blank, a resource record inherits the name from the previous record. In this case, the NS record inherits the value of @ in the SOA record, its previous record. This is the zone's domain, and the NS record specifies **turtle.mytrek.com** as the name server for this zone.

```
        IN   NS    turtle.mytrek.com.
```

Here the domain name is inherited. The entry can be read as the following. Notice the trailing period at the end of the domain name:

```
mytrek.com. IN  NS   turtle.mytrek.com.
```

Address Record

The following address records set up an address for the domain itself. This is often the same as the name server, in this case 192.168.0.1 (the IP address of **turtle.mytrek.com**). This enables users to reference the domain itself, rather than a particular host in it. A mail exchanger record follows that routes mail for the domain to the name server. Users can send mail to the **mytrek.com** domain and it will be routed to **turtle.mytrek.com**.

```
            IN   A    192.168.0.1
```

Here the domain name is inherited. The entry can be read as the following:

```
mytrek.com. IN  A    192.168.0.1
```

Mail Exchanger Record

The next records are mail exchanger (MX) records listing **turtle.mytrek.com** and **fast.mytrek.com** as holding the mail servers for this zone. You can have more than one mail exchanger record for a host. More than one host may exist through which mail can be routed. These can be listed in mail exchanger records for which you can set priority rankings (a smaller number ranks higher). In this example, if **turtle.mytrek.com** cannot be reached, its mail is routed through **rabbit.mytrek.com**, which has been set up also to handle mail for the **mytrek.com** domain:

```
        IN      MX      100     turtle.mytrek.com.
        IN      MX      150     rabbit.mytrek.com.
```

Again the domain name is inherited. The entries can be read as the following:

```
mytrek.com.    IN      MX  100   turtle.mytrek.com.
mytrek.com.    IN      MX  150   rabbit.mytrek.com.
```

Address Record with Host Name

The following resource record is an address record (A) that associates an IP address with the fully qualified domain name **turtle.mytrek.com**. The resource record name holds only **turtle** with no trailing period, so it is automatically expanded to **turtle.mytrek.com**. This record provides the IP address to which **turtle.mytrek.com** can be mapped.

```
turtle    IN     A     192.168.0.1
```

Inherited Names

Several resource records immediately follow that have blank names. These inherit their names from the preceding full record—in this case, **turtle.mytrek.com**. In effect, these records also apply to that host. Using blank names is an easy way to list additional resource records for the same host (notice that an apparent indent occurs). The first record is an information record, providing the hardware and operating system for the machine.

```
          IN     HINFO     PC-686 LINUX
```

Alias Records

If you are using the same machine to run several different servers, such as Web and FTP servers, you may want to assign aliases to these servers to make accessing them easier for users. Instead of using the actual domain name, such as **turtle.mytrek.com**, to access the Web server running on it, users may find that using the following is easier: for the Web server, **www.mytrek.com**; and for the FTP server, **ftp.mytrek.com**. You can implement such a feature using alias records. In the example zone file, one CNAME alias records exist for the **turtle.mytrek.com** machine: FTP. The next record implements an alias for **www**, using another address record for the same machine. None of the name entries ends in a period, so they are appended automatically with the domain name **mytrek.com**. **www.mytrek.com** and **ftp.mytrek.com** are aliases for **turtle.mytrek.com**. Users entering those URLs automatically access the respective servers on the **turtle.mytrek.com** machine.

Loopback Record

Address and mail exchanger records are then listed for the two other machines in this zone: **rabbit.mytrek.com** and **lizard.mytrek.com**. You could add HINFO, TXT, MINFO, or alias records for these entries.

IPv6 Zone File Example

This is the same zone file using IPv6 addresses. The addresses are unique-local (FC00), instead of global (3), providing private network addressing. The AAAA IPv6 address records are used.

Note: On Ubuntu, if your network does not use zones for private address space, you can redirect those addresses to an empty configuration file, **db.empty**. Load the RFC 1912 configuration file, **zones.rfc1912**, into the **named.conf.local** file using an **include** statement.

```
; Authoritative data for turle.mytrek.com, IPv6 version
;
$TTL 1d
@ IN SOA turtle.mytrek.com. hostmaster.turtle.mytrek.com. (
                              93071200 ; Serial number
                                 10800 ; Refresh 3 hours
                                  3600 ; Retry 1 hour
                               3600000 ; Expire 1000 hours
                              86400 ) ; Minimum 24 hours
             IN       NS        turtle.mytrek.com.
             IN       AAAA        FC00::8:800:200C:417A
             IN       MX    10  turtle.mytrek.com.
             IN       MX    15  rabbit.mytrek.com.

turtle       IN       AAAA        FC00::8:800:200C:417A
             IN       HINFO     PC-686 LINUX
ftp          IN       CNAME     turtle.mytrek.com.
www          IN       AAAA        FC00::8:800:200C:417A

rabbit       IN       AAAA        FC00::FEDC:BA98:7654:3210

lizard       IN       AAAA        FC00::E0:18F7:3466:7D
             IN       HINFO     MAC MACOS
```

Localhost zone file: named.localhost

The **db.local** zone file implements mapping for the local loopback interface known as localhost. This file includes support for both for IPv4 and for IPv6 addressing. The IPv4 address for localhost is **127.0.0.1**, and the IPv6 address is **::1**. These are special addresses that functions as the local address for your machine. It allows a machine to address itself. The IPv4 address has the type A and the address 127.0.0.1, whereas the IPv6 address has the type AAAA and the address ::1.

```
A       127.0.0.1
AAAA    ::1
```

The **db.local** zone file is shown here.

db.local

```
$TTL 604000
@       IN SOA @ localhost  root.localhost. (
                                    2        ; Serial
                                    604800   ; Refresh
                                    86400    ; Retry
                                    2419200; Expire
;                                   604800) ; Negative Cache TTL
@      IN     NS     localhost.
@      IN     A      127.0.0.1
@      IN     AAAA   ::1
```

Reverse Mapping File

Reverse name lookups are enabled using a reverse mapping file. *Reverse mapping* files map fully qualified domain names to IP addresses. This reverse lookup capability is unnecessary, but it is convenient to have. With reverse mapping, when users access remote hosts, their domain name addresses can be used to identify their own host, instead of only the IP address. The name of the file can be anything you want. On Ubuntu, it is usually the first part of the zone's domain address (the network part of a zone's IP address). For example, the reverse mapping file for a zone with the IP address of 192.168.0 is **db.192**. Its full pathname would be something like **/etc/bind/db.192**. For the localhost which has address 127.0.0.1, the reverse zone file is **db.127**. Two reverse lookup zones are setup for the broadcast zone, 0 and 255, in the **db.0** and **db.255** files.

IPv4 IN-ADDR.ARPA Reverse Mapping Format

In IPv4, the zone entry for a reverse mapping in the **named** configuration files use a special domain name consisting of the IP address in reverse, with an **in-addr.arpa** extension. This reverse IP address becomes the zone domain referenced by the @ symbol in the reverse mapping file. For example, the reverse mapping zone name for a domain with the IP address of **192.168.43** would be **43.168.192.in-addr.arpa**. In the following example, the reverse domain name for the domain address **192.168.0** is **168.192.in-addr.arpa**:

```
zone "168.192.in-addr.arpa" in {
          type master;
          file "db.192";
          };
```

A reverse mapping file begins with an SOA record, which is the same as that used in a forward mapping file. Resource records for each machine defined in the forward mapping file then follow. These resource records are PTR records that point to hosts in the zone. These must be actual hosts, not aliases defined with CNAME records. Records for reverse mapping begin with a reversed IP address. Each segment in the IP address is sequentially reversed. Each segment begins with the host ID, followed by reversed network numbers.

If you list only the host ID with no trailing period, the zone domain is automatically attached. In the case of a reverse mapping file, the zone domain as specified in the zone statement is the domain IP address backward. The 1 expands to 1.1.168.192. In the following example, **turtle** and **lizard** inherit the domain IP address, whereas **rabbit** has its address explicitly entered:

```
; reverse mapping of domain names 1.168.192.IN-ADDR.ARPA
;
$TTL 86400
@ IN SOA turtle.mytrek.com. hostmaster.turtle.mytrek.com.(
                        92050300 ; Serial (yymmddxx format)
                           10800 ; Refresh 3hHours
                            3600 ; Retry 1 hour
                         3600000 ; Expire 1000 hours
                         86400 ) ; Minimum 24 hours

@           IN    NS     turtle.mytrek.com.
1           IN    PTR    turtle.mytrek.com.
2.1.168.192 IN    PTR    rabbit.mytrek.com.
3           IN    PTR    lizard.mytrek.com.
```

IPv6 IP6.ARPA Reverse Mapping Format

In IPv6, reverse mapping can be handled either with the current IP6.ARPA domain format, or with the older IP6.INT format. With IP6.ARPA, the address is represented by a bit-level representation that places the hexadecimal address within brackets. The first bracket is preceded by a backslash. The address must be preceded by an *x* indicating that it is a hexadecimal address. Following the address is a number indicating the number of bits referenced. In a 128-bit address, usually the first 64 bits reference the network address and the last 64 bits are for the interface address. The following example shows the network and interface addresses for lizard.

```
FC00:0000:0000:0000:00E0:18F7:3466:007D  lizard IPv6 address
\[xFC00000000000000/64]                  lizard network address
\[x00E018F73466007D/64]                    lizard interface address
```

The zone entry for a reverse mapping in a **named** configuration file with an **IP6.ARPA** extension would use the bit-level representation for the network address.

```
zone "\[xfc00000000000000/64].IP6.ARPA" in {
          type master;
          file "fec.ip6.arpa";
          };
```

A reverse mapping file then uses the same bit-level format for the interface addresses.

```
$TTL 1d
@ IN SOA turtle.mytrek.com. hostmaster.turtle.mytrek.com.(
                        92050300 ; Serial (yymmddxx format)
                           10800 ; Refresh 3hHours
                            3600 ; Retry 1 hour
                         3600000 ; Expire 1000 hours
                         86400 ) ; Minimum 24 hours

@                             IN    NS     turtle.mytrek.com.
\[x00080800200C417A/64]       IN    PTR    turtle.mytrek.com.
\[xFEDCBA9876543210/64]       IN    PTR    rabbit.mytrek.com.
\[x00E018F73466007D/64]       IN    PTR    lizard.mytrek.com.
```

Localhost Reverse Mapping

A localhost reverse mapping file implements reverse mapping for the local loopback interface known as *localhost,* whose network address is 127.0.0.1. The localhost reverse mapping file name is uses the network part of the IP address, 127.0.0, and is named **db.127**. The address 127.0.0.1 is a special address that functions as the local address for your machine.

In the zone statement for this file in the **named.conf.default-zones** file, the name of the zone is **127.in-addr.arpa**. The zone entry is shown here:

```
zone "127.in-addr.arpa" {
          type master;
          file " /etc/bind/db.127";
          };
```

The name of the file used for the localhost reverse mapping file is **db.127**, though it can be any name. The zone file supports both IPv4 and IPv6 addresses.

```
;
; BIND reverse data file for local loopback interface
;
$TTL    604800
@       IN      SOA     localhost. root.localhost. (
                              1         ; Serial
                         604800         ; Refresh
                          86400         ; Retry
                        2419200         ; Expire
                         604800 )       ; Negative Cache TTL
;
@        IN      NS      localhost.
1.0.0    IN      PTR     localhost.
```

The NS record specifies the name server localhost should use. This file has a PTR record that maps the IP address to the localhost. The 1.0.0 used as the name expands to append the zone domain—in this case, giving you 1.0.0.127, a reverse IP address. The contents of the **db.127** file are shown here. Notice the trailing periods for localhost.

Subdomains and Slaves

Adding a subdomain to a DNS server is a simple matter of creating an additional master entry in the **named** configuration file, and then placing name server and authority entries for that subdomain in your primary DNS server's zone file. The subdomain, in turn, has its own zone file with its SOA record and entries listing hosts, which are part of its subdomain, including any of its own mail and news servers.

Subdomain Zones

The name for the subdomain could be a different name altogether or a name with the same suffix as the primary domain. In the following example, the subdomain is called **beach.mytrek.com**. It could just as easily be called **mybeach.com**. The name server to that domain is on the host **crab.beach.mytrek.com**, in this example. Its IP address is 192.168.0.33, and its zone file is **db.beach.mytrek.com**. The **beach.mytrek.com** zone file holds DNS entries for all the hosts being serviced by this name server. The following example shows zone entries:

```
zone "beach.mytrek.com" {
        type master;
        file "db.beach.mytrek.com";
        };

zone "1.168.192.IN-ADDR.ARPA" {
        type master;
        file "192.168.0";
        };
```

Subdomain Records

On the primary DNS server, in the example **turtle.mytrek.com**, you would place entries in the master zone file to identify the subdomain server's host and designate it as a name server. Such entries are also known as *glue records*. In this example, you would place the following entries in the **mytrek.com** zone file on **turtle.mytrek.com**:

```
beach.mytrek.com.    IN    NS    beach.mytrek.com.
beach.mytrek.com.    IN    A     192.168.0.33.
```

URL references to hosts serviced by **beach.mytrek.com** can now be reached from any host serviced by **mytrek.com**, which does not need to maintain any information about the **beach.mytrek.com** hosts. It simply refers such URL references to the **beach.mytrek.com** name server.

Slave Servers

A slave DNS server is tied directly to a master DNS server and periodically receives DNS information from it. You use a master DNS server to configure its slave DNS servers automatically. Any changes you make to the master server are automatically transferred to its slave servers. This transfer of information is called a *zone transfer.* Zone transfers are initiated automatically whenever the slave zone's refresh time is reached or the slave server receives a notify message from the master. The *refresh time* is the second argument in the zone's SOA entry. A notify message is sent automatically by the master whenever changes are made to the master zone's configuration files and the **named** daemon is restarted. In effect, slave zones are configured automatically by the master zone, receiving the master zone's zone files and making them their own.

Slave Zones

Using the previous examples, suppose you want to set up a slave server on **rabbit.mytrek.com**. Zone entries, as shown in the following example, are set up in the **named** configuration file for the slave DNS server on **rabbit.mytrek.com**. The slave server is operating in the same domain as the master, and so it has the same zone name, **mytrek.com**. Its SOA file is named **slave.mytrek.com**. The term "slave" in the filename is merely a convention that helps identify it as a slave server configuration file. The masters statement lists its master DNS server—in this case, 192.168.0.1. Whenever the slave needs to make a zone transfer, it transfers data from that master DNS server. The entry for the reverse mapping file for this slave server lists its reverse mapping file as **slave.192.168.0**.

```
zone "mytrek.com" {
        type slave;
        file "slave.mytrek.com";
        masters { 192.168.0.1;
        };

zone "1.168.192.IN-ADDR.ARPA" {
         type slave;
         file "slave.192.168.0";
         masters { 192.168.0.1;
         };
```

Slave Records

On the master DNS server, the master SOA zone file has entries in it to identify the host that holds the slave DNS server and to designate it as a DNS server. In this example, you would place the following in the **mytrek.com** zone file:

```
        IN        NS        192.168.0.2
```

You would also place an entry for this name server in the **mytrek.com** reverse mapping file:

```
        IN        NS        192.168.0.2
```

Controlling Transfers

The master DNS server can control which slave servers can transfer zone information from it using the allow-transfer statement. Place the statement with the list of IP addresses for the slave servers to which you want to allow access. Also, the master DNS server should be sure its notify option is not disabled. The notify option is disabled by a "notify no" statement in the options or zone **named** configuration entries. Simply erase the "no" argument to enable notify.

Incremental Zone Transfers

BIND supports incremental zone transfers (IXFR). Previously, all the zone data would be replaced in an update, rather than changes such as the addition of a few resource records simply being edited in. With incremental zone transfers, a database of changes is maintained by the master zone. Then only the changes are transferred to the slave zone, which uses this information to update its own zone files. To implement incremental zone transfers, you have to turn on the maintain-ixfr-base option in the options section.

```
maintain-ixfr-base yes;
```

You can then use the ixfr-base option in a zone section to specify a particular database file to hold changes.

```
ixfr-base "db.mytrek.com.ixfr";
```

IP Virtual Domains

IP-based virtual hosting allows more than one IP address to be used for a single machine. If a machine has two registered IP addresses, either one can be used to address the machine. If you want to treat the extra IP address as another host in your domain, you need only create an address record for it in your domain's zone file. The domain name for the host would be the same as your domain name. If you want to use a different domain name for the extra IP, however, you have to set up a virtual domain for it. This entails creating a new zone statement for it with its own zone file. For example, if the extra IP address is 192.168.0.42 and you want to give it the domain name **sail.com**, you must create a new zone statement for it in a **named** configuration file with a new zone file. The zone statement would look something like this. The zone file is called **sail.com**:

```
zone "sail.com" in {
        type master;
        file "sail.com";
        };
```

In the **db.sail.com** file, the name server name is **turtle.mytrek.com** and the e-mail address is **hostmaster@turtle.mytrek.com**. In the name server (NS) record, the name server is **turtle.mytrek.com.**

```
; Authoritative data for sail.com
;
$TTL 1d
@ IN SOA turtle.mytrek.com. hostmaster.turtle.mytrek.com. (
                              93071200 ; Serial (yymmddxx)
                                 10800 ; Refresh 3 hours
                                  3600 ; Retry 1 hour
                               3600000 ; Expire 1000 hours
                               86400 ) ; Minimum 24 hours

      IN     NS          turtle.mytrek.com.
      IN     MX   10     turtle.mytrek.com.
      IN     A           192.168.0.42 ;address of the sail.com domain

jib   IN     A          192.168.0.42
www   IN     A          jib.sail.com.
ftp   IN     CNAME      jib.sail.com.
```

This is the same machine using the original address that the name server is running as. **turtle.mytrek.com** is also the host that handles mail addressed to **sail.com** (MX). An address record then associates the extra IP address 192.168.0.42 with the **sail.com** domain name. A virtual host on this domain is then defined as **jib.sail.com**. Also, **www** and **ftp** aliases are created for that host, creating **www.sail.com** and **ftp.sail.com** virtual hosts.

In your reverse mapping file (**/var/named/1.168.192**), add PTR records for any virtual domains.

```
42.1.168.192     IN     PTR     sail.com.
42.1.168.192     IN     PTR     jib.sail.com.
```

You also have to configure your network connection to listen for both IP addresses on your machine.

Cache File

The *cache file* is used to connect the DNS server to root servers on the Internet. The file can be any name. On Ubuntu, the cache file is called **db.root**. The cache file is usually a standard file installed by your BIND software, which lists resource records for designated root servers for the Internet. The following example shows sample entries taken from the **db.root** file:

```
; formerly NS.INTERNIC.NET
;
. 3600000 IN NS A.ROOT-SERVERS.NET.
A.ROOT-SERVERS.NET.    3600000    A   198.41.0.4
;
; formerly NS1.ISI.EDU
;
. 3600000 NS B.ROOT-SERVERS.NET.
B.ROOT-SERVERS.NET.    3600000    A   128.9.0.107
```

If you are creating an isolated intranet, you need to create your own root DNS server until you connect to the Internet. In effect, you are creating a fake root server. This can be another server on your system pretending to be the root or the same name server.

Dynamic Update: DHCP and Journal Files

There are situations wherein you will need to have zones updated dynamically. Instead of manually editing a zone file to make changes in a zone, an outside process updates the zone, making changes and saving the file automatically. Dynamic updates are carried out both by master zones updating slave zones, and by DHCP servers providing IP addresses they generated for hosts to the DNS server.

A journal file is maintained recording all the changes made to a zone, having a **.jnl** extension. Should a system crash occur, this file is read to implement the most current changes. Should you manually want to update a dynamically updated zone, you will need to erase its journal file first; otherwise, your changes would be overwritten by the journal file entries.

You allow a zone to be automatically updated by specifying the **allow-update** option. This option indicates the host that can perform the update.

```
allow-update {turtle.mytrek.com;};
```

Alternatively, for master zones, you can create a more refined set of access rules using the **update-policy** statement. With the **update-policy** statement, you can list several grant and deny rules for different hosts and types of hosts.

TSIG Signatures and Updates

With BIND 9.*x*, TSIG signature names can be used instead of host names or IP addresses for both **allow-update** and **update-policy** statements (see the following sections on TSIG). Use of TSIG signatures implements an authentication of a host performing a dynamic update, providing a much greater level of security. For example, to allow a DHCP server to update a zone file, you would place an **allow-update** entry in the zone statement listed in a **named** configuration file.

The TSIG key is defined in a key statement, naming the key previously created by the **dnssec-keygen** command. The algorithm is HMAC-MD5, and the secret is the encryption key listed in the **.private** file generated by **dnssec-keygen**.

```
key mydhcpserver {
algorithm HMAC-MD5;
secret "ONQAfbBLnvWU9H8hRqq/WA==";
};
```

The key name can then be used in an **allow-update** or **allow-policy** statement to specify a TSIG key.

```
allow-update { key mydhcpserver;};
```

Manual Updates: nsupdate

You can use the update procedure to perform any kind of update you want. You can perform updates manually or automatically using a script. For DHCP updates, the DHCP server is designed to perform dynamic updates of the DNS server. You will need to configure the DHCP server appropriately, specifying the TSIG key to use and the zones to update.

You can manually perform an update using the **nsupdate** command, specifying the file holding the key with the **-k** option.

```
nsupdate -k myserver.private
```

At the prompt, you can use **nsupdate** commands to implement changes. You match on a record using its full or partial entry. To update a record, you would first delete the old one and then add the changed version, as shown here:

```
update delete  rabbit.mytrek.com.  A  192.168.0.2
update add  rabbit.mytrek.com.  A  192.168.0.44
```

DNS Security: Access Control Lists, TSIG, and DNSSEC

DNS security currently allows you to control specific access by hosts to the DNS server, as well as providing encrypted communications between servers and authentication of DNS servers. With access control lists, you can determine who will have access to your DNS server. The DNS Security Extensions (DNSSEC), included with BIND 9.*x*, provide private/public key–encrypted authentication and transmissions. TSIGs (transaction signatures) use shared private keys to provide authentication of servers to secure actions such as dynamic updates between a DNS server and a DHCP server.

Once you have configured DNSSEC you can enable it by placing the **dnssec-enable** option in the **/etc/bind/named.conf.options** file.

```
dnssec-enable yes;
```

Access Control Lists

To control access by other hosts, you use access control lists, implemented with the acl statement. Using allow and deny options with access control host lists enables you to deny or allow access by specified hosts to the name server. With allow-query, you can restrict queries to specified hosts or networks. Normally, this will result in a response saying that access is denied. You can further eliminate this response by using the blackhole option in the options statement.

You define an ACL with the acl statement followed by the label you want to give the list and then the list of addresses. Addresses can be IP addresses, network addresses, or a range of addresses based on CNDR notation. You can also use an ACL as defined earlier. The following example defines an ACL called **mynet**:

```
acl mynet { 192.168.0.1; 192.168.0.2; };
```

If you are specifying a range, such as a network, you also add exceptions to the list by preceding such addresses with an exclamation point (!). In the following example, the **myexceptions** ACL lists all those hosts in the 192.168.0.0 network, except for 192.168.0.3:

```
acl myexceptions {192.168.0.0; !192.168.0.3; };
```

Four default ACLs are already defined for you. You can use them wherever an option uses a list of addresses as an argument. These are any for all hosts, none for no hosts, localhost for all local IP addresses, and localnet for all hosts on local networks served by the DNS server.

In the next example, an ACL of **mynet** is created. Then in the **mytrek.com** zone, only these hosts are allowed to query the server. As the server has no slave DNS serves, zone transfers are disabled entirely. The blackhole option denies access from the myrejects list, without sending any rejection notice.

```
acl mynet { 192.168.0.0; };
acl myrejects { 10.0.0.44; 10.0.0.93; };

zone "mytrek.com" {
        type master;
        file "mytrek.com";
        allow-query { mynet; };
        allow-recursion { mynet; };
        allow-transfer { none; };
        blackhole {myrejects};
        };
```

Once a list is defined, you can use it with the allow-query, allow-transfer, allow-recursion, and blackhole options in a zone statement to control access to a zone. allow-query specifies hosts that can query the DNS server. allow-transfer is used for master/slave zones, designating whether update transfers are allowed. allow-recursion specifies those hosts that can perform recursive queries on the server. The blackhole option will deny contact from any hosts in its list, without sending a denial response.

Secret Keys

Different security measures will use encryption keys generated with the dnssec-keygen command. You can use dnssec-keygen to create different types of keys, including zone (ZONE), host (HOST), and user (USER) keys. You specify the type of key with the -n option. A zone key will require the name ZONE and the name of the zone's domain name. A zone key is used in DNSSEC operations. The following example creates a zone key for the **mytrek.com** zone:

```
dnssec-keygen -n ZONE mytrek.com.
```

To create a host key, you would use the HOST type. HOST keys are often used in TSIG operations.

```
dnssec-keygen -n HOST turtle.mytrek.com.
```

You can further designate an encryption algorithm (-a) and key size (-b). Use the -h option to obtain a listing of the dnssec-keygen options. Currently you can choose from RSA, DSA, HMAC-MD5, and DH algorithms. The bit range will vary according to the algorithm. RSA ranges from 512 to 4096, and HMAC-MD5 ranges from 1 to 512. The following example creates a zone key using a 768-bit key and the DSA encryption algorithm:

```
dnssec-keygen -a DSA -b 768 -n ZONE mytrek.com.
```

The dnssec-keygen command will create public and private keys, each in corresponding files with the suffixes **.private** and **.key**. The **.key** file is a KEY resource record holding the public key. For DNSSEC, the private key is used to generate signatures for the zone, and the public key is used to verify the signatures. For TSIG, a shared private key generated by the HMAC-MD5 algorithm is used instead of a public/private key pair.

DNSSEC

DNSSEC provides encrypted authentication to DNS. With DNSSEC, you can create a signed zone that is securely identified with an encrypted signature. This form of security is used primarily to secure the connections between master and slave DNS servers, so that a master server transfers update records only to authorized slave servers, and does so with a secure encrypted communication. Two servers that establish such a secure connection do so using a pair of public and private keys. In effect, you have a parent zone that can securely authenticate child zones, using encrypted transmissions. This involves creating zone keys for each child, and having those keys used by the parent zone to authenticate the child zones.

Zone Keys

You generate a zone key using the dnssec-keygen command and specifying the zone type, ZONE, with the -n option. For the key name, you use the zone's domain name. The following example creates a zone key for the **mytrek.com** zone:

```
dnssec-keygen -n ZONE mytrek.com.
```

You can further designate an encryption algorithm (-a) and a key size (-b). Use the -h option to obtain a listing of the dnssec-keygen options. Since you are setting up a public/private key pair, you should choose either the RSA or DSA algorithm. The bit range will vary according to the algorithm. RSA ranges from 512 to 4096, and DSA ranges from 512 to 1024. The following example creates a zone key using a 768-bit key and the DSA encryption algorithm:

```
dnssec-keygen -a DSA -b 768 -n ZONE mytrek.com.
```

The dnssec-keygen command will create public and private keys, each in corresponding files with the suffixes **.private** and **.key**. The private key is used to generate signatures for the zone, and the public key is used to verify the signatures. The **.key** file is a KEY resource record holding the public key. This is used to decrypt signatures generated by the corresponding private key. You add the public key to a DNS **named** configuration file using the `$INCLUDE` statement to include the **.key** file.

DNSSEC Resource Records

In the zone file, you then use three DNSSEC DNS resource records to implement secure communications for a given zone: KEY, SIG, and NXT. In these records, you use the signed keys for the zones you have already generated. The KEY record holds public keys associated with zones, hosts, or users. The SIG record stores digital signatures and expiration dates for a set of resource records. The NXT record is used to determine that a resource record for a domain does not exist. In addition, several utilities let you manage DNS encryption. With the **dnskeygen** utility, you generated the public and private keys used for encryption. **dnssigner** signs a zone using the zone's private key, setting up authentication.

To secure a DNS zone with DNSSEC, you first use **dnskeygen** to create public and private keys for the DNS zone. Then use **dnssigner** to create an authentication key. In the DNS zone file, you enter a KEY resource record in which you include the public key. The public key will appear as a lengthy string of random characters. For the KEY record, you enter in the domain name followed by the KEY and then the public key.

```
mytrek.com. KEY 0x4101 3 3 (
AvqyXgKk/uguxkJF/hbRpYzxZFG3x8EfNX38917GX6w7rlLy
BJ14TqvrDvXr84XsShg+OFcUJafNr84U4ER2dg6NrlRAmZA1
jFfV0UpWDWcHBR2jJnvgV9zJB2ULMGJheDHeyztM1KGd2oGk
Aensm74NlfUqKzy/3KZ9KnQmEpj/EEBr48vAsgAT9kMjN+V3
NgAwfoqgS0dwj5OiRJoIR4+cdRt+s32OUKsclAODFZTdtxRn
vXF3qYV0S8oewMbEwh3trXi1c7nDMQC3RmoY8RVGt5U6LMAQ
KITDyHU3VmRJ36vn77QqSzbeUPz8zEnbpik8kHPykJZFkcyj
jZoHT1xkJ1tk )
```

For authentication, you can sign particular resource records for a given domain or host. Enter the domain or host followed by the term SIG and then the resource record's signature.

```
mytrek.com. SIG KEY 3 86400 19990321010705 19990218010705 4932 com. (
Am3tWJzEDzfU1xwg7hzkiJ0+8UQaPtlJhUpQx1snKpDUqZxm
igMZEVk= )
```

The NXT record lets you negatively answer queries.

```
mytrek.com. NXT ftp.mytrek.com. A NS SOA MX SIG KEY NXT
```

Signing Keys

To set up secure communications between a parent (master) DNS server and a child (slave) DNS server, the public key then needs to be sent to the parent zone. There, the key can be signed by the parent. As you may have more than zone key, you create a keyset using the dnssec-makekeyset command. This generates a file with the extension **.keyset** that is then sent to the parent. The parent zone then uses the dnssec-signkey command to sign a child's keyset. This generates a file with the prefix **signedkey-**. This is sent back to the child and now contains both the child's keyset and the parent's signatures. Once the child has the **signedkey-** files, the dnssec-signedzone command can be used to sign the zone. The dnssec-signedzone command will generate a file with the extension **.signed**. This file is then included in a **named** configuration file with the INCLUDE operation. The trusted-keys statement needs to list the public key for the parent zone.

TSIG Keys

TSIG (transaction signatures) also provide secure DNS communications, but they share the private key instead of a private/public key pair. They are usually used for communications between two local DNS servers, and to provide authentication for dynamic updates such as those between a DNS server and a DHCP server.

Generating TSIG keys

To create a TSIG key for your DNS server, you use the **`dnssec-keygen`** command as described earlier. Instead of using the same keys you use for DNSSEC, you create a new set to use for transaction signatures. For TSIG, a shared private key is used instead of a public/private key pair. For a TSIG key you would use an HMAC-MD5 algorithm that generates the same key in the both the **.key** and **.private** files. Use the **`-a`** option to specify the HMAC-MD5 algorithm to use and the **`-b`** option for the bit size. (HMAC-MD5 ranges from 1 to 512.) Use the **`-n`** option to specify the key type, in this case HOST for the host name. The bit range will vary according to the algorithm. The following example creates a host key using a 128-bit key and the HMAC-MD5 encryption algorithm:

```
dnssec-keygen -a HMAC-MD5 -b 128 -n HOST turtle.mytrek.com
```

This creates a private key and a public key, located in the **.key** and **.private** files. In a TSIG scheme, both hosts would use the same private key for authentication. For example, to enable a DHCP server to update a DNS server, both would need the private (secret) key for a TSIG authentication. The HMAC-MD5 key is used as a shared private key, generating both the same private and public keys in the **.key** and **.private** files.

The Key Statement

You then specify a key in the **named** configuration file with the **`key`** statement. For the algorithm option, you list the HMAC-MD5 algorithm, and for the secret option, you list the private key. This key will be listed in both the **.private** and **.key** files. The preceding example would generate key and private files called **Kturtle.mytrek.com.+157.43080.key** and **Kturtle.mytrek.com.+157.43080.private**. The contents of the **.key** file consist of a resource record shown here:

```
turtle.mytrek.com. IN KEY 512 3 157 ONQAfbBLnvWU9H8hRqq/WA==
```

The contents of the private file show the same key along with the algorithm:

```
Private-key-format: v1.2
Algorithm: 157 (HMAC_MD5)
Key: ONQAfbBLnvWU9H8hRqq/WA==
```

Within the **named** configuration file, you then name the key using a **`key`** statement:

```
key myserver {
algorithm HMAC-MD5;
secret "ONQAfbBLnvWU9H8hRqq/WA==";
};
```

The key's name can then be used to reference the key in other named statements, such as **`allow-update`** statements:

```
allow-update myserver;
```

The DNS server or DHCP server with which you are setting up communication will also have to have the same key. See the earlier section "Dynamic Update: DHCP and Journal Files". For communication between two DNS servers, each would have to have a server statement specifying the shared key. In the following example, the **named.conf** file for the DNS server on 192.168.0.1 would have to have the following server statement to communicate with the DNS server on 10.0.0.1, using the shared myserver key. The **named.conf** file on the 10.0.0.1 DNS server would have to have a corresponding server statement for the 192.168.0.1 server.

```
server 10.0.0.1 {  keys (myserver;}; };
```

Split DNS: Views

BIND 9.*x* allows you to divide DNS space into internal and external views. This organization into separate views is referred to as split DNS. Such a configuration is helpful to manage a local network that is connected to a larger network, such as the Internet. Your internal view would include DNS information on hosts in the local network, whereas an external view would show only the part of the DNS space that is accessible to other networks. DNS views are often used when you have a local network that you want to protect from a larger network such as the Internet. In effect, you protect DNS information for hosts on a local network from a larger external network such as the Internet.

Internal and External Views

To implement a split DNS space, you need to set up different DNS servers for the internal and external views. The internal DNS servers will hold DNS information about local hosts. The external DNS server maintains connections to the Internet through a gateway, as well as manages DNS information about any local hosts that allow external access, such as FTP or Web sites. The gateways and Internet-accessible sites make up the external view of hosts on the network. The internal servers handle all queries to the local hosts or subdomains. Queries to external hosts, such as Internet sites are sent to the external servers, which then forward them on to the Internet. Queries sent to those local hosts that operate external servers such as Internet FTP and Web sites are sent to the external DNS servers for processing. Mail sent to local hosts from the Internet is handled first by the external servers, which then forward messages on to the internal servers. With a split DNS configuration, local hosts can access other local hosts, Internet sites, and local hosts maintaining Internet servers. Internet users, on the other hand, can access only those hosts open to the Internet (served by external servers) such as those with Internet servers like FTP and HTTP. Internet users can, however, send mail messages to any of the local hosts, internal and external.

You can also use DNS views to manage connections for a private network that may use only one Internet address to connect its hosts to the Internet. In this case, the internal view holds the private addresses (192.168.), and the external view connects a gateway host with an Internet address to the Internet. This adds another level of security, providing a result similar to IP masquerading.

Configuring Views

DNS views are configured with the allow statements such as allow-query and allow-transfer. With these statements, you can specify the hosts that a zone can send and receive queries and transfers to and from. For example, the internal zone could accept queries from other local hosts, but not from local hosts with external access such as Internet servers. The local Internet servers, though, can accept queries from the local hosts. All Internet queries are forwarded to the gateway. In the external configuration, the local Internet servers can accept queries from anywhere. The gateways receive queries from both the local hosts and the local Internet servers.

In the following example, a network of three internal hosts and one external host is set up into a split view. There are two DNS servers: one for the internal network and one for external access, based on the external host. In reality these make up one network but they are split into two views. The internal view is known as **mygolf.com**, and the external as **greatgolf.com**. In each configuration, the internal hosts are designated in ACL-labeled internals, and the external host is designated in ACL-labeled externals. Should you want to designate an entire IP address range as internal, you could simply use the network address, as in 192.168.0.0/24. In the options section, allow-query, allow-recursion, and **`allow-transfers`** restrict access within the network.

Split View Example

The following example shows only the configuration entries needed to implement an internal view (see next page). In the **mygolf.com** zone, queries and transfers are allowed only among internal hosts. The global **`allow-recursion`** option allows recursion among internals.

`Internal DNS server`

```
acl internals { 192.168.0.1; 192.168.0.2; 192.168.0.3; };
acl externals {10.0.0.1;};
options {
             forward only;
             forwarders {10.0.0.1;}; // forward to external servers
             allow-transfer { none; }; // allow-transfer to no one by default
             allow-query { internals; externals; };// restrict query access
             allow-recursion { internals; }; // restrict recursion to internals
              }
zone "mygolf.com" {
              type master;
              file "mygolf";
              forwarders { };
             allow-query { internals; };
             allow-transfer { internals; }
              };
```

In the configuration for the external DNS server, the same ACLs are set up for internals and externals. In the options statement, recursion is now allowed for both externals and internals. In the **mygolf.com** zone, queries are allowed from anywhere, and recursion is allowed for externals and internals. Transfers are not allowed at all.

```
External DNS server

acl internals { 192.168.0.1; 192.168.0.2; 192.168.0.3; };
acl externals {10.0.0.1;};
options {
               allow-transfer { none; }; // allow-transfer to no one
               allow-query { internals; externals; };// restrict query access
               allow-recursion { internals; externals }; // restrict recursion
               };

zone "greatgolf.com" {
               type master;
               file "greatgolf";
               allow-query { any; };
               allow-transfer { internals; externals; };
};
```

ubuntu

16. Network Auto-configuration with IPv6, DHCPv6, and DHCP

Many networks now provide either IPv6 autoconfiguration or the DHCP (Dynamic Host Configuration Protocol) service, which automatically provides network configuration for all connected hosts. Autoconfiguration can be either stateless, as in the case of IPv6, or stateful, as with DHCP. Stateless IPv6 autoconfiguration requires no independent server or source to connect to a network. It is a direct plug-and-play operation, where the hardware network interfaces and routers can directly determine the correct addresses. DCHP is an older method that requires a separate server to manage and assign all addresses. Should this server ever fail, hosts cannot connect.

With the DHCP protocol, an administrator uses a pool of IP addresses from which the administrator can assign an IP address to a host as needed. The protocol can also be used to provide all necessary network connection information such as the gateway address for the network or the netmask. Instead of having to configure each host separately, network configuration can be handled by a central DHCP server. The length of time that an address can be used can be controlled by means of leases, making effective use of available addresses. If your network is configuring your systems with DHCP, you will not have to configure it.

There are currently two versions of DHCP, one for the original IPv4 protocol and another, known as DHCPv6, for the IPv6 protocol, which includes information for dynamic configuration that the IPv4 protocol lacks. In this respect, the IPv4 protocol is much more dependent on DHCP than is IPv6.

IPv6 Stateless Autoconfiguration

In an IPv6 network, the IPv6 protocol includes information that can directly configure a host. With IPv4 you either had to configure each host manually or rely on a DHCP server to provide configuration information. With IPv6, configuration information is integrated into the Internet protocol directly. IPv6 address autoconfiguration is described in detail in RFC 2462.

IPv6 autoconfiguration capabilities are known as stateless, meaning that it can directly configure a host without recourse of an external server. Alternatively, DHCP, including DHCPv6, is stateful, where the host relies on an external DHCP server to provide configuration information. Stateless autoconfiguration has the advantage of hosts not having to rely on a DHCP server to maintain connections to a network. Networks can even become mobile, hooking into one subnet or another, automatically generating addresses as needed. Hosts are no longer tied to a particular DHCP server.

Generating the Local Address

To autoconfigure hosts on a local network, IPv6 makes use of the each network device's hardware MAC address. This address is used to generate a temporary address, with which the host can be queried and configured.

The MAC address is used to create a link-local address, one with a link-local prefix, **FE80::0**, followed by an interface identifier. The link-local prefix is used for physically connected hosts such as those on a small local network.

A uniqueness test is then performed on the generated address. Using the Neighbor Discovery Protocol (NDP), other hosts on the network are checked to determine whether another host is already using the generated link-local address. If no other host is using the address, the address is assigned for that local network. At this point the host has only a local address valid within the local physical network. Link-local addresses cannot be routed to a larger network.

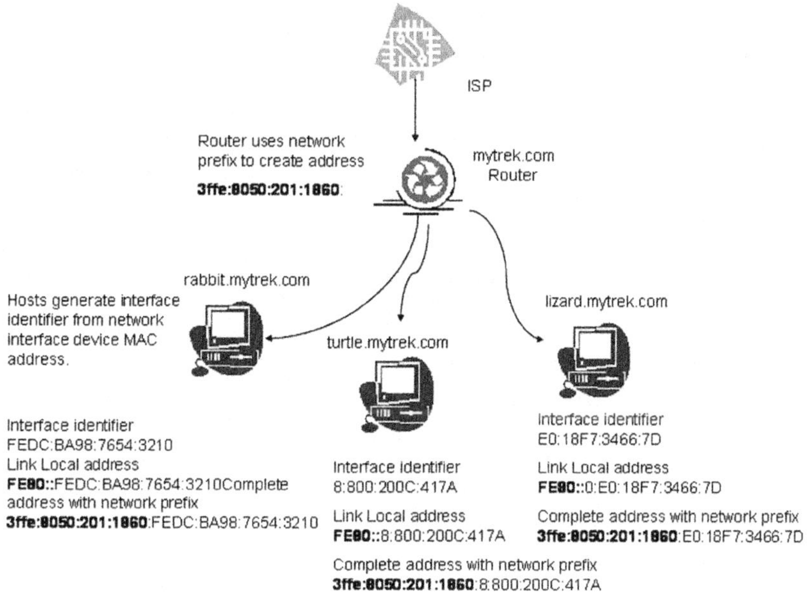

Figure 16-1: Stateless IPv6 address autoconfiguration

Generating the Full Address: Router Advertisements

Once the link-local address has been determined, the router for the network is queried for additional configuration information. The information can be stateful, stateless, or both. For stateless configuration, information such as the network address is provided directly, whereas for stateful configuration, the host is referred to a DHCPv6 server where it can obtain configuration information. The two can work together. Often the stateless method is used for addresses, and the stateful DHCPv6 server is used to provide other configuration information such as DNS server addresses.

In the case of stateless addresses, the router provides the larger network address, such as the network's Internet address. This address is then added to the local address, replacing the original link-local prefix, giving either a complete global Internet address or, in the case of private networks, unique-local addresses. Routers will routinely advertise this address information, though it can also be specifically requested. The NDP is used to query the information. Before the address is assigned officially, a duplicate address detection procedure checks to see if the address is already in use. The process depends on the router's providing the appropriate addressing information in the form of router advertisements. If there is no router, or there are no route advertisements, then a stateful method like DHCPv6 or manual configuration must be used to provide the addresses.

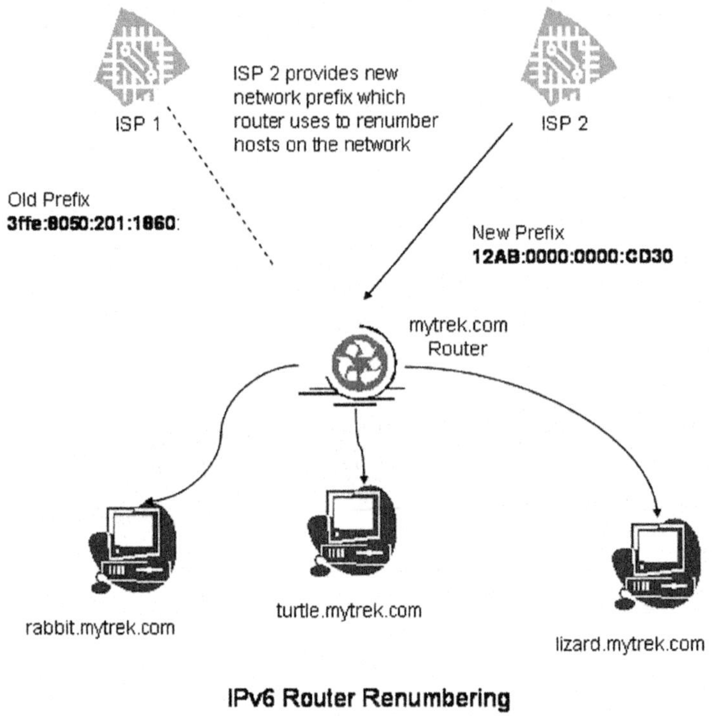

Figure 16-2: Router renumbering with IPv6 autoconfiguration

Figure 16-1 shows a network that is configured with stateless address autoconfiguration. Each host first determines its interface identifier using its own MAC hardware address to create a temporary link-local address for each host using the **FE80::0** prefix. This allows initial communication with the network's router. The router then uses its network prefix to create full Internet addresses, replacing the link-local prefix.

Router Renumbering

With IPv6, routers have the ability to renumber the addresses on their networks by changing the network prefix. Renumbering is carried out through the Router Renumbering (RR) Protocol. (See RFC 2894 for a description of router renumbering.) Renumbering is often used when a network changes ISP providers and requires that the net address for all hosts be changed (see Figure 16-2). It can also be used for mobile networks in which a network can be plugged in to different larger networks, renumbering each time.

With renumbering, routers place a time limit on addresses, similar to the lease time in DHCP, by specifying an expiration limit for the network prefix when the address is generated. To ease transition, interfaces still keep their old addresses as deprecated addresses, while the new addresses are first being used. The new addresses will be the preferred addresses used for any new connections, while deprecated addresses are used for older connections. In effect, a host can have two addresses, one deprecated and one preferred. This regeneration of addresses effectively renumbers the hosts.

Note: The IPv6 version of DHCP (DHCPv6) provides stateful autoconfiguration to those networks that still want a DHCP-like service on IPv6 networks. A version of the DHCPv6 server and client are available from the DHCPv6 project and located in the Ubuntu Universe repository as **wide-dhcpv6** collection of packages. You can find out more about the DHCPv6 project at **https://fedorahosted.org/dhcpv6/**. The server requires its own Wide DHCPv6 clients. Keep in mind that Ubuntu currently provides support for the ISC DHCP version 4.1 server, which integrates DHCPv6 support and has superseded officially the DHCPv6 project software, **https://www.isc.org/software/dhcp/new-features-4.1.0**.

Linux as an IPv6 Router: radvd

For a Linux system that operates as a router, you would use the **radvd** (Router ADVertisement Daemon) to advertise addresses, specifying a network prefix in the **/etc/radvd.conf** file (Ubuntu main repository). The **radvd** daemon will detect router network address requests from hosts, known as router solicitations, and provide them with a network address using a router advertisement. These router advertisements will also be broadcast to provide the network address to any hosts that do not send in requests. For **radvd** to work, you will have to turn on IPv6 forwarding. Use **sysctl** and set **net.ipv6.conf.all.forwarding** to 1. To start up the **radvd** daemon, you use the `radvd` startup script. To check the router addresses **radvd** is sending, you can use `radvdump`.

```
sudo service radvd start
```

You will have to configure the **radvd** daemon yourself, specifying the network address to broadcast. Configuration, though, is very simple, as the full address will be automatically generated using the host's hardware address. A configuration consists of interface entries, which in turn list interface options, prefix definitions, and options, along with router definitions if needed. The configuration is placed in the **/etc/radvd.conf** file, which will look something like this:

```
interface eth0 {
    AdvSendAdvert on;
        prefix fc00:0:0:0::/64
        {
        AdvOnLink on;
        AdvAutonomous on;
        };
};
```

This assumes one interface is used for the local network, **eth0**. This interface configuration lists an interface option (AdvSendAdvert) and a prefix definition, along with two prefix options (AdvOnLink and AdvAutonomous). To specify prefix options for a specific prefix, add them within parentheses following the prefix definition. The prefix definition specifies your IPv6 network address. If a local area network has its own network address, you will need to provide its IPv6 network prefix address. For a private network, such as a home network, you can use the unique-local IPv6 prefix, which operates like the IPv4 private network addresses, 192.168.0. The preceding example uses a unique-local address that is used for private IPv6 networks, fc00:0:0:0::, which has a length of 64 bits.

The AdvSendAdvert interface option turns on network address advertising to the hosts. The AdvAutonomous network prefix option provides automatic address configuration, and AdvOnLink simply means that host requests can be received on the specified network interface.

A second network interface is then used to connect the Linux system to an ISP or larger network. If the ISP supports IPv6, this is simply a matter of sending a router solicitation to the ISP router. This automatically generates your Internet address, using the hardware address of the network interface that connects to the Internet and the ISP router's advertised network address. In Figure 16-2, shown earlier, the **eth0** network interface connects to the local network, whereas **eth1** connects to the Internet.

DHCP

DHCP provides configuration information to systems connected to a TCP/IP network, whether the Internet or an intranet. The machines on the network operate as DHCP clients, obtaining their network configuration information from a DHCP server on their network. A machine on the network runs a DHCP client daemon that automatically receives its network configuration information from its network's DHCP server. The information includes its IP address, along with the network's name server, gateway, and proxy addresses, including the netmask. Nothing has to be configured manually on the local system, except to specify the DHCP server it should get its network configuration from. This has the added advantage of centralizing control over network configuration for the different systems on the network. A network administrator can manage the network configurations for all the systems on the network from the DHCP server.

A DHCP server also supports several methods for IP address allocation: automatic, dynamic, and manual. Automatic allocation assigns a permanent IP address for a host. Manual allocation assigns an IP address designated by the network administrator. With dynamic allocation, a DHCP server can allocate an IP address to a host on the network only when the host actually needs to use it. Dynamic allocation takes addresses from a pool of IP addresses that hosts can use when needed and releases them when they are finished.

The current version of DHCP supports the DHCP failover protocol, in which two DHCP servers support the same address pool. Should one fail, the other can continue to provide DHCP services for a network. Both servers are in sync and have the same copy of network support information for each host on the network. Primary and secondary servers in this scheme are designated with the primary and secondary statements.

A variety of DHCP servers and clients are available for different operating systems. The Ubuntu main repository provides DHCP version 4 software from the Internet Software Consortium (ISC) at **www.isc.org**. See **https://www.isc.org/software/dhcp/new-features-4.1.0**. It integrates support for both IPv4 and IPv6 addressing. The software available includes a DHCP server (**isc-dhcp-server**), common DHCP files (**isc-dhcp-common**), a client (**isc-dhcp-client**), and a relay agent (**isc-dhcp-relay**). Ubuntu no longer supports DHCP version 3.

```
sudo apt-get install isc-dhcp-server
```

Configuring DHCP Client Hosts

Configuring hosts to use a DHCP server is a simple matter of setting options for the host's network interface device, such as an Ethernet card. For a Linux host, you can use a distribution network tool to set the host to access a DHCP server automatically for network information. On a network tool's panel for configuring the Internet connection, you will normally find a check box for selecting DHCP. Clicking this box will enable DHCP.

Client support is carried out by the `dhclient` tool. When your network starts up, it uses `dhclient` to set up your DHCP connection. Though defaults are usually adequate, you can further configure the DHCP client using the **/etc/dhcp/dhclient.conf** file. Consult the **dhclient.conf** Man page for a detailed list of configuration options. Further configuration is provided in the **/etc/dhcp/dhclient-enter-hooks.d** and **/etc/dhcp/dhclient-exit-hooks.d** files for Avahi, Samba, the time server (NTP), and debugging. Check the **dhclient-script** man page for more details. Lease information on the DCHP connection is kept in the **/var/lib/dhcp/dhclient.leases** file. You can also directly run `dhclient` to configure DHCP connections.

```
dhclient
```

Configuring the DHCP Server

The DHCP sever package provided a single server, **dhcpd**, for both IPv4 addressing and for IPv6 addressing. Each form of addressing has a separate configuration file: for IPv4 it is **/etc/dhcp/dhcpd.conf**, and for IPv6 it is **/etc/dhcp/dhcpd6.conf**. Documentation for IPv6 configuration is integrated into the man pages for the DHCP server. See the man pages for **dhcpd.conf** for details on both IPv4 and the IPv6 addressing. The IPv6 sections are labeled DHCP6. The **dhcp-options** man page lists the DHCP/DHCP6 options. Any server runtime parameter can be set in the corresponding **/etc/default** files for the two methods of addressing: **/etc/default/dhcpd** and **/etc/default/dhcpd6**. Arguments are assigned to the DHCPDARGS variable.

For IPv4 addressing, **systemd** manages the DHCP server using the **isc-dhcp-server.service** unit file in the **/lib/systemd/system** directory. For IPv6 addressing it uses the **isc-dhcp-server6.service** unit file. The DHCP server is started after networking (After) and for the multi-user.target (WantedBy). It is started using the **/usr/sbin/dhcpd** command which reads configuration from **dhcpd.conf**. The **isc-dhcp-server6.service** unit file is the same except that the dhcpd command read the **dhcpd6.conf** file and has the option **-6** for IPv6.

isc-dhcp-server.service

```
[Unit]
Description=ISC DHCP Ipv4 server
Documentation=man:dhcpd(8)
Wants=network-online.target
After=network-online.target
After=time-sync.target
ConditionPathExists=/etc/default/isc-dhcp-server
ConditionPathExists=/etc/ltsp/dhcpd.conf
ConditionPathExists=/etc/dhcp/dhcpd.conf

[Service]
EnvironmentFile=/etc/default/isc-dhcp-server
RuntimeDirectory=dhcp-server
#Allow dhcp server to write lease and pid file as 'dhcpd' user
ExecStartPre=/bin/chown dhcpd:dhcpd /run/dhcp-server
#The leases file needs to be root:root even when dropping privileges
```

```
ExecStart=/bind/sh -ec '\
    CONFIG_FILE=/etc/dhcp/dhcpd.conf
    if [ -f /etc/ltsp/dhcpd.conf ]; then CONFIG_FILE=/etc/ltsp/dhcpd.conf; fi; \
    [ -e /var/ lib/dhcp/dhcpd.leases ] || touch /var/lib/hdcp/dhcpd.leases; \
    chown root:root /var/lib/dhcp  /var/lib/dhcp/dhcpd.leases*; \
    exec dhcpd -user dhcpd -group dhcpd -f -4 -pf /run/dhcp-server/dhcpd.pid -cf
$CONFIG_FILE $INTERFACES'

[Install]
WantedBy=multi-user.target
```

Use **`service`** command with the **`isc-dhcp-server`** or **`isc-dhcp-server6`** command with the **`start`**, **`restart`**, and **`stop`** options. The following examples start the dhcp server with either IPv4 or IPv6 addressing. Use the **`stop`** option to shut it down and **`restart`** to restart them.

```
sudo service isc-dhcp-server start
sudo service isc-dhcp-server6 start
```

Dynamically allocated IP addresses, known as leases, will be assigned for a given time. When a lease expires it can be extended, or a new one generated. Current leases are listed in the **dhcpd.leases** file located in the **/var/lib/dhcp** directory. A lease entry will specify the IP address and the start and end times of the lease along with the client's hostname.

/etc/dhcp/dhcpd.conf

The configuration file for the DHCP server is **/etc/dhcp/dhcpd.conf**. Here you specify parameters and declarations that define how different DHCP clients on your network are accessed by the DHCP server, along with options that define information passed to the clients by the DHCP server. These parameters, declarations, and options can be defined globally for certain sub-networks or for specific hosts. Global parameters, declarations, and options apply to all clients, unless overridden by corresponding declarations and options in subnet or host declarations. Technically, all entries in a **dhcpd.conf** file are statements that can be either declarations or parameters.

All statements end with a semicolon. Options are specified in **`options`** parameter statements. Parameters differ from declarations in that they define if and how to perform tasks, such as how long a lease is allocated. Declarations describe network features such as the range of addresses to allocate or the networks that are accessible. See Table 16-1 for a listing of commonly used declarations and options.

Declarations provide information for the DHCP server or designate actions it is to perform. For example, the **`range`** declaration is used to specify the range of IP addresses to be dynamically allocated to hosts:

```
range 192.168.0.5 192.168.0.128;
```

With parameters, you can specify how the server is to treat clients. For example, the **`default-lease-time`** declaration sets the number of seconds a lease is assigned to a client. The **`filename`** declaration specifies the boot file to be used by the client. The **`server-name`** declaration informs the client of the host from which it is booting. The **`fixed-address`** declaration can be used to assign a static IP address to a client. See the Man page for **dhcpd.conf** for a complete listing.

Entries	Description
Declarations	
`shared-network` *name*	Indicates if some subnets share the same physical network.
`subnet` *subnet-number netmask*	References an entire subnet of addresses.
`range [` *dynamic-bootp* `]` *low-address* `[` *high-address*`] ;`	Provides the highest and lowest dynamically allocated IP addresses.
`host` *hostname*	References a particular host.
`group`	Lets you label a group of parameters and declarations and then use the label to apply them to subnets and hosts.
`allow unknown-clients;` `deny unknown-clients;`	Does not dynamically assign addresses to unknown clients.
`allow bootp; deny bootp;`	Determines whether to respond to `bootp` queries.
`allow booting; deny booting;`	Determines whether to respond to client queries.
Parameters	
`default-lease-time` *time*`;`	Assigns length in seconds to a lease.
`max-lease-time` *time*`;`	Assigns maximum length of lease.
`hardware` *hardware-type hardware-address*`;`	Specifies network hardware type (Ethernet or token ring) and address.
`filename "`*filename*`";`	Specifies name of the initial boot file.
`server-name "`*name*`";`	Specifies name of the server from which a client is booting.
`next-server` *server-name*`;`	Specifies server that loads the initial boot file specified in the filename.
`fixed-address` *address* `[`, *address ...* `];`	Assigns a fixed address to a client.
`get-lease-hostnames` *flag*`;`	Determines whether to look up and use IP addresses of clients.
`authoritative;` `not authoritative;`	Denies invalid address requests.
`server-identifier hostname;`	Specifies the server.

Options	
`option subnet-mask` *ip-address* ;	Specifies client's subnet mask.
`option routers` *ip-address* [, *ip-address...*] ;	Specifies list of router IP addresses on client's subnet.
`option domain-name-servers` *ip-address* [, *ip-address...*] ;	Specifies list of domain name servers used by the client.
`option log-servers` *ip-address* [, *ip-address...*] ;	Specifies list of log servers used by the client.
`option host-name` *string* ;	Specifies client's hostname.
`option domain-name` *string* ;	Specifies client's domain name.
`option broadcast-address` *ip-address* ;	Specifies client's broadcast address.
`option nis-domain` *string* ;	Specifies client's Network Information Service domain.
`option nis-servers` *ip-address* [, *ip-address...*] ;	Specifies NIS servers the client can use.
`option smtp-server` *ip-address* [, *ip-address...*] ;	Lists SMTP servers used by the client.
`option pop-server` *ip-address* [, *ip-address...*] ;	Lists POP servers used by the client.
`option nntp-server` *ip-address* [, *ip-address...*] ;	Lists NNTP servers used by the client.
`option www-server` *ip-address* [, *ip-address...*] ;	Lists web servers used by the client.

Table 16-1: DHCP Declarations, Parameters, and Options

Options provide information to clients that they may need to access network services, such as the domain name of the network, the domain name servers that clients use, or the broadcast address. See the Man page for **dhcp-options** for a complete listing. This information is provided by `option` parameters as shown here:

```
option broadcast-address 192.168.0.255;
option domain-name-servers 192.168.0.1, 192.168.0.4;
option domain-name "mytrek.com";
```

Your **dhcpd.conf** file will usually begin with declarations, parameters, and options that you define for the network serviced by the DHCP server. The following example provides router (gateway), netmask, domain name, and DNS server information to clients. Additional parameters define the default and maximum lease times for dynamically allocated IP addresses.

```
option routers 192.168.0.1;
option subnet-mask 255.255.255.0;
option domain-name "mytrek.com ";
option domain-name-servers 192.168.0.1;
default-lease-time 600;
max-lease-time 7200;
```

With the subnet, host, and group declarations, you can reference clients in a specific network, particular clients, or different groupings of clients across networks. Within these declarations, you can enter parameters, declarations, or options that will apply only to those clients. Scoped declarations, parameters, and options are enclosed in braces. For example, to define a declaration for a particular host, use the **host** declaration as shown here:

```
host rabbit {
       declarations, parameters, or options;
       }
```

You can collect different subnet, global, and host declaration into groups using the **group** declaration. In this case, the global declarations are applied only to those subnets and hosts declared within the group.

Dynamic IPv4 Addresses for DHCP

Your DHCP server can be configured to select IP addresses from a given range and assign them to different clients. Given a situation where you have many clients that may not always be connected to the network, you can effectively service them with a smaller pool of IP addresses. IP addresses are assigned only when they are needed. With the **range** declaration, you specify a range of addresses that can be dynamically allocated to clients. The declaration takes two arguments, the first and last addresses in the range.

```
range 192.168.1.5 192.168.1.128;
```

For example, if you are setting up your own small home network, you would use a network address beginning with 192.168. The range would specify possible IP addresses with that network. So, for a network with the address 192.168.0.0, you place a **range** declaration along with any other information you want to give to your client hosts. In the following example, a range of IP addresses extending from 192.168.0.1 to 192.168.0.128 can be allocated to the hosts on that network:

```
range 192.168.0.5 192.168.0.128;
```

You should also define your lease times, both a default and a maximum:

```
default-lease-time 600;
max-lease-time 7200;
```

For a small, simple home network, you just need to list the **range** declaration along with any global options as shown here. If your DHCP server is managing several sub-networks, you will have to use the **subnet** declarations.

In order to assign dynamic addresses to a network, the DHCP server will require that your network topology be mapped. This means it needs to know what network addresses belong to a given network. Even if you use only one network, you will need to specify the address space for it. You define a network with the **subnet** declaration. Within this **subnet** declaration, you can specify any parameters, declarations, or options to use for that network. The **subnet** declaration informs the DHCP server of the possible IP addresses encompassed by a given subnet. This is determined by the network IP address and the netmask for that network. The next example defines a local network with address spaces from 192.168.0.0 to 192.168.0.255. The **range** declaration allows addresses to be allocated from 192.168.0.5 to 192.168.0.128.

```
subnet 192.168.1.0 netmask 255.255.255.0 {
         range 192.168.0.5 192.168.0.128;
 }
```

Versions of DHCP prior to 3.0 required that you even map connected network interfaces that are not being served by DHCP. Thus each network interface has to have a corresponding **subnet** declaration. Those not being serviced by DHCP don't have a **not authoritative** parameter as shown here (192.168.2.0 being a network not to be serviced by DHCP). In version 3.0 and later, DHCP simply ignores unmapped network interfaces:

```
subnet 192.168.2.0 netmask 255.255.255.0 {
      not authoritative;
}
```

The implementation of a very simple DHCP server for dynamic addresses is shown in the sample **dhcpd.conf** file that follows:

/etc/dhcp/dhcpd.conf

```
option routers 192.168.0.1;
 option subnet-mask 255.255.255.0;
 option domain-name "mytrek.com ";
 option domain-name-servers 192.168.0.1;

subnet 192.168.1.0 netmask 255.255.255.0 {
         range 192.168.0.5 192.168.0.128;
         default-lease-time 21600;
         max-lease-time 43200;
         }
```

DHCP Dynamic DNS Updates

For networks that also support a Domain Name Server, dynamic allocation of IP addresses currently needs to address one major constraint: DHCP needs to sync with a DNS server. A DNS server associates hostnames with particular IP addresses, whereas, in the case of dynamic allocation, the DHCP server randomly assigns its own IP addresses to different hosts. These may or may not be the same as the IP addresses that the DNS server expects to associate with a hostname. A solution to this problem is Dynamic DNS. With Dynamic DNS, the DHCP server is able to automatically update the DNS server with the IP addresses the DHCP server has assigned to different hosts. You can find detailed information about dynamic DNS in the **dhcpd.conf** Man page.

Note: Alternatively, if you want to statically synchronize your DHCP and DNS servers with fixed addresses, you configure DHCP to assign those fixed addresses to hosts. You can then have the DHCP server perform a DNS lookup to obtain the IP address it should assign, or you can manually assign the same IP address in the DHCP configuration file. Performing a DNS lookup has the advantage of specifying the IP address in one place, the DNS server.

The DHCP server has the ability to dynamically update BIND DNS server zone configuration files. You enable dynamic updates on a DNS server for a zone file by specifying the **allow-update** option for it in the **named.conf** file. Furthermore, it is strongly encouraged that you use TSIG signature keys to reference and authenticate the BIND and DHCP servers. Enabling the use of a TSIG key involves syncing configurations for both your DHCP and DNS servers. Both have to be configured to use the same key for the same domains. First you need to create a shared secret TSIG signature key using **dnssec-keygen**. In the DNS server, you place TSIG key declarations and **allow-update** entries in the server's **named.conf** file, as shown in this example:

```
key mydhcpserver {
algorithm HMAC-MD5;
secret "ONQAfbBLnvWU9H8hRqq/WA==";
};


zone "mytrek.com" {
       type master;
       file "mytrek.com";
       allow-update {key mydhcpserver;};
 };

zone "1.168.192.IN-ADDR.ARPA" {
       type master;
       file "192.168.0";
       allow-update {key mydhcpserver;};
};
```

In the DHCP server, you place a corresponding TSIG key declaration and **allow-update** entries in the server's **dhcpd.conf** file, as shown in this example. The **key** declaration has the same syntax as the DNS server. DHCP **zone** statements are then used to specify the IP address of the domain and the TSIG key to use. The domain names and IP addresses need to match exactly in the configuration files for both the DNS and DHCP servers. Unlike in a **named** configuration file, there are no quotes around the domain name or IP addresses in the **dhcpd.conf** file. In the **dhcpd.conf** file, the domain names and IP addresses used in the **zone** statement also need to end with a period, as they do in the DNS zone files. The **key** statement lists the key to use. Though the DHCP server will try to determine the DNS servers to update, it is recommended that you explicitly identify them with a primary statement in a **zone** entry.

```
key mydhcpserver {
    algorithm HMAC-MD5;
    secret "ONQAfbBLnvWU9H8hRqq/WA==";
    };

zone mytrek.com. {                  #DNS domain zone to update
       primary 192.168.0.1;         #address of DNS server
       key mydhcpserver;           #TSIG signature key
 };

zone 1.168.192.IN-ADDR.ARPA. {      #domain PTR zone to update
       primary 192.168.0.1;         #address of DNS server
       key mydhcpserver;            # TSIG signature key
};
```

To generate a fully qualified hostname to use in a DNS update, the DHCP server will normally use its own domain name and the hostname provided by a DHCP client (see the **dhcpd.conf** Man page for exceptions). Should you want to assign a specific hostname to a host, you can use the **ddns-hostname** statement to specify it in the host's hardware section. The domain name is specified in the **domain-name** option:

```
option domain-name "mytrek.com"
```

The DNS update capability can be turned on or off for all domains with the **ddns-update-style** statement. It is off by default. Set it to **yes** to turn it on. To turn off DNS updates for particular domains, you can use the **ddns-updates** statement. This is also on by default.

```
ddns-updates-style yes;
```

DHCP Subnetworks

If you are dividing your network space into several subnetworks, you can use a single DHCP server to manage them. In that case, you will have a **subnet** declaration for each subnetwork. If you are setting up your own small network, you use a network address beginning with 192.168. The range specifies possible IP addresses within that network so, for a network with the address 192.168.0.0, you create a **subnet** declaration with the netmask 255.255.255.0. Within this declaration, you place a **range** declaration along with any other information you want to give to your client hosts. In the following example, a range of IP addresses extending from 192.168.0.1 to 192.168.0.75 can be allocated to the hosts on that network:

```
subnet 192.168.0.0 netmask 255.255.255.0 {
 range 192.168.0.5 192.168.0.75;
}
```

You may want to specify different policies for each subnetwork, such as different lease times. Any entries in a **subnet** declaration will override global settings. So if you already have a global lease time set, a lease setting in a **subnet** declaration will override it for that subnet. The next example sets different lease times for different subnets, as well as different address allocations. The lease times for the first subnet are taken from the global lease time settings, whereas the second subnet defines its own lease times:

```
default-lease-time 21600;
max-lease-time 43200;

subnet 192.168.1.0 netmask 255.255.255.0 {
      range 192.168.0.5 192.168.0.75;
      }
subnet 192.168.1.128 netmask 255.255.255.252 {
      range 192.168.0.129 192.168.0.215;
      default-lease-time 56000;
      max-lease-time 62000;
       }
```

If your subnetworks are part of the same physical network, you need to inform the server of this fact by declaring them as shared networks. You do this by placing subnet declarations within a **shared-network** declaration, specifying the shared network's name. The name can be any descriptive name, though you can use the domain name. Any options specified within the **shared-**

network declaration and outside the subnet declarations will be global to those subnets. In the next example, the subnets are part of the same physical network and so are placed within a **shared-network** declaration:

```
shared-network mytrek.com
{
default-lease-time 21600;
max-lease-time 43200;
subnet 192.168.1.0 netmask 255.255.255.0 {
        range 192.168.0.5 192.168.0.75;
        }
subnet 192.168.1.128 netmask 255.255.255.252 {
        range 192.168.0.129 192.168.0.215;
        default-lease-time 56000;
        max-lease-time 62000;
        }
}
```

DHCP Fixed Addresses

Instead of using a pool of possible IP addresses for your hosts, you may want to give each one a specific address. Using the DHCP server still gives you control over which address will be assigned to a given host. However, to assign an address to a particular host, you need to know the hardware address for that host's network interface card (NIC). In effect, you need to inform the DHCP server that it has to associate a particular network connection device with a specified IP address. To do that, the DHCP server needs to know which network device you are referring to. You can identify a network device by its hardware address, known as its MAC address. To find out a client's hardware address, log in to the client and use the **ifconfig** command to find out information about your network devices. To list all network devices, use the **-a** option. If you know your network device name, you can use that. The next example will list all information about the first Ethernet device, **eth0**:

```
ifconfig eth0
```

This will list information on all the client's network connection devices. The entry (usually the first) with the term **HWaddr** will display the MAC address. Once you have the MAC address, you can use it on the DHCP server to assign a specific IP address to that device.

In the **dhcpd.conf** file, you use a **host** declaration to set up a fixed address for a client. Within the **host** declaration, you place a **hardware** option in which you list the type of network connection device and its MAC address. Then use the **fixed-address** parameter to specify the IP address to be assigned to that device. In the following example, the client's network device with a MAC address of 08:00:2b:4c:29:32 is given the IP address 192.168.0.2:

```
host rabbit {
            option host-name "rabbit.mytrek.com"
            hardware ethernet 08:00:2b:4c:29:32;
            fixed-address 192.168.0.2;
            }
```

You can also have the DHCP server perform a DNS lookup to obtain the host's IP address. This has the advantage of letting you manage IP addresses in only one place, the DNS server. Of course, this requires that the DNS server be operating so that the DHCP server can determine the IP address. For example, a proxy server connection (which can provide direct web access) needs just an IP address, not a DNS hostname, to operate. If the DNS server were down, the preceding example would still assign an IP address to the host, whereas the following example would not:

```
host rabbit {
            option host-name "rabbit.mytrek.com"
            hardware ethernet 08:00:2b:4c:29:32;
            fixed-address rabbit.mytrek.com;
            }
```

You can also use the **host** declaration to define network information for a diskless workstation or terminal. In this case, you add a **filename** parameter specifying the boot file to use for that workstation or terminal. Here the terminal called **myterm** obtains boot information from the server **turtle.mytrek.com**:

```
host myterm {
            option host-name "myterm.mytrek.com"
            filename "/boot/vmlinuz";
            hardware ethernet 08:00:2b:4c:29:32;
            server-name "turtle.mytrek.com";
            }
```

A common candidate for a fixed address is the DNS server for a network. Usually, you want the DNS server located at the same IP address, so that it can be directly accessed. The DHCP server can then provide this IP address to its clients.

17. Firewalls

Firewalls management tools

UFW and GUFW

FirewallD

IPtables, NAT, Mangle, and ip6tables

Packet Filtering

Network Address Translation (NAT)

Packet Mangling: the Mangle Table

IPtables Scripts

IPtables Masquerading

Most systems currently connected to the Internet are open to attempts by outside users to gain unauthorized access. Outside users can try to gain access directly by setting up an illegal connection, by intercepting valid communications from users remotely connected to the system, or by pretending to be valid users. Firewalls, encryption, and authentication procedures are ways of protecting against such attacks. A firewall prevents any direct unauthorized attempts at access, encryption protects transmissions from authorized remote users, and authentication verifies that a user requesting access has the right to do so. The current Linux kernel incorporates support for firewalls using the Netfilter (IPtables) packet filtering package. To implement a firewall, you simply provide a series of rules to govern what kind of access you want to allow on your system. If that system is also a gateway for a private network, the system's firewall capability can effectively help protect the network from outside attacks.

Web Site	Security Application
www.netfilter.org	Netfilter project, Iptables, and NAT
www.openssh.org	Secure Shell encryption
www.squid-cache.org	Squid Web Proxy server
web.mit.edu/Kerberos	Kerberos network authentication

Table 17-1: Network Security Applications

To provide protection for remote communications, transmission can be simply encrypted. For Linux systems, you can use the Secure Shell (SSH) suite of programs to encrypt any transmissions, preventing them from being read by anyone else. Kerberos authentication provides another level of security whereby individual services can be protected, allowing use of a service only to users who are cleared for access. Outside users may also try to gain unauthorized access through any Internet services you may be hosting, such as a Web site. In such a case, you can set up a proxy to protect your site from attack. For Linux systems, use Squid proxy software to set up a proxy to protect your Web server. Table 17-1 lists several network security applications commonly used on Linux.

Firewall management tools

You can choose from several different popular firewall management tools (see Table 17-2). Ubuntu now provides its own firewall configuration tool called the Uncomplicated Firewall (ufw). IPtables and ufw are on the Ubuntu main repository, and other firewall tools are in the Universe repository. You can also choose to use other popular management tools such as Fwbuilder. Gufw provides a desktop interface. Gufw is covered in this chapter, along with the underlying IPTables firewall application. Search Synaptic Package Manager for firewall to see a more complete listing. In addition you can use the FirewallD dynamic firewall, which uses a daemon instead of generating iptables commands.

Setting up a firewall with the Uncomplicated Firewall: ufw

The Uncomplicated Firewall, ufw, is now the official firewall application for Ubuntu. It provides a simple firewall that can be managed with a few command-line operations. Like all firewall applications, ufw uses IPTables to define rules and run the firewall. The ufw application is just a management interface for IPtables. Default IPtables rules are kept in before and after files, with added rules in user files. The IPtables rule files are held in the **/etc/ufw** directory. Firewall configuration for certain packages will be placed in the **/usr/share/ufw** directory. You can find out more about ufw at the Ubuntu Firewall site at **https://wiki.ubuntu.com/UncomplicatedFirewall** and at the Ubuntu firewall section in the Ubuntu Server Guide at **https://help.ubuntu.com/stable/serverguide/firewall.html**. The Server Guide also shows information on how to implement IP Masquerading on ufw.

Firewall	Description
IPTables	IPTables: netfilter, NAT, and mangle. **http://netfilter.org** (Main repository)
ufw	Uncomplicated Firewall, ufw. **https://wiki.ubuntu.com/UncomplicatedFirewall** (Ubuntu Main repository), also see Ubuntu Server Guide at **http://doc.ubuntu.com**.
Gufw	GNOME interface for Uncomplicated Firewall, ufw. **https://help.ubuntu.com/community/Gufw**
Fwbuilder	Firewall configuration tool, allow for more complex configuration **http://www.fwbuilder.org** (Universe repository)
Shorewall	Shoreline firewall (Universe repository)
FirewallD	Dynamic Firewall daemon, https://fedorahosted.org/firewalld/ (Universe repository)

Table 17-2: Ubuntu Firewall configuration tools

You can now manage the ufw firewall with either the **ufw** command or using the Gufw desktop tool.

The ufw **systemd** unit files manage static IPtables rules, much like System V scripts did in previous releases. The iptables command keeps firewall rules in **/etc/ufw/**. The ufw operation runs an **ufw-init** script to start and stop the firewall. Runtime configuration is read from **/etc/default/ufw**.

ufw.service

```
[Unit]
Description=Uncomplicated firewall
DefaultDependencies=no
Before=network.target

[Service]
Type=oneshot
RemainAfterExit=yes
ExecStart=/lib/ufw/ufw-init start quiet
ExecStop=/lib/ufw/ufw-init stop

[Install]
WantedBy=multi-user.target
```

ufw commands

IPtables firewall rules can be set up using **ufw** commands entered on the command line and in a Terminal window. Most users may only need to use **ufw** commands to allow or deny access by services like the Web server or Samba server. To check the current firewall status, listing those services allowed or blocked, use the status command.

```
sudo ufw status
```

Commands	Description
enable | disable	Turn the firewall on or off
status	Display status along with services allowed or denied.
logging on | off	Turn logging on or off
default allow | deny	Set the default policy, **allow** is open, whereas **deny** is restrictive
allow *service*	Allow access by a service. Services are defined in **/etc/services** which specify the ports for that service.
allow *port-number/protocol*	Allow access on a particular port using specified protocol. The protocol is optional.
deny *service*	Deny access by a service
delete *rule*	Delete an installed rule, use **allow**, **deny**, or **limit** and include rule specifics.
proto *protocol*	Specify protocol in **allow**, **deny**, or **limit** rule
from *address*	Specify source address in **allow**, **deny**, or **limit** rule
to *address*	Specify destination address in **allow**, **deny**, or **limit** rule
port *port*	Specify port in **allow**, **deny**, or **limit** rule for **from** and **to** address operations

Table 17-3: UFW firewall operations

If the firewall is not enabled, you will first have to enable it with the **enable** command.

```
sudo ufw enable
```

You can restart the firewall, reloading your rules, using the service command and the **ufw** option.

```
sudo service ufw restart
```

You can then add rules using allow and deny commands and their options as listed in Table 17-3. To allow a service, use the allow command and the service name. This is the name for the service listed in the **/etc/services** file. The following command allows the ftp service.

```
sudo ufw allow ftp
```

If the service you want is not listed in **/etc/services**, and you know the port and protocol it uses, you can specify the port and protocol directly. For example, the Microsoft Discovery Service, used by Samba, uses port 445 and protocol TCP.

```
sudo ufw allow 445/tcp
```

The status operation will then show what services are allowed.

```
sudo ufw status
To                  Action          From
21:tcp              ALLOW           Anywhere
21:udp              ALLOW           Anywhere
445:tcp             ALLOW           Anywhere
```

To remove a rule, prefix it with the **delete** command.

```
sudo ufw delete allow 445/tcp
```

A range of ports can be specified using the colon. Samba also uses the 137 and 138 ports with the UDP protocol.

```
sudo ufw allow 137:138/udp
```

Provided ports use the same protocol, you can list several in the same rule separated by commas. The Samba service uses both ports 445 and 135 with the TCP protocol.

```
sudo ufw allow 135,445/tcp
```

More detailed rules can be specified using address, port, and protocol commands. These are similar to the actual IPtables commands. Packets to and from particular networks, hosts, and ports can be controlled. The following denies SSH access (port 22) from host 192.168.03.

```
sudo ufw deny proto tcp from 192.168.03 to any port 22
```

UFW also supports connection rate limiting. Use the **limit** option in place of **allow**. With **limit**, connections are limited to 6 per 30 seconds on the specified port. It is meant to protect against brute force attacks.

The rules you add are placed in the **/lib/ufw/user.rules** file as IPTables rules (corresponding IPv6 rules are placed in the **user6.rules** file). ufw is just a front-end for **iptables-restore** which will read this file and set up the firewall using **iptables** commands. **ufw** will also have **iptables-restore** read the **before.rules** and **after.rules** files in the **/etc/ufw** directory. These files are considered administrative files that include needed supporting rules for your IPtables firewall. Administrators can add their own Iptables rules to these files for system specific features like IP Masquerading.

Note: The Ubuntu Server Guide shows information on how to implement IP masquerading on ufw (**https://help.ubuntu.com/stable/serverguide/firewall.html**).

The **before.rules** file will specify a table with the * symbol, as in ***filter** for the netfilter table (the corresponding IPv6 before rules are in the **before6.rules** file). For the NAT table you would use ***nat**. At the end of each table segment, a COMMIT command is needed to instruct ufw to apply the rules. Rules use **-A** for allow and **-D** for deny, assuming the **iptables** command. The following would implement IP Forwarding when placed at the end of the **before.rules** file (see Ubuntu firewall server documentation). This particular rule works on the first Ethernet device (eth0) for a local network (192.168.0.0/24).

```
# nat Table rules
*nat
:POSTROUTING ACCEPT [0:0]
# Forward traffic from eth1 through eth0.
-A POSTROUTING -s 192.168.0.0/24 -o eth0 -j MASQUERADE
# don't delete the 'COMMIT' line or these nat table rules won't be processed
COMMIT
```

Default settings for ufw are placed in **/etc/default/ufw**. Here you will find the default INPUT, OUTPUT, and FORWARD policies specified by setting associated variables, like DEFAULT_INPUT_POLICY for INPUT and DEFAULT_OUTPUT_POLICY for OUTPUT. The DEFAULT_INPUT_POLICY variable is set to DROP, making DROP the default policy for the INPUT rule. The DEFAULT_OUTPUT_POLICY variable is set to ACCEPT, and the DEFAULT_FORWARD_POLICY variable is set to DROP. To allow IP Masquerading, DEFAULT_FORWARD_POLICY would have to be set to ACCEPT. These entries set default policies only. Any user rules you have set up would take precedence.

Gufw

Gufw will initially open with the firewall disabled, with no ports configured. The application is locked initially. Click the unlock button in the lower right corner of the window. The Status button is set to off, and the shield image will be gray. To enable the firewall, just click the left side of the Status button, setting the status to on. The shield image will be colored and the firewall rules will be listed. Figure 17-1 shows the firewall enabled and several rules listed Samba ports. Rules for both IPv4 and IPv6 (**v6**) network protocols are listed.

Figure 17-1: Gufw

The Gufw dialog has a Firewall section and four tabs, Home, Rules, Report, and Log. The Firewall section has a Status button for turning the firewall on or off. There is a Profile menu for Home, Office, and Public configurations. The Incoming and Outgoing drop down menus for setting the default firewall rules. Options are Deny, Reject, or Allow, and are applied to incoming and outgoing traffic respectively. By default, incoming traffic is denied (Deny), and outgoing traffic is allowed (Allow). Rules you specified in the Rules tab will make exceptions, allowing only certain traffic in or out. Should you select the Allow option, the firewall accepts all incoming traffic. In this case you should set up rules to deny access to some traffic, otherwise the firewall becomes ineffective, allowing access to all traffic. The Report tab lists active services and ports such as the Samba server (smbd) on port 139. The Log tab list firewall notices. You can copy notices, as well as delete a log. The Home tab provides basic help on how to use Gufw.

To add a rule, click the plus button (+) on the lower left corner of the Rules tab to open the "Add rule" dialog, which has three tabs for managing rules: Preconfigured, Simple, and Advanced. The Preconfigured tab provides five menus: the first for the policy (Allow, Deny, Reject, and Limit), the second for the traffic direction (In or Out), the third for the category of the application and the fourth for a subcategory, and the fifth for the particular application or service for the rule. The main categories are Audio video, Games, Network, Office, and System. The Network category lists most network services like SSH, Samba, and FTP. Should there be a security issue with the rule, a warning is displayed.

Should you need modify the default rule for an application, you can click on the arrow button to open the Advanced tab for that rule.

Click the Add button to add the rule. Once added a port entry for the rule appears in the Rules section. In Figure 17-2 the Samba service has been selected and then added, showing up in the Rules section as "137,138/udp ALLOW IN Anywhere."

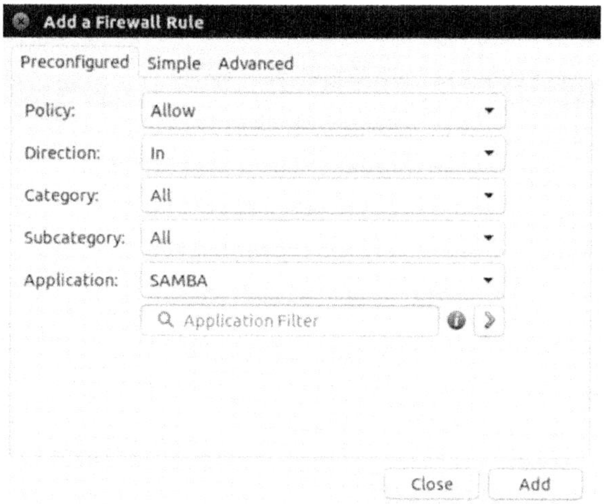

Figure 17-2: Gufw Preconfigured rules

Applications and services can also be blocked. To prevent access by the FTP service, you would first select Deny, then Service, and then the FTP entry.

Besides Allow and Deny, you can also choose a Limit option. The Limit option will enable connection rate limiting, restricting connections to no more than 6 every 30 seconds for a given port. This is meant to protect against brute force attacks.

Should there be no preconfigured entry, you can use the Simple tab to allow access to a port (see Figure 17-3). The first menu is for the rule (Allow, Deny, Reject, and Limit), and the second for the protocol (TCP, UDP, or both). In the Port text box you enter the port number.

Figure 17-3: Gufw Simple rules

On the Advanced tab you can enter more complex rules. You can set up allow or deny rules for tcp or udp protocols, and specify the incoming and outgoing host (ip) and port (see Figure 17-4).

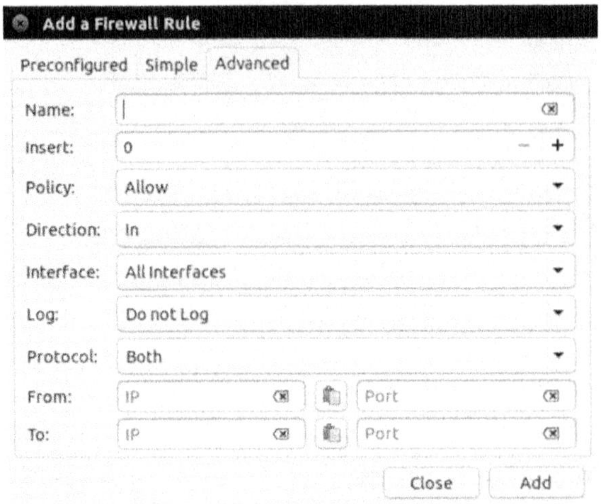

Figure 17-4: Gufw Advanced rules

If you decide to remove a rule, select it in the Rules section and then click the minus button on the lower left corner (-). To remove several rules, click and press Shift-click or use Ctrl-click to select a collection of rules, and then click the minus button.

You can edit any rule by selecting it and clicking the edit button (gear image) to open an "Update a Firewall Rule" dialog (see Figure 17-5). For a default or simple rule, you can only change a few options, but you can turn on logging.

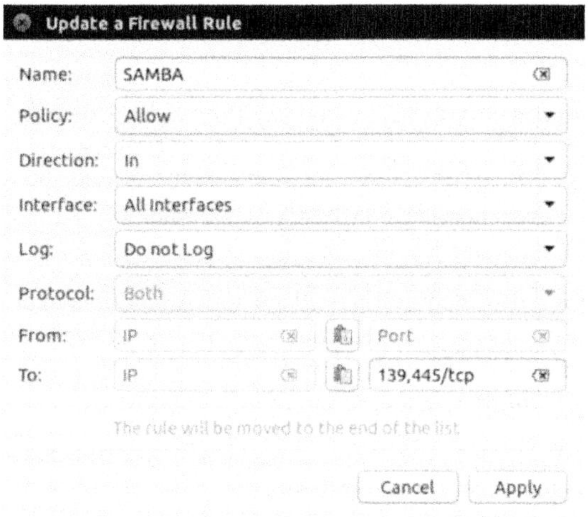

Figure 17-5: Gufw edit a rule

You can also create rules for detected active ports. Click on a port in the Listening Report section, and then click on the plus button at the bottom of that section. An "Add a Firewall Rule" dialog opens to the Advanced tab with the name of the service active on that port and the port number (see figure 17-6). You can change any of the options. The port number is already entered.

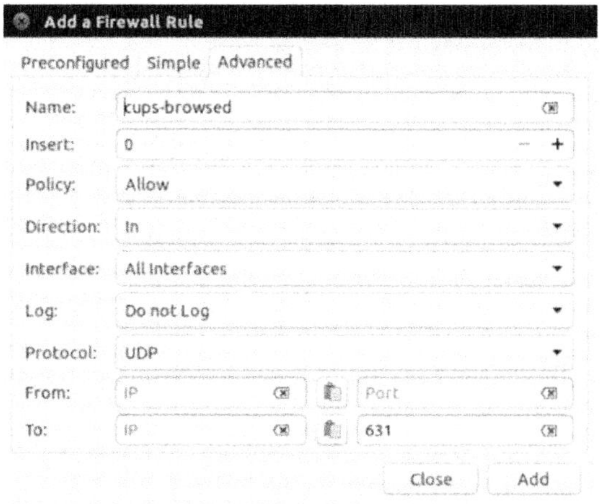

Figure 17-6: Gufw create a rule for an active port

IPtables, NAT, Mangle, and ip6tables

A good foundation for your network's security is to set up a Linux system to operate as a firewall for your network, protecting it from unauthorized access. You can use a firewall to implement either packet filtering or proxies. *Packet filtering* is the process of deciding whether a packet received by the firewall host should be passed on into the local network. The packet-filtering software checks the source and destination addresses of the packet and sends the packet on, if it's allowed. Even if your system is not part of a network but connects directly to the Internet, you can still use the firewall feature to control access to your system. Of course, this also provides you with much more security.

With proxies, you can control access to specific services, such as Web or FTP servers. You need a proxy for each service you want to control. The Web server has its own Web proxy, while an FTP server has an FTP proxy. Proxies can also be used to cache commonly used data, such as Web pages, so that users needn't constantly access the originating site. The proxy software commonly used on Linux systems is Squid.

An additional task performed by firewalls is network address translation (NAT). Network address translation redirects packets to appropriate destinations. It performs tasks such as redirecting packets to certain hosts, forwarding packets to other networks, and changing the host source of packets to implement IP masquerading.

Firewalls also can perform packet mangling, which modifies packet information to control operations like routing, connection size, and priority.

Note: The IP Chains package is the precursor to IPtables that was used on Linux systems running the 2.2 kernel. It is still in use on some Linux systems. The Linux Web site for IP Chains, which is the successor to ipfwadm used on older versions of Linux, is currently **www.netfilter.org/ipchains**. IP Chains is no longer included with many Linux distributions.

The Netfilter software package implements both packet filtering and NAT tasks for the Linux 2.4 kernel and above. The Netfilter software is developed by the Netfilter Project, which you can find out more about at **http://www.netfilter.org**.

Iptables

The command used to execute packet filtering and NAT tasks is iptables, and the software is commonly referred to as simply Iptables. Netfilter implements packet filtering and NAT tasks separately using different tables of rules. This approach streamlines the packet-filtering task, letting IPtables perform packet-filtering checks without the overhead of also having to do address translations. NAT operations are also freed from being mixed in with packet-filtering checks. You use the **iptables** command for packet filtering, NAT tasks, and packet mangling. Each operation has its own table of rules: filter for packet filtering, nat for NAT tasks, and mangle for packet mangling. For NAT you specify the NAT table with the **-t nat** option. For the mangle table you use the **-t mangle** option. The packet filtering is the default. It can be specified with the **-t filter** option, but it's usually left out, assuming that if a table is not specified it is a filter operation. In addition, netfilter also handles certain exemptions to connection tracking operations in a **raw** table.

On Ubuntu, firewall applications, such as ufw,will set up their own iptables files containing **iptables** commands. When these are run, they will set up the tables and rules used to filter, translate, and mangle packets. The iptables files are located at **/etc/ufw**. If you want to set up rules manually and start them automatically you can use the iptables-persistent service (**iptables-persistent** package). The iptables-persistent service will run IPtables rules using rules you have set up in the **/etc/iptables/rules** file. Use the **iptables-persistent** script to run **iptables-restore** to load rules from the rules file.

```
sudo service iptables-persistent start
```

ip6tables

The ip6tables command provides support for IPv6 addressing. It is identical to IPtables, except that it allows the use of IPv6 addresses instead of IPv4 addresses. Both filter and mangle tables are supported in ip6tables, but not NAT tables. The filter tables support the same options and commands as supported in IPtables. The mangle tables will allow specialized packet changes like those for IPtables, using PREROUTING, INPUT, OUTPUT, FORWARD, and POSTROUTING rules. Some extensions have ipv6 labels for their names, such as ipv6-icmp, which correspond to the IPtables icmp extension. The ipv6headers extension is used to select IPv6 headers.

arptables

The arptables tool allows you to manage rules for the IPv4 Address Resolution Protocol (ARP). The ARP is used on IPv4 local networks to discover the hardware address (MAC address) associated with an IP address. Once the association is made, connections can be made to that address. In this way, a host on a local network can detect and connect to another host. arptables sets up IPtables rules for controlling access between these hosts. The filter, mangle, and nat tables are supported. Install the arptables package. arptables has its own commands for saving and loading ARP rules, **arptables-restore** and **arptables-save**. It is used for managing transmissions on local networks.

ebtables

The ebtables tool manages rules for Ethernet bridges. Install the **ebtables** packages. Configuration files are **/etc/sysconfig/ebtables-config**. ebtables has its own startup script, **/etc/init.d/ebtables**, and uses **ebtables-save** and **ebtables-restore** to save and load ebtables rules.

xtables

xtables is an underlying framework that combines the code for iptables, ip6tables, and arptables. Firewall modules hook into this framework. Modules that connect directly to this framework begin the **xt** prefix.

Modules

Netfilter is designed to be modularized and extensible. Capabilities can be added in the form of modules such as the state module, which adds connection tracking. Most modules are loaded as part of the IPtables service. Others are optional; you can elect to load them before installing rules. The IPtables modules are located at **/lib/modules/***kernel-version***/kernel/net/ipv4/netfilter**, where *kernel-version* is your kernel number. For IPv6 modules, check the **ipv6/netfilter** directory. Modules that load automatically will have an **ipt_** prefix, and optional modules have just an **ip_** prefix. If you are writing you own iptables script, you would have to add **modprobe** commands to load optional modules directly.

The optional IPtables modules, also known as helper modules, are located in the **/lib/modules/***kernel-version***/kernel/net/netfilter** directory. Modules that apply to the netfilter table begin with the prefix **nf**, and those that apply to all tables begin with the prefix **ipt**. An example of a helper module is a connection tracking module that tracks packets that belong to an established connection, like an FTP download connection tracker module. The conntrack helper modules have the name conntrack, such as **nf_conntrack_ipv4.ko**.

Packet Filtering

Netfilter is essentially a framework for packet management that can check packets for particular network protocols and notify parts of the kernel listening for them. Built on the Netfilter framework is the packet selection system implemented by IPtables. With IPtables, different tables of rules can be set up to select packets according to differing criteria. Netfilter currently supports three tables: filter, nat, and mangle. Packet filtering is implemented using a filter table that holds rules for dropping or accepting packets. Network address translation operations such as IP masquerading are implemented using the NAT table that holds IP masquerading rules. The mangle table is used for specialized packet changes. Changes can be made to packets before they are sent out, when they are received, or as they are being forwarded. This structure is extensible in that new modules can define their own tables with their own rules. This also greatly improves efficiency. Instead of all packets checking one large table, they access only the table of rules they need.

IP table rules are managed using the iptables command. For this command, you will need to specify the table you want to manage. The default is the filter table, which does not need to be specified. You can list the rules you have added at any time with the -L and -n options, as shown next. The -n option says to use only numeric output for both IP addresses and ports, avoiding a DNS lookup for hostnames. You could, however, just use the -L option to see the port labels and hostnames:

```
iptables -L -n
```

Chains

Rules are combined into different chains. The kernel uses chains to manage packets it receives and sends out. A *chain* is simply a checklist of rules. These rules specify what action to take for packets containing certain headers. The rules operate with an if-then-else structure. If a packet does not match the first rule, the next rule is then checked, and so on. If the packet does not match any rules, the kernel consults chain policy. Usually, at this point the packet is rejected. If the packet does match a rule, it is passed to its target, which determines what to do with the packet. The standard targets are listed in Table 17-4. If a packet does not match any of the rules, it is passed to the chain's default target.

Targets

A *target* could, in turn, be another chain of rules, or even a chain of user-defined rules. A packet could be passed through several chains before finally reaching a target. In the case of user-defined chains, the default target is always the next rule in the chains from which it was called. This sets up a procedure or function-call-like flow of control found in programming languages. When a rule has a user-defined chain as its target, when activated, that user-defined chain is executed. If no rules are matched, execution returns to the next rule in the originating chain.

Tip: Specialized targets and options can be added by means of kernel patches provided by the Netfilter site. For example, the SAME patch returns the same address for all connections. A patch-o-matic option for the Netfilter make file will patch your kernel source code, adding support for the new target and options. You can then rebuild and install your kernel.

Target	Function
ACCEPT	Allow packet to pass through the firewall.
DROP	Deny access by the packet.
REJECT	Deny access and notify the sender.
QUEUE	Send packets to user space.
RETURN	Jump to the end of the chain and let the default target process it.

Table 17-4: IPtables Targets

Firewall and NAT Chains

The kernel uses three firewall chains: INPUT, OUTPUT, and FORWARD. When a packet is received through an interface, the INPUT chain is used to determine what to do with it. The kernel then uses its routing information to decide where to send it. If the kernel sends the packet to another host, the FORWARD chain is checked. Before the packet is actually sent, the OUTPUT chain is also checked. In addition, two NAT table chains, POSTROUTING and PREROUTING, are implemented to handle masquerading and packet address modifications. The built-in Netfilter chains are listed in Table 17-5.

Chain	Description
INPUT	Rules for incoming packets
OUTPUT	Rules for outgoing packets
FORWARD	Rules for forwarded packets
PREROUTING	Rules for redirecting or modifying incoming packets, NAT table only
POSTROUTING	Rules for redirecting or modifying outgoing packets, NAT table only

Table 17-5: Netfilter Built-in Chains

Adding and Changing Rules

You add and modify chain rules using the iptables commands. An iptables command consists of the command iptables, followed by an argument denoting the command to execute (see Table 17-6). For example, iptables -A is the command to add a new rule, whereas iptables -D is the command to delete a rule. The iptables commands are listed in Table 17-4.

Option	Function
-A *chain*	Appends a rule to a chain.
-D *chain* [*rulenum*]	Deletes matching rules from a chain. Deletes rule *rulenum* (1 = first) from *chain*.
-I *chain* [*rulenum*]	Inserts in *chain* as *rulenum* (default 1 = first).
-R *chain rulenum*	Replaces rule *rulenum* (1 = first) in *chain*.
-L [*chain*]	Lists the rules in *chain* or all chains.
-E [*chain*]	Renames a chain.
-F [*chain*]	Deletes (flushes) all rules in *chain* or all chains.
-R *chain*	Replaces a rule; rules are numbered from 1.
-Z [*chain*]	Zero counters in *chain* or all chains.
-N *chain*	Creates a new user-defined chain.
-X *chain*	Deletes a user-defined chain.
-P *chain target*	Changes policy on *chain* to *target*.

Table 17-6: IPtables Commands

The following command simply lists the chains along with their rules currently defined for your system. The output shows the default values created by iptables commands.

```
iptables -L -n
Chain input (policy ACCEPT):
Chain forward (policy ACCEPT):
Chain output (policy ACCEPT):
```

To add a new rule to a chain, you use -A. Use -D to remove it, and -R to replace it. Following the command, list the chain to which the rule applies, such as the INPUT, OUTPUT, or FORWARD chain, or a user-defined chain. Next, you list different options that specify the actions you want taken (most are the same as those used for IP Chains, with a few exceptions). The -s option specifies the source address attached to the packet, -d specifies the destination address, and the -j option specifies the target of the rule. The ACCEPT target will allow a packet to pass. The -i option indicates the input device and can be used only with the INPUT and FORWARD chains. The -o option indicates the output device and can be used only for OUTPUT and FORWARD chains. Table 17-6 lists several basic options.

IPtables Options

The IPtables package is designed to be extensible, and a number of options with selection criteria can be included with IPtables (see Table 17-7). For example, the TCP extension includes the --syn option that checks for SYN packets. The ICMP extension provides the --icmp-type option for specifying ICMP packets as those used in ping operations. The limit extension includes the --limit option, with which you can limit the maximum number of matching packets in a specified time period, such as a second.

Note: In IPtables commands, chain names have to be entered in uppercase, as with the chain names INPUT, OUTPUT, and FORWARD.

Option	Function
-p [!] *proto*	Specifies a protocol, such as TCP, UDP, ICMP, or ALL.
-s [!] *address*[/*mask*] [!] [*port*[:*port*]]	Source address to match. With the *port* argument, you can specify the port.
--sport [!] [*port*[:*port*]]	Source port specification. You can specify a range of ports using the colon, *port:port.*
-d [!] *address*[/*mask*] [!] [*port*[:*port*]]	Destination address to match. With the *port* argument, you can specify the port.
--dport [!][*port*[:*port*]]	Destination port specification.
--icmp-type [!] *typename*	Specifies ICMP type.
-i [!] *name*[+]	Specifies an input network interface using its name (for example, eth0). The + symbol functions as a wildcard. The + attached to the end of the name matches all interfaces with that prefix (eth+ matches all Ethernet interfaces). Can be used only with the INPUT chain.
-j *target* [port]	Specifies the target for a rule (specify [port] for REDIRECT target).
--to-source < *ipaddr*>[-< *ipaddr*>][: *port*- *port*]	Used with the SNAT target, rewrites packets with new source IP address.
--to-destination < *ipaddr*>[-< *ipaddr*>][: *port*- *port*]	Used with the DNAT target, rewrites packets with new destination IP address.
-n	Numeric output of addresses and ports, used with -L.
-o [!] *name*[+]	Specifies an output network interface using its name (for example, eth0). Can be used only with FORWARD and OUTPUT chains.
-t *table*	Specifies a table to use, as in -t nat for the NAT table.
-v	Verbose mode, shows rule details, used with -L.
-x	Expands numbers (displays exact values), used with -L.
[!] -f	Matches second through last fragments of a fragmented packet.
[!] -V	Prints package version.

`!`	Negates an option or address.
`-m`	Specifies a module to use, such as state.
`--state`	Specifies options for the state module such as NEW, INVALID, RELATED, and ESTABLISHED. Used to detect packet's state. NEW references SYN packets (new connections).
`--syn`	SYN packets, new connections.
`--tcp-flags`	TCP flags: SYN, ACK, FIN, RST, URG, PS, and ALL for all flags.
`--limit`	Option for the limit module (`-m limit`). Used to control the rate of matches, matching a given number of times per second.
`--limit-burst`	Option for the limit module (`-m limit`). Specifies maximum burst before the limit kicks in. Used to control denial-of-service attacks.

Table 17-7: IPtables Options

In the following example, the user adds a rule to the INPUT chain to accept all packets originating from the address 192.168.0.55. Any packets that are received (INPUT) whose source address (-s) matches 192.168.0.55 are accepted and passed through (-j ACCEPT):

```
iptables -A INPUT -s 192.168.0.55 -j ACCEPT
```

Accepting and Denying Packets: DROP and ACCEPT

There are two built-in targets: DROP and ACCEPT. Other targets can be either user-defined chains or extensions added on, such as REJECT. Two special targets are used to manage chains, RETURN and QUEUE. RETURN indicates the end of a chain and returns to the chain it started from. QUEUE is used to send packets to user space. The following example will drop all incoming packets from the **www.myjunk.com** site:

```
iptables -A INPUT -s www.myjunk.com -j DROP
```

You can turn a rule into its inverse with an ! symbol. For example, to accept all incoming packets except those from a specific address, place an ! symbol before the -s option and that address. The following example will accept all packets except those from the IP address 192.168.0.45:

```
iptables -A INPUT -j ACCEPT ! -s 192.168.0.45
```

You can specify an individual address using its domain name or its IP number. For a range of addresses, you can use the IP number of their network and the network IP mask. The IP mask can be an IP number or simply the number of bits making up the mask. For example, all of the addresses in network 192.168.0 can be represented by 192.168.0.0/225.255.255.0 or by 192.168.0.0/24. To specify any address, you can use 0.0.0.0/0.0.0.0 or simply 0/0. By default, rules reference any address if no -s or -d specification exists. The following example accepts messages coming in that are from (source) any host in the 192.168.0.0 network and that are going (destination) anywhere at all (the -d option is left out or could be written as -d 0/0):

```
iptables -A INPUT -s 192.168.0.0/24  -j ACCEPT
```

The IPtables rules are usually applied to a specific network interface such as the Ethernet interface used to connect to the Internet. For a single system connected to the Internet, you will have two interfaces, one that is your Internet connection, and a loopback interface (**lo**) for internal connections between users on your system. The network interface for the Internet is referenced using the device name for the interface. For example, the first Ethernet card with the device name would be referenced by the device name **eth0**. A modem using PPP protocols with the device name **ppp0** would have the name **ppp0**. In IPtables rules, you use the -i option to indicate the input device; it can be used only with the INPUT and FORWARD chains. The -o option indicates the output device and can be used only for OUTPUT and FORWARD chains. Rules can then be applied to packets arriving and leaving on particular network devices. In the following examples, the first rule references the Ethernet device **eth0**, and the second, the localhost:

```
iptables -A INPUT -j DROP -i eth0 -s 192.168.0.45
iptables -A INPUT -j ACCEPT  -i lo
```

User-Defined Chains

With IPtables, the FORWARD and INPUT chains are evaluated separately. One does not feed into the other. This means that if you want to completely block certain addresses from passing through your system, you will need to add both a FORWARD rule and an INPUT rule for them.

```
iptables -A INPUT -j DROP -i eth0 -s 192.168.0.45
iptables -A FORWARD -j DROP -i eth0 -s 192.168.0.45
```

A common method for reducing repeated INPUT and FORWARD rules is to create a user chain into which both the INPUT and FORWARD feed. You define a user chain with the -N option. The next example shows the basic format for this arrangement. A new chain is created called incoming (it can be any name you choose). The rules you would define for your FORWARD and INPUT chains are now defined for the incoming chain. The INPUT and FORWARD chains then use the incoming chain as a target, jumping directly to it and using its rules to process any packets they receive.

```
iptables -N incoming

iptables -A incoming -j DROP -i eth0 -s 192.168.0.45
iptables -A incoming -j ACCEPT  -i lo

iptables -A FORWARD -j incoming
iptables -A INPUT -j incoming
```

ICMP Packets

Firewalls often block certain Internet Control Message Protocol (ICMP) messages. ICMP redirect messages, in particular, can take control of your routing tasks. You need to enable some ICMP messages, however, such as those needed for ping, traceroute, and particularly destination-unreachable operations. In most cases, you always need to make sure destination-unreachable packets are allowed; otherwise, domain name queries could hang. Some of the more common

ICMP packet types are listed in Table 17-8. You can enable an ICMP type of packet with the --icmp-type option, which takes as its argument a number or a name representing the message. The following examples enable the use of echo-reply, echo-request, and destination-unreachable messages, which have the numbers 0, 8, and 3:

Number	Name	Required By
0	echo-reply	ping
3	destination-unreachable	Any TCP/UDP traffic
5	redirect	Routing if not running routing daemon
8	echo-request	ping
11	time-exceeded	traceroute

Table 17-8: Common ICMP Packets

```
iptables -A INPUT -j ACCEPT  -p icmp -i eth0 --icmp -type  echo-reply -d 10.0.0.1
iptables -A INPUT -j ACCEPT  -p icmp -i eth0 --icmp-type  echo-request -d 10.0.0.1
iptables -A INPUT -j ACCEPT  -p icmp -i eth0 --icmp-type destination-unreachable -d 10.0.0.1
```

Their rule listing will look like this:

```
ACCEPT      icmp --  0.0.0.0/0            10.0.0.1            icmp type 0
ACCEPT      icmp --  0.0.0.0/0            10.0.0.1            icmp type 8
ACCEPT      icmp --  0.0.0.0/0            10.0.0.1            icmp type 3
```

Ping operations need to be further controlled to avoid the ping-of-death security threat. You can do this several ways. One way is to deny any ping fragments. Ping packets are normally very small. You can block ping-of-death attacks by denying any ICMP packet that is a fragment. Use the -f option to indicate fragments.

```
iptables -A INPUT -p icmp -j DROP -f
```

Another way is to limit the number of matches received for ping packets. You use the limit module to control the number of matches on the ICMP ping operation. Use -m limit to use the limit module, and --limit to specify the number of allowed matches. 1/s will allow one match per second.

```
iptables -A FORWARD -p icmp --icmp-type echo-request -m limit --limit 1/s -j ACCEPT
```

Controlling Port Access

If your system is hosting an Internet service, such as a Web or FTP server, you can use IPtables to control access to it. You can specify a particular service by using the source port (--sport) or destination port (--dport) options with the port that the service uses. IPtables lets you use names for ports such as **www** for the Web server port. The names of services and the ports they use are listed in the **/etc/services** file, which maps ports to particular services. For a domain name server, the port would be **domain**. You can also use the port number if you want, preceding the number with a colon. The following example accepts all messages to the Web server located at 192.168.0.43:

```
iptables -A INPUT -d 192.168.0.43 --dport www -j ACCEPT
```

Common ports checked and their labels are shown here:

Service	Port Number	Port Label
Auth	113	auth
Finger	79	finger
FTP	21	ftp
NTP	123	ntp
Portmapper	111	sunrpc
Telnet	23	telnet
Web server	80	www

You can also use port references to protect certain services and deny others. This approach is often used if you are designing a firewall that is much more open to the Internet, letting users make freer use of Internet connections. Certain services you know can be harmful, such as Telnet and NTP, can be denied selectively. For example, to deny any kind of Telnet operation on your firewall, you can drop all packets coming in on the Telnet port, 23. To protect NFS operations, you can deny access to the port used for the portmapper, 111. You can use either the port number or the port name.

```
# deny outside access to portmapper port on firewall.
iptables -A arriving  -j DROP -p tcp -i eth0  --dport 111
# deny outside access to telnet port on firewall.
iptables -A arriving  -j DROP -p tcp -i eth0  --dport telnet
```

The rule listing will look like this:

```
DROP      tcp  --  0.0.0.0/0    0.0.0.0/0     tcp dpt:111
DROP      tcp  --  0.0.0.0/0    0.0.0.0/0     tcp dpt:23
```

One port-related security problem is access to your X server ports that range from 6000 to 6009. On a relatively open firewall, these ports could be used to illegally access your system through your X server. A range of ports can be specified with a colon, as in 6000:6009. You can also use x11 for the first port, x11:6009. Sessions on the X server can be secured by using SSH, which normally accesses the X server on port 6010.

```
iptables -A arriving  -j DROP -p tcp -i eth0 --dport 6000:6009
```

Packet States: Connection Tracking

One of the more useful extensions is the state extension, which can easily detect tracking information for a packet. Connection tracking maintains information about a connection such as its source, destination, and port. It provides an effective means for determining which packets belong to an established or related connection. To use connection tracking, you specify the state module first with -m state. Then you can use the --state option. Here you can specify any of the following states:

State	Description
NEW	A packet that creates a new connection
ESTABLISHED	A packet that belongs to an existing connection
RELATED	A packet that is related to, but not part of, an existing connection, such as an ICMP error or a packet establishing an FTP data connection
INVALID	A packet that could not be identified for some reason
RELATED+REPLY	A packet that is related to an established connection, but not part of one directly

If you are designing a firewall that is meant to protect your local network from any attempts to penetrate it from an outside network, you may want to restrict packets coming in. Simply denying access by all packets is unfeasible, because users connected to outside servers—say, on the Internet—must receive information from them. You can, instead, deny access by a particular kind of packet used to initiate a connection. The idea is that an attacker must initiate a connection from the outside. The headers of these kinds of packets have their SYN bit set on and their FIN and ACK bits empty. The state module's NEW state matches on any such SYN packet. By specifying a DROP target for such packets, you deny access by any packet that is part of an attempt to make a connection with your system. Anyone trying to connect to your system from the outside is unable to do so. Users on your local system who have initiated connections with outside hosts can still communicate with them. The following example will drop any packets trying to create a new connection on the **eth0** interface, though they will be accepted on any other interface:

```
iptables -A INPUT -m state --state NEW -i eth0 -j DROP
```

You can use the ! operator on the **eth0** device combined with an ACCEPT target to compose a rule that will accept any new packets except those on the **eth0** device. If the **eth0** device is the only one that connects to the Internet, this still effectively blocks outside access. At the same time, input operation for other devices such as your localhost are free to make new connections. This kind of conditional INPUT rule is used to allow access overall with exceptions. It usually assumes that a later rule, such as a chain policy, will drop remaining packets.

```
iptables -A INPUT -m state --state NEW ! -i eth0 -j ACCEPT
```

The next example will accept any packets that are part of an established connection or related to such a connection on the **eth0** interface:

```
iptables -A INPUT -m state --state ESTABLISHED,RELATED -j ACCEPT
```

Specialized Connection Tracking: ftp, irc, Amanda, tftp.

To track certain kinds of packets, IPtables uses specialized connection tracking modules. These are optional modules that you need to have loaded manually. To track passive FTP connections, you would have to load the ip_conntrack_ftp module. To add NAT table support, you would also load the ip_nat_ftp module. For IRC connections, you use ip_conntrack_irc and ip_nat_irc. There are corresponding modules for Amanda (the backup server) and TFTP (Trivial FTP).

If you are writing your own iptables script, you would have to add **modprobe** commands to load the modules.

```
modprobe ip_conntrack ip_conntrack_ftp ip_nat_ftp
modprobe ip_conntrack_amanda ip_nat_amanda
```

Network Address Translation (NAT)

Network address translation (NAT) is the process whereby a system will change the destination or source of packets as they pass through the system. A packet will traverse several linked systems on a network before it reaches its final destination. Normally, they will simply pass the packet on. However, if one of these systems performs a NAT operation on a packet, it can change the source or destination. A packet sent to a particular destination could have its destination address changed. To make this work, the system also needs to remember such changes so that the source and destination for any reply packets are altered back to the original addresses of the packet being replied to.

NAT is often used to provide access to systems that may be connected to the Internet through only one IP address. Such is the case with networking features such as IP masquerading, support for multiple servers, and transparent proxying. With IP masquerading, NAT operations will change the destination and source of a packet moving through a firewall/gateway linking the Internet to computers on a local network. The gateway has a single IP address that the other local computers can use through NAT operations. If you have multiple servers but only one IP address, you can use NAT operations to send packets to the alternate servers. You can also use NAT operations to have your IP address reference a particular server application such as a Web server (transparent proxy). NAT tables are not implemented for ip6tables.

Adding NAT Rules

Packet selection rules for NAT operations are added to the NAT table managed by the iptables command. To add a rule to the NAT table, you would have to specify the NAT table with the -t nat option as shown here:

```
iptables -t nat
```

With the `-L` option, you can list the rules you have added to the NAT table:

```
iptables -t nat -L -n
```

Adding the -n option will list IP addresses and ports in numeric form. This will speed up the listing, as iptables will not attempt to do a DNS lookup to determine the hostname for the IP address.

Nat Targets and Chains

In addition, there are two types of NAT operations: source NAT, specified as SNAT target, and destination NAT, specified as DNAT target. The SNAT target is used for rules that alter source addresses, and DNAT target, for those that alter destination addresses.

Three chains in the NAT table are used by the kernel for NAT operations. These are PREROUTING, POSTROUTING, and OUTPUT. PREROUTING is used for destination NAT (DNAT) rules. These are packets that are arriving. POSTROUTING is used for source NAT

(SNAT) rules. These are for packets leaving. OUTPUT is used for destination NAT rules for locally generated packets.

The targets valid only for the NAT table are shown here:

SNAT	Modify source address, use `--to-source` option to specify new source address.
DNAT	Modify destination address, use `--to-destination` option to specify new destination address.
REDIRECT	Redirect a packet.
MASQUERADE	IP masquerading.
MIRROR	Reverse source and destination and send back to sender.
MARK	Modify the Mark field to control message routing.

As with packet filtering, you can specify source (-s) and destination (-d) addresses, as well as the input (-i) and output (-o) devices. The -j option will specify a target such as MASQUERADE. You would implement IP masquerading by adding a MASQUERADE rule to the POSTROUTING chain:

```
iptables -t nat -A POSTROUTING -o eth0 -j MASQUERADE
```

To change the source address of a packet leaving your system, you would use the POSTROUTING rule with the SNAT target. For the SNAT target, you use the --to-source option to specify the source address:

```
iptables -t nat -A POSTROUTING -o eth0 -j SNAT --to-source 192.168.0.4
```

To change the destination address of packets arriving on your system, you would use the PREROUTING rule with the DNAT target and the --to-destination option:

```
iptables -t nat -A PRETROUTING -i eth0 -j DNAT --to-destination 192.168.0.3
```

Specifying a port lets you change destinations for packets arriving on a particular port. In effect, this lets you implement port forwarding. In the next example, every packet arriving on port 80 (the Web service port) is redirected to 10.0.0.3, which in this case would be a system running a Web server.

```
iptables -t nat -A PRETROUTING -i eth0 -dport 80 -j DNAT --to-destination 10.0.0.3
```

With the TOS and MARK targets, you can mangle the packet to control its routing or priority. A TOS target sets the type of service for a packet, which can set the priority using criteria such as normal-service, minimize-cost, or maximize-throughput, among others.

Nat Redirection: Transparent Proxies

NAT tables can be used to implement any kind of packet redirection, a process transparent to the user. Redirection is commonly used to implement a transparent proxy. Redirection of packets is carried out with the REDIRECT target. With transparent proxies, packets received can be automatically redirected to a proxy server. For example, packets arriving on the Web service port, 80, can be redirected to the Squid Proxy service port, usually 3128. This involves a command to redirect a packet, using the REDIRECT target on the PREROUTING chain:

```
# iptables -t nat -A PREROUTING -i eth1 --dport 80 -j REDIRECT --to-port 3128
```

Packet Mangling: the Mangle Table

The *packet mangling* table is used to actually modify packet information. Rules applied specifically to this table are often designed to control the mundane behavior of packets, like routing, connection size, and priority. Rules that actually modify a packet, rather than simply redirecting or stopping it, can be used only in the mangle table. For example, the TOS target can be used directly in the mangle table to change the Type of Service field to modifying a packet's priority. A TCPMSS target could be set to control the size of a connection. The ECN target lets you work around ECN black holes, and the DSCP target will let you change DSCP bits. Several extensions such as the ROUTE extension will change a packet, in this case, rewriting its destination, rather than just redirecting it.

The mangle table is indicated with the -t mangle option. Use the following command to see what chains are listed in your mangle table:

```
iptables -t mangle  -L
```

Several mangle table targets are shown here:

TOS	Modify the Type of Service field to manage the priority of the packet.
TCPMSS	Modify the allowed size of packets for a connection, enabling larger transmissions.
ECN	Remove ECN black hole information.
DSCP	Change DSCP bits.
ROUTE	Extension TARGET to modify destination information in the packet.

Note: The IPtables package is designed to be extensible, allowing customized targets to be added easily. This involves applying patches to the kernel and rebuilding it. See **www.netfilter.org** for more details, along with a listing of extended targets.

IPtables Scripts

Though you can enter IPtables rules from the shell command line, when you shut down your system, these commands will be lost. You will most likely need to place your IPtables rules in a script that can then be executed directly. This way you can edit and manage a complex set of rules, adding comments and maintaining their ordering.

To load the rules, use the **iptables-restore** script to read the IPtables commands from that file.

```
sudo iptables-restore < myfilter
```

The **iptables-save** command will save currently loaded firewall rules to a file of your choosing using the redirection operator, >. You could use this command to save a copy of rules set up by another firewall application like ufw, and then use that file as a basis for customizing firewall rules manually. You could then use **iptables-restore** to load your customized rules. The **iptables-save** command will save whatever rules are loaded currently, even those you may have entered directly using the **iptables** command.

```
sudo iptables-save > mycurrentfirewall
```

An IPtables Script Example: IPv4

You now have enough information to create a simple IPtables script that will provide basic protection for a single system connected to the Internet. The following script, **myfilter**, provides an IPtables filtering process to protect a local network and a Web site from outside attacks. This example uses IPtables and IPv4 addressing. For IPv6 addressing you would use ip6tables, which has corresponding commands, except for the NAT rules, which would be implemented as mangle rules.

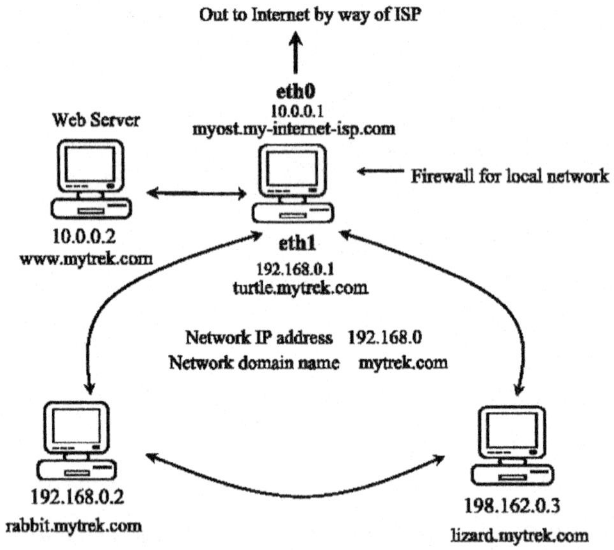

Figure 17-7 A network with a firewall

myfilter

```
# Firewall Gateway system IP address is 10.0.0.1 using Ethernet device eth0
# Private network address is 192.168.0.0 using Ethernet device eth1
# Web site address is 10.0.0.2
# turn off IP forwarding
echo 0 > /proc/sys/net/ipv4/ip_forward
# Flush chain rules
iptables -F INPUT
iptables -F OUTPUT
iptables -F FORWARD
# set default (policy) rules
iptables -P INPUT DROP
iptables -P OUTPUT ACCEPT
iptables -P FORWARD ACCEPT

# IP spoofing, deny any packets on the internal network that have an external source address
iptables -A INPUT -j LOG  -i eth1 \! -s 192.168.0.0/24
iptables -A INPUT -j DROP  -i eth1 \! -s 192.168.0.0/24
iptables -A FORWARD -j DROP  -i eth1 \! -s 192.168.0.0/24
# IP spoofing, deny any outside packets (any not on eth1) that have the
# source address of the internal network
iptables -A INPUT -j DROP \! -i eth1 -s 192.168.0.0/24
iptables -A FORWARD -j DROP \! -i eth1 -s 192.168.0.0/24
# IP spoofing, deny any outside packets with localhost address
# (packets not on the lo interface (any on eth0 or eth1) that have source address localhost)
iptables -A INPUT -j DROP  -i \! lo  -s  127.0.0.0/255.0.0.0
iptables -A FORWARD -j DROP  -i \! lo  -s  127.0.0.0/255.0.0.0

# allow all incoming messages for users on your firewall system
iptables -A INPUT -j ACCEPT  -i lo

# allow  communication to the Web server (address 10.0.0.2), port www
iptables -A INPUT  -j ACCEPT -p tcp -i eth0  --dport www -s 10.0.0.2
# Allow  established connections from Web servers to internal network
iptables -A INPUT -m state --state ESTABLISHED,RELATED -i eth0 -p tcp  --sport www -s
10.0.0.2 -d 192.168.0.0/24  -j ACCEPT
# Prevent new  connections from Web servers to internal network
iptables -A OUTPUT -m state --state  NEW -o eth0 -p tcp --sport www -d 192.168.0.0/24 -j DROP

# allow established and related outside communication to your system
# allow outside communication to the firewall, except for ICMP packets
iptables -A INPUT -m state --state ESTABLISHED,RELATED -i eth0 -p \! icmp -j ACCEPT
# prevent outside initiated connections
iptables -A INPUT -m state --state NEW -i eth0 -j DROP
iptables -A FORWARD -m state --state NEW -i eth0 -j DROP
# allow all local communication to and from the firewall on eth1  from the local network
iptables -A INPUT -j ACCEPT -p all -i eth1 -s 192.168.0.0/24

# Set up masquerading to allow internal machines access to outside network
iptables -t nat -A POSTROUTING -o eth0 -j MASQUERADE

# Accept ICMP Ping and Destination unreachable messages
# Others will be rejected by INPUT and OUTPUT DROP policy
iptables -A INPUT -j ACCEPT  -p icmp -i eth0 --icmp-type  echo-reply -d 10.0.0.1
iptables -A INPUT -j ACCEPT  -p icmp -i eth0 --icmp-type  echo-request -d 10.0.0.1
iptables -A INPUT -j ACCEPT -p icmp -i eth0 --icmp-type  destination-unreachable -d 10.0.0.1
# Turn on IP Forwarding
echo 1 > /proc/sys/net/ipv4/ip_forward
```

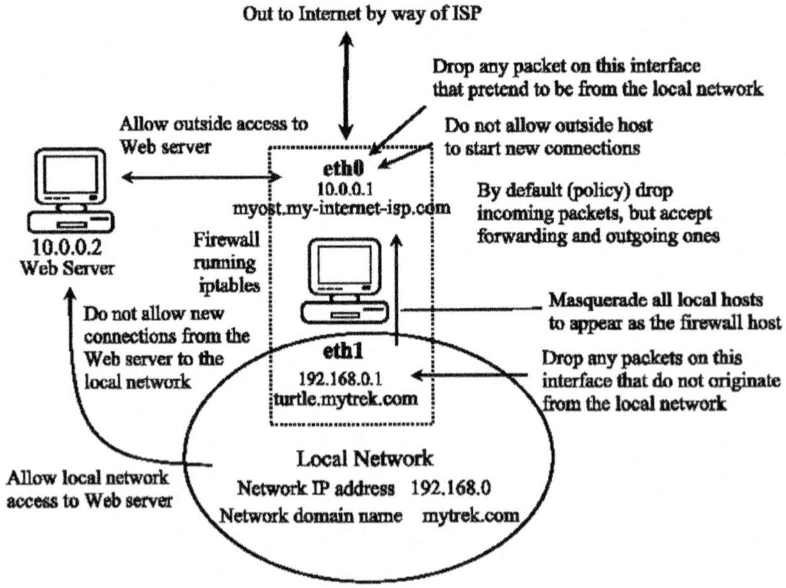

Figure 17-8: Firewall rules applied to a local network example

The script configures a simple firewall for a private network. In this configuration, all remote access initiated from the outside is blocked, but two-way communication is allowed for connections that users in the network make with outside systems. In this example, the firewall system functions as a gateway for a private network whose network address is 192.168.0.0 (see Figure 17-7). The Internet address is, for the sake of this example, 10.0.0.1. The system has two Ethernet devices: one for the private network (**eth1**) and one for the Internet (**eth0**). The gateway firewall system also supports a Web server at address 10.0.0.2. Entries in this example that are too large to fit on one line are continued on a second line, with the newline quoted with a backslash. The basic rules as they apply to different parts of the network are illustrated in Figure 17-8.

Initially, in the script you would clear your current IPtables with the flush option (-F), and then set the policies (default targets) for the non-user-defined rules. IP forwarding should also be turned off while the chain rules are being set:

```
echo 0 > /proc/sys/net/ipv4/ip_forward
```

Drop Policy

First, a DROP policy is set up for INPUT and FORWARD built-in IP chains. This means that if a packet does not meet a criterion in any of the rules to let it pass, it will be dropped. Then both IP spoofing attacks and any attempts from the outside to initiate connections (SYN packets) are rejected.

Outside connection attempts are also logged. This is a very basic configuration that can easily be refined to your own needs by adding IPtables rules.

```
iptables -P INPUT DROP
iptables -P OUTPUT ACCEPT
iptables -P FORWARD ACCEPT
```

IP Spoofing

One way to protect the private network from the IP spoofing of any packets is to check for any outside addresses on the Ethernet device dedicated to the private network. In this example, any packet on device **eth1** (dedicated to the private network) whose source address is not that of the private network (! -s 192.168.0.0) is denied. Also, check to see if any packets coming from the outside are designating the private network as their source. In this example, any packets with the source address of the private network on any Ethernet device other than for the private network (**eth1**) are denied. The same strategy can be applied to the local host.

```
# IP spoofing, deny any packets on the internal network
# that has an external source address.
iptables -A INPUT -j LOG  -i eth1 \! -s 192.168.0.0/24
iptables -A INPUT -j DROP  -i eth1 \! -s 192.168.0.0/24
iptables -A FORWARD -j DROP  -i eth1 \! -s 192.168.0.0/24
# IP spoofing, deny any outside packets (any not on eth1)
# that have the source address of the internal network
iptables -A INPUT -j DROP \! -i eth1 -s 192.168.0.0/24
iptables -A FORWARD -j DROP \! -i eth1 -s 192.168.0.0/24
# IP spoofing, deny any outside packets with localhost address
# (packets not on the lo interface (any on eth0 or eth1)
# that have the source address of localhost)
iptables -A INPUT -j DROP  -i \! lo  -s  127.0.0.0/255.0.0.0
iptables -A FORWARD -j DROP  -i \! lo  -s  127.0.0.0/255.0.0.0
```

Then, you would set up rules to allow all packets sent and received within your system (localhost) to pass.

```
iptables -A INPUT -j ACCEPT  -i lo
```

Server Access

For the Web server, you want to allow access by outside users but block access by anyone attempting to initiate a connection from the Web server into the private network. In the next example, all messages are accepted to the Web server, but the Web server cannot initiate contact with the private network. This prevents anyone from breaking into the local network through the Web server, which is open to outside access. Established connections are allowed, permitting the private network to use the Web server.

```
# allow  communication to the Web server (address 10.0.0.2), port www
iptables -A INPUT  -j ACCEPT -p tcp -i eth0  --dport www -s 10.0.0.2
# Allow  established connections from Web servers to internal network
iptables -A INPUT -m state --state ESTABLISHED,RELATED -i eth0 \
   -p tcp  --sport www -s 10.0.0.2 -d 192.168.0.0/24  -j ACCEPT
# Prevent new  connections from Web servers to internal network
iptables -A OUTPUT -m state --state  NEW -o eth0 -p tcp \
  --sport www -d 192.168.0.1.0/24  -j DROP
```

Firewall Outside Access

To allow access by the firewall to outside networks, you allow input by all packets except for ICMP packets. These are handled later. The firewall is specified by the firewall device, **eth0**. First, your firewall should allow established and related connections to proceed, as shown here. Then you would block outside access as described later.

```
# allow outside communication to the firewall,
# except for ICMP packets
iptables -A INPUT -m state --state ESTABLISHED,RELATED \
        -i eth0 -p \! icmp -j ACCEPT
```

Blocking Outside Initiated Access

To prevent outsiders from initiating any access to your system, create a rule to block access by SYN packets from the outside using the state option with NEW. Drop any new connections on the **eth0** connection (assumes only **eth0** is connected to the Internet or outside network).

```
# prevent outside initiated connections
iptables -A INPUT -m state --state NEW -i eth0 -j DROP
iptables -A FORWARD -m state --state NEW -i eth0 -j DROP
```

Local Network Access

To allow interaction by the internal network with the firewall, you allow input by all packets on the internal Ethernet connection, **eth1**. The valid internal network addresses are designated as the input source.

```
iptables -A INPUT -j ACCEPT -p all -i eth1 -s 192.168.0.0/24
```

Listing Rules

A listing of these **iptables** options shows the different rules for each option, as shown here:

```
$ iptables -L
Chain INPUT (policy DROP)
target   prot opt source           destination
LOG      all  -- !192.168.0.0/24  anywhere         LOG level warning
DROP     all  -- !192.168.0.0/24  anywhere
DROP     all  --  192.168.0.0/24  anywhere
DROP     all  --  127.0.0.0/8     anywhere
ACCEPT   all  --  anywhere         anywhere
ACCEPT   tcp  --  10.0.0.2         anywhere         tcp dpt:http
ACCEPT   tcp  --  10.0.0.2         192.168.0.0/24  state RELATED,ESTABLISHED tcp spt:http
ACCEPT  !icmp --  anywhere         anywhere         state RELATED,ESTABLISHED
DROP     all  --  anywhere         anywhere         state NEW
ACCEPT   all  --  192.168.0.0/24  anywhere
ACCEPT   icmp --  anywhere         10.0.0.1         icmp echo-reply
ACCEPT   icmp --  anywhere         10.0.0.1         icmp echo-request
ACCEPT   icmp --  anywhere         10.0.0.1         icmp destination-unreachable
Chain FORWARD (policy ACCEPT)
target   prot opt source           destination
DROP     all  -- !192.168.0.0/24  anywhere
DROP     all  --  192.168.0.0/24  anywhere
DROP     all  --  127.0.0.0/8     anywhere
```

```
DROP       all  --  anywhere          anywhere          state NEW

Chain OUTPUT (policy ACCEPT)
target    prot opt source             destination
DROP        tcp  --  anywhere          192.168.0.0/24  state NEW tcp spt:http
```

```
$ iptables -t nat -L
Chain PREROUTING (policy ACCEPT)
target      prot opt source       destination
Chain POSTROUTING (policy ACCEPT)
target      prot opt source       destination
MASQUERADE  all  --  anywhere      anywhere
Chain OUTPUT (policy ACCEPT)
target     prot opt source       destination
```

User-Defined Rules

For more complex rules, you may want to create your own chain to reduce repetition. A common method is to define a user chain for both INPUT and FORWARD chains, so that you do not have to repeat DROP operations for each. Instead, you would have only one user chain that both FORWARD and INPUT chains would feed into for DROP operations. Keep in mind that both FORWARD and INPUT operations may have separate rules in addition to the ones they share. In the next example, a user-defined chain called arriving is created. The chain is defined with the -N option at the top of the script:

```
iptables -N arriving
```

A user chain has to be defined before it can be used as a target in other rules. So, you have to first define and add all the rules for that chain, and then use it as a target. The arriving chain is first defined and its rules added. Then, at the end of the file, it is used as a target for both the INPUT and FORWARD chains. The INPUT chain lists rules for accepting packets, whereas the FORWARD chain has an ACCEPT policy that will accept them by default.

```
iptables -N arriving
iptables -F arriving
# IP spoofing, deny any packets on the internal network
# that has an external source address.
iptables -A arriving -j LOG  -i eth1 \! -s 192.168.0.0/24
iptables -A arriving -j DROP  -i eth1 \! -s 192.168.0.0/24
iptables -A arriving -j DROP \! -i eth1 -s 192.168.0.0/24
......................
# entries at end of script
iptables -A INPUT -j arriving
iptables -A FORWARD -j arriving
```

A listing of the corresponding rules is shown here:

```
Chain INPUT (policy DROP)
target    prot opt source          destination
arriving  all  --  0.0.0.0/0        0.0.0.0/0
Chain FORWARD (policy ACCEPT)
target    prot opt source          destination
arriving  all  --  0.0.0.0/0        0.0.0.0/0
Chain arriving (2 references)
target    prot opt source          destination
LOG       all  -- !192.168.0.0/24   0.0.0.0/0        LOG flags 0 level 4
DROP      all  -- !192.168.0.0/24   0.0.0.0/0
DROP      all  --  192.168.0.0/24   0.0.0.0/0
```

For rules where chains may differ, you will still need to enter separate rules. In the **myfilter** script, the FORWARD chain has an ACCEPT policy, allowing all forwarded packets to the local network to pass through the firewall. If the FORWARD chain had a DROP policy, like the INPUT chain, then you may need to define separate rules under which the FORWARD chain could accept packets. In this example, the FORWARD and INPUT chains have different rules for accepting packets on the **eth1** device. The INPUT rule is more restrictive. To enable the local network to receive forwarded packets through the firewall, you could enable forwarding on its device using a separate FORWARD rule, as shown here:

```
iptables -A FORWARD -j ACCEPT -p all -i eth1
```

The INPUT chain would accept packets only from the local network.

```
iptables -A INPUT -j ACCEPT -p all -i eth1 -s 192.168.0.0/24
```

Masquerading Local Networks

To implement masquerading, where systems on the private network can use the gateway's Internet address to connect to Internet hosts, you create a NAT table (-t nat) POSTROUTING rule with a MASQUERADE target.

```
iptables -t nat -A POSTROUTING -o eth0 -j MASQUERADE
```

Controlling ICMP Packets

In addition, to allow ping and destination-reachable ICMP packets, you enter INPUT rules with the firewall as the destination. To enable ping operations, you use both echo-reply and echo-request ICMP types, and for destination unreachable, you use the destination-unreachable type.

```
iptables -A INPUT -j ACCEPT  -p icmp -i eth0 --icmp-type echo-reply -d 10.0.0.1
iptables -A INPUT -j ACCEPT  -p icmp -i eth0 --icmp-type echo-request -d 10.0.0.1
iptables -A INPUT -j ACCEPT -p icmp -i eth0 --icmp-type destination-unreachable -d 10.0.0.1
```

At the end, IP forwarding is turned on again.

```
echo 1 > /proc/sys/net/ipv4/ip_forward
```

Simple LAN Configuration

To create a script to support a simple LAN without any Internet services like Web servers, you would not include rules for supporting those services. You would still need FORWARD and POSTROUTING rules for connecting your local hosts to the Internet, as well as rules governing interaction between the hosts and the firewall. To modify the example script to support a simple LAN without the Web server, remove the three rules governing the Web server. Leave everything else the same.

LAN Configuration with Internet Services on the Firewall System

Often, the same system that runs a firewall is also used to run Internet servers, like Web and FTP servers. In this case the firewall rules are applied to the ports used for those services. The example script dealt with a Web server running on a separate host system. If the Web server were, instead, running on the firewall system, you would apply the Web server firewall rules to the port that the Web server uses. Normally the port used for a Web server is 80. In the following example, the IPtables rules for the Web server have been applied to port www, port 80, on the firewall system. The modification simply requires removing the old Web server host address references, 10.0.0.2.

```
# allow  communication to the Web server, port www (port 80)
iptables -A INPUT  -j ACCEPT -p tcp -i eth0  --dport www
# Allow  established connections from Web servers to internal network
iptables -A INPUT -m state --state ESTABLISHED,RELATED -i eth0 \
   -p tcp  --sport www -d 192.168.0.0/24  -j ACCEPT
# Prevent new  connections from Web servers to internal network
iptables -A OUTPUT -m state --state  NEW -o eth0 -p tcp \
  --sport www -d 192.168.0.1.0/24 -j DROP
```

Similar entries could be set up for an FTP server. Should you run several Internet services, you could use a user-defined rule to run the same rules on each service, rather than repeating three separate rules per service. Working from the example script, you would use two defined rules, one for INPUT and one for OUTPUT, controlling incoming and outgoing packets for the services.

```
iptables -N inputservice
iptables -N outputservice
iptables -F inputservice
iptables -F outputservice

# allow  communication to the service
iptables -A inputservice  -j ACCEPT -p tcp -i eth0
# Allow  established connections from the service to internal network
iptables -A inputservice -m state --state ESTABLISHED,RELATED -i eth0 \
   -p tcp  -d 192.168.0.0/24  -j ACCEPT
# Prevent new  connections from service to internal network
iptables -A outputservice -m state --state  NEW -o eth0 -p tcp \
  -d 192.168.0.1.0/24 -j DROP
.....................
# Run rules for the Web server, port www (port 80)
iptables -A INPUT  --dport www -j inputservice
iptables -A INPUT  --dport www -j outputservice
# Run rules for the FTP server, port ftp (port 21)
iptables -A OUTPUT  --dport ftp -j inputservice
iptables -A OUTPUT  --dport ftp -j outputservice
```

IP Masquerading

On Linux systems, you can set up a network in which you can have one connection to the Internet that several systems on your network can use. This way, using only one IP address, several different systems can connect to the Internet. This method is called *IP masquerading,* where a system masquerades as another system, using that system's IP address. In such a network, one system is connected to the Internet with its own IP address, while the other systems are connected on a local area network (LAN) to this system. When a local system wants to access the network, it masquerades as the Internet-connected system, borrowing its IP address.

IP masquerading is implemented on Linux using the IPtables firewall tool. In effect, you set up a firewall, which you then configure to do IP masquerading. Currently, IP masquerading supports all the common network services—as does IPtables firewall—such as Web browsing, Telnet, and ping. Other services, such as IRC, FTP, and RealAudio, require the use of certain modules. Any services you want local systems to access must also be on the firewall system because request and response actually are handled by services on that system.

With IP masquerading, as implemented on Linux systems, the machine with the Internet address is also the firewall and gateway for the LAN of machines that use the firewall's Internet address to connect to the Internet. Firewalls that also implement IP masquerading are sometimes referred to as *MASQ gates.* With IP masquerading, the Internet-connected system (the firewall) listens for Internet requests from hosts on its LAN. When it receives one, it replaces the requesting local host's IP address with the Internet IP address of the firewall and then passes the request out to the Internet, as if the request were its own. Replies from the Internet are then sent to the firewall system. The replies the firewall receives are addressed to the firewall using its Internet address. The firewall then determines the local system to whose request the reply is responding. It then strips off its IP address and sends the response on to the local host across the LAN. The connection is transparent from the perspective of the local machines. They appear to be connected directly to the Internet.

Masquerading Local Networks

IP masquerading is often used to allow machines on a private network to access the Internet. These could be machines in a home network or a small LAN, such as for a small business. Such a network might have only one machine with Internet access, and as such, only the one Internet address. The local private network would have IP addresses chosen from the private network allocations (10., 172.16., or 192.168.). Ideally, the firewall has two Ethernet cards: one for an interface to the LAN (for example, **eth1**) and one for an interface to the Internet, such as **eth0**. The card for the Internet connection (**eth0**) would be assigned the Internet IP address. The Ethernet interface for the local network (**eth1**, in this example) is the firewall Ethernet interface. Your private LAN would have a network address like 192.168.0. Its Ethernet firewall interface (**eth1**) would be assigned the IP address 192.168.0.1. In effect, the firewall interface lets the firewall operate as the local network's gateway. The firewall is then configured to masquerade any packets coming from the private network. Your LAN needs to have its own domain name server, identifying the machines on your network, including your firewall. Each local machine needs to have the firewall specified as its gateway. Use separate interfaces for them, such as two Ethernet cards.

Masquerading NAT Rules

In Netfilter, IP masquerading is a NAT operation and is not integrated with packet filtering as in IP Chains. IP masquerading commands are placed on the NAT table and treated separately from the packet-filtering commands. Use IPtables to place a masquerade rule on the NAT table. First reference the NAT table with the -t nat option. Then add a rule to the POSTROUTING chain with the -o option specifying the output device and the -j option with the MASQUERADE command.

```
iptables -t nat -A POSTROUTING -o eth0 -j MASQUERADE
```

IP Forwarding

The next step is to turn on IP forwarding, either manually or by setting the **`net.ipv4.ip_forward`** variable in the **/etc/sysctl.conf** file and running **`sysctl`** with the **`-p`** option. IP forwarding will be turned off by default. For IPv6, use **`net.ipv6.conf.all.forwarding`**. The **/etc/sysctl.conf** entries are shown here:

```
net.ipv4.ip_forward = 1
net.ipv6.conf.all.forwarding = 1
```

You then run sysctl with the -p option.

```
sysctl -p
```

You can directly change the respective forwarding files with an **`echo`** command as shown here:

```
echo 1 > /proc/sys/net/ipv4/ip_forward
```

For IPv6, you would to use the forwarding file in the corresponding **/proc/sys/net/ipv6** directory, **conf/all/forwarding**.

```
echo 1 > /proc/sys/net/ipv6/conf/all/forwarding
```

Masquerading Selected Hosts

Instead of masquerading all local hosts as the single IP address of the firewall/gateway host, you could use the NAT table to rewrite addresses for a few selected hosts. Such an approach is often applied to setups where you want several local hosts to appear as Internet servers. Using the DNAT and SNAT targets, you can direct packets to specific local hosts. You would use rules on the PREROUTING and POSTROUTING chains to direct input and output packets.

For example, the Web server described in the previous example could have been configured as a local host to which a DNAT target could redirect any packets originally received for 10.0.0.2. Say the Web server was set up on 192.168.0.5. It could appear as having the address 10.0.0.2 on the Internet. Packets sent to 10.0.0.2 would be rewritten and directed to 192.168.0.5 by the NAT table. You would use the PREROUTING chain with the -d option to handle incoming packets and POSTROUTING with the -s option for outgoing packets.

```
iptables -t nat -A PREROUTING -d 10.0.0.2 --to-destination 192.168.0.5 -j DNAT
iptables -t nat -A POSTROUTING -s 192.168.0.5 --to-source 10.0.0.2 -j SNAT
```

Tip: Masquerading is not combined with the FORWARD chain. If you specify a DROP policy for the FORWARD chain, you will also have to specifically enable

FORWARD operation for the network that is being masqueraded. You will need both a POSTROUTING rule and a FORWARD rule.

Dynamic Firewall with FirewallD

FirewallD runs as a daemon implementing a dynamic firewall. Instead of loading rules offline from file, you add them directly to the FirewallD daemon. FirewallD is no supported by Ubuntu, but is available on the Ubuntu repository. It is the default firewall for Fedora and Suse Linux. For documentation see:

`http://fedoraproject.org/wiki/FirewallD`

FirewallD Zones

FirewallD sets up network zones to define the level of trust for different kinds of network connections (see Table 17-9). Each zone can have several connections, but a connection can belong only to one zone. FirewallD defines several zones, most of which you can change (mutable). The drop and block zones are immutable and designed to stop all incoming packets. The public, external, and dmz zones are designed for untrusted networks, exposing only part of your system. The work, home, and internal zone are used for trusted networks. The trusted zone (also immutable) allows all network connections.

Zone	Description
drop (immutable)	Deny all incoming connections, outgoing ones are accepted.
block (immutable)	Deny all incoming connections, with ICMP host prohibited messages issued.
trusted (immutable)	Allow all network connections
public	Public areas, do not trust other computers
external	For computers with masquerading enabled, protecting a local network
dmz	For computers publicly accessible with restricted access.
work	For trusted work areas
home	For trusted home network connections
internal	For internal network, restrict incoming connections

Table 17-9: FirewallD zones

Zone configurations are located in **/etc/firewalld/zones**. You can use **firewall-config** or **firewall-cmd** to manage your zones and add new ones. The default zone is set in the **/etc/firewalld.conf** configuration files by the DefaultZone variable. Initially it is set to public. The default and fallback zones are saved in **/lib/firewalld/zones**.

Zone files are saved a XML files which list the zone name and the services and ports allowed. Also any masquerade, ICMP, and port forwarding options.

Dynamic and Static Firewalls: FirewallD and the iptables command

Traditionally firewalls were static. You modified firewall rules and then restarted your firewall to load the rules. A dynamic firewall, such as FirewallD, can apply modified rules without restarting the firewall. Rules, however, have to be managed directly by the FirewallD daemon. You cannot use the **iptables** command to add firewall rules for the firewalld daemon. In fact, FirewallD does not user netfilter rules in the traditional sense. You do not list a set of rules that the firewall then reads, as you do with static firewalls like iptables. Instead, you use to **firewall-config** and **firewall-cmd** tools to directly configure your firewall.

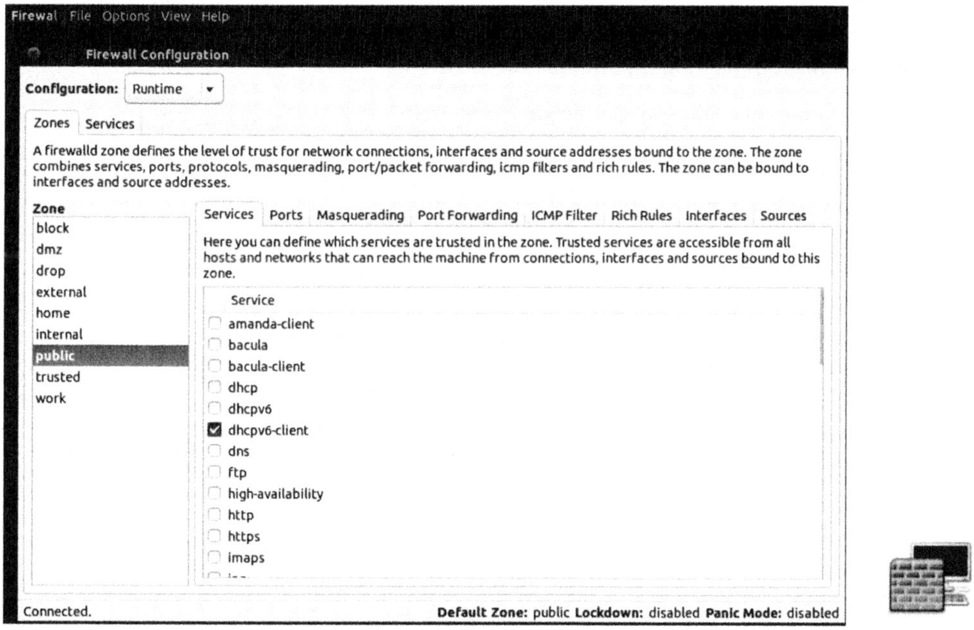

Figure 17-9: firewall-config: Runtime Configuration

Though not supported by Ubuntu directly, you can use the FirewallD dynamic firewall daemon to set up a firewall. You can disable and enable FirewallD manually using the **systemctl** command.

```
sudo systemctl enable firewalld
sudo systemctl disable firewalld
```

On Ubuntu, FirewallD is managed by the **firewalld** service script. You can start and stop it using the **service** command. You will have to start the FirewallD daemon in a terminal window with the following command.

```
sudo service firewalld start
```

You can stop it with a stop command.

```
sudo service firewalld stop
```

firewall-config

On the desktop, you can use the **firewalld-config** to configure Firewalld. You can also use **firewalld-cmd** command from the command line. To set up your firewall, run firewall-config (System | Firewall) (see Figure 17-9). The top button bar has a button to Reload your saved firewall.

With firewall-config you can configure either a Runtime or Permanent Configuration. Select one from the Configuration menu. The Runtime Configuration shows your current runtime set up, whereas a Permanent configuration does not take effect until you reload or restart. If you wish to edit your zones and services you need to choose the Permanent Configuration (see Figure 17-7). This view displays a zone toolbar for editing zone at the bottom of the zone scroll box, and an Edit button on the Services tab for editing service protocols, ports, and destination addresses.

Additional tabs can be displayed from the View menu for configuring ICMP types, and for adding firewall rules directly (Direct Configuration).

From the Options menu you can reload your saved firewall.

A firewall configuration is set up for a given zone, such as a home, work, internal, external, or public zone. Each zone can have its own configuration. Zones are listed in the Zone scroll box on the left side of the firewall-config window (see Figure 17-10). Select the one you want to configure. The firewall-config window opens to the default, Public. You can choose the default zone from the System Default Zone dialog (see Figure 17-11), which you open from the Options menu as "Change Default Zone."

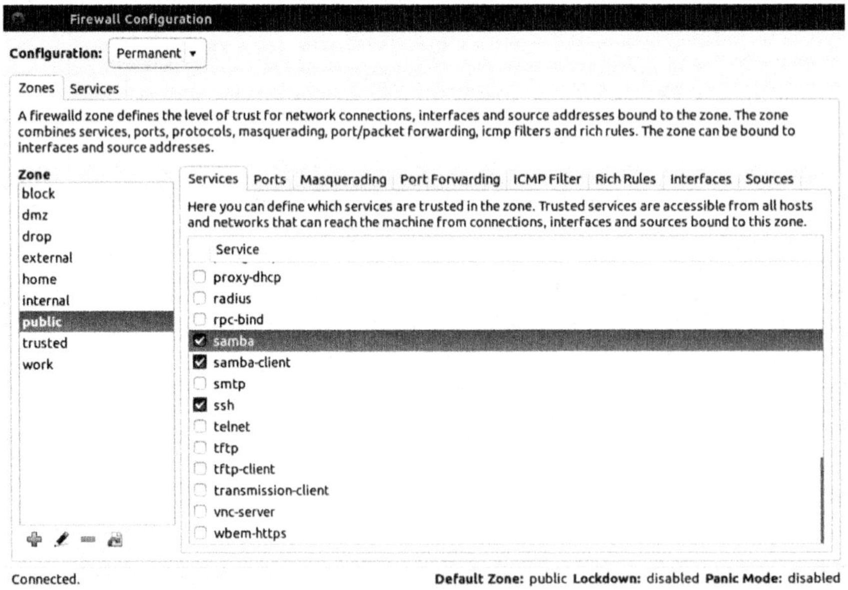

Figure 17-10: firewall-config: Permanent Configuration

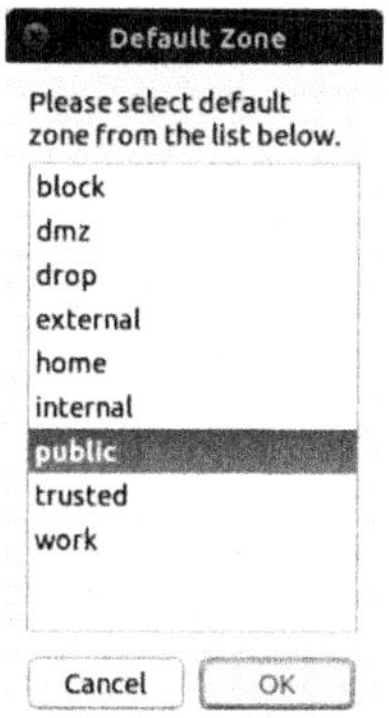

Figure 17-11: Default Zone

If you choose Permanent Configuration from the Current View Menu, a tool bar for zones is displayed below the Zone scroll box, as shown here. The plus button lets you add a zone, minus removes a zone. The pencil button lets you edit a zone. The add and edit buttons open the Base Zone Settings dialog, where you enter or edit the zone name, version, description, and the target (see Figure 17-12). The default target is ACCEPT. Other options are REJECT and DROP. The Load Zone Defaults button (yellow arrow) loads default settings, removing any you have made.

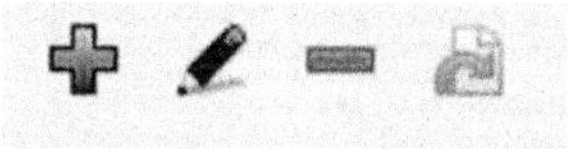

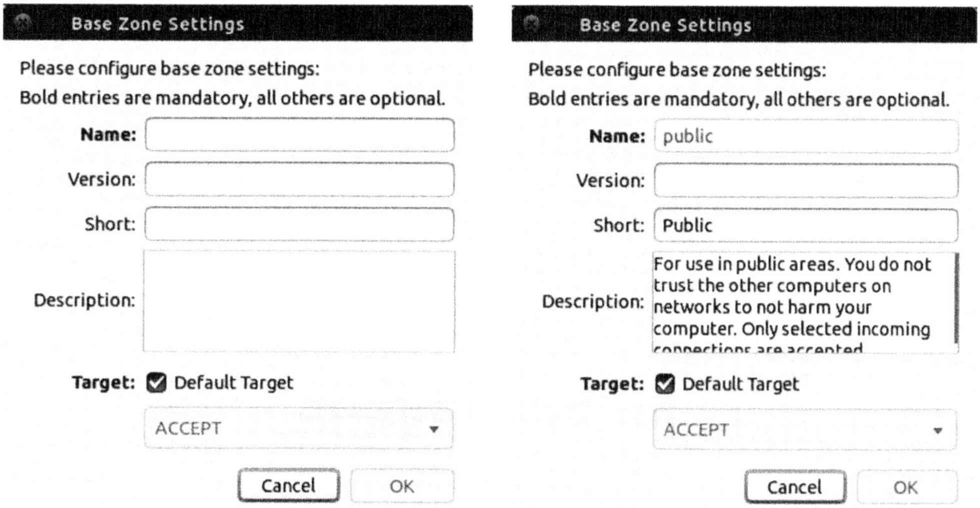

Figure 17-12: Base Zone Settings

Each zone, in turn, can have one or more network connections. From the Options menu choose "Change Zones of Connections" to open the Network Connections dialog where you can add a network connection.

For a given zone you can configure services, ports, masquerading, port forwarding, and ICMP filter (see Figure 17-8). A Linux system is often used to run servers for a network. If you are creating a strong firewall but still want to run a service such as a Web server, an FTP server, Samba desktop browsing, or SSH encrypted connections, you must specify them in the Services tab. Samba desktop browsing lets you access your Samba shares, like remote Windows file systems, from your GNOME or KDE desktops.

For a selected service, you can specify service settings such as ports and protocols it uses, any modules, and specific network addresses. Default settings are already set up for you such as port 139 for Samba, using the TCP protocol. To modify the settings for service, click the Services tab to open the Service Settings window (see Figure 17-13). Choose the service you want to edit from the Service scroll box at the left. For a given service you can then use the Ports and Protocols, Modules, and Destination tabs to specify ports, protocols, modules, and addresses. On the Ports and Protocols tab click the Add button to open the Port and/or Protocol dialog where you can add a port or port range, and choose a protocol from the Protocol menu (see Figure 17-14). On the Destination tab you can enter an IPv4 or IPv6 destination address for the service.

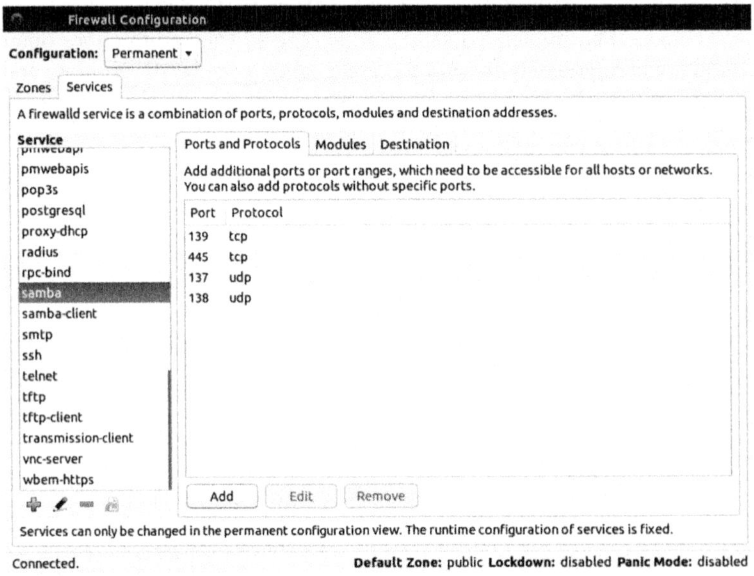

Figure 17-13: Service Settings

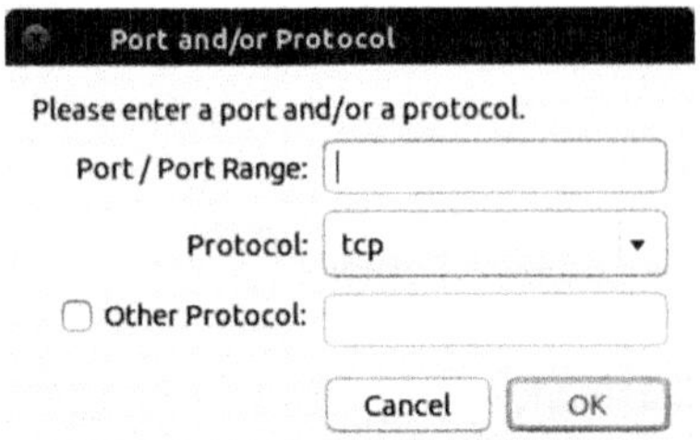

Figure 17-14: Service Protocols and Ports

The Ports tab lets you specify ports that you may want opened for certain services, like BitTorrent. Click the Add button to open a dialog where you can select the port number along with the protocol to control (tcp or udp), or enter a specific port number or range.

If your system is being used as gateway to the Internet for your local network, you can implement masquerading to hide your local hosts from outside access from the Internet. This, though, also requires IP forwarding which is automatically enabled when you choose masquerading. Local hosts will still be able to access the Internet, but they will masquerade as your gateway system. You would select for masquerading the interface that is connected to the Internet. Masquerading is available only for IPv4 networks, not IPv6 networks.

The Port Forwarding tab lets you set up port forwarding, channeling transmissions from one port to another, or to a different port on another system. Click the Add button to add a port, specifying its protocol and destination (see Figure 17-15).

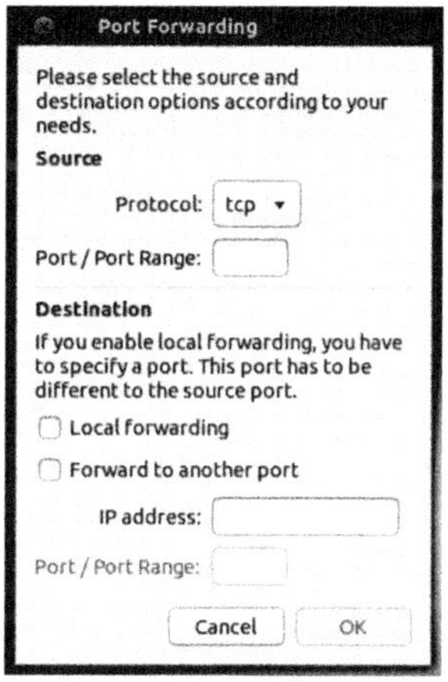

Figure 17-15: Port Forwarding

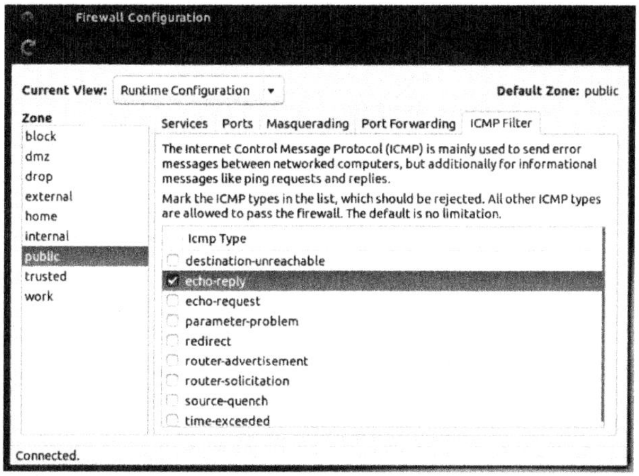

Figure 17-16: ICMP Filters

The ICMP Filters tab allows you to block ICMP messages. By default all ICMP messages are allowed. Blocking ICMP messages makes for a more secure system. Certain types of ICMP messages are often blocked as they can be used to infiltrate or overload a system, such as the ping and pong ICMP messages (see Figure 17-16).

If you have specific firewall rules to add, use the Direct Configuration tab (displayed from the View | Direct Configuration menu).

firewall-cmd

The firewall-cmd command works on a command line interface, using options to set features for different zone. Zone modification options such as **--add-service**, can be either runtime or permanent. Runtime changes are gone after a restart or reload. To make the changes permanent you add the **--permanent** option, making changes for a persistent configuration, instead of a runtime one.

Use the get options to display information about the firewall. The **--get-zones** option lists your zones, the **--get-services** option list services supported by the current zone, and the **--get-icmptypes** lists the ICMP types.

```
firewall-cmd --get-zones
firewall-cmd --get-services
firewall-cmd --get-icmptypes
```

The **--get-default-zone** option lists the default zone, and **--set-default-zone** sets up a new default zone.

```
firewall-cmd --set-default-zone  home
```

To find out what features have been enabled for a zone, use the **--list-all** option with a **--zone=** option to specify the zone.

```
firewall-cmd home --zone=home  --list-all
```

Zone are assigned network interfaces. There are interface options to add, remove, or change an interface. Use the query option to check if an interface belongs to a zone.

```
firewall-cmd --zone=home  --query-interface=eth0
```

The service, port, masquerade, icmp, and forwarding options can be either runtime or persistent (permanent). The **--service** options can add and remove services to a zone.

```
firewall-cmd -add-service=vsftp
```

To make the change permanent (persistent mode), add the **--permanent** option.

```
firewall-cmd --permanent -add-service=vsftp
```

The **--query-service** option checks to see if a service is enabled for a zone.

```
firewall-cmd --zone=home -query-service=http
```

The **--port** options are used to add, remove, or query ports.

```
firwall-cmd --zone=home --add-port=22
```

Add the **--permanent** option to make it permanent.

```
firwall-cmd --permanent --zone=home --add-port=22
```

The **--masquerade** option add, removes, and queries zones for masquerading.

```
firwall-cmd --zone=work --add-masquerade
```

The **--icmp-block** options add, remove, and query ICMP types.

```
firewall-cmd --zone=work --add-icmp-block=echo-reply
```

Should your firewall needs to use custom firewall rules, you can add, remove, and list them using the **--direct** option. These are rules written in the IPtables syntax. You have to specify the protocol, table, chain, and arguments. The following lists the rules you added to the netfilter table. The rules are not saved, and have to be added again each time you restart or reload. You could have a script of firewall-cmd rules to do this.

```
firewall-cmd --direct --get-rules ipv4 netfilter
```

The following adds a simple netfilter rule.

```
Firewall-cmd --direct -add-rule ipv4 netfilter INPUT  Deny
```

ubuntu

18. Administering TCP/IP Networks

TCP/IP Protocol Suite

IPv4 and IPv6

TCP/IP Network Addresses

IPv6 Addressing

IPv6 and IPv4 Coexistence Methods

TCP/IP Configuration Files

Domain Name Service (DNS)

Network Interfaces and Routes: ifconfig and route

Monitoring Your Network

Wireshark

Network Tools

Linux systems are configured to connect with networks that use the TCP/IP protocols. These are the same protocols used by the Internet and many local area networks (LANs). TCP/IP is a robust set of protocols designed to provide communications among systems with different operating systems and hardware. The TCP/IP protocols were developed in the 1970s as a special project of the Defense Advanced Research Projects Agency (DARPA) to enhance communications between universities and research centers. These protocols were originally developed on UNIX systems, with much of the research carried out at the University of California, Berkeley.

Linux, as a version of UNIX, benefits from much of this original focus on UNIX. Currently, the TCP/IP protocol development is managed by the Internet Engineering Task Force (IETF), which, in turn, is supervised by the Internet Society (ISOC). The ISOC oversees several groups responsible for different areas of Internet development, such as the Internet Assigned Numbers Authority (IANA), which is responsible for Internet addressing (see Table 18-1). Over the years, TCP/IP protocol standards and documentation have been issued in the form of Request for Comments (RFC) documents. Check the most recent RFCs for current developments at the IETF Web site at **http://www.ietf.org**.

TCP/IP Protocol Suite

The TCP/IP protocol suite consists of several different protocols, each designed for a specific task in a TCP/IP network. The three basic protocols are the Transmission Control Protocol (TCP), which handles receiving and sending out communications, the Internet Protocol (IP), which handles the actual transmissions, and the User Datagram Protocol (UDP), which also handles receiving and sending packets. The Internet Protocol (IP), which is the base protocol that all others use, handles the actual transmissions, handling the packets of data with sender and receiver information in each. The TCP protocol is designed to work with cohesive messages or data. This protocol checks received packets and sorts them into their designated order, forming the original message. For data sent out, the TCP protocol breaks the data into separate packets, designating their order. The UDP protocol, meant to work on a much more raw level, also breaks down data into packets but does not check their order. The TCP/IP protocol is designed to provide stable and reliable connections that ensure that all data is received and reorganized into its original order. UDP, on the other hand, is designed simply to send as much data as possible, with no guarantee that packets will all be received or placed in the proper order. UDP is often used for transmitting very large amounts of data of the type that can survive the loss of a few packets, for example, temporary images, video, and banners displayed on the Internet.

Other protocols provide various network and user services. The Domain Name Service (DNS) provides address resolution, the File Transfer Protocol (FTP) provides file transmission, and the Network File System (NFS) provides access to remote file systems. Table 18-2 lists the protocols in the TCP/IP suite. These protocols make use of either TCP or UDP to send and receive packets, which in turn uses the IP protocol for transmitting the packets.

In a TCP/IP network, messages are broken into small components, called datagrams, which are then transmitted through various interlocking routes and delivered to their destination computers. Once received, the datagrams are reassembled into the original message. Datagrams themselves can be broken down into smaller packets. The packet is the physical message unit actually transmitted among networks. Sending messages as small components has proven to be far more reliable and faster than sending them as one large, bulky transmission. With small components, if one is lost or damaged, only that component must be resent, whereas if any part of a large transmission is corrupted or lost, the entire message has to be resent.

Group	Title	Description
ISOC	Internet Society	Professional membership organization of Internet experts that oversees boards and task forces dealing with network policy issues **www.isoc.org**
IESG	The Internet Engineering Steering Group	Responsible for technical management of IETF activities and the Internet standards process **www.ietf.org/iesg.html**
IANA	Internet Assigned Numbers Authority	Responsible for Internet Protocol (IP) addresses **www.iana.org**
IAB	Internet Architecture Board	Defines the overall architecture of the Internet, providing guidance and broad direction to the IETF **www.iab.org**
IETF	Internet Engineering Task Force	Protocol engineering and development arm of the Internet **www.ietf.org**

Table 18-1: TCP/IP Protocol Development Groups

The configuration of a TCP/IP network on your Linux system is implemented using a set of network configuration files (see Table 18-6). Many of these files can be managed using network tools on your desktop like NetworkManager. You can also use more specialized programs, such as **netstat**, **ifconfig**, Wireshark, and **route**. Some configuration files are easy to modify yourself using a text editor. The **ifconfig** utility enables you to configure your network interfaces, adding new ones and modifying others. The **ifconfig** and **route** utilities are lower-level programs that require more specific knowledge of your network to use effectively. The **netstat** utility provides you with information about the status of your network connections. Wireshark is a network protocol analyzer that lets you capture packets as they are transmitted across your network, selecting those you want to check.

Zero Configuration Networking: Avahi and Link Local Addressing

Zero Configuration Networking (Zeroconf) allows the setup of non-routable private networks without the need of a DHCP server or static IP addresses. A Zeroconf configuration lets users automatically connect to a network and access all network resources, such as printers, without having to perform any configuration. On Linux, Zeroconf networking is implemented by Avahi (**http://avahi.org**), which includes multicast DNS (mDNS) and DNS service discovery (DNS-SD) support that automatically detects services on a network. IP addresses are determined using either IPv6 or IPv4 Link Local (IPv4LL) addressing. IPv4 Link Local addresses are assigned from the 168.254.0.0 network pool. Derived from Apple's Bonjour Zeroconf implementation, it is a free and open source version currently used by desktop tools, such as the GNOME virtual file system. Ubuntu implements full Zeroconf network support with the Avahi daemon that implements multicast DNS discover, and **avahi-autoipd** that provides dynamic configuration of local IPv4 addresses. Both are installed as part of the desktop configuration.

Transport	Description
TCP	Transmission Control Protocol; places systems in direct communication
UDP	User Datagram Protocol
IP	Internet Protocol; transmits data
ICMP	Internet Control Message Protocol; status messages for IP
Routing	**Description**
RIP	Routing Information Protocol; determines routing
OSPF	Open Shortest Path First; determines routing
Network Addresses	**Description**
ARP	Address Resolution Protocol; determines unique IP address of systems
DNS	Domain Name Service; translates hostnames into IP addresses
RARP	Reverse Address Resolution Protocol; determines addresses of systems
User Service	**Description**
FTP	File Transfer Protocol; transmits files from one system to another using TCP
TFTP	Trivial File Transfer Protocol; transfers files using UDP
Telnet	Remote login to another system on the network
SMTP	Simple Mail Transfer Protocol; transfers e-mail between systems
RPC	Remote Procedure Call; allows remote systems to communicate
Gateway	**Description**
EGP	Exterior Gateway Protocol; provides routing for external networks
GGP	Gateway-to-Gateway Protocol; provides routing between gateways
IGP	Interior Gateway Protocol; provides routing for internal networks
Network Service	**Description**
NFS	Network File System; allows mounting of file systems on remote machines
NIS	Network Information Service; maintains user accounts across a network
BOOTP	Boot Protocol; starts system using boot information on server for network
SNMP	Simple Network Management Protocol; provides status messages on TCP/IP configuration
DHCP	Dynamic Host Configuration Protocol; automatically provides network configuration information to host systems

Table 18-2: TCP/IP Protocol Suite

Avahi support tools like **avahi-browse** and **avahi-publish** are located in the **avahi-utils** package. Specialized tools like SSH and Shell tools are located in the **avahi-ui-tools** package. The KDE Zeroconf solution is also provided using Avahi (**kde-zeroconf**).

IPv4 and IPv6

Traditionally, a TCP/IP address is organized into four segments, consisting of numbers separated by periods. This is called the IP address. The IP address actually represents a 32-bit integer whose binary values identify the network and host. This form of IP addressing adheres to Internet Protocol, version 4, also known as IPv4. IPv4, the kind of IP addressing described here, is still in use.

Currently, version 6 of the IP protocol called Internet Protocol, IPv6, is replacing the older IPv4 version. IPv6 expands the number of possible IP addresses by using 128 bits. It is fully compatible with systems still using IPv4. IPv6 addresses are represented differently, using a set of eight 16-bit segments, each separated from the next by a colon. Each segment is represented by a hexadecimal number. A sample address would be:

```
FC00:0:0:0:800:BA98:7654:3210
```

Advantages of IPv6 include the following:

IPv6 features simplified headers that allow for faster processing.

IPv6 provides support for encryption and authentication along with virtual private networks (VPN), using the integrated IPsec protocol.

One of its most significant advantages lies in extending the address space to cover 2 to the power of 128 possible hosts (billions of billions). This extends far beyond the 4.2 billion supported by IPv4.

IPv6 supports stateless autoconfiguration of addresses for hosts, bypassing the need for DHCP to configure such addresses. Addresses can be generated directly using the MAC (Media Access Control) hardware address of an interface.

IPv6 supports Quality of Service (QoS) operations, providing sufficient response times for services like multimedia and telecom tasks.

Multicast capabilities are built into the protocol, providing direct support for multimedia tasks. Multicast addressing also provides that same function as IPv4 broadcast addressing.

More robust transmissions can be ensured with anycast addressing, where packets can be directed to an anycast group of systems, only one of which needs to receive them. Multiple DNS servers supporting a given network could be designated as an anycast group, of which only one DNS server needs to receive the transmission, providing greater likelihood that the transmissions will go through.

IPv6 provides better access for mobile nodes, like PDAs, notebooks, and cell phones.

TCP/IP Network Addresses

The traditional IPv4 TCP/IP address is organized into four segments, consisting of numbers separated by periods. Part of an IP address is used for the network address, and the other part is used to identify a particular interface on a host in that network. You should realize that IP addresses are assigned to interfaces—such as Ethernet cards or modems—and not to the host computer. Usually a computer has only one interface and is accessed using only that interface's IP address. In that regard, an IP address can be thought of as identifying a particular host system on a network, so the IP address is usually referred to as the host address.

In fact, though, a host system could have several interfaces, each with its own IP address. This is the case for computers that operate as gateways and firewalls from a local network to the Internet. One interface usually connects to a local network and another to the Internet using two Ethernet cards. Each interface (such as an Ethernet card) has its own IP address. Other Ethernet cards have their own IP addresses. If you use a modem to connect to an ISP, you would set up a Point-to-Point Protocol (PPP) interface that would also have its own IP address (usually dynamically assigned by the ISP).

IPv4 Network Addresses

The IP address is divided into two parts: one part identifies the network, and the other part identifies a particular host. The network address identifies the network of which a particular interface on a host is a part. Two methods exist for implementing the network and host parts of an IP address: the original class-based IP addressing and the current Classless Interdomain Routing (CIDR) addressing. Class-based IP addressing designates officially predetermined parts of the address for the network and host addresses, whereas CIDR addressing allows the parts to be determined dynamically using a netmask.

Class-Based IP Addressing

Originally, IP addresses were organized according to classes. On the Internet, IPc4 networks are organized into three classes depending on their size—classes A, B, and C. A class A network uses only the first segment for the network address and the remaining three for the host, allowing a great many computers to be connected to the same network. Most IP addresses reference smaller, class C, networks. For a class C network, the first three segments are used to identify the network, and only the last segment identifies the host. Altogether, this forms a unique address with which to identify any network interface on computers in a TCP/IP network. For example, in the IP address 192.168.1.72, the network part is 192.168.1 and the interface/host part is 72. The interface/host is a part of a network whose own address is 192.168.1.0.

In a class C network, the first three numbers identify the network part of the IP address. This part is divided into three network numbers, each identifying a subnet. Networks on the Internet are organized into subnets, beginning with the largest and narrowing to small subnetworks. The last number is used to identify a particular computer, referred to as a *host.* You can think of the Internet as a series of networks with subnetworks; these subnetworks have their own subnetworks. The rightmost number identifies the host computer, and the number preceding it identifies the subnetwork of which the computer is a part. The number to the left of that identifies the network the subnetwork is part of, and so on. The Internet address 192.168.187.4 references the fourth computer connected to the network identified by the number 187. Network 187 is a subnet to a larger network identified as 168. This larger network is itself a subnet of the network identified as 192. Here's how it breaks down:

192.168.187.4	IPv4 address
192.168.187	Network identification
4	Host identification

Netmask

Systems derive the network address from the host address using the netmask. You can think of an IP address as a series of 32 binary bits, some of which are used for the network and the remainder for the host. The *netmask* has the network set of bits set to 1s, with the host bits set to 0s (see Figure 18-1). In a standard class-based IP address, all the numbers in the network part of your host address are set to 255, and the host part is set to 0. This has the effect of setting all the binary bits making up the network address to 1s. This, then, is your netmask. So, the netmask for the host address 192.168.1.72 is 255.255.255.0. The network part, 192.168.1, has been set to 255.255.255, and the host part, 72, has been set to 0. Systems can then use your netmask to derive your network address from your host address. They can determine what part of your host address makes up your network address and what those numbers are.

For those familiar with computer programming, a bitwise AND operation on the netmask and the host address results in zeroing the host part, leaving you with the network part of the host address. You can think of the address as being implemented as a four-byte integer, with each byte corresponding to a segment of the address. In a class C address, the three network segments correspond to the first three bytes, and the host segment corresponds to the fourth byte. A netmask is designed to mask out the host part of the address, leaving the network segments alone. In the netmask for a standard class C network, the first three bytes are all 1s and the last byte consists of 0s. The 0s in the last byte mask out the host part of the address, and the 1s in the first three bytes leave the network part of the address alone. Figure 18-1 shows the bitwise operation of the netmask on the address 192.168.1.4. This is a class C address to the mask, which consists of twenty-four 1s making up the first three bytes and eight 0s making up the last byte. When it is applied to the address 192.168.1.4, the network address remains (192.168.1) and the host address is masked out (4), giving you 192.168.1.0 as the network address.

The netmask as used in Classless Interdomain Routing (CIDR) is much more flexible. Instead of having the size of the network address and its mask determined by the network class, it is determined by a number attached to the end of the IP address. This number simply specifies the size of the network address, how many bits in the address it takes up. For example, in an IP address whose network part takes up the first three bytes (segments), the number of bits used for that network part is 24—eight bits to a byte (segment). Instead of using a netmask to determine the network address, the number for the network size is attached to the end of the address with a slash, as shown here:

```
192.168.1.72/24
```

CIDR gives you the advantage of specifying networks that are any size bits, instead of only three possible segments. You could have a network whose addresses take up 14 bits, 22 bits, or even 25 bits. The host address can use whatever bits are left over. An IP address with 21 bits for the network can cover host addresses using the remaining 11 bits, 0 to 2,047.

Classless Interdomain Routing (CIDR)

The class-based organization of IP addresses is being replaced by the CIDR format. CIDR was designed for midsized networks, those between a class C, and classes with numbers of hosts greater than 256 and smaller than 65,534. A class C network–based IP address uses only one segment, an 8-bit integer, with a maximum value of 256. A class B network–based IP address uses two segments, which make up a 16-bit integer, whose maximum value is 65,534. You can think of an address as a 32-bit integer taking up four bytes, where each byte is 8 bits. Each segment conforms to one of the four bytes. A class C network uses three segments, or 24 bits, to make up its network address. A class B network, in turn, uses two segments, or 16 bits, for its address. With this scheme, allowable host and network addresses are changed an entire byte at a time, segment to segment. With CIDR addressing, you can define host and network addresses by bits, instead of whole segments. For example, you can use CIDR addressing to expand the host segment from 8 bits to 9, rather than having to jump it to a class B 16 bits (two segments).

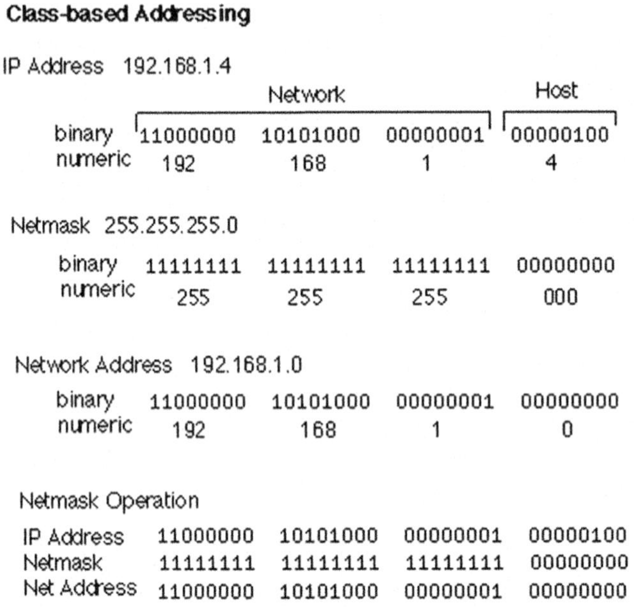

Figure 18-1: Class-based netmask operations

CIDR addressing notation achieves this by incorporating netmask information in the IP address (the netmask is applied to an IP address to determine the network part of the address). In the CIDR notation, the number of bits making up the network address is placed after the IP address, following a slash. For example, the CIDR form of the class C 192.168.187.4 IP address is

```
192.168.187.4/24
```

Figure 18-2 shows an example of a CIDR address and its network mask. The IP address is 192.168.1.6 with a network mask of 22 bits, 192.168.1.6/22. The network address takes up the first 22 bits of the IP address, and the remaining 10 bits are used for the host address. The host address is taking up the equivalent of a class-based IP address's fourth segment (8 bits) and 2 bits from the third segment.

Table 18-3 lists the different IPv4 CIDR network masks available along with the maximum number of hosts. Both the short forms and the full forms of the netmasks are listed.

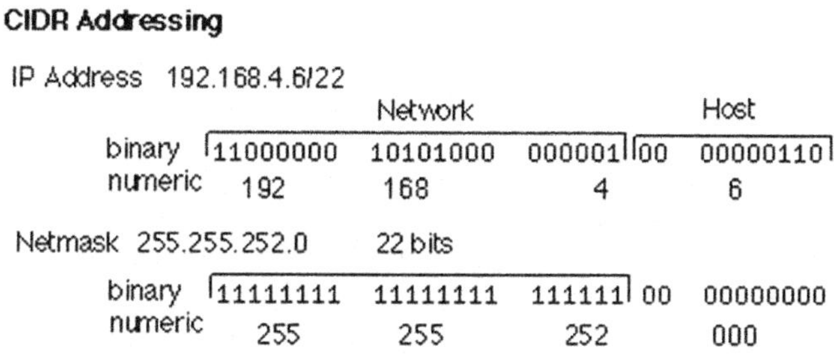

Figure 18-2: CIDR addressing

IPv4 CIDR Addressing

The network address for any standard class C IPv4 IP address takes up the first three segments, 24 bits. If you want to create a network with a maximum of 512 hosts, you can give them IP addresses where the network address is 23 bits and the host address takes up 9 bits (0–511). The IP address notation remains the same, however, using the four 8-bit segments. This means a given segment's number could be used for both a network address and a host address. Segments are no longer wholly part of either the host address or the network address. Assigning a 23-bit network address and a 9-bit host address means that the number in the third segment is part of the network address and the host address - the first 7 bits for the network and the last bit for the host. In this following example, the third number, 145, is used as the end of the network address and as the beginning of the host address:

```
192.168.145.67/23
```

This situation complicates CIDR addressing, and in some cases the only way to represent the address is to specify two or more network addresses. Check RFC 1520 at **www.ietf.org** for more details.

CIDR also allows a network administrator to take what is officially the host part of an IP address, and break it up into subnetworks with fewer hosts. This is referred to as subnetting. A given network will have its official IP network address recognized on the Internet or by a larger network. The network administrator for that network could, in turn, create several smaller networks within it using CIDR network masking. A classic example is to take a standard class C network with 254 hosts and break it up into two smaller networks, each with 64 hosts. You do this by using a CIDR netmask to take a bit from the host part of the IP address and use it for the subnetworks. Numbers within the range of the original 254 addresses whose first bit would be set to 1 would represent one subnet, and the others, whose first bit would be set to 0, would constitute the remaining network. In the network whose network address is 192.168.187.0, where the last segment is used for the hostnames, that last host segment could be further split into two subnets, each with its own hosts. For two subnets, you would use the first bit in the last 8-bit segment for the network. The remaining 7 bits could then be used for host addresses, giving you a range of 127 hosts per network. The subnet whose bit is set to 0 would have a range of 1 to 127, with a CIDR netmask of 25. The 8-bit segment for the first host would be 00000001. So, the host with the address of 1 in that network would have this IP address:

```
192.168.187.1/25
```

For the subnet where the first bit is 1, the first host would have an address of 129, with the CIDR netmask of 25, as shown here. The 8-bit sequence for the first host would be 10000001.

```
192.168.187.129/25
```

Note: A simple way to calculate the number of hosts a network can address is to take the number of bits in its host segment as a power of 2, and then subtract 2—that is, 2 to the number of host bits, minus 2. For example, an 8-bit host segment would be 2 to the power of 8, which equals 256. Subtract 2 (1 for the broadcast address, 255, and 1 for the zero value, 000) to leave you with 254 possible hosts.

Each subnet would have a set of 126 addresses, the first from 1 to 126, and the second from 129 to 254; 127 is the broadcast address for the first subnet, and 128 is the network address for the second subnet. The possible subnets and their masks that you could use are shown here:

Subnetwork	CIDR Address	Binary Mask
First subnet network address	.0/25	00000000
Second subnet network address	.128/25	10000000
First subnet broadcast address	.127/25	01111111
Second subnet broadcast address	.255/25	11111111
First address in first subnet	.1/25	00000001
First address in second subnet	.129/25	10000001
Last address in first subnet	.126/25	01111110
Last address in second subnet	.254/25	11111110

IPv6 CIDR Addressing

IPv6 CIDR addressing works much the same as with the IPv4 method. The number of bits used for the network information is indicated by number following the address. A host (interface) address could take up much more than the 64 bits that it usually does in an IPv6 address, making the network prefix (address) section smaller than 64 bits. How many bits that the network prefix uses is indicated by the following number. In the next example the network prefix (address) uses only the first 48 bits of the IPv6 address, and the host address uses the remaining 80 bits:

```
FC00:0000:0000:0000:FEDC:BA98:7654:3210/48
```

You can also use a two-colon notation (::) for the compressed version:

```
FC00::FEDC:BA98:7654:3210/48
```

Though you can use CIDR to subnet addresses, IPv6 also supports a subnet field that can be used for subnets.

Obtaining an IP Address

IP addresses are officially allocated by IANA, which manages all aspects of Internet addressing (**www.iana.org**). IANA oversees Internet Registries, which, in turn, maintain Internet addresses on regional and local levels. The Internet Registry for the Americas is the American Registry for Internet Numbers (ARIN), whose Web site is at **https://www.arin.net**. These addresses are provided to users by Internet service providers (ISPs). You can obtain your own Internet address from an ISP, or if you are on a network already connected to the Internet, your network administrator can assign you one. If you are using an ISP, the ISP may temporarily assign one from a pool it has on hand with each use.

Short Form	Full Form	Maximum Number of Hosts
/8	/255.0.0.0	16,777,215 (A class)
/16	/255.255.0.0	65,535 (B class)
/17	/255.255.128.0	32,767
/18	/255.255.192.0	16,383
/19	/255.255.224.0	8,191
/20	/255.255.240.0	4,095
/21	/255.255.248.0	2,047
/22	/255.255.252.0	1,023
/23	/255.255.254.0	511
/24	/255.255.255.0	255 (C class)
/25	/255.255.255.128	127
/26	/255.255.255.192	63
/27	/255.255.255.224	31
/28	/255.255.255.240	15
/29	/255.255.255.248	7
/30	/255.255.255.252	3

Table 18-3: CIDR IPv4 Network Masks

IPv4 Reserved Addresses

Certain numbers are reserved. The numbers 127, 0, and 255 cannot be part of an official IP address. The number 127 is used to designate the network address for the loopback interface on your system. The loopback interface enables users on your system to communicate with each other, within the system, without having to route through a network connection. Its network address would be 127.0.0.0, and its IP address is 127.0.0.1. For class-based IP addressing, the number 255 is a special broadcast identifier you can use to broadcast messages to all sites on a network. Using 255 for any part of the IP address references all nodes connected at that level. For example, 192.168.255.255 broadcasts a message to all computers on network 192.168, all its subnetworks, and their hosts. The address 192.168.187.255 broadcasts to every computer on the local network. If you use 0 for the network part of the address, the host number references a computer within your local network. For example, 0.0.0.6 references the sixth computer in your local network. If you want to broadcast to all computers on your local network, you can use the number 0.0.0.255. For CIDR IP addressing, the broadcast address may appear much like a normal IP address. As indicated in the preceding section, CIDR addressing allows the use of any number of bits to make up the IP address for either the network or the host part. For a broadcast address, the host part must have all its bits set to 1 (see Figure 18-3).

A special set of numbers is reserved for use on non-Internet Local Area Networks (LANs) (see RFC 1918). These are numbers that begin with the special network number 192.168 (for class C networks), as used in these examples. If you are setting up a LAN, such as a small business or a home network, you are free to use these numbers for your local machines. You can set up an intranet using network cards, such as Ethernet cards and Ethernet hubs, and then configure your machines with IP addresses starting from 192.168.0.1. The host segment can go up to 256. If you have three machines on your home network, you could give them the addresses 192.168.0.1, 192.168.0.2, and 192.168.0.3. You can implement Internet services, such as FTP, Web, and mail services, on your local machines and use any of the Internet tools to make use of those services. They all use the same TCP/IP protocols used on the Internet. For example, with FTP tools, you can transfer files among the machines on your network. With mail tools, you can send messages from one machine to another, and with a Web browser, you can access local Web sites that may be installed on a machine running its own Web servers. If you want to have one of your machines connected to the Internet or some other network, you can set it up to be a gateway machine. By convention, the gateway machine is usually given the address 192.168.0.1. With a method called *IP masquerading,* you can have any of the non-Internet machines use a gateway to connect to the Internet.

IPv4 Private Network Addresses	Network Classes
10.0.0.0	Class A network
172.16.0.0–172.31.255.255	Class B network
192.168.0.0	Class C network
127.0.0.0	Loopback network (for system self-communication)

Table 18-4: Non-Internet IPv4 Local Network IP Addresses

Numbers are also reserved for class A and class B non-Internet local networks. Table 18-4 lists these addresses. The possible addresses available span from 0 to 255 in the host segment of the address. For example, class B network addresses range from 172.16.0.0 to 172.31.255.255, providing you a total of 32,356 possible hosts. The class C network ranges from 192.168.0.0 to 192.168.255.255, providing you 256 possible subnetworks, each with 256 possible hosts. The network address 127.0.0.0 is reserved for a system's loopback interface, which allows it to communicate with itself, enabling users on the same system to send messages to each other.

Broadcast Addresses

The broadcast address allows a system to send the same message to all systems on your network at once. With IPv4 class-based IP addressing, you can easily determine the broadcast address using your host address: the broadcast address has the host part of your address set to 255.

The network part remains untouched. So the broadcast address for the host address 192.168.1.72 is 192.168.1.255 (you combine the network part of the address with 255 in the host part). For CIDR IP addressing, you need to know the number of bits in the netmask. The remaining bits are set to 1 (see Figure 18-3). For example, an IP address of 192.168.4.6/22 has a broadcast address of 192.168.7.255/22. In this case, the first 22 bits are the network address and the last 10 bits are the host part set to the broadcast value (all 1s).

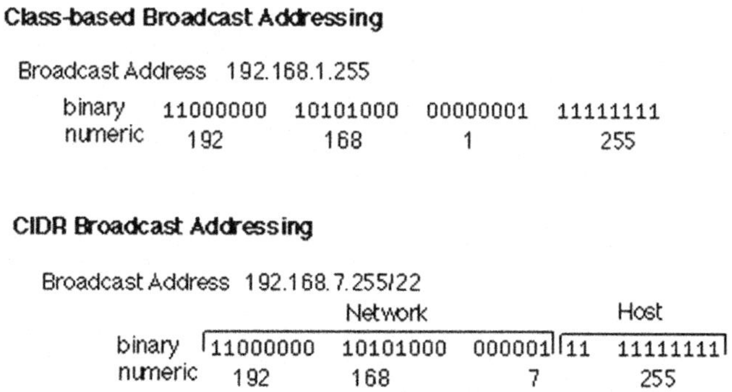

Figure 18-3: Class-based and CIDR broadcast addressing

In fact, you can think of a class C broadcast address as merely a CIDR address using 24 bits (the first three segments) for the network address, and the last 8 bits (the fourth segment) as the broadcast address. The value 255 expressed in binary terms is simply 8 bits that are all 1s. 255 is the same as 11111111.

IP Address	Broadcast Address	IP Broadcast Number	Binary Equivalent
192.168.1.72	192.168.1.255	255	11111111
192.168.4.6/22	192.168.7.255/22	7.255 (last 2 bits in 7)	1111111111

Gateway Addresses

Some networks have a computer designated as the gateway to other networks. All connections to and from a network to other networks pass through this gateway computer. Most local networks use gateways to establish a connection to the Internet. If you are on this type of network, you must provide the gateway address. If your network does not have a connection to the Internet, or a larger network, you may not need a gateway address. The gateway address is the address of the host system providing the gateway service to the network. On many networks, this host is given a host ID of 1, so the gateway address for a network with the address 192.168.0 would be 192.168.0.1, but this is only a convention. To be sure of your gateway address, ask your network administrator.

Name Server Addresses

Many networks, including the Internet, have computers that provide a Domain Name Service (DNS) that translates the domain names of networks and hosts into IP addresses. These are known as the network's *domain name servers.* The DNS makes your computer identifiable on a network, using your domain name, rather than your IP address. You can also use the domain names of other systems to reference them, so you needn't know their IP addresses. You must know the IP addresses of any domain name servers for your network, however. You can obtain the addresses from your system administrator (often more than one address exists). Even if you are using an ISP, you must know the address of the domain name servers your ISP operates for the Internet.

IPv6 Addressing

IPv6 addressing introduces major changes into the format and method of addressing systems under the Internet Protocol (see RFC 3513 at **www.ietf.org/rfc** or **www.faqs.org** for more details). There are several different kinds of addressing with different fields for the network segment. The host segment has been expanded to a 64-bit address, allowing direct addressing for a far larger number of systems. Each address begins with a type field specifying the kind of address, which will then determine how its network segment is organized. These changes are designed, not only to expand the address space, but to also provide greater control over transmissions at the address level.

Note: Ubuntu is distributed with IPv6 support already enabled in the kernel. Kernel support for IPv6 is provided by the IPv6 kernel module. Kernel configuration support can be found under Device Drivers | Networking Support | Networking Options | The IPv6 Protocol.

IPv6 Address Format

An IPv6 address consists of 128 bits, up from the 32 bits used in IPv4 addresses. The first 64 bits are used for network addressing, of which the first few bits are reserved for indicating the address type. The last 64 bits are used for the interface address, known as the interface identifier field. The amount of bits used for subnetting can be adjusted with a CIDR mask, much like that in IPv4 CIDR addressing (see the preceding section).

An IPv6 address is written as eight segments representing 16 bits each (128 bits total). To represent 16-bit binary numbers more easily, hexadecimal numbers are used. Hexadecimal numbers use 16 unique numbers, instead of the 8 used in octal numbering. These are 0–9, continuing with the characters A–F.

In the next example the first four segments represent the network part of the IPv6 address, and the following four segments represent the interface (host) address:

```
FC00:0000:0000:0000:0008:0800:200C:417A
```

You can cut any preceding zeros, but not trailing zeros, in any given segment. Segments with all zeros can be reduced to a single zero.

```
FC00:0:0:0:8:800:200C:417A
```

The loopback address used for localhost addressing can be written with seven preceding zeros and a 1.

```
0:0:0:0:0:0:0:1
```

Many addresses will have sequences of zeros. IPv6 supports a shorthand symbol for representing a sequence of several zeros in adjacent fields. This consists of a double colon (::). There can be only one use of the :: symbol per address.

```
FC00::8:800:200C:417A
```

The loopback address 0000000000000001 can be reduced to just the following:

```
::1
```

To ease the transition from IPv4 addressing to IPv6, a form of addressing incorporating IPv4 addresses is also supported. In this case, the IPv4 address (32 bits) can be used to represent the last two segments of an IPv6 address and can be written using IPv4 notation.

```
FC00::192.168.0.3
```

IPv6 Interface Identifiers

The identifier part of the IPv6 address takes up the second 64 bits, consisting of four segments containing four hexadecimal numbers. The interface ID is a 64-bit (four-segment) Extended Unique Identifier (EUI-64) generated from a network device's Media Access Control (MAC) address.

IPv6 Address types

There are three basic kinds of IPv6 addresses, unicast, multicast, and anycast.

A *unicast* address is used for a packet that is sent to a single destination.

An *anycast* address is used for a packet that can be sent to more than one destination.

A *multicast* address is used to broadcast a packet to a range of destinations.

IPv6 Addresses Format Prefixes and Reserved Addresses	Description
3	Unicast global addresses
FE8	Unicast link-local addresses, used for physically connected hosts on a network, used for DHCP equivalents.
FC00	Unicast unique-local addresses, comparable to IPv4 private addresses.
0000000000000001	Unicast loopback address (for system self-communication, localhost)
0000000000000000	Unspecified address
FF	Multicast addresses

Table 18-5: IPv6 Format Prefixes and Reserved Addresses

In IPv6, addressing is controlled by the format prefix that operates as a kind of address type. The format prefix is the first field of the IP address. The three major kinds of unicast network addresses are global, link-local, and unique-local. Global, unique-local, and link-local are indicated by their own format prefix (see Table 18-5).

Global addresses begin with the address type 3, unique-local with FE00, and link-local with FE8. Global addresses can be sent across the Internet.

Link-local addresses are used for physically connected systems on a local network. It is often used for DHCP addresses.

Unique-local can be used for any hosts on a local network. Unique-local addresses operate like IPv4 private addresses; they are used only for local access and cannot be used to transmit over the Internet.

In addition, IPv6 has two special reserved addresses. The address 0000000000000001 is reserved for the loopback address used for a system's localhost address, and the address 0000000000000000 is the unspecified address.

IPv6 Unicast Global Addresses

IPv6 global addresses currently use four fields: the format prefix, a global routing prefix, the subnet identifier, and the interface identifier. The format prefix for a unicast global address is 3 (3 bits). The global routing prefix references the network address (45 bits), and the subnet ID references a subnet within the site (16 bits).

IPv6 Unicast Local Use Addresses: Link-Local and Unique-Local Addresses

For local use, IPv6 provides both link-local and unique-local addresses. Link-local addressing is used for interfaces (hosts) that are physically connected to a network. This is usually a small local network. A link-local address uses only three fields, the format prefix **FE8** (10 bits), an empty field (54 bits), and the interface identifier (host address) (64 bits). In effect, the network section is empty.

IPv6 unique-local addresses have three fields: the format prefix (10 bits), the subnet identifier (54 bits), and the interface identifier (64 bits). Except for any local subnetting, there is no network address. The unique local address has a format prefix of **FC00**. The unique-local addresses (also known as unique local addresses) fulfill the same function as private addresses in IPv4 (192.168.0).

IPv6 Multicast Addresses

Multicast addresses have a format prefix of FF (8 bits) with flag and scope fields to indicate whether the multicast group is permanent or temporary, and whether it is local or global in scope. A group identifier (112 bits) references the multicast group. For the scope, 2 is link-local, 5 is unique-local, and E is global. In addition to their interface identifiers, hosts will also have a group ID that can be used as a broadcast address. You use this address to broadcast to the hosts. The following example will broadcast only to those hosts on the local network (5) with the group ID 101:

```
FF05:0:0:0:0:0:0:101
```

To broadcast to all the hosts in a link-local scope, you would use the broadcast address:

```
FF02:0:0:0:0:0:0:1
```

For a unique-local scope, a local network, you would use:

```
FF05:0:0:0:0:0:0:2
```

IPv6 and IPv4 Coexistence Methods

In the transition from IPv4 to IPv6, many networks will find the need to support both. Some will be connected to networks that use the contrary protocol, and others will connect through other network connections that use that protocol. There are several official IETF methods for providing IPv6 and IPv4 cooperation, which fall into three main categories:

Dual-stack Allows IPv4 and IPv6 to coexist on the same networks.

Translation Enables IPv6 devices to communicate with IPv4 devices.

Tunneling: Allows transmission from one IPv6 network to another through IPv4 networks as well as allowing IPv6 hosts to operate on or through IPv4 networks.

In the dual-stack methods both IPv6 and IPv4 addresses are supported on the network. Applications and DNS servers can use either to transmit data.

Translation uses NAT tables to translate IPv6 addresses to corresponding IPv4 address and vice versa, as needed. IPv4 applications can then freely interact with IPv6 applications. IPv6-to-IPv6 transmissions are passed directly through, enabling full IPv6 functionality.

Tunneling is used when one IPv6 network needs to transmit to another through an IPv4 network that cannot handle IPv6 addresses. With tunneling, the IPv6 packet is encapsulated within an IPv4 packet, where the IPv4 network then uses the outer IPv4 addressing to pass on the packet. Several methods are used for tunneling, as shown here, as well as direct manual manipulation:

6-over-4 Used within a network to use IPv4 multicasting to implement a virtual LAN to support IPv6 hosts, without an IPv6 router (RFC 2529)

6-to-4 Used to allow IPv6 networks to connect to and through a larger IPv4 network (the Internet), using the IPv4 network address as an IPv6 network prefix (RFC 3056)

Tunnel brokers Web-based services that create tunnels (RFC 3053)

TCP/IP Configuration Files

A set of configuration files in the **/etc** directory, shown in Table 18-6, are used to set up and manage your TCP/IP network. These configuration files specify such network information as host and domain names, IP addresses, and interface options. The IP addresses and domain names of other Internet hosts you want to access are entered in these files. If you configured your network during installation, you can already find that information in these files.

Identifying Hostnames: /etc/hosts

Without the unique IP address the TCP/IP network uses to identify computers, a particular computer cannot be located. Because IP addresses are difficult to use or remember, domain names are used instead. For each IP address, a domain name exists. When you use a domain name to reference a computer on the network, your system translates it into its associated IP address, which can then be used by your network to locate that computer.

Originally, every computer on the network was responsible for maintaining a list of the hostnames and their IP addresses. This list is still kept in the **/etc/hosts** file. When you use a domain name, your system looks up its IP address in the **hosts** file. The system administrator is responsible for maintaining this list. Because of the explosive growth of the Internet and the development of larger networks, the responsibility for associating domain names and IP addresses has been taken over by domain name servers. The **hosts** file is still used to hold the domain names and IP addresses of frequently accessed hosts, however. Your system normally checks your **hosts** file for the IP address of a domain name before taking the added step of accessing a name server.

Address	**Description**
Host address	IP address of your system; it has a network part to identify the network you are on and a host part to identify your own system
Network address	IP address of your network
Broadcast address	IP address for sending messages to all hosts on your network at once
Gateway address	IP address of your gateway system, if you have one (usually the network part of your host IP address with the host part set to 1)
Domain name server addresses	IP addresses of domain name servers your network uses
Netmask	Used to determine the network and host parts of your IP address
File	**Description**
/etc/hosts	Associates hostnames with IP addresses, lists domain names for remote hosts with their IP addresses
/etc/network/interfaces	Network interfaces
/etc/network	Network connection startup scripts for services
/etc/host.conf	Lists resolver options
/etc/nsswitch.conf	Name Switch Service configuration (see Chapter 11)
/etc/resolv.conf	Lists domain name server names, IP addresses (nameserver), and domain names where remote hosts may be located (search)
/etc/protocols	Lists protocols available on your system
/etc/services	Lists available network services, such as FTP and Telnet, and the ports they use

Table 18-6: TCP/IP Configuration Addresses and Files

The format of a domain name entry in the **hosts** file is the IP address followed by the domain name, separated by a space. You can then add aliases for the hostname. After the entry, on the same line, you can enter a comment. A comment is always preceded by a # symbol. You can already find an entry in your **hosts** file for localhost with the IP address 127.0.0.1; **localhost** is a special identification used by your computer to enable users on your system to communicate locally with each other. The domain name for the local host is **localhost.localdomain**. The IP address 127.0.0.1 is a special reserved address used by every computer for this purpose. It identifies what is technically referred to as a *loopback device.* The corresponding IPV6 localhost address is **::1**, which also has the domain name **localhost6.localdomain6** and the name **localhost6**. For compatibility it is also given the names **localhost** as well as **ip6-localhost** and **ip6-loopback**. You should never remove the **localhost** and **ip6-localhost** or **ip6-loopback** entries. A sample **/etc/hosts** file is shown here:

/etc/hosts

```
192.168.0.1        turtle.mytrek.com
192.168.0.2         rabbit.mytrek.com
192.168.34.56       pangol.mytrain.com
127.0.0.1          localhost.localdomain    localhost
::1                 turtle.mytrek.com localhost6.localdomain6  localhost6
127.0.1.1           turtle.mytrek.com

# The following lines are desirable for IPv6 capable hosts
::1     localhost ip6-localhost ip6-loopback
fe00::0 ip6-localnet
ff00::0 ip6-mcastprefix
ff02::1 ip6-allnodes
ff02::2 ip6-allrouters
ff02::3 ip6-allhosts
```

/etc/resolv.conf

The **/etc/resolv.conf** file holds the IP addresses for your DNS servers along with domains to search. A DNS entry will begin with the term nameserver followed by the name server's IP address. A search entry will list network domain addresses. Check this file to see if your network DNS servers have been correctly listed. If you have a router for a local network, DHCP will automatically place an entry for the router in this file and label the router's address as nameserver. The router in turn will reference your ISP's nameserver.

/etc/resolv.conf

```
search  mytrek.com   mytrain.com
nameserver  192.168.0.1
nameserver  192.168.0.1
```

/etc/network

The **/etc/network** directory holds network interface information used by ifup and ifdown to start up and shut down your networking. Subdirectories for the ifup and ifdown operations, like **if-up.d** and **if-down.d**, hold configuration scripts for certain network-related services, such as multicast DNS discover with Avahi, network time update, or remote file system mounting with NFS. The subdirectories included are **if-down.d, if-post-down.d**, **if-pre-up.d**, and **if-up.d**.

/etc/network/interfaces

Interfaces are defined in **/etc/network/interfaces** file, which usually holds only the configuration for the internal loopback interface. NetworkManager will handle all configurations for network interfaces such as your Ethernet card or wireless connection. A standard Ubuntu version defines the loopback interface, the local network interface for your computer. The auto command will automatically activate the network interface when you boot up.

```
auto lo
iface lo inet loopback
```

The **/etc/network/interfaces** file holds manual network configuration settings, such as those you set with Network Manager. Automatic configurations are also managed by NetworkManager. NetworkManager will run any **if-up** and **if-down** scripts in the **/etc/network** subdirectories.

Should you need to configure your connection manually, you could enter configuration entries directly by editing the **/etc/network/interfaces** file. The **iface** command defines the interface. Its arguments are the interface name, the protocol it uses (**inet** for IPv4 and **inet6** for IPv6), and the connection type: **static**, **dhcp**, **ppp** (dial-up), or **bootp**. Each protocol and connection type can support different options. Check the interface's man page for details.

The following example sets up a static IP address for the first Ethernet device, **eth0**, using the IPv4 protocol. The address entry specifies the IP address, along with netmask and gateway for the IP addresses for those servers:

```
auto eth0
iface eth0 inet static
address 192.168.0.5
netmask 255.255.255.0
gateway 192.168.0.1
```

Should you be using a DHCP server to set up your address information, you would specify **dhcp**:

```
auto eth0
iface eth0 inet dhcp
```

You use the **auto** entry to specify whether an interface should be started up with the **ifup -a** command. This command is run by the **/etc/init.d/networking** script, which is run when your system starts up and whenever you restart networking.

If you make changes, you can then restart the network services with the init networking script:

```
sudo /etc/init.d/networking restart
```

/etc/services

The **/etc/services** file lists network services available on your system, such as FTP and Telnet, and associates each with a particular port. Here, you can find out what port your Web server is checking or what port is used for your FTP server. You can give a service an alias, which you specify after the port number. You can then reference the service using the alias.

/etc/protocols

The **/etc/protocols** file lists the TCP/IP protocols currently supported by your system. Each entry shows the protocol number, its keyword identifier, and a brief description. See **http://www.iana.org/assignments/protocol-numbers** for a complete listing.

/etc/hostname and hostnamectl

The **/etc/hostname** file contains your hostname. You can use the **hostnamectl** command to display your current hostname and all information pertaining to it such as the machine ID, the kernel used, the architecture, chassis (type of computer), and the operating system (you can add the **status** option if you want). Three different kinds of hostnames are supported: static, pretty, and transient. You can set each with the **hostnamectl**'s **set-hostname** command with the corresponding type. The static hostname is used to identify your computer on the network (usually a fully qualified host name). You can use the **--static** option to set it. The pretty hostname is a descriptive host name made available to users on the computer. This can be set by **set-hostname** with the **--pretty** option. The transient host name is one allocated by a network service such as DHCP, and can be managed with the **--transient** option. Without options, the **set-hostname** command will apply the name to all the host name types.

```
hostnamectl set-hostname --pretty "my computer"
```

The **set-chassis** command sets the computer type, which can be desktop, laptop, server, tablet, handset, and vm (virtual system). Without a type specified it reverts to the default for the system. The **set-icon-name** sets the name used by the graphical applications for the host.

host.conf

Name servers are queried by resolvers. These are programs specially designed to obtain addresses from name servers. To use domain names on your system, a resolver must be set up. Your local resolver is configured with your **/etc/host.conf** and **/etc/resolv.conf** files.

Your **host.conf** file lists resolver options (shown in Table 18-7). Each option can have several fields, separated by spaces or tabs. You can use a **#** at the beginning of a line to enter a comment. The options tell the resolver what services to use. The order of the list is important. The resolver begins with the first option listed and moves on to the next in turn. You can find the **host.conf** file in your **/etc** directory, along with other configuration files.

Option	Description
`order`	Specifies sequence of name resolution methods: `hosts` Checks for name in the local **/etc/host** file `bind` Queries a DNS name server for an address `nis` Uses Network Information Service protocol to obtain an address
`alert`	Checks addresses of remote sites attempting to access your system; you turn it on or off with the `on` and `off` options
`nospoof`	Confirms addresses of remote sites attempting to access your system
`trim`	Checks your local host's file; removes the domain name and checks only for the hostname; enables you to use only a hostname in your host file for an IP address
`multi`	Checks your local hosts file; allows a host to have several IP addresses; you turn it on or off with the `on` and `off` options

Table 18-7: Resolver Options, host.conf

Your **host.conf** file will be set up already with a standard configuration for accessing most DNS services. The default **host.conf** file is shown here. The `order` option instructs your resolver first to look up names in your local **/etc/hosts** file, and then, if that fails, to query domain name servers. The system does not have multiple addresses.

/etc/host.conf

```
# The "order" line is only used by old versions of the C library.
order hosts,bind
# multiple addresses
multi on
```

Network Interfaces and Routes: ifconfig and route

Your connection to a network is made by your system through a particular hardware interface, such as an Ethernet card or a modem. Data passing through this interface is then routed to your network. The **ifconfig** command configures your network interfaces, and the **route** command sets up network connections accordingly. If you configure an interface with a network configuration tool like Network Manager, you needn't use **ifconfig** or **route**. However, you can configure interfaces directly using **ifconfig** and **route**, if you want. Every time you start your system, the network interfaces and their routes must be established. This is done automatically for you by NetworkManager. Interfaces and routes are set up when you start up your system by the **ifup** command run by the **/etc/init.d/networking** initialization file. The **ifup** command uses configuration settings in the **/etc/network/interfaces** file. Alternatively, you can run your own direct configuration with **ifconfig** and **route** commands.

Note: As an alternative to **ifconfig** and **route**, you can use **ip**. This is a tool provided by the **iproute** package. The syntax is much the same. Route commands use the **route** option, **ip route**. The **ifconfig** operations on addresses would use the **addr** option, **ip addr**.

Network Startup Script: /etc/init.d/networking

Your network interface is started up using the `networking` script in the **/etc/init.d** directory. This script will activate your network interface cards (NICs), as well as implement configuration information such as gateway, host, and name server identities. You can manually shut down and start your network interface using this script and the `restart`, `start`, or `stop` options, as well as NetworkManager. You can run the script with the `service` command. The following commands shut down and then start up your network interface:

```
sudo service networking stop
sudo service networking start
```

If you are changing network configuration, you will have to restart your network interface for the changes to take effect:

```
sudo service networking restart
```

To test if your interface is working, use the `ping` command with an IP address of a system on your network, such as your gateway machine. The `ping` command continually repeats until you stop it with a CTRL-C.

```
ping 192.168.0.1
```

ifconfig

The **ifconfig** command takes as its arguments the name of an interface and an IP address, as well as options. The **ifconfig** command then assigns the IP address to the interface. Your system now knows that such an interface exists, and that it references a particular IP address. In addition, you can specify whether the IP address is a host address or a network address. You can use a domain name for the IP address, provided the domain name is listed along with its IP address in the **/etc/hosts** file. The syntax for the **ifconfig** command is as follows:

```
ifconfig interface -host_net_flag address options
```

The *host_net_flag* can be either **-host** or **-net** to indicate a host or network IP address. The **-host** flag is the default. The **ifconfig** command can have several options, which set different features of the interface, such as the maximum number of bytes it can transfer (**mtu**) or the broadcast address. The **up** and **down** options activate and deactivate the interface. In the next example, the **ifconfig** command configures an Ethernet interface:

```
ifconfig eth0 192.168.0.1
```

Option	Description
Interface	Name of the network interface, such as **eth0** for the first Ethernet device or **ppp0** for the first PPP device (modem)
up	Activates an interface; implied if IP address is specified
down	Deactivates an interface
allmulti	Turns on or off the promiscuous mode; preceding hyphen (-) turns it off; this allows network monitoring
mtu *n*	Maximum number of bytes that can be sent on this interface per transmission
dstaddr *address*	Destination IP address on a point-to-point connection
netmask *address*	IP network mask; preceding hyphen (-) turns it off
broadcast *address*	Broadcast address; preceding hyphen (-) turns it off
point-to-point *address*	Point-to-point mode for interface; if address is included, it is assigned to remote system
hw	Sets hardware address of interface
Address	IP address assigned to interface

Table 18-8: The ifconfig Options

For a simple configuration such as this, **ifconfig** automatically generates a standard broadcast address and netmask. The standard broadcast address is the network address with the number 255 for the host address. For a class C network, the standard netmask is 255.255.255.0, whereas for a class A network, the standard netmask is 255.0.0.0. If you are connected to a network with a particular netmask and broadcast address, however, you must specify them when you use **ifconfig**. The option for specifying the broadcast address is **broadcast**; for the network mask, it is **netmask**. Table 18-8 lists several **ifconfig** options. In the next example, **ifconfig** includes the netmask and broadcast address:

```
ifconfig eth0 192.168.0.1 broadcast 192.168.0.255 netmask 255.255.255.0
```

Once you configure your interface, you can use **ifconfig** with the **up** option to activate it and with the **down** option to deactivate it. If you specify an IP address in an **ifconfig** operation, as in the preceding example, the **up** option is implied.

```
ifconfig eth0 up
```

Point-to-point interfaces such as Parallel IP (PLIP), Serial Line IP (SLIP), and Point-to-Point Protocol (PPP) require you to include the **pointopoint** option. A PLIP interface name is identified with the name **plip** with an attached number. For example, **plip0** is the first PLIP interface. SLIP interfaces use **slip0**. PPP interfaces start with **ppp0**. Point-to-point interfaces are those that usually operate between only two hosts, such as two computers connected over a modem. When you specify the **pointopoint** option, you need to include the IP address of the host. In the next example, a PLIP interface is configured that connects the computer at IP address 192.168.1.72 with one at 192.166.254.14. If domain addresses were listed for these systems in **/etc/hosts**, those domain names could be used in place of the IP addresses.

```
ifconfig plip0 192.168.1.72 pointopoint 192.166.254.14
```

If you need to, you can also use **ifconfig** to configure your loopback device. The name of the loopback device is **lo**, and its IP address is the special address 127.0.0.1. The following example shows the configuration:

```
ifconfig lo 127.0.0.1
```

The **ifconfig** command is useful for checking on the status of an interface. If you enter the **ifconfig** command along with the name of the interface, information about that interface is displayed:

```
ifconfig eth0
```

To see if your loopback interface is configured, you can use **ifconfig** with the loopback interface name, **lo**:

Routing

A packet that is part of a transmission takes a certain *route* to reach its destination. On a large network, packets are transmitted from one computer to another until the destination computer is reached. The route determines where the process starts and to what computer your system needs to send the packet for it to reach its destination. On small networks, routing may be static—that is, the route from one system to another is fixed. One system knows how to reach another, moving through fixed paths. On larger networks and on the Internet, however, routing is dynamic. Your system knows the first computer to send its packet off to, and then that computer takes the packet from there, passing it on to another computer, which then determines where to pass it on. For dynamic routing, your system needs to know little. Static routing, however, can become complex because you have to keep track of all the network connections.

Your routes are listed in your routing table in the **/proc/net/route** file. To display the routing table, enter **`route`** with no arguments (the **`netstat -r`** command will also display the routing table):

```
$ route
Kernel routing table
Destination Gateway     Genmask       Flags Metric Ref Use  Iface
192.168.0.0    *         255.255.255.0 U     0        0 0    etho
192.168.0.0    *         255.255.255.0 U     0        0 0    wlan0
link-local     *         255.255.0.0   U     1000     0 0    etho
default     192.168.0.1  0.0.0.0       UG    0        0 0    eth0
```

Each entry in the routing table has several fields, providing information such as the route destination and the type of interface used. The different fields are listed in Table 18-9.

With the **`add`** argument, you can add routes either for networks with the **`-net`** option or with the **`-host`** option for IP interfaces (hosts). The **`-host`** option is the default. In addition, you can then specify several parameters for information, such as the netmask (**`netmask`**), the gateway (**`gw`**), the interface device (**`dev`**), and the default route (**`default`**). If you have more than one IP interface on your system, such as several Ethernet cards, you must specify the name of the interface using the **`dev`** parameter. If your network has a gateway host, you use the **`gw`** parameter to specify it. If your system is connected to a network, at least one entry should be in your routing table that specifies the default route. This is the route taken by a message packet when no other route entry leads to its destination. The following example is the routing of an Ethernet interface:

```
route add 192.168.1.2 dev eth0
```

Field	Description
Destination	Destination IP address of the route
Gateway	IP address or hostname of the gateway the route uses; `*` indicates no gateway is used
Genmask	The netmask for the route
Flags	Type of route: U = up, H = host, G = gateway, D = dynamic, M = modified
Metric	Metric cost of route
Ref	Number of routes that depend on this one
Window	TCP window for AX.25 networks
Use	Number of times used
Iface	Type of interface this route uses

Table 18-9: Routing Table Entries

If your system has only the single Ethernet device as your IP interface, you could leave out the **`dev eth0`** parameter:

```
route add 192.168.1.2
```

You can delete any route you establish by invoking **`ifconfig`** with the **`del`** argument and the IP address of that route, as in this example:

```
route del 192.168.1.2
```

For a gateway, you first add a route to the gateway interface, and then add a route specifying that it is a gateway. The address of the gateway interface in this example is 192.168.1.1:

```
route add 192.168.1.1
route add default gw 192.168.1.1
```

If you are using the gateway to access a subnet, add the network address for that network (in this example, 192.168.23.0):

```
route add -net 192.168.23.0 gw dev eth1
```

To add another IP address to a different network interface on your system, use the **ifconfig** and **route** commands with the new IP address. The following command configures a second Ethernet card (**eth1**) with the IP address 192.168.1.3:

```
ifconfig eth1 192.168.1.3
route add 192.168.1.3 dev eth1
```

Tip: InfiniBand is often used as a replacement for local network connections. Check the Linux InfiniBand Project at **http://infiniband.sourceforge.net**.

Monitoring Your Network: ping, netstat, tcpdump, Ettercap, Wireshark, and Nagios

Several applications are available on Linux to let you monitor your network activity. Graphical applications like EtherApe, Ettercap, and Wireshark provide detailed displays and logs to let you analyze and detect network usage patterns. Other tools like **ping**, **netstat**, and **traceroute** offer specific services. Table 18-10 lists various network information tools.

The EtherApe, Ettercap, and Wireshark tools can be accessed on the Applications | Internet menu (Applications | Internet). Tools like **ping**, **traceroute**, and **netstat** can be accessed from Applications | Administration | Network Tools, or they can be run individually on a command line (Terminal window). EtherApe provides a simple graphical display for your protocol activity. The Preferences dialog lets you set features like the protocol to check and the kind of traffic to report.

GNOME Network Tools: gnome-nettool

The GNOME Nettool utility (**gnome-nettool**) provides a GNOME interface for network information tools, like the ping and traceroute operations as well as Finger, Whois, and Lookup for querying users and hosts on the network (see Figure 18-4). Nettool is installed by default and is accessible from Applications | Other | Network Tools. The first tab, Devices, describes your connected network devices, including configuration and transmission information about each device, such as the hardware address and bytes transmitted. Both IPv4 and IPv6 host IP addresses are listed.

```
sudo apt-get install gnome-nettool
```

You can use the ping, finger, lookup, whois, and traceroute operations to find out status information about systems and users on your network. The ping operation is used to check if a remote system is up and running. You use finger to find out information about other users on your network, seeing if they are logged in or if they have received mail. The traceroute tool can be used to track the sequence of computer networks and systems your message passed through on its way to you. Whois will provide domain name information about a particular domain, and Lookup will provide both domain name and IP addresses. Netstat shows your network routing (addresses used) and active service (open ports and the protocols they use). Port Scan lists the ports and services they use on a given connection (address); use 12.0.0.1 for your local computer.

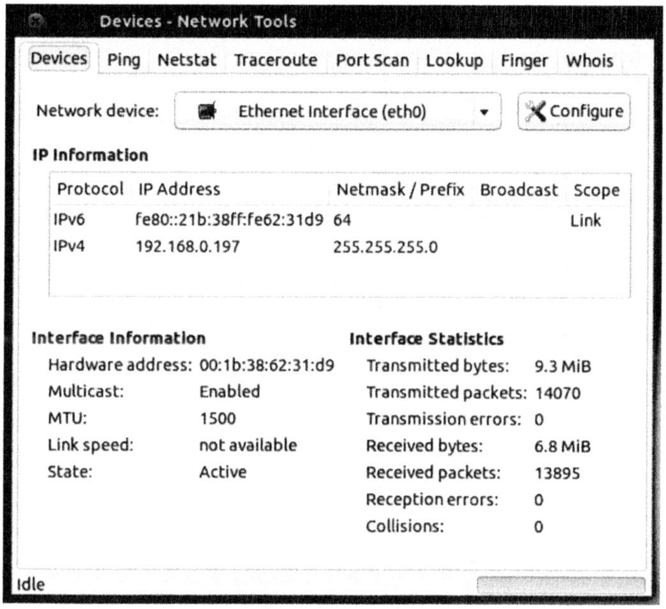

Figure 18-4: Gnome network tool

Network Information: ping, finger, traceroute, and host

You can use the **ping**, **finger**, **traceroute**, and **host** commands to find out status information about systems and users on your network. The **ping** command is used to check if a remote system is up and running. You use **finger** to find out information about other users on your network, seeing if they are logged in or if they have received mail; **host** displays address information about a system on your network, giving you a system's IP and domain name addresses; and **traceroute** can be used to track the sequence of computer networks and systems your message passed through on its way to you.

ping

The **ping** command detects whether a system is up and running. **ping** takes as its argument the name of the system you want to check. If the system you want to check is down, **ping** issues a timeout message indicating a connection could not be made. The ping program sends a request to the host for a reply. The host then sends a reply back, and it is displayed on your screen. The ping program continually sends such a request until you stop it with a **break** command, by pressing CTRL-C. You see one reply after another scroll by on your screen until you stop the program. If ping cannot access a host, it issues a message saying the host is unreachable. If ping fails, it can indicate that your network connection is not working—only the particular interface, a basic configuration problem, or a bad physical connection. The ping utility uses the ICMP, discussed in Chapter 17. Networks may block these protocols as a security measure, also preventing ping from working. A ping failure may simply indicate a security precaution on the part of the queried network.

Network Information Tools	Description
ping	Detects whether a system is connected to the network.
finger	Obtains information about users on the network.
who	Checks what users are currently online.
whois	Obtains domain information.
host	Obtains network address information about a remote host.
traceroute	Tracks the sequence of computer networks and hosts your message passes through.
wireshark	Protocol analyzer to examine network traffic.
gnome-nettool	GNOME interface for various network tools including ping, finger, and traceroute.
mtr and xmtr	My traceroute combines both ping and traceroute operations (Traceroute on System Tools menu).
EtherApe	Analyze protocol activity
Ettercap	Sniffer program for man-in-middle attacks
netstat	Real time network status monitor
tcpdump	Capture and save network packets
Nagios	Nagios network monitoring, **nagio3** packages, **/etc/nagios3** configuration directory, **http://localhost/nagios3** browser access

Table 18-10: Network Tools

To use ping, enter ***ping*** and the name of the host. The next example checks to see if **www.ubuntu.com** is up and connected to the network:

```
$ ping www.ubuntu.com
PING www.ubuntu.com (91.189.94.8) 56(84) bytes of data.
64 bytes from jujube.canonical.com (91.189.94.8): icmp_seq=1 ttl=48 time=609 ms
64 bytes from jujube.canonical.com (91.189.94.8): icmp_seq=2 ttl=48 time=438 ms
64 bytes from jujube.canonical.com (91.189.94.8): icmp_seq=3 ttl=48 time=568 ms
^C
--- www.ubuntu.com ping statistics ---
4 packets transmitted, 3 received, 25% packet loss, time 3554ms
rtt min/avg/max/mdev = 438.939/539.125/609.885/72.824 ms
```

You can also use **ping** with an IP address instead of a domain name. With an IP address, **ping** can try to detect the remote system directly without having to go through a domain name server to translate the domain name to an IP address. This can be helpful for situations where your network's domain name server may be temporarily down and you want to check if a particular remote host on your network is connected.

```
ping 91.189.94.8
```

finger and who

You can use the **finger** command to obtain information about other users on your network and the **who** command to see what users are currently online on your system. The **who** and **w** commands lists all users currently connected, along with when, how long, and where they logged in. The **w** command provides more detailed information. It has several options for specifying the level of detail. The **who** command is meant to operate on a local system or network; **finger** can operate on large networks, including the Internet, though most systems block it for security reasons.

host

With the **host** command, you can find network address information about a remote system connected to your network. The information usually consists of a system's IP address, domain name address, domain name nicknames, and mail server. This information is obtained from your network's domain name server. For the Internet, this includes all systems you can connect to over the Internet.

The **host** command is an effective way to determine a remote site's IP address or URL. If you have only the IP address of a site, you can use **host** to find out its domain name. For network administration, an IP address can be helpful for making your own domain name entries in your **/etc/host** file. That way, you needn't rely on a remote domain name server (DNS) for locating a site.

```
$ host gnomefiles.org
gnomefiles.org has address 67.18.254.188
gnomefiles.org mail is handled by 10 mx.zayda.net.

$ host 67.18.254.188
188.254.18.67.in-addr.arpa domain name pointer gnomefiles.org.
```

traceroute

Internet connections are made through various routes, traveling through a series of interconnected gateway hosts. The path from one system to another could take different routes, some of which may be faster than others. For a slow connection, you can use **traceroute** to check the route through which you are connected to a host, monitoring the speed and the number of intervening gateway connections a route takes. The **traceroute** command takes as its argument the hostname or IP addresses for the system whose route you want to check. Options are available for specifying parameters like the type of service (**-t**) or the source host (**-s**). The **traceroute** command will return a list of hosts the route traverses, along with the times for three probes sent to each gateway. Times greater than five seconds are displayed with a asterisk, *.

```
traceroute rabbit.mytrek.com
```

You can also use the mtr or xmtr tools to perform both ping and traces (Traceroute on the System Tools menu).

Ettercap

Ettercap is a sniffer program designed to detect Man in the Middle attacks. In this kind of attack, packets are detected and modified in transit to let an unauthorized user access a network. You can use either its graphical interface or its command line interface. Ettercap can perform Unified sniffing on all connections, or Bridged sniffing on a connection between network interfaces. Ettercap uses plugins for specific tasks, like dos_attack to detect Denial of Service attacks and dns-spoof for DNS spoofing detection. Check the plugins Help tab, or enter **ettercap -P list** for a complete listing. Ettercap can be run in several modes, including a text mode, a command line cursor mode, a script mode using commands in a file, and even as a daemon logging results automatically.

Wireshark

Wireshark is a network protocol analyzer that lets you capture packets transmitted across your network, selecting and examining those from protocols you want to check. You can examine packets from particular transmissions, displaying the data in readable formats. You can access Wireshark from Applications | Internet | Wireshark. The Wireshark interface displays three panes: a listing of current packets, the protocol tree for the currently selected packet, a display of the selected packets contents. The first pane categorizes entries by time, source, destination, and protocol, with button headers for each. To sort a set of entries by a particular category, you click its header. For example, group entries by protocol, click the Protocol button; for destinations, click the Destination button.

Capture Options

To configure Wireshark, you select the Options entry from the Capture menu (Capture | Options). This opens an options window where you can select the network interface to watch. Here you can also select options, such as the file in which to hold your captured information and a size limit for the capture, along with a filter to screen packets. With the promiscuous mode selected, you can see all network traffic passing through that device, whereas with it off, you will see only those packets destined for that device. You can then click the start button to start Wireshark. To stop and start Wireshark, you select the Stop and Start entries on the Capture menu.

The Capture Files options lets you select a file to save your capture in. If no file is selected, then data is simply displayed in the Wireshark window. If you want to keep a continuous running snapshot of your network traffic, you can use ring buffers. These are a series of files that are used to save captured data. When they fill up, the capture begins saving again to the first file, and so on. Check "Use multiple files" to enable this option.

Limit lets you set a limit for the capture packet size.

Capture Filter lets you choose the type of protocol you want to check.

Display Options control whether packets are displayed in real time on the Wireshark window.

"Enable network name resolution" enables the display of host and domain names instead of IP addresses, if possible.

Wireshark Filters

A filter lets you select packets that match specified criteria, such as packets from a particular host. Criteria are specified using expressions supported by the Packet Capture Library and implemented by **tcpdump**. Wireshark filters use expressions similar to those used by the **tcpdump** command. Check the **tcpdump** Man page for detailed descriptions.

You can set up either a Search filter in the Find tab (Edit menu) to search for certain packets, or set up a Capture Filter in the Options tab (Capture menu) to select which packets to record. The filter window is the same for both. On the filter window you can select the protocol you want to search or capture. The Filter name and string will appear in the Properties segment. You can also enter your own string, setting up a new filter of your own. The string must be a filter expression.

To create a new filter, enter the name you want to give it in the Filter Name box. Then in the Filter String box, enter the filter expression, like **icmp**. Then click New. Your new filter will appear in the list. To change a filter, select it and change its expression in the Filter String box, then click Change.

A filter expression consists of an ID, such as the name or number of host, and a qualifier. Qualifiers come in three types: type, direction, and protocol. The type can reference the host, network, or port. The type qualifiers are **host**, **net**, and **port**. Direction selects either source or destination packets, or both. The source qualifier is **src**, and the destination qualifier is **dst**. With no destination qualifier, both directions are selected. Protocol lets you specify packets for a certain protocol. Protocols are represented using their lowercase names, such as **icmp** for ICMP. For example, the expression to list all packets coming in from a particular host would be **src host** *hostname,* where *hostname* is the source host. The following example will display all packets from the 192.168.0.3 host:

```
src host 192.168.0.3
```

Using just **host** will check for all packets going out as well as coming in for that host. The **port** qualifier will check for packets passing through a particular port. To check for a particular protocol, you use the protocol name. For example, to check for all ICMP packets you would use the expression

```
icmp
```

There are also several special qualifiers that let you further control your selection. The **gateway** qualifier lets you detect packets passing through a gateway. The **broadcast** and **multi-cast** qualifiers detect packets broadcast to a network. The **greater** and **less** qualifiers can be applied to numbers such as ports or IP addresses.

You can combine expressions into a single complex Boolean expression using **and**, **or**, or **not**. This lets you create a more refined filter. For example, to capture only the ICMP packets coming in from host 192.168.0.2, you can use

```
src host 192.168.0.3 and icmp
```

tcpdump

Like Wireshark, **tcpdump** will capture network packets, saving them in a file where you can examine them. **tcpdump** operates entirely from the command line. You will have to open a terminal window to run it. Using various options, you can refine your capture, specifying the kinds of packets you want. **tcpdump** uses a set of options to specify actions you want to take, which include limiting the size of the capture, deciding which file to save it to, and choosing any filter you want to apply to it. Check the **tcpdump** Man page for a complete listing of options.

The **-i** option lets you specify an interface to listen to.

With the **-c** option, you can limit the number of packets to capture.

Packets will be output to the standard output by default. To save them to a file, you can use the **-w** option.

You can later read a packet file using the **-r** option and apply a filter expression to it.

The **tcpdump** command takes as its argument a filter expression that you can use to refine your capture. Wireshark uses the same filter expressions as **tcpdump** (see the filters discussion in Wireshark).

netstat

The netstat program provides real-time information on the status of your network connections, as well as network statistics and the routing table. The **netstat** command has several options you can use to bring up different sorts of information about your network.

```
$ netstat
Active Internet connections
Proto Recv-Q Send-Q Local Address Foreign Address (State) User
tcp 0 0 turtle.mytrek.com:01 pangol.mytrain.com.:ftp ESTABLISHED dylan
Active UNIX domain sockets
Proto RefCnt Flags Type State Path
unix 1 [ ACC ] SOCK_STREAM LISTENING /dev/printer
unix 2 [ ] SOCK_STREAM CONNECTED /dev/log
unix 1 [ ACC ] SOCK_STREAM LISTENING /dev/nwapi
unix 2 [ ] SOCK_STREAM CONNECTED /dev/log
unix 2 [ ] SOCK_STREAM CONNECTED
unix 1 [ ACC ] SOCK_STREAM LISTENING /dev/log
```

The **netstat** command with no options lists the network connections on your system. First, active TCP connections are listed, and then the active domain sockets are listed. The domain sockets contain processes used to set up communications among your system and other systems. You can use **netstat** with the **-r** option to display the routing table, and **netstat** with the **-i** option displays the uses of the different network interfaces.

nagios3

Ubuntu also supports Nagios, the enterprise level network monitoring software. You can install Nagios with the **nagios3** package. All dependent Nagios packages will be selected and installed, including **nagios3-doc** for documentation and nagios-plugins for servers like DNS, MySQL, and NTP. To install you can use **apt-get**, **aptitude**, or, from the desktop, the Synaptic Package Manager.

```
sudo apt-get install nagios3
```

Make sure that the nagios3 server is running. If not enter the following at the command line or in a terminal window to start it.

```
sudo service nagios3 start
```

When you install nagios, you will be prompted to enter an administrative password. A Debconf dialog will appear labeled "Configuring nagios3-cgi", with prompts to enter the password and repeat the password. This is the password you will use to access Nagios.

You then open your browser and access your nagios interface with the following URL.

```
http://localhost/nagios3
```

You will be prompted to enter a user and password. Use the user **nagiosadmin** and the password you were prompted to enter when you installed nagios.

```
nagiosadmin
```

The Nagios Web interface is then displayed as shown in Figure 18-5.

Using the links listed on the left sidebar you can then display different monitoring information like the service status for hosts on your network (see Figure 18-6). It is possible to run nagios from the command line using the **lynx** Web browser.

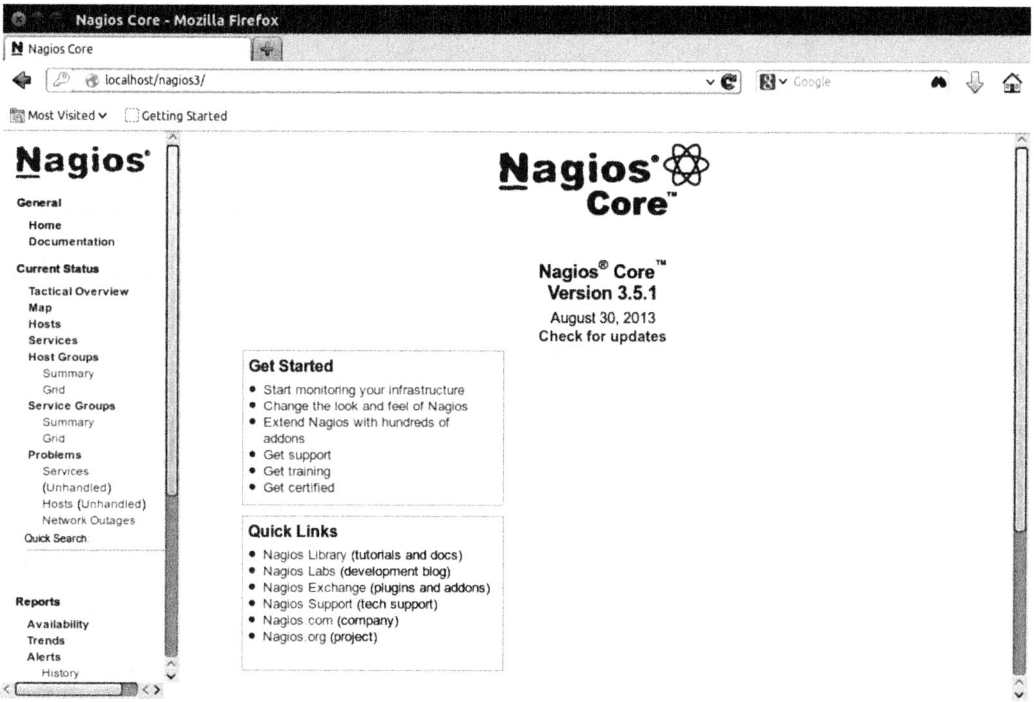

Figure 18-5: Nagios 3 network monitoring Web interface

Configuration files for nagios3 are located at **/etc/nagios3**, and the configuration files for different plugins are located at **/etc/nagios-plugins/config**. The main configuration file is **nagios.cfg**, an editable text file with detailed comments for each directive. The **apache2.conf** file sets up script aliases mapping nagios to the nagios3 directories and files. An AuthUserFile directive specifies that the Nagios Web page user and password file is **/etc/nagios3/htpasswd.users**.

You can later create or change the nagios user and password with the following command entered in a terminal window. You will be prompted to enter a new password twice.

```
sudo htpasswd -c /etc/nagios3/htpasswd.users nagiosadmin
```

The Nagios application and plugins are supported directly by Ubuntu as part of the main repository. Nagios also provides a remote plugin server that allows Nagios plugins to run on remote hosts. The Nagios Remote Plugin Executor server (NRPE) is part of the Universe repository. Install both the **nagios-nrpe-server** and the **nagios-nrpe-plugin** packages.

```
sudo apt-get install nagios-nrpe-server nagios-nrpe-plugin
```

The NRPE server script is **nagios-nrpe-server**.

```
sudo service nagios-nrpe-server start
```

The configuration files for the NRPE server are located at **/etc/nagios**.

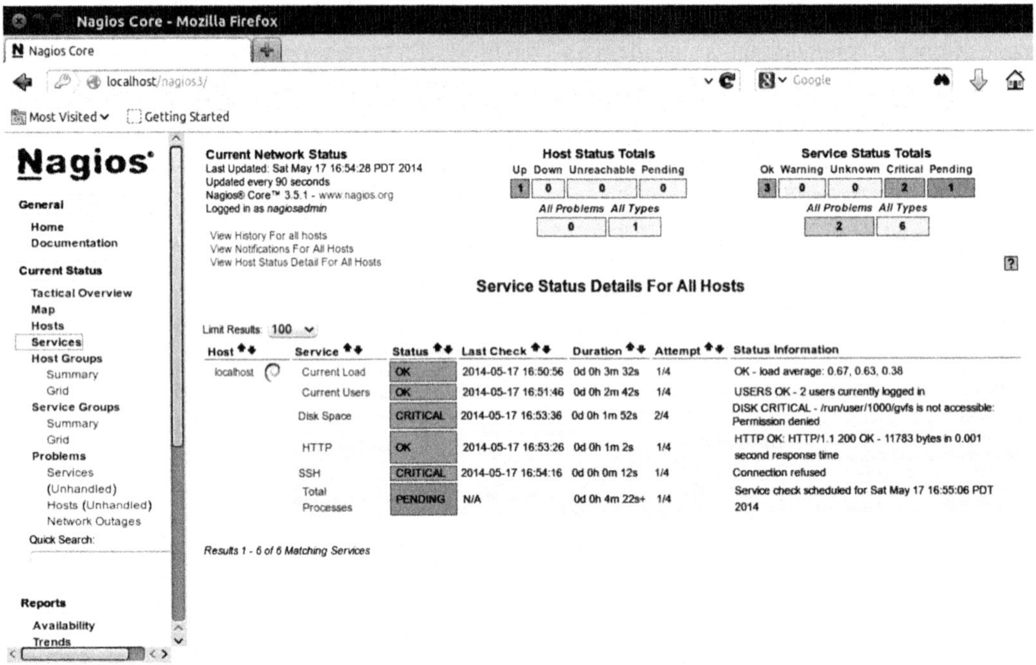

Figure 18-6: Nagios 3 network monitoring Service Status

Part 5: Shells

Shells
Files and Directories
Shell Variables and Scripts
Shell Configuration

19. Shells

The Command Line

History

Filename Expansion: *, ?, [ ]

Standard Input/Output and Redirection

The shell is a command interpreter that provides a line-oriented interactive and non-interactive interface between the user and the operating system. You enter commands on a command line; they are interpreted by the shell and then sent as instructions to the operating system (the command line interface is accessible from GNOME and KDE through a Terminal windows – Applications lens /Accessories filter). You can also place commands in a script file to be consecutively executed, much like a program. This interpretive capability of the shell provides for many sophisticated features. For example, the shell has a set of file expansion characters that can generate filenames. The shell can redirect input and output, as well as run operations in the background, freeing you to perform other tasks.

Shell	Web Site
`www.gnu.org/software/bash`	BASH Web site with online manual, FAQ, and current releases
`www.gnu.org/software/bash/manual/bash.html`	BASH online manual
`www.zsh.org`	Z shell Web site with referrals to FAQs and current downloads.
`www.tcsh.org`	TCSH Web site with detailed support including manual, tips, FAQ, and recent releases
`www.kornshell.com`	Korn shell site with manual, FAQ, and references

Table 19-1: Linux Shells

Several different types of shells have been developed for Linux: the Bourne Again shell (BASH), the Korn shell, the TCSH shell, and the Z shell. All shells are available for your use, although the BASH shell is the default. You only need one type of shell to do your work. Ubuntu Linux includes all the major shells, although it installs and uses the BASH shell as the default. If you use the command line shell, you will be using the BASH shell unless you specify another. This chapter discusses the BASH shell, which shares many of the same features as other shells.

You can find out more about shells at their respective Web sites as listed in Table 19-1. Also, a detailed online manual is available for each installed shell. Use the **`man`** command and the shell's keyword to access them, **bash** for the BASH shell, **ksh** for the Korn shell, **zsh** for the Z shell, and **tsch** for the TSCH shell. For example, the command **`man bash`** will access the BASH shell online manual.

Note: You can find out more about the BASH shell at **www.gnu.org/software/bash**. A detailed online manual is available on your Linux system using the **`man`** command with the **`bash`** keyword.

The Command Line

The Linux command line interface consists of a single line into which you enter commands with any of their options and arguments. From GNOME or KDE, you can access the command line interface by opening a terminal window (Applications | Accessories | Terminal). Should you start Linux with the command line interface, you will be presented with a BASH shell command line when you log in.

By default, the BASH shell has a dollar sign ($) prompt, but Linux has several other types of shells, each with its own prompt (like % for the C shell). The root user will have a different prompt, the #. A shell *prompt,* such as the one shown here, marks the beginning of the command line:

```
$
```

You can enter a command along with options and arguments at the prompt. For example, with an **-l** option, the **ls** command will display a line of information about each file, listing such data as its size and the date and time it was last modified. In the next example, the user enters the **ls** command followed by a **-l** option. The dash before the **-l** option is required. Linux uses it to distinguish an option from an argument.

```
$ ls -l
```

If you wanted only the information displayed for a particular file, you could add that file's name as the argument, following the **-l** option:

```
$ ls -l mydata
-rw-r--r-- 1 chris weather 207 Feb 20 11:55 mydata
```

Tip: Some commands can be complex and take some time to execute. When you mistakenly execute the wrong command, you can interrupt and stop such commands with the interrupt key—CTRL-C.

You can enter a command on several lines by typing a backslash just before you press ENTER. The backslash "escapes" the ENTER key, effectively continuing the same command line to the next line. In the next example, the **cp** command is entered on three lines. The first two lines end in a backslash, effectively making all three lines one command line.

```
$ cp -i \
mydata \
/home/george/myproject/newdata
```

You can also enter several commands on the same line by separating them with a semicolon (;). In effect the semicolon operates as an execute operation. Commands will be executed in the sequence in which they are entered. The following command executes an **ls** command followed by a **date** command.

```
$ ls ; date
```

You can also conditionally run several commands on the same line with the **&&** operator. A command is executed only if the previous command is true. This feature is useful for running several dependent scripts on the same line. In the next example, the **ls** command is run only if the **date** command is successfully executed.

```
$ date && ls
```

TIP: Command can also be run as arguments on a command line, using their results for other commands. To run a command within a command line, you encase the command in back quotes.

Movement Commands	Operation
CTRL-F, RIGHT-ARROW	Move forward a character
CTRL-B, LEFT-ARROW	Move backward a character
CTRL-A or HOME	Move to beginning of line
CTRL-E or END	Move to end of line
ALT-F	Move forward a word
ALT-B	Move backward a word
CTRL-L	Clear screen and place line at top
Editing Commands	**Operation**
CTRL-D or DEL	Delete character cursor is on
CTRL-H or BACKSPACE	Delete character before the cursor
CTRL-K	Cut remainder of line from cursor position
CTRL-U	Cut from cursor position to beginning of line
CTRL-W	Cut previous word
CTRL-C	Cut entire line
ALT-D	Cut the remainder of a word
ALT-DEL	Cut from the cursor to the beginning of a word
CTRL-Y	Paste previous cut text
ALT-Y	Paste from set of previously cut text
CTRL-Y	Paste previous cut text
CTRL-V	Insert quoted text, used for inserting control or meta (Alt) keys as text, such as CTRL-B for backspace or CTRL-T for tabs
ALT-T	Transpose current and previous word
ALT-L	Lowercase current word
ALT-U	Uppercase current word
ALT-C	Capitalize current word
CTRL-SHIFT-_	Undo previous change

Table 19-2: Command Line Editing Operations

Command Line Editing

The BASH shell, which is your default shell, has special command line editing capabilities that you may find helpful as you learn Linux (see Table 19-2). You can easily modify commands you have entered before executing them, moving anywhere on the command line and inserting or deleting characters. This is particularly helpful for complex commands.

You can press CTRL-F or the RIGHT ARROW key to move forward a character, or the CTRL-B or LEFT ARROW key to move back a character. CTRL-D or DEL deletes the character the cursor is on, and CTRL-H or BACKSPACE deletes the character preceding the cursor. To add text, you use the arrow keys to move the cursor to where you want to insert text and type the new characters.

You can even cut words with the CTRL-W or ALT-D key, and then press the CTRL-Y key to paste them back in at a different position, effectively moving the words. As a rule, the CTRL version of the command operates on characters, and the ALT version works on words, such as CTRL-T to transpose characters and ALT-T to transpose words. At any time, you can press ENTER to execute the command. For example, if you make a spelling mistake when entering a command, rather than re-entering the entire command, you can use the editing operations to correct the mistake. The actual associations of keys and their tasks, along with global settings, are specified in the **/etc/inputrc** file.

The editing capabilities of the BASH shell command line are provided by Readline. Readline supports numerous editing operations. You can even bind a key to a selected editing operation. Readline uses the **/etc/inputrc** file to configure key bindings. This file is read automatically by your **/etc/profile** shell configuration file when you log in. Users can customize their editing commands by creating an **.inputrc** file in their home directory (this is a dot file). It may be best to first copy the **/etc/inputrc** file as your **.inputrc** file and then edit it. **/etc/profile** will first check for a local **.inputrc** file before accessing the **/etc/inputrc** file. You can find out more about Readline in the BASH shell reference manual at **www.gnu.org/manual/bash**.

Command and Filename Completion

The BASH command line has a built-in feature that performs command line and file name completion. Automatic completions can be effected by pressing the TAB key. If you enter an incomplete pattern as a command or filename argument, you can press the TAB key to activate the command and filename completion feature, which completes the pattern. A directory will have a forward slash (/) attached to its name. If more than one command or file has the same prefix, the shell simply beeps and waits for you to press the TAB key again. It then displays a list of possible command completions and waits for you to add enough characters to select a unique command or filename. For situations where you know multiple possibilities are likely, you can just press the ESC key instead of two TABs. In the next example, the user issues a `cat` command with an incomplete filename. When the user presses the TAB key, the system searches for a match and, when it finds one, fills in the filename. The user can then press ENTER to execute the command.

```
$ cat pre <tab>
$ cat preface
```

The automatic completions also work with the names of variables, users, and hosts. In this case, the partial text needs to be preceded by a special character, indicating the type of name. A listing of possible automatic completions follows:

Filenames begin with any text or /.

Shell variable text begins with a $ sign.

User name text begins with a ~ sign.

Host name text begins with a @.

Commands, aliases, and text in files begin with normal text.

Variables begin with a **$** sign, so any text beginning with a dollar sign is treated as a variable to be completed. Variables are selected from previously defined variables, like system shell variables. User names begin with a tilde (~). Host names begin with a @ sign, with possible names taken from the **/etc/hosts** file. For example, to complete the variable HOME given just $HOM, simply press a tab key.

```
$ echo $HOM <tab>
$ echo $HOME
```

If you entered just an **H**, then you could press TAB twice to see all possible variables beginning with H. The command line is redisplayed, letting you complete the name.

```
$ echo $H <tab> <tab>
$HISTCMD $HISTFILE $HOME $HOSTTYPE HISTFILE  $HISTSIZE $HISTNAME
$ echo $H
```

You can also specifically select the kind of text to complete, using corresponding command keys. In this case, it does not matter what kind of sign a name begins with.

Command (CTRL-R for listing possible completions)	Description
TAB	Automatic completion
TAB TAB or ESC	List possible completions
ALT-/, CTRL-R-/	Filename completion, normal text for automatic
ALT-$, CTRL-R-$	Shell variable completion, $ for automatic
ALT-~, CTRL-R-~	User name completion, ~ for automatic
ALT-@, CTRL-R-@	Host name completion, @ for automatic
ALT-!, CTRL-R-!	Command name completion, normal text for automatic

Table 19-3: Command Line Text Completion Commands

For example, the pressing ALT-~ will treat the current text as a user name. Pressing ALT-@ will treat it as a host name, and ALT-$, as a variable. Pressing ALT-! will treat it as a command. To display a list of possible completions, press the CTRL-X key with the appropriate completion key, as in CTRL-X-$ to list possible variable completions. See Table 19-3 for a complete listing.

History

The BASH shell keeps a *history list,* of your previously entered commands. You can display each command, in turn, on your command line by pressing the UP ARROW key. Press the DOWN ARROW key to move down the list. You can modify and execute any of these previous commands when you display them on the command line.

Tip: The ability to redisplay a command is helpful when you've already executed a command you had entered incorrectly. In this case, you would be presented with an error message and a new, empty command line. By pressing the UP ARROW key, you can redisplay the previous command, make corrections to it, and then

History Events

In the BASH shell, the *history utility* keeps a record of the most recent commands you have executed. The commands are numbered starting at 1, and a limit exists to the number of commands remembered—the default is 500. The history utility is a kind of short-term memory, keeping track of the most recent commands you have executed. To see the set of your most recent commands, type **history** on the command line and press ENTER. A list of your most recent commands is then displayed, preceded by a number.

```
$ history
1 cp mydata today
2 vi mydata
3 mv mydata reports
4 cd reports
5 ls
```

Each of these commands is technically referred to as an event. An *event* describes an action that has been taken—a command that has been executed. The events are numbered according to their sequence of execution. The most recent event has the highest number. Each of these events can be identified by its number or beginning characters in the command.

The history utility lets you reference a former event, placing it on your command line so you can execute it. The easiest way to do this is to use the UP ARROW and DOWN ARROW keys to place history events on the command line, one at a time. You needn't display the list first with **history**. Pressing the UP ARROW key once places the last history event on the command line. Pressing it again places the next history event on the command line. Pressing the DOWN ARROW key places the previous event on the command line.

You can use certain control and meta keys to perform other history operations like searching the history list. A meta key is the ALT key, and the ESC key on keyboards that have no ALT key. The ALT key is used here. Pressing ALT-< will move you to the beginning of the history list; ALT-N will search it. CTRL-S and CTRL-R will perform incremental searches, display matching commands as you type in a search string. Table 19-4 lists the different commands for referencing the history list.

Tip: If more than one history event matches what you have entered, you will hear a beep, and you can then enter more characters to help uniquely identify the event.

You can also reference and execute history events using the **!** history command. The ! is followed by a reference that identifies the command. The reference can be either the number of the event or a beginning set of characters in the event. In the next example, the third command in the history list is referenced first by number and then by the beginning characters:

```
$ !3
mv mydata reports
$ !mv my
mv mydata reports
```

History Commands	**Description**
CTRL-N or DOWN ARROW	Moves down to the next event in the history list
CTRL-P or UP ARROW	Moves up to the previous event in the history list
ALT-<	Moves to the beginning of the history event list
ALT->	Moves to the end of the history event list
ALT-N	Forward Search, next matching item
ALT-P	Backward Search, previous matching item
CTRL-S	Forward Search History, forward incremental search
CTRL-R	Reverse Search History, reverse incremental search
`fc` *event-reference*	Edits an event with the standard editor and then executes it **Options** **-l** List recent history events; same as **history** command **-e** *editor event-reference* Invokes a specified editor to edit a specific event
History Event References	
`!`*event num*	References an event with an event number
`!!`	References the previous command
`!`*characters*	References an event with beginning characters
`!?`*pattern*`?`	References an event with a pattern in the event
`!-`*event num*	References an event with an offset from the first event
`!`*num-num*	References a range of events

Table 19-4: History Commands and History Event References

You can also reference an event using an offset from the end of the list. A negative number will offset from the end of the list to that event, thereby referencing it. In the next example, the fourth command, **`cd mydata`**, is referenced using a negative offset, and then executed. Remember that you are offsetting from the end of the list—in this case, event 5—up toward the beginning of the list, event 1. An offset of 4 beginning from event 5 places you at event 2.

```
$ !-4
vi mydata
```

To reference the last event, you use a following !, as in **`!!`**. In the next example, the command **`!!`** executes the last command the user executed—in this case, **`ls`**:

```
$ !!
ls
mydata today reports
```

Filename Expansion: *, ?, [ ]

Filenames are the most common arguments used in a command. Often you will know only part of the filename, or you will want to reference several filenames that have the same extension or begin with the same characters. The shell provides a set of special characters that search out, match, and generate a list of filenames. These are the asterisk, the question mark, and brackets (`*`, `?`, `[]`). Given a partial filename, the shell uses these matching operators to search for files and expand to a list of filenames found. The shell replaces the partial filename argument with the expanded list of matched filenames. This list of filenames can then become the arguments for commands such as **`ls`**, which can operate on many files. Table 19-5 lists the shell's file expansion characters.

Matching Multiple Characters

The asterisk (`*`) references files beginning or ending with a specific set of characters. You place the asterisk before or after a set of characters that form a pattern to be searched for in filenames.

If the asterisk is placed before the pattern, filenames that end in that pattern are searched for. If the asterisk is placed after the pattern, filenames that begin with that pattern are searched for. Any matching filename is copied into a list of filenames generated by this operation.

In the next example, all filenames beginning with the pattern "doc" are searched for and a list generated. Then all filenames ending with the pattern "day" are searched for and a list is generated. The last example shows how the `*` can be used in any combination of characters.

```
$ ls
doc1 doc2 document docs mydoc monday tuesday
$ ls doc*
doc1 doc2 document docs
$ ls *day
monday tuesday
$ ls m*d*
monday
$
```

Filenames often include an extension specified with a period and followed by a string denoting the file type, such as **.c** for C files, **.cpp** for C++ files, or even **.jpg** for JPEG image files. The extension has no special status, and is only part of the characters making up the filename. Using the asterisk makes it easy to select files with a given extension. In the next example, the asterisk is used to list only those files with a **.c** extension. The asterisk placed before the **.c** constitutes the argument for **`ls`**.

```
$ ls *.c
calc.c main.c
```

You can use `*` with the **`rm`** command to erase several files at once. The asterisk first selects a list of files with a given extension, or beginning or ending with a given set of characters, and then it presents this list of files to the **`rm`** command to be erased. In the next example, the **`rm`** command erases all files beginning with the pattern "doc":

```
$ rm doc*
```

Common Shell Symbols	Execution
ENTER	Execute a command line.
;	Separate commands on the same command line.
`` `command` ``	Execute a command.
$(command)	Execute a command.
[]	Match on a class of possible characters in filenames.
\	Quote the following character. Used to quote special characters.
|	Pipe the standard output of one command as input for another command.
&	Execute a command in the background.
!	History command.
File Expansion Symbols	**Execution**
*	Match on any set of characters in filenames.
?	Match on any single character in filenames.
[]	Match on a class of characters in filenames.
Redirection Symbols	**Execution**
>	Redirect the standard output to a file or device, creating the file if it does not exist and overwriting the file if it does exist.
>!	The exclamation point forces the overwriting of a file if it already exists.
<	Redirect the standard input from a file or device to a program.
>>	Redirect the standard output to a file or device, appending the output to the end of the file.
Standard Error Redirection Symbols	**Execution**
2>	Redirect the standard error to a file or device.
2>>	Redirect and append the standard error to a file or device.
2>&1	Redirect the standard error to the standard output.

Table 19-5: Shell Symbols

Tip: Use the `*` file expansion character carefully and sparingly with the `rm` command. The combination can be dangerous. A misplaced `*` in an `rm` command without the `-i` option could easily erase all the files in your current directory. The `-i` option will first prompt the user to confirm whether the file should be deleted.

Matching Single Characters

The question mark (?) matches only a single incomplete character in filenames. Suppose you want to match the files **doc1** and **docA**, but not the file **document**. Whereas the asterisk will match filenames of any length, the question mark limits the match to one extra character. The next example matches files that begin with the word "doc" followed by a single differing letter:

```
$ ls
doc1 docA document
$ ls doc?
doc1 docA
```

Matching a Range of Characters

Whereas the * and ? file expansion characters specify incomplete portions of a filename, the brackets ([]) enable you to specify a set of valid characters to search for. Any character placed within the brackets will be matched in the filename. Suppose you want to list files beginning with "doc", but only ending in *1* or *A*. You are not interested in filenames ending in *2* or *B*, or any other character. Here is how it's done:

```
$ ls
doc1 doc2 doc3 docA docB docD document
$ ls doc[1A]
doc1 docA
```

You can also specify a set of characters as a range, rather than listing them one by one. A dash placed between the upper and lower bounds of a range of characters selects all characters within that range. The range is usually determined by the character set in use. In an ASCII character set, the range "a-g" will select all lowercase alphabetic characters from *a* through *g*, inclusive. In the next example, files beginning with the pattern "doc" and ending in characters *1* through *3* are selected. Then, those ending in characters *B* through *E* are matched.

```
$ ls doc[1-3]
doc1 doc2 doc3
$ ls doc[B-E]
docB docD
```

You can combine the brackets with other file expansion characters to form flexible matching operators. Suppose you want to list only filenames ending in either a **.c** or **.o** extension, but no other extension. You can use a combination of the asterisk and brackets: `* [co]`. The asterisk matches all filenames, and the brackets match only filenames with extension **.c** or **.o**.

```
$ ls *.[co]
main.c  main.o  calc.c
```

Matching Shell Symbols

At times, a file expansion character is actually part of a filename. In these cases, you need to quote the character by preceding it with a backslash (\) to reference the file. In the next example, the user needs to reference a file that ends with the ? character, called **answers?**. The ? is, however, a file expansion character and would match any filename beginning with "answers" that has one or more characters. In this case, the user quotes the ? with a preceding backslash to reference the filename.

```
$ ls answers\?
answers?
```

Placing the filename in double quotes will also quote the character.

```
$ ls "answers?"
answers?
```

This is also true for filenames or directories that have white space characters like the space character. In this case you could either use the backslash to quote the space character in the file or directory name, or place the entire name in double quotes.

```
$ ls My\ Documents
My Documents
$ ls "My Documents"
My Documents
```

Generating Patterns

Though not a file expansion operation, `{}` is often useful for generating names that you can use to create or modify files and directories. The braces operation only generates a list of names. It does not match on existing filenames. Patterns are placed within the braces and separated with commas. Any pattern placed within the braces will be used to generate a version of the pattern, using either the preceding or following pattern, or both. Suppose you want to generate a list of names beginning with "doc", but ending only in the patterns "ument", "final", and "draft". Here is how it's done:

```
$ echo doc{ument,final,draft}
document docfinal docdraft
```

Since the names generated do not have to exist, you could use the `{}` operation in a command to create directories, as shown here:

```
$ mkdir {fall,winter,spring}report
$ ls
fallreport springreport winterreport
```

Standard Input/Output and Redirection

The data in input and output operations are organized like a file. Data input at the keyboard is placed in a data stream arranged as a continuous set of bytes. Data output from a command or program is also placed in a data stream and arranged as a continuous set of bytes. This input data stream is referred to in Linux as the *standard input,* while the output data stream is called the *standard output.* A separate output data stream reserved solely for error messages is called the *standard error.*

Because the standard input and standard output have the same organization as that of a file, they can easily interact with files. Linux has a redirection capability that lets you easily move data in and out of files. You can redirect the standard output so that, instead of displaying the output on a screen, you can save it in a file. You can also redirect the standard input away from the keyboard to a file, so that input is read from a file instead of from your keyboard.

When a Linux command is executed that produces output, this output is placed in the standard output data stream. The default destination for the standard output data stream is a device—in this case, the screen. *Devices,* such as the keyboard and screen, are treated as files. They receive and send out streams of bytes with the same organization as that of a byte-stream file. The screen is a device that displays a continuous stream of bytes. By default, the standard output will send its data to the screen device, which will then display the data.

For example, the `ls` command generates a list of all filenames and outputs this list to the standard output. Next, this stream of bytes in the standard output is directed to the screen device. The list of filenames is then printed on the screen. The `cat` command also sends output to the standard output. The contents of a file are copied to the standard output, whose default destination is the screen. The contents of the file are then displayed on the screen.

Command	**Execution**
ENTER	Execute a command line
;	Separate commands on the same command line
command\ *opts args*	Enter backslash before carriage return to continue entering a command on the next line
\` *command* \`	Execute a command
Special Characters for Filename Expansion	**Execution**
*	Match on any set of characters
?	Match on any single characters
[]	Match on a class of possible characters
\	Quote the following character. Used to quote special characters
Redirection	**Execution**
command > *filename*	Redirect the standard output to a file or device, creating the file if it does not exist and overwriting the file if it does exist
command < *filename*	Redirect the standard input from a file or device to a program.
command >> *filename*	Redirect the standard output to a file or device, appending the output to the end of the file
command 2> *filename*	Redirect the standard error to a file or device
command 2>> *filename*	Redirect and append the standard error to a file or device
command 2>&1	Redirect the standard error to the standard output in the Bourne shell
command >& *filename*	Redirect the standard error to a file or device in the C shell
Pipes	**Execution**
command | *command*	Pipe the standard output of one command as input for another command

Table 19-6: The Shell Operations

Redirecting the Standard Output: > and >>

Suppose that instead of displaying a list of files on the screen, you would like to save this list in a file. In other words, you would like to direct the standard output to a file rather than the screen. To do this, you place the output redirection operator, the greater-than sign (>), followed by the name of a file on the command line after the Linux command. Table 19-6 lists the different ways you can use the redirection operators. In the next example, the output of the `ls` command is redirected from the screen device to a file:

```
$ ls -l *.c > programlist
```

The redirection operation creates the new destination file. If the file already exists, it will be overwritten with the data in the standard output. You can set the **noclobber** feature to prevent overwriting an existing file with the redirection operation. In this case, the redirection operation on an existing file will fail. You can overcome the **noclobber** feature by placing an exclamation point after the redirection operator. You can place the **noclobber** command in a shell configuration file to make it an automatic default operation. The next example sets the **noclobber** feature for the BASH shell and then forces the overwriting of the **oldarticle** file if it already exists:

```
$ set -o noclobber
$ cat myarticle >! oldarticle
```

Although the redirection operator and the filename are placed after the command, the redirection operation is not executed after the command. In fact, it is executed before the command. The redirection operation creates the file and sets up the redirection before it receives any data from the standard output. If the file already exists, it will be destroyed and replaced by a file of the same name. In effect, the command generating the output is executed only after the redirected file has been created.

In the next example, the output of the `ls` command is redirected from the screen device to a file. First the `ls` command lists files, and in the next command, `ls` redirects its file list to the **listf** file. Then the `cat` command displays the list of files saved in **listf**. Notice the list of files in **listf** includes the **listf** filename. The list of filenames generated by the `ls` command includes the name of the file created by the redirection operation—in this case, **listf**. The **listf** file is first created by the redirection operation, and then the `ls` command lists it along with other files. This file list output by `ls` is then redirected to the **listf** file, instead of being printed on the screen.

```
$ ls
mydata intro preface
$ ls > listf
$ cat listf
mydata intro listf preface
```

Tip: Errors occur when you try to use the same filename for both an input file for the command and the redirected destination file. In this case, because the redirection operation is executed first, the input file, because it exists, is destroyed and replaced by a file of the same name. When the command is executed, it finds an input file that is empty.

You can also append the standard output to an existing file using the >> redirection operator. Instead of overwriting the file, the data in the standard output is added at the end of the file. In the next example, the **myarticle** and **oldarticle** files are appended to the **allarticles** file. The **allarticles** file will then contain the contents of both **myarticle** and **oldarticle**.

```
$ cat myarticle >> allarticles
$ cat oldarticle >> allarticles
```

The Standard Input

Many Linux commands can receive data from the standard input. The standard input itself receives data from a device or a file. The default device for the standard input is the keyboard. Characters typed on the keyboard are placed in the standard input, which is then directed to the Linux command. Just as with the standard output, you can also redirect the standard input, receiving input from a file rather than the keyboard. The operator for redirecting the standard input is the less-than sign (<). In the next example, the standard input is redirected to receive input from the **myarticle** file, rather than the keyboard device (use CTRL-D to end the typed input). The contents of **myarticle** are read into the standard input by the redirection operation. Then the `cat` command reads the standard input and displays the contents of **myarticle**.

```
$ cat < myarticle
hello Christopher
How are you today
$
```

You can combine the redirection operations for both standard input and standard output. In the next example, the `cat` command has no filename arguments. Without filename arguments, the `cat` command receives input from the standard input and sends output to the standard output. However, the standard input has been redirected to receive its data from a file, while the standard output has been redirected to place its data in a file.

```
$ cat < myarticle > newarticle
```

Redirecting the Standard Error: >&, 2>, |&

When you execute commands, it is possible for an error to occur. You may give the wrong number of arguments or some kind of system error could take place. When an error occurs, the system will issue an error message. Usually such error messages are displayed on the screen along with the standard output. Error messages are placed in another standard byte stream called the standard error. In the next example, the cat command is given as its argument the name of a file that does not exist, **myintro**. In this case, the `cat` command will simply issue an error. Redirection operators are listed in Table 19-6.

```
$ cat myintro
cat : myintro not found
```

Because error messages are in a separate data stream from the standard output, this means that if you have redirected the standard output to a file, error messages will still appear on the screen for you to see. Though the standard output may be redirected to a file, the standard error is still directed to the screen. In the next example, the standard output of the `cat` command is redirected to the file **mydata**. The standard error, containing the error messages, is still directed toward the screen

```
$ cat myintro > mydata
cat : myintro not found
```

Like the standard output, you can also redirect the standard error. This means that you can save your error messages in a file for future reference. This is helpful if you need to save a record of the error messages. Like the standard output, the standard error's default destination is the display. Using special redirection operators, you can redirect the standard error to any file or device that you choose. If you redirect the standard error, the error messages will not be displayed on the screen. You can examine them later by viewing the contents of the file in which you saved them.

All the standard byte streams can be referenced in redirection operations with numbers. The numbers 0, 1, and 2 reference the standard input, standard output, and standard error respectively. By default an output redirection, >, operates on the standard output, 1. You can modify the output redirection to operate on the standard error by preceding the output redirection operator with the number 2, `2>`. In the next example, the `cat` command again will generate an error. The error message is redirected to the standard byte stream represented by number 2, the standard error.

```
$ cat nodata 2> myerrors
$ cat myerrors
cat : nodata not found
```

You can also append the standard error to a file by using the number 2 and the redirection append operator, >>. In the next example, the user appends the standard error to the **myerrors** file, which then functions as a log of errors.

```
$ cat nodata 2>> myerrors
$ cat compls 2>> myerrors
$ cat myerrors
cat : nodata not found
cat : compls not found
$
```

To redirect both the standard output as well as the standard error, you would need a separate redirection operation and file for each. In the next example, the standard output is redirected to the file **mydata**, and the standard error is redirected to **myerrors**. If nodata were to exist, then **mydata** would hold a copy of its contents.

```
$ cat nodata 1> mydata 2> myerrors
cat myerrors
cat : nodata not found
```

If, however, you want to save a record of your errors in the same file as that used for the redirected standard output, you need to redirect the standard error into the standard output. You can reference a standard byte stream by preceding its number with an ampersand. `&1` references the standard output. You can use such a reference in a redirection operation to make a standard byte stream a destination file. The redirection operation `2>&1` redirects the standard error into the standard output. In effect, the standard output becomes the destination file for the standard error. Conversely the redirection operation `1>&2` would redirect the standard input into the standard error.

Pipes: |

You may encounter situations in which you need to send data from one command to another. In other words, you may want to send the standard output of a command to another command, rather than to a destination file. Suppose you want to send a list of your filenames to the printer to be printed. You need two commands to do this: the **ls** command to generate a list of filenames and the **lpr** command to send the list to the printer. In effect, you need to take the output of the **ls** command and use it as input for the **lpr** command. You can think of the data as flowing from one command to another. To form such a connection in Linux, you use what is called a *pipe.* The *pipe operator* (|, the vertical bar character) placed between two commands forms a connection between them. The standard output of one command becomes the standard input for the other. The pipe operation receives output from the command placed before the pipe and sends this data as input to the command placed after the pipe. As shown in the next example, you can connect the **ls** command and the **lpr** command with a pipe. The list of filenames output by the **ls** command is piped into the **lpr** command.

```
$ ls | lpr
```

You can combine the **pipe** operation with other shell features, such as file expansion characters, to perform specialized operations. The next example prints only files with a **.c** extension. The **ls** command is used with the asterisk and ".c" to generate a list of filenames with the **.c** extension. Then this list is piped to the **lpr** command.

```
$ ls *.c | lpr
```

In the preceding example, a list of filenames was used as input, but what is important to note is that pipes operate on the standard output of a command, whatever that might be. The contents of whole files, or even several files, can be piped from one command to another. In the next example, the **cat** command reads and outputs the contents of the **mydata** file, which are then piped to the **lpr** command:

```
$ cat mydata | lpr
```

Linux has many commands that generate modified output. For example, the **sort** command takes the contents of a file and generates a version with each line sorted in alphabetic order. The **sort** command works best with files that are lists of items. Commands such as **sort** that output a modified version of its input are referred to as *filters.* Filters are often used with pipes. In the next example, a sorted version of **mylist** is generated and piped into the **more** command for display on the screen. The original file, **mylist**, has not been changed and is not sorted. Only the output of **sort** in the standard output is sorted.

```
$ sort mylist | more
```

The standard input piped into a command can be more carefully controlled with the standard input argument (-). When you use the dash as an argument for a command, it represents the standard input.

20. Working with files and directories

Linux Files

The File Structure

Listing, Displaying, and Printing Files: ls, cat, more, less, and lpr

Managing Directories: mkdir, rmdir, ls, cd, pwd

File and Directory Operations: find, cp, mv, rm, ln

Archiving and Compressing Files

In Linux, all files are organized into directories that, in turn, are hierarchically connected to each other in one overall file structure. A file is referenced not according to just its name, but also according to its place in this file structure. You can create as many new directories as you want, adding more directories to the file structure. The Linux file commands can perform sophisticated operations, such as moving or copying whole directories along with their subdirectories. You can use file operations such as find, cp, mv, and ln to locate files and copy, move, or link them from one directory to another. Desktop file managers, such as Konqueror and Nautilus used on the KDE and GNOME desktops, provide a graphical user interface to perform the same operations using icons, windows, and menus (see Chapters 3). This chapter will focus on the commands you use in the shell command line to manage files, such as cp and mv. However, whether you use the command line or a desktop file manager, the underlying file structure is the same.

Though not part of the Linux file structure, there are also special tools you can use to access Windows partitions and floppy disks. These follow much the same format as Linux file commands.

Archives are used to back up files or to combine them into a package, which can then be transferred as one file over the Internet or posted on an FTP site for easy downloading. The standard archive utility used on Linux and UNIX systems is tar, for which several desktop graphical front ends exist. You have several compression programs to choose from, including GNU zip (gzip), Zip, bzip, and compress.

Linux Files

You can name a file using any letters, underscores, and numbers. You can also include periods and commas. Except in certain special cases, you should never begin a filename with a period. Other characters, such as slashes, question marks, or asterisks, are reserved for use as special characters by the system and should not be part of a filename. Filenames can be as long as 256 characters. Filenames can also include spaces, though to reference such filenames from the command line, be sure to encase them in quotes. On a desktop like GNOME or KDE you do not need to use quotes.

You can include an extension as part of a filename. A period is used to distinguish the filename proper from the extension. Extensions can be useful for categorizing your files. You are probably familiar with certain standard extensions that have been adopted by convention. For example, C source code files always have a **.c** extension. Files that contain compiled object code have an **.o** extension. You can, of course, make up your own file extensions. The following examples are all valid Linux filenames. Keep in mind that to reference the name with spaces on the command line, you would have to encase it in quotes as "New book review":

```
preface
chapter2
9700info
New_Revisions
calc.c
intro.bk1
New book review
```

Special initialization files are also used to hold shell configuration commands. These are the hidden, or dot, files, which begin with a period. Dot files used by commands and applications have predetermined names, such as the **.mozilla** directory used to hold your Mozilla data and configuration files. Recall that when you use ls to display your filenames, the dot files will not be displayed. To include the dot files, you need to use ls with the **-a** option.

The **ls -l** command displays detailed information about a file. First, the permissions are displayed, followed by the number of links, the owner of the file, the name of the group to which the user belongs, the file size in bytes, the date and time the file was last modified, and the name of the file. Permissions indicate who can access the file: the user, members of a group, or all other users. The group name indicates the group permitted to access the file object. The file type for **mydata** is that of an ordinary file. Only one link exists, indicating the file has no other names and no other links. The owner's name is **chris**, the same as the login name, and the group name is **weather**. Other users probably also belong to the **weather** group. The size of the file is 207 bytes, and it was last modified on February 20 at 11:55 A.M. The name of the file is **mydata**.

If you want to display this detailed information for all the files in a directory, simply use the ls -l command without an argument.

```
$ ls -l
-rw-r--r-- 1 chris weather 207 Feb 20 11:55 mydata
-rw-rw-r-- 1 chris weather 568 Feb 14 10:30 today
-rw-rw-r-- 1 chris weather 308 Feb 17 12:40 monday
```

All files in Linux have one physical format, a byte stream, which is simply a sequence of bytes. This allows Linux to apply the file concept to every data component in the system. Directories are classified as files, as are devices. Treating everything as a file allows Linux to organize and exchange data more easily. The data in a file can be sent directly to a device such as a screen because a device interfaces with the system using the same byte-stream file format used by regular files.

This same file format is used to implement other operating system components. The interface to a device, such as the screen or keyboard, is designated as a file. Other components, such as directories, are themselves byte-stream files, but they have a special internal organization. A directory file contains information about a directory, organized in a special directory format. Because these different components are treated as files, they can be said to constitute different *file types.* A character device is one file type. A directory is another file type. The number of these file types may vary according to your specific implementation of Linux. Five common types of files exist, however: ordinary files, directory files, first-in first-out (FIFO) pipes, character device files, and block device files. Although you may rarely reference a file's type, it can be useful when searching for directories or devices.

Although all ordinary files have a byte-stream format, they may be used in different ways. The most significant difference is between binary and text files. Compiled programs are examples of binary files. However, even text files can be classified according to their different uses. You can have files that contain C programming source code or shell commands, or even a file that is empty. The file could be an executable program or a directory file. The Linux file command helps you determine what a file is used for. It examines the first few lines of a file and tries to determine a classification for it. The file command looks for special keywords or special numbers in those first few lines, but it is not always accurate. In the next example, the file command examines the contents of two files and determines a classification for them:

```
$ file monday reports
monday: text
reports: directory
```

If you need to examine the entire file byte by byte, you can do so with the od (octal dump) command, which performs a dump of a file. By default, it prints every byte in its octal representation. However, you can also specify a character, decimal, or hexadecimal representation. The od command is helpful when you need to detect any special character in your file or if you want to display a binary file.

The File Structure

Linux organizes files into a hierarchically connected set of directories. Each directory may contain either files or other directories. In this respect, directories perform two important functions. A *directory* holds files, much like files held in a file drawer, and a directory connects to other directories, much as a branch in a tree is connected to other branches. Because of the similarities to a tree, such a structure is often referred to as a *tree structure.*

The Linux file structure branches into several directories beginning with a root directory, /. Within the root directory, several system directories contain files and programs that are features of the Linux system. The root directory also contains a directory called **/home** that contains the home directories of all the users in the system. Each user's home directory, in turn, contains the directories the user has made for their own use. Each of these can also contain directories. Such nested directories branch out from the user's home directory.

Note: The user's home directory can be any directory, though it is usually the directory that bears the user's login name. This directory is located in the directory named **/home** on your Linux system. For example, a user named **dylan** will have a home directory called **dylan** located in the system's **/home** directory. The user's home directory is a subdirectory of the directory called **/home** on your system.

Home Directories

When you log in to the system, you are placed within your home directory. The name given to this directory by the system is the same as your login name. Any files you create when you first log in are organized within your home directory. Within your home directory, you can create more directories. You can then change to these directories and store files in them. The same is true for other users on the system. Each user has a home directory, identified by the appropriate login name. Users, in turn, can create their own directories.

You can access a directory either through its name or by making it your working directory. Each directory is given a name when it is created. You can use this name in file operations to access files in that directory. You can also make the directory your working directory. If you do not use any directory names in a file operation, the working directory will be accessed. The working directory is the one from which you are currently working. When you log in, the working directory is your home directory, which usually has the same name as your login name. You can change the working directory by using the cd command to move to another directory.

Pathnames

The name you give to a directory or file when you create it is not its full name. The full name of a directory is its pathname. The hierarchically nested relationship among directories forms paths and these paths can be used to identify and reference any directory or file uniquely or absolutely. Each directory in the file structure can be said to have its own unique path. The actual name by which the system identifies a directory always begins with the root directory and consists of all directories nested below that directory.

In Linux, you write a pathname by listing each directory in the path separated from the last by a forward slash. A slash preceding the first directory in the path represents the root. The pathname for the **chris** directory is **/home/chris**. If the **chris** directory has a subdirectory called **reports**, then the full the pathname for the **reports** directory would be **/home/chris/reports**. Pathnames also apply to files. When you create a file within a directory, you give the file a name. The actual name by which the system identifies the file, however, is the filename combined with the path of directories from the root to the file's directory. As an example, the pathname for **monday** is **/home/chris/reports/monday** (the root directory is represented by the first slash). The path for the **monday** file consists of the root, **home**, **chris**, and **reports** directories and the filename **monday**.

Directory	Function
/	Begins the file system structure, called the *root*.
/home	Contains users' home directories.
/bin	Holds all the standard commands and utility programs.
/usr	Holds those files and commands used by the system; this directory breaks down into several subdirectories.
/usr/bin	Holds user-oriented commands and utility programs.
/usr/sbin	Holds system administration commands.
/usr/lib	Holds libraries for programming languages.
/usr/share/doc	Holds Linux documentation.
/usr/share/man	Holds the online Man files.
/var/spool	Holds spooled files, such as those generated for printing jobs and network transfers.
/sbin	Holds system administration commands for booting the system.
/var	Holds files that vary, such as mailbox files.
/dev	Holds file interfaces for devices such as the terminals and printers (dynamically generated by udev, do not edit).
/etc	Holds system configuration files and any other system files.

Table 20-1: Standard System Directories in Linux

Pathnames may be absolute or relative. An *absolute pathname* is the complete pathname of a file or directory beginning with the root directory. A *relative pathname* begins from your working directory; it is the path of a file relative to your working directory. The working directory is the one you are currently operating in. Using the previous example, if **chris** is your working directory, the relative pathname for the file **monday** is **reports/monday**. The absolute pathname for **monday** is **/home/chris/reports/monday**.

The absolute pathname from the root to your home directory can be especially complex and, at times, even subject to change by the system administrator. To make it easier to reference, you can use the tilde (~) character, which represents the absolute pathname of your home directory. You must specify the rest of the path from your home directory. In the next example, the user references the **monday** file in the **reports** directory. The tilde represents the path to the user's home directory, **/home/chris**, and then the rest of the path to the **monday** file is specified.

```
$ cat ~/reports/monday
```

System Directories

The root directory that begins the Linux file structure contains several system directories that contain files and programs used to run and maintain the system. Many also contain other subdirectories with programs for executing specific features of Linux. For example, the directory **/usr/bin** contains the various Linux commands that users execute, such as lpl. The directory **/bin** holds system level commands. Table 20-1 lists the basic system directories.

Listing, Displaying, and Printing Files: ls, cat, more, less, and lpr

One of the primary functions of an operating system is the management of files. You may need to perform certain basic output operations on your files, such as displaying them on your screen or printing them. The Linux system provides a set of commands that perform basic file-management operations, such as listing, displaying, and printing files, as well as copying, renaming, and erasing files. These commands are usually made up of abbreviated versions of words. For example, the `ls` command is a shortened form of "list" and lists the files in your directory. The `lpr` command is an abbreviated form of "line print" and will print a file. The `cat`, `less`, and `more` commands display the contents of a file on the screen. Table 20-2 lists these commands with their different options. When you log in to your Linux system, you may want a list of the files in your home directory. The `ls` command, which outputs a list of your file and directory names, is useful for this. The `ls` command has many possible options for displaying filenames according to specific features.

Displaying Files: cat, less, and more

You may also need to look at the contents of a file. The `cat` and `more` commands display the contents of a file on the screen. The name `cat` stands for *concatenate.*

```
$ cat mydata
computers
```

The `cat` command outputs the entire text of a file to the screen at once. This presents a problem when the file is large because its text quickly speeds past on the screen. The `more` and `less` commands are designed to overcome this limitation by displaying one screen of text at a time. You can then move forward or backward in the text at your leisure. You invoke the `more` or `less` command by entering the command name followed by the name of the file you want to view (**less** is a more powerful and configurable display utility).

```
$ less mydata
```

When **more** or **less** invoke a file, the first screen of text is displayed. To continue to the next screen, you press the F key or the SPACEBAR. To move back in the text, you press the B key. You can quit at any time by pressing the Q key.

Command or Option	Execution
`ls`	This command lists file and directory names.
`cat` *filenames*	This filter can be used to display a file. It can take filenames for its arguments. It outputs the contents of those files directly to the standard output, which, by default, is directed to the screen.
`more` *filenames*	This utility displays a file screen by screen. Press the SPACEBAR to continue to the next screen and **q** to quit.
`less` *filenames*	This utility also displays a file screen by screen. Press the SPACEBAR to continue to the next screen and **q** to quit.
`lpr` *filenames*	Sends a file to the line printer to be printed; a list of files may be used as arguments. Use the **-P** option to specify a printer.
`lpq`	Lists the print queue for printing jobs.
`lprm`	Removes a printing job from the print queue.

Table 20-2: Listing, Displaying, and Printing Files

Printing Files: lpr, lpq, and lprm

With the printer commands such as **lpr** and **lprm**, you can perform printing operations such as printing files or canceling print jobs (see Table 20-2). When you need to print files, use the **lpr** command to send files to the printer connected to your system. In the next example, the user prints the **mydata** file:

```
$ lpr mydata
```

If you want to print several files at once, you can specify more than one file on the command line after the **lpr** command. In the next example, the user prints out both the **mydata** and **preface** files:

```
$ lpr mydata preface
```

Printing jobs are placed in a queue and printed one at a time in the background. You can continue with other work as your files print. You can see the position of a particular printing job at any given time with the lpq command, which gives the owner of the printing job (the login name of the user who sent the job), the print job ID, the size in bytes, and the temporary file in which it is currently held.

If you need to cancel an unwanted printing job, you can do so with the **lprm** command, which takes as its argument either the ID number of the printing job, or the owner's name. It then removes the print job from the print queue. For this task, `lpq` is helpful, for it provides you with the ID number and owner of the printing job you need to use with `lprm`.

Managing Directories: mkdir, rmdir, ls, cd, pwd

You can create and remove your own directories, as well as change your working directory, with the `mkdir`, `rmdir`, and `cd` commands. Each of these commands can take as its argument the pathname for a directory. The `pwd` command displays the absolute pathname of your working directory. In addition to these commands, the special characters represented by a single dot, a double dot, and a tilde can be used to reference the working directory, the parent of the working directory, and the home directory, respectively. Taken together, these commands enable you to manage your directories. You can create nested directories, move from one directory to another, and use pathnames to reference any of your directories. Those commands commonly used to manage directories are listed in Table 20-3.

Command	**Execution**
`mkdir` *directory*	Creates a directory.
`rmdir` *directory*	Erases a directory.
`ls -F`	Lists directory name with a preceding slash.
`ls -R`	Lists working directory as well as all subdirectories.
`cd` *directory name*	Changes to the specified directory, making it the working directory. **cd** without a directory name changes back to the home directory: **$ cd reports**
`pwd`	Displays the pathname of the working directory.
directory name / filename	A slash is used in pathnames to separate each directory name. In the case of pathnames for files, a slash separates the preceding directory names from the filename.
`..`	References the parent directory. You can use it as an argument or as part of a pathname. **$ cd ..** **$ mv ../larisa oldarticles**
`.`	References the working directory. You can use it as an argument or as part of a pathname. **$ ls .**
~ / pathname	The tilde is a special character that represents the pathname for the home directory. It is useful when you need to use an absolute pathname for a file or directory: **$ cp monday ~/today**

Table 20-3: Directory Commands

Creating and Deleting Directories

You create and remove directories with the `mkdir` and `rmdir` commands. In either case, you can also use pathnames for the directories. In the next example, the user creates the directory **reports**. Then the user creates the directory **articles** using a pathname:

```
$ mkdir reports
$ mkdir /home/chris/articles
```

You can remove a directory with the `rmdir` command followed by the directory name. In the next example, the user removes the directory **reports** with the `rmdir` command:

```
$ rmdir reports
```

To remove a directory and all its subdirectories, you use the `rm` command with the `-r` option. This is a very powerful command and could easily be used to erase all your files. You will be prompted for each file. To simply remove all files and subdirectories without prompts, add the `-f` option. The following example deletes the **reports** directory and all its subdirectories:

```
rm -rf reports
```

Displaying Directory Contents

You have seen how to use the `ls` command to list the files and directories within your working directory. To distinguish between file and directory names, however, you need to use the `ls` command with the `-F` option. A slash is then placed after each directory name in the list.

```
$ ls
weather reports articles
$ ls -F
weather reports/ articles/
```

The `ls` command also takes as an argument any directory name or directory pathname. This enables you to list the files in any directory without first having to change to that directory. In the next example, the `ls` command takes as its argument the name of a directory, **reports**. Then the `ls` command is executed again, only this time the absolute pathname of **reports** is used.

```
$ ls reports
monday tuesday
$ ls /home/chris/reports
monday tuesday
$
```

Moving Through Directories

The `cd` command takes as its argument the name of the directory to which you want to move. The name of the directory can be the name of a subdirectory in your working directory or the full pathname of any directory on the system. If you want to change back to your home directory, you need to enter only the `cd` command by itself, without a filename argument.

```
$ cd reports
$ pwd
/home/chris/reports
```

Referencing the Parent Directory

A directory always has a parent (except, of course, for the root). For example, in the preceding listing, the parent for **reports** is the **chris** directory. When a directory is created, two entries are made: one represented with a dot (.), and the other with double dots (..). The dot represents the pathnames of the directory, and the double dots represent the pathname of its parent directory. Double dots, used as an argument in a command, reference a parent directory. The single dot references the directory itself.

You can use the single dot to reference your working directory, instead of using its pathname. For example, to copy a file to the working directory retaining the same name, the dot can be used in place of the working directory's pathname. In this sense, the dot is another name for the working directory. In the next example, the user copies the **weather** file from the **chris** directory to the **reports** directory. The **reports** directory is the working directory and can be represented with the single dot.

```
$ cd reports
$ cp /home/chris/weather .
```

The .. symbol is often used to reference files in the parent directory. In the next example, the `cat` command displays the **weather** file in the parent directory. The pathname for the file is the .. symbol (for the parent directory) followed by a slash and the filename.

```
$ cat ../weather
raining and warm
```

Tip: You can use the `cd` command with the `..` symbol to step back through successive parent directories of the directory tree from a lower directory.

File and Directory Operations: find, cp, mv, rm, ln

As you create more and more files, you may want to back them up, change their names, erase some of them, or even give them added names. Linux provides several file commands that you can use to search for files, copy files, rename files, or remove files (see Table 20-5). If you have a large number of files, you can also search them to locate a specific one. The commands are shortened forms of full words, consisting of only two characters. The `cp` command stands for "copy" and copies a file, `mv` stands for "move" and renames or moves a file, `rm` stands for "remove" and erases a file, and `ln` stands for "link" and adds another name for a file, often used as a shortcut to the original. One exception to the two-character rule is the `find` command, which performs searches of your filenames to find a file. All these operations can be handled by the GUI desktops, like GNOME and KDE.

Searching Directories: find

Once a large number of files have been stored in many different directories, you may need to search them to locate a specific file, or files, of a certain type. The `find` command enables you to perform such a search from the command line. The `find` command takes as its arguments directory names followed by several possible options that specify the type of search and the criteria for the search; it then searches within the directories listed and their subdirectories for files that meet these criteria. The `find` command can search for a file by name, type, owner, and even the time of the last update.

```
$ find directory-list -option criteria
```

The **-name** option has as its criteria a pattern and instructs **find** to search for the filename that matches that pattern. To search for a file by name, you use the **find** command with the directory name followed by the **-name** option and the name of the file.

```
$ find directory-list -name filename
```

The **find** command also has options that merely perform actions, such as outputting the results of a search. If you want **find** to display the filenames it has located, you simply include the **-print** option on the command line along with any other options. The **-print** option is an action that instructs **find** to write to the standard output the names of all the files it locates (you can also use the **-ls** option instead to list files in the long format). In the next example, the user searches for all the files in the **reports** directory with the name **monday**. Once located, the file, with its relative pathname, is printed.

```
$ find reports -name monday -print
reports/monday
```

The **find** command prints out the filenames using the directory name specified in the directory list. If you specify an absolute pathname, the absolute path of the found directories will be output. If you specify a relative pathname, only the relative pathname is output. In the preceding example, the user specified a relative pathname, **reports**, in the directory list. Located filenames were output beginning with this relative pathname. In the next example, the user specifies an absolute pathname in the directory list. Located filenames are then output using this absolute pathname.

```
$ find /home/chris  -name monday -print
/home/chris/reports/monday
```

Tip: Should you need to find the location of a specific program or configuration file, you could use **find** to search for the file from the root directory. Log in as the root user and use **/** as the directory. This command searched for the location of the **more** command and files on the entire file system: **find / -name more -print**.

Searching the Working Directory

If you want to search your working directory, you can use the dot in the directory pathname to represent your working directory. The double dots would represent the parent directory. The next example searches all files and subdirectories in the working directory, using the dot to represent the working directory. If your working directory is your home directory, this is a convenient way to search through all your own directories. Notice that the located filenames that are output begin with a dot.

```
$ find . -name  weather -print
./weather
```

Command or Option	Execution
`find`	Searches directories for files according to search criteria. This command has several options that specify the type of criteria and actions to be taken.
`-name` *pattern*	Searches for files with the *pattern* in the name.
`-lname` *pattern*	Searches for symbolic link files.
`-group` *name*	Searches for files belonging to the group *name*.
`-gid` *name*	Searches for files belonging to a group according to group ID.
`-user` *name*	Searches for files belonging to a user.
`-uid` *name*	Searches for files belonging to a user according to user ID.
`-size` *numc*	Searches for files with the size *num* in blocks. If **c** is added after *num,* the size in bytes (characters) is searched for.
`-mtime` *num*	Searches for files last modified *num* days ago.
`-newer` *pattern*	Searches for files modified after the one matched by *pattern.*
`-context` *scontext*	Searches for files according to security context (SE Linux).
`-print`	Outputs the result of the search to the standard output. The result is usually a list of filenames, including their full pathnames.
`-type` *filetype*	Searches for files with the specified file type. File type can be **b** for block device, **c** for character device, **d** for directory, **f** for file, or **l** for symbolic link.
`-perm` *permission*	Searches for files with certain permissions set. Use octal or symbolic format for permissions.
`-ls`	Provides a detailed listing of each file, with owner, permission, size, and date information.
`-exec` *command*	Executes command when files found.

Table 20-4: The find Command

You can use shell wildcard characters as part of the pattern criteria for searching files. The special character must be quoted, however, to avoid evaluation by the shell. In the next example, all files (indicated by the asterisk, *) with the **.c** extension in the **programs** directory are searched for and then displayed in the long format using the `-ls` action:

```
$ find programs -name '*.c' -ls
```

Locating Directories

You can also use the `find` command to locate other directories. In Linux, a directory is officially classified as a special type of file. Although all files have a byte-stream format, some files, such as directories, are used in special ways. In this sense, a file can be said to have a file type. The `find` command has an option called `-type` that searches for a file of a given type. The `-type` option takes a one-character modifier that represents the file type. The modifier that represents a directory is a **d**. In the next example, both the directory name and the directory file type are used to search for the directory called **travel**:

```
$ find /home/chris -name travel -type d -print
/home/chris/articles/travel
$
```

File types are not so much different types of files, as they are the file format applied to other components of the operating system, such as devices. In this sense, a device is treated as a type of file, and you can use **find** to search for devices and directories, as well as ordinary files. Table 20-4 lists the different types available for the **find** command's **-type** option.

You can also use the find operation to search for files by ownership or security criteria, like those belonging to a specific user or those with a certain security context. The **-user** option lets to locate all files belonging to a certain user. The following example lists all files that the user **chris** has created or owns on the entire system. To list those just in the users' home directories, you would use **/home** for the starting search directory. This would find all those in a user's home directory as well as any owned by that user in other user directories.

```
$ find / -user chris -print
```

Copying Files

To make a copy of a file, you simply give **cp** two filenames as its arguments (see Table 20-5). The first filename is the name of the file to be copied—the one that already exists. This is often referred to as the *source file.* The second filename is the name you want for the copy. This will be a new file containing a copy of all the data in the source file. This second argument is often referred to as the *destination file.* The syntax for the **cp** command follows:

```
$ cp source-file destination-file
```

In the next example, the user copies a file called **proposal** to a new file called **oldprop**:

```
$ cp proposal oldprop
```

You could unintentionally destroy another file with the **cp** command. The **cp** command generates a copy by first creating a file and then copying data into it. If another file has the same name as the destination file, that file is destroyed and a new file with that name is created. By default, Ubuntu configures your system to check for an existing copy by the same name (**cp** is aliased with the **-i** option). To copy a file from your working directory to another directory, you need to use that directory name as the second argument in the **cp** command. In the next example, the **proposal** file is overwritten by the **newprop** file. The **proposal** file already exists.

```
$ cp newprop proposal
```

You can use any of the wildcard characters to generate a list of filenames to use with **cp** or **mv**. For example, suppose you need to copy all your C source code files to a given directory. Instead of listing each one individually on the command line, you could use an * character with the **.c** extension to match on and generate a list of C source code files (all files with a **.c** extension). In the next example, the user copies all source code files in the current directory to the **sourcebks** directory:

```
$ cp *.c sourcebks
```

If you want to copy all the files in a given directory to another directory, you could use * to match on and generate a list of all those files in a **cp** command. In the next example, the user copies all the files in the **props** directory to the **oldprop** directory. Notice the use of a **props** pathname preceding the * special characters. In this context, **props** is a pathname that will be appended before each file in the list that * generates.

```
$ cp props/* oldprop
```

You can, of course, use any of the other special characters, such as ., ?, or []. In the next example, the user copies both source code and object code files (**.c** and **.o**) to the **projbk** directory:

```
$ cp *.[oc] projbk
```

When you copy a file, you can give the copy a name that is different from the original. To do so, place the new filename after the directory name, separated by a slash.

```
$ cp filename directory-name/new-filename
```

Command	Execution
cp *filename filename*	Copies a file. **cp** takes two arguments: the original file and the name of the new copy. You can use pathnames for the files to copy across directories:
cp -r *dirname dirname*	Copies a subdirectory from one directory to another. The copied directory includes all its own subdirectories:
mv *filename filename*	Moves (renames) a file. The **mv** command takes two arguments: the first is the file to be moved. The second argument can be the new filename or the pathname of a directory. If it is the name of a directory, then the file is literally moved to that directory, changing the file's pathname:
mv *dirname dirname*	Moves directories. In this case, the first and last arguments are directories:
ln *filename filename*	Creates added names for files referred to as links. A link can be created in one directory that references a file in another directory:
rm *filenames*	Removes (erases) a file. Can take any number of filenames as its arguments. Literally removes links to a file. If a file has more than one link, you need to remove all of them to erase a file:

Table 20-5: File Operations

Moving Files

You can use the **mv** command to either rename a file or to move a file from one directory to another. When using **mv** to rename a file, you simply use the new filename as the second argument. The first argument is the current name of the file you are renaming. If you want to rename a file when you move it, you can specify the new name of the file after the directory name. In the next example, the **proposal** file is renamed with the name **version1**:

```
$ mv proposal version1
```

As with **cp**, it is easy for **mv** to erase a file accidentally. When renaming a file, you might accidentally choose a filename already used by another file. In this case, that other file will be erased. The **mv** command also has an -i option that checks first to see if a file by that name already exists.

You can also use any of the special characters to generate a list of filenames to use with **mv**. In the next example, the user moves all source code files in the current directory to the **newproj** directory:

```
$ mv *.c newproj
```

If you want to move all the files in a given directory to another directory, you can use * to match on and generate a list of all those files. In the next example, the user moves all the files in the **reports** directory to the **repbks** directory:

```
$ mv reports/* repbks
```

Note: The easiest way to copy files to a CD-R/RW or DVD-R/RW disc is to use the built-in Nautilus burning capability. Just insert a blank disk, open it as a folder, and drag-and-drop files on to it. You will be prompted automatically to burn the files.

Copying and Moving Directories

You can also copy or move whole directories at once. Both **cp** and **mv** can take as their first argument a directory name, enabling you to copy or move subdirectories from one directory into another (see Table 20-5). The first argument is the name of the directory to be moved or copied, and the second argument is the name of the directory within which it is to be placed. The same pathname structure used for files applies to moving or copying directories.

You can just as easily copy subdirectories from one directory to another. To copy a directory, the **cp** command requires you to use the **-r** option, which stands for "recursive." It directs the **cp** command to copy a directory, as well as any subdirectories it may contain. In other words, the entire directory subtree, from that directory on, will be copied. In the next example, the **travel** directory is copied to the **oldarticles** directory. Now two **travel** subdirectories exist, one in **articles** and one in **oldarticles**.

```
$ cp -r articles/travel oldarticles
$ ls -F articles
/travel
$ ls -F oldarticles
/travel
```

Erasing Files and Directories: the rm Command

As you use Linux, you will find the number of files you use increases rapidly. Generating files in Linux is easy. Applications such as editors, and commands such as **cp**, can easily be used to create files. Eventually, many of these files may become outdated and useless. You can then remove them with the **rm** command. The **rm** command can take any number of arguments, enabling you to list several filenames and erase them all at the same time. In the next example, the file **oldprop** is erased:

```
$ rm oldprop
```

Be careful when using the **rm** command, because it is irrevocable. Once a file is removed, it cannot be restored (there is no undo). With the **-i** option, you are prompted separately for each file and asked whether you really want to remove it. If you enter **y**, the file will be removed. If you enter anything else, the file is not removed. In the next example, the **rm** command is instructed to erase the files **proposal** and **oldprop**. The **rm** command then asks for confirmation for each file. The user decides to remove **oldprop,** but not **proposal**.

```
$ rm -i proposal oldprop
Remove proposal? n
Remove oldprop? y
$
```

Links: the ln Command

You can give a file more than one name using the **ln** command. You might do this because you want to reference a file using different filenames to access it from different directories. The added names are often referred to as *links.* Linux supports two different types of links, hard and symbolic. Hard links are literally another name for the same file, whereas symbolic links function like shortcuts referencing another file. Symbolic links are much more flexible and can work over many different file systems, while hard links are limited to your local file system. Furthermore, hard links introduce security concerns, as they allow direct access from a link that may have public access to an original file that you may want protected. Links are usually implemented as symbolic links.

Symbolic Links

To set up a symbolic link, you use the **ln** command with the **-s** option and two arguments: the name of the original file and the new, added filename. The **ls** operation lists both filenames, but only one physical file will exist.

```
$ ln -s original-file-name added-file-name
```

In the next example, the **today** file is given the additional name **weather**. It is just another name for the **today** file.

```
$ ls
today
$ ln -s today weather
$ ls
today weather
```

You can give the same file several names by using the **ln** command on the same file many times. In the next example, the file **today** is assigned the names **weather** and **weekend**:

```
$ ln -s today weather
$ ln -s today weekend
$ ls
today weather weekend
```

If you list the full information about a symbolic link and its file, you will find the information displayed is different. In the next example, the user lists the full information for both **lunch** and **/home/george/veglist** using the **ls** command with the **-l** option. The first character in the line specifies the file type. Symbolic links have their own file type, represented by an **l**. The file type for **lunch** is **l**, indicating it is a symbolic link, not an ordinary file. The number after the term "group" is the size of the file. Notice the sizes differ. The size of the **lunch** file is only 4 bytes. This is because **lunch** is only a symbolic link—a file that holds the pathname of another file—and a pathname takes up only a few bytes. It is not a direct hard link to the **veglist** file.

```
$ ls -l lunch /home/george/veglist
lrw-rw-r-- 1 chris group 4 Feb 14 10:30 lunch
-rw-rw-r-- 1 george group 793 Feb 14 10:30 veglist
```

To erase a file, you need to remove only its original name (and any hard links to it). If any symbolic links are left over, they will be unable to access the file. In this case, a symbolic link would hold the pathname of a file that no longer exists.

Hard Links

You can give the same file several names by using the **ln** command on the same file many times. To set up a hard link, you use the **ln** command with no **-s** option and two arguments: the name of the original file and the new, added filename. The **ls** operation lists both filenames, but only one physical file will exist.

```
$ ln original-file-name added-file-name
```

In the next example, the **monday** file is given the additional name **storm**. It is just another name for the **monday** file.

```
$ ls
today
$ ln monday storm
$ ls
monday storm
```

To erase a file that has hard links, you need to remove all its hard links. The name of a file is actually considered a link to that file—hence the command **rm** that removes the link to the file. If you have several links to the file and remove only one of them, the others stay in place and you can reference the file through them. The same is true even if you remove the original link—the original name of the file. Any added links will work just as well. In the next example, the **today** file is removed with the **rm** command. However, a link to that same file exists, called **weather**. The file can then be referenced under the name **weather**.

```
$ ln today weather
$ rm today
$ cat weather
The storm broke today
and the sun came out.
$
```

Archiving and Compressing Files

Archives are used to back up files or to combine them into a package, which can then be transferred as one file over the Internet or posted on an FTP site for easy downloading. The standard archive utility used on Linux and Unix systems is tar, for which several GUI front ends exist. You have several compression programs to choose from, including GNU zip (gzip), Zip, bzip, and compress. Table 20-6 lists the commonly used archive and compressions applications.

Applications	Description
tar	Archive creation and extraction **www.gnu.org/software/tar/manual/tar.html**
FileRoller (Archive Manager)	GNOME front end for tar and gzip/bzip2
gzip	File, directory, and archive compression **www.gnu.org/software/gzip/manual/**
bzip2	File, directory, and archive compression **www.gnu.org/software/gzip/manual/**
zip	File, directory, and archive compression

Table 20-6: Archive and Compression Applications

Archiving and Compressing Files with File Roller

GNOME provides the File Roller tool (accessible from the Accessories menu, labeled Archive Manager) that operates as a GUI front end to archive and compress files, letting you perform Zip, gzip, tar, and bzip2 operation using a GUI interface. You can examine the contents of archives, extract the files you want, and create new compressed archives. When you create an archive, you determine its compression method by specifying its filename extension, such as **.gz** for gzip or **.bz2** for bzip2. You can select the different extensions from the File Type menu or enter the extension yourself. To both archive and compress files, you can choose a combined extension like .tar.bz2, which both archives with tar and compresses with bzip2. Click Add to add files to your archive. To extract files from an archive, open the archive to display the list of archive files. You can then click Extract to extract particular files or the entire archive.

Tip: File Roller can also be use to examine the contents of an archive file easily. From the file manager, right-click the archive and select Open With Archive Manager. The list of files and directories in that archive will be displayed. For subdirectories, double-click their entries. This method also works for DEB software files, letting you browse all the files that make up a software package.

Archive Files and Devices: tar

The tar utility creates archives for files and directories. With tar, you can archive specific files, update them in the archive, and add new files as you want to that archive. You can even archive entire directories with all their files and subdirectories, all of which can be restored from the archive. The tar utility was originally designed to create archives on tapes. (The term "tar" stands for tape archive. However, you can create archives on any device, such as a floppy disk, or you can create an archive file to hold the archive.) The tar utility is ideal for making backups of your files or combining several files into a single file for transmission across a network (File Roller is a GUI interface for tar). For more information on tar, check the man page or the online man page at **www.gnu.org/software/tar/manual/tar.html**.

Note: As an alternative to tar, you can use pax, which is designed to work with different kinds of Unix archive formats such as cpio, bcpio, and tar. You can extract, list, and create archives. The pax utility is helpful if you are handling archives created on Unix systems that are using different archive formats.

Commands	**Execution**
`tar` *options files*	Backs up files to tape, device, or archive file.
`tar` *options*f *archive_name filelist*	Backs up files to a specific file or device specified as *archive_name*. *filelist*; can be filenames or directories.
Options	
`c`	Creates a new archive.
`t`	Lists the names of files in an archive.
`r`	Appends files to an archive.
`U`	Updates an archive with new and changed files; adds only those files modified since they were archived or files not already present in the archive.
`--delete`	Removes a file from the archive.
`w`	Waits for a confirmation from the user before archiving each file; enables you to update an archive selectively.
`x`	Extracts files from an archive.
`m`	When extracting a file from an archive, no new timestamp is assigned.
`M`	Creates a multiple-volume archive that may be stored on several floppy disks.
`f` *archive-name*	Saves the tape archive to the file archive name, instead of to the default tape device. When given an archive name, the `f` option saves the tar archive in a file of that name.
`f` *device-name*	Saves a tar archive to a device such as a floppy disk or tape. **/dev/fd0** is the device name for your floppy disk; the default device is held in **/etc/default/tar-file**.
`v`	Displays each filename as it is archived.
`z`	Compresses or decompresses archived files using gzip.
`j`	Compresses or decompresses archived files using bzip2.

Table 20-7: File Archives: tar

Displaying Archive Contents

Both file managers in GNOME and KDE have the capability to display the contents of a tar archive file automatically. The contents are displayed as though they were files in a directory. You can list the files as icons or with details, sorting them by name, type, or other fields. You can even display the contents of files. Clicking a text file opens it with a text editor, and an image is displayed with an image viewer. If the file manager cannot determine what program to use to display the file, it prompts you to select an application. Both file managers can perform the same kinds of operations on archives residing on remote file systems, such as tar archives on FTP sites. You can obtain a listing of their contents and even read their readme files. The Nautilus file manager (GNOME) can also extract an archive. Right-click the Archive icon and select Extract.

Creating Archives

On Linux, tar is often used to create archives on devices or files. You can direct tar to archive files to a specific device or a file by using the f option with the name of the device or file. The syntax for the tar command using the f option is shown in the next example. The device or filename is often referred to as the archive name. When creating a file for a tar archive, the filename is usually given the extension **.tar**. This is a convention only and is not required. You can list as many filenames as you want. If a directory name is specified, all its subdirectories are included in the archive.

```
$ tar optionsf archive-name.tar directory-and-file-names
```

To create an archive, use the c option. Combined with the f option, c creates an archive on a file or device. You enter this option before and right next to the f option. Notice no dash precedes a tar option. Table 20-7 lists the different options you can use with tar. In the next example, the directory **mydir** and all its subdirectories are saved in the file **myarch.tar**. In this example, the **mydir** directory holds two files, **mymeeting** and **party**, as well as a directory called **reports** that has three files: **weather**, **monday**, and **friday**.

```
$ tar cvf myarch.tar mydir
mydir/
mydir/reports/
mydir/reports/weather
mydir/reports/monday
mydir/reports/friday
mydir/mymeeting
mydir/party
```

Extracting Archives

The user can later extract the directories from the tape using the x option. The xf option extracts files from an archive file or device. The tar extraction operation generates all subdirectories. In the next example, the xf option directs tar to extract all the files and subdirectories from the tar file **myarch.tar**:

```
$ tar xvf myarch.tar
mydir/
mydir/reports/
mydir/reports/weather
mydir/reports/monday
mydir/reports/friday
mydir/mymeeting
mydir/party
```

You use the r option to add files to an already-created archive. The r option appends the files to the archive. In the next example, the user appends the files in the **letters** directory to the **myarch.tar** archive. Here, the directory **mydocs** and its files are added to the **myarch.tar** archive:

```
$ tar rvf myarch.tar mydocs
mydocs/
mydocs/doc1
```

Updating Archives

If you change any of the files in your directories you previously archived, you can use the u option to instruct tar to update the archive with any modified files. The tar command compares the time of the last update for each archived file with those in the user's directory and copies into the archive any files that have been changed since they were last archived. Any newly created files in these directories are also added to the archive. In the next example, the user updates the **myarch.tar** file with any recently modified or newly created files in the **mydir** directory. In this case, the **gifts** file was added to the **mydir** directory.

```
tar uvf myarch.tar mydir
mydir/
mydir/gifts
```

If you need to see what files are stored in an archive, you can use the tar command with the t option. The next example lists all the files stored in the **myarch.tar** archive:

```
tar tvf myarch.tar
drwxr-xr-x root/root 0 2000-10-24 21:38:18 mydir/
drwxr-xr-x root/root 0 2000-10-24 21:38:51 mydir/reports/
-rw-r--r-- root/root 22 2000-10-24 21:38:40 mydir/reports/weather
-rw-r--r-- root/root 22 2000-10-24 21:38:45 mydir/reports/monday
-rw-r--r-- root/root 22 2000-10-24 21:38:51 mydir/reports/friday
-rw-r--r-- root/root 22 2000-10-24 21:38:18 mydir/mymeeting
-rw-r--r-- root/root 22 2000-10-24 21:36:42 mydir/party
drwxr-xr-x root/root 0 2000-10-24 21:48:45 mydocs/
-rw-r--r-- root/root 22 2000-10-24 21:48:45 mydocs/doc1
drwxr-xr-x root/root 0 2000-10-24 21:54:03 mydir/
-rw-r--r-- root/root 22 2000-10-24 21:54:03 mydir/gifts
```

Note: To backup files using several CD/DVD-ROMs, you would first create a split archive, one consisting of several files, using the -M option, the multi-volume option. The tape size for an ISO DVD would be specified with the tape-length option, --tape-length=2294900.

Compressing Archives

The tar operation does not perform compression on archived files. If you want to compress the archived files, you can instruct tar to invoke the gzip utility to compress them. With the lowercase z option, tar first uses gzip to compress files before archiving them. The same z option invokes gzip to decompress them when extracting files.

```
$ tar czf myarch.tar.gz mydir
```

To use bzip instead of gzip to compress files before archiving them, you use the j option. The same j option invokes bzip to decompress them when extracting files.

```
$ tar cjf myarch.tar.bz2 mydir
```

Remember, a difference exists between compressing individual files in an archive and compressing the entire archive as a whole. Often, an archive is created for transferring several files at once as one tar file. To shorten transmission time, the archive should be as small as possible. You can use the compression utility gzip on the archive tar file to compress it, reducing its size, and then send the compressed version. The person receiving it can decompress it, restoring the tar file. Using gzip on a tar file often results in a file with the extension **.tar.gz**. The extension **.gz** is added to a compressed gzip file. The next example creates a compressed version of **myarch.tar** using the same name with the extension **.gz**:

```
$ gzip myarch.tar
$ ls
$ myarch.tar.gz
```

Instead of retyping the **tar** command for different files, you can place the command in a script and pass the files to it. Be sure to make the script executable. In the following example, a simple **myarchprog** script is created that will archive filenames listed as its arguments.

myarchprog

```
tar  cvf   myarch.tar      $*
```

A run of the **myarchprog** script with multiple arguments is shown here:

```
$ myarchprog mydata preface
mydata
preface
```

Archiving to Tape

If you have a default device specified, such as a tape, and you want to create an archive on it, you can simply use tar without the f option and a device or filename. This can be helpful for making backups of your files. The name of the default device is held in a file called **/etc/default/tar**. The syntax for the tar command using the default tape device is shown in the following example. If a directory name is specified, all its subdirectories are included in the archive.

```
$ tar option directory-and-file-names
```

In the next example, the directory **mydir** and all its subdirectories are saved on a tape in the default tape device:

```
$ tar c mydir
```

In this example, the **mydir** directory and all its files and subdirectories are extracted from the default tape device and placed in the user's working directory:

```
$ tar x mydir
```

Note: There are other archive programs you can use such as cpio, pax, and shar. However, tar is the one most commonly used for archiving application software.

File Compression: gzip, bzip2, and zip

Several reasons exist for reducing the size of a file. The two most common are to save space or, if you are transferring the file across a network, to save transmission time. You can effectively reduce a file size by creating a compressed copy of it. Anytime you need the file again, you decompress it. Compression is used in combination with archiving to enable you to compress whole directories and their files at once. Decompression generates a copy of the archive file, which can then be extracted, generating a copy of those files and directories. File Roller provides a GUI interface for these tasks. For more information on gzip, check the man page or the online man page at **www.gnu.org/software/gzip/manual/**. For bzip2 also check its man page or the online documentation at **www.bzip.org/docs.html.**

Compression with gzip

Several compression utilities are available for use on Linux and Unix systems. Most software for Linux systems uses the GNU gzip and gunzip utilities. The gzip utility compresses files, and gunzip decompresses them. To compress a file, enter the command gzip and the filename. This replaces the file with a compressed version of it with the extension **.gz**.

Option	Execution
`-c`	Sends compressed version of file to standard output; each file listed is separately compressed: `gzip -c mydata preface > myfiles.gz`

`-d`	Decompresses a compressed file; or you can use gunzip:
	`gzip -d myfiles.gz`
	`gunzip myfiles.gz`

`-h`	Displays help listing.
`-l` *file-list*	Displays compressed and uncompressed size of each file listed: `gzip -l myfiles.gz.`
`-r` *directory-name*	Recursively searches for specified directories and compresses all the files in them; the search begins from the current working directory. When used with `gunzip`, compressed files of a specified directory are uncompressed.
`-v` *file-list*	For each compressed or decompressed file, displays its name and the percentage of its reduction in size.
-*num*	Determines the speed and size of the compression; the range is from –1 to –9. A lower number gives greater speed but less compression, resulting in a larger file that compresses and decompresses quickly. Thus –1 gives the quickest compression but with the largest size; –9 results in a very small file that takes longer to compress and decompress. The default is –6.

Table 20-8: The gzip Options

```
$ gzip mydata
$ ls
mydata.gz
```

To decompress a gzip file, use either gzip with the -d option or the command gunzip. These commands decompress a compressed file with the **.gz** extension and replace it with a decompressed version with the same root name but without the **.gz** extension. When you use gunzip, you needn't even type in the **.gz** extension; gunzip and gzip -d assume it. Table 20-8 lists the different gzip options.

```
$ gunzip mydata.gz
$ ls
mydata
```

Tip: On your desktop, you can extract the contents of an archive by locating it with the file manager and double-clicking it. You can also right-click and choose Open with Archive Manager. This will start the File Roller application, which will open the archive, listing its contents. You can then choose to extract the archive. File Roller will use the appropriate tools to decompress the archive (bzip2, zip, or gzip) if compressed, and then extract the archive (tar).

You can also compress archived tar files. This results in files with the extensions **.tar.gz**. Compressed archived files are often used for transmitting extremely large files across networks.

```
$ gzip myarch.tar
$ ls
myarch.tar.gz
```

You can compress tar file members individually using the tar z option that invokes gzip. With the z option, tar invokes gzip to compress a file before placing it in an archive. Archives with members compressed with the z option, however, cannot be updated, nor is it possible to add to them. All members must be compressed, and all must be added at the same time.

The compress and uncompress Commands

You can also use the compress and uncompress commands to create compressed files. They generate a file that has a **.Z** extension and use a different compression format from gzip. The compress and uncompress commands are not that widely used, but you may run across **.Z** files occasionally. You can use the uncompress command to decompress a **.Z** file. The gzip utility is the standard GNU compression utility and should be used instead of compress.

Compressing with bzip2

Another popular compression utility is **bzip2**. It compresses files using the Burrows-Wheeler block-sorting text compression algorithm and Huffman coding. The command line options are similar to gzip by design, but they are not exactly the same. (See the bzip2 Man page for a complete listing.) You compress files using the bzip2 command and decompress with bunzip2. The bzip2 command creates files with the extension **.bz2**. You can use bzcat to output compressed data to the standard output. The bzip2 command compresses files in blocks and enables you to specify their size (larger blocks give you greater compression). As when using gzip, you can use bzip2 to compress tar archive files. The following example compresses the **mydata** file into a bzip compressed file with the extension **.bz2**:

```
$ bzip2 mydata
$ ls
mydata.bz2
```

To decompress, use the bunzip2 command on a bzip file:

```
$ bunzip2 mydata.bz2
```

Using Zip

Zip is a compression and archive utility modeled on PKZIP, which was used originally on DOS systems. Zip is a cross-platform utility used on Windows, Mac, MS-DOS, OS/2, Unix, and Linux systems. Zip commands can work with archives created by PKZIP and can use Zip archives. You compress a file using the zip command. This creates a Zip file with the **.zip** extension. If no files are listed, zip outputs the compressed data to the standard output. You can also use the - argument to have zip read from the standard input. To compress a directory, you include the -r option. The first example archives and compresses a file:

```
$ zip mydata
$ ls
mydata.zip
```

The next example archives and compresses the **reports** directory:

```
$ zip -r reports
```

A full set of archive operations is supported. With the -f option, you can update a particular file in the Zip archive with a newer version. The -u option replaces or adds files, and the -d option deletes files from the Zip archive. Options also exist for encrypting files, making DOS-to-Unix end-of-line translations and including hidden files.

To decompress and extract the Zip file, you use the unzip command.

```
$ unzip mydata.zip
```

ubuntu

21. Shell Variables and Scripts

Shell Variables

Environment Variables

Control Structures

A shell script combines Linux commands in such a way as to perform a specific task. The different kinds of shells provide many programming tools that you can use to create shell scripts. You can define variables and assign values to them. You can also define variables in a script file, and have a user interactively enter values for them when the script is executed. The shell provides loop and conditional control structures that repeat Linux commands or make decisions on which commands you want to execute. You can also construct expressions that perform arithmetic or comparison operations. All these shell programming tools operate in ways similar to those found in other programming languages, so if you're already familiar with programming, you might find shell programming simple to learn.

The BASH, TCSH, and Z shells are types of shells. You can have many instances of a particular kind of shell. A shell, by definition, is an interpretive environment within which you execute commands. You can have many environments running at the same time, of either the same or different types of shells; you have several shells running at the same time that are of the BASH shell type, for example.

This chapter will cover the basics of creating a shell script using the BASH and TCSH shells, the shells used on most Linux systems. You will learn how to create your own scripts, define shell variables, and develop user interfaces, as well as learn the more difficult task of combining control structures to create complex programs. Tables throughout the chapter list shell commands and operators, while numerous examples show how they are implemented.

Usually, the instructions making up a shell program are entered into a script file that can then be executed. You can even distribute your program among several script files, one of which will contain instructions on how to execute others. You can think of variables, expressions, and control structures as tools you can use to bring together several Linux commands into one operation. In this sense, a shell program is a new and complex Linux command that you have created.

The BASH shell has a flexible and powerful set of programming commands that allows you to build complex scripts. It supports variables that can be either local to the given shell or exported to other shells. You can pass arguments from one script to another. The BASH shell has a complete set of control structures, including loops and if statements, as well as case structures, all of which you'll learn about as you read this book. All shell commands interact easily with redirection and piping operations that allow them to accept input from the standard input or send it to the standard output. Unlike the Bourne shell, the first shell used for UNIX, BASH incorporates many of the features of the TCSH and Z shells. Arithmetic operations in particular are easier to perform in BASH.

Shell Variables

Within each shell, you can enter and execute commands. You can further enhance the capabilities of a shell using shell variables. A shell variable lets you hold data that you can reference over and over again as you execute different commands within a shell. For example, you can define a shell variable to hold the name of a complex filename. Then, instead of retyping the filename in different commands, you can reference it with the shell variable.

You define variables within a shell, and such variables are known as *shell variables.* Some utilities, such as the Mail utility, have their own shells with their own shell variables. You can also create your own shell using *shell scripts.* You have a user shell that becomes active as soon as you log in. This is often referred to as the *login shell.* Special system-level parameter variables are defined within this login shell. Shell variables can also be used to define a shell's environment.

Note: Shell variables exist as long as your shell is active—that is, until you exit the shell. For example, logging out will exit the login shell. When you log in again, any variables you may need in your login shell must be defined again.

Definition and Evaluation of Variables: =, $, set, unset

You define a variable in a shell when you first use the variable's name. A variable's name may be any set of alphabetic characters, including the underscore. The name may also include a number, but the number cannot be the first character in the name. A name may not have any other type of character, such as an exclamation point, an ampersand, or even a space. Such symbols are reserved by the shell for its own use. Also, a variable name may not include more than one word. The shell uses spaces on the command line to distinguish different components of a command such as options, arguments, and the command name.

You assign a value to a variable with the assignment operator (=). You type the variable name, the assignment operator, and then the value assigned. Do not place any spaces around the assignment operator. The assignment operation poet = Virgil, for example, will fail. (The C shell has a slightly different type of assignment operation.) You can assign any set of characters to a variable. In the next example, the variable poet is assigned the string Virgil:

```
$ poet=Virgil
```

Once you have assigned a value to a variable, you can use the variable name to reference the value. Often you use the values of variables as arguments for a command. You can reference the value of a variable using the variable name preceded by the $ operator. The dollar sign is a special operator that uses the variable name to reference a variable's value, in effect evaluating the variable. Evaluation retrieves a variable's value, usually a set of characters. This set of characters then replaces the variable name on the command line. Wherever a $ is placed before the variable name, the variable name is replaced with the value of the variable. In the next example, the shell variable poet is evaluated and its contents, Virgil, is used as the argument for an echo command. The echo command simply echoes or prints a set of characters to the screen.

```
$ echo $poet
Virgil
```

You must be careful to distinguish between the evaluation of a variable and its name alone. If you leave out the **$** operator before the variable name, all you have is the variable name itself. In the next example, the **$** operator is absent from the variable name. In this case, the **echo** command has as its argument the word *poet*, and so prints out *poet*:

```
$ echo poet
poet
```

The contents of a variable are often used as command arguments. A common command argument is a directory pathname. It can be tedious to retype a directory path that is being used over and over again. If you assign the directory pathname to a variable, you can simply use the evaluated variable in its place. The directory path you assign to the variable is retrieved when the variable is evaluated with the **$** operator. The next example assigns a directory pathname to a variable, and then uses the evaluated variable in a copy command. The evaluation of **ldir** (which is **$ldir**) results in the pathname **/home/chris/letters**. The copy command evaluates to **cp myletter /home/chris/letters**.

```
$ ldir=/home/chris/letters
$ cp myletter $ldir
```

You can obtain a list of all the defined variables with the **set** command. If you decide you do not want a certain variable, you can remove it with the **unset** command. The **unset** command undefines a variable.

Variable Values: Strings

The values that you assign to variables may consist of any set of characters. These characters may be a character string that you explicitly type in or the result obtained from executing a Linux command. In most cases, you will need to quote your values using either single quotes, double quotes, backslashes, or back quotes. Single quotes, double quotes, and backslashes allow you to quote strings in different ways. Back quotes have the special function of executing a Linux command and using its results as arguments on the command line.

Quoting Strings: Double Quotes, Single Quotes, and Backslashes

Variable values can be made up of any characters. However, problems occur when you want to include characters that are also used by the shell as operators. Your shell has certain metacharacters that it uses in evaluating the command line. A space is used to parse arguments on the command line. The asterisk, question mark, and brackets are metacharacters used to generate lists of filenames. The period represents the current directory. The dollar sign, **$**, is used to evaluate variables, and the greater-than and less-than characters , > <, are redirection operators. The ampersand, **&**, is used to execute background commands and the bar pipes output. If you want to use any of these characters as part of the value of a variable, you first need to quote them. Quoting a metacharacter on a command line makes it just another character. It is not evaluated by the shell.

You can use double quotes, single quotes, and backslashes to quote such metacharacters. Double and single quotes allow you to quote several metacharacters at a time. Any metacharacters within double or single quotes are quoted. A backslash quotes the single character that follows it.

If you want to assign more than one word to a variable, you need to quote the spaces separating the words. You can do so by enclosing all the words within double quotes. You can think of this as creating a character string to be assigned to the variable. Of course, any other metacharacters enclosed within the double quotes are also quoted.

In the following first example, the double quotes enclose words separated by spaces. Because the spaces are enclosed within double quotes, they are treated as characters, not as delimiters used to parse command line arguments. In the second example, double quotes also enclose a period, treating it as just a character. In the third example, an asterisk is also enclosed within the double quotes. The asterisk is considered just another character in the string and is not evaluated.

```
$ notice="The meeting will be tomorrow"
$ echo $notice
The meeting will be tomorrow

$ message="The project is on time."
$ echo $message
The project is on time.

$ notice="You can get a list of files with ls *.c"
$ echo $notice
You can get a list of files with ls *.c
```

Double quotes, however, do not quote the dollar sign, the operator that evaluates variables. A `$` operator next to a variable name enclosed within double quotes will still be evaluated, replacing the variable name with its value. The value of the variable will then become part of the string, not the variable name. There may be times when you want a variable within quotes to be evaluated. In the next example, the double quotes are used so that the winner's name will be included in the notice.

```
$ winner=dylan
$ notice="The person who won is $winner"
$ echo $notice
The person who won is dylan
```

On the other hand, there may be times when you do not want a variable within quotes to be evaluated. In that case you have to use the single quotes. Single quotes suppress any variable evaluation and treat the dollar sign as just another character. In the next example, single quotes prevent the evaluation of the winner variable.

```
$ winner=dylan
$ result='The name is in the $winner variable'
$ echo $result
The name is in the $winner variable
```

If, in this case, the double quotes were used instead, an unintended variable evaluation would take place. In the next example, the characters "$winner" are interpreted as a variable evaluation.

```
$ winner=dylan
$ result="The name is in the $winner variable"
$ echo $result
The name is in the dylan variable
```

You can always quote any metacharacter, including the `$` operator, by preceding it with a backslash. The use of the backslash is to quote ENTER keys (newlines). The backslash is useful when you want to both evaluate variables within a string and include $ characters. In the next example, the backslash is placed before the **$** in order to treat it as a dollar sign character: \$. At the same time the variable `$winner` is evaluated because the double quotes that are used do not quote the `$` operator.

```
$ winner=dylan
$ result="$winner won \$100.00"
$ echo $result
dylan won $100.00
```

Quoting Commands: Single Quotes

There are, however, times when you may want to use single quotes around a Linux command. Single quotes allow you to assign the written command to a variable. If you do so, you can then use that variable name as another name for the Linux command. Entering in the variable name, preceded by the `$` operator on the command line, will execute the command. In the next example, a shell variable is assigned the characters that make up a Linux command to list files, `'ls -F'`. Notice the single quotes around the command. When the shell variable is evaluated on the command line, the Linux command it contains will become a command line argument, and it will be executed by the shell.

```
$ lsf='ls -F'
$ $lsf
mydata /reports /letters
$
```

In effect you are creating another name for a command, like an alias.

Values from Linux Commands: Back Quotes

Although you can create variable values by typing in characters or character strings, you can also obtain values from other Linux commands. To assign the result of Linux command to a variable, you first need to execute the command. If you place a Linux command within back quotes (`) on the command line, that command is first executed and its result becomes an argument on the command line. In the case of assignments, the result of a command can be assigned to a variable by placing the command within back quotes first to execute it. The back quotes can be thought of as an expression consisting of a command to be executed whose result is then assigned to the variable. The characters making up the command itself are not assigned. In the next example, the command **`ls *.c`** is executed and its result is then assigned to the variable **`listc.`** **`ls *.c`**, which generates a list of all files with a **.c** extension. This list of files is then assigned to the **`listc`** variable.

```
$ listc=`ls `*.c`
$ echo $listc
main.c prog.c lib.c
```

Keep in mind the difference between single quotes and back quotes. Single quotes treat a Linux command as a set of characters. Back quotes force execution of the Linux command. There may be times when you accidentally enter single quotes when you mean to use back quotes. In the following first example, the assignment for the **`lscc`** variable has single quotes, not back quotes, placed around the **`ls *.c`** command. In this case, **`ls *.c`** are just characters to be assigned to the variable **`lscc`**. In the second example, back quotes are placed around the **`ls *.c`** command, forcing evaluation of the command. A list of filenames ending in **.c** is generated and assigned as the value of **`lscc`**.

```
$ lscc='ls *.c'
$ echo $lscc
ls *.c

$ lscc=`ls *.c`
$ echo $lscc
main.c  prog.c
```

Shell Scripts: User-Defined Commands

You can place shell commands within a file and then have the shell read and execute the commands in the file. In this sense, the file functions as a shell program, executing shell commands as if they were statements in a program. A file that contains shell commands is called a *shell script.*

You enter shell commands into a script file using a standard text editor such as the Vi editor. The **sh** or **.** command used with the script's filename will read the script file and execute the commands. In the next example, the text file called **lsc** contains an **ls** command that displays only files with the extension **.c**:

lsc

```
ls *.c
```

A run of the **lsc** script is shown here:

```
$ sh lsc
main.c calc.c
$ . lsc
main.c calc.c
```

Executing Scripts

You can dispense with the **sh** and **.** commands by setting the executable permission of a script file. When the script file is first created by your text editor, it is given only read and write permission. The **chmod** command with the **+x** option will give the script file executable permission. Once it is executable, entering the name of the script file at the shell prompt and pressing ENTER will execute the script file and the shell commands in it. In effect, the script's filename becomes a new shell command. In this way, you can use shell scripts to design and create your own Linux commands. You need to set the permission only once.

In the next example, the **lsc** file's executable permission for the owner is set to on. Then the **lsc** shell script is directly executed like any Linux command.

```
$ chmod u+x lsc
$ lsc
main.c calc.c
```

You may have to specify that the script you are using is in your current working directory. You do this by prefixing the script name with a period and slash combination, as in **./lsc**. The period is a special character representing the name of your current working directory. The slash is a directory pathname separator. The following example shows how to execute the **lsc** script:

```
$ ./lsc
main.c calc.c
```

Script Arguments

Just as any Linux command can take arguments, so also can a shell script. Arguments on the command line are referenced sequentially starting with 1. An argument is referenced using the **$** operator and the number of its position. The first argument is referenced with **$1**, the second, with **$2**, and so on. In the next example, the **lsext** script prints out files with a specified extension.

The first argument is the extension. The script is then executed with the argument **c** (of course, the executable permission must have been set).

lsext

```
ls *.$1
```

A run of the **lsext** script with an argument is shown here:

```
$ lsext c
main.c calc.c
```

In the next example, the commands to print out a file with line numbers have been placed in an executable file called **lpnum**, which takes a filename as its argument. The **cat** command with the **-n** option first outputs the contents of the file with line numbers. Then this output is piped into the **lpr** command, which prints it. The command to print out the line numbers is executed in the background.

lpnum

```
cat -n $1 | lpr &
```

A run of the **lpnum** script with an argument is shown here:

```
$ lpnum mydata
```

You may need to reference more than one argument at a time. The number of arguments used may vary. In **lpnum**, you may want to print out three files at one time and five files at some other time. The **$** operator with the asterisk, **$***, references all the arguments on the command line. Using **$*** enables you to create scripts that take a varying number of arguments. In the next example, **lpnum** is rewritten using **$*** so that it can take a different number of arguments each time you use it:

lpnum

```
cat -n $* | lpr &
```

A run of the **lpnum** script with multiple arguments is shown here:

```
$ lpnum mydata preface
```

Environment Variables

When you log in to your account, your Linux system generates your user shell. Within this shell, you can issue commands and declare variables. You can also create and execute shell scripts. However, when you execute a shell script, the system generates a subshell. You then have two shells, the one you logged in to and the one generated for the script. Within the script shell you can execute another shell script, which will then have its own shell. When a script has finished execution, its shell terminates and you enter back to the shell from which it was executed. In this sense, you can have many shells, each nested within the other.

Variables that you define within a shell are local to it. If you define a variable in a shell script, then, when the script is run, the variable is defined with that script's shell and is local to it. No other shell can reference it. In a sense, the variable is hidden within its shell.

To illustrate this situation more clearly, the next example will use two scripts, one of which is called from within the other. When the first script executes, it generates its own shell. From within this shell, another script is executed which, in turn, generates its own shell. In the next example, the user first executes the **dispfirst** script, which displays a first name. When the **dispfirst** script executes, it generates its own shell and then, within that shell, it defines the `firstname` variable. After it displays the contents of `firstname`, the script executes another script: **displast**. When **displast** executes, it generates its own shell. It defines the `lastname` variable within its shell and then displays the contents of `lastname`. It then tries to reference `firstname` and display its contents. It cannot do so because `firstname` is local to **dispfirst's** shell and cannot be referenced outside it. An error message is displayed indicating that for the **displast** shell, `firstname` is an undefined variable.

dispfirst

```
firstname="Charles"
echo "First name is $firstname"

displast
```

displast

```
lastname="Dickens"

echo "Last name is $lastname"
echo "$firstname $lastname"
```

The run of the **dispfirst** script is shown here:

```
$ dispfirst
First name is Charles
Last name is Dickens
 Dickens
sh: firstname: not found
```

If you want the same value of a variable, used both in a script's shell and a subshell, you can simply define the variable twice, once in each script, and assign it the same value. In the previous example, there is a `myfile` variable defined in **dispfile** and in **printfile**. The user executes the **b** script, which first displays the list file with line numbers. When the **dispfile** script executes, it generates its own shell and then, within that shell, it defines the `myfile` variable. After it displays the contents of the file, the script then executes another script **printfile**. When **printfile** executes, it generates its own shell. It defines its own `myfile` variable within its shell and then sends a file to the printer.

What if you want to define a variable in one shell and have its value referenced in any subshell? For example, what if you want to define the `myfile` variable in the **dispfile** script and have its value, "List", referenced from within the **printfile** script, rather than explicitly defining another variable in **printfile**? Since variables are local to the shell they are defined in, there is no way you can do this with ordinary variables. However, there is a type of variable called an *environment variable* that allows its value to be referenced by any subshells. Environment variables constitute an environment for the shell and any subshell it generates, no matter how deeply nested.

dispfile

```
myfile="List"

echo "Displaying $myfile"
pr -t -n $myfile
```

printfile

```
printfile

myfile="List"

echo "Printing $myfile"
lp $myfile &
```

The run of the **dispfile** script is shown here:

```
$ dispfile
Displaying List
1 screen
2 modem
3 paper
Printing List
```

You can define environment variables in the three major types of shells: Bourne, Korn, and C. However, the strategy used to implement environmental variables in the Bourne and Korn shells is very different from that of the C shell. In the Bourne and Korn shells, environmental variables are exported. That is to say, a copy of an environmental variable is made in each subshell. In a sense, if the `myfile` variable is exported, a copy is automatically defined in each subshell for you. In the C shell, on the other hand, an environmental variable is defined only once and can be directly referenced by any subshell.

Shell Environment Variables

In the Bourne, BASH, and Korn shells, an environment variable can be thought of as a regular variable with added capabilities. To make an environment variable, you apply the `export` command to a variable you have already defined. The `export` command instructs the system to define a copy of that variable for each new shell generated. Each new shell will have its own copy of the environment variable. This process is called exporting variables.

In the next example, the variable `myfile` is defined in the **dispfile** script. It is then turned into an environment variable using the `export` command. The `myfile` variable will consequently be exported to any subshells, such as that generated when **printfile** is executed.

dispfile

```
myfile="List"
export myfile

echo "Displaying $myfile"
pr -t -n $myfile

printfile
```

printfile

```
echo "Printing $myfile"
lp $myfile &
```

The run of the **dispfile** script is shown here:

```
$ dispfile
Displaying List
1 screen
2 modem
3 paper
Printing List
```

When **printfile** is executed it will be given its own copy of `myfile` and can reference that copy within its own shell. You no longer need to explicitly define another `myfile` variable in **printfile**.

It is a mistake to think of exported environment variables as global variables. A new shell can never reference a variable outside of itself. Instead, a copy of the variable with its value is generated for the new shell. You can think of exported variables as exporting their values to a shell, not themselves. For those familiar with programming structures, exported variables can be thought of as a form of call-by-value.

Control Structures

You can control the execution of Linux commands in a shell script with control structures. Control structures allow you to repeat commands and to select certain commands over others. A control structure consists of two major components: a test and commands. If the test is successful, then the commands are executed. In this way, you can use control structures to make decisions as to whether commands should be executed.

Two different kinds of control structures are used: *loops*, which repeat commands, and *conditions*, which execute commands when certain conditions are met. The BASH shell has three loop control structures—**`while`**, **`for`**, and **`for-in`**—and two condition structures—**`if`** and **`case`**. The control structures have as their test the execution of a Linux command. All Linux commands return an exit status after they have finished executing. If a command is successful, its exit status will be 0. If the command fails for any reason, its exit status will be a positive value referencing the type of failure that occurred. The control structures check to see whether the exit status of a Linux command is 0 or some other value. In the case of the **`if`** and **`while`** structures, if the exit status is a 0 value, the command was successful and the structure continues.

Test Operations

With the test command, you can compare integers and strings, and even perform logical operations. The command consists of the keyword test, followed by the values being compared, separated by an option that specifies what kind of comparison is taking place. The option can be thought of as the operator, but it is written, like other options, with a minus sign and letter codes. For example, -eq is the option that represents the equality comparison. Two string operations, however, actually use an operator instead of an option. When you compare two strings for equality, you use the equal sign (=). For inequality you use !=. Table 21-1 lists some of the commonly used options and operators used by test. The syntax for the test command is shown here:

```
test value -option value
test string = string
```

Integer Comparisons	Function
-gt	Greater-than
-lt	Less-than
-ge	Greater-than-or-equal-to
-le	Less-than-or-equal-to
-eq	Equal
-ne	Not-equal
String Comparisons	
-z	Tests for empty string
=	Equal strings
!=	Not-equal strings
Logical Operations	
-a	Logical AND
-o	Logical OR
!	Logical NOT
File Tests	
-f	File exists and is a regular file
-s	File is not empty
-r	File is readable
-w	File can be written to, modified
-x	File is executable
-d	Filename is a directory name

Table 21-1: BASH Shell Test Operators

The next example compares two integer values to determine whether they are equal. In this case, the equality option, -eq, should be used. The exit status of the test command is examined to determine the result of the test operation. The shell special variable `$?` holds the exit status of the most recently executed Linux command.

```
$ num=5
$ test $num -eq 10
$ echo $?
1
```

Instead of using the keyword test for the test command, you can use enclosing brackets. The command test `$greeting = "hi"` can be written as

```
$ [ $greeting = "hi" ]
```

Similarly, the command test `$num -eq 10` can be written as

```
$ [ $num -eq 10 ]
```

The brackets themselves must be surrounded by white space: a space, tab, or enter. Without the spaces, the code is invalid.

Conditional Control Structures

The BASH shell has a set of conditional control structures that allow you to choose what Linux commands to execute. Many of these are similar to conditional control structures found in programming languages, but there are some differences. The if condition tests the success of a Linux command, not an expression. Furthermore, the end of an if-then command must be indicated with the keyword fi, and the end of a case command is indicated with the keyword esac. The condition control structures are listed in Table 21-2.

The **`if`** structure places a condition on commands. That condition is the exit status of a specific Linux command. If a command is successful, returning an exit status of 0, then the commands within the **`if`** structure are executed. If the exit status is anything other than 0, the command has failed and the commands within the **`if`** structure are not executed. The **`if`** command begins with the keyword **`if`** and is followed by a Linux command whose exit condition will be evaluated. The keyword **`fi`** ends the command.

The **`elsels`** script in the next example executes the **`ls`** command to list files with two different possible options, either by size or with all file information. If the user enters an s, files are listed by size; otherwise, all file information is listed.

elsels

```
echo Enter s to list file sizes,
echo       otherwise all file information is listed.
echo -n "Please enter option: "
read choice
if [  "$choice" = s  ]
    then
        ls -s
    else
            ls -l
fi
echo Good-bye
```

Condition Control Structures: `if`, `else`, `elif`, `case`	**Function**
if *command* **then** *command* **fi**	**if** executes an action if its test command is true.

if *command* **then**
command
else
command
fi
	if-else executes an action if the exit status of its test command is true; if false, the **else** action is executed.

if *command* **then**
command
elif *command* **then**
command
else
command
fi
	elif allows you to nest **if** structures, enabling selection among several alternatives; at the first true **if** structure, its commands are executed and control leaves the entire **elif** structure.

case *string* **in** *pattern)* *command;;* **esac**	**case** matches the string value to any of several patterns; if a pattern is matched, its associated commands are executed.
command **&&** *command*	The logical AND condition returns a true 0 value if both commands return a true 0 value; if one returns a nonzero value, then the AND condition is false and also returns a nonzero value.
command || *command*	The logical OR condition returns a true 0 value if one or the other command returns a true 0 value; if both commands return a nonzero value, then the OR condition is false and also returns a nonzero value.
! *command*	The logical NOT condition inverts the return value of the command.
Loop Control Structures: `while`, `until`, `for`, `for-in`, `select`	
while *command* **do** *command* **done**	**while** executes an action as long as its test command is true.
until *command* **do** *command* **done**	**until** executes an action as long as its test command is false.
for *variable* **in** *list-values* **do** *command* **done**	**for-in** is designed for use with lists of values; the variable operand is consecutively assigned the values in the list.

for *variable* **do** *command* **done**	**for** is designed for reference script arguments; the variable operand is consecutively assigned each argument value.
select *string* **in** *item-list* **do** *command* **done**	**select** creates a menu based on the items in the *item-list*; then it executes the command; the command is usually a **case**.

Table 21-2: BASH Shell Control Structures

A run of the program follows:

```
$ elsels
Enter s to list file sizes,
otherwise all file information is listed.
Please enter option: s
total 2
   1 monday     2 today
```

Loop Control Structures

The while loop repeats commands. A while loop begins with the keyword while and is followed by a Linux command. The keyword do follows on the next line. The end of the loop is specified by the keyword done. The Linux command used in while structures is often a test command indicated by enclosing brackets.

The for-in structure is designed to reference a list of values sequentially. It takes two operands: a variable and a list of values. The values in the list are assigned one by one to the variable in the for-in structure. Like the while command, the for-in structure is a loop. Each time through the loop, the next value in the list is assigned to the variable. When the end of the list is reached, the loop stops. Like the while loop, the body of a for-in loop begins with the keyword do and ends with the keyword done. The **cbackup** script makes a backup of each file and places it in a directory called **sourcebak**. Notice the use of the * special character to generate a list of all filenames with a **.c** extension.

cbackup

```
for backfile in *.c
do
    cp $backfile sourcebak/$backfile
 echo $backfile
done
```

A run of the program follows:

```
$ cbackup
io.c
lib.c
main.c
$
```

The **for** structure without a specified list of values takes as its list of values the command line arguments. The arguments specified on the command line when the shell file is invoked become a list of values referenced by the **for** command. The variable used in the for command is set automatically to each argument value in sequence. The first time through the loop, the variable is set to the value of the first argument. The second time, it is set to the value of the second argument.

ubuntu

22. Shell Configuration

Shell Configuration Files

Configuration Directories and Files

Aliases

Controlling Shell Operations

Environment Variables and Subshells: export

Configuring Your Shell with Shell Parameters

Four different major shells are commonly used on Linux systems: the Bourne Again shell (BASH), the AT&T Korn shell, the TCSH shell, and the Z shell. The BASH shell is an advanced version of the Bourne shell, which includes most of the advanced features developed for the Korn shell and the C shell. TCSH is an enhanced version of the C shell, originally developed for BSD versions of UNIX. The AT&T UNIX Korn shell is open source. The Z shell is an enhanced version of the Korn shell. Although their UNIX counterparts differ greatly, the Linux shells share many of the same features. In UNIX, the Bourne shell lacks many capabilities found in the other UNIX shells. In Linux, however, the BASH shell incorporates all the advanced features of the Korn shell and C shell, as well as the TCSH shell. All four shells are available for your use, though the BASH shell is the default.

Command	Description
`bash`	BASH shell, **/bin/bash**
`bsh`	BASH shell, **/bin/bsh** (link to **/bin/bash**)
`sh`	BASH shell, **/bin/sh** (link to **/bin/bash**)
`tcsh`	TCSH shell, **/usr/tcsh**
`csh`	TCSH shell , **/bin/csh** (link to **/bin/tcsh**)
`ksh`	Korn shell, **/bin/ksh** (also added link **/usr/bin/ksh**)
`zsh`	Z shell, **/bin/zsh**

Table 22-1: Shell Invocation Command Names

The BASH shell is the default shell for most Linux distributions. If you are logging in to a command line interface, you will be placed in the default shell automatically and given a shell prompt at which to enter your commands. The shell prompt for the BASH shell is a dollar sign (**$**). In the GUI interface, such as GNOME or KDE, you can open a terminal window that will display a command line interface with the prompt for the default shell (BASH). Though you log in to your default shell or display it automatically in a terminal window, you can change to another shell by entering its name. Entering tcsh invokes the TCSH shell, bash the BASH shell, ksh the Korn shell, and zsh the Z shell. You can leave a shell by pressing CTRL-D or using the exit command. You only need one type of shell to do your work. Table 22-1 shows the different commands you can use to invoke different shells. Some shells have added links you can use to invoke the same shell, like **sh** and **bsh**, which link to and invoke the **bash** command for the BASH shell.

This chapter describes common features of the BASH shell, such as aliases, as well as how to configure the shell to your own needs using shell variables and initialization files. The other shells share many of the same features and use similar variables and configuration files.

Though the basic shell features and configurations are shown here, you should consult the respective online manuals and FAQs for each shell for more detailed examples and explanations.

Shell Initialization and Configuration Files

Each type of shell has its own set of initialization and configuration files. The TCSH shell uses **.login**, **.tcshrc**, and **.logout** files in place of **.profile**, **.bashrc**, and **.bash_logout**. The Z shell has several initialization files: **.zshenv**, **.zlogin**, **.zprofile**, **.zschrc**, and **.zlogout**. See Table 22-2 for a listing. Check the Man pages for each shell to see how they are usually configured. When you install a shell, default versions of these files are automatically placed in the users' home directories. Except for the TCSH shell, all shells use much the same syntax for variable definitions and assigning values (TCSH uses a slightly different syntax, described in its Man pages).

Filename	Function
BASH Shell	
.profile	Login initialization file
.bashrc	BASH shell configuration file
.bash_logout	Logout name
.bash_history	History file
/etc/profile	System login initialization file
/etc/bash.bashrc	System BASH shell configuration file
/etc/profile.d	Directory for specialized BASH shell configuration files
/etc/bash_completion	Completion options for applications
TCSH Shell	
.login	Login initialization file
.tcshrc	TCSH shell configuration file
.logout	Logout file
Z Shell	
.zshenv	Shell login file (first read)
.zprofile	Login initialization file
.zlogin	Shell login file
.zshrc	Z shell configuration file
.zlogout	Logout file
Korn Shell	
.profile	Login initialization file
.kshrc	KORN shell configuration file

Table 22-2: Shell Configuration Files

Configuration Directories and Files

Applications often install configuration files in a user's home directory that contain specific configuration information, which tailors the application to the needs of that particular user.

This may take the form of a single configuration file that begins with a period, or a directory that contains several configuration files. The directory name will also begin with a period. For example, Mozilla installs a directory called **.mozilla** in the user's home directory that contains configuration files. On the other hand, many mail applications uses a single file called **.mailrc** to hold alias and feature settings set up by the user, though others like Evolution also have their own, **.evolution**. Most single configuration files end in the letters **rc**. **FTP** uses a file called **.netrc**. Most newsreaders use a file called **.newsrc**. Entries in configuration files are usually set by the application, though you can usually make entries directly by editing the file. Applications have their own set of special variables to which you can define and assign values. You can list the configuration files in your home directory with the ls -a command.

Aliases

You can use the alias command to create another name for a command. The alias command operates like a macro that expands to the command it represents. The alias does not literally replace the name of the command; it simply gives another name to that command. An alias command begins with the keyword alias and the new name for the command, followed by an equal sign and the command the alias will reference.

Note: No spaces should be placed around the equal sign used in the `alias` command.

In the next example, list becomes another name for the ls command:

```
$ alias list=ls
$ ls
mydata today
$ list
mydata today
$
```

If you want an alias to be automatically defined, you have to enter the alias operation in a shell configuration file. On Ubuntu, aliases are defined in either the user's **.bashrc** file or in a **.bash_aliases** file. To use a **.bash_aliases** file, you have to first uncomment the commands in the .bashrc file that will read the **.bash_aliases** file. Just edit the **.bashrc** file and remove the preceding # so it appears like the following:

```
if [ -f ~/.bash_aliases ]; then
    . ~/.bash_aliases
fi
```

You can also place aliases in the **.bashrc** file directly. Some are already defined, though commented out. You can edit the **.bashrc** file and remove the # comment symbols from those lines to activate the aliases.

```
# some more ls aliases
alias ll='ls -l'
alias la='ls -A'
alias l='ls -CF'
```

Aliasing Commands and Options

You can also use an alias to substitute for a command and its option, but you need to enclose both the command and the option within single quotes. Any command you alias that contains spaces must be enclosed in single quotes as well. In the next example, the alias lss references the ls command with its -s option, and the alias **lsa** references the ls command with the -F option. The ls command with the -s option lists files and their sizes in blocks, and ls with the -F option places a slash after directory names. Notice how single quotes enclose the command and its option.

```
$ alias lss='ls -s'
$ lss
mydata 14   today  6   reports  1
$ alias lsa='ls -F'
$ lsa
mydata today reports/
$
```

Aliases are helpful for simplifying complex operations. In the next example, **listlong** becomes another name for the ls command with the -l option (the long format that lists all file information), as well as the -h option for using a human-readable format for file sizes. Be sure to encase the command and its arguments within single quotes so that they are taken as one argument and not parsed by the shell.

```
$ alias listlong='ls -lh'
$ listlong
-rw-r--r--    1 root   root   51K  Sep  18  2008 mydata
-rw-r--r--    1 root   root   16K  Sep  27  2008 today
```

Aliasing Commands and Arguments

You may often use an alias to include a command name with an argument. If you execute a command that has an argument with a complex combination of special characters on a regular basis, you may want to alias it. For example, suppose you often list just your source code and object code files—those files ending in either a **.c** or **.o**. You would need to use as an argument for ls a combination of special characters such as *.[co]. Instead, you can alias ls with the .[co] argument, giving it a simple name. In the next example, the user creates an alias called lsc for the command ls.[co]:

```
$ alias lsc='ls *.[co]'
$ lsc
main.c main.o lib.c lib.o
```

Aliasing Commands

You can also use the name of a command as an alias. This can be helpful in cases where you should use a command only with a specific option. In the case of the rm, cp, and mv commands, the -i option should always be used to ensure an existing file is not overwritten. Instead of always being careful to use the -i option each time you use one of these commands, you can alias the command name to include the option. In the next example, the rm, cp, and mv commands have been aliased to include the -i option:

```
$ alias rm='rm -i'
$ alias mv='mv -i'
$ alias cp='cp -i'
```

The alias command by itself provides a list of all aliases that have been defined, showing the commands they represent. You can remove an alias by using the **unalias** command. In the next example, the user lists the current aliases and then removes the lsa alias:

```
$ alias
lsa=ls -F
list=ls
rm=rm -i
$ unalias lsa
```

Controlling Shell Operations

The BASH shell has several features that enable you to control the way different shell operations work. For example, setting the noclobber feature prevents redirection from overwriting files. You can turn these features on and off like a toggle, using the set command. The set command takes two arguments: an option specifying on or off and the name of the feature. To set a feature on, you use the -o option, and to set it off, you use the +o option. Here is the basic form:

```
$ set -o feature          turn the feature on
$ set +o feature          turn the feature off
```

Features	Description
`$ set -+o` *feature*	BASH shell features are turned on and off with the `set` command; `-o` sets a feature on and `+o` turns it off: `$ set -o noclobber` *set noclobber on* `$ set +o noclobber` *set noclobber off*
`ignoreeof`	Disables CTRL-D logout
`noclobber`	Does not overwrite files through redirection
`noglob`	Disables special characters used for filename expansion: `*`, `?`, `~`, and `[]`

Table 22-3: BASH Shell Special Features

Three of the most common features are ignoreeof, noclobber, and noglob. Table 22-3 lists these different features, as well as the set command. Setting ignoreeof enables a feature that prevents you from logging out of the user shell with CTRL-D. CTRL-D is not only used to log out of the user shell, but also to end user input entered directly into the standard input. CTRL-D is used often for the Mail program or for utilities such as cat. You can easily enter an extra CTRL-D in such circumstances and accidentally log yourself out. The ignoreeof feature prevents such accidental logouts. In the next example, the ignoreeof feature is turned on using the set command with the -o option. The user can then log out only by entering the logout command.

```
$ set -o ignoreeof
$ CTRL-D
Use exit to logout
$
```

Environment Variables and Subshells: export

When you log in to your account, Linux generates your user shell. Within this shell, you can issue commands and declare variables. You can also create and execute shell scripts. When you execute a shell script, however, the system generates a subshell. You then have two shells: the one you logged in to and the one generated for the script. Within the script shell, you can execute another shell script, which then has its own shell. When a script has finished execution, its shell terminates and you return to the shell from which it was executed. In this sense, you can have many shells, each nested within the other. Variables you define within a shell are local to it. If you define a variable in a shell script, then, when the script is run, the variable is defined with that script's shell and is local to it. No other shell can reference that variable. In a sense, the variable is hidden within its shell.

Shell Variables	Description
BASH	Holds full pathname of BASH command
BASH_VERSION	Displays the current BASH version number
GROUPS	Groups that the user belongs to
HISTCMD	Number of the current command in the history list
HOME	Pathname for user's home directory
HOSTNAME	The hostname
HOSTTYPE	Displays the type of machine the host runs on
OLDPWD	Previous working directory
OSTYPE	Operating system in use
PATH	List of pathnames for directories searched for executable commands
PPID	Process ID for shell's parent shell
PWD	User's working directory
RANDOM	Generates random number when referenced
SHLVL	Current shell level, number of shells invoked
UID	User ID of the current user

Table 22-4: Shell Variables, Set by the Shell

You can define environment variables in all types of shells, including the BASH shell, the Z shell, and the TCSH shell. The strategy used to implement environment variables in the BASH shell, however, is different from that of the TCSH shell. In the BASH shell, environment variables are exported. That is to say, a copy of an environment variable is made in each subshell. For example, if the EDITOR variable is exported, a copy is automatically defined in each subshell for you. In the TCSH shell, on the other hand, an environment variable is defined only once and can be directly referenced by any subshell.

In the BASH shell, an environment variable can be thought of as a regular variable with added capabilities. To make an environment variable, you apply the export command to a variable you have already defined. The export command instructs the system to define a copy of that variable for each new shell generated. Each new shell will have its own copy of the environment variable. This process is called exporting variables. To think of exported environment variables as global variables is a mistake. A new shell can never reference a variable outside of itself. Instead, a copy of the variable with its value is generated for the new shell.

Configuring Your Shell with Shell Parameters

When you log in, Linux will set certain parameters for your login shell. These parameters can take the form of variables or features. See the previous section "Controlling Shell Operations" for a description of how to set features. Linux reserves a predefined set of variables for shell and system use. These are assigned system values, in effect, setting parameters. Linux sets up parameter shell variables you can use to configure your user shell. Many of these parameter shell variables are defined by the system when you log in. Some parameter shell variables are set by the shell automatically, and others are set by initialization scripts, described later. Certain shell variables are set directly by the shell, and others are simply used by it. Many of these other variables are application specific, used for such tasks as mail, history, or editing. Functionally, it may be better to think of these as system-level variables, as they are used to configure your entire system, setting values such as the location of executable commands on your system, or the number of history commands allowable. See Table 22-4 for a list of those shell variables set by the shell for shell-specific tasks; Table 22-5 lists those used by the shell for supporting other applications.

A reserved set of keywords is used for the names of these system variables. You should not use these keywords as the names of any of your own variable names. The system shell variables are all specified in uppercase letters, making them easy to identify. Shell feature variables are in lowercase letters. For example, the keyword HOME is used by the system to define the HOME variable. HOME is a special environment variable that holds the pathname of the user's home directory. On the other hand, the keyword noclobber is used to set the noclobber feature on or off.

Shell Parameter Variables

Many of the shell parameter variables automatically defined and assigned initial values by the system when you log in can be changed, if you wish. However, some parameter variables exist whose values should not be changed. For example, the HOME variable holds the pathname for your home directory. Commands such as cd reference the pathname in the HOME shell variable to locate your home directory. Some of the more common of these parameter variables are described in this section.

Other parameter variables are defined by the system and given an initial value that you are free to change. To do this, you redefine them and assign a new value. For example, the PATH variable is defined by the system and given an initial value; it contains the pathnames of directories where commands are located. Whenever you execute a command, the shell searches for it in these directories. You can add a new directory to be searched by redefining the PATH variable yourself, so that it will include the new directory's pathname.

Still other parameter variables exist that the system does not define. These are usually optional features, such as the EXINIT variable that enables you to set options for the Vi editor. Each time you log in, you must define and assign a value to such variables. Some of the more common parameter variables are SHELL, PATH, PS1, PS2, and MAIL. The SHELL variable holds the pathname of the program for the type of shell you log in to. The PATH variable lists the different directories to be searched for a Linux command. The PS1 and PS2 variables hold the prompt symbols. The MAIL variable holds the pathname of your mailbox file. You can modify the values for any of these to customize your shell.

Note: You can obtain a listing of the currently defined shell variables using the `env` command. The `env` command operates like the `set` command, but it lists only parameter variables.

Using Initialization Files

You can automatically define parameter variables using special shell scripts called initialization files. An *initialization file* is a specially named shell script executed whenever you enter a certain shell. You can edit the initialization file and place in it definitions and assignments for parameter variables. When you enter the shell, the initialization file will execute these definitions and assignments, effectively initializing parameter variables with your own values. For example, the BASH shell's **.profile** file is an initialization file executed every time you log in. It contains definitions and assignments of parameter variables. However, the **.profile** file is basically only a shell script, which you can edit with any text editor such as the Vi editor; changing, if you wish, the values assigned to parameter variables.

In the BASH shell, all the parameter variables are designed to be environment variables. When you define or redefine a parameter variable, you also need to export it to make it an environment variable. This means any change you make to a parameter variable must be accompanied by an export command. You will see that at the end of the login initialization file, **.profile**, there is usually an export command for all the parameter variables defined in it.

Your Home Directory: HOME

The HOME variable contains the pathname of your home directory. Your home directory is determined by the parameter administrator when your account is created. The pathname for your home directory is automatically read into your HOME variable when you log in. In the next example, the echo command displays the contents of the HOME variable:

```
$ echo $HOME
/home/chris
```

The HOME variable is often used when you need to specify the absolute pathname of your home directory. In the next example, the absolute pathname of **reports** is specified using HOME for the home directory's path:

```
$ ls $HOME/reports
```

Command Locations: PATH

The PATH variable contains a series of directory paths separated by colons. Each time a command is executed, the paths listed in the PATH variable are searched, one by one, for that command. For example, the cp command resides on the system in the directory **/bin**. This directory path is one of the directories listed in the PATH variable. Each time you execute the cp command, this path is searched and the cp command located. The system defines and assigns PATH an initial set of pathnames. In Linux, the initial pathnames are **/bin** and **/usr/bin**.

Shell Variables	Description
BASH_VERSION	Displays the current BASH version number
CDPATH	Search path for the `cd` command
EXINIT	Initialization commands for Ex/Vi editor
FCEDIT	Editor used by the history `fc` command.
GROUPS	Groups that the user belongs to
HISTFILE	The pathname of the history file
HISTSIZE	Number of commands allowed for history
HISTFILESIZE	Size of the history file in lines
HOME	Pathname for user's home directory
IFS	Interfield delimiter symbol
IGNOREEOF	If not set, EOF character will close the shell. Can be set to the number of EOF characters to ignore before accepting one to close the shell (default is 10)
INPUTRC	Set the **inputrc** configuration file for Readline (command line). Default is current directory, **.inputrc**. Most Linux distributions set this to **/etc/inputrc**
KDEDIR	The pathname location for the KDE desktop
LOGNAME	Login name
MAIL	Name of specific mail file checked by Mail utility for received messages, if MAILPATH is not set
MAILCHECK	Interval for checking for received mail
MAILPATH	List of mail files to be checked by Mail for received messages
HOSTTYPE	Linux platforms, such as i686, x86_64, or ppc
PROMPT_COMMAND	Command to be executed before each prompt.
HISTFILE	The pathname of the history file
PS1	Primary shell prompt
PS2	Secondary shell prompt
SHELL	Pathname of program for type of shell you are using
TERM	Terminal type
TMOUT	Time that the shell remains active awaiting input
USER	Username
UID	Real user ID (numeric)

Table 22-5: System Environment Variables Used by the Shell

The shell can execute any executable file, including programs and scripts you have created. For this reason, the PATH variable can also reference your working directory; so, if you want to execute one of your own scripts or programs in your working directory, the shell can locate it. No spaces are allowed between the pathnames in the string. A colon with no pathname specified references your working directory. Usually, a single colon is placed at the end of the pathnames as an empty entry specifying your working directory. For example, the pathname **//bin:/usr/bin:** references three directories: **/bin**, **/usr/bin**, and your current working directory.

```
$ echo $PATH
/bin:/usr/sbin:
```

You can add any new directory path you want to the PATH variable. This can be useful if you have created several of your own Linux commands using shell scripts. You can place these new shell script commands in a directory you create, and then add that directory to the PATH list. Then, no matter what directory you are in, you can execute one of your shell scripts. The PATH variable will contain the directory for that script, so that directory will be searched each time you issue a command.

You add a directory to the PATH variable with a variable assignment. You can execute this assignment directly in your shell. In the next example, the user **chris** adds a new directory, called **bin,** to the PATH. Although you could carefully type in the complete pathnames listed in PATH for the assignment, you can also use an evaluation of PATH—$PATH—in its place. In this example, an evaluation of HOME is also used to designate the user's home directory in the new directory's pathname. Notice the last colon, which specifies the working directory:

```
$ PATH=$PATH:$HOME/mybin:
$ export PATH
$ echo $PATH
/bin:/usr/bin::/home/chris/mybin
```

If you add a directory to PATH yourself while you are logged in, the directory will be added only for the duration of your login session. When you log back in, the login initialization file, **.profile**, will again initialize your PATH with its original set of directories. The **.profile** file is described in detail a bit later in this chapter. To add a new directory to your PATH permanently, you need to edit your **.profile** file and find the assignment for the PATH variable. Then, you simply insert the directory, preceded by a colon, into the set of pathnames assigned to PATH.

Specifying the BASH Environment: BASH_ENV

The BASH_ENV variable holds the name of the BASH shell initialization file to be executed whenever a BASH shell is generated. For example, when a BASH shell script is executed, the BASH_ENV variable is checked, and the name of the script that it holds is executed before the shell script. The BASH_ENV variable usually holds **$HOME/.bashrc**. This is the **.bashrc** file in the user's home directory. (The **.bashrc** file is discussed later in this chapter.) You can specify a different file if you wish, using that instead of the **.bashrc** file for BASH shell scripts.

Configuring the Shell Prompt

The PS1 and PS2 variables contain the primary and secondary prompt symbols, respectively. The primary prompt symbol for the BASH shell is a dollar sign ($). You can change the prompt symbol by assigning a new set of characters to the PS1 variable. In the next example, the shell prompt is changed to the -> symbol:

```
$ PS1='->'
-> export PS1
->
```

The following table lists the codes for configuring your prompt:

Prompt Codes	Description
`\!`	Current history number
`\$`	Use `$` as prompt for all users except the root user, which has the `#` as its prompt
`\d`	Current date
`\#`	History command number for just the current shell
`\h`	Hostname
`\s`	Shell type currently active
`\t`	Time of day in hours, minutes, and seconds.
`\u`	Username
`\v`	Shell version
`\w`	Full pathname of the current working directory
`\W`	Name of the current working directory
`\\`	Displays a backslash character
`\n`	Inserts a newline
`\[ \]`	Allows entry of terminal specific display characters for features like color or bold font
nnn	Character specified in octal format

You can change the prompt to be any set of characters, including a string, as shown in the next example:

```
$ PS1="Please enter a command: "
Please enter a command: export PS1
Please enter a command: ls
mydata /reports
Please enter a command:
```

The PS2 variable holds the secondary prompt symbol, which is used for commands that take several lines to complete. The default secondary prompt is >. The added command lines begin with the secondary prompt instead of the primary prompt. You can change the secondary prompt just as easily as the primary prompt, as shown here:

```
$ PS2="@"
```

Like the TCSH shell, the BASH shell provides you with a predefined set of codes you can use to configure your prompt. With them you can make the time, your username, or your directory pathname a part of your prompt. You can even have your prompt display the history event number of the current command you are about to enter. Each code is preceded by a \ symbol: \w represents the current working directory, \t the time, and \u your username; \! will display the next history event number. In the next example, the user adds the current working directory to the prompt:

```
$ PS1="\w $"
/home/dylan $
```

The codes must be included within a quoted string. If no quotes exist, the code characters are not evaluated and are themselves used as the prompt. PS1=\w sets the prompt to the characters \w, not the working directory. The next example incorporates both the time and the history event number with a new prompt:

```
$ PS1="\t \! ->"
```

The default BASH prompt is **\s-\v\$** to display the type of shell, the shell version, and the $ symbol as the prompt. Some distributions have changed this to a more complex command consisting of the user name, the hostname, and the name of the current working directory. A sample configuration is shown here. A simple equivalent is shown here with @ sign in the hostname and a $ for the final prompt symbol. The home directory is represented with a tilde (~).

```
$ PS1="\u@\h:\w$"
richard@turtle.com:~$
```

Ubuntu also includes some complex prompt definitions in the **.bashrc** file to support color prompts and detect any remote user logins.

Specifying Your News Server

Several shell parameter variables are used to set values used by network applications, such as web browsers or newsreaders. NNTPSERVER is used to set the value of a remote news server accessible on your network. If you are using an ISP, the ISP usually provides a Usenet news server you can access with your newsreader applications. However, you first have to provide your newsreaders with the Internet address of the news server. This is the role of the NNTPSERVER variable. News servers on the Internet usually use the NNTP protocol. NNTPSERVER should hold the address of such a news server. For many ISPs, the news server address is a domain name that begins with **nntp**. The following example assigns the news server address **nntp.myservice.com** to the NNTPSERVER shell variable. Newsreader applications automatically obtain the news server address from NNTPSERVER. Usually, this assignment is placed in the shell initialization file, **.profile**, so that it is automatically set each time a user logs in.

```
NNTPSERVER=news.myservice.com
export NNTPSERVER
```

Configuring Your Login Shell: .profile

The **.profile** file is the BASH shell's login initialization file. It is a script file that is automatically executed whenever a user logs in. The file contains shell commands that define system environment variables used to manage your shell. They may be either redefinitions of system-defined variables, or definitions of user-defined variables. For example, when you log in, your user shell needs to know what directories hold Linux commands. It will reference the **PATH** variable to find the pathnames for these directories. However, first, the **PATH** variable must be assigned those pathnames. In the **.profile** file, an assignment operation does just this. Because it is in the **.profile** file, the assignment is executed automatically when the user logs in.

.profile

```
# ~/.profile: executed by the command interpreter for login shells.
# This file is not read by bash(1), if ~/.bash_profile or ~/.bash_login
# exists.
# see /usr/share/doc/bash/examples/startup-files for examples.
# the files are located in the bash-doc package.

# the default umask is set in /etc/profile
#umask 022

# if running bash
if [ -n "$BASH_VERSION" ]; then
    # include .bashrc if it exists
    if [ -f "$HOME/.bashrc" ]; then
      . "$HOME/.bashrc"
    fi
fi

# set PATH so it includes user's private bin if it exists
if [ -d "$HOME/bin" ] ; then
    PATH="$HOME/bin:$PATH"
fi
```

Exporting Variables

Any new parameter variables you may add to the **.profile** file, will also need to be exported, using the export command. This makes them accessible to any subshells you may enter. You can export several variables in one export command by listing them as arguments. The **.profile** file contain no variable definitions, though you can add ones of your own. In this case, the **.profile** file would have an export command with a list of all the variables defined in the file. If a variable is missing from this list, you may be unable to access it. The **.bashrc** file contain a definition of the **HISTCONTROL** variable, which is then exported. You can also combine the assignment and export command into one operation as shown here for NNTPSERVER:

```
export NNTPSERVER=news.myservice.com
```

Variable Assignments

A copy of the standard **.profile** file, provided for you when your account is created, is listed in the next example. Notice how PATH is assigned. PATH is a parameter variable the system has already defined. PATH holds the pathnames of directories searched for any command you enter. The assignment PATH="$PATH:$HOME/bin" has the effect of redefining PATH to include your **bin** directory within your home directory so that your **bin** directory will also be searched for any commands, including ones you create yourself, such as scripts or programs.

Should you want to have your current working directory searched also, you can use any text editor to add another PATH line in your **.profile** file PATH="$PATH:". You would insert a colon : after PATH. In fact, you can change this entry to add as many directories as you want to search. Making commands automatically executable in your current working directory could be a security risk, allowing files in any directory to be executed, instead of in certain specified directories. An example of how to modify your **.profile** file is shown in the following section.

```
PATH="$PATH:"
```

Editing Your BASH Profile Script

Your **.profile** initialization file is a text file that can be edited by a text editor, like any other text file. You can easily add new directories to your PATH by editing **.profile** and using editing commands to insert a new directory pathname in the list of directory pathnames assigned to the PATH variable. You can even add new variable definitions. If you do so, however, be sure to include the new variable's name in the export command's argument list. For example, if your **.profile** file does not have any definition of the EXINIT variable, you can edit the file and add a new line that assigns a value to EXINIT. The definition EXINIT='set nu ai' will configure the Vi editor with line numbering and indentation. You then need to add EXINIT to the export command's argument list. When the **.profile** file executes again, the EXINIT variable will be set to the command set nu ai. When the Vi editor is invoked, the command in the EXINIT variable will be executed, setting the line number and auto-indent options automatically.

.profile

```
# ~/.profile: executed by the command interpreter for login shells.
# This file is not read by bash(1), if ~/.bash_profile or ~/.bash_login
# exists.
# see /usr/share/doc/bash/examples/startup-files for examples.
# the files are located in the bash-doc package.

# the default umask is set in /etc/profile
#umask 022

# if running bash
if [ -n "$BASH_VERSION" ]; then
    # include .bashrc if it exists
    if [ -f "$HOME/.bashrc" ]; then
     . "$HOME/.bashrc"
    fi
fi

# set PATH so it includes user's private bin if it exists
if [ -d "$HOME/bin" ] ; then
    PATH="$HOME/bin:$PATH"
fi

HISTSIZE=30
NNTPSERVER=news.myserver.com
EXINIT='set nu ai'
PS1="\w \$"
export PATH HISTSIZE EXINIT PS1 NNTPSERVER
```

In the following example, the user's **.profile** has been modified to include definitions of EXINIT and redefinitions of PATH, PS1, and HISTSIZE. The PATH variable has the ending colon added to it that specifies the current working directory, enabling you to execute commands that may be located in either the home directory or the working directory. The redefinition of HISTSIZE reduces the number of history events saved, from 1,000 defined in the system's **.profile** file, to 30. The redefinition of the PS1 parameter variable changes the prompt to just show the pathname of the current working directory. Any changes you make to parameter variables within your **.profile** file override those made earlier by the system's **.profile** file. All these parameter variables are then exported with the export command.

Manually Re-executing the .profile script

Although the **.profile** script is executed each time you log in, it is not automatically re-executed after you make changes to it. The **.profile** script is an initialization file that is executed *only* whenever you log in. If you want to take advantage of any changes you make to it without having to log out and log in again, you can re-execute the **.profile** script with the dot (.) command. The **.profile** script is a shell script and, like any shell script, can be executed with the . command.

```
$ . .profile
```

Alternatively, you can use the source command to execute the **.profile** initialization file or any initialization file such as **.login** used in the TCSH shell or **.bashrc**.

```
$ source .profile
```

System Shell Profile Script

Your Linux system also has its own profile file that it executes whenever any user logs in. This system initialization file is simply called **profile** and is found in the **/etc** directory, **/etc/profile**. This file contains parameter variable definitions the system needs to provide for each user. On Ubuntu, the **/etc/profile** script checks the /etc/profile.d directory for any shell configuration scripts to run, and then runs the **/etc/bash.baschrc** script, which performs most of the configuration tasks.

The number of configuration settings needed for different applications would make the **/etc/profile** file much too large to manage. Instead, application task-specific aliases and variables are placed in separate configuration files located in the **/etc/profile.d** directory. There are corresponding scripts for both the BASH and C shells. The BASH shell scripts are run from **/etc/profile** with the following commands. A **for** loop sequentially accesses each script and executes it with the dot (.) operator.

```
for i in /etc/profile.d/*.sh; do
  if [ -r $i ]; then
    . $i
  fi
done
```

For a basic install, you will have only the **gvfs-bash-completion.sh** script. As you install other shells and application there may be more. The **/etc/profile.d** scripts are named for the kinds of tasks and applications they configure. Files run by the BASH shell end in the extension **.sh**, and those run by the C shell have the extension **.csh**. The **/etc/profile** script will also check first if the **PS1** variable is defined before running any **/etc/profile.d** scripts.

A copy of part of the system's **profile** file follows

/etc/profile

```
# /etc/profile: system-wide .profile file for the Bourne shell (sh(1))
# and Bourne compatible shells (bash(1), ksh(1), ash(1), ...).

if [ "$PS1" ]; then
  if [ "$BASH" ] && [ "$BASH != "/bin/sh" ]; then
    PS1='\u@\h:\w\$ '
    if [ -f /etc/bash.bashrc ]; then
      . /etc/bash.bashrc
    fi
  else
    if [ "`id -u`" -eq 0 ]; then
      PS1='# '
    else
      PS1='$ '
    fi
  fi
fi

# The default umask is now handled by pam_umask.
# See pam_umask(8) and /etc/login.defs.

if [ -d /etc/profile.d ]; then
  for i in /etc/profile.d/*.sh; do
    if [ -r $i ]; then
      . $i
    fi
  done
  unset i
fi
```

Configuring the BASH Shell: .bashrc

The **.bashrc** script is a configuration file executed each time you enter the BASH shell or generate any subshells. If the BASH shell is your login shell, **.bashrc** is executed along with your **.profile** script when you log in. If you enter the BASH shell from another shell, the **.bashrc** script is automatically executed, and the variable and alias definitions it contains will be defined. If you enter a different type of shell, the configuration file for that shell will be executed instead. For example, if you were to enter the TCSH shell with the tcsh command, the **.tcshrc** configuration file would be executed instead of **.bashrc**.

The User .bashrc BASH Script

The **.bashrc** shell configuration file is actually executed each time you generate a BASH shell, such as when you run a shell script. In other words, each time a subshell is created, the **.bashrc** file is executed. This has the effect of exporting any local variables or aliases you have defined in the **.bashrc** shell initialization file. The **.bashrc** file usually contains the definition of aliases and any feature variables used to turn on shell features. Aliases and feature variables are locally defined within the shell. But the **.bashrc** file defines them in every shell. For this reason, the **.bashrc** file usually holds aliases and options you want defined for each shell. As an example of how you can add your own aliases and options, aliases for the **rm**, **cp**, and **mv** commands and the shell **noclobber** and **ignoreeof** options have been added to the example shown here. For the root user **.bashrc**, the **rm**, **cp**, and **mv** aliases have already been included in the root's **.bashrc** file.

The **.bashrc** file will check for aliases in a **.bash_aliases** file and run **/etc/bash_completion** for command completion directives.

The **.bashrc** file will set several features including history, prompt, alias, and command completion settings. The **HISTCONTROL** directive is defined to ignore duplicate commands and lines beginning with a space (**ignoreboth**). The history file is appended to, and the history size and history file sizes are set to 1000 and 2000.

```
# don't put duplicate lines or lines starting with space in the history
# See bash(1) for more options
HISTCONTROL=ignoreboth

# append to the history file, don't overwrite it
shopt -s histappend

# for setting history length see HISTSIZE and HISTFILESIZE in bash(1
HISTSIZE=1000
HISTFILESIZE=2000
```

Several commands then define terminal display features and command operations, including the shell prompt, beginning with **PS1=**.

The code for reading the user's **.bash_aliases** script is included. Possible aliases are also provided, some of which are commented. You can remove the comment symbols, #, to activate them. Aliases that provide color support for the **ls**, **grep**, **fgrep**, and **egrep** commands are listed. An alert alias is also provided which notifies you of long running commands.

```
# enable color support of ls and also add handy aliases
if [ -x /usr/bin/dircolors ]; then
    test -r ~/.dircolors && eval "$(dircolors -b ~/.dircolors)" || eval
"$(dircolors -b)"
    alias ls='ls --color=auto'
    #alias dir='dir --color=auto'
    #alias vdir='vdir --color=auto'

    alias grep='grep --color=auto'
    alias fgrep='fgrep --color=auto'
    alias egrep='egrep --color=auto'
fi

# some more ls aliases
#alias ll='ls -alF'
#alias la='ls -A'
#alias l='ls -CF'

# Add an "alert" alias for long running commands. Use like so:
# sleep 10; alert
alias alert='notify-send --urgency=low -i "$([ $? = 0 && echo terminal || echo
error)" "$(history | tial -n1 | sed -e '\''s/^\s*[0-
9]\+\s*//;s/[;&|]\s*alert$//'\'')"'
```

```
# Alias definitions.
# You may want to put all your additions into a separate file like
# ~/.bash_aliases, instead of adding them here directly.
# See /usr/share/doc/bash-doc/examples in the bash-doc package.

#if [ -f ~/.bash_aliases ]; then
#     . ~/.bash_aliases
#fi
```

The **.bash_completion** file is then read to set up command completion options:

```
# enable programmable completion features (you don't need to enable
# this, if it's already enabled in /etc/bash.bashrc and /etc/profile
# sources /etc/bash.bashrc).
if [ -f /etc/bash_completion ]; then
   . /etc/bash_completion
fi
```

You can add any commands or definitions of your own to your **.bashrc** file. If you have made changes to **.bashrc** and you want them to take effect during your current login session, you need to re-execute the file with either the . or the **source** command:

```
$ . .bashrc
```

The System /etc/bash.bashrc BASH Script

Ubuntu also has a system **bashrc** file executed for all users, called **bash.bashrc**. Currently the **/etc/bash.bashrc** file sets the default shell prompt, updates the window size, identifies the root directory, and checks whether a user is authorized to use a command. The **bash.bashrc** file is shown here:

```
# System-wide .bashrc file for interactive bash(1) shells.

# To enable the settings / commands in this file for login shells as well,
# this file has to be sourced in /etc/profile.

# If not running interactively, don't do anything
[ -z "$PS1" ] && return

# check the window size after each command and, if necessary,
# update the values of LINES and COLUMNS.
shopt -s checkwinsize

# set variable identifying the chroot you work in (used in the prompt below)
if [ -z "$debian_chroot" ] && [ -r /etc/debian_chroot ]; then
    debian_chroot=$(cat /etc/debian_chroot)
fi
# set a fancy prompt (non-color, overwrite the one in /etc/profile)
PS1='${debian_chroot:+($debian_chroot)}\u@\h:\w\$ '

# sudo hint
if [ ! -e $HOME/.sudo_as_admin_successful ] && [ ! -e "$HOME/.hushlogin" ]; then
    case " $(groups) " in *\ admin\ *)
```

```
    if [ -x /usr/bin/sudo ]; then
      cat <<-EOF
      To run a command as administrator (user "root"), use "sudo <command>".
      See "man sudo_root" for details.

      EOF
    fi
    esac
fi

# if the command-not-found package is installed, use it
if [ -x /usr/lib/command-not-found -o -x /usr/share/command-not-found/command-
not-found ]; then
        function command_not_found_handle {
                # check because c-n-f could've been removed in the meantime
                if [ -x /usr/lib/command-not-found ]; then
                  /usr/bin/python /usr/lib/command-not-found -- "$1"
                    return $?
                elif [ -x /usr/share/command-not-found/command-not-found ]; then
                  /usr/bin/python /usr/share/command-not-found/command-not-found
-- "$1"
                    return $?
                else
                  printf "%s: command not found\n" "$1" >&2
                  return 127
                fi
        }
fi
```

Though commented out, the file also includes statements to set the title of a terminal window to the user, hostname, and directory, as well as to enable bash completion.

The BASH Shell Logout File: .bash_logout

The **.bash_logout** file is also a configuration file, but it is executed when the user logs out. It is designed to perform any operations you want to occur whenever you log out. Instead of variable definitions, the **.bash_logout** file usually contains shell commands that form a kind of shutdown procedure—actions you always want taken before you log out. One common logout command is to clear the screen and then issue a farewell message.

As with **.profile**, you can add your own shell commands to **.bash_logout**. In fact, the **.bash_logout** file is not automatically set up for you when your account is first created. You need to create it yourself, using the Vi or Emacs editor. You could then add a farewell message or other operations. The default **.bash_logout** file includes instructions to invoke the **clear_console** command to clear the screen.

.bash_logout

```
# ~/.bash_logout: executed by bash(1) when login shell exits.
# when leaving the console clear the screen to increase privacy

    if [ "$SHLVL" = 1 ]; then
            [ -x /usr/bin/clear_console ] && /usr/bin/clear_console -q
    fi
```

Table Listing

Figure Listing

Index

B

C

D

E

F

G

H

I

J

K

L

M

O

P

Q

R

S

V

W

Z

CPSIA information can be obtained at www.ICGtesting.com
Printed in the USA
BVOW09s0209180615

405168BV00005B/31/P

9 781936 280988